Spencer L. Allen

The Splintered Divine

Studies in Ancient Near Eastern Records

General Editor:
Gonzalo Rubio

Editors:
Nicole Brisch, Petra Goedegebuure, Markus Hilgert, Amélie Kuhrt, Peter Machinist, Piotr Michalowski, Cécile Michel, Beate Pongratz-Leisten, D. T. Potts, Kim Ryholt

Volume 5

Spencer L. Allen

The Splintered Divine

A Study of Ištar, Baal, and Yahweh Divine Names and Divine Multiplicity in the Ancient Near East

DE GRUYTER

ISBN 978-1-5015-1575-0
e-ISBN (PDF) 978-1-61451-236-3
e-ISBN (EPUB) 978-1-5015-0022-0
ISSN 2161-4415

Library of Congress Cataloging-in-Publication Data
A CIP catalog record for this book has been applied for at the Library of Congress.

Bibliographic information published by the Deutsche Nationalbibliothek
The Deutsche Nationalbibliothek lists this publication in the Deutsche Nationalbibliografie; detailed bibliographic data are available on the Internet at http://dnb.dnb.de.

This volume is text- and page-identical with the hardback published in 2015.
Typesetting: Meta Systems Publishing & Printservices GmbH, Wustermark
Printing and binding: Hubert & Co. GmbH & Co. KG, Göttingen
♾ Printed on acid-free paper
Printed in Germany

www.degruyter.com

In Memoriam
Grover "Buddy" Dyer
Whose teaching led me to a career in
Biblical and ancient Near Eastern Studies.

Preface

Each of the following should be addressed at least once in the main body of *The Splintered Divine*, but I think it would be to everyone's benefit if I spell out the different writing conventions that I adopted for this book here at the beginning. For my dissertation readers who have an electric manuscript available to them, I could place an explanation at the first occurrence of a convention in one or more chapters and let them use a find function to locate that explanation easily. However, now that you are reading a physical copy of this book, such functions are not available. So, the following are my clarifications:

First, because the book's subtitle refers to itself as *A Study of Ištar, Baal, and Yahweh Divine Names*, I should explain how I identify divine names or portions of them. Throughout this book I use the phrases "first name," "last name," and "full name" to refer to portions of a divine name so that I can zero-in on a specific deity. "First name" refers to the individual deity's personal name, which is typically the first name in European naming traditions, and these are the names that most people think of when they think about Near Eastern deities. We refer to the names Marduk and Assur as the first (and only) names of these two deities, and like Marduk and Assur, most Near Eastern deities only have a first name. The name Ištar is a first name, but as I argue it is one that is commonly shared by many different goddesses. Because this first name was shared by several entities, the different ones had to be distinguished through the addition of "last names," which is typically the family name in European naming traditions. Most of the last names explored in this study are usually considered geographic epithets by modern scholars. As may be expected at this point, a "full name" is the combination of a first name and a last name that marks a specific deity. Admittedly, the phraseology behind "first name" and "last name" is inexactly applied to ancient Near Eastern deities, just as any metaphor or analogy is inexact. However, these phrases are used here because they efficiently relate the distinctions between an individual deity's personal name and its geographic name.[1] For example, the divine full

1 Michael Hundley wisely shortened my "first name" and "last name" phraseology in his book *Gods in Dwellings* to "forename" and "surname," respectively (Michael B. Hundley, *Gods in Dwellings: Temples and Divine Presence in the Ancient Near East*, ed. Amélie Kuhrt, SBLWAW Supplement Series 3 [Atlanta: Society of Biblical Literature, 2013], 268). I have retained the wordier first and last name phraseology for two reasons: to correspond with the usage in my dissertation and other earlier publications, and because I only learned of Hundley's usage after this manuscript was completed.

names Ištar-of-Nineveh and Ištar-of-Arbela share the common first name Ištar, whereas Baal-of-Ṣidon and Astarte-of-Ṣidon share the common last name (of-)Ṣidon. Occasionally, I use the term "nickname" to indicate a first name that is not actually a divine personal name. Usually this is in reference to the name Baal as a substitute for the personal divine name Hadad. I also use the phrase "divine name formula" to refer to a first name that has been followed by an epithet that is more than just a geographic identifier, e.g., Ištar//Lady-of-Nineveh.

Second, although it may be obvious at this point, I use dashes to indicate that a particular first name (or nickname) and last name represent a full name, such as Ištar-of-Nineveh. Similarly, two parallel lines (//) are used to indicate that a divine name and an epithet are acting together as a divine name formula and retaining the force of a full name. Usually the epithet following the parallel lines consists of more than one word or a simple geographic name, such as Lady-of-Nineveh in Ištar//Lady-of-Nineveh. With reference to the cuneiform evidence, these parallel lines indicate that the first name is preceded by a divine determinative, but the epithet is not. If an epithet is preceded by a divine determinative, then this is used to differentiate the epithet from the first name, which means that we are discussing two distinct divine entities. As will be clear, this slants-and-dash punctuation becomes necessary when a long list of divine names and epithets appear together because it makes the distinctiveness of divine entities more readily recognizable. Consider, for example, the following list of divine names derived from SAA 2 2 vi 6–20:

> Assur, Anu, Antu, Enlil, Mullissu, Ea, Damkina, Sîn, Ningal, Šamaš, Aya, Adad, Šala, Marduk, Zarpānītu, Nabû, Tašmētu, Ninurta, Gula, Uraš, Bēlet-ekalli, Zababa, Bau, Nergal, Laṣ, Madānu, Ningirsu, Ḫumḫummu, Išum, Erra, Nusku, Ištar//Lady-of-Nineveh, Ištar//Lady-of-Arbela, Adad-of-Kurbail, Hadad-of-Aleppo, Palil, and the Sebittu.

In this list of 37 divine names, we can quickly and clearly see that Ištar//Lady-of-Nineveh is contrasted with Ištar//Lady-of-Arbela and the other 35 deities without considering the possibility that Lady-of-Nineveh and Lady-of-Arbela are listed independently of the first name Ištar. In contrast to this slants-and-dash punctuation, I have placed quotation marks around geographic epithets and avoid a dash to connect the first name from the epithet when they are not actually functioning as a last name. For example, the phrase "God of Israel" is an epithet of Yahweh in Psalm 68:36, but it is neither Yahweh's last name nor part of his divine name formula in that verse.

Third, throughout this book, I tend to write out a Mesopotamian deity's name according by its Neo-Assyrian spelling because most of the cuneiform texts that were involved in this study belong to the Neo-Assyrian period. Thus,

I write the Akkadian name Anu instead of the Sumerian An/AN or the Old Babylonian Anum. Similarly, the Neo-Assyrian first name Mullissu is used instead of the Sumerian Ninlil, and I regularly refer to the Mesopotamian moon-god as Sîn instead of Nanna/NANNA, the sun-god as Šamaš instead of Utu/UTU, and Ištar instead of Inanna/INANNA, although I will occasionally write the Akkadian and Sumerian together, e.g., Nanna/Sîn. However, I use the Sumerian first name Enlil instead of the Neo-Assyrian Illil because the former is often used in Neo-Assyrian scholarship and "Illil" looks and sounds silly when repeated three-times fast.

Fourth, the people at De Gruyter have graciously decided to print a few pages with colored ink (I would like to thank Gonzalo Rubio and John Whitley for defending this idea). I believe that this quickly and meaningfully simplifies many of the tables and lists in the book in a way that variations of black ink with italics and underlining could never do. In these tables and lists, the chief deities **Aššur**, **Marduk**, and **Nabû** and their consorts appear in a bold **black**; members of Triad 1 (i.e., **Anu**, **Enlil**, and **Ea**) and their consorts appear in bold **blue**; members of Triad 2 (i.e., **Sîn**, **Šamaš**, and **Adad**) and their consorts appear in bold **red**; warrior (or other male) gods appear in bold **green**; goddesses appear in bold **pink**; other deities, including deified objects appear in bold **yellow**; and celestial objects (e.g., planets/stars) appear in bold **orange**. Also, within these tables, if a deity's consort is placed immediately after the deity, not only is her name written in the same color, but her name is indented to indicate that her position in the list is dependent upon his status.

Fifth, regarding composite god lists that have been compiled from embedded god lists (EGLs, which list three or more divine names), the divine name Marduk usually precedes the divine name Nabû. However, there are many instances in which Nabû precedes Marduk in EGLs or when the two deities are invoked as a pair in a blessing. When I create a composite god list from multiple texts, as I do throughout chapter 3.3 and the appendix, the text or line numbers are italicized if the name Nabû immediately precedes Marduk. For example, **SAA 13 126:*4*** indicates that the divine name Nabû precedes Marduk in that tablet and line, whereas **SAA 2 6:17–18** indicates that Marduk precedes Nabû. Also, whenever I create a composite god list, I provide a footnote with the texts used to compile that list. On occasion, when discussing a divine name that has been partially or wholly reconstructed in a text used to create the composite, I place the tablet in square brackets to indicate that it represents a lacuna. For example, in the following list of tablets that contain EGLs, much of SAA 18 74, 197, and 200 are reconstructed, whereas the other tablets are largely extant: SAA 18 24, 68, 70, 73, [74], 124, 192, 193, 194, 195, [197], 199, [200], 201, 202, and 204.

Sixth, as Daniel Richter observes, “the logic of polytheism excludes the possibility of the existence of another pantheon; by virtue of their divinity, all gods are necessarily part of the same divine pantheon.”[2] Thus, there was only one pantheon as far as any ancient polytheist would have been concerned, regardless of his nationality or whether he revered a particular deity revered by another person, people, or empire. However, rather than use the world “pantheon” literally as a reference to all of the gods revered by any and all people, I occasionally use it to describe a particular subset of deities that a particular population actively revered or invoked. Typically, I use “pantheon” like this when I respond to or describe previous scholarship that uses the word in such a colloquial manner. For instance, while a technical definition of “Assyrian pantheon” would include “all deities” (literally *pan-theon*) that the Assyrians worshipped, those they encountered from other peoples, and other deities that they had yet to meet, the colloquial definition occasionally used in this study focuses on those deities revered in official state rituals and invoked in treaties during a particular period. In this way, my usage of “Neo-Assyrian pantheon” is shorthand for “the subset of gods that the Neo-Assyrians revered,” which is in contrast with, say, the “Hittite pantheon,” or “the subset of gods that the Hittites revered,” even though I recognize that both the Neo-Assyrians and the Hittites themselves would have recognized the divinity of untold other deities in a way akin to the Athenians whom Paul criticized in Acts 17:23 for maintaining an altar “to an unknown god” just in case.

Now that this is all settled, you are ready to enjoy *The Splintered Divine*.

---

2 Daniel S. Richter, *Cosmopolis: Imagining Community in Late Classical Athens and the Early Roman Empire* (Oxford: Oxford University Press, 2011), 209.

Acknowledgments

A world of gratitude is owed to the several people who helped me transform my dissertation into this book. I would especially like to thank Profs. Jeffrey H. Tigay and Grant Frame at the University of Pennsylvania for the tireless hours they invested in this project during the dissertation stage and their continued support in the past three years. While researching and writing this topic, I often wondered if I should consider myself a Biblicist dabbling in Assyriology or an Assyriologist dabbling in Bible, so it was extremely helpful having one advisor to help me focus on Assyriological matters when I was in a Bible mode and another to help me focus on biblical matters when I was in an Assyriology mode. With their complementary help, as well as the help of the two anonymous reviewers in 2013, the two halves should be recognizable as an integrated whole. I would also like to thank Prof. Barry Eichler of Yeshiva University, whose instruction and feedback were most invaluable during the topic's planning stages. The entirety of this book is built upon the foundation that he caused me to set. I would also like to thank Barbara N. Porter of Harvard University for allowing me to pursue this topic of study after stumbling upon her article "Ishtar of Nineveh and her Collaborator, Ishtar of Arbela, in the Reign of Assurbanipal."

Transforming the study into a monograph means that I now owe a new world of gratitude to Gonzalo Rubio of Pennsylvania State University, the editor for the Studies in Ancient Near Eastern Records series. In addition to his own thorough and helpful comments that added to my revisions, he made sure that I had access to an array of primary and secondary sources to improve my arguments. I would also like to thank JoAnn Scurlock of Elmhurst College, Richard Beal of the Oriental Institute at the University of Chicago, Shalom Holtz of Yeshiva University, Jeffrey Stackert of the University of Chicago Divinity School, and Joshua Jeffers of the University of Pennsylvania for helping me chase down other materials and references that are not available in my local Arkansas libraries and for discussing issues relating to divine multiplicity over the past several years. Michael Hundley of Georgetown University deserves special thanks for encouraging me to cut out most of the polemical attitudes that appeared in the earlier version and for encouraging me to finish the revisions for this book, which is to say ridiculing me until it was done and citing it many times in his recent publications. Mark S. Smith of New York University, Jeremy Hutton of University of Wisconsin-Madison, and Philip C. Schmitz of Eastern Michigan University have all been kind enough to send me their past and current scholarship since I began my revisions. These articles have allowed me to refine my arguments in the Baal and Yahweh chapters by exposing me to new data and new theories concerning those data. I appreciate the academic dialogue that we have begun, and I look forward to continued agreements and disagreements in the future. Thomas Paradise of the University of Arkansas graciously volunteered to create four new maps for this book. In a very literal way, they add a sense of place to a discussion about place names, and they look great.

I am also indebted to numerous others who offered feedback on Biblical Studies and Assyriology topics, who offered feedback on topics beyond these disciplines, who promoted my scholarship at conferences and in print, or who offered computer/technical assistance during my preparation for this project: Wiebke Meinhold of the University of Heidelberg; Shawn Z. Aster of Bar-Ilan University; Michael Carasik of the University of Pennsylvania; Sarah Griffis of Harvard University; Robert St. Hilaire of Niagra University; Benjamin Zeller of Lake Forest College; Daniel Levine of the University of Arkansas; Steven Holloway of the American Theological Library Association; Bruce Wells of Saint Joseph's University; Bernd U. Schipper of the Humoldt-Universität zu Berlin and Harvard Divinity School and Daniel Schwemer of the University of Würzburg at *Die Welt des Orients*; William R. Osborne of the College of the Ozarks and Russell L. Meek of Midwestern Baptist Theological Seminary at the *Journal for the Evangelical Study of the Old Testament*; Robbie F. Castleman of John Brown University; Robert L. Skaggs of the Art Institute of Chicago; Mark Pearrow of the Massachusetts Institute of Technology; and Melissa Pearrow of the University of Massachusetts-Boston. A special thanks to Florian Ruppenstein of De Gruyter and his team in Berlin for typesetting and patiently correcting the final version of this book. A general appreciation is also extended to my many professors, teaching assistants, and fellow graduate students at the University of Pennsylvania, the Hebrew University of Jerusalem, and Harvard Divinity School. I should probably thank the thousands of people who downloaded my dissertation from ScholarlyCommons, many of whom sent me helpful ideas and articles, but I will thank them more when they buy this book; after all, it's revised, new, and improved.

There are many others at the University of Pennsylvania who also made the dissertation, and thus the book, possible: David Stern, Richard Zettler, Erle Leichty, Jamie Novotny, Ilona Zsonlay, Phil Jones, Judah Kraut, Linda Greene, Peggy Guinan, Diane Moderski, and Chrissy Walsh. I am also grateful for the material support provided by the University of Pennsylvania while I was a William Penn fellow; by the Ellis Fellowship Fund; and by Valerie Ross, Patrick Wehner, and the Critical Writing Fellowship at Penn.

I am especially thankful to my friends who have encouraged and supported me throughout the writing process: Raphael Cunniff, J. J. Shirley, and their family in Philadelphia, PA; Safdar and Samala Akbar and their family in Frederick, MD; Eleanor and Jason Pearrow and their parents in Dedham, MA; Jason Bolden, Sarah Keith-Bolden, and their family in Little Rock, AR; Jolene Phelps and the rest of the Theology Pub at the All Saints Church of Bentonville, AR: Mary and Wayne Stewart, Ralph Kunz, Paul Stuckey, and Sandy Wylie; Rev. Carl McCormack and my weekly Monday School class at the First Presbyterian Church, Rogers, AR; and Rev. Sandra Wanasek and my weekly Biblical Studies 101 class at the First United Methodist Church, Rogers, AR.

Throughout this book, I stress time and again that the names placed at the end of a list are the least important names in that list unless indicated otherwise. Realizing this, some readers could be tempted to think about generalizing this rule and notice that I am ending these acknowledgements with my family. Hopefully, the reader will remember that the first names that don't need last names or geographic epithets are generally more important and that I am intentionally stressing them here. So, thank you to those who need no further specification: my mother Barbara; my father Barry and Sammi; my sister Katie and Matt; Michael and Denice, Melanie, Brian, Vu, Chris, Brock, and Greg. Finally, I would like to extend a "best-for-last thank you" to my wonderful wife whose help made this book possible and conclude with the name that I want everyone to remember: Laura.

Spencer L. Allen
Rogers, AR
July 2014

Contents

Abbreviations

A	tablets in the collections of the Oriental Institute, University of Chicago.
AB	*Anchor Bible Commentary Series*. Edited by W. F. Albright and D. N. Freedman. New York, 1964.
ABC	Assyrian and Babylonian Chronicles. Edited by A. Kirk Grayson. Texts from Cuneiform Sources 5. Locust Valley: J. J. Augustin, 1975.
ABD	*Anchor Bible Dictionary*. Edited by David Noel Freedman. 6 vols. New York: Doubleday, 1992.
ADD	*Assyrian Deeds and Documents*. Edited by C. H. W. Johns. 4 vols. Cambridge, 1898–1923.
AfO	*Archiv für Orientforschung*
AJSL	*American Journal of Semitic Languages and Literatures*
AMT	*Assyrian Medical Texts from the originals in the British Museum.*
ANEP	*The Ancient Near East in Pictures Relating to the Old Testament*. Edited by James B. Pritchard. Princeton: Princeton University Press, 1954.
ANET	*Ancient Near Eastern Texts Relating to the Old Testament*. Edited by James B. Pritchard. Princeton: Princeton University Press, 1969.
AnOr	Analecta orientalia
AnSt	*Anatolian Studies*
AOAT	Alter Orient und Altes Testament
AoF	*Altorientalische Forschungen*
ARAB	*Ancient Records of Assyria and Babylonia*. Edited by Daniel D. Luckenbill. 2 vols. Chicago: University of Chicago Press, 1926–1927.
ARET	*Archivi Reali di Ebla*
ARM	Archives royales de Mari
ARMT	Archives royales de Mari, transcrite et traduite
Arnaud Emar	*Recherches au pays d'Aštata: Emar. 6/3: Textes sumériens et accadiens: texte*. Edited by Arnaud, D. Paris, 1986.
AS	Assyriological Studies
BAM	*Die babylonisch-assyrische Medizin in Texten und Untersuchungen*. Edited by Franz Köcher. 7 vols. Berlin, 1963 ff.
BAR	*Biblical Archaeological Review*
BASOR	*Bulletin of the American Schools of Oriental Research*
BDB	Brown, F., S. R. Driver, and C. A. Briggs, *A Hebrew and English Lexicon of the Old Testament*. Oxford, 1962.
BiOr	*Bibliotheca Orientalis*
BIWA	Beiträge zum Inschriftenwerk Assurbanipals*: Die Prismenklassen A, B, C = K, D, E, F, G, H, J und T sowie andere Inschriften: Mit einem Beitrag von Andreas Fuchs*. Edited by R. Borger. Wiesbaden, 1996.
BLei	Khirbet Beit Lei inscriptions in Dobbs-Allsopp, *et al*. New Haven, 2005
BM	tablets in the collections of the British Museum
BMS	*Babylonian Magic and Sorcery – being "The Prayers of the Lifting of the Hand."* Edited by Leonard W. King. London, 1896.
BWL	*Babylonian Wisdom Literature*. Edited by Wilfred. G. Lambert. Oxford, 1960.
BZAW	*Beihefte zur Zeitschrift für die alttestamentliche Wissenschaft*
CAD	*The Assyrian Dictionary of the Oriental Institute of the University of Chicago*. Edited by I. J. Gelb, *et al*. 21 volumes. Chicago, 1956 ff.

CBQMS	Catholic Biblical Quarterly Monograph Series
CdB	*Cahiers de Byrsa*
CHANE	Culture and History of the Ancient Near East
CIG	*Corpus inscriptionum graecarum*. Edited by A. Boeckh. 4 vols. Berlin, 1828–1877.
CIL	*Corpus inscriptionum latinarum*. 17 vols. Berolini, 1862 ff.
CIS	*Corpus inscriptionum semiticarum*. 5 vols. Parisiis, 1881 ff.
CNI	Carsten Niebuhr Institute of Near Eastern Studies
COS	*Context of Scripture*. Edited by William W. Hallo. 3 vols. Leiden, 2003.
CSMS Bulletin	*Canadian Society for Mesopotamian Studies Bulletin*
CTH	*Catalogue des texts Hittites*. Edited by Emmanuel Laroche. Paris, 1971.
DBH	Dresdner Beiträge zur Hethitologie
DNWSI	*Dictionary of the North-West Semitic Inscriptions*. Edited by Jacob Hoftijzer and Karel Jongeling. 2 vols. Leiden, 1995.
DPS	Diagnostic and Prognostic Series.
EA	El-Amarna tablets. According to the edition of Jörgen A. Knudtzon. *Die El-Amarna-Tafeln*. Aalen, 1964.
Faist	*Alltagstexts aus neuassyrischen Archiven und Bibliotheken der Stadt Assur*. Edited by Betina Faist. Studien zu den Assur-Texten 3. Wiesbaden: Harrassowtiz Verlag, 2007)
FRLANT	Forschungen zur Religion und Literatur des Alten und Neuen Testaments
GAB	The *Götteradressbuch* of Aššur
HANES	History of the Ancient Near Eastern Studies
HdO	Handbuch der Orientalistik
HSAO	Heidelberger Studien zum Alten Orient
HSM	Harvard Semitic Monographs
HSS	Harvard Semitic Studies
HTR	*Harvard Theological Review*
HUCA	*Hebrew Union College Annual*
IEJ	*Israel Exploration Journal*
JA	*Journal asiatique*
JANER	*Journal of Near Eastern Religions*
JAOS	*Journal of the American Oriental Society*
JBL	*Journal of Biblical Literature*
JCS	*Journal of Cuneiform Studies*
JESOT	*Journal for the Evangelical Study of the Old Testament*
JNES	*Journal of Near Eastern Studies*
JSOT	*Journal for the Study of the Old Testament*
K	tablets in the Kouyunjik collection of the British Museum
KAI	*Kanaanäische und Aramäische Inschriften*. Edited by Herbert Donner and Wolfgang Röllig. 3 vols. Wisebaden, 1962 ff. (5th ed., 2002).
KAH 2	*Keilschrifttexte aus Assur historischen Inhalts 2*. Edited by Otto. Schroeder. Deutsche Orient-Gesellschaft. WVDOG 37. Worcester: Yare Egyptology, 1922.
KAR	*Keilschrifttexte aus Assur religiösen Inhalts*. Edited by Erich Ebeling. Leipzig, 1919–1923.
KAV	*Keilschrifttexte aus Assur verschiedenen Inhalts*. Edited by Otto Schroeder. Leipzig, 1920.
KBo	*Keilschrifttexte aus Boghazköi*. Leipzig, 1916–1980.

KJV	King James Version
KTU^2	*The Cuneiform Alphabetic Texts from Ugarit (Die keilalphabetischen Texte aus Ugarit), Ras Ibn Hani and other Places*. Edited by M. Dietrich, O. Loretz, and J. Sanmartín. Münster, 1995.
KUB	*Keilschrifturkunden aus Boghazköi*. Berlin, 1921 ff.
KUSATU	*Kleine Untersuchungen zur Sprache des Alten Testaments und seiner Umwelt*
LCL	Loeb Classical Library
LH	The Laws of Ḫammurapi
LKA	*Literarische Keilschrifttexte aus Assur*. Edited by Franz. Köcher and L. Rost. Berlin, 1953.
Lozachmeur	*La Collection Clermont-Genneau: Ostraca, épigraphs sur jarred, étiquettes de bois*. Edited by Hélène Lozachmeur. 2 vols. Paris, 2006.
LXX	Septuagint (the Greek Old Testament)
Lyon	*Keilschrifttext Sargon's Königs von Assyrien (722-705 v. Chr.) nach den Orginalen neu herausgegeben, umschrieben, üebersetzt und erklärt*. Edited by D. G. Lyon. Assyriologische Bibliothek 5. Leipzig: J. C. Hinrichs, 1883.
MARV	Mittelassyrische Rechtsurkunden und Verwaltungstexte. Berlin, 1976–1982.
MM	tablets in the collection of the Monserrat Museum
MT	Masoretic Text
MVAG	*Mitteilungen der Vorderasiatisch-Aegyptischen Gesellschaft*. Vols. 1–44. 1896–1939.
*Nav**	Naveh inscriptions in Dobbs-Allsopp, *et al.* New Haven, 2005
NBC	tablets in the Nies Babylonian Collection, Yale University
Nbn.	*Inschriften von Nabonidus, König von Babylon*. Edited by Johann N. Strassmaier. Leipzig, 1889.
NCBT	tablets in the Newell Collection of Babylonian Tablets, Yale University
ND	field numbers of the tablets excavated at Nimrud (Kalḫu/Calaḫ)
NJPS	*Tanakh: The Holy Scriptures: The New JPS Translation according to the Traditional Hebrew Text*
NPNF	A Select Library of Nicene and Post-Nicene Fathers of the Christian Church, 2nd series
NRSV	New Revised Standard Version
OLA	Orientalia Lovaniensia Analecta
Or NS	*Orientalia* (Nova Series)
PBS	Publications of the Babylonian Section, University Museum, University of Pennsylvania. 16 vols. Philadelphia, 1911–1930.
PE	*Praeparatio evangelica. = Philo of Byblos: The Phoenician History; Introduction, Critical Texts, Translation, and Notes*. Edited by Harold W. Attridge and Robert A. Oden CBQMS 9. Washington, D.C.: Catholic Biblical Association of America, 1981.
PEQ	*Palestine Exploration Quarterly*
PNA	*The Prosopography of the Neo-Assyrian Empire*. Vol. 1/1–3/1. Finland, 1998–2002.
PRU	*Le palais royal d'Ugarit*
PTS	tablets in the collections of the Princeton Theological Seminary
RA	*Revue d'assyriologie et d'archélogie orientale*
RB	*Revue biblique*
RIMA	The Royal Inscriptions of Mesopotamia, Assyrian Periods.

RIMB	The Royal Inscriptions of Mesopotamia, Babylonian Periods.
RIME	The Royal Inscriptions of Mesopotamia, Early Periods.
RINAP	The Royal Inscriptions of the Neo-Assyrian Period.
RlA	*Reallexikon der Assyriologie und vorderasiatischen Archäologie.*
RS	Ras Shamra
SAA	State Archives of Assyria.
SAAB	State Archives of Assyria Bulletin.
SAALT	State Archives of Assyria Literary Texts.
SAAS	State Archives of Assyria Studies.
Samr	Samaria inscriptions in Dobbs-Allsopp, *et al.* New Haven, 2005
SCCNH	Studies on the Civilization and Culture of Nuzi and the Hurrians
Schneider	Schneider, Nikolaus. *Die Drehem- und Djohatexte im Kloster Monserrat.* AnOr 7. Rome, 1932.
SMN	Museum siglum of the Semitic Museum of the Harvard University (Nuzi Tablets)
StBoT	Studien zu den Bogazköy-Texten (Wiesbaden 1965 ff.)
STT	*The Sultantepe Tablets.* Edited by Oliver R. Gurney and J. J. Finkelstein. 2 vols. London, 1957–1964.
Studi Orientalistici	*Studi Orientalistici in onore di Giorgio Levi Della Vida.* 2 vols. Rome, 1956.
SWU	*Spätbabylonische Wirtschaftstexte aus Uruk.* Edited by H. Freydank. Berlin, 1971.
TAD	*Textbook of Aramaic Documents from Ancient Egypt.* Edited by B. Porten and A. Yardeni. 4 vols. Jerusalem, 1986–1999.
TBER	*Textes babyloniens d'époque récente.* Edited by J.-M. Durand. Paris, 1981.
TCL	Textes cunéiforms.Musée du Louvre
TDOT	*Theological Dictionary of the Old Testament.* Edited by G. J. Botterweck, *et al.* 15 vols. Grand Rapids, 2003 ff.
TH	tablets in the collection of the British Museum
TM	Find siglum Tell Mardikh
TSSI	*Textbook of Syrian Semitic Inscriptions.* Edited by John C. L. Gibson. 3 vols. Oxford, 1971–1982.
TuL	*Tod und Leben nach den Vorstellungen der Babylonier.*
UF	*Ugarit-Forschungen*
UVB	*Vorläufige Bericht über die ... Ausgrabungen in Uruk-Warka*
VAT	Vorderasiatische Abteilung Tontafel. Vorderasiatisches Museum, Berlin
VS	*Vorderasiatische Schriftdenkmäler der Königlichen Museen zu Berlin.* Edited by F. Delitzsch. Berlin, 1907 ff.
VT	*Vetus Testamentum*
VTE	Vassal Treaty of Esarhaddon (= SAA 2 6, "Esarhaddon's Succession Treaty")
WVDOG	Wissenschaftliche Veröffentlichung der Deutschen Orient-Gesellschaft
WSS	*Corpus of West Semitic Stamp Seals.* Edited by N. Avigad. Jerusalem, 1997.
YBC	tablets in the Babylonian Collection, Yale University Library
YOS	Yale Oriental Series, Babylonian Texts
ZA	*Zeitschrift für Assyriologie*
ZÄS	*Zeitschrift für ägyptische Sprache und Alterntumskunde*
ZAW	*Zeitschrift für die Alttestamentliche Wissenschaft*
ZPE	*Zeitschrift für Papyrologie und Epographik*

Additional Abbreviations

§ (§)	paragraph(s)
B.C.E.	Before the Common Era
b. e.	bottom edge (of a tablet)
ca.	circa
C.E.	Common Era
cf.	*confer*, compare
col(s).	column(s)
DN	divine name
e.g.	*exempli gratia*, for example
et al.	*et alii*, and others
EGL	embedded god list
esp.	especially
GN	geographic name
i.e.	*id est*, that is
l(l).	line(s)
l. e.	left edge (of a tablet)
n(n).	note(s)
no(s).	number(s)
obv.	obverse (front) of a tablet
p(p).	page(s)
PN	personal name
r.	reverse
r. e.	right edge (of a tablet)
RN	royal name
TN	temple name
v(v).	verse(s)
var.	variant reading
vol(s).	volume(s)

Keys to Signs Used in transliteration and translation:

( )	special remark or supplied words in translation
[x]	restored passage of damaged sign(s)
⸢x⸣	partially damaged sign(s)
⟨x⟩	missing sign(s)
xx . xx	word divider in alphabetic script inscriptions
x.x	sign divider for Sumerian logograms in Akkadian inscriptions

0 Introduction

0.1 Ištar-of-Nineveh and Ištar-of-Arbela

In her 2004 article, Barbara N. Porter examines *Assurbanipal's Hymn to the Ištars of Nineveh and Arbela* and claims that the hymn's narrative and grammar make it clear that "the text itself is quite clearly a two-goddess hymn."[1] Although the hymn's colophon is dedicated to one particular goddess who is addressed as the Lady-of-Nineveh (^{d}*be-let* ^{uru}*ni-na-a*, SAA 3 3 r. 19), the hymn begins by invoking and exalting two divine entities who are identified as the patron goddesses ("lady," *bēlet*) of Nineveh and Arbela:

> ^{1}*šu-uš-qa-a šu-uš-ri-ḫa* ^{d}*be-let* ^{uru}*ni-na-a* ^{2}*šur-ba-a na-'i-i-da* ^{d}*be-let* ^{uru}*arba-il*$_{3}$ ^{3}*ša*$_{2}$ *ina* DINGIR^{meš} GAL^{meš} *ša*$_{2}$*-ni-na la i-ša*$_{2}$*-a*
>
> Raise up (and) glorify Lady-of-Nineveh, exalt (and) praise Lady-of-Arbela, who have no equal among the great gods. (SAA 3 3:1–3, Alasdair Livingston's translation, modified slightly)[2]

These opening lines also contain grammatical constructions that indicate that the goddesses are separate and distinct entities. This plurality is indicated by the feminine-plural verb *īšâ* (*i-ša*$_{2}$*-a*, "have") rather than the common-singular form of the verb *īšu*. Elsewhere in the hymn, feminine-plural suffixes appear on nouns in three successive lines – "their names" (*zi-kir-ši-na*, l. 4), "their cult centers" (*ma-ḫa-za-ši-na*, l. 5), and "their lips" (*šap-te-ši-na*, l. 6) – and three more appear shortly thereafter. Assurbanipal even literally refers to his patronesses Lady-of-Nineveh and Lady-of-Arbela as "my Ištars/*ištar*s" (^{d}*iš*$_{8}$*-tar*$_{2}$^{meš}*-ia*, r. 5),[3] after crediting them for his military success and the spread of his fame (ll. 18–22).

Porter notes that the distinctiveness of these two goddesses is further highlighted by their separate roles in the creation of the king.[4] Lady-of-Nineveh is referred to as his birth mother (*um-mu a-li-ti-ia*, "the mother who bore me," SAA 3 3 r. 14), and Lady-of-Arbela is called his creator (⸢*ba*!⸣-[*ni*]-⸢*ti-ia*⸣ *taq-*

---

1 Barbara N. Porter, "Ishtar of Nineveh and Her Collaborator, Ishtar of Arbela, in the Reign of Assurbanipal," *Iraq* 66 (2004): 41.

2 Unless otherwise indicated, all translations are my own.

3 Admittedly, "my Ištars" may be translated as a common noun, meaning "my goddesses," rather than a plural proper noun (*CAD* I/J, *ištaru*), which is reflected in Livingstone's translation: "my goddesses" (SAA 3 3 r. 5; Alasdair Livingstone, *Court Poetry and Literary Miscellanea*, SAA 3 [Helsinki: Neo-Assyrian Text Corpus Project, 1989]).

4 Porter, "Ishtar of Nineveh," 41.

ba-a TI.LA *da-ra-a-te*, "my creator who decreed eternal life for me," r. 14–16). According to Porter, the former goddess could be understood as his divine birth mother in the hymn, and the latter should be thought of as responsible for shaping him in a more abstract way.[5] These distinct roles also appear in other texts. For instance, the Ninevite goddess, known elsewhere as Queen-of-Nineveh (^{d}*šar-rat* NINA^{ki}, SAA 3 13 r. 6–8) or Queen Mullissu (LUGAL ^{d}NIN.LIL$_2$, SAA 9 7:2), is the goddess who suckled the young prince Assurbanipal, whereas the Arbelite goddess served as his nurse or nanny (SAA 9 7 r. 6b).[6]

In her brief survey, Porter notes that multiple Ištars are named in royal inscriptions and treaties by other kings, including Esarhaddon of Assyria and Cyrus of Persia, indicating that this phenomenon of distinct Ištar goddesses extends beyond this one particular hymn of praise attributed to Assurbanipal near the end of Assyrian hegemony. In addition to the already mentioned localized Ištar goddesses of Nineveh and Arbela, other localized Ištar goddesses who were revered in the seventh century B.C.E. include Lady-of-the-Kidmuri-Temple, Assyrian-Ištar, and Assur's consort Mullissu, as well as (the unspecified) Ištar.[7] Some Ištar goddesses are named according to specific circumstances (e.g., Goddess-of-Battle or -of-Oaths), and others are named according to specific locations, such as Lady-of-Nineveh and Lady-of-Arbela. Sometimes these localized Ištar goddesses are presented as acting together, and sometimes they are presented as acting independently of each other. Because of this variability in the evidence from the seventh-century, Porter calls upon Assyriologists to be aware of and sensitive to the significance of these epithets. It might have been the case, she suggests, that other ancient scribes could have recognized and revered distinct and co-existent Ištar goddesses, just as the scribe-king recognized and revered two localized Ištar

5 Porter suggests that this type of creating may refer to the shaping of an individual in the womb, as opposed to incubating a child as a birth mother does (Porter, "Ishtar of Nineveh," 42).

6 Porter, "Ishtar of Nineveh," 42. Like SAA 3 3, SAA 9 7 r. 6 refers to the Ninevite goddess as "mother" (AMA-*šu$_2$-ni*), whereas the Arbelite goddess is simply the one who nurses him (*ta-ri-su-ni*). In subsequent lines, r. 7 ff., the Ninevite goddess, addressed here as Mullissu (ll. 2, 12, r. 6), further elaborates her role as the prince's wet nurse. The complex set of relationships between the divine names Mullissu, Ištar, Queen, and Lady – especially as they relate to the Ninevite goddesses – are discussed throughout chapter 4.

7 The *tākultu*-ritual texts also list Ištar goddesses with additional geographic epithets, non-geographical epithets, and divine names that appear to fuse multiple deities traditionally considered distinct, like fusing Ištar with Assur to get the divine name Assur-Ištar (Porter, "Ishtar of Nineveh," 43–44).

goddesses who were each "an independent force acting in Assurbanipal's life alongside other Ištars."[8]

0.2 Divine Names and Divine Multiplicity

Traditionally, scholars have understood gods or goddesses who shared a common name as locally venerated manifestations of an individual deity known by that name. The geographic epithets are often interpreted as secondary data about local manifestations of that one deity rather than as specific and essential information that defines the manifestation as divine entities all their own.[9] In the past two decades, however, this traditional interpretation has been challenged in a few publications, like Porter's, which have posited that each of these manifestations was envisioned as a deity in its own right, independent of any other god or goddess sharing the same divine name.[10] The scopes of these publications haves been extremely narrow, and no comprehensive study has yet proposed a methodology by which the distinctiveness of these manifestations can be demonstrated; the extent to which this multiplicity phenomenon was common to ancient Near Eastern religious traditions; or the manner in which multiple manifestations of specific gods were understood in ancient societies. This book aims to help fill this gap

---

8 Porter, "Ishtar of Nineveh," 44.

9 In discussions about Classical and ancient Near Eastern deities, "manifestations" is often used to describe the materialized form that a deity takes, such as a cult statue, celestial body, or another visual/physical appearance. The term is also used to denote the indication of the existence of a particular god or goddess who is thought to be interacting with the human world, which is to say that the deity's actions are manifest in the physical world even when the deity's physical form is not revealed. Because we will ultimately conclude that deities who have a common divine name but different geographical epithets are *not* manifestations of one singular deity but are separate deities, in this book we use the word "manifestation" only when discussing previous scholarship and earlier treatments of divine names with geographic epithets. Otherwise, we refer to the deities in question as "Ištar goddess/es," "Baal deity/ies," and similar terms to denote distinct and independent deities.

10 See, for example, Wiebke Meinhold, *Ištar in Aššur: Untersuchung eines Lokalkultes von ca. 2500 bis 614 v. Chr.*, AOAT 367 (Münster: Ugarit-Verlag, 2009); see chapter 4, "Die Rolle Ištars im Pantheon der Stadt Aššur," 185–223, for a series of discussions on the various Ištar goddesses at Assur. For treatments of Baal deities, see Paolo Xella, *Baal Hammon: Recherches sur l'identité et l'histoire d'un dieu phénico-punique*, Contributi alla storia della religione fenicio-punica 1 (Rome: Consiglio Nazionale Delle Ricerche, 1991) and Herbert Niehr, *Ba'alšamem: Studien zu Herkunft, Geschichte und Rezeptionsgeschichte eines phönizischen Gottes*, OLA 123 (Leuven: Peeters, 2003).

in scholarship as it examines whether ancient Near Eastern deities who shared a common divine name (or "first name") but with different appended epithets (or "last name") were manifestations of a singular god or whether they were independent gods in their own right. Admittedly, the phraseology behind "first name" and "last name" is inexactly applied to ancient Near Eastern deities, just as any metaphor or analogy is inexact. However, these phrases are used here because they efficiently relate the distinctions between an individual deity's personal name, which is typically the so-called "first name" in European naming traditions, and the individual's family name, which is typically the "last name." Thus, the divine "full names" Ištar-of-Nineveh and Ištar-of-Arbela share the common first name "Ištar," whereas Baal-of-Ṣidon and Astarte-of-Ṣidon share the common last name "(of-)Ṣidon."

Not all geographic last names represent city names, as are the cases for Ištar-of-Nineveh and Ištar-of-Arbela, whose last names were cities of strategic importance in the Neo-Assyrian Empire (see Chapter 3.4). Many of the geographic last names encountered in Neo-Assyrian and Northwest Semitic inscriptions do correspond to cities, but several refer to geographic regions or mountains, such as Baal-of-Ṣapun, whose last name represents the deity's mythical home on Mount Ṣapun rather than a place where his devotees worship him. Similarly, many scholars have identified the geographic last names of Yahweh-of-Teman and Yahweh-of-Samaria as regions rather than cities (see Chapter 6.2 and 6.3). In Hittite inscriptions, we see that various non-city locations could be used as geographic last names, including: IŠKUR-of-the-Market, IŠKUR-of-the-Ruin-Mound, and Ištar-of-the-Countryside. In Neo-Assyrian texts, the name of a deity's temple could also serve as the geographic element in that god's last name. Among those deities whose temple name served as last names are Lady-of-Eanna, who was a localized Ištar goddess at Uruk, and Lady-of-Kidmuri, who was a localized Ištar goddess at Nineveh. We will also include Heaven within this group of geographic last names, although "cosmic geography" might be a more precise phrase for such a location.[11] Heaven appears frequently as a geographic epithet and as an occasional last name for deities in Akkadian, Hittite, Aramaic, Phoenician, Punic, and Hebrew texts. There is, for example, an Ištar-of-Heaven in Akkadian sources, an IŠKUR-of-Heaven in Hittite sources, a Baal-of-Heaven (= Baal-Šamêm) in Akkadian, Aramaic, Phoenician and Punic sources, and the Hebrew epithet "God of Heaven," which serves as an epithet for Yahweh in Psalm 136:26 and Ezra 7:12,

---

11 For a full discussion on the geography of Heaven in Mesopotamian sources, see Wayne Horowitz, *Mesopotamian Cosmic Geography*, Mesopotamian Civilizations 8 (Winona Lake: Eisenbrauns, 1998), 243–267.

21, and 34. In the case of city, temple, and some regional geography-based names, the deity in question typically had an active cult presence at that place, which was usually run by members of the priestly class, and the deity was thought to reside there. In the case of cosmic geography-based names, such as mythical mountain homes on earth or an abode in Heaven (or in the heavens), the deity was still thought to reside where his or her last name indicated, but other divine beings were thought to play the role that the human priestly class played on earth.

In addition to Ishtar-of-Nineveh, Ištar-of-Arbela, Ištar-of-Heaven, and the various other localized Ištar goddesses found in seventh-century Assyrian inscriptions, there are several Hittite diplomatic treaties that mention deities with the first name Ištar (whose equivalent name in Hurrian was Šaušga), each having different last names. For example, the treaty between Šuppiluliuma I of Ḫatti and Ḫuqqana of Ḫayasa lists, "Ištar, Ištar-of-the-Countryside, Ištar-of-Nineveh, and Ištar-of-[Ḫattarina]" (*CTH* 42, § 8, A i 48–59, Gary Beckman's translation).[12] Hittite treaties also list up to 32 different storm-gods (IŠKUR deities) as divine witnesses, as is the case in the same Šuppiluliuma treaty with Ḫuqqana: "IŠKUR-of-Heaven, IŠKUR-of-Ḫatti, IŠKUR-of-Aleppo, IŠKUR-of-Arinna, IŠKUR-of-Zippalanda ... IŠKUR-of-the-Army, IŠKUR-of-the-Market, etc." (§ 7, A i 41–47, Beckman's translation).[13] At Ugarit, Baal-of-Ṣapun received offerings in the same texts as Baal-of-Aleppo (e.g., *KTU*[2] 1.148:26–27). Other Northwest Semitic inscriptions are notable for referring to major deities in association with very specific geographical epithets: these include Baal-Ṣidon (*KAI* 14:18), Astarte in-Ṣidon (*KAI* 14:16), Astarte-of-Kition (*KAI* 37:5), and Tannit in-Lebanon (*KAI* 81:1), although not all of these geographic associations actually represent deities with last names.[14]

Somewhat unexpectedly discovered in the mid-1970s, a handful of late ninth- or early eighth-century B.C.E. Hebrew texts from the eastern Sinai refer to a Yahweh-of-Samaria and a Yahweh-of-Teman, the region to the south or southeast of Judah:

[1]ברכת. אתכמ. [2]ליהוה. שמרנ. ולאשרתה

I bless you by Yahweh-of-Samaria and by his ašerah/Ašerah. (*Meshel* 3.1:1b-2)

12 Gary Beckman, *Hittite Diplomatic Texts*, SBLWAW 7 (Atlanta: Scholars Press, 1999), 29.

13 Beckman, *Hittite Diplomatic Texts*, 28.

14 For a fuller discussion on the difference between "of-Ṣidon" and "in-Ṣidon," see chapter 5.6 and Spencer L. Allen, "An Examination of Northwest Semitic Divine Names and the *Bet*-locative," *JESOT* 2 (2013): 75–76 and 80–82; cf. P. Kyle McCarter, "Aspects of the Religion of the Israelite Monarchy: Biblical and Epigraphic Data," in *Ancient Israelite Religion: Essays in Honor*

[5]ברכתכ. לי[6]הוה תמנ[7]ולאשרתה

I bless you by [Ya]hweh-of-Teman and by his ašerah/Ašerah. (*Meshel* 3.6:5–7)

The Kuntillet ʻAjrud (Ḥorvat Teman, see Map 1) texts represent an exciting aspect of ancient Israelite religion, but they belong to a very small corpus of texts from which to derive conclusions about ancient conceptions of local Yahwehs.

Although the eastern Sinai is geographically remote from the heartland of the Assyrian Empire, the Neo-Assyrian inscriptions with their multiple Ištar goddesses and the Hebrew texts with their different Yahweh deities are products of the same Neo-Assyrian imperial period. For this and many other reasons, the insights obtained from a thorough examination of the full names of Ištar goddesses can aid our understanding of the Yahweh full names uncovered at Kuntillet ʻAjrud. Israelite and Judahite religion and culture are distinct from the contemporary Assyrian religion and culture – indeed, Israelite religion and culture might have been distinct from contemporary Judahite religion and culture – so all conclusions drawn about Neo-Assyrian conceptions of Ištar and localized Ištar goddesses cannot be applied *a priori* to monarchic period conceptions of Yahweh or localized Yahweh deities. The methodology that has been created to examine Neo-Assyrian conceptions of multiple Ištar goddesses must be refined before it can be applied to potential Yahweh deities in Israelite texts because the number of gods officially revered by the Neo-Assyrians was substantially larger than the contemporary Israelites and Judahites. This refining process is demonstrated with other Near Eastern gods and cultures, such as the Baal deities from second-millennium Ugaritic texts and from first-millennium Phoenician, Punic, and Aramaic texts. The various Northwest Semitic goddesses mentioned in Ugaritic, Phoenician, Punic, and Ammonite texts are also helpful in demonstrating this refining process.

0.3 Outline and Method

This book investigates the issue of divine singularity and multiplicity as it relates to commonly shared divine names, or first names, in the ancient Near East. It focuses primarily on the first name Ištar in Mesopotamia, Baal in the Levant, and Yahweh in and around Israel, and it is structured in response to a

of Frank Moore Cross, eds. Patrick D. Miller, Paul D. Hanson, and S. Dean McBride (Philadelphia: Fortress, 1987), 140–142.

seemingly simple question "What or who was a god?" Over the course of six chapters this one question is further unpacked into three lengthier questions: How did the ancients define what it meant to be a god – or more pragmatically, what kind of treatment did a personality or object need in order to be considered a god by the ancients? In what ways are deities with both first and last names treated differently from deities with only first names? Under what circumstances are deities with common first names and different last names recognizable as distinct independent deities? The conclusions drawn about localized deities and their common first names are specific to each divine full name and are based on the data and texts available for each divine full name.

This book consists of six chapters, along with this introduction and the conclusion, and each chapter addresses one or more of these questions. For the most part, chapter 1 focuses on the first question and is rooted in modern theory and discussions about ancient conceptions about the divine and the privileging of ancient scholarly texts over state documents. The remainder of the book, chapters 2–6, focuses on the latter two questions and is rooted in the empirical analyses of ancient texts from ancient Assyria, Anatolia, Syro-Palestine, and the Mediterranean world.

Chapter 1, *Considering Multiplicity and Defining Deity*, briefly surveys the assumptions made about divine names and syncretism and how these assumptions have and have not changed over time. The survey begins with George Barton's studies from the early 1890s that equate every goddess known as Ištar – as well as goddesses whose names resemble the name Ištar or who share common attributes or epithets associated with Ištar – and then moves to consider more recent studies from the late-twentieth and early twenty-first centuries that build upon or react against Barton's conclusions.

Several scholars have recently challenged this traditional view of minimizing multiplicity in Mesopotamia because they have begun to redefine the meaning of "god" by contrasting modern notions of divinity with ancient ones found in Mesopotamian texts. Not only did Mesopotamian gods not need to be anthropomorphic to be considered divine entities, but they also did not need to be animate to be gods. The perceived active role that inanimate, non-anthropomorphic objects played in maintaining the order of the universe was important enough to the ancient Mesopotamians that they readily deified them. Offering lists indicate that statues, crowns, drums, and other cult objects were treated in much the same way in temple rites as were the divine personalities that we today more easily recognize as gods, like Anu or Inanna/Ištar. Additionally, some omen texts indicate that the moon-god Sîn could be considered distinct from the celestial lunar disk and Ištar could be considered distinct from the planet Venus, and cultic texts suggest that both an anthropomorphic god and a statue of that god could simultaneously receive separate offerings and have distinct divine names. If Mesopotamian priests and astronomers distinguished between a deity's personality and a physical representation of that same deity and, in some cases, treated both like deities, then it is not unreasonable for us to entertain the idea that goddesses who shared a first name but had distinct last names were distinct deities. Following this chapter, a brief excursus focuses on the term "Syncretism" and its different meanings in different religious traditions of the ancient Near East.

Chapter 2, *Comparative Insights*, differs from the other chapters because it focuses on religious traditions that are outside of the Mesopotamian heartland and the Levant, namely, Roman Catholicism and ancient Hittite religious traditions. This chapter looks forward to chapters 3–6 in two ways. First, the occasional appearances of madonnine multiplicity in the Roman Catholic traditions, especially in modern, popular Italian traditions, suggest methodological criteria for chapter 3 to help us determine when or whether localized Ištar goddesses with different last names should be considered distinct. Although she is not a deity and definitely not multiple in official Roman Catholic thought, there are long-held traditions among the Catholic laity that recognize multiple and independent madonnas. Of particular interest are the coexistent "sister" madonnas who visit each other's churches during processionals and those madonnine images that perform miracles to attract attention to themselves (as opposed to the heavenly Madonna Mary or other madonnine images). Likewise, the Hittite material suggests methodological criteria for chapter 3 regarding polytheistic traditions that more closely resemble Assyrian religious traditions. The Hittite portion of this chapter primarily considers the distinctiveness of independent storm-gods (IŠKUR deities), tutelary-gods (LAMMAs), and Ištar goddesses. Whether the Hittite scribal tradition used the Sumerian logograms IŠKUR, LAMMA, and IŠTAR/ŠAUŠGA to designate deities' shared first names, or if these functioned more like titles or categorical labels is also discussed. The chapter ends with an examination of the Hittite practice of dividing a god and how this relates to the larger issue of Hittite multiplicity.

With chapter 3, *The Divine Hierarchy and Embedded God Lists (EGLs)*, the focus begins with a consideration of the lexical god-list tradition in Mesopotamia and then turns to the empirical analysis of Akkadian state and administrative texts. The methodology presented here makes use of embedded god lists (EGLs) that are found in various texts and genres from the Neo-Assyrian period that served pragmatic purposes: royal inscriptions, divine witness lists, blessings and curses found in treaties and letters, and cultic offering and ritual texts. EGLs range in length from three to three dozen divine names, and the divine names in these EGLs are typically found in a consistent order that reflects a regular hierarchy of the gods. The examination of several EGLs indicates that deities who have both first and last names were treated in the same manner as deities with only first names, except that their geographic last names functioned as a necessary component of these gods' identities. For example, Assur and Šamaš both commonly appear in EGLs, usually near the beginning. Assur invariably appears before Šamaš, which indicates that he outranks Šamaš in the Assyrian divine hierarchy. In contrast, when Ištar-of-Nineveh and Ištar-of-Arbela appear together in EGLs, they typically appear near the end, indicating their relatively low status in the hierarchy. What is significant is that throughout these EGLs, Ištar-of-Nineveh is treated as distinct from Ištar-of-Arbela as is Assur from Šamaš or any other deity in the list. Together, the observation that deities with last names have a relatively low rank and that higher-ranking deities only appear once in an EGL argue against the possibility that these multiple localized Ištar goddesses are really just local manifestations of one overarching Ištar who has a relatively high rank among the Assyrian gods. If the singular Ištar had been such a high-ranking goddess that she deserved to be addressed more than her divine peers, her name would have appeared earlier in these EGLs, reflecting such an important rank.

Chapter 4, *The Ištar Goddesses of Neo-Assyrians*, continues chapter 3's discussion of the Ištar-multiplicity issue that Porter brought to the foreground in her 2004 article. It also more closely analyses localized Ištar goddesses appearing in the EGLs by looking at the different cuneiform signs used to write their names and the other names by which these goddesses were known. Although the first name Ištar could function as a common noun meaning "goddess" (*ištaru*) in Akkadian, this does not appear to be the case in the EGLs examined. When the name Ištar appears in an EGL with a geographic epithet, it is distinctly a first name, as opposed to a title or nickname. The chapter also pays special attention to Ištar-of-Nineveh, Ištar-of-Arbela, Mullissu, Assyrian-Ištar, and two other goddesses who were not named Ištar. Anunītu and Dīrītu had historical ties to the first name Ištar, but over time these goddesses received non-Ištar first names and appear to have been considered distinct from the name Ištar in the cultic realm.

Chapter 5, *Geographic Epithets in the West*, follows the methodology set forth in chapter 3 and applies it to the different EGLs from Syro-Palestinian texts from the second millennium B.C.E. into the early first millennium C.E., where local populations revered substantially fewer deities than did their second millennium or Neo-Assyrian counterparts. The first name Baal functioned as both a typical divine first name – often a nickname for deities historically known as Hadad – and, occasionally, as a title (i.e., a lower-case-b *baal*) indicating that the deity was the "lord" or "master" of the geographic region or cult represented by the last name.[15] This chapter also explores the meaning of, and grammatical possibilities behind, various divine names and geographic epithets associated with goddesses of the Levant.

Finally, chapter 6, *A Kuntillet ʻAjrud Awakening*, surveys the Yahweh full names discovered at Kuntillet ʻAjrud and several other full names that scholars have subsequently proposed as representing either distinct or semi-independent Yahweh deities in ancient Israel and Judah. Because there are no definitive EGLs in the biblical or in extra-biblical Hebrew texts, analogy and syntax serve as the primary forms of investigation for potential Yahwistic multiplicity. The forms of the Neo-Assyrian and Northwest Semitic deities' full names are compared with those proposed for potential localized Yahweh deities. Unlike the positive conclusions that are drawn about the multiplicity of Hittite deities, the several Neo-Assyrian Ištar goddesses, and the Northwest Semitic Baal deities, no data point conclusively to the perceived coexistence of multiple, independent localized Yahweh deities by ancient Israelites. This need not mean that the scribes responsible for the texts and graffiti who invoked a Yahweh with a specific last name only believed in the existence of one singular and solitary Yahweh. Indeed, the fact that these scribes used phraseology so similar to that used in Akkadian, Hittite, Ugaritic, Phoenician, Punic, Neo-Punic, Aramaic, and Ammonite texts could suggest that the Yahweh deities invoked by each scribe were tied to specific locale or cult and might have been specified with a last name in order to distinguish them from other potential localized Yahweh deities. However, unlike their Neo-Assyrian and other counterparts, these scribes only appealed to one Yahweh at a time rather than contrast multiple localized Yahweh deities in a single text. For this reason, we cannot determine whether or not any Israelites who encountered the names

---

15 The divine first name Hadad is attested in third-millennium B.C.E. texts as ^{d}'a_3-*da* at Ebla, in second-millennium texts as *hd* at Ugarit, and in a fourth-century C.E. Greek text as Ἀδάδῳ at Cyprus. Despite the slightly different pronunciations that are indicated by these and various other spellings, each is rendered "Hadad" in English in order to highlight the fact that all represent the same divine name. In Akkadian and Hittite texts, the divine name is represented by the logogram ^{d}IŠKUR, which scholars translate as "Adad" for Sumerian and Akkadian texts but leave as IŠKUR for Hittite texts because they often do not know which divine names/names is/are represented by the logogram in Hittite. To avoid confusion the logogram ^{d}10, which also indicates storm-gods in Hittite texts, has also been "translated" as IŠKUR throughout this book.

Similarly, the divine first name or nickname Baal is attested with several different spellings and pronunciations from third-millennium B.C.E. Ebla to third-century C.E. Carthage and fourth-century C.E. Cyprus, but "Baal" has been retained as the English translation, whereas "Bēl" is used to denote the divine nickname of the Mesopotamian deity Marduk in cuneiform sources.

Yahweh-of-Samaria and Yahweh-of-Teman would have recognized them as distinct and independent deities. We can argue that if their Assyrian and Phoenician contemporaries had encountered these texts, they would likely have recognized that Yahweh-of-Samaria and Yahweh-of-Teman were two distinct deities.

This book concludes by summarizing the findings and exploring the implications of the preceding chapters. In particular, the conclusion compares the findings suggestive of multiple, independent localized Ištar goddesses and Baal deities with the lack of evidence for multiple, independent localized Yahweh deities.

1 Considering Multiplicity and Defining Deity

One might think that a plain-sense reading of the seventh-century *Assurbanipal's Hymn to the Ištars of Nineveh and Arbela* (SAA 3 3) would cause one to conclude, without reservation, that the entity identified in the text as Lady-of-Nineveh was a distinct and separate entity from the other, who was identified as Lady-of-Arbela. Not only does this hymn use feminine-plural verbs and pronominal suffixes throughout its approximately forty lines, but the undeniably plural noun "goddesses" (^{d}*iš*$_{8}$-*tar*$_{2}$^{meš}-*ia*, r. 5) is also used to describe Assurbanipal's objects of praise, and this would not change if we instead translated "goddesses" as the plural proper noun "Ištars." Likewise, one goddess is described as a birth mother, while the other is referred to as "my creator" (⸢*ba*$^{!}$⸣-[*ni*]-⸢*ti-ia*⸣, r. 14). Semantically, "mother" and "creator" may overlap, and both terms are feminine, so we could easily expect that these terms refer to the same woman if they referred to a human person. However, the entities addressed here as "mother" and "creator" are decidedly not human, so these terms are not necessarily redundant in reference to the divine world as they would be to ours; a divine creator could easily be distinct from a divine mother.[1] A third way by which this hymn distinguishes between Lady-of-Nineveh and Lady-of-Arbela is its reference to the Emašmaš-temple and the Egašankalamma-temple (l. 10), which belonged to the patron goddesses of Nineveh and Arbela, respectively.[2]

Together the plural vocabulary and syntax, dual roles, and two corresponding places of worship should all indicate to the reader that Assurbanipal was praising more than one deity, each of whom he respectfully called "Lady" rather than calling them by their divine first names. With this in

---

1 Akkadian *bānû*/*bānītu* may be used to describe the forming/creating of an individual (or deity) by either a male or female deity or even by a human father (*CAD* B, *bānû* A). Alejandro F. Botta notes that the goddess Bānit, whom he identifies with (the unspecified) Ištar, was revered by Arameans in Elephantine (Alejandro F. Botta, "Outlook: Aramaeans Outside of Syria: Egypt," in *The Aramaeans in Ancient Syria*, ed. Herbert Niehr, HdO 106 [Leiden: Brill, 2014], 369 n. 32 and 373 n. 63). This goddess had a temple dedicated to her (e.g., *TAD* A2.2:1, 4, and 12; and A2.4:1), and her name served as the theophoric element in Aramaean personal names (e.g., Bānit-sar, Bānit-sar-el, and Makki-Bānit). Furthermore, André Lemaire has recently identified an Aramaic graffito from Tarsus (ca. 700 B.C.E.) bearing the personal name Ṣil-Bānit (André Lemaire, "Outlook: Aramaeans Outside of Syria: Anatolia," in *The Aramaeans in Ancient Syria*, ed. Herbert Niehr, HdO 106 [Leiden: Brill, 2014], 321).

2 Andrew R. George, *House Most High*: *The Temple Lists of Ancient Mesopotamia*, Mesopotamian Civilizations 5 (Winona Lake, IN: Eisenbrauns, 1993), 121 (no. 742) and 90 (no. 351).

mind, Porter's central thesis and conclusion that Lady-of-Nineveh and Lady-of-Arbela are two distinct goddesses should be so obvious that the article need never have been developed, presented at the *49th Rencontre Assyriologique Internationale* in London in 2003, and published along with the conference's proceedings in *Iraq* 66 the following year. The fact that Porter even considered arguing for a plain-sense reading of SAA 3 3 as a hymn praising two distinct goddesses itself suggests that the dominant opinions held by Assyriologists were based on the assumption that in the polytheistic system that operated during the Neo-Assyrian period Lady-of-Nineveh was actually the same goddess as Lady-of-Arbela. Because Lady-of-Nineveh and Lady-of-Arbela can be considered the respective titles or epithets for a local Ninevite goddess known as Ištar and a local Arbelite goddess also known as Ištar, it was generally assumed that these two localized Ištars represented the one goddess Ištar whose geographic allegiance was unspecified. Because both ladies had also been called by the divine name Ištar, they were both the same Ištar.

1.1 An Early History of Identifying and Equating Divine Names

Porter's "Ishtar of Nineveh and her Collaborator, Ishtar of Arbela, in the Reign of Assurbanipal" needed to be developed and written precisely because there was a long and influential history of dismissing localized Ištar goddesses as distinct and individual deities. Consider, for instance, George Barton's work from the early 1890s, the two-part essay "The Semitic Ištar Cult."[3] Barton developed two methodological approaches in order to demonstrate that there were fewer distinct Ištar goddesses than the available geographic epithets permitted. This is not to say that Barton's conclusions are the sole foundation upon which subsequent scholarship identified each localized Ištar goddess with other Ištar goddesses – indeed, he initially allowed for the existence of a few distinct Ištar goddesses – but his investigations of the many localized Ištars do reveal, at minimum, a frame of mind from which modern examinations of Mesopotamian religious traditions stem.

Barton surveyed "the great mass of material extant in the Assyrian language" and concluded that these texts needed to be classified in order to reconstruct the history of Ištar in Mesopotamian religious thought.[4] His interest

3 George A. Barton, "Semitic Ištar Cult," *Hebraica* 9 (1893): 131–165; and George A. Barton, "The Semitic Ištar Cult (Continued)," *Hebraica* 10 (1893–1894): 1–74.
4 Barton, "Semitic Ištar Cult," (1893): 131.

in this classification arose primarily in response to the three main localized Ištar goddesses from the Neo-Assyrian period, namely, Ištar-of-Nineveh, Ištar-of-Arbela, and Assyrian-Ištar. In order to optimize his potential history or histories of these potential divine personalities, he employed two separate methodologies. The first relied upon his assumed link between each localized goddess and her cult at that place, and it assumed that each of these three Ištar goddesses possessed her own unique personality and characteristics. Barton began this first line of inquiry with the premise that each Ištar goddess was independent of the others until he uncovered texts to demonstrate otherwise. This process was aided by his belief that a text could be traced to a particular temple (TN) or to a particular city (GN). After ascertaining each text's provenance, he identified the Ištar from that text as specifically Ištar-of-TN/GN. He then sorted the texts into three different collections according to their cults of origin (i.e., Nineveh, Arbela, and Assur) and used each collection to reconstruct an individual personality for each local Ištar goddess.

Barton based his second methodological approach on the texts' historical settings rather than their geographical associations. This tactic downplayed the need to determine each text's provenance before deciding to which Ištar the text referred because, he argued, provenance and origins were irrelevant compared to *when* the text was written.[5] This also allowed him to avoid another primary assumption of the first methodology because he no longer needed to assume that localized Ištars had distinct personalities. Because his second methodology depended on royal inscriptions and administrative texts rather than cultic or mythic texts to isolate potentially distinct Ištars, Barton presumed that each king invoked the Ištar who was worshipped in his capital city rather than any other potential Ištar. This meant that texts from Sennacherib's reign that happen to mention (the unspecified) Ištar must have implicitly meant Ištar-of-Nineveh because Nineveh was Sennacherib's imperial capital. Barton inferred that if the king had meant to address a different Ištar, then he would have expressly indicated this in the inscription.[6] This allowed, for example, Barton to treat the myth *Ištar's Descent* (and, secondarily, other texts discussing Ištar and her divine paramour Tammuz) as a myth specifically about Ištar-of-Nineveh because this material was recovered from Assurbanipal's library in Nineveh.[7] Barton considered this second methodology the

5 Barton, "Semitic Ištar Cult," (1893): 131.

6 Barton, "Semitic Ištar Cult," (1893): 131.

7 Barton, "Semitic Ištar Cult," (1893): 150 and 153. While he recognized that the tradition behind this myth predated Assurbanipal and the establishment of Nineveh as the Assyrian capital, Barton lacked the ancient Sumerian version of the myth and so was unable to provide a more definite period or place for its composition.

more reliable of the two because it provided "a tangible rather than a speculative basis on which to rest, and in investigations of such antiquity such a basis should always be sought."[8] This "speculative basis" was the idea that drove this first methodological inquiry: divine personalities were distinct enough to distinguish accurately between two gods.

Barton began his dual-approach reconstruction for divine personalities with the goddess Ištar-of-Nineveh because he believed that she was first worshipped by Assurnāṣirpal I, a king whom Barton dated to the Old Assyrian period in the early second millennium.[9] Although we know now that this king reigned from Assur during the eleventh century, Barton was forced to consider Assurnāṣirpal's prayer to Ištar a Ninevite text about the Ninevite Ištar goddess because of the copy's provenance.[10] This prayer referred to this Ištar as Lady-of-Nineveh (*be-let* ^{uru}NINA, *AfO* 25 38:5) and the goddess Who-Resides-(in)-the-Emašmaš-temple (*a-ši-bat* e_2*-maš-maš*, l. 3).[11] This Ištar-of-Nineveh was also called Sîn's daughter and the beloved sister of Šamaš (DUMU.MUNUS ^{d}30 *ta-li-mat* ^{d}*šam-ši*, l. 6), as well as the wife of the supreme god Assur (*na-ra-mi*$_3$*-ki* AD DINGIR^{meš} ... *q*[*u*$^?$*-ra*]*-du* ^{d}*aš-šur*, *AfO* 25 42:81). Elsewhere in this psalm, Assurnāṣirpal claimed to be the one who introduced the worship of Ištar to the people of Assyria, who had previously neither known or recognized her divinity (UN^{meš} KUR ^{d}*aš-šur*^{ki} *ul i-da-ni-ma ul im-da-ḫa-ra* AN-*ut-ki*, *AfO* 25 39:24), which Barton rightly regarded as a pious hyperbole.[12]

Like the extant copy of the prayer to Ištar-of-Nineveh, the remainder of the material available to Barton belonged to the Neo-Assyrian period.[13] Although no texts from Assurnāṣirpal II's reign explicitly identified a goddess by the full name Ištar-of-Nineveh, statements made about Ištar in the available texts indicated to Barton that she was a warrior goddess and Assurnāṣirpal's patron

---

8 Barton, "Semitic Ištar Cult," (1893): 131.

9 Barton, "Semitic Ištar Cult," 135. Barton dated Assurnāṣirpal I's reign to ca. 1800 B.C.E.

10 Barton, "Semitic Ištar Cult," (1893): 135. Barton noted that the psalm only survived as a Neo-Assyrian copy from Assurbanipal's library.

11 Wolfram von Soden, "Zwei Königsgebete an Ištar aus Assyrien," *AfO* 25 (1974): 38; and Barton, "Semitic Ištar Cult," (1893): 132–133.

12 Barton, "Semitic Ištar Cult," (1893): 151.

13 Barton mentioned texts from Assur-rēš-iši I's reign, ca. 1150, and an earlier reference to Ištar in a letter from Tušratta of Mitanni to Amenhotep III of Egypt (i.e., EA 23), ca. 1400, but he was forced to overlook them because he could not definitively determine to which city or shrine – and, thus, to which Ištar – these texts referred. This was no problem for him, however, because he claimed that neither text added to his knowledge of Ištar (Barton, "Semitic Ištar Cult," [1893]: 137).

goddess (e.g., RIMA 2 A.0.101.1 i 70).[14] The earliest text available to Barton that explicitly named an Ištar-of-Nineveh was from the end of the eighth century, from Sennacherib's reign.[15] Significantly, Sennacherib was the king who moved the Assyrian capital to Nineveh, and this was also, according to Barton, when Ištar-of-Nineveh joined Assur as a chief deity of the Assyrian Empire.[16]

Compared to the numerous texts that Barton found and associated with Ištar-of-Nineveh, texts invoking other Neo-Assyrian Ištars were limited, so Barton concluded little more about their personalities than the fact that these Ištars were also warrior goddesses. When Barton moved beyond personalities and looked instead to the relationships among the deities, he concluded that Assyrian-Ištar was Assur's consort during Tiglath-Pileser I's reign from his capital city Assur, and Ištar-of-Nineveh was Assur's consort during Sennacherib's reign at Nineveh.[17] Because Barton was able to identify each Ištar as Assur's wife, he established that these two goddesses were actually one: "We may hence infer that the myths connected with these two Ištars were the same."[18] Conversely, he found that Ištar-of-Arbela had her own mythology and familial relationships that he interpreted as contradicting those of Ištar-of-Nineveh/Assyrian-Ištar. Because she had no known consort, he tentatively recognized her as a deity distinct from Ištar-of-Nineveh/Assyrian Ištar.[19] His conclusion that Ištar-of-Arbela was distinct from Ištar-of-Nineveh/Assyrian-

---

14 Barton, "Semitic Ištar Cult," (1893): 136; see also RIMA 2 A.0.101.1 i 70: *ina qi*$_2$*-bit aš-šur* ^{d}INANNA DINGIR^{meš} GAL^{meš} EN^{meš}*-ia* TA ^{uru}*ni-nu-a at-tu-muš*, "By the command of Assur (and) Ištar, the great gods, my lords, I departed from Nineveh."

15 Barton, "Semitic Ištar Cult," (1893): 138–139.

16 Barton, "Semitic Ištar Cult," (1893): 152. Barton noted that Ištar-of-Nineveh was already "classed with Aššur as one of the two first gods of the land" (ibid., 151–152) when she first reappeared in Assurnāṣirpal II's annals, but it was Sennacherib who first described her as a chief deity.

17 Because Barton recognized Assur as the capital of Assyria between 1800 and 885, he considered any unspecified reference to Ištar from this period as a reference to Assyrian-Ištar (Barton, "Semitic Ištar Cult," [1893]: 151).

18 Barton, "Semitic Ištar Cult," (1893): 158.

19 Barton, "Semitic Ištar Cult," (1893): 165. Barton noted that Ištar-of-Uruk was the daughter of Anu and Antu, whereas Ištar-of-Nineveh and Ištar-of-Arbela were identified as the daughters of Sîn and Assur, respectively (Barton, "Semitic Ištar Cult (Continued)," [1894]: 14). Barton did not use this distinct parentage to distinguish Ištar-of-Uruk from Ištar-of-Nineveh. Instead, he had already identified the two goddesses because he found mythological texts discussing the city of Uruk in Assurbanipal's library in Nineveh. To correct for the distinctive parentage for one goddess, Barton concluded that the newer, Ninevite goddess was borrowed from the older Ištar cult in Uruk, and her divine heritage was modified accordingly (Barton, "Semitic Ištar Cult," (1893): 154; and Barton, "Semitic Ištar Cult (Continued)," [1894]: 68).

Ištar was also based on her relatively late appearance in the Assyrian texts because the earliest text that was available to Barton with the name Ištar-of-Arbela was from Sennacherib's reign. However, in his second article, Barton offhandedly indicated that Ištar-of-Nineveh/Assyrian-Ištar and Ištar-of-Arbela were actually the same Ištar: "*She* (Ištar) is called, moreover, the subjugator, indicating that among them *she* was, in one of her phases at least, a goddess of war, as *she* was at Nineveh, Arbela, and Erech (Uruk)."[20] Indeed, throughout his second essay, Barton used the name Ištar generically, indicating that he had actually equated each localized Ištar goddess with the others, despite the conclusions reached in the previous article.

Elsewhere in the second installment of his essay, Barton examined the goddess Ištar-of-Babylon, whose antiquity was indicated by a hymn that he dated to ca. 2000.[21] In this hymn, Ištar-of-Babylon was a mother goddess who was merciful to those who appealed to her in times of stress, and it was this particular Ištar goddess whom Barton identified with the planet Venus.[22] Based on the actions and epithets attributed to Ištar-of-Babylon, he first concluded that this hymn portrayed a distinct Ištar from Ištar-of-Nineveh. However, in the same way that he revised his initial assessment that Ištar-of-Arbela was distinct from Ištar-of-Nineveh, he reversed his decision to interpret Ištar-of-Babylon as a unique and distinct Ištar goddess. He did this by introducing yet another equation: Ištar-of-Babylon was Zarpānītu, who was really Ištar-of-Nineveh:

> When we remember that Zarpanit was a mother goddess, and that as the wife of Marduk, the chief Babylonian deity, she occupied the same position in Babylon that Ištar did at Nineveh, the conclusion cannot be escaped that Ištar and Zarpanit were one.[23]

Curiously, he never explicitly claimed that Ištar-of-Babylon and Ištar-of-Nineveh were one. Zarpānītu was Marduk's spouse in various texts, and Ištar-of-Babylon was his paramour in others, so Barton concluded that the name Zarpānītu was an epithet for Ištar-of-Babylon.[24] Rather than allow for the

---

20 Barton, "Semitic Ištar Cult," (1893): 164; and Barton, "Semitic Ištar Cult (Continued)," (1894): 27 (emphasis mine).

21 Barton, "Semitic Ištar Cult (Continued)," (1894): 15.

22 Barton, "Semitic Ištar Cult (Continued)," (1894): 22. Barton credited Babylon and its astrological reputation for associating Ištar-of-Babylon with Venus.

23 Barton, "Semitic Ištar Cult (Continued)," (1894): 21.

24 Barton, "Semitic Ištar Cult (Continued)," (1894): 22. Furthermore, the fact that he concluded that Ištar-of-Babylon and Zarpānītu were one is all the more surprising given that he knew of other texts wherein Zarpānītu and Nanaya, whom he also equated with Ištar(-of-Babylon), were asked to intercede with Ištar on the supplicant's behalf. See now Andrew R. George, *Babylonian Topographical Texts*, OLA 40 (Leuven: Department Orientalistiek, 1992), 411, where he discusses the equation of Lady(Ištar)-of-Babylon with Zarpānītu.

possibility that Marduk had two consorts, Barton equated the two goddesses. As the quote above indicates, he also recognized another commonality between Ištar-of-Babylon and Ištar-of-Nineveh: both were the spouse of the local chief deity. Although he never explicitly said that Ištar-of-Nineveh was Ištar-of-Babylon, the fact that the former was the wife of the Assyrian chief deity and the latter was the wife of the Babylonian chief deity still managed to serve as compelling evidence that the two goddesses were the same.[25]

In addition to his willingness to backtrack previous conclusions because of shared paramours and attributes, Barton's diachronic analysis of the Ištar goddesses is problematic because of his willingness to draw conclusions from limited evidence. He equated distinct goddesses (or distinct divine names) with each other even when one text was from the late third-millennium (according to his own chronology) and another was from the middle of the first millennium. This might have seemed necessary to him given the relatively sparse material available to him in his day, but this tactic – drawing conclusions about a deity by borrowing from texts representing multiple periods and provenances – skewed his results. Diachronic studies of deities are helpful and necessary because they can provide reconstructed personalities and cultic histories, but the additional information that diachronic studies provide can confound results if scholars expect a uniform treatment of a deity or a divine name by its devotees over the millennia, as Barton did.

1.2 Toward Minimizing Multiplicity

Barton's willingness to recognize different divine names as representing the same deity (e.g., Zarpānītu was Ištar-of-Babylon, whom, incidentally, he also identified with Nanaya) and to identify various goddesses named Ištar with one another has not been limited to the early days of Assyriology. Influential scholars of the late twentieth and early twenty-first centuries have also demonstrated a tendency to identify multiple divine names with a particular deity, especially when the divine first names match, as is the case with the various localized Ištar names. In some instances, this tendency is the product of the scholar's desire to retroject theological speculations from a later period

25 Barton, "Semitic Ištar Cult," (1893): 151–152. Curiously, the fact that the celebrated fifth-century historian Herodotus mentioned that Ištar was called Μύλιττα (= Mullissu) at Babylon was not part of Barton's decision to equate Ištar-of-Babylon with Ištar-of-Nineveh (Barton, "Semitic Ištar Cult (Continued)," [1894]: 22). Instead, Barton identified Herodotus' Mullissu with Assyrian-Mulittu, or Assyrian-Mullissu.

onto earlier periods. Often, this occurs when two or more deities are identified in first-millennium texts and the equation is assumed to be meaningful in early second-millennium Akkadian texts or even third-millennium Sumerian texts. Other times, this desire to equate deities results because scholars view the history of Mesopotamian religion as part of a larger progression from a collection of unorganized village- or city-based pantheons to a monotheistic, or nearly monotheistic, imperialistic or supra-regional pantheon. Of course, when scholars blatantly overstate their case for the identification of any or all deities, there is usually an appropriate amount of resistance to the conclusions, but often the more subtle identifications and equations are left unchallenged, or accepted.

In his 1975 article, "The Historical Development of the Mesopotamian Pantheon: A Study in Sophisticated Polytheism,"[26] Wilfred G. Lambert first summarized how the gods revered in various Sumerian villages and cities were organized into a regional pantheon to avoid redundancy and to reduce the overall number of potential deities in southern Mesopotamia. It was during this early period, for example, that the Sumerian deities Ninurta (of Nippur) and Ningirsu (of Girsu) were identified with each other because they were both considered the son of Enlil and shared other common characteristics.[27] Believing that that these two gods had been identified with each other at such an early stage in Mesopotamian history, he concluded that Ninurta and Ningirsu had always been (or should have always been) identified as the same deity in the Sumerian mind. Because the divine name Ningirsu means "Lord of Girsu" in Sumerian, Lambert suggested that the name Ningirsu might have represented a localized title or epithet for the god Ninurta in the city of Girsu, which is, of course, entirely plausible. Of particular interest to us and our multiplicity-of-Ištar topic, when Lambert considered the possibility that Ninurta and Ningirsu had always represented a singular deity, he used the Ištars of Nineveh and Arbela as an analogy: "Either the two were always understood to be one, like Ištar of Nineveh and Ištar of Arbela from Assyria, or their equating results from taking an overall view of the pantheon and identifying similar gods."[28] Effectively, Lambert declared that Ištar-of-Nineveh had always been the same goddess as Ištar-of-Arbela. He revived this declara-

26 W. G. Lambert, "The Historical Development of the Mesopotamian Pantheon: A Study in Sophisticated Polytheism," in *Unity and Diversity: Essays in the history, literature, and religion of the ancient Near East*, eds. H. Goedicke and J. J. M. Roberts (Baltimore: Johns Hopkins University Press, 1975), 191–200.
27 Lambert, "Historical Development," 193.
28 Lambert, "Historical Development," 193.

tion three decades later at the *49th Rencontre Assyriologique Internationale* – the same conference where Porter presented her paper on these two Ištar goddesses – when he noted that the two goddesses were addressed in the plural in *Assurbanipal's Hymn to the Ištars of Nineveh and Arbela* (SAA 3 3).[29] In his paper, "Ištar of Nineveh," he noted that the question of whether these divine names represent multiple goddesses or a single goddess should be asked, and he provided a handful of texts that seemed to distinguish them, but he never actually attempted to answer the question. If asked for a definitive answer, he might have allowed for their distinctiveness by the end of the Neo-Assyrian period, but he noted more than once that texts that address Ištar-of-Nineveh use "extravagant language which is not very informative in the matter which would have been of interest to us," which is to say that he did not consider Ištar-of-Nineveh distinct from other localized Ištar goddesses.[30]

Lambert also believed that the early reorganization of various local Sumerian gods into a regional pantheon inevitably led to the creation of the lexical god-list tradition in Mesopotamia. These lexical lists, he suggested, were used by ancient theologians, or scholar-scribes, to identify different divine names as representing an individual deity.[31] Lambert also offered the eventual creation of the so-called syncretistic hymns of praise as evidence for a restructuring of the Mesopotamian pantheon, but he recognized that the theological force behind these hymns had a limited audience, referring to them as a "harmless hyperbole."[32] Supposedly syncretistic in nature, these hymns provided the gods Marduk and Ninurta (and the goddess Nanaya) with alternative names that belonged to otherwise independent deities (see Tables 1.1–1.4) and made a first-millennium progression toward monotheism possible in Mesopotamia because these other divine names were identified with Marduk or Ninurta or were identified as specific aspects of them. For Lambert, the strongest evidence for this progression toward monotheism in Mesopotamia

---

29 W. G. Lambert, "Ištar of Nineveh," *Iraq* 66 (2004): 35. Unlike Porter, Lambert did not recognize the difference between Ištar-of-Nineveh as Assurbanipal's mother and Ištar-of-Arbela as the creator: "It deals mostly with the wonders worked by the two goddesses for Ashurbanipal and does not get involved in the characters of the deities, nor the question of how the two can both be his mother" (ibid., 37).

30 Lambert, "Ištar of Nineveh," 37.

31 Lambert, "Historical Development," 193. For example, he noted elsewhere that Ištar-of-Nineveh was one "in a long list of Ištars" listed in TCL 15 10, an early Old Babylonian lexical god list (Lambert, "Ishtar of Nineveh," 36).

32 "Hymns of praise to deities even say that there exists no other god than the one being addressed. This is not monotheism, but harmless hyperbole" (Lambert, "Historical Development," 194).

was the *Syncretistic Hymn to Marduk* (Erich Ebeling, *KAR* 25 ii 3–16) because numerous major deities were said to be mere attributes of Marduk (e.g., Anu is your royalty, l. 3; see Table 1.1).[33] Notably, Lambert recognized that this hymn was not fully monotheistic in nature because it still revered Marduk's wife Zarpānītu alongside him.[34]

To be fair, Lambert did distinguish the world of the syncretistic hymns, lexical god lists, and other theologically speculative texts that could be considered the products of scholar-scribes from the world of the larger lay population that he assumed was oblivious to these texts. With their limited audience, he doubted that any of the theological innovations (e.g., the statement that Šamaš should be identified with Marduk or reduced to being an aspect of Marduk) contained in such texts could have led to a "major public uproar."[35] Furthermore, he also assumed that these texts had little-to-no influence on cultic activities. Esoteric equations and the theologically speculative texts that contained them belonged to the scholar-scribes' world alone, even if Lambert believed that these scholar-scribes were the ones responsible for the inevitable progression toward monotheism.

Perhaps the most spirited discussion of emergent monotheism and, thus, the over-identification of various deities with one another in ancient Mesopotamia comes from Simo Parpola. Whereas most Assyriologists (including Lambert) accept that Assyrian religion was a polytheistic religion, Parpola has suggested that Assyrian religion was neither exclusively nor primarily polytheistic but "*essentially monotheistic*," and he argues that this is expressed especially well in the Neo-Assyrian period.[36] In a manner reminiscent of Lambert's interpretation of the *Syncretistic Hymn to Marduk*, Parpola views the numerous and varied divine names of the Assyrian deities as mere attributes of "*the only*

---

33 In 1997, Lambert revisited what he described in 1975 as the progression toward monotheism in Mesopotamian religion and surmised that the lay population in Mesopotamia was unaware of this monotheism. Lambert conceded that the identification of deities – or to use his phraseology, the "swallowing up" of one god by another – went on without expressed outrage from the public because these identifications likely did not change religious practice. Even though Šamaš is identified as another name or aspect of Marduk in the text, both the cults of Šamaš and Marduk continued their rituals as they had before its composition (Wilfred G. Lambert, "Syncretism and Religious Controversy in Babylonia," AoF 24 [1997]: 159).

34 Lambert, "Historical Development," 198.

35 Lambert, "Syncretism," 159.

36 Simo Parpola, "Monotheism in Ancient Assyria," in *One God or Many? Concepts of Divinity in the Ancient World*, ed. Barbara N. Porter, Transactions of the Casco Bay Assyriological Institute 1 (Casco Bay Assyriological Institute, 2000), 165 (italics in the original); and Simo Parpola, *Assyrian Prophecies*, SAA 9 (Helsinki: Helsinki University Press, 1997), XIII–CXXI.

true God," whom he interprets to be a transcendent entity.[37] In contrast to Lambert, Parpola argues that this monotheistic tendency was not limited to the theological speculations of an elite priestly group or scholar-scribes; instead, the transcendent Assur was recognized as an imperial and universal deity by most of the lay Assyrian population and by Assyria's vassals and their people.[38] Furthermore, for Parpola, the Akkadian phrases "the great gods" (*ilānū rabûtu* or DINGIR^{meš} GAL^{meš}) and "Assur and the great gods," along with several other variations, can even be understood as references to the monotheistic god Assur.

Parpola's assumptions and claims have been rightly challenged more than once,[39] but our present concern revolves less around his retrojecting the origins of Jewish and Christian mysticism into the eighth century B.C.E. and more around his interest in identifying, equating, or otherwise reducing divine multiplicity. By treating each divine name as a manifestation of the same single deity, Parpola leaves no room to concern himself with the distinction between Ištar-of-Nineveh, Ištar-of-Arbela, or any other potentially localized Ištar goddess. Even though the prophets who delivered the oracles collected in *Assyrian Prophecies* (SAA 9; the same volume in which he lays out his argument for a singular transcendent Assur) attributed their messages to more than one divine name (see chapter 4.5), Parpola considers all of them the same goddess: "Irrespective of her mythological role, the most common notions attached to Ištar (and other goddesses equated with her) in Mesopotamian texts are purity, chastity, prudence, wisdom and beauty."[40] Again, all of these goddesses who are really Ištar are also the god Assur: "Ištar, who in oracles addresses the king as her child, is *Aššur revealed in his mother aspect.*"[41]

37 Parpola, "Monotheism," 166 (italics in the original).
38 Parpola suggests that evidence of this can be found within the credo of the Esarhaddon's Succession Treaty (SAA 2 6:393–394): "in the future and forever Aššur shall be your god, and Assurbanipal shall be your lord," which he argues is drastically similar in tone to the Islamic credo, "There is no god except Allah, and Muhammad is his envoy" (Parpola, "Monotheism," 167).
39 Jerrold Cooper notes that Parpola is overly excited throughout his earlier essays on the subject and that he fails to notice his need to read the tenets of these later religions back into Assyrian religious thought (Jerrold S. Cooper, "Assyrian Prophecies, the Assyrian Tree, and the Mesopotamian Origins of Jewish Monotheism, Greek Philosophy, Christian Theology, Gnosticism, and Much More," *JAOS* 120 [2000]: 440–442). For another critique of Parpola's conjectures, see also Eckart Frahm, "Wie „christlich“ war die assyrische Religion? Anmerkungen zu Simo Parpolas Edition der assyrischen Prophetien," *WdO* 31 (2000/2001): 31–45.
40 Parpola, *Assyrian Prophecies*, XXIX.
41 Parpola, *Assyrian Prophecies*, XXVI (all emphasis in the original).

Parpola's musings on Ištar as a precursor to Jewish, Christian, and Gnostic mysticism have not been embraced by the larger Assyriological community, but the identification of one Ištar goddess with another is not among the problems discussed regarding Parpola's theories.

For reasons completely different from Lambert's interest in the Mesopotamian progression toward monotheism and Parpola's belief that this progression was completed during the Neo-Assyrian period, Amar Annus unapologetically telescopes numerous divine personalities from different regions, periods, and mythologies in order to create a synthesis of a divine being that Mesopotamian believers worshipped as "the abstract object" Ninurta.[42] In his study of the god Ninurta, Annus boldly states that his:

> methodology includes philology in the largest sense; the presentation tries to be descriptive and synthetic. There are many problems in dealing with Ninurta because his identity is fluid. *I think that the author must look for the divine personality itself and not care about names.* Ninurta is actually one name of the deity sharing many attributes with other Mesopotamian gods: both Nanna/Sin and Ninurta/Ningirsu are first-born sons of Enlil endowed with kingship ... Ninurta shares with the weather gods Iškur/Adad his thunderous weapons ... *He is identical with* Nabu as the divine scribe and holder of the tablets of destinies, with Nergal he shares his strength, with Šamaš his position as divine judge. (emphasis mine)[43]

He treats Ninurta this way because he perceives the deity's fluid nature. Because he looks too closely at the similarities within his collection of deities, he loses the distinction between them, and they become nothing more than generic deities. In his search for a divine personality, he creates a numinous caricature built from interchangeable gods. For instance, because the god of war and farming in the *Lugal-e* Epic is Enlil's son, he is the moon-god Nanna/Sîn, who is Enlil's first-born in the *Enlil and Ninlil* myth. Also, when Ninurta retrieves the Tablet of Destinies on behalf of his father Enlil, he is Nabû who holds the tablet as the scribe and son of the Babylonian chief deity Marduk.

---

42 Amar Annus, *The God Ninurta in the Mythology and Royal Ideology of Ancient Mesopotamia*, SAAS 14 (Helsinki: Neo-Assyrian Text Corpus Project: 2002), 2.

43 Annus, *Ninurta*, 4. It is noteworthy that Annus refers to his methodology as philological "in the largest sense," both descriptive and synthetic, which produces a methodology that ultimately concludes that Ninurta "is identical with Nabu" (ibid., 4). Elsewhere, he concludes that Ninurta's loss in popularity coincides with the rise of Nabû within the divine hierarchy (ibid., 46–47). That one deity's rise could occur at the expense of another should be conceptually antithetical to the identification of the two gods. However, because he focuses on "the divine figure behind all these names" (i.e., Ninurta, Nabû, Adad, Nergal, and Zababa) that "persevered unchanged" instead of on the gods themselves (ibid., 46–47), Annus is able to distinguish the deities while simultaneously equating them.

While previous scholars, such as Lambert and Jerrold Cooper, have identified Ninurta with Ningirsu as a matter of fact,[44] there is a significant difference between identifying two (or even three) gods who share many similar attributes and a common divine lineage and identifying one god with other gods because of a shared attribute. The former practice is at least native to Mesopotamia, as with the Ninurta-Ningirsu example. Annus's willingness to identify multiple gods with one another because of one or two similar characteristics, however, is an intentional exaggeration of native Mesopotamian speculative theology. Moreover, it suggests that he would interpret the two divine epithets in *Assurbanipal's Hymn to the Ištars of Nineveh and Arbela* (SAA 3 3), namely, Lady-of-Nineveh and Lady-of-Arbela, as representative of a singular Ištar goddess, despite the hymn's morphology and syntax. It was precisely this climate of scholarship, as represented by Annus and Parpola (and to a lesser extent Barton and Lambert), wherein distinct divine names or epithets could be used to identify deities with one another, to which Porter responded in her 2004 article about the separate and distinct localized Ištar goddesses.

However, despite Porter's article, this climate of reducing divine multiplicity continues. Employing a geography-based methodology reminiscent of Barton's, Ilona Zsolnay has recently identified Ištars according to their non-geographic epithets and mapped the provenience of the texts containing those epithets. In doing so, she has isolated three Ištar epithets from royal inscriptions: 1) *bēlet qabli u tāḫāzi* (Sovereign-of-Combat-and-Battle), the Ištar who led the king's army, provided him with weapons, and associated with Assur, Adad, and Ninurta; 2) *bēlet šamê u erṣeti* (Sovereign-of-Heaven-and-Earth), the Ištar who commanded the king in battle and associated with Assur, Enlil, Šamaš, and Adad as they cooperatively led the king's army; and 3) *bēlet ninua* (Sovereign-of-Nineveh), the Ištar who resembled *bēlet šamê u erṣeti* but acted alone or only with Assur.[45] Elsewhere, she recognizes that there were "no fewer than eight active manifestations for Ištar," each with her own specific region, associated deities, and typical activities: (the unspecified)

44 See, for example, Jerrold S. Cooper, *The Return of Ninurta to Nippur*: an-gim dím-ma (AnOr 52; Rome: Pontificium Institutum Biblicum, 1978); and W. G. Lambert, "Ancient Mesopotamian Gods: Superstition, Philosophy, Theology," *Révue de l'histoire religions* 207 (1990): 120. Lambert also includes Zababa in this equation because all three are referred to as the chief son of Enlil.

45 Zsolnay's translations have been retained here for these titles but have been modified to fit the epithet formatting used throughout my study (Ilona Zsolnay, "The Function of Ištar in the Assyrian Royal Inscriptions: A Contextual Analysis of the Actions Attributed to Ištar in the Inscriptions of Ititi through Šalmaneser III" [Ph.D. diss., Brandeis University, 2009], 85).

Ištar, Ištar//*bēlet-Ninua*, Ištar//*bēlet-tāḫāzi*, Dinītu, Ištar//*bēlet-qabli-u-tāḫāzi*, Ištar//*bēlet-šamê-u-erṣeti*, Ištar//*bēlet-tēšê*, and *Šarrat-Niphi*.[46] Despite delineating the geographic and chronological boundaries for these different epithets, Zsolnay ultimately concludes that all of them were aspects of a singular Ištar goddess: "each of these designations represents a different manifestation of the goddess."[47] For Zsolnay, the epithets and their associated characteristics definitely served to highlight what populations from different regions thought of the ethereal (i.e., non-tangible) Ištar, but she ultimately dismisses the possibility that these manifestations represent distinct localized Ištar goddesses.

Although we might not connect him directly with Barton and his methodologies, but more with Lambert, Parpola, and Annus, a final voice for consideration that has been making itself heard in numerous discussions of divine multiplicity in ancient Assyria and the rest of the Near East belongs to Benjamin Sommer.[48] Sommer argues for the distinctiveness of divine manifestations – be they multiple Adad deities, multiple Baal deities, multiple Ištar goddesses, or deities associated with other first names – but like Zsolnay and many others, he ends up concluding that there was really only one deity who was represented by the various divine-first-and-last-name combinations. He acknowledges and follows Porter's treatment of Ištar-of-Nineveh and Ištar-of-Arbela as they cooperatively but independently acted as Assurbanipal's mother and nurse, but Sommer still concludes that these two Ištars were the same Ištar: "she appears fragmented – not self-contradictory, but manifesting herself as separate beings in separate places."[49] He stresses that his observed fragmentation is not the result of an overly-simplistic diachronic study or the syncretization of localized goddesses into one Ištar; rather, it is the nature of Assyrian and other Near Eastern deities to exert their "fluidity" into "discrete conscious" selves so that "a single deity could exist simultaneously in several bodies."[50] For Sommer, a divine attribute that distinguished the ancient Near Eastern deity from human beings was the fact that the deity could be present in several places at the same moment, pouring, as it were, some of its essence

46 Zsolnay, "Function of Ištar," 211. Two parallel lines (//) are used here and elsewhere to indicate that a proper name and epithet are acting together with the force of a single full name (e.g., Ištar//Lady-of-Nineveh).
47 Zsolnay, "Function of Ištar," 209.
48 Benjamin Sommer, *The Bodies of God and the World of Ancient Israel* (Cambridge: Cambridge University Press, 2009).
49 Sommer, *Bodies of God*, 14–15.
50 Sommer, *Bodies of God*, 12.

into a particular physical manifestation.[51] There was no one-to-one correspondence because the deity was too great to be contained in any statue: "the *ṣalmu* ('image') was a body of the god, but it did not exhaust that god's being; it was itself a god, assimilated into the heavenly god yet physically a distinct thing."[52] Thus, a singular deity's multiple bodies – or multiple localized full names – demonstrated not the limits of the deity but the limits of the Mesopotamians' ability to express their experience of the divine.[53]

Admittedly, Sommer's brief discussion of Near Eastern deities only serves as an introduction to his main topic, the bodies of the God in the Hebrew Bible and later interpretative traditions that dealt with the biblical data. Because his analysis reveals a bias for monotheistic traditions over polytheistic ones – as did Lambert's and, even more so, Parpola's bias – the more glaring problem is that Sommer willingly and simultaneously recognizes distinct forms of a particular deity (typically Ištar and, to a lesser extent, Baal) and uses those distinct forms to lead him into a discussion of one singular deity by that name. (His discussion on the singular nature of different Greek deities, however, is worthwhile because the Classical concept of divinity more closely fits his paradigm than do the Mesopotamian and Levantine concepts.[54])

1.3 Toward Maximizing Multiplicity

If Barton's early conclusions have influenced subsequent scholars to recognize distinct divine names and epithets as representing a singular deity (e.g., the divine name Zarpānītu is an epithet of Ištar), the interest he simultaneously displayed in examining individual names and epithets and the methodologies that he employed to study them have also inspired continued interest in divine identities. Indeed, there have been several attempts over the past thirty years aiming to understand the divine names behind Ištar and other goddesses from the ancient Near Eastern world. Notable among these are Ilse Wegner's *Gestalt und Kult der Ištar-Šawuška in Kleinasien*, Gary Beckman's article "Ištar of Nineveh Reconsidered," and Weibke Meinhold's *Ištar in Assur: Untersuchung eines Lokalkultes von ca. 2500 bis 614 v. Chr.*, each of which analyze specific

51 Sommer, *Bodies of God*, 24.
52 Sommer, *Bodies of God*, 23.
53 Sommer, *Bodies of God*, 36.
54 Sommer, *Bodies of God*, 30–36.

regions or cities and the related localized Ištar goddesses.[55] Moreover, studies about Ištar goddesses in the Babylonian world or any particular Babylonian city, such as Paul-Alain Beaulieu's valuable *The Pantheon of Uruk During the Neo-Babylonian Period* – which, despite its name, provides an excellent survey of the deities revered in and around Uruk from the fourth millennium into the first millennium – and Jennie Myers' "The Pantheon of Sippar: A Diachronic Study," are welcome contributions to the development of localized Ištar goddesses.[56]

Indeed, the real significance and benefit of Barton's studies lie in the groundwork he laid with his methodologies. While the studies by Wegner, Beckman, and Meinhold depend less on the potential link between a king's capital city and the nearest Ištar than did Barton's, they all lean on his central premise that an otherwise unspecified Ištar could be identified as the localized Ištar, especially when the localized Ištar has a cultic presence in that city and a strong association with her geographic epithet. For example, Wegner briefly uses Barton's methodology when she suggests that Assyrian-Ištar ("assyrischen Ištar") should be identified with the Hittite goddess Ištar- or Šaušga-of-Šamuḫa.[57] Unless she is using "assyrischen Ištar" as a reference to *any* Ištar cult in Assyria, rather than the specific localized goddess typically identified as ^{d}Ištar *aš-šu*$_{(2)}$*-ri-tu* in the cuneiform, Wegner bases this choice

---

55 Ilse Wegner, *Gestalt und Kult der Ištar-Šawuška in Kleinasien*, AOAT 36 (Kevelaer: Butzon und Bercker, 1981); Gary Beckman, "Ištar of Nineveh Reconsidered," *JCS* 50 (1998): 1–10; and Meinhold, *Ištar in Aššur*.

56 Paul-Alain Beaulieu, *The Pantheon of Uruk During the Neo-Babylonian Period*, Cuneiform Monographs 23 (Leiden: Brill, 2003); and Jennie Myers, "The Pantheon at Sippar: A Diachronic Study" (Ph.D. diss., Harvard University, 2002). When discussing offerings at the temple, Beaulieu carefully distinguishes each entity from the others as receiving offerings; however, regarding the relationship between Inanna/Ištar, Nanaya, and other goddesses, he displays syncretistic tendencies. For instance, Beaulieu states that Inanna/Ištar's identification with Nanaya "was a basic tenet of Babylonian theology from very early times. There are very few hymns to Nanaya from the late periods which do not contain at least some trace of it" (ibid., 186–187). This tenet is then revealed in first-millennium poetry, which usually includes syncretistic tendencies. Along with late copies of hymnal and liturgical traditions, the *Hymn of Nanâ*, the *Hymn to the City of Arbela*, and the *Hymn in Praise of Uruk* suggest that Nanaya was a form of Ištar (see Erica Reiner, "A Sumero-Akkadian Hymn of Nanâ," *JNES* 33 [1974]: 221–236; and SAA 3 3, 8, and 9). Beaulieu also mentions a possible identification of Nanaya with Urkittu in the *Nanaya Hymn of Assurbanipal* (SAA 3 5), which "seems to equate her with Urkittu (i.e., Urkayītu)," if Urkittu is best interpreted as an epithet there (Beaulieu, *Pantheon of Uruk*, 187 and n. 56). Despite this ancient identification, Beaulieu says elsewhere that Nanaya was "second only to Ištar in the local divine hierarchy" of first-millennium Uruk, appearing alongside her in legal documents and official correspondence (ibid., 187).

57 Wegner, *Gestalt und Kult*, 160.

upon the idea that the Assyrian merchants worshipped their familiar Ištar who hailed from Assur. Likewise, Beckman applies a form of this methodology in his analysis of early second-millennium Ištars when he suggests that these same Assyrian traders at Kaneš worshipped specifically the goddess known as Assyrian-Ištar. Because his survey of second-millennium Ištars revealed that "we have no indication that Ištar of Aššur (i.e., Assyrian-Ištar) was ever called Šaušga (i.e., the Hurrian and Hittite equivalent to the Akkadian word Ištar)," he concludes that any inscription from the Kaneš corpus that addresses a deity as Ištar or Šaušga must "refer to the goddess of the political capital" (i.e., Assyrian-Ištar in Assur) and not Ištar- or Šaušga-of-Nineveh.[58] Thus, Beckman recognizes that these ancient Assyrians did not identify Ištar-of-Nineveh with Assyrian-Ištar.

More recently, Meinhold applied a form of Barton's methodology and suggested that any unspecified Ištar found in second-millennium Assyrian texts should be identified with Assyrian-Ištar. After all, Assyrian-Ištar was from the capital city.[59] Meinhold also notes that during the seventh century, when Nineveh was the Assyrian capital, Ištar-of-Nineveh was increasingly recognized as Assur's wife Mullissu.[60] This seventh-century identification of Ištar-of-Nineveh with Mullissu was a limited phenomenon, meaning that only those people living in Nineveh (and perhaps those who lacked a localized Ištar of their own) would have identified Ištar-of-Nineveh with Mullissu.[61] By the same token, Meinhold concludes that the residents of Arbela likely identified Ištar-of-Arbela with Assur's consort Mullissu. Ištar-of-Arbela was the wife of Assur in Arbela because the identification of Ištar-of-Nineveh with Mullissu did not interfere with the local Arbelite identification of Ištar-of-Arbela with Mullissu. Although no texts explicitly refer to Ištar-of-Arbela as the wife or beloved of Assur, the fact that Meinhold explores the equation of localized and distinct Ištar goddesses with another goddess itself suggests that Meinhold entertains the idea that Ištar-of-Nineveh and Ištar-of-Arbela were conceived of as distinct and separate goddesses in the Neo-Assyrian period.[62]

---

58 Beckman, "Ištar of Nineveh," 2 n. 21. Wegner's position that Assyrian-Ištar is Šaušga-of-Šamuḫa need not be in conflict with Beckman's comment that Assyrian-Ištar is nowhere identified with Šaušga because Beckman is specifically referring to Ištar-of-Nineveh when he discusses Šaušga. Notably, Wegner does not supply any references to link the two goddesses; her theory seems to be one of speculation.

59 Meinhold, *Ištar in Aššur*, 183 f.

60 Meinhold, *Ištar in Aššur*, 203 f.

61 Meinhold, *Ištar in Aššur*, 202.

62 In contrast, Pongratz-Leisten observes, "The equation of Mullissu with an Ištar hypostasis is restricted to the figure of Ištar of Nineveh who indeed might be addressed as 'the mother who bore me' (*umma alittīja*)" (Beate Pongratz-Leisten, "When the Gods are Speaking: Toward

Like Meinhold, Beate Pongratz-Leisten considers the possibility that localized Ištar goddesses coexisted as distinct deities, but her interest focuses on the supra-regional status of the deities representing distinct ethno-linguistic entities. She brings up the topic of Ištars as part of her larger discussion linking patron deities to their cities:

> This close association between city and patron deity implied that in ancient Near Eastern religions the local hypostases of a particular deity, when venerated in another city, did not necessarily merge with the respective deity of the local cult of that particular city. This is the case with the various hypostases of Ishtar as, for instance, in the cult of Assur, where she was venerated as Ištar-Aššurītu, Ištar-Anunītu (originally from Akkade), Bēlate-ekalli, Šarrat-nipha (Queen-of-the-Rising-Star), and Ištar-ša-Ninua (Ishtar-of-Nineveh). All these goddesses had their own sanctuaries and their own groups of deities with which they were associated in the city of Assur.[63]

Of these mentioned Ištar hypostases, she is especially interested in Ištar-of-Nineveh and the fact that this goddess could be venerated in a different region while retaining the geographic epithet "-of-Nineveh." She notes that worship of this specific goddess was incorporated into the Hittite cultic system in Ḫatti because Ištar-of-Nineveh could not be identified with another goddess, or as Pongratz-Leisten puts it, Ištar-of-Nineveh "possessed specific and non-transferrable power, which could not be substituted by another divinity."[64] The unique set of rituals and divine associations back home in Nineveh, as well as the political and ethno-linguistic barriers that separated the Hurrians and Hittites from the Assyrians in the second millennium, meant that the Assyrian entity known as Ištar-of-Nineveh could not be fused with any particular Hittite divine personalities or did not closely resemble any already known Ištar/Šaušga goddess in Ḫatti.[65] Concluding her case study of Ištar-of-Nineveh as a foreign goddesses revered in Ḫatti, Pongratz-Leisten comments that more research on these localized Ištar goddesses and other localized divine personalities needs to be conducted.[66]

Defining the Interface between Polytheism and Monotheism," in *Propheten in Mari, Assyrien und Israel*, ed. Matthias Köckert and Martti Nissinen, FRLANT 201 [Göttingen: Vandenhoeck & Ruprecht, 2003], 166.

63 Beate Pongratz-Leisten, "Comments on the Translatability of Divinity: Cultic and Theological Responses to the Presence of the Other in the Ancient Near East," in *Les représentations des dieux autres*, eds. Corinne Bonnet, Amandine Declercq, and Iwo Slobodzianek, Supplemento a Mythos 2. Rivista di Storia delle Religioni (Caltanisseta: Salvatore Sciascia Editore, 2012), 90.

64 Pongratz-Leisten, "Comments on the Translatability," 93.

65 Pongratz-Leisten, "Comments on the Translatability," 102.

66 Pongratz-Leisten, "Comments on the Translatability," 93.

JoAnn Scurlock's analysis of Ištar goddesses, based on texts compiled in the Diagnostic and Prognostic Series (DPS), also follows Barton's methodology in that she examines the mythical familial relationships of a given localized Ištar in much the same manner as Barton had when he determined whether to distinguish individual Ištars.[67] Barton initially insisted that Ištar-of-Arbela was not Ištar-of-Nineveh because the former was the daughter of Assur, whereas the latter was Assur's spouse. Likewise, he argued that Ištar-of-Nineveh was Assyrian-Ištar because both goddesses were Assur's wife. Similarly, Scurlock distinguishes Ištar-of-Ḫarrān, the daughter of Sîn, from Assyrian-Ištar, the daughter of Assur, and from Ištar-of-Uruk, the daughter of Anu.[68]

Using each localized Ištar goddess's divine parentage, Scurlock examines each diagnosis-prognosis entry that mentions an unspecified Ištar and identifies other deities that are also associated with that disease. Then, she determines which city was most closely associated with those deities. For example, when one diagnosis-prognosis pairing in the DPS blames Ištar for fevers and skin lesions, Scurlock concludes that this Ištar must have been Ištar-of-Ḫarrān because her father Sîn and brother Šamaš were also responsible for such ailments, and Sîn (or Moon-God) was the patron deity of Ḫarrān.[69] In other instances, another deity is explicitly mentioned within the same diagnosis with Ištar, or two different divine names appear as variants in different copies of a particular diagnosis, and Scurlock determines the relevant city and relevant localized Ištar goddess according to the other deity's patron city. Both of these can be illustrated by diagnoses invoking the divine names Marduk and Ištar:

> DIŠ NA *ina* KI.NA$_2$-*šu*$_2$ LUḪ.LUḪ-*ut* ŠA$_3$-*šu*$_2$ *e-šu-u ina* KI.NA$_3$-*šu*$_2$ *re-ḫu-su* DU-*ak* NA BI DIB-*ti* ^{d}AMAR.UTU *u* ^{d}EŠ$_4$.DAR UGU-*šu*$_2$ GAL$_3$-*ši ana* TI-*šu*$_2$
>
> If a person continually jerks in his bed, his heart (beat) is confused, (and) his semen flows in his bed, the anger of Marduk and Ištar is upon that person, to cure him(19.112 = *BAM* 205:12′–21′ / / *STT* 95:16–18 / / *STT* 280 ii 1–3, Scurlock's translation)

---

67 JoAnn Scurlock and Burton Andersen, *Diagnoses in Assyrian and Babylonian Medicine: Ancient Sources, Translations, and Modern Medical Analyses* (Urbana: University of Illinois Press, 2005).

68 Scurlock and Andersen, *Diagnoses*, 523. In addition to distinguishing these Ištars from one another because of their divine relationships, Scurlock also uses the nature of prognoses associated with both Ištar and other deities to distinguish potential Ištar goddesses (ibid., 488–481, 523 and 761 n. 319).

69 Scurlock and Andersen, *Diagnoses*, 488–491 and 523.

DIŠ *ina* SAG ŠA$_3$-*šu*$_2$ [*di-ik-šu*$_2$ GAR-*su-ma ur*]-*qa*$_2$ ŠUB-*a* ŠU ^{d}AMAR.UTU : ŠU ^{d}15 GAM

If [a needling pain is firmly established] in his upper abdomen (epigastrium) (and) he is unevenly colored with ⸢yellow spots⸣, "hand" of Marduk (var. "hand" of Ištar); he will die. (19.113 = DPS XIII B i 42′ / / F 4, Scurlock's translation)[70]

With Scurlock's methodology, because these diagnoses for sexually transmitted diseases link Marduk and Ištar, an explanation should be sought to explain this link. In this case, Scurlock suggests that Marduk and Ištar were paramours, which makes sense given the sexual nature of the disease, and because Marduk is most closely associated with Babylon, this means that the Ištar mentioned in this diagnosis-prognosis should be identified as Ištar-of-Babylon.[71]

Scurlock's methodology for locating these Ištars according to their acquaintance deities is appealing; however, any conclusions drawn from these results should remain tentative and be considered as secondary evidence when they complement conclusions already obtained from geographic and toponymic analyses of divine names.[72] Fortunately, because using the methodology that we lay out in chapters 3 and 4 reveals so much evidence to demonstrate that Ištar-of-Nineveh and Ištar-of-Arbela are distinct from each other and other Ištar goddesses, Scurlock's use of the DPS can, indeed, be used as supporting evidence for still another genre of text and group of scribes that distinguish between the goddesses.

1.4 Agency, Names, Offerings, and Rituals

On the one hand, the idea that any potential goddess referred to as Ištar should be identified with or equated to any other goddess named Ištar seems straight

70 Scurlock and Andersen, *Diagnoses*, 459.

71 Scurlock and Andersen, *Diagnoses*, 523 and 761 n. 319. Curiously, even though the DPS only mentions (the unspecified) Ištar and Arbilītu/Urbilītu, Scurlock notes that the *āšipu* (doctor-scribe) who collected these diagnoses assigned different diseases to particular Ištar goddesses. Assyrian-Ištar was never responsible for disease; Ištar-of-Ḫarrān was responsible for fevers and skin lesions; Ištar-of-Babylon, for sexually transmitted diseases; and Ištar-of-Uruk, for infantile spasms (Scurlock and Andersen, *Diagnoses*, 523).

72 For instance, Arbilītu/Urbilītu, which is likely another name for Ištar-of-Arbela (see chapter 4.4), is the only Ištar goddess specifically linked to a toponym in the DPS, and no other diagnostic statements explicitly associate another Ištar goddess with another city; only the name Ištar appears in a given diagnosis and prognosis entry.

Scurlock and Andersen provide a few instances from DPS (4.1 = 5.76, concerning venereal disease; 13.268, concerning peripheral neuropathy; 14.26 = 19.151, concerning abdominal wounds; and 19.155, concerning gangrene) in which the divine name Ištar is spelled ^{d}*dil-bat* –

forward, even axiomatic, especially given the long history of identifying and equating divine names and personalities with each other. After all, cursory readings of the various Akkadian myths only refer to one Ištar goddess, just as they refer to the one sky-god Anu and the one moon-god Sîn. Furthermore, each ancient community presumably recognized that the Ištar it worshipped and to whom it gave offerings at the local cult was the same goddess worshipped by other communities. On the other hand, while these ideas may seem axiomatic, several recent Assyriological studies have helped redefine our understanding of polytheistic notions of the divine and can be extrapolated to argue that localized Ištar goddesses were viewed as distinct deities in ancient Mesopotamia. Likewise, Thorkild Jacobsen observed that ancient myths did not reflect the theology of the lay population but the cultic reality of the priests and scholar-scribes, so we should be mindful that any conclusions that we draw from myths about the Mesopotamian gods are not necessarily reflective of every Mesopotamian's theological outlook.[73]

---

a reference to Ištar as the planet Venus – instead of the typical numeric spelling ^{d}15. The diseases associated with Dilbat are typical of diseases expected to be associated with an Ištar goddess as both a love goddess and warrior goddess.

73 One such example of an ancient myth that has been modified to reflect a newer cultic reality is the Sumerian myth *Inanna's Descent*. As a folk story, Inanna's Descent relates the story of Inanna's trip to strip her sister Ereškigal of her rule over the netherworld, and in her travels she strips herself naked to gain access. Inanna fails and is released only when Dumuzi and his sister Geštinanna are taken captive in her place, each spending half a year in the netherworld. According to Jacobsen, on the story's mythical level, Inanna's travels to the netherworld and her subsequent capture by Ereškigal, who hangs her up as a slab of meat, represents the fate of sheep: after the grass dies, they are shorn for their wool, and then they are butchered and left in cold storage (Thorkild Jacobsen, *The Harps that Once ... Sumerian Poetry in Translation* [New Haven: Yale University Press, 1987b], 205). Likewise, the second half of the myth explains the seasonal effects on livestock and agriculture: Dumuzi's reappearance from the netherworld each year represents the resurgence of sheep in the freshly grown grasslands in the spring, and Geštinanna's reappearance in autumn represents the culmination of the grape harvest.

The myth also works on a third level, the cultic one. At the beginning of the story as Inanna prepares to descend into the netherworld, she travels throughout the land of Sumer. First she goes to Uruk and forsakes her Eanna-temple. Then she goes to Bad-Tibira to forsake her Emuškalamma-temple; then to Zabalam and her Giguna-temple; then Adab and the Ešara-temple; then Nippur and her Ebaragdurgara-temple; then Kiši and her Hursagkalamma-temple; and finally Akkad and her Eulmaš-temple. These seven cities and their respective temples were the major Inanna cult centers, moving northward from Uruk (W. Leemans, *Ishtar of Lagaba and her Dress* [Studia ad tabulas cuneiformas collectas a F.M.Th. de Liagre Böhl pertinentia 1/1; Leiden: Brill, 1953], 32; and Jacobsen *Harps that Once*, 207 n. 2), and her travels reflect the goddess's cult-statue making its ritual journey from her primary temple in Uruk to Akkad and beyond to the mountains, which represent the netherworld (Stephanie Dalley,

These studies have challenged traditional understandings of polytheism in the ancient Near East because they reassess the nature of polytheistic divinity from the ground up rather than from the top down. Instead of using Assur, Marduk, and other famous Mesopotamian deities, whom we imagine as anthropomorphic in nature, and conforming our concept of divinity around them, these newer studies begin by asking the question "what is a god?" or, as Victor Hurowitz once challenged Mark S. Smith in Akkadian terminology, "what is an *ilu*?"[74] As many of these recent studies suggest, and what Hurowitz and Smith were entertaining with this question, ancient Mesopotamians considered an *ilu* an entity that could: intentionally impose its influence on the universe; possess its own unique name, which was preceded by a divine determinative; deserve food offerings and other gifts from humanity; and participate in cult and state rituals. Each of these definitions allows for the inclusion of localized Ištar goddesses, like Ištar-of-Nineveh and Ištar-of-Arbela.

Pongratz-Leisten has recently noted that historians of religion tend to over emphasize the role of specific gods in their examinations of polytheistic systems at the expense of a general understanding of the divine world.[75] All of the attention that scholars have focused on the major gods, who tend to be presented as anthropomorphic entities, has caused modern scholars both to misunderstand these deities' role in polytheistic religious systems and to exclude non-anthropomorphic entities from the divine realm. She also states that the establishment of order (i.e., the opposite of destruction and chaos) should be studied as the true focus of polytheistic systems, not specific deities.[76] By focusing on order as a concept, she concludes that the role and purpose of the deity was to help maintain the cosmic order. The gods are best understood as the universe's custodians rather than the universe's sovereigns,

---

Myths from Mesopotamia: Creation, The Flood, Gilgamesh, and Others [Oxford: Oxford University Press, 1998], 154; and G. Buccellati, "The Descent of Inanna as a Ritual Journey to Kutha?" Syro-Mesopotamian Studies 4 [1982]: 3–7). On this third level, when she removes her garments, jewelry, and makeup, her actions do not represent a "not taking it with you" attitude about death or the end of the shearing season; rather, the undressing and redressing mimics the actions of the priests taking off and later putting back on the cult-statue's refineries during various cultic ceremonies.

74 Mark S. Smith, *The Origins of Biblical Monotheism: Israel's Polytheistic Background and the Ugaritic Texts* (Oxford: Oxford University Press, 2001), 6.

75 Beate Pongratz-Leisten, "Divine Agency and Astralization of the Gods in Ancient Mesopotamia in *Reconsidering the Concept of Revolutionary Monotheism*, ed. Beate Pongratz-Leisten (Winona Lake: Eisenbrauns, 2011), 140.

76 Beate Pongratz-Leisten, "A New Agenda for the Study of the Rise of Monotheism," in *Reconsidering the Concept of Revolutionary Monotheism*, ed. Beate Pongratz-Leisten (Winona Lake: Eisenbrauns, 2011), 25.

or even its components. Instead of identifying gods as personifications of the natural world, gods should be viewed as the personalities responsible for maintaining the cosmic order in their respective realms.[77] For instance, rather than viewing the sun-god Šamaš as the actual sun that illuminates the world during the day, Pongratz-Leisten's approach to polytheism would define Šamaš as the intentional personality who controls the sun and, thereby, maintains the cosmic order by properly exercising this control. Likewise, the storm-god Adad is not in each storm as much as he intentionally uses his will to control the storms and maintain order here on earth. Of course, it would be going too far to suggest that the sun-god Šamaš simply was not the sun at all or that Adad was never in the storm, but her point is that the deities are more than what we consider the natural world; they also influence the movements of the natural world, but they still serve a higher purpose.

This modified understanding of polytheism also demands that we expand the concept of divinity beyond the traditional major gods to "all kinds of cultic paraphernalia, statues, symbols, and celestial bodies."[78] Although we might be inclined to suggest that these physical and inanimate objects lacked discernable personalities – especially compared to anthropomorphic deities known to us in various myths, hymns, and prayers[79] – these objects all played essential roles in maintaining order in the minds of ancient Mesopotamians. These roles might be markedly different from the roles attributed to the anthropomorphic deities, but Assyrian priests, kings, and the lay population believed that these roles were necessary. Even if these objects functioned primarily as mediators between the human world and the divine world or as boundary markers delineating the different realms of divine order, in doing so these cult objects demonstrated divine agency and, thereby, acted like gods.[80] Moreover, by applying a combined cognitive science and history of religions perspective on the concept of agency, Pongratz-Leisten provides the psycho-

77 Pongratz-Leisten, "Divine Agency," 144.
78 Pongratz-Leisten, "Divine Agency," 140.
79 Barbara N. Porter, "Introduction," in *What is a God? Anthropomorphic and Non-Anthropomorphic Aspects of Deity in Ancient Mesopotamia*, ed. Barbara N. Porter, Transactions of the Casco Bay Assyriological Institute 2 (Winona Lake: Casco Bay Assyriological Institute, 2009), 1. Like Pongratz-Leisten, Porter's own survey of modern treatments of Mesopotamia divinity concludes that Mesopotamian deities have been treated too anthropomorphically in scholarship, primarily because of modern interest in myths, hymns, and prayers. In contrast, Jean Bottéro explicitly states that to determine what a god can do, scholars should turn to hymns and prayers (Jean Bottéro, *Religion in Ancient Mesopotamia*, trans. T. L. Fagan [Chicago: University of Chicago, 2001], 59).
80 Pongratz-Leisten, "Divine Agency," 148.

logical drive behind this ancient desire to attribute agency to inanimate cult objects and explains that once human beings attribute agency to any inanimate object, they will subsequently attribute additional human properties to the object, such as intentionality or other humanlike behaviors. This is as true for ancient Mesopotamians as it is for twenty-first century scholars:

> Recent research in evolutionary biology, cognitive psychology, and cognitive religion has shown that the tendency to impute human attributes such as will, intention, agency, and responsiveness to inanimate entities is an abiding feature of human cognition ... [W]e intuitively assume that agents have minds.[81]

Thus, Pongratz-Leisten defines deity in the polytheistic systems of ancient Mesopotamia as entities that could act with intention. Form, function, size, and mobility are irrelevant to her definition of deity; agency is what counts.

Despite her new definition of divinity in the ancient Near East, Pongratz-Leisten still distinguishes the traditional major gods, the anthropomorphic ones (e.g., Assur and Marduk), from the gods constituting the cultic paraphernalia. She dubs the former gods "primary agents" and the latter "secondary agents," noting that the secondary agents tend to be more tangible than primary agents, but she notes that she makes this distinction more for the benefit of modern scholars than as a reflection of ancient theology.[82] She

---

81 Pongratz-Leisten, "Divine Agency," 145. According to Tremlin, "Agents are looked upon as much more than things that can move and instigate actions. Our knowledge of agents links physical casualty to *mental* causality" (Todd Tremlin, *Minds and Gods: The Cognitive Foundations of Religion* [New York: Oxford University Press, 2010], 68 [italics in the original]). Notably, neither Tremlin nor Pongratz-Leisten limit this willingness to attribute agency or other humanlike behaviors to inanimate objects to ancient Mesopotamians or polytheists in general; all humans, including modern Westerners, are susceptible to such projections.

82 Pongratz-Leisten, "Divine Agency," 146. Michael Hundley, who agrees that "inert non-anthropomorphic" objects should be recognized as deities, denies that cult objects possess "personality or agency" and instead focuses on the aura of potency and fear that they can inspire (Michael Hundley, "Here a God, There a God: An Examination of the Divine in Ancient Mesopotamia," AoF 40 [2013], 77). Hundley offers the example of a divinized cultic bed that received the same offerings that Assur, Nabû, and Marduk normally received: regular sheep offerings ($^{13'}$UD^{meš} *ša* ^{giš}NA$_2$ *ina* ŠA$_3$-*bi-ni* UDU.*da-ri-u*$_2$ $^{r.1}$*ina* IGI *i-na-su-hu*, SAA 1 55:13′-r. 1). In a previous letter by the same author, Ṭâb-šar-Assur mentioned that the bed would soon be set up in the temple and ceremonially decorated and washed, a custom also applied to the cult statues of the great gods (for a fuller discussion on this bed, see Barbara N. Porter, "Blessings from a Crown, Offerings to a Drum: Were There Non-Anthropomorphic Deities in Ancient Mesopotamia?" in *What is a God? Anthropomorphic and Non-Anthropomorphic Aspects of Deity in Ancient Mesopotamia*, ed. Barbara N. Porter, Transactions of the Casco Bay Assyriological Institute 2 [Winona Lake: Casco Bay Assyriological Institute, 2009], 192 f.). Hundley notes that people even feared the bed in the same way they feared the god to whom the bed belongs (Hundley, "Here a God," 77; and Porter, "Blessings," 193).

contends that the secondary agents are distinct from the primary agents, but she also admits that "a supplicant might have blurred the distinction in the past, just as in modern times."[83] Not only did these inanimate deities, or cult objects or secondary agents, express their divinity to the Mesopotamian population by intentionally demonstrating their ability to help maintain cosmic order, the Mesopotamians reciprocated by treating them in the same manner they treated the traditional major gods, the primary agents. Like their ethereal, anthropomorphic counterparts, the tangible divine cult objects and other secondary agents also received offerings, they participated in other cult rituals, and they had their own unique names that differentiated them from other divine entities.

Although Pongratz-Leisten could argue that this book and its expressed interest in various Ištar, Baal, and other entities, focus too much on specific anthropomorphic gods, one aim of this book is to expand the definition of deity in the ancient Near East to include not just non-anthropomorphic deities – as Pongratz-Leisten and others rightly have – but to include also a multiplicity of distinct and separate anthropomorphic deities who share a common first name, which is itself an area that she says elsewhere needs further research.[84] To this end, by continuing our treatment of secondary agents as distinct divine entities in ancient Mesopotamia, we set the stage to then demonstrate that localized Ištar goddesses and other same-named deities individually partook in divinity as distinct members of the divine realm. After all, like the traditional major gods and the divine cult objects, they, too, received offerings, participated in cult and other rituals, and had their own unique names, and they were viewed as agents responsible for maintaining the cosmic order.

Armed with a cognitive science- and phenomenological-based theory about divine agency and the maintenance of cosmic order, we can now examine how ritual and other cultic texts treat both primary agents and

83 Pongratz-Leisten, "Divine Agency," 146. In his review of Pongratz-Leisten's essay, Hundley argues for a divine continuum of agency along which anthropomorphic deities (i.e., primary agents), cult statues, emblems, and other objects (i.e., secondary agents) would be placed rather than a simple dichotomous division: "the designators 'primary' and 'secondary' at times mandate an excessive divide between the categories (e.g., between the god and statue), while conflating the wide range of agents in the second category (e.g., although both are 'secondary' agents, the enlivened statue is the god in the human sphere, while a divine weapon serves as a more distant way to [establish the] presence [of] the deity)" (Michael Hundley, review of *Reconsidering the Concept of Revolutionary Monotheism* by ed. Beate Pongratz-Leisten, *RBL* [http://www.bookreviews.org] [2012]: 4).
84 Pongratz-Leisten, "Comments on the Translatability," 93.

secondary agents, or anthropomorphic and non-anthropomorphic entities, as equally divine. For example, the Assyrian ritual texts K 252 and *STT* 88 provide more than one example of how the Neo-Assyrians priests treated various divine entities, ranging in form from anthropomorphic statues to crowns, stars, lions, temple doors, locks, and city gates. Our understanding of these and other similar ritual texts is limited, but possible interpretations are still available as they relate to the deity or deities named. First, as *STT* 88 i 17′–20′ demonstrates, the names of non-anthropomorphic cult objects could be preceded by the same divine determinative as were the names of anthropomorphic cult statues to designate the following divine:

> 17′ ^{d}*a-šur* ^{d}*a-gu-u* 18′ ^{d}*šu-šam* 19′ *aš-šur* ^{d}*laḫ-mu*^{meš} 20′ *aš-šur* ^{d}DI.KU$_{5}$^{meš}
>
> 17′ Assur, Crown, 18′ Šušam, 19′ Assur-of-the-Laḫmu, 20′ (and) Assur-Dayyānu. (*STT* 88 i)

The chief deity of the Assyrian Empire Assur was marked as divine with the same symbol as the crown listed after him, so in this regard Assur and his crown are equally divine. As Porter observes, Assur's crown appeared in multiple texts, and its name could be written multiple different ways (e.g., "Crown": ^{d}AGA, AGA, MEN$_{2}$, ^{d}*a-gu-u*, and *a-gu-u*; or "Lord-Crown": ^{d}EN AGA and EN AGA), but significantly the name was often preceded by a divine determinative to signify its divine status.[85] Not only could non-anthropomorphic and inanimate objects have a divine determinative placed before their name, so could nonphysical abstract concepts and medical conditions. Epilepsy (*bennu*) appeared in ancient texts with a divine determinative (^{d}*bennu*), so we recognize that it, too, was considered a divine entity in ancient Mesopotamia.[86] To our modern minds, objects and diseases may seem inferior when compared to anthropomorphic deities, but ancient scribes used the same divine determinatives to indicate that "they were not seen as entities of a truly different type," despite our potential modern misgivings.[87]

In addition to the placement of a divine determinative to indicate divine status, ritual texts also indicate that the anthropomorphic cult statues of anthropomorphic deities could be considered distinct. Often this is indicated through the use of distinct names. For example, the Assyrian ritual text K 252 ii 26–30 provides a list of ten divine names, each of which is preceded by a

85 Porter, "Introduction," 5–6; see Brigitte Menzel, *Assyrische Tempel*, Studia Pohl. Series Maior 20 (Rome: Biblical Institute, 1981), 2:T113–125, nos. 53 and 54, and 2:57* n. 698.
86 Porter, "Blessings," 158; and Pongratz-Leisten, "Divine Agency," 146–147; cf. Bottéro, *Religion*, 62–63.
87 Porter, "Blessings," 159.

divine determinative, and ll. 31–32 states that these ten names represent the gods of this particular temple:

26	^{d}30 ^{d}UTU.ALAM ^{d}UTU	Sîn, Šamaš-the-cult-statue, Šamaš
27	^{d}NIN.GAL ^{d}*a-a*	Ningal, Aya
28	^{d}BU.NE.NE ^{d}EN.TI	Bunene, Ebiḫ
29	^{d}*kit-tu*$_4$ ^{d}*u*$_2$*-mu*	Kittu, Umu
30	^{d}*ta-am-ba-a-a*	Tambâya
31	DINGIR^{meš} *ša*$_2$ E$_2$ ^{d}30 ^{d}UTU	Gods of the temple of Sîn (and) Šamaš
32	*ša*$_2$ ^{uru}ŠA$_3$.URU	of the Inner City.[88]

Of particular interest here are the repetition of the divine name Šamaš in l. 26 and the absence of other repeated divine names. What does it mean when a deity is named along with his statue in a list that does not otherwise repeat names, which appears to be the case for Šamaš and Šamaš-the-cult-statue? One potential interpretation is that the sun-god Šamaš had two cult statues, whereas the other deities only had one. However, this interpretation still allows for multiple theological possibilities: Were these two distinct physical forms of

88 The interpretation of K 252 ii 26 as a line providing three divine names is primarily based on ll. 18 and 20 earlier in this text. In each of these lines, the goddesses' names (i.e., Nipḫu and Nūru) are followed by ALAM, giving the appearance that ALAM is an element in the goddesses' full names. The same impression is given in column i, where the divine name Kippat-māti appears twice, once without the ALAM element and once with it (^{11} ^{d}*kip-pat*-KUR ^{12} ^{d}*kip-pat*-KUR ALAM, K 252 i). This is precisely how *CAD* interprets these divine names (*CAD* Ṣ, *ṣalmu* mng. a1′d′) when they appear in Frankena's *Tākultu* edition of that text (see Rintje Frankena, *Tākultu: de Sacrale Maaltijd in Het Assyrische Ritueel: Met een overzicht over de in Assur Vereerde Goden* [Leiden: Brill, 1954]). Elsewhere in this text, the scribe regularly added a divine determinative to ALAM when the word appears to be independent of other divine names (e.g., i 15, 25 [partially reconstructed], 32 [plural], ii 2 [⌜^{d}⌝*ṣal-mu*], v 31, and 32).

In a variant text, however, ALAM typically received a divine determinative regardless of whether ALAM appeared independently or as an element in a full name. For example, instead of K 252 ii 20's ^{d}*nu-ru* ALAM, *STT* 88 ii 45 lists ^{d}*nu-*⌜*ru*⌝ ^{d}[ALAM] (the Nipḫu $^{(d)}$ALAM in l. 43 is only a proposed reconstruction), which suggests two distinct divine names. Likewise, in its parallel account of our primary line of interest, *STT* 88 ii 50–51 appears to list four divine names instead of three: Sîn, Šamaš, Ṣalmu, and Šamaš once again (^{50} ^{d}30 ^{d}UTU ^{51} ^{d}A[LAM] ⌜^{d}⌝UTU). In addition to having its own determinative marker, ALAM has also been severed from the preceding UTU with its placement at the start of a new line. Graphically, the impetus behind this change is easily explained: two determinatives and two other signs are placed on each line for balance. Theologically, however, the implications of this arrangement are much more difficult to discern. If, indeed, four divine names are listed, why was Šamaš's name repeated? If ^{d}ALAM should be interpreted as an element for the first ^{d}UTU's full name, why has it been separated? If ^{d}ALAM should be understood as an element for the second ^{d}UTU, why is this instance the only one in which ALAM precedes the other element in the divine name?

the god that could still be equated? Were these two names (i.e., Šamaš-the-cult-statue and Šamaš) both physical representatives of the same god in that temple? Or could it mean something else entirely? For instance, what if Šamaš-the-cult-statue was the only physical object mentioned within a list of nine ethereal divine entities? If nothing else, we can confidently conclude from this text that the divine entity listed as Šamaš-the-cult-statue (^{d}UTU.ALAM) and the divine entity listed as (the unspecified) Šamaš (^{d}UTU) were entirely separate forms that functioned independently but were related to each other through their Šamaš associations. We may not know how these two differed from each other in a physical sense, but the context in which we find Šamaš-the-cult-statue and Šamaš suggests to us that they were, in fact, theologically distinct, just as each was theologically distinct from the other divine entities represented in the text: Sîn, Ningal, Aya, Bunene, Ebiḫ, Kittu, Umu, and Tambâya (ll. 26–30). Likewise, whether Pongratz-Leisten would consider just Šamaš-the-cult-statue or both it and (the unspecified) Šamaš as secondary agents representing the ethereal, primary agent Šamaš may be unclear, but we could expect that she would consider both divine names as divine agents regardless of their physical nature.[89]

In another text, BM 119282, seven different cult statues of Marduk, which were located in different temples or shrines around Babylon, reinforce the idea that a cult statue was distinct from the ethereal deity. Although not every statue's name is extant in BM 119282, the very fact that each cult statue had its own name is significant. Moreover, in contrast to K 252 ii 26, where the secondary agent Šamaš-the-cult-statue includes the primary agent's name, these seven different names did not include the divine name Marduk. The cult statue of Marduk (literally, "image-of-Bēl") that was placed in Ea's temple was named Magruš ([*ṣal-mu* ^{d}EN *ša*$_2$ E$_2$] ⸢^{d}⸣*e*$_2$*-a* ^{d}*ma-ag-ru-uš šum*$_3$*-šu*$_2$, BM 119282:1), and the statue that was placed in Ninurta-of-the-Courtyard's temple was named Asarre (^{d}*asar-re šum*$_3$*-šu*$_2$, l. 3).[90] Each statue might have served as a

---

89 Pongratz-Leisten, "Divine Agency," 146; see also Hundley, review, 4. Jacobsen long ago observed and concluded that the cult image is not the god (Thorkild Jacobsen, "Graven Image," in *Ancient Israelite Religion: Essays in Honor of Frank Moore Cross*, eds. Patrick D. Miller, Paul D. Hanson, and S. Dean McBride [Philadelphia: Fortress, 1987], 22). According to an inscription from the reign of Nabû-apal-iddina in the ninth century, the cult image of Šamaš was identified as distinct from the god Šamaš during the mouth washing ritual, as indicated by the statement in the text that the statue's mouth was washed "before Šamaš." (*ma-ḫar* ^{d}*Šamaš*, ibid., 22).

90 The first half of l. 1 has been reconstructed, but its reconstruction can be considered reliable because the first few signs of the first seven lines all start out *ṣal-mu* ^{d}EN *ša*$_2$ (A. R. George, "Marduk and the Cult of the Gods of Nippur at Babylon," *Or* NS 66 [1997]: 65).

focal point for Marduk's divinity at each temple or shrine, at least according to the author of BM 119282, but each name also serves as a reminder that its bearer was uniquely divine, as indicated by the divine determinative placed before the unique name of each statue (e.g., ^{d}Magruš, ^{d}Asalluḫi, and ^{d}Asarre). Moreover, according to Gebhard Selz, these unique divine names also indicate that these statues participated in specific induction ceremonies during which these names were conferred.[91] These statues might have contained or reflected Marduk's divinity within the cult, but they had their own claim to divinity because they had a divine name, which was preceded by a divine determinative and was bestowed upon them during an official temple rite.

Moving from the cultic and ritualistic realm into the cosmic realm allows us to consider the importance of unique divine names on another type of secondary agents, stars and planets.[92] As part of her discussion on celestial divination, Francesca Rochberg notes that those gods who were associated with celestial bodies (e.g., the moon-god Sîn with the moon, and Ištar with the planet Venus) could be differentiated from those same heavenly bodies.[93] This differentiation is principally expressed in an omen's metaphoric language. For example, one omen protasis mentioned that the visible lunar disk (i.e., the moon in the sky) wore a crown:

> [5]1 30 *ina* IGI.LAL-*šu*$_2$ AGA *a-pir* [6]LUGAL *a-ša*$_2$*-ri-*⟨*du*⟩*-tu*$_2$ DU-*ak*
>
> If the moon at its appearance wears a crown: the king will reach the highest rank. (SAA 8 10:5–6)

91 Gebhard Selz, "The Holy Drum, the Spear, and the Harp. Towards an Understanding of the Problems of Deification in the Third Millennium Mesopotamia," in *Sumerian Gods and Their Representations*, ed. I. L. Finkel (Gröningen: Styx Publications, 1997), 176–178.
92 Pongratz-Leisten, "Divine Agency," 174.
93 Francesca Rochberg, *The Heavenly Writing: Divination: Divination, Horoscopy, and Astronomy in Mesopotamian Culture* (Cambridge: Cambridge University Press, 2004), 171–180, esp. 176; see also Francesca Rochberg, "'The Stars Their Likenesses': Perspectives on the Relation Between Celestial Bodies and Gods in Ancient Mesopotamia," in *What is a God? Anthropomorphic and Non-Anthropomorphic Aspects of Deity in Ancient Mesopotamia*, ed. Barbara N. Porter, Transactions of the Casco Bay Assyriological Institute 2 (Winona Lake: Casco Bay Assyriological Institute, 2009), 89; and Francesca Rochberg, "The Heavens and the Gods in Ancient Mesopotamian: The View from a Polytheistic Cosmology," in *Reconsidering the Concept of Revolutionary Monotheism*, ed. Beate Pongratz-Leisten (Winona Lake: Eisenbrauns, 2011), 124–130.

Likewise, Jan Assmann notes that the Egyptian "Solar Phases Hymn" refers to the sun as the celestial object rather than the sun-god (Jan Assmann, *Egyptian Solar Religion in the New Kingdom: Re, Amun and the Crisis of Polytheism*, trans. A. Alock [London: Kegan Paul International, 1995], 42).

This statement need not mean that the moon-god Sîn had a crown on his anthropomorphic yet ethereal head.[94] Instead, anticipating Pongratz-Leisten's agency terminology, Rochberg argues that this incongruous situation "may be explained in terms of the attribution of agency only to the gods, who were therefore not viewed as constituting the signs, but as producing the signs."[95] The moon as a lunar disk was the moon-god Sîn's signal to the omen reader in this situation; it was not necessarily the moon-god himself. Acting on behalf of a deity or as a sign from the deity does not mean acting as or being that deity. In the world of astrology and omens, the focus was on the communication with the divine, which could be provided through the observable formation of constellations, the moon, and the planets or through sheep exta. We should think of the lunar disk as the medium of the god Sîn's communication with humanity, like we do the sheep's liver, rather than as the moon-god presenting himself to humanity. Applying Pongratz-Leisten's agency model to Rochberg's situation, the primary divine agent Sîn was presented as intentionally controlling the lunar disk as part of his role in maintaining cosmic order, and as the secondary divine agent, the lunar disk served as the divine medium, making divine-human socialization possible.[96]

Allowing for this distinction between the deity and the celestial body plays an important role in our examination of Ištar goddesses in the Neo-Assyrian period. For example, one possible reading of a celestial omen protasis suggests that the planet Venus was envisioned as having a beard: SU_6 (*ziqnu*) *zaq-na-at* (ACh Suppl. Ištar 33:41).[97] If the planet Venus was thought of as necessarily and wholly Ištar, then we should interpret such an omen as though it literally suggested that the goddess Ištar was occasionally a bearded anthropomorphic entity. However, if we allow for a distinction between the goddess and the

---

94 Rochberg, "Personifications and Metaphors in Babylonian Celestial Omina," *JAOS* 116 (1996): 480; and Rochberg, *Heavenly Writing*, 180. See also SAA 8 113:5 for another reference to the moon and its crown.

95 Rochberg, "Personifications," 482; and Rochberg, *Heavenly Writing*, 176. In her own discussion of divine agency and objects associated with the divine, Pongratz-Leisten notes, "Moon, sun, and planets were considered part of the composite nature of the divinity and, therefore, agents acting on behalf of the divinity" (Pongratz-Leisten, "Divine Agency," 186).

96 Pongratz-Leisten, "Divine Agency," 148.

97 Rochberg notes that the logogram SU_6 may also be read as *nabāṭu* ("to become radiant"), which is a reading that would circumvent any complicated interpretation or explanation of Ištar as an androgenic deity with a beard (Rochberg, "Personifications," 480). Although "beard" is the primary meaning of *ziqnu*, *CAD* Z suggests that the word can also be used metaphorically for light. Lambert translated *mu-šaḫ-miṭ ziq-nat ur-ri* literally as "(Šamaš) [w]ho sets aglow the *beard* of light" (*BWL* 126, l. 18), but *CAD* prefers the translation "(Šamaš) who makes glow the rays of light (literally, the beard of light)" (*CAD* Z, *ziqnu* mng. c).

planet just as we allow for the distinction between the moon-god and the moon, then this protasis can be interpreted as a visual metaphor and a sign provided by a goddess who does not need a shave.[98] The ethereal Ištar is the primary agent, whereas the visible planet Venus is the secondary agent who serves as her messages' divine medium to the human world.

Just as importantly, this perceived distinction between the anthropomorphic yet ethereal Ištar and the celestial Venus also explains the fact that different names are usually used to differentiate the deity from the planetary body.[99] For example, when the planet Venus was mentioned in omen texts, the planet was more often designated as $^{mul/d}$*dil-bat* rather than a more common designation for Ištar, such as ^{d}*iš-tar*, ^{d}INANNA, ^{d}ININ, or ^{d}15.[100] Similarly, the name for the planet Jupiter, the planet most commonly associated with Marduk, was typically written out as ^{d}SAG.ME.GAR in omens rather than using Marduk's more common designation ^{d}AMAR.UTU or his nickname Bēl.[101] This is not to deny that the names ^{d}*dil-bat* and ^{d}SAG.ME.GAR (occasionally occurring with divine determinatives) could serve as alternative names for Ištar and Marduk outside of astrological or omen corpora; rather, as Rochberg observes, these decidedly different designations for the planets and gods underscore for us the ancient differentiation between the celestial object and the deity in the astrologers' and diviners' mind.[102]

Additionally, the fact that the planet Jupiter was generally addressed by its own name, a name that lacks an explicit Marduk element, is reminiscent of

---

98 Just as Rochberg has demonstrated that Sîn and the moon could function separately in omen texts, Porter argues that the goddess Ištar and the planet Venus (Dilbat) were envisioned as acting independently of each other, even though the planet Venus was typically understood to be a celestial aspect of the goddess Ištar (Barbara N. Porter, "The Anxiety of Multiplicity: Concepts of Divinity as One and Mandy in Ancient Assyria," in *One God or Many? Concepts of Divinity in the Ancient World*, ed. Barbara N. Porter, Transactions of the Casco Bay Assyriological Institute 1 [Casco Bay Assyriological Institute, 2000], 274).

99 Admittedly, the same cannot be said as convincingly for the moon-god Sîn and the lunar disk. Although celestial divination texts most frequently indicate the lunar disk with the logogram ^{d}30, a number which refers to the heavenly body's approximately 30-day cycle, ^{d}30 is often used in place of other logographic or syllabographic spellings of the name Sîn to address the moon-god in other textual genres, including state treaties and personal names (Rochberg, "Personifications," 480).

100 Rochberg, "Personifications," 480.

101 To further mark the distinctiveness between Marduk and his celestial aspect Jupiter, it should be noted that Marduk could also be identified with other stars and that Jupiter could be associated with other deities (Rochberg, "The Heavens," 126–127).

102 Rochberg, "Personifications," 479; Rochberg, *Heavenly Writing*, 168; and Pongratz-Leisten, "Divine Agency," 147.

Marduk's cult statues Magruš, Asalluḫi, and Asarre in BM 119282, whose names also lack an explicit Marduk element. In ancient Mesopotamia, the cult statues and planets shared much in common. Both cult statues and planets are visual, physical (if not actually tangible) objects that can be contrasted with the intangible and ethereal anthropomorphic deities. Both were thought to act as secondary agents, and possessing agency meant that both cult statues and planets could receive additional humanlike attributes. Both could receive prayers and hymns. On the one hand, prayers were addressed to the lunar disk in the night sky (e.g., *Šuilla* prayers to Sîn), and hymns praised the moon-god Sîn by describing the visual attributes of the lunar disk (e.g., Enḫeduanna's hymns to Sîn). On the other hand, a devotee could pray in front of a statue in the temple as a form of worship. In both instances, the efficacy of the prayers and hymns offered to the celestial bodies and cult statues only demanded that these visible objects act as the channels through which the human could address the primary deity.[103] Furthermore, and quite importantly, cult statues and planets had their own distinct names, which were marked with the divine determinative in order to indicate their divine status. Celestial bodies, like their earth-bound cultic counterparts, were gods.

As mentioned above, BM 119282:1–7 explicitly names seven cult statues that served as secondary agents for Marduk, and Selz observed that these seven names further imply that each statue participated in an induction ceremony at its respective shrines.[104] In addition to naming ceremonies, cult statues partook in various other temple rites, including mouth-opening and mouth-washing rites, which bestowed a sense of cultic purity on them.[105] According to the Neo-Assyrian rituals known as *mīs pî* ("washing the mouth") – versions of which have be uncovered in places as diverse as Assur, Nineveh, Calaḫ,

103 Rochberg, "The Stars Their Likenesses," 90.
104 Selz, "Holy Drum," 177–179.
105 Selz, "Holy Drum," 177–179; Beate Pongratz-Leisten, "Reflections on the Translatability of the Notion of Holiness," in *Of God(s), Trees, Kings, and Scholars: Neo-Assyrian and Related Studies in Honour of Simo Parpola*, eds. Mikko Luukko, Saana Svärd, and Raija Mattila, Studia Orientalia 106 [Helsinki: Finnish Oriental Society, 2009], 422. Pongratz-Leisten challenges modern scholars to reconsider the sacred/holy-profane dichotomy that has been anachronistically imposed upon biblical and ancient Near Eastern texts (ibid., 410). In place of this dichotomy, she suggests that the Mesopotamians viewed temples, cult objects, rituals, and priestly attendants as pure or clean because they had been selected by divine ancients and cleansed or purified through washing rituals or extispicy (ibid., 422). These pure people, places, and things are to be distinguished from other people, places, and things specifically because they had been chosen and cleansed; nothing was inherently pure in the Mesopotamian religious world without participation in purification rites.

Babylon, Sippar, Nippur, Uruk, Sultantepe, and Hama – the cult statue was divine and was born in heaven and was definitely not produced by human craftsmen.[106] According to the Nineveh Ritual Tablet, when the priest recited the incantation, entitled "Born in heaven by his own power," he reassured the statue of its divine origin, claiming that it was created by divine, not human, hands.[107] After having been declared free of human origin and contamination, the anthropomorphic statue was recognized as the god it was.

The ancient Mesopotamians washed and opened the mouths of anthropomorphic cult statues, but they also performed these same rituals on non-

---

106 Smith, *Origins*, 184.

107 Christopher Walker and Michael Dick, *The Induction of the Cult Image in Ancient Mesopotamia: The Mesopotamian Mīs Pî Ritual: Transliteration, Translation, and Commentary*, SAALT 1 [Helsinki: The Neo-Assyrian Text Corpus Project, 2001], 63:133 and 66:183–184. By thoroughly examining the *mīs pî*-ritual texts, Christopher Walker and Michael Dick have also attempted to define the relationship between the cult image and the god (ibid., 14). Accepting that the relationship between the statue and deity likely differed according to time and place in ancient Mesopotamia, they compare the relationship to the "Eucharistic Presence":

> To Orthodox and Roman Catholics the bread and wine during the Eucharistic ritual become the real presence of the Divine Jesus, while still subsisting under the appearance of bread and wine. Obviously the Eucharistic species are not coterminous with Jesus, so that the Eucharistic Presence can be found simultaneously in Churches throughout the world. Nor would the destruction of the consecrated bread and wine entail the destruction of Jesus (ibid., 7).

First, the deity could theoretically be present in more than one statue in a given moment, depending on the number of temples devoted to that deity; and second, the destruction of a statue did not mean the destruction of the deity it represented.

This second point can become complicated. In the *Erra Epic*, when the god Marduk was dirtied as a result of his cult image becoming dirtied and covered (I 180; Dalley, *Myths from Mesopotamia*, 290), the god left the image, but he also abdicated his rule, so Erra promised to act as the interim ruler. Similarly, according to *Marduk's Ordeal* (SAA 3 34 and 35), which dates to Sennacherib's reign, the exiled Marduk statue corresponded to the real exile of the deity Marduk from Babylon, who was then relocated to Assur. A third text, from Assurbanipal's reign, suggests that cult images in damaged sanctuaries rendered a god or goddess powerless: [62]*eš-re-e-ti* KUR ELAM-*ma*^{ki} [63]*a-di la ba-še-e* *u*$_2$-*šal-pit* [64] DINGIR^{meš}-*šu* ^{d}15^{meš}-*šu*$_2$ *am-na-a a-na za-qi*$_2$-*qi*$_2$ ("I desecrated the sanctuaries of the land of Elam until it was nothing and counted their gods and goddesses as ghosts," *BIWA* 55 A vi 62–64). Just as the cult image represented the deity, the destruction of the sanctuary that housed the images represented the defeat of the deity, who, in this case, was powerless to stop Assurbanipal. All of these texts indicate that there was a relationship between the deity and the image. According to Dick, "The cult image is the effective manifestation of the god," but the cult image is not coterminous with the deity it represents (Michael Dick, review of *Die Theologie der Bilder: Herstellung und Einweihung von Kultbildern in Mesopotamien und die alttestamentliche Bilderpolemik*, by Angelika Berlejung, *JAOS* 120 [2000]: 258).

anthropomorphic objects that lacked discernable mouths.[108] Focusing on Ur III ritual texts, Selz found that there was no distinctive feature that separated cult statues from other cult objects, including tiaras, crowns, and statues of the king.[109] Cult objects often resided in the temples alongside the more anthropomorphic cult statues; they displayed a divine name on them; they partook in rituals; and they received offerings.[110] Moreover, various cult objects received votive gifts, and crowns were also created to decorate steles, and drums received crowns and necklaces.[111] Selz especially stresses the importance of naming harps as independent entities because "[t]he importance that names had for the peoples of the ancient Near East cannot be overestimated."[112] The name made the god. Following Selz's analysis, if we accept that cult statues were themselves divine, then we must also accept that non-anthropomorphic cult objects that were offered similar treatment were also divine.

Although Selz's survey of cult objects was limited to the late third millennium, we also have similar evidence for such a treatment of non-anthropomorphic cult objects from the Neo-Assyrian period. Specifically, Assur's crown was a cult object whose name, like the names of cult statues, could be preceded by a divine determinative (see *STT* 88 i 17′, above). As Porter observes, we learn from other texts that Assur's crown, also known as Lord-Crown, could receive its own offering and seemed to operate separately from Assur.[113] According to ritual text A 125, on the sixteenth of the month of Šabāṭu, the king was supposed to light a censer to Assur's cult statue and then set up an offering table in front of Lord-Crown. The king would then present "water for the hands" separately for Assur and for Lord-Crown ([19]A^{meš} [ŠU^{II}] [20][*a-na*] EN AG[A] ⌜*uq-ṭar-rib*⌝, A 125 i 19–20).[114] In this text, the non-anthropomorphic object is treated remarkably similar to the anthropomorphic cult statue in this portion of the ritual, even though the crown only had (presumably) metaphorical hands. This ritual is all the more fascinating because the king would begin

108 Selz, "Holy Drum," 177.
109 Selz, "Holy Drum," 167.
110 Selz, "Holy Drum," 184. Selz notes that the Ur III tablets under discussion include both offerings and votive texts. The former genre generally contains a greater list of gods than the latter, but the treatment of major gods and cult objects is similar in both genres (ibid., 173).
111 Selz, "Holy Drum," 175–176.
112 Selz, "Holy Drum," 178.
113 Porter, "Blessings," 186 n. 119.
114 Menzel, *Assyrische Tempel*, 2:T32–33, no. 24 i 17–23 and ii 19′–25′.

the ritual by wearing Lord-Crown on his head, and as the ritual progressed (and the literal and figurative hands had been washed), Lord-Crown (ii 22′) was presented as an offering to Assur and Mullissu.[115] The object that served as the offering at the conclusion of the ritual was the same object that received offerings during the ritual.

In a clear demonstration of this non-anthropomorphic deity's agency, another ritual text lists Lord-Crown among fifteen other deities who themselves make offerings before Assur (A 485 + 3109).[116] In her analysis of Lord-Crown, Porter concludes that Lord-Crown was closely associated with the imperial god Assur and that it abstractly represented Assur's sovereignty or command, but she stresses that the crown was not identified or equated with Assur.[117] Lord-Crown was a lesser deity – a secondary agent using Pongratz-Leisten's terminology – who operated independently of but in coordination with the primary agent and that deity's cult statue. It was divine, but its divinity depended upon another.[118] Significantly, the primary agent Assur appears to affect the non-anthropomorphic Lord-Crown in the same way he and other deities affect their anthropomorphic cult statues. As the Lord-Crown-example texts indicate, the resemblance between the treatment of cult objects in the late third millennium and the treatment of cult objects in the early first millennium is clear, and both of these treatments suggest that the Mesopotamians recognized these objects' divine status. Each cult object was thought to participate in the divine because each object had a share in maintaining the cosmic order through cultic rites, each object was explicitly labeled divine through use of a unique divine name that was preceded by a divine determinative, and each object received offerings and human reverence.

If we concede that cult objects, which were dependent upon the agency of ethereal gods and goddesses and received offerings and other divine benefits, were recognized as distinct deities by ancient Mesopotamians, then accepting that localized Ištar goddesses were also considered distinct and separate deities is not an unreasonable conclusion. Localized Ištar goddesses were expected to act as agents in state treaties, personal letters between the king and his court, and in Assurbanipal's hymn. In many of these instances, the goddesses Ištar-of-Nineveh and Ištar-of-Arbela are invoked in curses and are asked to implement these curses when someone transgresses the treaty. For

115 Porter, "Blessings," 186.
116 Menzel, *Assyrische Tempel*, 2:T44, no. 28 r. 19–24.
117 Porter, "Blessings," 188.
118 Porter, "Blessings," 191; see also Pongratz-Leisten, "Divine Agency," 146; and Hundley, "Here a God," 79.

example, in *Assurbanipal's Treaty with Babylonian Allies* (SAA 2 9), Ištar//Who-Resides-(in)-Arbela is charged with subjugating the transgressor by breaking his bow and making him crouch at his enemies' feet (r. 24′–25′). Just by threatening this curse, anyone reading or hearing this treaty would have recognized that this goddess helped maintain the cosmic order. When Adad-šumu-uṣur invoked Ištar-of-Nineveh, Ištar-of-Arbela, and Ištar-of-Kidmuri in his letter to the king (SAA 10 197:10–12), he included each goddess because each one played a role in effecting the blessings. When Assurbanipal praised Lady-of-Nineveh and Lady-of-Arbela and described them as his mother and nurse in SAA 3 3, he was extolling their capacities as royal caregivers, agents who maintain cosmic order by nurturing the king.

Similarly, as each cult statue, cult object, and planet had its own unique name to distinguish it from the ethereal deity, each localized Ištar goddess had her own unique name – or sets of name formulas – that distinguished her from (the unspecified) Ištar and other Ištar goddesses. Although the first name Ištar does act as a proper noun in the divine full names Ištar-of-Nineveh and Ištar-of-Arbela – as opposed to the common noun *ištaru* meaning "goddess" – the Ištar portion of these names are the interchangeable elements; the geographic names are not. Consider the different ways that the Ninevite goddess could be addressed in Assyrian inscriptions: ^{d}Ištar-of-Nineveh, ^{d}Ištar//Who-Resides-(in)-Nineveh, ^{d}Lady-of-Nineveh, ^{d}Queen-of-Nineveh, ^{d}Ištar//Lady-of-Nineveh, or possibly ^{d}Ninua'ītu. The common elements are the geographic element and the divine determinative. Venus ($^{d/mul}$*dil-bat*) is not the same name as ^{d}Ištar in celestial divination texts; ^{d}Magruš and ^{d}Asarre are not the same name as ^{d}Marduk in BM 119282; and ^{d}UTU.ALAM is a not the same name as ^{d}UTU in K 151 ii 26; likewise, ^{d}Ištar-of-Nineveh is not the same name as ^{d}Ištar or ^{d}Ištar-of-Arbela in SAA 3 3 or SAA 10 197.

Finally, non-anthropomorphic cult objects participated in cult rites and received offerings in the cult and were, thus, treated like gods. Likewise, Neo-Assyrian inscriptions indicate that Ištar-of-Nineveh and Ištar-of-Arbela (and other localized Ištar goddesses) participated in cult rites and received offerings. According to BM 121206 ix from Sennacherib's reign (705–681), a cult statue representing Ištar-of-Nineveh was arranged so that it was ahead of a cult statue representing Nusku (^{d}15 NINA^{ki} SAG ^{d}PA.TUG$_{2}$, l. 11′). Ištar-of-Nineveh is the only localized Ištar goddess involved in that particular ritual, but she was still referred to specifically as Ištar-of-Nineveh. Later in this same text, Ištar-of-Heaven, Ištar-of-Nineveh, Ištar-of-Arbela, and Assyrian-Ištar, as well as Mullissu, are each included in another ritual (ix 27′–34′). Consider also the large corpus of legal texts from the eight and seventh centuries that explicitly discusses the real possibility of placing monies "in the lap" (*ina bur-ki*) of Ištar-of-Nineveh and Ištar-of-Arbela (see Table 4.1 and chapter 4.1) and the fact that the *Akītu*-festival and its accompanying rituals were celebrated in Arbela in honor of Ištar-of-Arbela.[119]

In addition to these few inscriptions offered here that attest to the treatment of localized Ištar goddesses as deities, several hundred other texts can and will be presented as further evidence that these goddesses were considered divine in the Neo-Assyrian period. Of course, few if any Assyriologists would argue that Ištar-of-Nineveh or Ištar-of-Arbela was not divine; instead, the argument would be that neither of these two is necessarily a separate and distinct goddess, likely agreeing with what Lambert wrote in 1975: "Either the two were always understood to be one, like Ištar of Nineveh and Ištar of Arbela from Assyria, or their equating results from taking an overall view of the pantheon and identifying similar gods."[120] They are "manifestations" or "representations" of Ištar in the same way a cult statue in a given temple or shrine is just another manifestation or representation of the ethereal goddess. However, it is precisely this notion that this book challenges – a process that not only includes arguing for their individuality but also for reminding us that cult statues and other cult objects were themselves seen as separate and distinct deities in ancient Mesopotamia – and hundreds of inscriptions will be offered as evidence for the distinctiveness of these and other localized Ištars in Mesopotamian religious thought (and localized Baal deities in Levantine thought).

1.5 Conclusions

Porter's analysis of Assurbanipal's hymn to Lady-of-Nineveh and Lady-of-Arbela concluded that the seventh-century Assyrian king recognized that these two divine ladies were two distinct divine entities. Although Porter's conclusion are based on a plain-sense, or literal, reading of Assurbanipal's texts and his use of feminine-plural morphology and grammar, the idea that these two

---

119 Beate Pongratz-Leisten, Ina Šulmi Īrub: *die Kulttopographische und ideologische Programmatik der akīitu-Prozession in Babylonien und Assyrien im 1. Jahrtausend v. Chr*, Baghdader Forschungen 16 (Hainz am Rhein: Philipp von Zabern, 1994), 80; and Annus, *Ninurta*, 90–91; see also Elnathan Weissert, "Royal Hunt and Royal Triumph in a Prism Fragment of Ashurbanipal (82-5-22, 2)," in *Assyria 1995*: *Proceedings of the 10th Anniversary Symposium of the Neo-Assyrian Text Corpus Project, Helsinki, September 7–11, 1995*, eds. Simo Parpola and R. M. Whiting (Helsinki: Neo-Assyrian Text Corpus Project, 1997), 339–358.
120 Lambert, "Historical Development," 193.

ladies were actually two distinct divine entities is in conflict with mainstream Assyriological thought. In the late nineteenth century, Barton had determined that Ištar-of-Nineveh and Ištar-of-Arbela, as well as various other localized Ištar goddesses and other goddesses whose name lacked any Ištar element, were ultimately conceived of by ancient Mesopotamians as different manifestations of one ethereal Ištar. Following in Barton's wake, even if they did not adopt all of his methodologies and underlying assumptions, several prominent scholars of the twentieth and twenty-first century have likewise determined that Ištar-of-Nineveh and Ištar-of-Arbela represent manifestations of a singular Assyrian goddess. Some of these conclusions might have been based on identifications like those made by Barton, while still others were based on syncretistic texts or theological speculations produced by scholar-scribes, and still others seem to have been derived from Classical Greco-Roman or Christian conceptions of the divine. Other scholars have entertained the possibility that localized Ištar goddesses were considered distinct in the minds of some ancient devotees, especially when their data included inscriptional evidence from outside the Mesopotamian heartland (i.e., Hurrian and Hittite inscriptions that mention the goddess Šaušga), but, for the most part, their conclusions were not as boldly stated as Porter's.

In contrast to these previous studies that were primarily interested in ethereal anthropomorphic deities, Pongratz-Leisten and others like, Selz, Rochberg, and Porter, have begun to shift our focus away from the traditional major gods toward minor non-anthropomorphic deities. These crowns, harps, drum, planets, cult statues, and even diseases may pale in comparison to ethereal yet superhuman deities, but as Pongratz-Leisten argues this did not prevent them from being divinized in the ancient world and receiving the benefits of that divinization. Because these entities possessed their own agency and intention, the ancient scribes recognized as gods the many non-anthropomorphic deities that they kept in the temples and celestial bodies that they observed in the heavens. The scribes used their native word "god" (DINGIR/*ilu*) to describe them, addressed them like they did the anthropomorphic gods in blessings and prayers, performed rituals on and with them, and allowed them to reside in temples and receive food offerings.[121] Because they were treated like and recognized as gods by the ancients, these objects should be granted divine status by modern scholars. Finally, because localized Ištar goddesses received the same treatment as these non-anthropomorphic deities and the anthropomorphic cult statues, if we are willing to

121 Porter, "Blessings," 161.

expand our concept of the ancient Mesopotamian notion of divinity to include cult objects and statues, we should also be willing to expand our notion to include these localized Ištar goddesses and other comparable deities.

Excursus: "Syncretism"

In Egyptological circles, the word "syncretism" has a special usage that does not correspond to that of the Classics, Assyriology and biblical studies. According to the *Oxford Encyclopedia of Ancient Egypt*, "syncretism" describes the coexistence or cooperation of two or more gods for either political or theological reasons.[122] Whereas in Assyriological and biblical studies we tend to think of syncretism as the identification of deities from two distinct political entities or ethno-linguistic cultures, within Egyptological discussions, however, the two (or more) gods involved in a particular syncretism were often native Egyptian gods who could continue to be distinguished from each other. For example, the syncretism of Re with Atum was thought to form a deity identified specifically as Re-Atum rather than a deity Re who could also be called Atum (or vice versa), as was the case for Zeus and Jupiter in the Classical world or for Ninurta and Ningirsu in late third-millennium Sumer. The earliest attested example of this Egyptian form of syncretism dates to the 4th Dynasty (ca. 26–25th centuries B.C.E.).[123] This Egyptian style of syncretism was temporary – even if "temporary" represented hundreds or thousands of years of Egyptian religious history – and each original god retained his or her original characteristics during the syncretism.[124] According to John Baines,

122 U. H. Luft, "Religion," in *The Oxford Encyclopedia of Ancient Egypt*, ed. Donald Redford (Oxford: Oxford University Press, 2001), 3:142.
123 Erik Hornung, *Conceptions of God in Ancient Egypt: The One and the Many*, trans. J. Baines (Ithaca: Cornell University Press, 1982), 92. The combined divine name Re-Atum, which James Allen translates as "Sun Atum" appears several times in *The Resurrection Ritual*, a segment of the Pyramid Texts of Unis, the last king of the Fifth Dynasty (ca. 2353–2323; James P. Allen, *The Ancient Egyptian Pyramid Texts*, ed. P. Der Manuelian, SBLWAW 23 [Atlanta: Society of Biblical Literature, 2005], 442). This text was located in the burial chamber and south-side passage of the pyramid: "Re-Atum will not give you to Osiris: he will not claim your mind, he will not have control of your heart. Re-Atum will not give you to Horus: he will not claim your mind, he will not have control of your heart" (ibid., 32 § 148) and "Re-Atum, this Unis has come to you—an imperishable akh" (ibid., 33 § 150; Allen's translation, modified slightly).
124 John Baines, "Egyptian Deities in Context: Multiplicity Unity and the Problem of Change," in *One God or Many? Concepts of Divinity in the Ancient World*, ed. Barbara N. Porter, Transactions of the Casco Bay Assyriological Institute 1 (Casco Bay Assyriological Institute, 2000), 33.

such syncretisms can be seen as creating new deities out of the existing ones, but a better explanation would interpret this phenomenon as a way to express or isolate particular aspects of a deity for the worshipper.[125] When Egyptians paired the two deities, the second-named deity typically outranked the first, but the iconography of this new deity, as well as the mode of address to the new deity, was based upon the first deity named.[126] According to Erik Hornung, this form of syncretism became more common during the Middle Kingdom, with additional examples including Sobek-Re and Khnum-Re, and, Amun-Re.[127] In each of these instances, because Re is the second-named deity, we learn that Re was considered greater than the gods Sobek, Khnum, and Amun. The ancient Egyptians recognized that these other gods continued to exist, but as a result of these syncretisms the Egyptians also recognized that Sobek, Khnum, and Amun highlighted specific aspects of Re's personality.

Theologically, the Egyptian meaning and usage of syncretism closely resembles metaphoric interpretations of BM 47406, the *Syncretic Hymn to Marduk*, and the *Syncretic Hymn to Ninurta*.[128] For instance, Lambert had advanced BM 47406 as evidence for a series of identifications that resulted in a qualified monotheism in Babylon because "the compiler wished us to see Marduk as the sole possessor of power in the universe: all other powers of nature were but mere aspects of him."[129] The obverse of this text contains a 14-line hymn, wherein the first column names a deity, the second names Marduk, and the third column describes how Marduk's nature relates to the deity in column one. For example, "Zababa : (is) Marduk : of warfare. Enlil : (is) Marduk : of lordship and consultations. Nabû : (is) Marduk : of accounting" (ll. 5–7; see Table 1.2). For Lambert, this hymn represented the end of "the tidying up of an originally unwieldy (Mesopotamian) pantheon" because these gods were presented as mere aspects of Marduk, even though he admitted that this attempt at monotheism proved unsuccessful by not garnering the broad support "which it deserved."[130] If we interpret BM 47406 metaphorically, then the statement, "Zababa (is) Marduk of warfare," does not mean that Zababa's

125 Baines, "Egyptian Deities," 31.
126 Baines, "Egyptian Deities," 32. Baines notes that the sun-god Re was the most commonly syncretized Egyptian deity, and his name was typically the second name of a newly paired syncretization. He also notes other syncretisms wherein these patterns do not hold; for instance, in the triple-deity syncretization Ptah-Sokar(-Osiris), Ptah was the primary deity of import.
127 Hornung, *Conceptions of God*, 92.
128 See, for example, Porter, "Anxiety," 253 f.
129 Lambert, "Historical Development," 198.
130 Lambert, "Historical Development," 197 and 199.

divine personality has been absorbed by Marduk; instead, it means that Marduk is himself as great a warrior god as Zababa. Likewise, "Enlil (is) Marduk of lordship and consultations," should be interpreted to mean that Marduk reached what had been Enlil's level of sovereignty among the gods, and not that the once-powerful Enlil is now nothing more than an aspect of Marduk. Thus, Zababa and Enlil become to Marduk in Babylon as Sobek, Khnum, and Amun were to Re in the Middle Kingdom of Egypt. The same holds true for the *Syncretic Hymn to Marduk* (*KAR* 25 ii 3–16, see also Foster, *Before the Muses*, 692). The statement "Sîn is your divinity, Anu is your sovereignty" (l. 3) does not mean that Sîn and Anu had been identified with Marduk or reduced an aspect of him. Such a metaphoric reading would instead have us interpret the line as describing the extraordinary magnitude of Marduk's divinity: regarding his divinity, Marduk is equal to Sîn, whose own divinity we can consider *par excellence*, and regarding his sovereignty, Marduk is as powerful or as important in the divine hierarchy as the ancient high-god Anu, an idea already suggested by Porter.[131] Again, Sîn and Anu illuminate ancient speculations of Marduk in the same way Sobek, Khnum, and Amun illuminate Re. Such readings allow other gods to continue to exist in Mesopotamian thought, but they remind us that Marduk's qualities are as great each of these other gods' strongest or most important qualities.

Another valid reading of *Syncretic Hymn to Marduk* would examine these deities not as metaphors but as delegates of Marduk's power. The same can be said about Ninurta, who is also the subject of a so-called syncretic hymn, the *Syncretic Hymn to Ninurta* (Ebeling, *KAR* 102:10–33; see also Foster, *Before the Muses*, 713). This twelfth-century Assyrian hymn, which continued as part of the scribal curriculum into the eighth and seventh centuries with "the status of a minor classic,"[132] equates other deities with various parts of Ninurta's body: "Your eyes, lord, are Enlil and Mullissu" (l. 11). The arrangement begins with Ninurta's head and works down to his navel, with thirty-three different gods equated with parts of Ninurta's body in the extant text (see Table 1.3). Although they are all described as parts of Ninurta, these deities are recognized as objects of worship in their own right; they are still gods. Thus, like the *Syncretic Hymn to Marduk* and BM 47406, this hymn to Ninurta lacks a syncretistic or identification force, despite its modern title.[133] Indeed, the fact that Šamaš appears multiple times in this hymn to Ninurta – once as Ninurta's face, once as his eyelid, and once as his eyebrow (*KAR* 102:10, 13, and 14) –

131 Porter, "Anxiety," 253 f.
132 Porter, "Anxiety," 241.
133 Porter, "Anxiety," 250.

emphasizes the numerous qualities that any one deity can express, and this repeated use of Šamaš emphasizes the continuing importance of Šamaš himself in Assyrian theology. For these reasons, we should recognize that this hymn to Ninurta provides a glimpse into the author's Assyrian-based conception of the divine world, in that it names almost three dozen important Assyrian deities.[134] Moreover, it does not deny the continued existence of Šamaš or the others any more than the Sobek-Re, Khnum-Re, and Amun-Re syncretisms deny the continued existence of Sobek, Khnum, and Amun when they have been syncretized with Re; rather, they clarify the concepts surrounding Re.

In the same way that a Egyptian god's iconography revealed his characteristics or attributes rather than his actual physical (albeit ethereal) form, the deities with whom another Egyptian god could be syncretized reveal his or her characteristics and attributes. Following Hornung's and Baines's interpreta-

---

134 Like BM 47406 and the two syncretic hymns, a final hymn worth mentioning here is one that actually is suggestive of divine identification: the *Sumero-Akkadian Hymn of Nanâ* (K 3933). Erica Reiner reports that this Neo-Assyrian text is unusual because it is one of only a handful of Akkadian texts wherein a deity boasts about his or her own accomplishments, and it is unique because the goddess Nanaya herself proclaims to be other goddesses (Reiner, "Sumero-Akkadian," 221). In the first strophe, the deity identifies herself as Inanna/Ištar from the cities Borsippa, Uruk, Daduni, and Babylon, and she concludes with the refrain: *a-na-ku-ma* ^{d}*na-na-a*, which Reiner interprets as "still I am Nanâ":

> i 1 [gašan]-mu ^{d}EN.ZU ^{d}inanna na-i-nim-gi u$_3$-tu-da šu-a-ab-dil-e-ne
> 2 [*m*]*a-rat* ^{d}30 *te-li-tu*$_2$ *a-ḫat* ^{d}*ša*$_2$*-m*[*aš t*]*a-lim-tu*$_2$ *ina bar*$_2$*-sipa*^{ki} *ḫa-am-ma-ku*
> 3 [*ina*] UNUG^{ki} *ḫa-ri-ma-ku ina* ^{uru}*da-x-*[*x t*]*u-la-a kub-bu-ta-ku*
> 4 [*ina*] *bābili zi-iq-na zaq-*[*na-ku*] ⸢*a*⸣*-na-ku-ma* ^{d}*na-na-a*
>
> My Lady, Sin, Inanna, born of ..., similarly$^{(?)}$ / I am the same$^{(?)}$
> Wise daughter of Sin, beloved sister of Šamaš, I am powerful in Borsippa,
> I am a hierodule in Uruk, I have heavy breasts in Daduni,
> I have a beard in Babylon, still I am Nanâ. (K 3933, Reiner's translation; Reiner, "Sumero-Akkadian," 224)

The rhetorical force of this hymn's more than 20 strophes can be summarized as "they call me (some) DN, but I am still Nanâ" (ibid., 222). Despite this recurrent equating theme, using this text as evidence for a reduction in the number of Babylonian goddesses during the late Babylonian period is an over-extension of the data (see Table 1.4 for a list of goddesses equated with Nanaya in this hymn). Instead, this hymn should be interpreted like these other theologically speculative hymns because it intentionally emphasizes one deity in terms of others, like the Marduk and Ninurta syncretic hymns and BM 47406. The fact that the Sumerian lines of this text, which Reiner describes as an "artificial Sumerian" that "def[ies] translation" (ibid., 222), do not correspond with the Akkadian lines would suggest that it was intended for a small audience, such as the priests at Nanaya's cult or just within the scholar-scribe circles. Thus, this, like BM 47406 and the other syncretistic hymns need not be interpreted as evidence for minimizing the divine.

tion – both of whom follow Hans Bonnet – because syncretism was about revealing the nature of the deity's character and attributes and not about the deity's existence at a particular time or place, multiple syncretisms could simultaneously exist independently of each other.[135] Entities invoked as Amun-Re, Min-Re, Khnum-Re, or Re-Atum could be thought of as coexisting alongside Re without conflict, and the character and attributes of Re's divine presence was more accurately revealed to the devotee through exposure to all of these divine forms.

Hornung states that the clearest example of this kind of syncretism comes from the Ramessid-period tomb of Nofretiri. The iconography of the two deities is represented in the form of a ram-headed mummy, representing both Re (ram-headed) and Osiris (mummified), as the accompanying text declares, "Re enters into Osiris and Osiris enters into Re daily, and the combination is dissolved again daily" (Theban Tomb 290, Hornung's translation).[136] As the text indicates, the personalities of Re and Osiris remain distinct from each other – because this syncretism only takes place at night – and two individual deities survive intact as individuals. One deity does not disappear or cease to exist independently because it was incorporated by the other; he simply serves to highlight an aspect of the other deity. In the case of Osiris-Re, the netherworld deity Osiris represents the sun-god Re during his nightly travels through the *duat*, the Egyptian netherworld.[137]

Hornung describes this special form of syncretism of Egyptian deities as "inhabiting":

> These syncretisms may be interpreted as meaning that Egyptians recognize Re in all these very different gods as soon as they encounter them as creator gods ... It is also clear that every deity whom another deity "inhabits" acquires an extended nature and sphere of action. But all these formulations are no more than initial attempts to grasp the meaning of syncretism.[138]

He suggests that scholarly terms common to other fields of religious studies should be rejected because they lack the specialized nuance that "inhabiting"

---

135 Baines, "Egyptian Deities," 33; and Hans Bonnet, "On Understanding Syncretism," trans. J. Baines, *Or* NS 68 (1999): 189.

136 Hornung, *Conceptions of God*, 95. Hornung provides a reproduction of the Osiris-Re iconography on p. 94. According to Baines, this particular syncretism and its accompanying iconography were so unusual that "they could not ... be decoded without the text" (Baines, "Egyptian Deities," 34).

137 Leonard H. Lesko, "Ancient Egyptian Cosmogonies and Cosmology," in *Religion in Ancient Egypt: Gods, Myths, and Personal Practice*, ed. Bryon E. Shafer (Ithaca: Cornell University Press, 1991), 119 f.

138 Hornung, *Conceptions of God*, 92.

provides.[139] Terms such as equating, fusing, identifying, and especially syncretism, suggest a phenomenon that is too permanent for Hornung's interpretation of this Egyptian concept. For instance, when we think of the syncretism of Classical gods, like with Zeus and Jupiter or with Aphrodite and Venus, we tend not to entertain the idea or possibility that Zeus once existed independently of Jupiter, and we do not anticipate a moment in the future when Zeus and Jupiter will go their separate ways; we simply equate Zeus with Jupiter. In the theological world of ancient Egypt, in contrast, a given inhabiting could cease potentially at any moment, and the two original deities would become as distinct from each other as they had been before the inhabiting. This is what the text written in Nofretiri's tombs suggests: each morning the inhabiting divine entity Osiris-Re becomes two distinct deities, namely, Osiris and Re. Put another way, the metaphorical relationship that Osiris-Re represents during the solar disk's nightly trip through the *duat* is no longer relevant after the morning.

Because the term syncretism represents a vastly different phenomenon in regards to ancient Egyptian religion than it does in Mesopotamian and Classical religious traditions, any Assyriologist or Biblicist should be careful when using this term. This difference also heightens our sensitivity to the numerous usages and nuances that term "syncretism" can have in various fields of religious studies. In fact, recognizing this difference does two things for the Assyriologist. First, it requires the Assyriologist to focus on how "syncretism" is used in Classical terms, which focuses on the identification of two divine names from two different ethno-linguistic cultures as representing the same deity. Using Lambert's example given above, can we say that the originally distinct entities represented by the divine (Sumerian) names Ninurta and Ningirsu were actually syncretized, or were they simply identified or equated with each other at some point in Sumerian (pre)history? Although Lambert argued that they had always been the same in the Sumerian mind, if they were not, then syncretism is not the appropriate term to use. Second, the Egyptian concept of inhabiting encourages us to reconsider the so-called syncretic hymns (e.g., the *Syncretic Hymn to Marduk* and the *Syncretic Hymn to Ninurta*) in light of a metaphorical – as opposed to strictly theological – interpretation. Just as Osiris-Re provides a nuance for understanding Re's passing through Osiris' netherworld during his nightly journey, so does saying

139 Hornung, *Conceptions of God*, 91. Here Hornung is refining a discussion on inhabiting originally proposed in Hans Bonnet, "Zum Verständnis des Synkretismus," *ZÄS* 75 (1939): 40–52.

"Zababa is Marduk of warfare" or "Šamaš is Ninurta's face" provide an more tangible explanation of Marduk's and Ninurta's divine natures.

For these reasons, when we discuss whether Assyrian or Levantine divine entities with distinct divine names were treated as one or multiple gods by their respective devotees, "identification," "identified with," and "equated with" have been adopted throughout this book in place of "syncretism" or "syncretized." Returning to Lambert's example, we would not say that Ninurta was syncretized with Ningirsu sometime in third-millennium Sumer; rather, we would say that Ninurta was identified with Ningirsu at that time. Likewise, modern scholars often claim that Assur, the Assyrian chief deity of the second and first millennia, had been syncretized with Enlil, who was the Sumerian chief deity in the third and second millennia.[140] Although Assur and Enlil did, in fact, come from two different ethno-linguistic cultures, the two deities were rarely, if ever, identified with each other, much less successfully syncretized. As I have argued elsewhere, Tukultī-Ninurta I did commission material that seems to have equated Assur with Enlil, such as ll. 36′–37′ and 52′–53′ of *A Psalm to Aššur for Tukultī-Ninurta I* (Ebeling, *KAR* 128+).[141] However, this Assur-is-Enlil experiment as one divine being was inconsistently applied during Tukultī-Ninurta's reign, as demonstrated by the fact that they were treated as two distinct deities in his own royal inscriptions, such as in RIMA 1 A.0.78.27:2–4 and elsewhere. Moreover, this supposed equation between Assur and Enlil (and between Assur and the Assyrian-Enlil) was neglected by most other Assyrian kings until the end of the Assyrian empire in the late seventh century.[142] The temporality of the relationship expressed by Tukultī-Ninurta in the thirteenth century should not be interpreted as a sign of syncretism between the two deities any more than the statement "Anu is (Marduk's) sovereignty" in the *Syncretic Hymn to Marduk*; rather, it simply defines the Assyrian chief deity Assur as a sovereign deity who would head the divine hierarchy with as much (or more) effectiveness as Enlil had previously.

---

140 Alasdair Livingstone, "New Dimensions in the Study of Assyrian Religion," in *Assyria 1995: Proceedings of the 10th Anniversary Symposium of the Neo-Assyrian Text Corpus Project, Helsinki, September 7–11, 1995*, eds. Simo Parpola and R. M. Whiting (Helsinki: Neo-Assyrian Text Corpus Project, 1997), 167; Menzel, *Assyrische Tempel*, 1:65 and 2:64* n. 812; George, *Babylonian Topographical Texts*, 185–186; Amar Annus, *Ninurta*, 39; and B. Landsberger, and K. Balkan, "Die Inschrift des assyrischen Königs Īriṣum, gefunden in Kültepe 1948," *Belleten* 14 (1950): 251.

141 Spencer L. Allen, "Aššur and Enlil in Neo-Assyrian Documents," in *Organization, Representation, and Symbols of Power in the Ancient Near East Proceedings of the 54th Rencontre Assyriologique Internationale Proceedings of the 54th Rencontre Assyriologique Internationale at Würzburg 20–25 July 2008*, ed. G. Wilhelm (Winona Lake: Eisenbrauns, 2012), 404.

142 Allen, "Aššur and Enlil," 400–405, esp. 401.

In contrast, when an inscription or a set of inscriptions actually does suggest that two divine names represent deities who had similar attributes or dominion over the same natural realms and who represent two different ethno-linguistic cultures, then we may refer to these divine names as having been syncretized. Thus, we could interpret Philo of Byblos' statements regarding the syncretism between the Greek Hermes and the Egyptian Thoth (*Preparatio evangelica* 1.9.24), the Greek Zeus and the Phoenician Baal-Šamêm (1.10.7), and the Greek Aphrodite was the Phoenician Astarte (1.10.32),[143] and we would still view the relationship between the Sumerian Inanna and the Akkadian Ištar as syncretized. Likewise, we can interpret the Greek-Phoenician bilingual text that mentions Athena (Ἀθηνᾷ, l. 1) in the Greek text and Anat (ענת, l. 1) in the complementary Phoenician portion as an identification of two deities and recognition of their syncretistic relationship (*KAI* 42). Finally, we can probably also assume that the Neo-Punic author of *KAI* 176, who addressed the male deity by the Greek name Kronos (ΚΡΟΩΙ, l. 1) and female deity by the Semitic name Tannit (ΘΕΝΝΕΙΘ, ll. 1–2), recognized that his Kronos was the same divine entity also known as Baal-Ḥamān (see chapter 5.5), which is a syncretism that was also recognized by Sophocles (Sophocles, *Andromeda*, fragment 126) and Philo of Byblos (*Preparatio evangelica* 1.10.44). We need not, as Ted Kaizer recently observed, "avoid the term 'syncretism,'" like many scholars recently have "because of its notorious implication of an arbitrary 'melting pot.'"[144] After all, the word "syncretism" still works within its academic Classical usage as long as we use the term carefully and limit the way that we use it.

143 Mark S. Smith, *God in Translation: Deities in Cross-Cultural Discourse in the Biblical World* (Grand Rapids: Eerdmans, 2010), 253; and Harold W. Attridge and Robert A. Oden, *Philo of Byblos: The Phoenician History: Introduction, Critical Texts, Translation, and Notes*, CBQMS 9 (Washington, D. C.: Catholic Biblical Association of America, 1981), 28–29, 40–41, and 62–63. Similarly, we can still accept Herodotus syncretistic observation that Greek Aphrodite was also the Egyptian goddess Hathor (*Herodotus* 2.41.5c) and his claim that nearly all of Greece's gods actually came from Egypt (2.50).

144 Ted Kaizer, "Identifying the Divine in the Roman Near East," in Panthée: *Religious Transformations in the Graeco-Roman Empire*, eds. Laurent Bricault and Corinne Bonnet. Religions in the Graeco-Roman World 177 (Leiden: Brill, 2013), 115.

2 Comparative Insights

Before continuing with our study of Mesopotamian (and Levantine) conceptions of the divine and divine names, a survey of similar phenomena in non-Mesopotamian cultures and religious traditions is in order. Specifically, the non-Mesopotamian cultures under discussion include the veneration of multiple madonnine images in first millennium (C.E.) Christianity and nineteenth- and twentieth-century Italian Catholicism, and it includes examinations of various groups or classes of deities worshipped during the second half of the second millennium (B.C.E.) in Hittite Anatolia, an area beyond the Mesopotamian heartland but still within its sphere of influence. This survey is instructive because it provides us with glimpses into other cultures and how they dealt with the equation, identification, and/or syncretization of supernatural entities – be they canonized intercessors in Christianity or divine entities in Hittite religion – as they relate to localized divine entities associated with a specific first name. The potential conceptual differences between these cultures and Mesopotamia (and the Levant) also allow us to consider our methodology. Thirdly, a comparative survey is specifically necessary for our topic of divine multiplicity and splintered personalities because several Assyriological and biblical scholars have already appealed to these (and other) cultures, religions, and geographies in order to illustrate Near Eastern conceptions of the divine.

Of course, because the Hittites themselves were influenced by Mesopotamia and Assyria and because they exerted their own influence upon Assyria and the northern Levant – as discussed in chapter 4.3, the goddess Ištar-of-Nineveh could potentially represent bidirectional influence – we rightly expect scholars to look to the religious traditions of ancient Anatolia. The less obvious comparison is the Christian one because of its distance in both time and space, as well as the fact that Christianity is a monotheistic religion, but scholars have informed their writings by addressing the nature of multiple entities who share common names or origins, such as Porter who ended her article on Ištar-of-Nineveh and Ištar-of-Arbela with a reference to an anecdote about multiple madonnas.[1] Regardless of how obvious these comparative choices are, both the Christian and Hittite religious traditions deal with supernatural entities that are addressed by various names and epithets or are described as taking on various distinct forms.

1 Porter, "Ishtar of Nineveh," 44 n. 16.

2.1 The Multiple Manifestations of the Madonna

In their search of modern analogues to explain ancient conceptions of the divine, a few scholars have been tempted to discuss the treatment of Mary, the Blessed Virgin, in Roman Catholic lay tradition. For instance, as part of his attempt to explain the relationship between Zeus-the-Accomplisher and Zeus-the-Kindly in ancient Greece, Hugh Lloyd-Jones appealed to his own personal experiences and "remembers how in some parts of Italy villagers have been known to stone the Madonna of their neighbours."[2] Lloyd-Jones used this violent confrontation between madonnine shrines, each of which had its own particular name for its preferred madonna, to suggest that ancient Greek deities were also associated with specific cult titles at various sites. Thus, Zeus-the-Accomplisher would have been revered at a different shrine or by a different community than Zeus-the-Kindly. Edwyn Bevan also mentioned madonnine manifestations in his attempt to explain Greek religion. In particular, he noted the goddess Hera's ability to animate more than one image at a time without being limited to any or all of those images, which is a statement that anticipates those by Jacobsen and Pongratz-Leisten in Assyriology and by Sommer in biblical and Classical studies.[3] In much the same way Zeus-the-Kindly and Zeus-the-Accomplisher reminded Lloyd-Jones about madonnine images in Italy, so, too, did Hera's statues remind Bevan of the way nineteenth- and twentieth-century Italian peasants treated their local madonnas:

> If any peasant were pressed to explain his beliefs, he would probably say that the Mother of God who lives in heaven works miracles on the earth through her images, and that his local image is a more favoured instrument for the Madonna than the Madonna of another district.[4]

Both scholars pointed to the Italian infighting over the madonnas, but each drew a slightly different conclusion about the Madonna that they represented. Bringing this analogy into Classical Greek religious tradition, Lloyd-Jones suggested that those who venerated one Zeus might not have accepted the legitimacy of the competing Zeus, whereas Bevan painted any potential rivalry as being about hierarchical status rather than legitimacy. More intriguing,

2 Hugh Lloyd-Jones, "Ancient Greek Religion," *APSP* 145 (2001): 462.

3 Jacobsen, "Graven Image," 18; Pongratz-Leisten, "Divine Agency," 146; and Sommer, *Bodies of God*, 30–35.

4 Edwyn Bevan, *Holy Images: An Inquiry into Idolatry and Image-Worship in Ancient Paganism and in Christianity* (London: G. Allen & Unwin, 1940), 20.

however, is how each scholar used their similar Italian examples to present a different conclusion about the nature of Classical deities and polytheistic tolerance. For Lloyd-Jones, the different epithets and cults represent "not quite the same" Zeus, but for Bevan, the images of Hera are ultimately local mascots of the same heavenly being.[5]

In addition to this observed Italian infighting, the anecdote about the education of an ex-seminarian in Montegrano is occasionally presented by scholars to highlight the multiplicity of Madonna in Italian religious thought. In her discussion of Ištar-of-Arbela and Ištar-of-Nineveh, Porter recounts the ex-seminarian's encounter with an elderly woman: "When a young candidate for the priesthood instructed an elderly woman that there is only one Madonna, she replied scornfully, 'You studied with the priests for eight years and you haven't even learned the differences between the Madonnas!'"[6] This anecdote is meant to highlight the perceived distinctiveness of the five madonnas that have been venerated in Montegrano despite the fact that the official or orthodox position is that each madonna is really a representative of the Madonna, Jesus' mother Mary. As the woman might have recounted, these five madonnas are:

> (1) the Madonna of Pompei, whose miracles are well known in Montegrano; (2) the Madonna of Carmine, whose feast is celebrated in a nearby town; (3) the Madonna of Peace, who is honored in Montegrano with a feast and with a statue erected after World War I and to whom mothers prayed for their sons at war; (4) the Madonna of Assunta, the protector of one of the Montegrano churches; and (5) The Madonna Addolorata, most commonly identified with the mother of Christ.[7]

Because the elderly woman embraces the idea of multiple madonnas, this anecdote also tells us that the lay population viewed these multiple madonnas as distinct yet complementary entities, which is in sharp contrast with Lloyd-Jones's and Bevan's examples and what their perceived cultic competition suggests. This anecdote also exemplifies the original definition of *Volksfrömmigkeit*, "folk religion," because it preserves the supposed differences between the official doctrine of the Catholic Church, represented by the ex-seminarian, and the beliefs of the European peasant lay population, represented by the woman.[8]

---

5 Lloyd-Jones, "Ancient Greek Religion," 462; and Bevan, *Holy Images*, 21.

6 Porter, "Ishtar of Nineveh," 44 n. 16.

7 Edward Banfield, *The Moral Basis of a Backward Society* (Glencoe: The Free Press, 1958), 131.

8 Rainer Albertz, "Household in the ancient Near East," in *Household and Family Religion in Antiquity*, eds. J. Bodel and S. Olyan (Malden: Blackwell, 2008), 91. Regarding these different religious systems in the ancient Near East, Karel van der Toorn prefers the implicit label non-

This relatively short list of the Montegrano madonnas that was originally offered by Edward Banfield is revealing. These five madonnas include both descriptive and geographic epithets, including two epithets that represent madonnas who were venerated in Montegrano even though they originated elsewhere (i.e., Madonna-of-Pompei and Madonna-of-Carmine) and are not themselves native to the community.[9] The other three are descriptive epithets that refer to characteristics of *the* Madonna, namely, Mary. Madonna-of-Peace was thought to answer prayers for a soldiers' safety during times of war, and Madonna-of-Assunta (Madonna-of-the-Assumption) was said to play a similar role as the protector of local churches. Finally, Madonna-Addolorata (Madonna-Laden-with-Sorrow) represented the Virgin Mary who suffers on account of the death of her son.[10]

Notably, of these five separate madonnas, none of their epithets portrays a known biblical event, and only two of the five (e.g., the assumption and the suffering madonnas) represent extra-biblical, ancient Catholic traditions. This corresponds well with Michael Carroll's comment regarding madonnine images in Italy to whom miracles are attributed. Venerated madonnine images are typically not those depicting a biblical narrative or popular Catholic tradition; instead, they are static in nature, recalling no particular narrative.[11] It may be

official religion sphere as "family religion" instead of the traditional. According to van der Toorn, family religion includes personal piety, women's religious practices, and some forms of magic, which were often condemned by official religion. "Family religion" may be a bit vague given the various forms of religion encompassed within it, but it is more useful than *Volksfrömmigkeit* and its English equivalents because these suggest that non-official or popular religions are degenerated forms of religious practice or that they are necessarily derivative forms of official religious practice. For a fuller explanation for choosing "family religion" over "domestic," "personal, "individual," or "private" religion as the counterpart of "official religion" and for choosing "official religion" over "city" or "royal" religion, see Karel van der Toorn, *Family Religion in Babylonia, Syria, and Israel: Continuity and Change in the Forms of Religious Life* (SHCANE 7; Leiden: Brill, 1996), 1–11, esp. 2–3.

9 According to Michael Carroll, geographic epithets are the second most common type of epithets that Italians have attributed to Mary; the primary type reveals her willingness to dispense favors (Michael Carroll, *Madonnas that Maim: Popular Catholicism in Italy since the Fifteenth Century* [Baltimore: Johns Hopkins University Press, 1992], 62).

10 Michael Carroll, *Veiled Threats: The Logic of Popular Catholicism in Italy* (Baltimore: Johns Hopkins University Press, 1996), 93.

11 Carroll, *Veiled Threats*, 28–29. In this regard, Carroll notes that madonnine images holding or nursing an infant are not actually references to biblical stories: "True, the madonna and child who appear in a miraculous image are often engaged in some recognizable activity (e.g., the madonna is gazing at the child, the madonna is nursing the child, the child is touching the madonna's cheek, etc.), but these activities are not associated with a commonly known story." (ibid., 28)

purely coincidental that Carroll's statement concerning miraculous images also mildly applies to our brief textual analysis of the five epithets at Montegrano, but both observations direct us toward the same potential conclusion: madonnas who do not explicitly direct the individual to the Madonna Mary can more easily be viewed as distinct from her and are more likely to receive veneration.

The capacity to view these madonnas with different epithets, or last names, as distinct and independent madonnas is not limited to the city of Montegrano in southern Italy. In 1786, the Synod of Pistoia warned people against investing intrinsic value in any madonnine image by singling it out in contrast with other imagines and exaggerating its role as a mediator:

> ... the holy Synod wants you to fully eradicate the harmful custom of distinguishing certain images, especially (those) of the Virgin with special titles and names.[12]

Moreover, in an attempt to enforce the rulings of the Synod of Pistoia, Leopold II actually limited the number of images any particular church could display of the Madonna:

> No church will be lawfully permitted to keep more than one image of any saint, and of the Blessed Virgin, in particular. The different images and the different titles have raised and nourished a thousand problems and a thousand strange ideas among the people, *as though there were different Blessed Marys because she is invoked under different titles.*[13]

As a result of distinguishing between the physically distinct and separate madonnine images in a given church, Leopold noticed that people were attributing individuality to particular images. He thought that multiple imagines could distract people from the fact that there was only one true Madonna, but he was not concerned with competing factions of devotees within the church as Lloyd-Jones and Bevan might have been. Notice, however, that Leopold gave little concern to the possibility that a single madonnine image would be problematic in any way. We can entertain the idea that people could have venerated a single image of the Blessed Mary in a manner that

---

12 "... vuole il santo Sindodo, che ti tolga assatto il pernicioso costume di distinguere certe date Imagini, specialmente della Vergine con titoli e nomi particolari" (*Atti e decreti del concilio diocesano di Pistoia dell'anno 1786* [Florence: L. S. Olschki Editore, 1986], 1:202, ll. 22–25).

13 "Non sarà parimente lecito tenere nella stessa chiesa più d'un' imagine dell'istesso santo e particolarmente della Vergine Santissima. Le diverse immagini e I diversi titoli hanno suscitato e nudrito mille inconvenienti e mille strane idee nel popolo, come se fosse una diversa persona Maria Santissima, perchè è invocata sotto diversi titoli" (emphasis mine; S. Ricci, *Memorie di Scipinoe de'Ricci*: *Vescovo di Prato e Pistoia* [Florence: Felice Le Monnier, 1865], 2:337–338; see also, 2:322–323).

undermined strict tenets of Catholic monotheistic, but Leopold was not worried about this.

Similarly, a few decades prior to the Synod of Pistoria, the pastor of the Diocese of Asti recorded in 1742 that the 296 families who comprised the community of Priocca, Italy, venerated four distinct madonnas; the 322 families in Monticello venerated seven madonnas; and the 506 families of Canale venerated 13.[14] However, a list with a mere four or thirteen madonnas pales in comparison to the list of epithets derived from prayers, confraternities, or papal indulgences. Each of the following epithets has been officially approved by the Catholic Church (which officially recognizes that each represents the same personality):

> Immaculate-Conception, the-Name-of-Mary, the-Immaculate-Heart-of-Mary, Our-Lady-of-the-Blessed-Sacrament, Our-Lady-of-Lourdes, Our-Lady-of-Fatima, Our-Lady-of-Guadalupe, Our-Lady-of-Miracles, Queen-of-the-Rosary, Mother-of-Sorrows, Our-Lady-of-the-Angels, Our-Lady-of-Perpetual-Help, Our-Lady-Help-of-Christians, Our-Lady-of-Mt-Carmel, Our-Lady-of-Reparation, Our-Lady-of-Mercy, Our-Lady-of-Compassion, Our-Lady-Help-of-the-Sick, Our-Lady-of-Hope.[15]

This list of epithets is far from complete, but as a set these madonnine epithets tend not to reference specific biblical or traditional Catholic stories, which would increase the possibility that a given epithet inspires its own shrine, or is considered separate and distinct from the other madonnine images and the one officially recognized Madonna.[16] Giacomo Medica's sample of 697 Marian sanctuaries in Italy alone revealed 397 unique titles, which indicates the vast potentiality of the veneration of distinct madonnas in Italy.[17] Indeed, the possibility that a given madonnine epithet or title could spawn its own shrine is further increased because each epithet represents a distinct madonnine identity with a distinct sanctuary, festivals, processions, prayers, rituals, confraternities, and shrine. Moreover, many of the madonnas represented by these epithets have their own iconography to distinguish them visually from

14 Carroll, *Madonnas that Maim*, 60.

15 Michael Carroll, *Catholic Cults & Devotions: A Psychological Inquiry* (Montreal: McGill-Queen's University Press, 1989), 155, modified slightly.

16 Carroll, *Veiled Threats*, 29.

17 G. Medica, *I santuari mariani d'Italia* (Torino: Leumann, 1965); and Carroll, *Madonnas that Maim*, 62. Medica distinguishes between the various different primary manifestations of the Madonna in his index, identifying each one as SM (Santa Maria, "Saint Mary"), MS (Maria Santissima, "Blessed Mary"), Md (Madonna, "My Lady"), BV (Beata Vergine, "Blessed Virgin"), NS (Nostra Signora, "Our Lady"), ND (Notre Dame, "Our Lady" [French]), and Rg (Regina, "Queen"; Medica, *I santuari mariani d'Italia*, 749).

other madonnas. For instance, Madonna-del-Rosario is always depicted holding a rosary and appears with San Domenico, whereas Madonna-di-Monte-Berico is a pudgy Madonna when compared to the others.[18] Taken together, it is not difficult to imagine each madonna having a unique personality.

Significantly, in addition to each potentially distinct madonna, who could be seen as having her own distinct feasts, processions, and offerings, some madonnine images are recognized by devotees as undeniably distinct. This view of madonnine distinctiveness was explicitly revealed through a set of interviews with respondents from the Meszzogiorno region in the 1970s, some of whom described the different madonnas as "sisters":

> You have the idea of a group of friends, brothers, or sisters; for example, the various figures of the Madonna are connected through the idea of sisters or of friends, which is considered its own real society ...[19]

This notion of kinship among images was apparently so pervasive throughout Italy that madonnine multiplicity can be described as *imparentamento delle madonne* ("causing the madonnas to become relatives of one another").[20] Moreover, kinship terminology can be traced back to the cathedral at Melfi in 1635. As part of a good-weather ritual, the cathedral's madonna statue would visit two other churches during its procession through the city streets. The cathedral's madonna had to stop at these churches because the people of Melfi recognized that the other churches contained madonnine images that were related to her. These three madonnine images were related to each other precisely because each one was associated with the official Mary recognized by the Catholic Church.[21]

In many ways, these sister images and their temporal co-existence in ritual resemble the Neo-Assyrian cultic processions and rituals that explicitly list Ištar-of-Arbela and Ištar-of-Nineveh (and Ištar-of-Heaven and Assyrian-Ištar)

---

18 Carroll, *Madonnas that Maim*, 63. Medica's illustration of Madonna-di-Monte-Berico at Venice (Medica, *I santuari mariani d'Italia*, 189) is not nearly as pudgy as Carroll (or a Google-image search for this madonna) suggests.

19 "Si ha l'idea del gruppo di amici o di fratelli o di sorelle, per esempio le varie figure di madonne sono collegate con l'idea delle sorelle o delle amiche per cui si determina un vero e proprio sociogramma ..." (Gino Provitera, "L'edicola votive e le sue funzioni," in *Questione meridionale, religione, e classi subalterne*, ed. F. Saija [Napoli: Guida, 1978], 343).

20 Carroll, *Madonnas that Maim*, 66. Carroll cites an Italian study by Cleto Corrain and Pierluigi Zampini, which provides the verb "to cause to become relatives of one another" (Cleto Corrain and Pierluigi Zampinim, *Documenti etnografici e folkloristici nei diocesani italiani* [Bologna: Forni, 1970], 150).

21 Carroll, *Madonnas that Maim*, 66.

as co-participants, including those rituals contained in BM 121206 xi. Although the three sister madonnas from Melfi and their counterparts throughout the rest of Italy were physical images – at least as far as the official church theology was concerned – that were intended to direct the devotee's direction heavenward, we could rightly apply Pongratz-Leisten's "secondary agent" phraseology to this situation. This is not to say that the Italian lay population treated the images like gods or to deride them for acting like pagans, as *Volksfrömmigkeit* scholars might have done in the nineteenth and twentieth centuries[22]; instead, it reminds us that we should be willing to accept that all people, ourselves included, instinctually attribute human minds and personalities to objects that we identify or recognize as agents, and in this particular Italian tradition these madonnine agents act as intercessors for the divine.[23] If we consider each Neo-Assyrian cult statue a divine agent worthy of individual veneration because it represented the ethereal deity and so helped maintain cosmic order, then each sister madonna in Melfi and elsewhere was worthy of individual veneration because it, too, was envisioned as actively manipulating the world for the benefit of the devotee. Specifically, in Italy, madonnine images were thought to manipulate the world in two different ways: serving as intercessors between humanity and the divine and performing miracles for the faithful.

Mary, like each of the canonized saints, serves as intercessor between humanity and God.[24] In addition to telling God what the person needs, this role also allows her (or any other saints) to obtain these benefits from God for

---

22 Jacques Berlinerblau, *Official Religion and Popular Religion in Pre-exilic Ancient Israel* (Cincinnati: Department of Judaic Studies, University of Cincinnati, 2000), 6–7.

23 Pongratz-Leisten, "Divine Agency," 145; and Carroll, *Catholic Cults*, 154.

24 Elizabeth A. Johnson, "Saints and Mary," in *Systematic Theology: Roman Catholic Perspectives*, eds. F. Schüssler Fiorenza and J. Galvin (Minneapolis: Fortress, 1991), 2:150; and Richard P. McBrien, *Catholicism* (Minneapolis: Winston, 1980), 2:873–874 and 891–892. Johnson notes that when the Romans persecuted Christians, saints and martyrs served as Christ's followers who were the mediators between the living and the dead (Johnson, "Saints and Mary," 2:149). Officially, these early martyrs and saints were supposed to serve as revered examples of faithful and devoted Christians for those who felt persecuted, and church statements have stressed this role numerous times in the past two millennia. See, for example, chapter 8 in the Second Vatican Council's *Dogmatic Constitution on the Church*: "The Role of the Blessed Virgin Mary, Mother of God, in the Mystery of Christ and the Church" (McBrien, *Catholicism*, 2:882–883; and Johnson, "Saints and Mary," 2:157–158). Likewise, McBrien still makes a point to emphasize Mary and the saints' role as models rather than mediators: "it is not because Mary and the saints have the power of influence with God that they are objects of veneration and devotion. Rather it is because the grace of God has triumphed *in them*" (McBrien, *Catholicism*, 2:891; italics in the original).

the person. As a result, the faithful see Mary as a power broker for the divine. Officially, the plethora of madonnine epithets and titles are all linked to this one particular Mary, each exalting her attributes but never distracting the faithful from the true source of the benefits, namely, God. This delineated role was attested already in the Second Council of Nicaea in 787:

> For by so much more frequently as [Christ, Mary, the angels and the saints] are seen in artistic representation, by so much more readily are men lifted up to the memory of their prototypes, and to a longing after them; and to these should be given due salutation and honorable reverence, not indeed that true worship of faith which pertains alone to the divine nature; but to these, as to the figure of the precious and life-giving Cross and to the Book of the Gospels and to the other holy objects, incense and lights may be offered according to ancient pious custom. (The Decree of the Holy, Great, Ecumenical Synod, the Second of Nicaea, vol.7, col. 552 [NPNF^2 14:550])

Images of Mary, according to the council, were intended to remind the individual of the reverence due the "prototype" of "our undefiled Lady the Holy Mother of God," Mary, who was a member of the community of holy Catholic saints, but she was not supposed to have been worshipped by the individual because only God should receive worship.[25] As reminders, the madonnine images were not to be thought of as possessing any efficacy themselves (or act as secondary agents) because according to official doctrine such conceptions would be tantamount to idolatry or fetishism.[26] However, because humans have a tendency to assign mindfulness to an object that they consider to already possess efficacy or agency, that inanimate object can easily become an object worth venerating. Thus, Mary could derive her efficacy or agency by playing this intercessor role, but the tangible madonnine image in front of the faithful is also credited with the same efficacy. It was this predisposition towards granting inanimate objects personhood that the Second Council of Nicaea tried to thwart or, at least, minimize, and this is also why several centuries later the Reformers Ulrich Zwingli and John Calvin feared the intermediary role that madonnine (and other) images played for the laity and why they shied away from them.[27] As intercessors, the images possessed agency, which inevitably gave them a life of their own.

25 Johnson, "Saints and Mary," 2:151.

26 McBrien defines fetishism as the identification of the sacred object with the divine in Christianity (McBrien, *Catholicism*, 1:257), and he defines idolatry as the worshipping of a physical object rather than the divine entity it is meant to represent (i.e., God; ibid., 1:xiv). In this specific case at Nicaea, the images in the churches became idols because they received worship that should have been directed to God.

27 McBrien, *Catholicism*, 2:877. This is not to say that the Reformers wholly rejected the veneration of saints, including Mary. Instead, Johnson notes, Lutherans thanked God for Mary

Although Mary may serve as intercessor on behalf of the divine, many individual madonnine images, especially in Italy, are thought to perform miracles for the faithful, and their power is not thought to be dependent upon God or Christ.[28] The faithful also believe that the closer they physically are to the madonna, the more likely it is that she will grant their requests.[29] From the image's perspective, the person's proximity relates to the amount of veneration the image receives. Of course, the possibility that a madonnine image could generate its own power is very much in contrast with orthodox Catholic belief that views the image as a prototype of Mary who is due honor but should ultimately redirect worship to the divine.[30] However, in Italian lay piety these images are, in fact, viewed as independently powerful entities. Indeed, they are thought to crave veneration, and they are believed to exchange favors or grant miracles in order to initiate or continue a following at their shrines.[31] Carroll notes that some madonnine-image shrines began because an image was said to have cured a blind, lame, or deaf individual, but more often, he notes, madonnine images intentionally seek to attract or keep people's attention through supernatural means.[32] For example, an image that has decided it wants to be venerated will bleed, cry, sweat, talk, change color, or make itself surrounded by light in order to appear supernatural and catch a passer-by's attention and, thus, his or her devotion. This madonnine-image desire for self-promotion has long been discussed by devotional commentators, as D. Cesare D'Engenio Caracciolo's early seventeenth-century account demonstrates:

> Thirty-four years ago there was an image of the Madonna-of-Pietà that was painted on the wall of the garden of Fransesco di Sangro, Duke of Torremaggiore. *Not wanting to be held with so little respect*, it began to dispense a great quantity of miracles.[33]

---

and the saints, who served as model Christians whose piety and devotion to God should be imitated (Johnson, "Saints and Mary," 2:152). What the Reformers rejected was the invocation of Mary and the saints as mediators between humankind and God, a role that they considered to be Christ's alone.

28 Carroll, *Veiled Threats*, 28. Carroll notes, "Virtually every investigator who has studied popular Catholicism in Italy has concluded that the saints and madonnas of Italy are seen as more powerful than Christ. Italian madonnas, in other words, do not derive their power from anyone, and certain not from Christ; they themselves have power." (ibid., 28)

29 Carroll, *Veiled Threats*, 46.

30 Johnson, "Saints and Mary," 2:152; and McBrien, *Catholicism*, 2:1065.

31 Carroll, *Veiled Threats*, 37 f. and 45.

32 Carroll, *Veiled Threats*, 37 f.

33 "Sono già 34.anni, che nel muro della parte del giardino di Fransesco di Sangro Duca di Torremaggiore stava dipinta l'Imagine della Madonna della Pietà, la qual no volle con si poca riuerenza esser tenuta, cominciando à risplender di grandiffimi miracoli ..." (D. Cesare D'Engenio, *Napoli Sacra* [Napoli: Ottavio Beltrano, 1623], 262, emphasis mine.)

He readily attributed the miracle to the image rather than the Madonna when he stated that the image desired more respect than it had been receiving. Although D'Engenio's statement does not explicitly contrast the Madonna-of-Pietà image at the Church of S. Maria della Sanità at Naples with other madonnine images, the treatment of and reverence given specifically to this one individual image suggests that devotees would not mistakenly credit another madonnine image. The possibility that Mary or another image other than the one in the Duke of Torremaggiore's garden would have received credit for these miracles undermines the reason that Madonna-of-Pietà granted miracles in the first place, to garner attention and devotion at her particular shrine.

Whether a particular madonnine image was credited with agency because she was thought to be a conduit to the divine as an intercessor or because she performed miracles through her own powers, the cognitive reality underlying both options meant that the image possessed agency and deserved to be credited with intentionality and a human personality. Inanimate objects came to be viewed as alive despite official theology, and Carroll has offered his theory that the Catholic Church as an institution often encourages local madonnine shrines and their images.[34] Contrary to the concerns to Leopold II and the members of the Synod of Pistoia and the Second Council of Nicaea, the Church has and does tacitly sanction a splintering of madonnas from the one official Madonna. This is because the promotion of local madonnine shrines benefits both the local population and the larger church body. In the same way that a church's relic collection can encourage the local congregation, promote pilgrimages, and stimulate the locale as a locus of political power, churches benefit from their active madonnine shrines.[35] Pilgrims may travel to shrines and leave donations, and the local faithful may give more than they

---

34 Carroll, *Madonnas that Maim*, 164. According to Carroll, no madonnine cult can survive without the official support of the church (Carroll, *The Cult of the Virgin Mary: Psychological Origins* [Princeton: Princeton University Press, 1986], 222). As one example of this need for official church encouragement, Carroll notes that in post-Reformation times, the popular madonnine cult Our-Lady-of-Walsingham in Britain was quickly razed and the associated feminine entity morphed into the-Witch-of-Walsingham. With Protestant zeal leading the church in England, the pro-Madonna, Catholic clergy were purged, and the cult died out (ibid., 221).

35 Robert Markus, "How on Earth Could Places Become Holy?" *JECS* 2 (1994): 271; Jonathan Sumption, *The Age of Pilgrimage: the Medieval Journey to God* (Mahwah: Hidden Spring, 2003), 32–34; and Joan Carroll Cruz, *Relics: The Shroud of Turin, the True Cross, the Blood of Januarius ... History, Mysticism, and the Catholic Church* (Huntington: Our Sunday Visitor, 1984), 5.

would have otherwise, but the real advantage of local madonnine shrines is the religious autonomy that they provide.[36] Often these shrines exist in rural or dilapidated areas, and the object of devotion becomes a point of pride for the locals, who no longer need to look to the regional or urban center for religious instruction because the shrine and its clergy now serves as their center. Indeed, this seems to have been the motivation behind the Madonna-of-Pietà shrine in Naples. Madonna-of-Pietà had been discovered in a church where a bishop had been buried more than a millennium earlier in 450 C.E., but by the sixteenth century, the building was in disrepair, serving as the home and shop for a sword-making family.[37] Only after the Dominicans took over the building in 1577, did Madonna-of-Pietà's make its presence known by performing miracles, granting favors, and reestablishing the building as a church.

It is highly unlikely that the madonnine images, which were created to serve as prototypical pictorial representations of Mary, were believed to be independent agents of power only in the eighth, sixteenth, and eighteenth centuries when the Second Council of Nicaea met, the Church of S. Maria della Sanità reestablished itself, and Leopold II and the Synod of Pistoia aimed to limit the number of madonnine images a church could have in it. Rather, they were likely believed to have been agents of power, at least in some fashion, throughout the two millennia of Christian history. As such, the preceding discussion of the various celebrated and venerated madonnas, most of which were in Italy, does not attempt to suggest that these examples are representative of Catholicism, in general, or even a majority or substantial minority of faithful Catholics. Rather, it serves to illustrate issues surrounding multiplicity, the power of names, and agency, and it demonstrates how conceptions held by members of a lay population can differ from theological speculations and official theology embraced by the clergy (or scholar-scribes).

Regarding multiplicity, contrary to what Lloyd-Jones and Bevan concluded about Italian madonnine plurality, the shrines dedicated to each madonna and the people venerating them are not locked in struggles over the legitimacy or place in the hierarchy of a shrine or cult. Instead, we have seen that different madonnine images can be thought to exist simultaneously without issue. This fits with Carroll's conclusions about Italian madonnine plurality:

---

36 William Christian, *Local Religion in Sixteenth-Century Spain* (Princeton: Princeton University Press, 1981), 91; and Carroll, *Cult of the Virgin Mary*, 133.

37 Carroll, *Veiled Threats*, 38–40. Other accounts of Madonna-of-Pietà's origin story provide different occupants and uses for the building.

> Italian Catholics don't really venerate simply "Mary" under some particular title. They venerate simultaneously a *range* of "Marys," each designated by a separate title, each venerated at a different time of the year (since all madonnas have different feast days), and each addressed in at least slightly different prayers. Though there is no denying that all these Marys are perceived to be linked in some way, they are to a large extend considered to be separate and distinct. (Carroll, *Catholic Cults*, 161)

Indeed, as the processions through seventeenth-century Melfi indicate, not only do these separate and distinct madonnas get along, vocabulary has been invented to celebrate their plurality: *imparentamento delle madonne*. These madonnas are sisters.

Also of particular interest is the fact that the Synod of Pistoia and, especially, Leopold II wanted to limit the number of madonnine images, names, and titles available in a given church. Leopold was less concerned that people would inappropriately venerate images, the primary interest discussed in relation to the Second Council of Nicaea, than that they would acknowledge or venerate a multiplicity of madonnine images. He was also concerned with the fact that each madonnine image had its own name, a marker that he recognized as further transforming an inanimate object into an animate agent. The multiplicity of names and objects "raised and nourished a thousand problems and a thousand strange ideas among the people" because the unique titles given to each image made them appear even more distinct from each other than they would have been otherwise. This would be no less true even if everyone involved understood that each named madonnine image was created with the purpose of reminding everyone of the same Mary. Magruš, Asarre, and the other five images of Bēl listed in BM 119282 each had its own name, yet each was recognized as a divine agent on its own; likewise, the varied and various madonnine images in Italy each had her own name that contributed to her individuality and agency. Of course, unique rituals, festivals, prayers, processions, and other features for each separate madonna only increased the likelihood that these images would be venerated as separate and distinct not only from each other, their sister madonnas, but from the Mary to whom they are supposed to redirect attention. Several factors also helped increase the lay population's belief that madonnine images possessed their own agency: miracles and favors can be attributed to specific madonnine images; those madonnas actually desire and seek out veneration; and a closer proximity to an image intensifies the chances of a miracle's occurrence. These madonnas were undeniably separate and distinct, and they wanted people's individual – not undivided – attention, without regard to competing madonnas or to the official one Madonna, Mary.

2.2 Hittite Multiplicity

The second stop on our comparative survey of multiplicity is both geographically and chronologically closer to ancient Mesopotamia, the Hittite religious traditions of second-millennium B.C.E. Anatolia. Hittite religious traditions are admittedly distinct in many ways from the neighboring Mesopotamian religious traditions. The Hittites spoke an Indo-European language rather than Sumerian or a Semitic language, and the topography and climate in Anatolia were quite different from those of the alluvial plain of ancient Iraq. Despite this, the Hittites were undeniably influenced by their Mesopotamian neighbors, as evidenced by their adoption of Sumerian logograms to identify their deities instead of writing the native names out syllabically, which is why the actual names of many Hittite gods are unknown today.[38] Moreover, the genres of the Hittite texts examined below (e.g., state treaties, ritual texts, and royal inscriptions) often resemble their generic Akkadian counterparts. Like the Akkadian texts surveyed in chapters 3 and 4, these Hittite texts contain several embedded god lists (EGLs) that reveal a distinct divine realm that includes numerous entries that share first names (or titles).

For the Mesopotamians, a plethora of names and epithets for one deity was acceptable and celebrated as a means of illumining an important aspect of the deity; after all, the more names that a deity could embrace, the more awe that the deity could inspire. The most famous representative of this is the fifty names attributed to Marduk in the final two tablets of the Babylon creation epic *Enūma eliš* VI–VII. The opposite appears to have been true for the Hittites, whose religious sentiment "was not into theological speculation and contemplation, but practical, pragmatic, functional, and expedient" issues, at least until the reign of Ḫattušili III in the first half of the thirteenth century.[39]

The Hittite subset of gods officially revered by the state continued expanding as new territories were encountered or conquered, which is exemplified by King Tudḫaliya who brought Goddess-of-the-Night (DINGIR GE_6), or at least an allomorph of her, from her temple in Kizzuwatna into the Hittite-controlled

38 Because the first names of so many Hittite deities were written with Sumerian logograms, we often do not know those deities' first names in Hittite. It might be that the Sumerian logograms served to indicate the type – rather than first name – of the deities in question that were being discussed, regardless of what signs appeared in individual inscriptions. For example, IŠKUR = a storm-god; UTU = a sun-god; $UTU.MI_2$ = a sun-goddess; and LAMMA = a tutelary deity

39 Trevor Bryce, *Life and Society in the Hittite World* (Oxford: Oxford University Press, 2002), 145.

Šamuḫa.[40] In this case, Goddess-of-the-Night originated in Kizzuwatna, an independent country that Tudḫaliya did not conquer, and she was added to the Hittite cultic system as a symbol of hope for their peaceful future.[41] However, when the Hittites did conquer other lands, in order to integrate them securely into the empire, they removed cult statues from their cities of origin and transferred them to the imperial capital Ḫattuša for veneration. This act was thought to demonstrate respect for the deities and symbolize the defeated deities' acknowledgement of their takeover by the Hittite foreigners. Beckman refers to this type of incorporation into the empire's official cultic system as "agglutinated" rather than "assimilated" because new deities are added rather than identified with deities already included in it, and Itamar Singer stressed that the Hittite treatment of these cult statues indicated Hittites supplication to deities previously revered only by foreign peoples.[42]

According to Hilary Deighton, the Hittite practice of integrating a deity into their cultic system as a new or unique god rather than identifying it with an already revered deity was one of the "major oddities" of Hittite religion.[43] Because of the Hittite's agglutinative practice, or additive nature, the Hittites could boast of their "thousand gods" (*LI.IM* DINGIR^{meš}, *KBo* 18 77:18–19), which Trevor Bryce has described as "an extreme form of polytheism."[44]

---

40 Jared L. Miller, "Setting up the Goddess of the Night Separately," in *Anatolian Interfaces: Hittites, Greeks, and their Neighbors: Proceedings of an International Conference on Cross-cultural Interaction, September 17-19, 2004, Emory University, Atlanta, GA*, eds. Billie Jean Collins, Mary R. Bachvarova, and Ian Rutherford (Oxford: Oxbow Books, 2008), 68; see also Richard H. Beal, "Dividing a God," in *Magic and Ritual in the Ancient World*, eds. Paul Mirecki and Marvin Meyer (Leiden: Brill, 2002), 197–208. Miller and Beal both observe that Muršili's inscription does not adequately identify which King Tudḫaliya is being discussed because the text simply refers to the previous king as "my forefather" or "my ancestor." Beal argues for an identification with Tudḫaliya II after ruling out Tudḫaliya III, who was Muršili's actual grandfather, whereas Miller prefers Tudḫaliya I (Beal, "Dividing a God," 199 n. 15; and Jared Miller, *Studies in the Origins, Development and Interpretation of the Kizzuwatna Rituals*, StBoT 46 [Wiesbaden: Harrassowitz, 2004], 350–356).

41 Beal, "Dividing a God," 199.

42 Gary Beckman, "Pantheon. A. II. Bei den Hethitern," *RlA* 10/3–4 (2004) 308; and Itamar Singer, "'The Thousand Gods of Hatti': The Limits of an Expanding Pantheon," in *Concepts of the Other in Near Eastern Religions*, eds. I. Alon, I. Gruenwald, and I. Singer (Leiden: Brill, 1994), 86–87.

43 Hilary Deighton, *The 'Weather-God' in Hittite Anatolia: An Examination of the Archaeological and Textual Sources* (Oxford: British Archaeological Reports International Series, 1982), 109.

44 Bryce, *Life and Society*, 135. Restorations of the phrase "a thousand gods" can also be found in letter nos. 34b (HKM 29) and 85 in H. A. Hoffner's *Letters from the Hittite Kingdom*, ed. G. Beckman, SBLWAW 15 (Atlanta: SBL, 2009). Similarly, in the Telipinu myth, the sun-god hosted a feast for the thousand deities, but they were not satiated because Telipinu soon disappeared, causing the vegetation, trees, pastures, and springs to dry and bringing famine

Other peoples' gods became new Hittite gods, and the *Puḫanu Chronicle* from the Old Hittite period illustrates this agglutinative practice through a dialogue between IŠKUR-of-Aleppo and the king's emissary (*CTH* 16b). Only when IŠKUR-of-Aleppo felt that the Hittites had properly respected his divinity would he allow them to rule over the newly conquered city of Aleppo. This was indicated by the charge that he gave to Puḫanu: "The male gods of Storm-god [IŠKUR] sent me to the King (saying): 'Go (and) find the Great Ones and let the Great Ones say to the King: "You have shown me respect, (therefore) I have come"'" (Singer's translation).[45] According to the chronicle, the Hittites captured Aleppo because the local gods invited them, not simply because the Hittites had a mighty military. Likewise, when Šuppiluliuma conquered Carchemish in the fourteenth century, he respectfully made sure that no one desecrated the local temples, and the local goddess Kubaba, the Great-Lady-of-Carchemish, was soon agglutinated into the Hittite cultic system at Ḫattuša.[46] As a result of the Hittite's theological agglutination, foreign deities retained their earlier personalities while residing in Ḫatti, even when the new gods closely resembled established Hittite gods, and the number of officially revered deities continued to grow. Eventually, the Hittite cultic system came to consist of mostly foreign gods, including at least 25 Ištar goddesses and numerous storm-gods, two of which were known along with their consorts as "IŠKUR-of-Aleppo- and Ḫebat-of-Aleppo-of-Ḫattuša" and "IŠKUR-of-Aleppo- and Ḫebat-of-Aleppo-of-Šamuḫa" (*KUB* 6 45 i 43 and 51).[47]

In order to combat this ever expanding cultic system, a divine restructuring was attempted by Ḫattušili III's wife Queen Puduḫepa during the middle of the thirteenth century, relatively late in the history of the Hittite Empire. In practice, her reform meant that her son King Tudḫaliya IV needed to make sure that local temples were in good condition so that the local people did not feel isolated from their gods.[48] Benefiting from the peace with Egypt that had been

---

in the land (*The Disappearance of the Storm God*, § 5 [A i 16–21; H. A. Hoffner, *Hittite Myths*, ed. G. Beckman, SBLWAW 2 [Atlanta: Scholars Press, 1998), 21]).

45 Singer, "Thousand Gods," 87.

46 Singer, "Thousand Gods," 88.

47 See Singer, "Thousand Gods," 82 and 88; and Beckman, "Ištar of Nineveh Reconsidered," 3. Pongratz-Leisten has noted that "the concept of 'foreign god' 'or the god of the Other' was of limited significance in the cognitive world of the ancients" (Pongratz-Leitsten, "Comments on the Translatability," 85), but the our-god versus foreign-god dichotomy is very real in the Hittite and Neo-Assyrian treaty traditions (see, for example, Tables 2.8, 3.10, and 3.12 and 3.13).

48 Laroche claimed that Tudḫaliya began his reign as a co-regent with his mother Puduḫepa after the death of his father Ḫattušili III (Laroche, "Le Panthéon de Yazilikaya," *JCS* 6 [1952]: 122). For this reason, the religious reforms that date to his reign can also be attributed to the queen mother.

established by his predecessors, Tudḫaliya was able to focus on these religious reforms and their potential ramifications. He commissioned deputies to survey cult sites throughout Anatolia and to take inventory of cultic equipment, personnel, and the various local ceremonies, and he brought many of these same rituals, cults, and deities to the capital to be worshipped in the Great Temple that he had constructed.[49]

Despite Puduḫepa's attempts, her reforms probably did not affect the organization of local cults or the identification of comparable deities in any real way. She might have boasted in her prayer that the sun goddess UTU.MI-of-Arinna had been successfully identified with Ḫebat and worshipped as part of her campaign to link Hurrian with Hittite deities:

> O UTU.MI-of-Arinna//My-Lady//Queen-of-all-the-Lands! In Hatti you gave yourself the name UTU.MI-of-Arinna, but the land which you made, that of the cedar, there you gave yourself the name Hebat. (*Puduhepa's Prayer to the Sun-goddess of Arinna and her Circle for the Well-being of Ḫattusili*; *CTH* 384, Singer's translation, modified slightly)[50]

However, according to Singer, separate cults for both goddesses continued to be maintained, even at the same localities, and the vast multiplicity of independent and distinct deities remained.[51]

In fact, the bas-reliefs and texts from Yazilikaya, near Ḫattuša, which were completed during Tudḫaliya IV's reign, argue against the divine streamlining process that Puduḫepa claimed to have imagined and reconstructed. One the one hand, Yazilikaya suggests that she successfully identified the Hurrian IŠKUR (Tešub) and UTU.MI-of-Arinna with the Hittite (unspecified) IŠKUR and Ḫebat, even if they were worshipped as separate deities elsewhere in the empire. Also, because Tešub/IŠKUR and UTU.MI-of-Arinna/Ḫebat appear in the center of the bas-relief and the gazes of all the other deities face them, we can conclude that these two were Puduḫepa's and her son's chief deities. On the other hand, the tenth tablet of the Hurrian-Hittite *itkalzi*-ritual, which is comparable to the iconography of the bas-reliefs, indicates that two storm-gods (ll. 41–42) and two Šaušga, the Hurrian and Hittite equivalent for Ištar,

49 Piotr Taracha, *Religions of Second Millennium Anatolia* (Wiesbaden: Barrassowitz, 2009), 133.

50 Itamar Singer, *Hittite Prayers*, ed. H. A. Hoffner, SBLWAW 11 (Atlanta: Society of Biblical Literature, 2002), 102. Two parallel lines (//) are used here and elsewhere to indicate that a proper name and epithet are acting together (e.g., UTU.MI-of-Arinna//My-Lady//Queen-of-all-the-Lands and Ištar//Lady-of-Nineveh). With reference to the cuneiform evidence, these parallel lines indicate that the first name is preceded by a divine determinative, but the epithet is not.

51 Singer, "Thousand Gods," 90.

goddesses (ll. 38 and 56) were depicted in the bas-reliefs.[52] Although the Hurrian storm-god Tešub may have been identified with a Hittite storm-god, as indicated by ^{d}10 in the text (*JCS* 6 121, l. 42), a second storm-god is shown standing behind the first in the reliefs and is identified as IŠKUR-of-Ḫattuša (^{d}10 ḫa^{ki}, l. 41) in the corresponding text of the *itkalzi*-ritual.[53] Additionally, the Šaušga in l. 38 is located among a collection of several male deities (ll. 30–35 and 39–42), accompanied by her entourage members Ninatta and Kulitta (ll. 36–37).[54] This group of deities corresponds to the left portion of the bas-reliefs. The second Šaušga name in l. 56 is the last of a series of goddess divine names (ll. 43 ff.), which corresponds to the right portion of the bas-reliefs, even though this Šaušga is no longer visible.[55] Because multiple storm-god and Šaušga deities were maintained in the Yazilikaya bas-reliefs, not even this supposed paradigm of Puduḫepa's Hurrian-Hittite identifications reflects a full religious reform.

Her reform might have equated Hurrian deities with their Hittite counterparts in the official state religion in a very specific and limited way, but it did little to minimize the multiplicity of deities who shared common divine first names – the storm-gods, the tutelary deities, and the Ištar/Šaušga goddesses – to which we now turn. Actually, divine "first name" may not always be the most accurate description of the cuneiform representing Hittite deities because the cuneiform signs often seem to refer to a function or class of Hittite deities rather than a particular deity's first name. If so, then a better designation for Hittite uses of ^{d}IŠKUR (= 10 = U), ^{d}LAMMA, and ^{d}IŠTAR would be "divine label," reflecting how the Hittites categorized their gods according

---

52 Taracha, *Religions of Second Millennium Anatolia*, 95.

53 Laroche, "Panthéon de Yazilikaya," 121. Laroche supplied the logogram AN/DINGIR and interpreted l. 42 as a reference specifically to Tešub-of-Heaven (see Table 2.1).

54 Robert Alexander accepts that the goddess on right is Ištar/Šaušga (compare *JCS* 6 121, l. 56 in Lacroche, "Panthéon de Yazilikaya," 121), but he claims that the goddess on the left (i.e., the position comparable to l. 38) is a warrior goddess "with a dual sexual nature" (Robert Alexander, "Šaušga and the Hittite Ivory from Megiddo," *JNES* 50 [1991]: 173; see Table 2.1).

55 This presence of two Ištar/Šaušga goddesses in the bas-relief at Yazilikaya is curious because this would make it the only divine designation that was repeated in the corresponding text of the *itkalzi*-ritual; after all, the unspecified storm-god (^{d}10, l. 42) is distinguished from the localized storm-god by the addition of an epithet (^{d}10 *ḫa*^{uru}, l. 41). Laroche noted this peculiarity at the end of his discussion by commenting on the absence of "^{d}IB = the Hurrian Ninurta" (Laroche, "Panthéon de Yazilikaya," 121 n. 51). Note, however, that Laroche retained a question mark at the beginning of l. 56 (see Table 2.1), indicating the presence of a sign that could have potentially modified Šaušga's name in l., 56 distinguishing it from the Šaušga in l. 38.

to the role they played. Of these three potential designations, two divine labels best demonstrate this: the storm-gods and the tutelary deities.

Originally, the Hittite scribes used the logogram IŠKUR to represent their storm-god, who was honored as the Hittite chief deity; however, because syllabically written divine names are quite uncommon in Hittite texts, the specific personal name of even the most important Hittite storm-god is still uncertain to us. Thus, although Daniel Schwemer has noted that the Hattic storm-god was named Taru, a word meaning "to be powerful" or "to overcome," this deity's primary epithet and designation as head of the Hittite hierarchy was simply IŠKUR-of-Heaven.[56] The deity's worship spread throughout the Hittite empire, with numerous local cults named in Hittite texts. Moreover, Philo H. J. Houwink ten Cate says that about 140 towns had their own storm-god cult, and according to Schwemer, many of these local deities were considered sons of the great IŠKUR-of-Heaven, including IŠKUR-of-Nerik and IŠKUR-of-Ziplanda.[57] Many of these local storm-gods "were established as gods in their own right" and had their own personal divine names, such as Telipinu, Piḫaimmi, and Piḫammi.[58]

56 Daniel Schwemer, "The Storm-Gods of the Ancient Near East: Summary, Synthesis, Recent Studies: Part II," *JANER* 8 (2008), 15, 18, and 20. Alberto Green equates the Hittite IŠKUR-of-Heaven with IŠKUR-of-Ḫatti (Alberto R. W. Green, *The Storm-God in the Ancient Near East*, Biblical and Judaic Studies 8 [Lake Winona: Eisenbrauns, 2003], 131–132).

57 Philo H. J. Houwink ten Cate, "The Hittite Storm God: His Role and his Rule According to Hittite Cuneiform Sources," in *Natural Phenomena: Their Meaning, Depiction, and Description in the Ancient Near East*, ed. D. J. W. Meijer (Amsterdam: North-Holland, 1992), 84; and Schwemer, "Storm-Gods: Part II," 21. Schwemer notes that these two localized storm-gods, IŠKUR-of-Nerik and IŠKUR-of-Ziplanda, were equated in the imperial period.

58 According to Deighton, Telipinu and IŠKUR-of-Nerik had much in common (Deighton, *'Weather-God,'* 71). Both Telipinu and IŠKUR(^{d}10)-of-Nerik were sons of (the unspecified) IŠKUR (i.e., ^{d}10). IŠKUR-of-Nerik was the son of UTU.MI$_2$-of-Arinna, and Telipinu was also associated with her. Moreover, each was associated with Mt. Ḫulla, and the mythology of both gods involved the drying up of springs.

Similarly, Schwemer typically does not interpret multiple localized storm-gods as indicating separate distinct deities, but he does recognize the distinctions between Piḫaimmi and Piḫammi, who were sons of another storm-god (Schwemer, "Storm-Gods: Part II," 22 and n. 57; see also *Chicago Hittite Dictionary P*, *piḫaimmi*, and *piḫammi*). Otherwise, he considers the storm-god titles with non-geographic epithets as manifestations of Taru:

> The same embedding in the pantheon as son-gods was also then applied to some of the many aspectually differentiated manifestations of **the** storm-god; typical examples of such aspectually differentiated manifestations of **the** storm-god include the storm-god "of thunder", "of the meadow", "of the (the king's) person", "of the market", "of the army", "of the oath" etc. (Schwemer, "Storm-Gods: Part II," 21, emphasis mine)

Many of these numerous storm-gods, however, had very different characteristics and backgrounds, and subsuming them all under the general storm-god category IŠKUR does them a disservice. Many of these storm-gods were from the pre-Hittite layers of religious tradition from the third and early second millennia, and they each represented the nature of the water and weather that was local to each cult site's geography, climate, and community.[59] As a result of these differing climatic and geographic differences, each deity had different characteristics, and any common features between them were more a function of each deity's association with water than a common storm-god heritage, and for this reason many scholars prefer to refer to Hittite storm-gods as "weather gods."[60] For example, some storm- or weather-god differences include the peaceful attributes of the Anatolian terrestrial/chthonic water-god Taru, who was associated with aquifers and who could act as the divine herder of the winds, and the Hurrian celestial storm-god Tešub, who was associated with thunder, lightning, and rain.[61]

Regardless, these various kinds of water-, weather-, or storm-gods were all labeled IŠKUR or 10 in the cuneiform texts, including the Hurrian god Tešub, the Akkadian god Adad, and the Northwest Semitic god Hadad.[62] Although they all shared the same labels, scholars have identified between five and eight separate types of Hittite storm-god.[63] Of these, Houwink ten Cate's analysis of Hittite storm-god epithets is the most pertinent and instructive for us. The first

---

59 Green, *Storm-God*, 89–91.

60 See, for example, J. G. Macqueen, "Nerik and its Weather God," *AnSt* 30 [1980]: 179–187; and Deighton, *The 'Weather-God' in Hittite Anatolia: An Examination of Archaeological and Textual Sources* (1982).

61 Green, *Storm-God*, 130 f.

62 Over time, the logogram ᵈ10 – the "unequivocal Sumerian logogram for the Semitic Adad" (Green, *Storm-God*, 131) – replaced ᵈIŠKUR as the preferred storm-gods sign, and by the mid-fifteenth century, ᵈ10 became the standard logogram for Hittite storm-gods. This change coincided with the Hittite empire's rise as a dominant political power in the region and reflected their interests in war and domination, which coincided with Semitic Adad's role as a warrior god (Deighton, *'Weather-God,'* 50).

Despite this common cuneiform designation, the many Hittite storm-gods had nothing in common with the Semitic god Adad (Deighton, *'Weather-God,'* 49–50). In comparison to the Hittite storm-god tradition, Adad's character was a destructive one, even though he was also associated with life-giving rain in addition to death-inflicting floods. Green notes that in later Hittite tradition, IŠKUR-of-Heaven was associated with Mesopotamian Adad (Green, *Storm-God*, 149).

63 Özgüç's classification system with eight categories was determined by iconography (Deighton, *'Weather-God,'* 37), and Houwink ten Cate has five categories that relate to the storm-god epithets (Houwink ten Cate, "Hittite Storm God," 85).

of his five categories describes deities who were defined by forces of nature: e.g., IŠKUR-of-lightning, IŠKUR-of-clouds, IŠKUR-of-rain, IŠKUR-of-dew, and IŠKUR-of-growing.[64] The second category defines these deities in terms of human characteristics or by their relationship with mankind, including IŠKUR-of-the-head, which reveals god's relationship with the king. The third category defines the deity in relation to non-city geography, such as IŠKUR-of-the-field. The fourth comprises topography within the city: e.g., IŠKUR-of-the-temple, IŠKUR-of-the-house, IŠKUR-of-the-market, and IŠKUR-of-the-palace. Finally, the fifth category of epithets deals with warfare and political authority: e.g., IŠKUR-of-the-army-camp, IŠKUR-of-the-coadjutor, IŠKUR-of-the-alliance, and IŠKUR-of-the-fastening. Stressing the importance of unique names, Houwink ten Cate claimed that each epithet represented a distinct deity because these epithets – whether they are adjectival or participial in nature – "have been personified."[65]

Storm-gods with geographic epithets, Houwink ten Cate's third and fourth categories, comprise a large portion of storm-gods in Hittite inscriptions. Of the 21 storm-gods listed in the divine witness section of Šuppiluliuma I's treaty with Ḫuqqana of Ḫayasa (*CTH* 42; see Table 2.2), most epithets associate a deity with a city: e.g., IŠKURs-of-Aleppo, IŠKUR-of-Arinna, and IŠKUR-of-Nerik. IŠKUR-of-Heaven is the first storm-god in *CTH* 42, and following him are eight geographically identified storm-gods and two warfare-themed storm-gods, IŠKUR-of-the-Army and IŠKUR-of-the-Market. Following another spurt of city-based storm-gods is IŠKUR-of-the-Ruin-Mound, a deity with a non-city geographic epithet. In all, *CTH* 42 lists sixteen localized Anatolian storm-gods – seventeen if we include IŠKUR-of-Heaven – and four others, which is only slightly higher than the fourteen localized storm-gods and three storm-gods with non-geographical epithets listed in *CTH* 53 and 62 (see Table 2.3 for a collection of IŠKUR gods from other treaties).

In addition to treaties and ritual texts, storm-gods with geographic epithets also appeared in other genres, such as prayers. For instance, King Muršilil II named multiple storm-gods in his personal prayers, and he selected each deity to aid with a particular problem. Muršili became king in the fourteenth century because a plague killed off much of the Hittite population, including his two royal predecessors, his father Šuppiluliuma I and his brother Arnuwanda II.[66] The plague lasted twenty years, and Muršili concluded that it was sent in response to his father's political misdeeds. In order to stop the plague, Muršili

64 Houwink ten Cate, "Hittite Storm God," 85.
65 Houwink ten Cate, "Hittite Storm God," 109.
66 Gary Beckman, "Plague Prayers of Muršili II," in *COS* 1.60:156.

first performed the ritual bloodshed that his predecessors had neglected, but this did not work, so he prayed for forgiveness and relief from the plague. He addressed his first prayer to all the Hittite deities:

> O [all of] you [male deities], all female deities, [all] male deities of the oath, [all] female deities of the oath, [all] primeval [deities], all [male] deities and all female deities who were summoned to assembly for witnessing an oath in this [matter]! O mountains, rivers, springs, and underground watercourses! I, Muršili, your priest and servant, have now pled my case before you. O gods, my lords, [listen] for me to my concern about which I present you my justification. (*First Prayer of Muršili, COS* 1.60:156; *CTH* 378, Beckman's translation)

This appeal reflects the extreme polytheism of the Hittite tradition, but the prayer was not answered, so the king tried again. This time, Muršili specifically petitioned IŠKUR-of-Ḫatti because he believed that Šuppiluliuma's transgressions had angered his particular god:

> O IŠKUR-of-Ḫatti//My-Lord, and gods, my lords – so it happens: People always sin. My father sinned and transgressed the word of IŠKUR-of-Ḫatti, my lord .... Because I have confessed the sin of my father, let the souls of IŠKUR-of-Ḫatti, my lord, and of the gods, my lords, again be appeased. May you be well-disposed toward me once more. Send the plague away from Ḫatti again .... I repeatedly plead my case [to you], IŠKUR-of-Ḫatti, my lord. Save me! (*Second Prayer of Muršili, COS* 1.60:157; *CTH* 378, Beckman's translation, modified slightly)

He directed a third prayer to UTU.MI-of-Arinna, a fourth to a plethora of deities residing throughout the empire, and a fifth to several gods; however, he singled out only one individual male deity in the second prayer because he believed that only he had been personally offended. This individual deity was specifically and explicitly named as IŠKUR-of-Ḫatti, and his name appeared more than two dozen times in the second prayer.[67]

In another prayer, Muršili responded to an oracle from which he learned that a particular storm-god was responsible for his "withered" speech, the result of a minor stroke that the king suffered after the stresses of constant warfare, continued plague, and emotional family crises:

> Thus speaks My Sun Muršili, the Great King: "I travelled to Til-Kunnu ... A storm burst forth and the IŠKUR thundered terrifyingly. I was afraid. Speech withered in my mouth, and my speech came forth somewhat haltingly. I neglected this plight entirely. But as the

67 The deity is addressed as (the unspecified) IŠKUR three times in the prayer, one of which has been restored. Approximately three of the twenty-six occurrences of IŠKUR-of-Ḫatti have been partially or totally restored.

> years followed one another, the cause of my plight began to appear in my dreams. And in my sleep the god's hand fell upon me, and my mouth went sideways. I consulted the oracles, and IŠKUR-of-Manuzziya was ascertained (as responsible for my plight)." (*CTH* 486:1–10, Bryce's translation, modified slightly)[68]

As he indicated, Muršili implicitly understood that a storm-god was responsible for his affliction because a thunder storm originally triggered the problem, but such a generality did not satisfy the king. He was determined to find out exactly who this god was. He sought oracular advice, offered up a "substitute ox" at a storm-god's temple in Kumme, and wore the clothes that he wore when his ailment first occurred.[69] As a result, Muršili discovered that IŠKUR-of-Manuzziya was the offended deity, so he made sure that IŠKUR-of-Manuzziya was satisfied and would heal him. Unfortunately, no extant text reports whether the ritual offering and prayer was effective or confirms that IŠKUR-of-Manuzziya was actually the god responsible for Muršili's stroke, but his prayer highlights how important a Hittite storm-god's last name, or epithet, was in identifying him among the crowd of Hittite storm-gods. The king appealed to IŠKUR-of-Ḫatti when he was the responsible party, and he appealed to IŠKUR-of-Manuzziya when he was. Anything less specific did not suffice.

In sum, in the Hittite world, many deities were identified as storm-gods. This collection of storm-gods included deities representing numerous local, regional, and ethnic origins, and these storm-gods represented several different types of water-, weather-, and storm-related phenomena. As Hittite hegemony expanded from Ḫattuša throughout Anatolia and into northern Syria, new local storm-gods were typically not identified with one another, although some did establish filial connections with each other. Instead, new cults were established in the capital and the new deities' geographic origins functioned as their last names, distinguishing each individual storm-god from the others in ritual texts, treaties, and royal inscriptions. Making distinctions between gods was important, as Muršili's prayers demonstrate.

Hittite scribes did not just label storm-gods by function or class with a particular cuneiform sign or signs, like IŠKUR, 10, and U; they also labeled tutelary, or protective, deities as a class with the logogram LAMMA. Protective deities were not unique to Hittite tradition. LAMMA and the related ALAD are both Sumerian words, and both logograms also have Akkadian equivalents, *lamassu* and *šēdu*, which represent the spirits that watched or guarded over

---

68 Trevor Bryce, *The Kingdom of the Hittites* (Oxford: Oxford University Press, 1999), 239.
69 Bryce, *Kingdom*, 239–240.

particular individuals, places, or activities, or served as patron deities.[70] In Hittite texts, the LAMMA-sign functioned as a common noun, as it did in Sumerian and Akkadian, but in most occurrences it also served as the title of a specific unnamed deity, standing alone or accompanied by an epithet.[71] Some Hittite inscriptions even refer to the multiplicity of LAMMA deities by addressing them as a collective group. The phrase *A.NA ŠUM*$^{\text{!-ḫi.a}}$ ^{d}LAMMA *ḫu-u-ma-an-da-aš* ("to the names of all the tutelary deities," *KUB* 2 1 i 42, McMahon's translation) appears in the *Festival for all the Tutelary Deities*, and ^{d}LAMMA$^{\text{ḫi.a}}$ ("the tutelary deities," *KUB* 5 1 ii 94–95) appears in an oracle revealed during a military campaign. So, we can liken LAMMA to a deity's first name, but it seems to operate more like a label for a deity or as a class of deity than an actual first name; however, we can still treat the epithets like last names.

In his study of Hittite tutelary deities, Gregory McMahon has identified four distinct categories.[72] The first group includes those whose unique divine first name we know (e.g., Zithariya or Karzi). Those in the second group were only identified by the tutelary logogram LAMMA. Those in the third group were identified as a LAMMA and had a geographic epithet (e.g., ^{d}LAMMA-^{uru}Karaḫna), and those in the fourth group had a non-geographic epithet (e.g., ^{d}LAMMA-^{kuš}*kuršaš*, The-tutelary-deity-of-the-hunting-bag). Most LAMMA deities had some sort of epithet, so they belonged to the final two categories.[73] Because most of our Hittite sources come from Ḫattuša, LAMMA deities from other regions played relatively minor roles in the festivals and cult activities recorded at the capital, but it is because of these later ritual texts that McMahon was able to detect these four groups of LAMMA deities.[74]

McMahon suggests that the Hittites inherited their numerous named and unnamed LAMMA deities from the political fragmentation of the early second millennium.[75] As with the numerous localized IŠKUR gods, the Hittites

---

70 Greogry McMahon, *The Hittite State Cult of the Tutelary Deities*, AS 25 (Chicago: The Oriental Institute of the University of Chicago, 1991), 2; *CAD* L, *lamassu* mng. 1; and *CAD* Š/2, *šēdu* A mng. 1.

71 McMahon, *Hittite State Cult*, 28. LAMMA deities included both male and female deities, as indicated in Muwatalli's prayer to IŠKUR-Piḫaššašši (*KUB* 6 45 + *KUB* 30 14 ii 5–6), which addresses a tutelary deity from Karaḫna, whose actual name Ala was spelled out and preceded by a feminine determinative (f): ^{df}*a-la-a-aš* (ibid., 12).

72 McMahon, *Hittite State Cult*, 4–5.

73 McMahon, *Hittite State Cult*, 10.

74 McMahon, *Hittite State Cult*, 33–35; and Taracha, *Religions of Second Millennium Anatolia*, 85.

75 McMahon, *Hittite State Cult*, 212.

included each new LAMMA that they encountered in their cultic system, they provided them offerings in the state cult, and they invoked them as treaty witnesses. As the Hittite Empire expanded, most localized LAMMA deities became less prominent in official texts and rituals, possibly as a result of the increased Hurrian influence in the Hittite cult.[76] By the late Empire Period, all the LAMMA deities, including (the unspecified) LAMMA and LAMMA-of-Ḫatti – who were privileged to be the only two LAMMA deities addressed in Muršili II's fifth plague prayer (following an unspecified LAMMA; see *CTH* 379; *KUB* 31 121 + *KUB* 48 111) – were portrayed as part of the collection of lower-level deities in treaties and ritual texts. In contrast, during the Old and Middle Hittite periods, the unspecified LAMMA had been a member of an elite Hittite triad, along with (the unspecified) IŠKUR and UTU.MI.[77] However, as the divine witness list in Šuppiluliuma I's treaty with Ḫuqqana of Ḫayasa (*CTH* 42, § 7) indicates, the class of LAMMA deities was eventually demoted. The treaty's witness list begins with UTU-of-Heaven and UTU.MI-of-Arinna, several IŠKUR gods with geographic and non-geographic epithets, and two Ḫebat goddesses before identifying any LAMMA deities (see Table 2.2). When the first LAMMA finally appears in this witness list, it is (the unspecified) LAMMA who begins a set of eight LAMMA deities, but his was the 26th divine name in this treaty. Another indication that the LAMMA deities had been demoted as a class is the fact that no kings from the later periods identified any LAMMA deity as their special patron protective god: Muršili II depended upon UTU.MI$_2$-of-Arinna; Muwatalli depended upon (the unspecified) IŠKUR; and Ḫattušili III depended upon Šaušga-of-Šamuḫa.[78] Even Tudḫaliya IV – the king who sponsored the

76 McMahon, *Hittite State Cult*, 323 and 212.

77 McMahon, *Hittite State Cult*, 32. The Hittite triad – (the unspecified) UTU, IŠKUR, and LAMMA – appears in both state-sponsored rituals, such as the *Totenritual and the Ritual by the Enemy Border* (*KUB* 39 33 iii 7–9 and *KUB* 4 1 i 3), and in "private" rituals, like the one of Pupuwanni (*CTH* 408; *KUB* 41 3:20′–22′) or the *Prayer of Arnuwanda and Ašmunikal* (*CTH* 375; FHL 3 + *KUB* 31 123:9).

The tutelary deity known as LAMMA-of-Ḫatti remained an important deity and appeared in more texts than any other localized LAMMA in the later period (McMahon, *Hittite State Cult*, 34; see also Taracha, *Religions of Second Millennium Anatolia*, 84–85 and 95). Even in this late period, LAMMA-of-Ḫatti's special status is made clear when we compare him to other localized LAMMA deities. For instance, he was included in an offering list from the *Festival of Ištar-of-Šamuḫa* (*KUB* 27 1 i 64–67) and in a list of Hurrian deities (*KUB* 34 102+ ii 11–15′, iii 32′–35′; ibid., 35).

78 McMahon, *Hittite State Cult*, 51–52; and Taracha, *Religions of Second Millennium Anatolia*, 165.

Festival for All the Tutelary Deities in the second half of the thirteenth century – depended upon Šarruma for protection rather than any particular LAMMA.[79]

Despite the group's collective demotion in the later period, Tudḫaliya IV did commission LAMMA-focused rituals. In fact, the texts belonging to the *Festival for All the Tutelary Deities* enumerates more LAMMA deities than are known from all other sources. McMahon speculates that the scribe who was responsible for this festival created many of these otherwise unattested LAMMA divine names because he wanted "new tutelary deities to protect everything the writer can think of."[80] According to McMahon, if the LAMMA deities whose names are only known from this festival were revered here for the first time, then these texts provide insight into the religious speculations of the Hittite scribes and scholars: "The Hittite penchant for seeking out and worshiping all possible manifestations of the divine is illustrated beautifully by this experiment in diversification."[81] Apparently, gods could be invented to suit all possible needs of the Hittite king, his people, and the empire, but we should assume that the scribe must have believed that these LAMMA deities had already existed and that they did not invent gods for the sole sake of venerating them. However, if any creative license was involved, it does indicate that the LAMMA deities were more important as a class of deity than as individuals.[82]

Two paragraphs of the *Festival for All the Tutelary Deities* (*KUB* 2 1, §§ 31′–32′) provide a list of LAMMA deities who received two large oxen as a group (2 ⌜GUD GAL⌝ *A-NA ŠUM*$^{\text{!ḫi.a}}$, *KUB* 2 1 i 42; see Table 2.4), and § 33′ is a list of LAMMA deities who shared the common name or title Ala (^{d}*a-a-la-aš ŠUM*$^{\text{ḫi.a}}$-*aš ḫu-u-ma-an-da-aš*, "to all the names of Ala," iii 27), each of which had an additional epithet. As a group, the Ala deities received one cow and three billy-goats-of-the-countryside (1 GUD.AB$_2$ *gi-im-ma-ra-uš* 3 MAŠ$_2$.GAL, iii 26). All together, more than one hundred deities were listed in these three paragraphs: "a total of 112 names of LAMMA" (ŠU.NIGIN 1 *ME* 12 *ŠUM*$^{\text{ḫi.a}}$ ^{d}LAMMA, 2.1 iii 25, McMahon's translation). Notably, many of the Ala deities repeated characteristics and epithets belonging to LAMMA deities in the earlier paragraphs, which may indicate that LAMMA and Ala deities formed divine couples or that each specific type of tutelary deity controlled a different area of protection.[83]

79 The festival is described in a text (preserved in two copies) that mentions King Tudḫaliya IV, but McMahon suggests that festival's origins predate this king (McMahon, *Hittite State Cult*, 140).
80 McMahon, *Hittite State Cult*, 83.
81 McMahon, *Hittite State Cult*, 83.
82 McMahon, *Hittite State Cult*, 84.
83 McMahon, *Hittite State Cult*, 138.

Regardless, the scope of objects and places that these deities were expected to protect was quite broad, yet individually specific, signifying the importance that each one deity was thought to play in protecting the Hittite king and his empire or maintaining the cosmic order.

In addition to these offering lists, another festival – the *Festival of Individual Offerings* (*KBo* 11 40, among others[84]; see Table 2.5) – closely parallels the *Festival for All the Tutelary Deities*. Whereas the *Festival for All the Tutelary Deities* presents each group of LAMMA deities a single offering, the *Festival of Individual Offerings* presents each LAMMA its own offering: one *tuḫurai*-bread, one type of flesh offering, one *talaimi*-jug of beer to the LAMMA-of-X (e.g., [1 ^{ninda}*t*]*u-u-ḫu-ra-i* 1 ^{uzu}*da-a-an-ḫa-aš-ti* GUD ZAG [1 ^{du}]^{g}*ta-la-i-mi-iš* KAŠ [^{uru}*tu-u*]*t-tu-wa-aš* ^{d}LAMMA-ri, *KBo* 11 40 § 13′ i 5′–7′, McMahon's translation). Many but not all of the deities in the *Festival of Individual Offerings* also appeared in the *Festival for All the Tutelary Deities*: about thirty LAMMA divine names are extant; several more should probably be reconstructed in the broken lines; and there are no less than twelve extant Ala deities (see Table 2.4).[85] More often than not, lines drawn on the tablet separate each divine name and the offerings it received from the other divine names and their offerings, which seem to indicate further that each deity was considered distinct from the others.

Just as the Hittite scribal tradition used the logograms IŠKUR and 10 to label their numerous storm-gods and used epithets as last names to differentiate them, so, too, they used the logogram ^{d}LAMMA and epithets to designate and differentiate tutelary deities. Some LAMMA deities had their own unique first names and were only recognizable as LAMMA deities because of the context, such as Zithariya, Karzi, and Ḫapantaliya, who are divine witnesses in the treaty between Muršili II and Manapa-Tarḫund (*CTH* 68, see Table 2.6). Some LAMMA deities had no unique first name and their last names were either conceptual or geographic epithets; and still others were addressed upon by the first name or label Ala instead of LAMMA and also had conceptual or geographic last names. Regardless, all of them were LAMMA deities, and the ancient Hittite scribes differentiated all of them from each other by using their full names.

Ritual texts from Tudḫaliya IV's reign are not the only sources for long lists of Hittite gods following Puduḫepa's reforms; Hittite diplomatic texts, treaties, and prayers also provide evidence for the multiplicity of types of gods in Hittite religion. Among these are the monumental bas-reliefs at Yazilikaya and the

---

84 McMahon, *Hittite State Cult*, 117.
85 See McMahon, *Hittite State Cult*, 120–127.

corresponding portion of the *itkalzi*-ritual text that reflect the multiplicity of storm-gods and of Šaušga goddesses. Before examining these other Hittite texts, a brief overview regarding the function of god lists and their arrangement in the Hittite treaties is in order. Michael Barré divides the deities in the divine witness lists in the Hittite treaties into three separate categories: high gods, associated deities, and non-cultic witnesses.[86] This three-part structure took its final shape sometime in the middle of the fourteenth century during either the reign of Tudḫaliya III or his son Šuppiluliuma I as the Hittite cultic system expanded with the incorporation of Kizzuwatna and Šamuḫa into the empire.[87] The final category includes both deified objects and olden gods, and it is typically separated from the first two groups by a ruled line and a summary statement encompassing "all the gods of the Ḫatti and all the gods of the land."[88] Barré characterizes the olden gods as those with a netherworldly nature and notes that the Mesopotamian queen of the netherworld, Ereškigal, appears as the head of this collection.[89] The Mesopotamian deities Anu, Enlil, and their consorts also appear in this group, which is why his label "olden gods" is preferable to "netherworld."[90] Others in the non-cultic group include rivers, mountains, clouds, day and night, and other deified objects. According to Barré, the distinction between the high gods and the associated deities is also easily defined. Specifically, the associated group begins with (the unspecified) LAMMA, who is often separated from the high gods by a ruled line in the tablet. After (the unspecified) LAMMA, the associated gods appear in the following order: oath god(desse)s, deities in the "circle of Ištar," Zababa and other warrior gods, and other local gods who are listed before the summary statement.[91]

Barré's categorization of the divine witness lists in Hittite treaties is quite helpful, both for our understanding the overall nature of the Hittite divine hierarchy and for aiding our analysis of lengthy divine-name lists, especially when the Hittite treaties are compared to Levantine and Mesopotamian

---

86 See chapter 3.3 and 3.4 for a full discussion of the god lists in treaties. See also Michael L. Barré, *The God-List in the Treaty between Hannibal and Philip V of Macedonia: a study in Light of the Ancient Near Eastern Treaty Tradition* (Baltimore: Johns Hopkins University Press, 1983), 30–37, for his treatment of specifically Hittite treaties and their god lists.

87 Taracha, *Religions of Second Millennium Anatolia*, 82–83.

88 Barré, *God-List*, 32.

89 Barré, *God-List*, 27.

90 Barré, *God-List*, 32. Taracha notes that these Mesopotamian deities were incorporated into the Hurrian traditions in the third millennium, whence they joined the Hittite traditions in the second millennium (Taracha, *Religions of Second Millennium Anatolia*, 120).

91 Barré, *God-List*, 9 and 33.

treaties. Because they divided the highest gods from the associated gods, often with a physical line on the tablet, and placed the olden gods near the end of the god lists, the Hittites unambiguously distinguished a number of deities whom we might have otherwise considered high gods from the other deities. Following Barré observed classification, we can see that the treaty between Šuppiluliuma I of Ḫatti and Ḫuqqana of Ḫayasa (*CTH* 42; Table 2.2) includes three subunits to the high gods section: two chief deities (i.e., UTU-of-Heaven and UTU.MI$_2$-of-Arinna), a large assortment of storm-gods, and two Ḫebat goddesses. By simplifying the divine witness lists and isolating the associated-gods group, Barré's categories highlight the prominent features of the associated gods group: most of the gods in this group were identifiable only by their (often) geographic last name. His divisions also highlight the similar treatment that the LAMMA deities, the Ištar goddesses, and the warrior gods receive. The divine name "Ištar" or "Šaušga" appears to function in the same manner as the titles or labels do for the storm-gods and tutelary deities. Furthermore, like the LAMMA deities and storm-gods, their divine names often use the formula DN-of-GN (see Table 2.3 for a collection of Šaušga goddesses from other treaties).[92] While it may be true that the first name Ištar really represented the divine name Šaušga instead of Ištar itself, a better interpretation might be that the logogram IŠTAR functioned as a label for a class or category of goddesses in the same way that LAMMA and IŠKUR referred to categories of tutelary deities and storm-gods. More than just resembling LAMMA and IŠKUR by comprising a category of deity, the arrangement of the individual divine names in the Ištar group also matches those in the tutelary- and storm-god groups. For instance, the first goddess mentioned in these treaties was usually either (the unspecified) Ištar or Ištar-of-Heaven. Because Barré has demonstrated that the overall structure of the divine witness list reflects a hierarchy of deities, and because the unspecified member of the LAMMA group appears first in both treaties and ritual contexts, we can accept that the first divine name in each

92 Although the divine name and category IŠTAR first appeared in an early fourteenth-century treaty between Arnuwanda I and Ašmunikkal of Kaška (*CTH* 139 ii 10), it was during Šuppiluliuma I's reign that IŠTAR first appeared in the treaties with some force. Šuppiluliuma's treaty included five distinct Ištar goddesses (*CTH* 42 A ii 48–59; see Table 2.2). This is the same number of Ištar goddesses that appeared in Tudḫaliya IV's treaty with Kurunta of Tarḫuntassa near the end of the thirteenth century (*CTH* 106, Table 2.10). However, only three of these Ištar goddesses are common to both treaties: Ištar-of-the-Countryside, Ištar-of-Nineveh, and Ištar-of-Ḫattarina. (The unspecified) Ištar in Šuppiluliuma's treaty was absent in Tudḫaliya's treaty, as was the goddess Ištar//Queen-of-Heaven. In their places were the localized Ištar goddesses, Ištar-of-Šamuḫa and Ištar-of-Lawazantiya, who appear first and third among the Ištar goddesses in Tudḫaliya's treaty.

group was the most important of its class, including (the unspecified) Ištar in the Ištar group. This makes sense because any deity or entity that could be identified by its title or label without further qualification must have been important.[93] Thus, the names of the five goddesses who have been introduced by the logogram IŠTAR in Šuppiluliuma I's treaty could be read as "THE Šaušga-Goddess, Šaušga-Goddess-of-the-Countryside, Šaušga-Goddess-of-Nineveh, [Šaušga-Goddess]-of-Ḫattarina, (and) Šaušga-Goddess//Queen-of-Heaven" (see Table 2.2). These five goddesses, along with Ninatta, Kulitta, and others, belonged to what Laroche called the "circle of Ištar."[94]

As a label, the logogram IŠTAR does not appear to simply mark the deity's female gender. The goddess Aya precedes all of the Ištar goddesses in Šuppiluliuma I's treaty and lacks such a label, so she does not appear to be included within this Ištar/Šaušga class of goddesses. The IŠTAR label seems to specify a particular class or type of Hittite goddess, and because Hittite and Hurrian traditions associated Ištar goddesses with love and war, perhaps this class of goddess represented a class of warrior goddesses, love goddesses, or both. The two Šaušga goddesses represented on the Yazilikaya bas-reliefs and its corresponding text of the *itkalzi*-ritual might point to both these categories. One appears among the men (*JCS* 6 121:38), suggestive of the goddess category's warlike qualities, and another appears among the goddesses (l. 56), suggestive of this category's love qualities (see Table 2.1). Iconography associated with the Ištar/Šaušga goddesses included winged-goddesses and goddesses standing on lions, the latter of which symbolized the martial nature of this class of goddess.[95] Moreover, Ištar- or Šaušga-of-Šamuḫa acted in military affairs. In his apology, Ḫattušili III appealed to this goddess, along

---

93 Richard Beal notes that the unspecified titles, like "*the* Ištar/Šaušga," refer to particular individual deities and do not serve as headings for the subsequent list of titles with specific epithets (Richard Beal, personal communication, 02/08/2010). By his reckoning, if the unspecified titles had simply been included as introductions or categorical labels, the preferred method of citation would have been something like "all the Šaušgas" (Šaušga$^{meš/ḫi.a}$ *ḫumanteš/dapianteš*), which resembles the treatments of LAMMA deities in ritual texts presented by McMahon (above).

94 Emmanuel Laroche, "Panthéon national et pantheons locaux chez les Hourttites," *Or* NS 45 (1976): 97.

95 Volkert Haas, *Geschichte der hethitschen Religion* (Leiden: Brill, 1994), 500. As the Yazilikaya bas-reliefs demonstrate, Ḫebat and other deities (e.g., her son Šarruma [see Emmanuel Laroche, "Le Dieu Anatolien Sarrumma," Syria 40 (1963): 277]) could also be depicted as standing on lions, but the lion was associated with Ištar throughout Mesopotamian history and in Hittite tradition (Elizabeth Douglas Van Buren, "The *ṣalmê* in Mesopotamian Art and Religion," *Or* NS 10 [1941]: 67; and Rainer. M. Boehmer, "Die Datierung des Puzur/Kutik-Inšušinak und einige sich daraus ergebende Konsequenzen," *Or* NS 35 [1966]: 373–374).

with her brother IŠKUR-of-Nerik, when he challenged his nephew and ultimately usurped the throne:

> Out of regard for the love of my brother I did not react at all and during seven years I complied. He, however, sought my destruction at divine and human behest and he took away from me Ḫakpiš and Nerik. Now I no longer complied and I became hostile to him, I did not commit a moral offence by revolting against him on the chariot or by revolting against him within (his) house. (No,) in a manly way I declared to him: "You opposed me. You (are) Great King, whereas I (am) king of the single fortress that you left me. So come! Ištar-of-Šamuḫa and the Storm-God-of-Nerik will judge us." (*Apology of Ḫattušili III, COS 1.77:203; CTH* 81, § 10c, iii 62–79, Th. P. J. van den Hout's translation)[96]

The two gods were called to judge between the two men by determining the outcome of this (military) trial.[97]

Another goddess associated with the military was Išḫara – whom Laroche counted among the "circle of Ištar," and Volkert Haas reckons Šaušga – a virgin goddess who resembles Inanna/Ištar, Anat, Aphrodite, and Artemis.[98] Išḫara was herself associated with the military in Hittite tradition, serving as a "deity of the oath" (*NIŠ DINGIR*) in the *First Soldiers' Oath* (*COS* 1.66:166; *CTH 427*), and she earned one of the few epithets that the Hittites doled out within their treaties' witness lists (see, for example, Tables 2.7 and 2.8): Queen-of-the-Oath(s). This military association is also highlighted by Išḫara's position in these treaties. In *CTH* 68, 69, and 106 (see Tables 2.7 through 2.10), not only was Išḫara awarded this epithet, but she appears immediately after Ninatta and Kulitta (the most famous members of the Ištar entourage in Hurrian and Hittite tradition) and prior to (the unspecified) Warrior-God in *CTH* 68 and 69.[99] Thus, on the one hand, she was linked to or associated with the Ištar/Šaušga goddesses, and on the other hand, she was connected to the male warrior gods.

Together, all this suggests that Išḫara could be interpreted as a goddess belonging to the IŠTAR category but who went by a personal name rather than

96 In *KBo* 4 29 ii 1–8 (*CTH* 85.1), Ḫattušili III issued the same challenge but dropped the geographic epithets for the storm-god: "You are a Great King, while I am a small king. Let us go in judgment before the IŠKUR//My-Lord and Šaušga//My-Lady. If you prevail in the trial, they will raise you; but if I prevail in the trial they will raise me" (Mario Liverani's translation, modified slightly; Mario Liverani, *International Relations in the Ancient Near East, 1600–1100 BC* [New York: Palgrave, 2001], 105).

97 Elsewhere, Ḫattušili III declared himself the beloved of UTU.MI$_2$-of-Arinna, IŠKUR-of-Nerik, and Ištar-of-Šamuḫa (*KBo* 4 28 = *CTH* 88). Ištar-of-Šamuḫa was also the goddess for whom his wife Puduḫepa served as priestess.

98 Haas, *Geschichte der hethitschen Religion*, 340.

99 The Moon-God, his consort Ningal, and the Deity-of-Arusna interrupt this flow in *CTH* 106 (see Tables 2.9 and 2.10).

a categorical title (with or without a supplemental last name). In this regard, she differed from the goddesses known as Ištar- or Šaušga-of-Nineveh and Ištar- or Šaušga-of-the-Countryside, and even from (the unspecified) Šaušga. Applying the four categories that McMahon established for LAMMA deities to the IŠTAR class of goddess, Išḫara could be considered an IŠTAR of the first category, those who have unique divine first names. (The unspecified) Ištar represents the second category because she has no epithet, and Ištar-of-Nineveh represents the third category because her epithet is geographic.[100] In this regard, Išḫara is to the IŠTAR category what the tutelary deity Zithariya is to the LAMMA category, a deity who could be invoked without explicit mention of the category to which the deity belonged. This is not to suggest that Išḫara was necessarily identified, equated, or syncretized with any particular Ištar goddess, as several scholars have claimed.[101] Actually, this suggestion runs completely counter to any identification between them. Instead of being equated with any Ištar/Šaušga goddess, we should recognize that Išḫara was a goddess associated with other similar goddesses, including one known only as (the unspecified) Ištar/Šaušga and others known chiefly by the label or title IŠTAR with their unique last names.

Because the Hittite tendency towards an extreme polytheism allowed or demanded the individuality of localized deities sharing a common name or label, and because the Hittite scribal convention used logograms to represent classes or groups of Hittite deities (e.g., LAMMA and IŠKUR), it would be reasonable to conclude that there was a category of IŠTAR goddesses in Hittite thought. The Hittites recognized the individuality and distinctiveness of these IŠTAR goddesses by giving them unique divine names, offerings, and agency, so we, too, should interpret these goddesses as existing specifically and

---

100 Likewise, the storm-gods in the divine witness lists also fall into these same four categories. Piḫaimmi, Šeri, and Ḫurri are storm-gods with unique divine first names; (the unspecified) IŠKUR received no further explanation; IŠKUR-of-Ḫatti and IŠKUR-of-Nerik were localized storm-gods with geographic epithets; and IŠKUR-of-Help and IŠKUR-of-Lightning were identified by non-geographic epithets.

101 See, for example, Taracha, *Religions of Second Millennium Anatolia*, 86; and Ichiro Nakata (Ichiro Nakata, "Deities in the Mari Texts: Complete Inventory of All the Information on the Deities Found in the Published Old Babylonian Cuneiform Texts from Mari" [Ph.D. diss., Columbia University, 1974], 80) in reference to Old Babylonian identifications of the goddesses, and Livingstone (Alasdair Livingstone, *Mystical and Mythological Explanatory Works of Assyrian and Babylonian Scholars* [Oxford: Clarendon Press, 1986], 234) for a Neo-Assyrian period identification between the goddesses. Likewise, Haas includes Išḫara in the same virgin goddess category as Inanna/Ištar, Anat, Aphrodite, and Artemis (Haas, *Geschichte der hethitschen Religion*, 340).

individually in the minds of the Hittite kings and other devotees. Like their cohorts the IŠKUR gods and LAMMA deities, these IŠTAR goddesses were recognized by the state as "associated gods," to use Barré's terminology, marking them as members of the official religion both individually and collectively. To suggest otherwise not only runs against the official state-sponsored position, but it also ignores the structural integrity of the witness lists in official state documents.

The Hittite subset of officially revered deities has been said to exhibit polytheism in an extreme fashion by boasting of a thousand deities, and these deities were even referred to as "the Thousand Gods (who) are now summoned to assembly" in Ḫattušili III's treaty with Ulmi-Teššup (*CTH* 106; see Table 2.9). At first glance, it appears that many of these deities shared first names. Upon closer inspection, however, it becomes clear that what would be considered first names in Sumerian or Akkadian texts might actually have been group labels in Hittite texts that designated the deities' categorical type. IŠKUR and LAMMA make more sense interpreted as labels rather than divine first names, and the individual deities baring these labels were differentiated by the epithets that comprised their last names. The designation IŠTAR might function in a similar way, but this collection of goddesses was significantly smaller – four or five as opposed to twenty or more – than the IŠKUR and LAMMA groups. The inescapable fact remains that there were numerous deities in the surviving cuneiform texts known as IŠKUR-of-X, LAMMA-of-X, and IŠTAR-of-X, and on several occasions deities with the same label were contrasted with one another, indicating that they were distinct deities.

Before concluding our discussion of multiplicity in the Hittite world, we should return to the topic of Hittite agglutination. As mentioned above, King Tudḫaliya brought a goddess known as Goddess-of-the-Night (DINGIR GE_6) to Šamuḫa from Kizzuwatna. According to Richard Beal, the goddess was never removed from Kizzuwatna and brought to Šamuḫa; she remained at her place of origin in Kizzuwatna and was introduced to her new temple at Šamuḫa.[102] Because this one deity was said to have existed simultaneously in two very different locations and worshipped by two different peoples at the same time, Muršili II's report of his ancestor Tudḫaliya's actions (*KUB* 32 133 i 1–10) have been offered as evidence in the larger multiplicity debate.[103] Ḫattušili III's similar actions in which he divided Šaušga-of-Šamuḫa and added a cult site

102 Beal, "Dividing a God," 199 and 208.

103 See, for example, Pongratz-Leisten's discussion about this text, related texts, and their possible implications (Pongratz-Leisten, "Comments on the Translatability," 91–92).

for her at Urikina (*KUB* 21 17 ii 5–8) has likewise been offered.[104] The third text that deals with this issue is *Adlocation of the Goddess of the Night*, and like Muršili's report, this text also revolves around Goddess-of-the-Night. In contrast to the other two inscriptions, this inscription preserves the process involved in rebuilding the new temple and cultic paraphernalia, the five days of ritual activities and offerings, and the declaration that is made to invite the deity into the new temple on the fifth day. Significantly, we learn that the new cult statue was supposed to be "identical in every respect to the statue of the goddess which already exists" (*KUB* 29 4 + *KBo* 24 86, § 1).[105] The new statue, the temple, and the goddess's belongings were expected to match everything already in Kizzuwatna in order to make her feel at home in this otherwise new and foreign land Šamuḫa. She was not a generic deity who would accept offerings or rites just because they were carried out in her temple. She had specific expectations that were as unique to her as was her name. Meeting her expectations was so important that Muršili's complaint about the manner in which Tudḫaliya treated her focused on the fact that Tudḫaliya had not worshipped her correctly:

> When my forefather, Tudḫaliya, Great King, split Goddess-of-the-Night from the temple of Goddess-of-the-Night in Kizzuwatna and worshipped her separately in a temple in Šamuḫa, those rituals and obligations which he determined in the temple of Goddess-of-the-Night – it came about, however, that the wooden tablet scribes and the temple personnel began incessantly to alter them – I, Muršili, Great King, have re-edited them from the tablets. (*KUB* 32 133 i 1–7, Miller's translation, modified slightly)[106]

To alter her proper forms of worship was to corrupt her worship, of which Muršili said Tudḫaliya was guilty; Tudḫaliya might as well have been worshipping another goddess. As Pongratz-Leisten observes, Goddess-of-the-Night

> possessed a particular personality not to be fused with other hypostases …. The evidence demonstrates that the local manifestation of a particular goddess possessed specific and non-transferable power, which could not be substituted by another divinity.[107]

104 Beal, "Dividing a God," 199; Miller, "Setting up the Goddess," 68; and Pongratz-Leisten, "Comments on the Translatability," 92.

105 Beal, "Dividing a God," 202; see also Billie Jean Collins' translation of this text (*Establishing a new Temple for the Goddess of the Night*, *COS* 1.70:173–177; *CTH* 481). Beal notes that the new statue was given a red shawl, whereas the old statue had a white one (Beal, "Dividing a God," 202).

106 Miller, "Setting up the Goddess," 70.

107 Pongratz-Leisten, "Comments on the Translatability," 93; see also Miller, "Setting up the Goddess," 67.

Goddess-of-the-Night was matchless among the divine and could not be identified with any local goddess, which is why Jared Miller is correct to doubt that this deity should be identified with (the unspecified) Šaušga, Šaušga-of-Šamuḫa, or any other known deity.[108] If she was interchangeable or identifiable with any of the established deities in Šamuḫa, then she would not have needed her own new temple, specific cultic paraphernalia, and rites.

In spite of the ritualistic details preserved in the *Adlocation of the Goddess of the Night*, the declaration that is made on the fifth day of the ritual has been of particular interest to scholars:

> Honored deity! Preserve your being, but divide your divinity! Come to that new temple, too, and take yourself the honored place! And when you make your way, then take yourself only that place! (§ 22, Miller's translation)[109]

In response to this pronouncement, Miller entertains the possibility that this speech made sure that Goddess-of-the-Night entered the correct temple and did not wander off to the wrong place, but the reference to a divided divinity is why this text has been offered up in discussions on Hittite multiplicity. The idea that a single deity could divide herself in order to be worshipped in two different places without exhausting her divinity is not in conflict with anything already presented in the current discussion on Hittite polytheism or our larger discussion on Mesopotamian, or specifically Neo-Assyrian, polytheism. Nothing in the *Adlocation of the Goddess of the Night* and the other, similar inscriptions suggests that the original goddess has been contrasted with the goddess at the new location, so we can confidently identify the original goddess with the new goddess; they are one and the same. What these texts do not do, however, is support the identification of two goddesses who share a divine first name but who have different last names. For example, the fact that Šaušga-of-Šamuḫa was thought to divide her divinity at least once does not mean that Šaušga-of-Šamuḫa could or should be identified with (the unspecified) Šaušga, Šaušga-of-Nineveh or any other localized Šaušga goddess. Šaušga-of-Šamuḫa is not the same deity as Šaušga-of-Nineveh because Šaušga-of-Šamuḫa is not the same divine full name as Šaušga-of-Nineveh. If Šaušga-of-Nineveh or Šaušga-of-Šamuḫa had originated from (the unspecified) Šaušga as a result of an *Adlocation*-like ritual, we would expect such a text to identify the original goddess as Šaušga and the newer goddess as Šaušga-of-Nineveh or Šaušga-of-Šamuḫa.

---

108 Miller, "Setting up the Goddess," 70–71.
109 Miller, "Setting up the Goddess," 67.

Significantly, in the inscriptions that deal with this dividing phenomenon, the original goddess had the identical name as the new goddess. In *Adlocation of the Goddess of the Night* and Muršili's report, the original deity was addressed as Goddess-of-the-Night, and the newer deity was also be addressed as Goddess-of-the-Night. I should note, however, that Muršili refers to the new temple in Šamuḫa twice as "Temple of Goddess-of-the-Night(-)of-Šamuḫa (E_2 DINGIR GE_6 ^{uru}*ša-mu-ḫa*, *KUB* 32 133 i 7 and 9) and once as just "Temple of Goddess-of-the-Night" (E_2 DINGIR GE_6, l. 5).[110] Whether the geographic epithet in ll. 7 and 9 refers to the temple's location or functions as part of the deity's name is unclear, but its inconsistent appearance suggests that the epithet might not have been an essential part of the deity's identity. Similarly, when Ḫattušili III added a goddess to the cultic system at Urikina, the original deity was addressed as Šaušga-of-Šamuḫa, and the newer deity was also addressed as Šaušga-of-Šamuḫa. The identical divine full name reflects the identical divine personality in same manner that the identical cult objects, rites, and offerings reflect the same personality. This text and the people involved in it recognized that this one goddess was worshipped in two different locations, Šamuḫa and Urikina, without issue. Thus, this text fits very well with the larger theme of the book: specific divine names make the deity different from other similarly named deities.

2.3 Conclusions

This survey of proposed comparable examples of splintered divinity in Catholic and Hittite religious traditions has found two appropriate comparisons concerning multiplicity in Mesopotamian and Levantine religious traditions. The first involves the treatment of madonnine images in (primarily Italian) Catholic tradition, wherein sister madonnas are contrasted with one another by the lay population and are further distinguished by unique festivals, offerings, rituals, and images. Despite these contrasts, each madonnine image is also recognized as having a relationship with the singular Madonna Mary. The second comparison, drawn from Hittite state religion, suggests that Mesopotamian logograms that represent divine first names in Assyria seem to be able to function as labels rather than first names for Hittite deities. For example, it may be that IŠKUR represents a class or group of deities that were storm-gods, LAMMA represents a class of tutelary deities, and IŠTAR represents

110 Miller, *Studies in the Origins*, 312.

a class of goddesses who were known to Hittites as Šaušga. Unlike the IŠKUR gods and LAMMA deities, which more clearly represent classes rather than personal divine names, the logogram IŠTAR could have represented the personal divine name Šaušga instead of a class of Ištar or Šaušga goddesses. This is enlightening, as will be discussed in chapter 4, 5, and 6, because some Akkadian and Northwest Semitic first names could or should be interpreted as categorical labels that actually mask the deities' real first names, such as *baal* ("master" or "lord") and *ištar* ("goddess"). Because Baal can be interpreted as a common noun that served as a title rather than a name, many scholars accept that there were independent and distinct Baal deities who should not be identified with either the Mesopotamian storm-god Adad or the Levantine storm-god Hadad. Whether or not IŠKUR, LAMMA, and IŠTAR represent labels or actual names, we do find that each deity was typically distinguished from the others through use of a divine last name, which was often, but not always, a geographic epithet. However, some deities needed no last names. Just as unique divine names marked cult statues and cult objects as distinct from the ethereal yet anthropomorphic (e.g., unspecified) deities in chapter one, these first and last name combinations serve as unique divine names for the Hittites deities and the madonnine images. The importance of unique divine names as markers for unique divine entities was further supported by our examination of the *Adlocation of the Goddess of the Night* and other similar texts. In agreement with the rest of our survey, these texts reinforce the idea that a unique name marks the deity as unique, even if the deity has been divided and worshipped simultaneously in two different temples or regions.

Despite the inexact comparisons between these non-Mesopotamian religious traditions and Mesopotamian traditions – or perhaps because of the many inexact comparisons – insights about what constitutes distinct manifestations of a divine name have been revealed. This is especially true as it relates to the avowed coexistence, cooperation, and/or interaction of the distinctly named deities – or, in the case of the madonnas, entities – as opposed to the confusing or contradictory rites and rituals that are specific to one particular entity. For this reason, when examining Akkadian and other Mesopotamian, and Levantine texts, special focus will be placed on the coexistence, cooperation, and/or interaction of distinct Ištar, Baal, and other deities sharing common first names.

3 The Divine Hierarchy and Embedded God Lists (EGLs)

Porter's argument for the distinction between Ištar-of-Nineveh and Ištar-of-Arbela came from Assurbanipal's hymn in which he explicitly contrasted the two divine entities, using different names and attributes to distinguish the two goddesses from one another. She notes that he also made the point to use plural pronouns, nouns, adjectives, and verbs to indicate that he was referring to multiple deities. On the one hand, *Assurbanipal's Hymn to the Ištars of Nineveh and Arbela* (SAA 3 3) is a poem that reflects the theological interests or speculations of a well-trained scribe-king, so his distinction between the goddesses could have been limited to him.[1] On the other hand, this is by no means the only inscription that places the divine name Ištar-of-Nineveh alongside Ištar-of-Arbela, as hundreds of Neo-Assyrian texts do just this. However, these other inscriptions rarely employ feminine-plural morphology to indicate explicitly that multiple Ištar goddesses are under discussion. When they do, often there are other goddesses with distinct divine first names that confound the interpretation. If we could demonstrate that Ištar-of-Nineveh and Ištar-of-Arbela had been explicitly contrasted with each other in the minds of the lay or non-clergy population (as we did with the various madonnine entities), or if we could demonstrate that the various localized Ištar goddesses represented distinct entities in large lists of divine names (as we did with the Hittite inscriptions), then we would have a solid reason to generalize Assurbanipal's theological speculations that are contained in SAA 3 3 as representative of the larger lay Neo-Assyrian population.

The first genre that probably comes to mind in Assyriology when someone mentions a large list of divine names is the lexical god-list genre, a genre that developed over the course of more than two thousand years in ancient Mesopotamia. Moreover, as Gonzalo Rubio notes, our earliest lexical god lists

---

1 Assurbanipal had been trained as a scribe and boasted of his scribal proficiency, including his mastery of esoteric knowledge. For example, in his annals, the king counts himself among the scholars as he proclaims:

> ix*a-na-ku* ^{m}*an-šar*$_2$-DU$_3$-A *qe*$_2$*-reb-šu*$_2$ *a-ḫu-uz ne*$_2$*-me-qi*$_2$ ^{d}AG ^{32}*kul-lat ṭup-šar-ru-u-ti ša gi-mir um-ma* ^{33}*ma-la ba-šu-u*$_2$ GAL$_2$*-u iḫ-ze-šu*$_2$*-nu a-ḫi-iṭ*
>
> I Assurbanipal seized within it the wisdom of Nabû; I investigated their learnings – all of the scribal craft of the totality of the scholars, all things that exist. (*BIWA* 16 A i 31–33)

Given his father Esarhaddon's obsessive interest in omens and the divinatory arts, it is little wonder that Assurbanipal was trained as a scribe and made to learn the secrets of what greatly interested his father.

were discovered outside of cultic settings in houses that contained other scholarly texts, so lexical god lists do not represent cultic points of view, even if the theological interests of scholar-scribes differ from those of the lay population.[2] Unfortunately, the nature of the lexical god-list tradition in Mesopotamia prevents us from determining whether two divine names in that list are contrasted with each other or even considered distinct from each other. The most famous lexical god lists, such as AN : *Anum*, might not reflect a true syncretistic attempt like we find in Classical religious traditions, but one of its functions was to provide alternative names and epithets for deities, which is to say that AN : *Anum* does equate or identify different divine names with each other. For this reason, we must turn to other texts to distill the desired, large god lists in order to determine if or when localized Ištar goddesses were thought of as distinct deities. Secondly, the structure of most lexical god lists makes it difficult, if not impossible, to determine the relative ranks of gods included within the list; however, as we discussed in chapter 2.2, Barré and others have observed that the relative ranks of deities can be easily derived from treaties and other non-lexical texts. This means that we should be able to examine god lists that are contained in treaties and other state documents in order to determine whether there were multiple distinct Ištar goddesses officially revered by the Neo-Assyrian state. Indeed, when we look outside of the lexical god list tradition, we find that are there hundreds of texts from which to examine a large list of divine names for contrasting purposes, and we find that these inscriptions are so numerous that their representations can be generalized – if not to the whole lay population – to a significantly large portion of the lay population.

3.1 Moving Away from Lexical God Lists

The lexical god-list tradition in Mesopotamia resembles other lexical-list traditions in many ways, but it was much more varied in nature.[3] Whereas typical lexical lists tend to be relatively stable in their arrangement, when we consider the lexical god lists, the genre's lack of homogeneity is apparent in many ways. For example, over time the general nature of arrangement drastically changes. In the Early Dynastic god lists of the third millennium, the

2 Gonzalo Rubio, "Gods and Scholars: Mapping the Pantheon in Early Mesopotamia," in *Reconsidering the Concept of Revolutionary Monotheism*, ed. Beate Pongratz-Leisten (Winona Lake: Eisenbrauns, 2011), 106.
3 Rubio, "Gods and Scholars," 97.

divine names were primarily arranged according to the shape and sound of the logograms, but the arrangements took on a more theological, or mythographic, stance in the Old Babylonian god lists of the early second millennium.[4] Moreover, the addition of second and third columns in the middle of the second millennium represents yet another fundamental change in lexical god lists. In addition to differences in arrangement principles, differences in content are readily noticeable. This is especially true when one considers the different god lists from the Early Dynastic, the Ur III, and the Old Babylonian periods. For example, only 52 divine names of the 421 extant names in the Fāra (SF 1) god list (from a list that probably contained about 600) correspond to any of the approximately 300 known divine names in the roughly contemporary Abū Ṣalābīḫ (IAS 82–90) god lists (from a probable 430 names). Moreover, these lists have no obvious relationship with the god lists from the Old Babylonian period, such as the Nippur List, the Weidner List, and the Genouillac List. Despite this tradition of heterogeneity among early lexical god lists, one particular god-list tradition does appear to have become the standard lexical god list in the second half of the second millennium, AN : *Anum*, a six-tablet collection of 1970 divine names to which a seventh tablet was later added.[5]

One primary objective of AN : *Anum* and its 1970 divine names was to preserve the organization of the divine hierarchy from Old Babylonian god lists, such as TCL 15 10, the longest Old Babylonian witness to the Genouillic List tradition.[6] Another intended purpose behind the AN : *Anum* god list and its two-column layout was to define how divine names related to each other. Keeping the primary divine name of interest in the right-hand column, the material in the left-hand column explains that divine name in some way. The entry in the left-hand column could provide another name by which the deity was known, it could provide the deity's occupation, or it could classify the deity as a member of another deity's family or entourage. Of all its purposes,

4 Rubio, "Gods and Scholars," 99.

5 Some copies of AN : *Anum* (e.g., YBC 2401) contain the contents of the six tablets on a single tablet (Richard Litke, *A Reconstruction of the Assyro-Babylonian God-lists, AN: ^{d}A-NU-UM and AN: ANU ŠÁ AMĒLI*, Texts from the Babylonian Collection 3 [New Haven: Yale Babylonian Collection, 1998], 4), providing a reliable template upon which to properly arrange the six-tablet arrangement. This also serves as a map for joining smaller fragments back into a reconstructed composite text (ibid., 17–18).

6 Rubio, "Gods and Scholars," 98; Wilfred G. Lambert, "Götterlisten," *RlA* 3/6 (1969), 478; and Lambert, "Historical Development," 195; see also H. de Genouillac, "Grande liste de noms divins sumériens," *RA* 20 (1923): 89–106.

as Rubio notes, AN : *Anum* was not intended to serve as a syncretistic text that equated distinct divine names as representing a single deity:

> It is important to note that AN : *Anum* has nothing to do with a hypothetical process of syncretism, such as the *translation Graeca*, in which Greek gods were equated with Roman gods on the basis of shared features (e.g., Zeus and Jupiter, Artemis and Diana).[7]

When AN : *Anum* provides different names for a deity, these were supposed to be identifying just the one deity in terms of another divine name.

While the dual-column nature of AN : *Anum* accelerates our understanding of the relationship expressed between the succeeding lines of the list (e.g., the new entry belongs to the entourage of the previous entry), the overall structure of the series is more complex. Like its predecessor the Genouillac List tradition found in TCL 15 10, this series consists of several units comprising a major deity's family and his entourage. Each unit begins with the common name of its main deity, and each subsequent line provides other names by which the deity was known. Eventually, the deity's consort is introduced, along with her alternative names, and their offspring and entourage complete the unit. For example, the sky-god Anu and his entourage, including his vizier Papsukkal, begin the series with the explanatory note AN : *Anum*, which means "(the Sumerian logogram) AN is (the Akkadian deity) Anu" (I i). Anu and his entourage are followed by Enlil and his entourage, which begins at I 148 and includes his consort Mullissu (l. 176) and his son Ninurta (l. 205). These are followed by Ea and his entourage, which begins at II 129 and includes his consort Damkina (l. 173), his son Marduk (l. 185) and his consort (l. 236), and their son Nabû (l. 242 ff.) and his wife (l. 247; see Table 3.1). Because Anu, Enlil, and Ea represent Mesopotamia's three olden high gods, AN : *Anum* is thought to reflect the "perceived hierarchy" of the divine world in ancient Mesopotamia.[8]

If AN : *Anum* does reveal a hierarchy of a proposed divine world, as is typically assumed, untangling this hierarchy is actually much more complicated than typically assumed. Drawing inferences about the divine hierarchy from AN : *Anum* is problematic because the rank of those deities who

7 Rubio, "Gods and Scholars," 98. Because Rubio considers "providing alternative names" for a deity something separate from the identification of deities with one another (e.g., the Greek Zeus is the Roman Jupiter), this means that he considers such entries as descriptive of divine equations that had taken place in ancient times and that these equations are not in conflict with the theology of the list's contemporary lay population (e.g., Ninurta of Nippur is Ningirsu of Girsu).

8 Rubio, "Gods and Scholars," 99.

belong to another deity's family or entourage cannot be easily compared to the rank of a deity from yet another entourage. Although the order of the primary deities in AN : *Anum* consists of Anu, Enlil (with Ninurta in his entourage), Ninhursag, Ea (with Marduk in his entourage), Sîn, Šamaš, Adad, and Ištar (see Table 3.1), we cannot determine the nature of the hierarchical relationship between Ninurta and Marduk or between Marduk and Sîn. Using only AN : *Anum* or other lexical god lists, the following questions remain unanswerable: Does Ninurta, a member of Enlil's family and entourage, outrank Marduk, a member of Ea's family and entourage, because the former's father appears to outrank the latter's father? Does Sîn outrank Marduk because he is a primary deity, whereas Marduk is simply a member of his father's unit? Does the subordinated deity Marduk outrank the primary deity Sîn because his father Enlil outranks Sîn? For that matter, does Marduk's own son Nabû outrank Sîn either because he belongs to Enlil's and Marduk's entourages, which precede Sîn's entourage? Does Ningal, the consort of the primary deity Sîn, outrank Nabû, the grandson of the primary deity Enlil? Does Anu's vizier Papsukkal outrank either Ninurta or Marduk? As one can imagine, these types of questions could continue indefinitely. The only relative ranks that we can derive from AN : *Anum*'s hierarchy with any certainty include the absolute ranks of the primary deities according to their ordinal appearance (e.g., Anu, Enlil, Ea, and then Sîn) and the ranks within a particular subunit (e.g., Ea, Marduk, Nabû). In contrast, the relative rankings of these lesser gods are confounded and impossible to determine reliably using AN : *Anum* or any other lexical god list.

Similarly, the related series AN : *Anu* : *ša amēli* ("An is the Anu of man"), which is an expanded form of AN : *Anum* that first appeared in the Middle Assyrian period,[9] shows even less interest in helping modern scholars produce an absolute divine hierarchy in Mesopotamia. This series consists of about 160 divine names but focuses on only 19 major deities (see Table 3.2), and its list of deities differs significantly when compared to AN : *Anum*.[10] Instead of placing Ea nearer his usual cohorts Anu and Enlil close to the beginning of the list, as AN : *Anum* does, AN : *Anu* : *ša amēli* places Ea closer to the end. Ea

9 Rubio, "Gods and Scholars," 98.

10 Litke, *A Reconstruction*, 15. In addition to the two-column format of AN : *Anum*, this series contains a third column, written in Akkadian, that explains the relationship between the names in the first two columns, specifying when the first name is to be identified with the second name. For example, the first line, AN : *Anu* : *ša amēli* (AN | AN | LU$_2$), states that the divine name Anu represents the god of a man, while line two, ^{d}DI.⌜MEŠ⌝ : *Anu* : *ša*$_2$ *sinništi*(SAL), means that the divine name Dimeš represents the god of a woman.

only appears in ll. 119–148 (of 157 lines), following lengthy units devoted to Sîn, Šamaš, Adad, Papsukkal, Ninurta, Nergal, Ištar, Nisaba, Sumuqan, Marduk, and Nabû. To complicate matters, however, the compiler's arrangement sends mixed signals because even though Ea's appearance occurs late in AN : *Anu : ša amēli*, the section devoted to him is roughly three times the size of the individual units representing Anu and Enlil. How a deity's ordinal rank in this series relates to the number of lines allotted to him is, therefore, unclear; the attention placed on Ea in his thirty lines surely suggests he enjoyed a higher rank than his late ordinal position would suggest, even if he does appear after his son Marduk and grandson Nabû in AN : *Anu : ša amēli*. In addition to his late placement, Ea's separation from Anu and Enlil here is all the more peculiar given not only his own antiquity and seniority among the gods but because Anu, Enlil, and Ea are often presented as a unified triad. Because of these irregularities that are inherent to AN : *Anu : ša amēli*, the benefits of using this or any other lexical god list to glean an actual divine hierarchy remain questionable.

3.2 The Last Are Least

In her study on Ištar's function in Assyrian royal inscriptions, Zsolnay discusses the arrangement of divine names in invocations spanning the fourteenth to eighth centuries and draws some conclusions about the hierarchy created by their arrangement. She rightly rejects Tammi Schneider's claim that the divine names in these royal inscriptions were derived from AN : *Anum* during Tiglath-pileser I's reign.[11] She observes both a lack of correlation between the AN : *Anum* order and the arrangement in Assyrian invocations and the fact that there was no fixed tradition to determine which deities should be included in an Assyrian inscription or what epithets were affixed to a divine name. Moreover, the deity Assur never appears in AN : *Anum*, which complicates the supposed correlation further.[12] Zsolnay does note that when deities do appear in a given Assyrian inscription, a standard order is evident (and exceptions to this order are easily explainable), but it simply is not based on the lexical god list tradition.[13] Because Šalmaneser III's inscriptions that

11 Zsolnay, "Function of Ištar," 151–152; see Tammi J. Schneider, "A New Analysis of the Royal Annals of Shalmaneser III" [Ph.D diss., University of Pennsylvania, 1991], 254, table 2.
12 Porter, "Anxiety of Multiplicity," 221.
13 Zsolnay, "Function of Ištar," 148. Zsolnay notes that in several royal inscriptions from the fourteenth to eighth centuries, Assur is the only divine name included.

Zsolnay examined are chronologically closest to the Sargonid texts in which we are primarily interested, the arrangement of the divine names in Šalmaneser's inscriptions are:

RIMA 3 A.0.102.2 i 1–3a	**RIMA 3 A.0.102.6 i 1–7**	**RIMA 3 A.0.102.10 i 1–5**	**RIMA 3 A.0.102.14 1–13 (the "Black Obelisk")**
Š III: A	Š III: B	Š III: C	Š III: D[14]
Assur	Assur	Assur	Assur
Anu	Anu	Anu	Anu
Enlil	Enlil	Enlil	Enlil
Ea	Ea		Ea
Sîn	Sîn		[Sîn]
		Adad	⌜Adad⌝
Šamaš	Šamaš		Šamaš
			[Mardu]k
	Ninurta	Ninurta	Ninurta
			Nergal
			Nusku
			Mullissu
Ištar	Ištar	Ištar	Ištar
		Ea	
		Sîn	
		Marduk.	

As can be seen, among these consistencies is the placement of the divine name Assur at the beginning of the list, which we might expect given that he is the Assyrian chief deity, but we would not expect this if AN : *Anum* provided the organizing standard order.

The standard order that Zsolnay observed leads her to agree with Victor Hurowitz and Joan Goodnick Westenholz's proposal that the final divine name in a series of divine names can belong to the most important deity in that list.[15] Their conclusion is partially based on *LKA* 63:35′–43′, a poem from Tiglath-pileser I's reign, which contains an atypical series of divine names in which

14 This table is derived from the last four rows in Zsolnay's "Chart A" (Zsolnay, "Function of Ištar," 153 n. 299 and 154). Zsolnay's treatments of these inscriptions are on pages 168, 169, 172, and 171, respectively.

15 Zsolnay, "Function of Ištar," 153–154; and Victor Hurowitz and Joan Goodnick Westenholz, "*LKA* 63: A Heroic Poem in Celebration of Tiglath-Pileser I's Musru-Qumanu Campaign," *JCS* 42 (1990): 38.

Assur seemingly appears as the first *and* last deity: (Assur) / Enlil / Ištar / Ninurta / Nusku / Adad / (Assur).[16] As indicated here by the parentheses, qualifications are needed to explain the series: "Assur appears before and after the god list, but not in its immediate context."[17] However, Assur is not actually named in this five-member series (i.e., Enlil / Ištar / Ninurta / Nusku / Adad), so he should not be considered a member of the series. As we will see in a moment, although we might expect Adad's name to appear before Ninurta's and Nusku's in a series of divine names in a royal inscription, the arrangement of the divine names in *LKA* 63 should not be considered evidence for an EGL's "crescendo," or a progression in which each new deity outranks the previous one from Nusku to Adad to Assur, as Hurowitz and Westenholz suggested.[18] With *LKA* 63 in mind, the idea that the final divine name in an series of divine names can be the most important deity allows Zsolnay to elevate the status of (the unspecified) Ištar in royal inscriptions from the reigns of Tukultī-Ninurta I through Šalmaneser III. Because (the unspecified) Ištar appears near or at the end of the series in Šalmaneser's royal inscriptions, Zsolnay finds it "inconceivable that Ištar, one of the great deities of the Assyrian empire, was considered a lesser deity than Nusku, who may appear two deities before her in certain invocations."[19] Instead of allowing the given order to reflect the relative status of each divine name and accept that (the unspecified) Ištar was not one of the three or four most important deities in the official Middle and Neo-Assyrian divine hierarchy, she seeks an alternative explanation that involves (the unspecified) Ištar's celestial and warrior aspects. Zsolnay suggests that because Ištar was Venus, she was grouped with Sîn and Šamaš in the heavens in RIMA 3 A.0.102.2 i 1–3a, and because she was a warrior goddess, she was paired with fellow warrior god Ninurta in A.0.102.6 i 1–7.[20]

---

16 Hurowitz and Westenholz, "*LKA* 63," 37.

17 Hurowitz and Westenholz, "*LKA* 63," 38. Hurowitz and Westenholz suggest that Assur is present in this series' context because he is the "heir of Ešarra" (*apil-ešarra*) who is alluded to in the king's name prior to the series (*LKA* 63:35′) and because he is so closely associated with "the king" who is mentioned again after the series (l. 43′).

18 Hurowitz and Westenholz, "*LKA* 63," 38; and Zsolnay, "Function of Ištar," 154 n. 300. There are Sargonid-period exceptions in which the divine names for Ninurta and Nusku are listed before Adad. In SAA 12 93, Ninurta is listed before Adad in a series of divine names inscribed on a donation to the god Ninurta (see also Tables 3.3 and 3.4, along with the relevant footnotes). In SAA 13 188:4–5, Nusku is listed before Šamaš, if the proposed reconstruction is accepted, but this is because Nusku is included as an immediate member of Sîn and Ningal's entourage. Likewise, Ninurta and/or Nusku appear before Adad in several of the lexical god lists from the Old Babylonian period.

19 Zsolnay, "Function of Ištar," 154.

20 Zsolnay, "Function of Ištar," 170.

Similarly, she reanalyzes the series of divine names in RIMA 3 A.0.102.10 i 1–5 and A.0.102.14:1–13 to reflect thematic groupings rather than hierarchies. According to Zsolnay, the three groups of divine names in A.0.102.10 i 1–5 include three majestic gods (i.e., Assur, Anu, Enlil), three other gods (i.e., Adad, Ninurta, Ištar), and three wisdom gods (i.e., Ea, Sîn, Marduk).[21] However, such complicated explanations are *ad hoc* in nature and do not help us understand the true nature of the listed divine names or the hierarchy that they actually represent.

Momentarily entertaining the idea that Ištar-of-Nineveh and Ištar-of-Arbela should be identified with (the unspecified) Ištar, we could apply Zsolnay's theory and consider the possibility that Ištar was the second most important Neo-Assyrian deity because the divine names Ištar-of-Nineveh and Ištar-of-Arbela are typically the last two names provided in Esarhaddon's royal inscriptions. Likewise, when (the unspecified) Ištar is the only Ištar goddess in a divine name series, her name is usually the last divine name listed (see Tables 3.3 and 3.4; the occasional exception is noted). If we were to identify Assyrian-Ištar (^{d}15 *aš-šu-ri-tu*) with (the unspecified) Ištar, Ištar's name is again the last divine name in these series that are found in many state documents that have been collected in SAA 12 (see Table 3.5a; the series in SAA 12 10 r. 6′–9′ is a notable exception). This final position for either the singular Ištar or multiple localized Ištar goddesses is also usually true for the series of divine names found in the letters that are collected in SAA 10, 13, 16, and 18 (see Table 3.6 and its first two endnotes for a full listing of relevant texts; SAA 10 286:3–7 [Table 3.7] and 197:7–13 [Table 3.8] are notable exceptions).

Identifying each and every localized Ištar goddess with (the unspecified) Ištar gives us the results to place that Ištar at the end of *most* series of divine names in seventh-century inscriptions. Nevertheless, there are numerous and

---

21 Zsolnay, "Function of Ištar," 172–173. The late appearance of Ea, Sîn, and Marduk in RIMA A.0.102.10 i 1–5 is, admittedly, unexpected, but it also undermines Zsolnay's argument that the final deity is of utmost importance. Likewise, Marduk's position in the middle of the series in A.0.102.14:1–13 (as well as in the series represented in "Chart B"; ibid., 154) is unremarkable. Finally, Zsolnay goes to great lengths to argue a thematic organization for the divine name series in A.0.102.14:1–13 (ibid., 172; see also 160–164), but her explanations are too complicated in comparison to Barré's observed model. Zsolnay's explanation for Mullissu's position in A.0.102.14 is particularly problematic because Mullissu is the twelfth of thirteen great gods in this series, but Zsolnay suggests that her penultimate position corresponds to Enlil's second position in the series (ibid., 163). Mullissu's epithet does indeed describe her as Enlil's spouse, but Enlil's is the third, not second, divine name in this series, so there is no correspondence with Mullissu in that regard. To correct this, Zsolnay proposes that Anu and Enlil have been presented as a combined deity in the inscription (ibid., 160).

significant exceptions that should give us pause and prevent us from concluding that the final deity in a series is the second most important Neo-Assyrian deity. In addition to the series in the letters SAA 10 197 and 286, where Ninurta, Nergal, and their consorts appear after the localized Ištar goddesses, it is not uncommon for other divine names to follow them in Assyrian state treaties. Gula appears after Ištar-of-Arbela in the curse section in Esarhaddon's Succession Treaty (SAA 2 6, see Table 3.9), and this is probably also true in Esarhaddon's treaty with King Baal of Tyre (SAA 2 5 iv 2′–3′, see Table 5.4). Similarly, Adad-of-Kurbail, Hadad-of-Aleppo, and *Palil* all appear after Ištar// Lady-of-Arbela, in Assur-nērārī V's treaty with Mati'-ilu of Arpad (SAA 2 2 vi 16–19; see Table 3.10), and several divine names follow the four Ištar goddesses listed in Sennacherib's Succession treaty (SAA 2 3 7′–11′ and r. 2′–5′; cf. BM 121206 ix 27′–34′; see Table 3.11).[22]

Another look at the series of divine names in SAA 2 2 vi 6–26 not only shows why an Ištar goddess at the end of series should not be interpreted as a particularly important Assyrian deity – i.e., second only to Assur – it demonstrates why Ištar-of-Nineveh should not be identified with Ištar-of-Arbela in this or any other Neo-Assyrian inscription. The arrangement of divine names in this eighth-century treaty adheres to Barré's ideal pattern: the Assyrian chief deity without a consort, the members of Triad 1 (i.e., Anu, Enlil, and Ea) and their consorts, the members of Triad 2 (i.e., Sîn, Šamaš, and Adad) and their consorts, the Babylonian chief deities (i.e., Marduk and Nabû) and their consorts, warrior gods (three with consorts and six without consorts), a collection of goddesses, another three gods, and the Sebittu (see Table 3.10).[23] The fact that the Sebittu, the seven Pleiades, are present in this series is significant because Barré notes that the Sebittu invariably conclude the series of divine names in treaties (see also Table 3.12 for the Aramaic text of the treaty Sefire i A [*KAI* 222] between two non-Assyrian states, in which the Sebittu conclude the group of Assyrian divine names).[24] Were we to treat the divine name in a series' final position as the second most important deity, as Zsolnay proposes, then the Sebittu would be more deserving of this high status than any of the Ištar goddesses because the Sebittu are invariably last when they appear in a series of divine names. Despite this, nothing from the inscriptions

22 Two parallel lines (//) are used here and elsewhere to indicate that a proper name and epithet are acting together with the force of a full name (e.g., Ištar//Lady-of-Nineveh and Ištar// Lady-of-Arbela). With reference to the cuneiform evidence, these parallel lines indicate that the first name is preceded by a divine determinative, but the epithet is not.

23 Barré, *God-List*, 9.

24 Barré, *God-List*, 19 and 25–26.

examined indicate that the Sebittu were considered among the highest ranked deities in the Neo-Assyrian period.

The late placement of the two Ištar goddesses, namely, Ištar-of-Nineveh and Ištar-of-Arbela, is telling in another regard: they appear immediately before two male deities with geographic last names: Adad-of-Kurbail and Hadad-of-Aleppo.[25] The fact that the four deities with geographic last names appear together near the end of this EGL in SAA 2 2 is significant. On the one hand, the inclusion of these four cities indicates the special reverence these cities were granted in the Neo-Assyrian period, but on the other hand, their placement near the end of the Assyrian EGL suggests that these deities were less important than those deities who did not have last names. The storm-god Hadad-of-Aleppo had been venerated in the West from the mid-third millennium into the first millennium, and the invocation of his geographic last name was at least as vital to his identity as his first name (see chapter 5.3 and Map 3). Aleppo had been a politically and culturally significant city in the West in the third and second millennia, but it was no longer a city of military or political importance during the Neo-Assyrian period.[26] Despite the fact that the city was no longer a military or political force, Šalmaneser III saw it fitting to offer a sacrifice to Hadad-of-Aleppo (^{d}IŠKUR *ša*^{uru}*ḫal-man*, RIMA 3 A.0.102.2 ii 87) in the middle of the ninth century while campaigning in the West.[27] Steven Holloway stresses the significance of this offering because Hadad-of-Aleppo is one of only two deities outside of Assyria, Babylonia, and Ḫarrān to whom an Assyrian king claims to have offered a sacrifice.[28] Alternatively, the case could be made that Hadad-of-Aleppo was included because Assur-nērārī V's treaty was with Mati'-ilu of Arpad, a city that neighbors Aleppo.[29] This possibility should be rejected; however, because Hadad-of-Aleppo's

25 The cuneiform for the first name of Adad-of-Kurbail is the same as that for Hadad-of-Aleppo: ^{d}IŠKUR. The different spellings of their names in English reflect the convention used in chapter 5: Adad represents a deity's Assyrian or Mesopotamian background, whereas Hadad represents a Northwest Semitic background.

26 Edward Lipiński, *The Aramaeans: Their Ancient History, Culture, Religion*, OLA 100 (Leuven: Peeters, 2000), 207; see also Pongratz-Leisten, "Comments on the Translatability," 89. As late as the 14th century, Aleppo's political significance was demonstrated when Šuppiluliuma I designated the city as one of his two viceregal seats, and this influence continued through the end of the Hittite Empire (Trevor Bryce, *The World of the Neo-Hittite Kingdoms: A Political and Military History* [Oxford: Oxford University Press, 2012], 52).

27 Holloway, *Aššur is King! Aššur is King!: Religion in the Exercise of Power in the Neo-Assyrian Empire*, CHANE 10 (Leiden: Brill, 2002), 89.

28 Holloway, *Aššur is King*, 342 n. 146. The other deity is Marduk//Who-Resides-(in)-Til-Assuri, and his offering was from Tiglath-pileser III.

29 Lipiński, *Aramaeans*, 208; Holloway, *Aššur is King*, 343.

pre-Sebittu position indicates that he was considered an Assyrian deity rather than an Arpadian one (see Table 3.10). He has intentionally been integrated to the collection of Assyrian deities at the expense of the local Aramaic collection, and his pre-Sebittu position in the Sefire treaty reinforces this fact (see Tables 3.12 and 3.13). Hadad-of-Aleppo might have been important to Mati'-ilu of Arpad, but his historical significance from the Assyrian perspective overrode his inclusion as an Arpadian deity,[30] a fact whose significance cannot be overstressed: Hadad-of-Aleppo could not be included in twice because no deity was included twice in either SAA 2 2 vi 6–26 or *KAI* 222:8–12.

In contrast to the historical significance of Hadad-of-Aleppo's divinity, the three deities with Kurbail, Nineveh, and Arbela as geographic epithets represent cities that played key roles in the Neo-Assyrian Empire. According to Pongratz-Leisten, each of these cities was important enough to the empire to receive "special financial and theological promotion(s)," which included hosting an *Akītu*-festival for the city's patron deity.[31] As he did with Hadad-of-Aleppo, Šalmaneser III also revered the storm-god Adad-of-Kurbail, as indicated by his life-sized statue that the king installed at Kurbail (RIMA 3 A.0.102.12:34–41). Although the dedicatory inscription never actually addresses the deity as "Adad-of-Kurbail," the epithet Who-Resides-(in)-Kurbail (*a-šib* ^{uru}*kur-ba-il*$_3$, l. 8) appears near the end of a long series of epithets praising him. Using our standard divine-full-name and epithet punctuation, this inscription would be written out: Adad//Epithet-1//Epithet-2//Epithet-3//...//Who-Resides-(in)-Kurbail. We should not over interpret this on a theological level, however. Holloway suggests that the patronage that Šalmaneser and later kings provided this deity "was probably an echo of the prerogatives of Mitannian kingship," the second-millennium empire that revered several important weather- or storm-gods, rather than genuine theological interest on the part of Assyria.[32] He dismisses statue and the *Akītu*-festivals as little more than political theater because the public shows of support for Adad-of-Kurbail were designed to help Assyria lay claim to the Kumme region and win over the local elites.[33] To this end, they

30 Barré, *God-Lists*, 19 and 25–26.

31 Beate Pongratz-Leisten, "The Interplay of Military Strategy and Cultic Practice in Assyrian Politics," in *Assyria 1995: Proceedings of the 10th Anniversary Symposium of the Neo-Assyrian Text Corpus Project, Helsinki, September 7–11, 1995*, eds. Simo Parpola and R. M. Whiting (Helsinki: Neo-Assyrian Text Corpus Project, 1997), 251 and 264. The other Assyrian cities that hosted *Akītu*-festivals are Assur, Kilizi, and Ḫarrān.

32 Holloway, *Aššur is King*, 340. J. N. Postgate notes that the earliest attestation of the city name Kurbail is from Salmaneser III's reign (J. N. Postgate, "Kurba'il," *RlA* 6/5–6 [1983], 367).

33 Holloway claims that apart from the cults in Babylonia and Ḫarrān, the Neo-Assyrian kings interest in non-Assyrian local cults was "strictly secular and pragmatic" (Holloway, *Aššur is King*, 342). Regarding Kurbail specifically, he states that during the ninth and eighth centuries,

publically worshipped the Adad who resided in Kurbail, a city whose location – north of Nineveh, near Arbela, somewhere along the Urarṭu border – made it a politically and economically important city in the ninth century.[34] Similarly, J. N. Postgate has speculated that the city might have served as a military center for the northern frontier.[35] Kurbail's continued importance for the Neo-Assyrians was demonstrated by the fact that it eventually became the capital of its Neo-Assyrian province and the inclusion of the city's temple to Adad in the Sargonid-period *Götteradressbuch* of Assur (GAB) after the entry for Ištar-of-Arbela's temple: E_2 ^{d}EN-*kur-ba-il*$_3$ ("the temple of Lord-of-Kurbail," GAB § 4, l. 179).[36]

Returning to localized Ištar goddesses, the cities Nineveh and Arbela had belonged to the Assyrian core since the fourteenth century.[37] Because of their location within the empire's core, they benefited in the early ninth century when Assurnāṣirpal II moved the capital from Assur to the centrally located Calaḫ because the move facilitated trade, transportation, accessibility, and high-speed communication throughout the region, especially to these two economic, cultic, and cultural capitals (see Map 2).[38] Šalmaneser III's imperial consolidation and his creation of a standing army that was distributed around the empire also seemed to benefit these cities while weakening the nobles in Assur.[39] Prior to becoming the Assyrian capital during Sennacherib's reign and

---

Adad-nērārī II, Adad-nērārī III, and the Urarṭian emperors Išpuinu and Menua had each used Kurbail and Kumme cults to rally local support for their larger political and economic gain.

34 Holloway, *Aššur is King*, 341 and 140 n. 202; and Pongratz-Leisten, "Interplay of Military," 247. Pongratz-Leisten notes that this city, probably near the Urarṭian border, originated in the ninth century during Šalmaneser III's reign.

35 Postgate, "Kurba'il," 368.

36 Actually, Lord-of-Kurbail is credited with two temples in the GAB: ^{179}E-kilib-kurkurra-duldul : House which overwhelms all the lands : the temple of Bēl-Kurbail ^{180}E-dur-ḫenunna : House, abode of plenty : the temple of Bēl-Kurbail (^{179}e$_2$.kilib.kur.kur.ra.dul$_6$.dul$_6$: *bītu ša*$_2$ nap-ḫar mātāti kat$_3$-mu-{šu$_2$} : *bīt* ^{d}EN-^{uru}*kur-ba-il*$_3$ ^{180}e$_2$.dur$_2$.ḫe$_2$.nun.na : *bītu šu-bat nu-uḫ-ši* : *bīt* EN-^{uru}*kur-ba-il*$_3$, GAB § 4, George's transliteration and translation; Andrew R. George, *Babylonian Topographical Texts*, 180–181; see also Menzel, *Assyrische Tempel*, 2:T163, no. 64).

37 Karen Radner, "The Assur-Nineveh-Arbela Triangle: Central Assyria in the Neo-Assyrian Period," in *Between the Cultures: The Central Tigris Region from the 3rd to the 1st Millennium BC: Conference at Heidelberg, January 22nd – 24th, 2009*, ed. Peter Miglus and Simone Mühl (Heidelberg: Heidelberger Orientverlag, 2011), 321. Nineveh in Nurrugum and Arbela in Qabra had each belonged to independent kingdoms in the eighteenth century before Šamšī-Adad of Ekallatum brought them into his empire (ibid., 322).

38 Radner, "Assur-Nineveh-Arbela," 323–324.

39 Karen Radner, "The Neo-Assyrian Empire," in *Imperien und Reiche in der Weltgeschichte: Epochenübergreifende und gloablhistorische Vergleiche, Teil 1: Imperien des Altertums, Mittel-*

growing because of the hundreds of thousands of people he relocated to the city, Nineveh's location made the city an ideal regional hub because it was situated along the overland routes from the Taurus Mountains and it controlled an important ford across the Tigris River.[40] Its location also prompted Tiglath-pileser III, Šalmaneser V, and Sargon II to use Nineveh for their westward expansions.[41] For these reasons and because Ištar-of-Nineveh's temple, the Emašmaš-temple, was the oldest place of worship in the country, this warrior goddess's political impact on the empire means that she earned her local *Akītu*-festival celebrations.[42] Likewise, the warrior and prophecy goddess Ištar-of-Arbela earned the *Akītu*-festival celebrations at Arbela and Milqia. Located on the eastern part of the Assyrian core on the western periphery of the Zagros Mountains, Arbela controlled the various routes into Iran and served as a military base for invasions into Urarṭu.[43]

Each of these four deities, Ištar-of-Nineveh, Ištar-of-Arbela, Adad-of-Kurbail, and Hadad-of-Aleppo deserved mention in Assur-nērārī's treaty with Mati'-ilu of Arpad (SAA 2 2 vi 15–18) along with the great Neo-Assyrian gods because of either their ancient theological significance, their patron cities' political and military significance, or both. Although these four patron deities were rewarded with inclusion in the treaty, the scribes responsible for the divine witness list felt that they needed to be distinguished from other deities with whom they shared a first name. Unlike other Neo-Assyrian treaties, two of these patron deities shared a name with someone other than an Ištar, namely, (the unspecified) Adad, who was already listed in SAA 2 2 vi 8–9. However, even though they were important enough to be included among the Assyrian gods, the fact remains that Adad-of-Kurbail and Hadad-of-Aleppo appear near the bottom of that series of divine names, following the two localized Ištar goddesses and preceding only the Sebittu. Their late appearances suggest that geographic last names mark the deity as having a relatively low status.[44] (Recall that in Hittite treaties, the divine names of localized storm-gods are

alterliche und frühneuzeitliche Imperien (Wiesbaden: Harrassowitz Verlag, 2014), 105–106 and 108.

40 Radner, Assur-Nineveh-Arbela," 327.

41 Radner, "Assur-Nineveh-Arbela," 321 and 326.

42 F. Mario Fales, *L'impero Assiro*: *Storia e Amministrazione* (*IX-VII Secolo A.C.*), Collezione storica (Rome: Editori Laterza, 2001), 37.

43 Rader, "Assur-Nineveh-Arbela," 321; Holloway, *Aššur is King*, 191 and 275; and Pongratz-Leisten, "Interplay of Military," 249–251.

44 Similarly, the localized Ištar-of-Arbela and Adad-of-Kurbail appear near the end of the Assyrian Temple List in GAB § 4, ll. 178–180 (Menzel, *Assyrische Tempel*, 2:T163, no. 64; see also George, *Babylonian Topographical Texts*, 180–181).

often listed after the unspecified storm-god; see Tables 2.2 and 2.6 through 2.10.) Pressing the significance of the late appearances even further, we could argue that late appearances of the localized Ištar goddesses and storm-gods indicate that the multiplicity of deities with shared names actually dilutes the theological significance of that name.[45] Perhaps (the unspecified) Ištar or even Ištar-of-Nineveh alone would have been important enough to deserve a higher position in the Neo-Assyrian divine hierarchy, but the addition of another Ištar, usually Ištar-of-Arbela and sometimes others, not only reduces the rarity of the divine name but also reduces the theological importance of each deity bearing that common name.[46]

Zsolnay argues that (the non-localized) Ištar could appear as the final deity in any series of divine names in royal inscriptions and yet still maintain her elevated status because the goddess's epithets proclaim her position as "the most supreme deity in the pantheon."[47] Throughout these royal inscriptions, (the non-localized) Ištar was identified as a warrior goddess with three distinct epithets – *bēlet tēšê* (Sovereign-of-Frenzy), *mušarriḫat qablāte* ([She]//Who-Quickens-Combats), and *bēlet qabli u tāḫāzi* (Sovereign-of-Combat and-Battle) – and other epithets that marked her as the supreme deity – *ašaritti ilāni* (Preeminent-among-the-Gods) and *ašaritti šamê u erṣeti* (Preeminent-of-Heaven-and-Earth).[48] These epithets do indeed testify to the warrior goddess's importance in Assyria, but they need not indicate that she was the supreme goddess, second only overall to Assur. However, this still seems to be an unlikely interpretation of the typically late appearance of the divine name Ištar within series of divine names, especially when the name Mullissu is also included. The warrior goddess's late appearance in the royal inscriptions that Zsolnay examined, along with the late appearance of Ištar-of-Nineveh and Ištar-of-Arbela in state treaties and other genres of text, reflects her (or their) relatively low status alongside the other Neo-Assyrian deities. Epithets might provide pertinent information about a deity and his or her nature, but they do not seem to improve that deity's status. If they did, we would find that (the

45 Cf. Hundley, "Here a God," 96 and n. 146.

46 This possibility is explored further below for Ištar goddesses, but the presence of two storm-gods, namely, Adad-of-Kurbail and Hadad-of-Aleppo, does not appear to have diminished the theological importance of (the unspecified) Adad in SAA 2 2 vi 6–20, which may be indicative of the perceived differences between these two IŠKURs and (the unspecified) Adad.

47 Zsolnay, "Function of Ištar," 177. Of all the invocations contained in royal inscriptions examined in her study, Zsolnay notes that there are only two instances in which Ištar's is not the final divine name mentioned, one of which she considers a scribal error (ibid., 176).

48 Zsolnay's translations have been retained for Ištar's epithets, modified slightly (Zsolnay, "Function of Ištar," 177).

unspecified or any other) Ištar would precede most of her male counterparts and Mullissu more often in series of divine names (see Table 3.14).

3.3 Building Composite God Lists

Zsolnay was correct to mine the series of divine names in these to yield a divine hierarchy, and methodologically she was off to a good start, but her unwillingness to accept the straight-forward implications that those inscriptions revealed complicated her interpretation and caused her to produce inaccurate conclusions, including the idea that Ištar was the second most important deity according to Neo-Assyrian scribes. Regardless of her conclusions, using the divine names in those inscriptions to build a hierarchy is much easier than trying to build a hierarchy from the lexical god lists. Like Zsolnay, we can avoid the unanswerable questions and other problems regarding the divine hierarchy that we encountered in the lexical god-list tradition if we adopt a theocentric – rather than political – view of Neo-Assyrian treaties, royal inscriptions, administrative documents, and court correspondence. By adopting this view, we can see that the series of divine names contained within these inscriptions appear to resemble lexical god lists. Typically, the series in which we are interested are derived from divine witness lists, blessings, curses, and strings of royal epithets, and most of the divine names appear alone (or occasionally in pairs) in each repetitive literary unit. Consider, for example, the chain of divine names and epithets contained in this royal inscription from Esarhaddon's reign:

> **Assur**, father of the gods, who loves my priesthood; **Anu** powerful, pre-eminent, who called my name; **Enlil**, sublime lord, who establishes my reign; **Ea**, wise, the knowing one, who fixes my destinies; **Sîn**, shining light, who makes my omens favorable; **Šamaš**, judge of heaven and the earth, who settles my decisions; **Adad**, terrifying lord, who makes my troops prosper; **Marduk**, prince of the Igigū and Anuna, who makes my kingship great; **Ištar**, lady of battle, who walks by my side; the **Sebittu**, the valiant ones, who destroy my enemies (RINAP 4, Esar. 98:1–10)

By ignoring the epithets, the following list of divine names is produced: Assur / Anu / Enlil / Ea / Sîn / Šamaš / Adad / Marduk / Ištar / Sebittu. Because of the regular and predictable placement of the divine names within these literary units – be they phrases, sentences, or paragraphs – the observed literary pattern allows us to reconstruct the names into a sequential list of gods. Depending on the text's genre, the god lists that are derived from – or found to be embedded within – a text are not always arranged in an obviously meaningful manner; however, more often than not the arrangements of the divine names within these texts reveal theological insights. Chief among these insights are the hierarchical rankings of the Neo-Assyrian deities and the perspective from which to claim definitively that each individual entry was recognized by its author as a distinct and separate entry. Because the divine names and their arrangement must be distilled from the larger contents and contexts of a given inscription, the list of divine names derived from this collection of diverse non-lexical genres are "embedded god lists" (EGLs) in order to easily differentiate them from the traditional "lexical god lists" or "god lists."

As we saw with Zsolnay's four EGLs in Šalmaneser's inscriptions, the series of divine names derived from EGLs are typically rather short, often containing three to ten members.[49] These shorter lists allow us to determine the relative rank of any two deities, which we could not do using the lexical god lists. Moreover, in contrast to the lexical god-list tradition, EGLs contained in royal inscriptions and other non-lexical genres rarely include a deity's extended entourage, at most they are limited to a consort and their divine child, who may have his own consort. In short, because EGLs are short, they are simpler to use. However, the main potential drawback to using EGLs from these sources is also their limited size; deities cannot be ranked against each other if they do not appear in the same EGLs. Fortunately, we can easily correct this drawback by collecting multiple EGLs and creating composite god lists with any and all deities of interest combined in an easily ranked hierarchy. Because the general arrangement of divine names in EGLs within royal inscriptions, treaties and other administrative documents, and letters from the ninth through seventh centuries appears to be relatively stable over time and across genres, the composite god lists that EGLs produce and their common anchor points present us with reliable hierarchies of Neo-Assyrian deities.

Anchor points are those divine names that appear in corresponding positions in multiple EGLs. Some anchor points are absolute, such as Assur's primary position in each of the three EGLs found in the following table (RINAP 4, Esar. 1 ii 30–39, ii 56 and Esar. 98:1–10).[50] Likewise, Ištar's position

49 In his examination of god lists in the Near Eastern treaty traditions, Barré defines god lists as requiring a minimum of three divine names (Barré, *God-List*, 6), a characteristic that has been applied to the embedded god lists examined in chapters 3 through 5.

50 "Absolute" should not be confused with "invariable." As an absolute anchor point, Assur can be said to be definitively first in a given EGL, like RINAP 4, Esar. 1 ii 30–39, regardless of whether he is first in other EGLs. Likewise, Ištar, Nabû, and the Sebittu can all be designated as absolute anchor points for their respective EGLs because they definitively complete the EGLs in which they appear.

as the last deity in Esar. 1 ii 30–39 is an absolute anchor point, as is the Sebittu's position in Esar. 98:1–10. If divine names that serve as absolute anchor points in separate EGLs appear together in one EGL, as Ištar and the Sebittu do when Esar. 98:1–10 is included, their relative positions can be determined. However, when two absolute anchor points from different EGLs do not appear together in another EGL, then the relative position between those two divine names cannot be determined with any degree of certainty. For instance, given only the two EGLs in Esar. 1 ii 30–39 and Esar. 1 ii 56, we cannot be certain of the relative status of Ištar with Nabû. In contrast to absolute anchor points are relative anchor points, which reflect the relationships between deities within an EGL. For example, Šamaš precedes Marduk/Bēl in each EGL below, so he outranks Marduk in a relative fashion. Together, the absolute and relative anchor points that are common to the EGLs allow us to build composite god lists by inserting the remaining divine names into the composite god list according to their relative positions in the individual EGLs. As the table shows, the EGLs found in some royal inscriptions of the Neo-Assyrian king Esarhaddon share many common anchor points from which to build a composite god list:

RINAP 4, Esar. 1 ii 30–39	RINAP 4, Esar. 1 ii 56	RINAP 4, Esar. 98:1–10	Anchor Points	Composite A
Assur	**Assur**	**Assur**	**Assur**	**Assur**
		Anu		**Anu**
		Enlil		**Enlil**
		Ea		**Ea**
Sîn	**Sîn**	**Sîn**	**Sîn**	**Sîn**
Šamaš	**Šamaš**	**Šamaš**	**Šamaš**	**Šamaš**
		Adad		**Adad**
Marduk	**Bēl**	**Marduk**	**Marduk**	**Marduk**
	Nabû			**Nabû**
Nergal				**Nergal**
Ištar		Ištar	Ištar	Ištar
		the **Sebittu**	the **Sebittu**	the **Sebittu**.[51]

51 In EGLs and tables in Akkadian and Sumerian texts, chief deities (i.e., **Aššur**, **Marduk**, and **Nabû**) and their consorts appear in a bold **black**; members of Triad 1 (i.e., **Anu**, **Enlil**, and **Ea**) and their consorts appear in bold **blue**; members of Triad 2 (i.e., **Sîn**, **Šamaš**, and **Adad**) and their consorts appear in bold **red**; warrior (or other male) gods appear in bold **green**; goddesses appear in pink; other deities, including deified objects appear in bold **yellow**; and celestial objects (e.g., planets/stars) appear in bold **orange**.

The EGLs in RINAP 4, Esar. 1 ii 30–39 and ii 56 and Esar. 98:1–10 have many anchor points. Two notable differences are present between them. The first is that the divine name Marduk is interchangeable with his title Bēl, and it should be noted here that this Marduk/Bēl interchange represents the only nickname substitution that regularly occurs within EGLs for male deities.[52] Otherwise, only goddesses are regularly identified by an epithet or title (e.g., Bēltiya, Lady-of-GN, or Queen-of-GN) instead of by their common first names. The second notable difference is the group of concluding deities in each EGL, which in the EGLs above includes all of those deities those following Marduk. Nergal and Ištar end the EGL in Esar. 1 ii 30–39, and Nabû ends the list in Esar.1 ii 56. Theoretically, in the absence of another EGL that includes both Nabû and Nergal, the relationship between Nabû and Nergal cannot be determined (just as the relationship between Ištar and the Nabû could not be determined). Even with the addition of Esar. 98:1–10, which lacks both Nabû and Nergal, their relative ranks still cannot be determined. For graphic simplicity – and because we know his status relative to Nergal and Ištar from other EGLs (e.g., Esar. 133:10) – Nabû has been placed before Nergal in our exemplar Composite A. However, if Esar. 1 ii 30–39 and ii 56 and Esar. 98:1–10 were the only information available for compiling a composite god list, Nabû could be placed before Nergal, after Ištar, or between the two deities with equal uncertainty. Finally, Composite A provides a fairly simple new god list with an easily decided final entry, the Sebittu, who appear after Ištar and conclude Esar. 98:1–10; however, remember that Nabû's status in this composite relative to Nergal, Ištar, and the Sebittu is indeterminable given the presented available data.

Numerous other EGLs can be added to Composite A, with each new EGL added by aligning absolute and relative anchor names in order to maintain the proper status of each deity in relation to the others. Generally, new EGLs tend to conform quite well to the existing composite god list, which suggests that these EGLs produce reliable hierarchies. For example, the EGL from RINAP 4, Esar. 133:10 includes only those deities already present in Composite A and lacks only the Sebittu; however, it does provide additional information because it places Nabû between Marduk and Nergal: Assur / Anu / Enlil / Ea / Sîn / Šamaš / Adad / Marduk / Nabû / Nergal / Ištar. Additional EGLs fill in more gaps, often including goddesses by pairing them with their consorts: Esar. 1 ii 16–18 lists Mullissu after Assur; Esar. 105 v 24–25 lists Zarpānītu between her consort Marduk and their son Nabû; and Esar. 12:13 lists Ningal and Aya after

52 Nabû is identified solely as "*mār*-Bēl" in a four-member EGL (Assur / Bēl / *mār*-Bēl / Ištar) in l. 14 of an Esarhaddon text from Uruk (RIMB 2 B.6.31.15), which follows an eleven-member EGL beginning in l. 10.

their respective consorts, Sîn and Šamaš.[53] The addition of Esar. 1 ii 16–18 creates two potential minor problems, however. The first problem already exists in Esar. 1 ii 16–18 itself: the inclusion of both Mullissu and Ištar, whom many modern scholars seem to consider the same goddess in their treatments of Neo-Assyrian deities, within the same EGL. The second problem exists only when Esar. 1 ii 16–18 is integrated into the composite god list because it lists Nabû before his father Marduk:

RINAP 4, Esar. 133:10 (plus Composite A)	**RINAP 4, Esar. 105 v 24–25**	**RINAP 4, Esar. 1 ii 16–18**	**Composite B**
Assur		**Assur**	**Assur**
		Mullissu	**Mullissu**
Anu			Anu
Enlil			Enlil
Ea			Ea
Sîn		Sîn	Sîn
Šamaš		Šamaš	Šamaš
Adad			Adad
Marduk	**Marduk**	***Nabû***	**Marduk**
	Zarpānītu		**Zarpānītu**
Nabû	**Nabû**	***Marduk***	**Nabû**
Nergal			Nergal
Ištar		Ištar	Ištar
the Sebittu			the Sebittu.[54]

Neither problem is so difficult as to prevent us from continuing to build a composite god list for Esarhaddon's royal inscriptions. The Mullissu-is-Ištar identification issue is dealt with in chapter 4.5, but for now it can be ignored because the two divine names are not related to each other. The Nabû-Marduk issue, however, slightly challenges the methodology, but it must be noted that Nabû never precedes Marduk in any Esarhaddon royal inscription when

53 Esarhaddon paired these divine names by providing himself with royal epithets, which can be used to create the EGL in RINAP 4, Esar. 1 ii 12 and 16–18: "I am Esarhaddon, king of the universe, king of Assyria ... the creation of Assur (and) Mullissu, the beloved of Sîn and Šamaš, the chosen one of Nabû (and) Marduk, the favorite of Ištar, the queen, the desired one of the great gods."

54 The divine names Nabû and Marduk appear in italics in the column representing the EGL in RINAP 4, Esar. 1 ii 16–18. Throughout this study, the tablet and line number are written in italics to indicate that Nabû's name is listed before Marduk's in an EGL: e.g., SAA 13 *126:4*.

Zarpānītu is also present. Because our composite god list includes Zarpānītu, Marduk rightfully maintains his position before his son Nabû in Composite B. Notably, letters written by Assyrian scribes often reflect a preference for listing Nabû before Marduk when the two deities are invoked together in blessings, but Babylonian scribes more consistently list the Babylonian chief deity first and Nabû second.[55] This particular irregularity in the treatment of these gods' relative status in EGLs is even observable within a given tablet; in SAA 13 92, Nabû-šumu-iddina lists Nabû before Marduk in a blessing (l. 5), and then he proceeds with another blessing that includes Marduk, Nabû, and Nergal in that specific order (l. 7).

When we add the EGL from RINAP 4, Esar. 1 ii 45–46 to our composite god list, we further complicate matters because we have now created a list that includes (the unspecified) Ištar and two localized Ištar goddesses.

Composite B	RINAP 4, Esar. 1 ii 45–46	Composite C[56]
Assur	**Assur**	**Assur**
Mullissu		**Mullissu**
Anu		Anu
Enlil		Enlil
Ea		Ea
Sîn		Sîn
Šamaš	Šamaš	Šamaš
Adad		Adad
Marduk	**Bēl**	**Marduk**
Zarpānītu		**Zarpānītu**
Nabû	**Nabû**	**Nabû**
Nergal		Nergal
Ištar		⟨Ištar⟩
	Ištar-of-Nineveh	Ištar-of-Nineveh
	Ištar-of-Arbela	Ištar-of-Arbela
the Sebittu		the Sebittu.

55 Barbara N. Porter, "What the Assyrians Thought the Babylonians Thought about the Relative Status of Nabû and Marduk in the Late Assyrian Period," *Assyria 1995: Proceedings of the 10th Anniversary Symposium of the Neo-Assyrian Text Corpus Project, Helsinki, September 7–11, 1995*, eds. Simo Parpola and R. M. Whiting (Helsinki: Neo-Assyrian Text Corpus Project, 1997), 255; and Parpola, SAA 10, XXV–XXVI.

56 When a consort is listed immediately after her husband in an EGL or composite god list, her name is indented by three spaces. When the goddess is not listed immediately following her husband, her name is justified to the left like the other divine names. Compare, for example, Mullissu's name in Table 3.9. iii and 3.15, both of which reflect EGLs from Esarhaddon's Succession Treaty (SAA 2 6).

It is important to note that Esar. 1 ii 45–46 lacks (the unspecified) Ištar, as do most EGLs that include Ištar goddesses with geographic last names. Because the Ištar in Composite B and the two Ištars in Esar. 1 ii 45–46 appear at or near the end of each individual EGL, the relative status between (the unspecified) Ištar and either of the other two cannot presently be determined.[57] For graphic convenience, we will always give priority to (the unspecified) Ištar in the composite god lists, and her name will be placed within angle brackets, ⟨ ⟩, in order to indicate that she is not competing for rank with the localized Ištar goddesses who are listed below her in the composite god list. On the rare occasion in which a scribe included (the unspecified) Ištar in an EGL that also contained localized Ištar goddesses (e.g., SAA 2 6:414–465; SAA 3 34:72–73 and [35:70]), (the unspecified) Ištar's name is *not* placed within angle brackets.

Table 3.14 represents the results of performing this compilation algorithm as needed with those EGLs found in royal inscriptions for Tiglath-pileser III, Sargon II, Sennacherib, Esarhaddon, and Assurbanipal. The occasional irregularity does occur in an individual EGL when compared to other EGLs, and complications are noted in the table and explained.[58] Not only does Table 3.14 demonstrate that the hierarchy of the gods is relatively static over the course of the century from the start of Tiglath-pileser III's reign to the close of Assurbanipal's, but this hierarchy also closely resembles the hierarchy found in the treaty curse lists (see Table 3.9), which makes sense given the fact that royal inscriptions and the curse lists found within imperial treaties are both commissioned by the kings. In short, following Barré's observation that the sequence of deities that are listed between Anu and Adad is regular in Neo-Assyrian treaties and royal inscriptions, the hierarchy begins with Assur, the chief deity of Assyria; continues with the Triad 1 deities (i.e., Anu, Enlil, and Ea, who are noticeably absent in both Tiglath-pileser III's and Assurbanipal's royal inscriptions' EGLs) and their consorts; the Triad 2 deities (i.e., Sîn, Šamaš, and Adad) and their consorts; the Babylonian chief deities (i.e., Marduk and Nabû) and their consorts.[59] The hierarchy then ends with the warrior (and other male) gods and goddesses, and concludes with the Sebittu. Other minor

57 Depending on the context of a given royal inscription, (the unspecified) Ištar could reasonably be identified as either one of the two (or even both?) geographic-specific goddesses listed. Such identifications must be done only when context warrants it rather than being universally applied according to the text's provenance or according to the king's capital city as Barton had suggested in the 1890s (see the discussion of Barton and his methodologies in chapter 1.1).

58 When the arrangement of divine names is in disagreement within a set of EGLs, the divine name that occurs first in more of the extant EGLs is placed first in the composite god list.

59 Barré, *God-List*, 9.

gods make infrequent appearances in EGLs, but rarely do they disturb the standard pattern given here.

3.4 Witness-List Traditions

Although a scribe could list an individual deity or group of deities in a royal inscription or in a series of curses, one could argue that these gods have been selected because they represented interests of the state rather than because they were actually distinct deities, which is what Holloway might suggest in regard to Kurbail. Their inclusion could be thought of as reflecting the political realities of the empire rather than real theological concerns.[60] For example, Esarhaddon's choice to include Ištar-of-Arbela in his succession treaty's curses (SAA 2 6:459 f.) after Mullissu-of-Nineveh could highlight his interest in promoting the city Arbela along with her priests and cult in the city. The city was important to the empire, and securing the morale and continued support of its citizens was taken seriously by promoting the city's patron deity along with the other great deities honored in the imperial cults. The fact that she was the same deity as the already named goddess from Nineveh is irrelevant because invoking only (the unspecified) Ištar would not excite local Arbelites and Ninevites as strongly as explicitly naming their city would. Because the name Ištar was associated with both cities, this suggests not that she was more than one goddess but that this double association more effectively encouraged or honored the local population and its troops.

This argument, however, is not tenable for the inclusion of multiple deities sharing a divine name in EGLs that appear in the blessing sections of personal letters or in witness lists. In regard to personal letters, Marduk-šallim-aḫḫē's and Urdu-Nabû's decisions to invoke both Ištar-of-Nineveh and Ištar-of-Arbela when they blessed the king did not promote a particular Ištar goddess and her local cult in the same way that an inclusion in a royal inscription or curse list would have. Perhaps the scribes had been indoctrinated by the propaganda in the royal inscriptions and/or had decided to toe the theological line portrayed in those royal inscriptions whenever they had an audience before the king, but it is also possible that they considered Ištar-of-Nineveh and Ištar-of-Arbela as distinct enough to effect a more beneficial blessing than only invoking one Ištar could. Such an interpretation allows the modern scholar to interpret the scribes' writings according to word choice. After all, invoking or addressing

60 See, for example, Holloway, *Aššur is King*, 343.

more deities – which also includes ensuring that the deities were physically present in statue form at the treaty or oath ceremony – gave a blessing more effective power than invoking fewer deities.[61] Additionally, the larger number of deities included in a blessing could instill honor upon either the blesser, whose increased status was indicated by the number of deities to whom he could appeal, or upon the blessed, whose increased status was also indicated by the larger number of named deities.

Likewise, the motivation to include additional divine names in a witness list suggests an increased status for those invoking the deities, and it increased the likelihood that the human participants would be intimidated by them and so fulfill their responsibilities.[62] The inclusion of a deity or a divine name in a witness list is treated here, as elsewhere, as a reflection of that deity's ability to enforce the treaty. It is worth noting that the witness lists in the Neo-Assyrian treaty tradition include substantially more deities than do the witness lists in lesser state documents, such as tablets concerning grants, decrees, and gifts. Because a treaty between a king and his vassal or between a king and his equal was more important than any decree promising a loyal subject a tax-free exemption for his land, we should expect that its witness list should be more involved and expansive. For instance, the divine witness list in Esarhaddon's Succession Treaty (SAA 2 6; Table 3.15) consists of 23 divine names, and the treaty between Assur-nērārī V and Mati'-ilu of Arpad (SAA 2 2; Table 3.10) comprises over three dozen Assyrian deities, as well as eight extant non-Assyrian divine names. In contrast, the number of divine names listed in grants, decrees, gifts, and private documents is generally six or fewer (see Tables 3.5a and 3.5b), and typically only four or five deities appear in the grants and decrees: Assur, Enlil, Adad, Bēr, and Assyrian-Ištar.[63]

The Akkadian treaty between Assur-nērārī V and Mati'-ilu of Arpad provides a lengthy EGL in the form of an adjuration or witness list (SAA 2 2 vi 6–26), and

61 Holloway, *Aššur is King*, 175; Theodore J. Lewis, "The Identity and Function of El/Baal Berith," *JBL* 115 (1996): 404; and Ulla Koch-Westenholz, *Mesopotamian Astrology: an Introduction to Babylonian and Assyrian Celestial Divination*, CNI Publications 19 (Denmark: Museum Tusculanum Press, 1995), 118.

62 Admittedly, residents from Arbela would surely have been excited to learn that their goddess had been called as a witness in an important treaty and responded positively – that is, if they would have ever learned of it – but it may be too cynical an explanation to accept that the kings' divine witness lists were motivated more by political expediency than by religious convictions.

63 The inclusion of these four or five deities as witnesses in these texts is a tradition that continued from the reigns of Adad-nērārī III and Tiglath-pileser III in the eighth century (e.g., SAA 12 13, 14, 69, 75, and 85) through to Assur-etel-ilāni's reign in the 620s (e.g., SAA 12 35, 36, 40, and 41).

its oath takers swore (*tamû*) by a list of deities that represents an ideal EGL.[64] The Assyrian chief deity Assur begins the list and is followed by Triads 1 and 2 and the Babylonian chief deities, each with their primary consorts (see Table 3.10). The scribe's use of KI.MIN indicates how the scribe thought the gods were to be paired. Rather than appearing at the end of each line following a collection of divine names, KI.MIN typically appears after each pair of deities, who are often a divine couple. Exceptions to this pairing do occur; for example, the two male deities Madānu and Ningirsu were paired. Other exceptions include the isolation of a several deities, each appearing with his or her own KI.MIN-signs: Assur, Ištar-of-Nineveh, Ištar-of-Arbela, Adad-of-Kurbail, Hadad-of-Aleppo, and *Palil*.[65]

Closely resembling the EGL in SAA 2 2 is a witness list of gods named in another treaty entered into by Mati'-ilu of Arpad, this time with the ruler of an otherwise unknown land, Barga'yah of KTK (Sefire i A [*KAI* 222]).[66] The resemblance between these two lists resides primarily in the pairing that the Sefire treaty incorporates into the god lists through the use of repeated *wqdm* ("and in the presence of"; see Table 3.12), just as several deities are paired by a following KI.MIN in SAA 2 2 (e.g., ^{d}*a-nu-um an-tum* KI.MIN ^{d}BAD ^{d}NIN.LIL$_2$ KI.MIN, SAA 2 2 vi 7; see Table 3.10 and 3.13). Despite this similarity, however, the actual composition of the two EGLs is somewhat different. Whereas SAA 2 2 lacks a consort for the chief deity Assur, Sefire i A (*KAI* 222) pairs Assur with Mullissu at the beginning of the list, and it places the Babylonian chief deities and their consorts next, just like many Assyrian EGLs (e.g., the curse lists in SAA 2 1 and 9, or the blessing-lists in SAA 13 10 and 102).[67] However, the Sefire EGL lacks all Triad 1 deities and their consorts, and it lists the first two members of Triad 2 and their respective consorts after the warrior god Nergal and his consort Laṣ (see Tables 3.12 and 3.13). After NKR, KD'H, and a group of deities referred to collectively as "all the gods of the open country and cultivated ground" (*kl 'lhy rḥbh w'dm*[...], Sefire i A 10), Hadad-of-Aleppo and the Sebittu appear at the end of this list of Assyrian deities, just as they do in SAA 2 2.[68] The enigmatic

64 *CAD* T, *tamû* mng. 3b1′.

65 The Sumerian divine name IGI.DU has been read as Palil. Because this reading is uncertain, the name is written in italics.

66 Gibson, *TSSI* 2, 28–29.

67 The restoration of Assur rather than Enlil in this lacuna in Sefire i A 7 (*KAI* 222) is based on Barré's analysis of the text (Michael L. Barré, "The First Pair of Deities in the Sefire I God-List," *JNES* 44 [1985]: 210).

68 Barré notes:

> One should note that with the exception of the supreme gods ([DN] *wmlš*), *nr*, and possibly *kd'h*, all the deities named in Sf1 [i.e., Sefire i A (*KAI* 222)] up to and including the Sebetti are also listed in the contemporary treaty A/M [i.e., SAA 2 2]; but none of those listed after

pairing of 'El and 'Elyon begins the list of deities in the Sefire treaty, which includes Heaven, Earth, the Abyss, Springs, Day, and Night.

As may be expected, the resemblance among the witness EGLs in Neo-Assyrian treaties is higher than between the two Mati'-ilu treaties.[69] Unfortunately, however, the only surviving witness or adjuration EGLs in the treaties are found in SAA 2 2 and 6, which together – along with SAA 12 10 – provide a composite divine witness list that is noticeably similar to other composite god lists presented thus far (see Table 3.16). Naturally, because both these treaty EGLs follow the expected divine hierarchy for the Neo-Assyrian period, their composite god list does as well: Assyrian chief deity, Triad 1, Triad 2, Babylonian chief deities and their consorts, warrior (and other male) gods and goddesses, and the Sebittu. Moreover, the hierarchy within this composite god list is very similar to those found in the royal inscription EGLs. Between these two treaties alone, this composite god list is the most comprehensive Neo-Assyrian one collected for this study. Indeed, perhaps only two or three significant divine names or relationships are missing from this list.[70]

---

the Sebetti in Sf1 is found in A/M. This is another reason for seeing the major break in the god-list after the Sebetti." (Barré, *God-List*, 25)

These discrepancies can now be reduced because Barré successfully argued that the divine name Assur belongs in the supreme deity's lacuna in his 1985 article (Barré, "First Pair," 210). Furthermore, he notes that *mlš* should be interpreted as Mullissu (ibid., 205). Mullissu may not be paired with Assur in SAA 2 2, as she is in Sefire i A, but she does appear in both. Now, a third deity may also be removed from this list of discrepancies because Parpola and Watanabe have tentatively identified the divine name *Nur* with Šamaš's consort Aya (^{d}*a-a*, SAA 2 2 vi 9), as indicated by their English translation of the line: "Ditto by Šamaš and *Nur*!" However, if Barré meant to tag the third divine name as *nkr* rather than *nr*, then two new divine names still occur in Sefire i A that are missing in SAA 2 2.

69 Barré notes that royal inscriptions from north Syria, including the Panamuwa and Bir-Rakib inscriptions (*KAI* 214–215) and Sefire (*KAI* 222), show a highly consistent collection of god lists (Barré, *God-List*, 9).

70 It should be noted that this composite god list (Table 3.16) lacks an explicit pairing of the chief Assyrian deity with Mullissu as his consort; instead, of the two Mullissus that appear in this list, the first is explicitly included as Enlil's consort because of SAA 2 2 vi 7. The second Mullissu should be interpreted as Assur's consort, but this is not stated explicitly in SAA 2 6:16–19. Mullissu follows Assur in the curse list EGL (SAA 2 6:414–418), and she appears first among the independent goddesses in the witness list in l. 19, where she precedes Šerū'a, who was probably understood as Assur's second wife when the treaty was written (Meinhold, *Ištar in Aššur*, 218).

The absence of Nanaya in this composite god list is also apparent compared to other composite god lists. Another possibly significant absence is that of the localized Ištar goddess Lady-of-Kidmuri, who does appear in EGLs found in royal inscription and personal letters. (The absence of Ištar-of-Heaven is noticeable, but this goddess is likely already included in SAA 2 6:13 and 428 as Venus. For a discussion on the identification of Ištar-of-Heaven with the

Unlike the other EGL traditions, the divine witness-list tradition has an earthly counterpart against which its structure and hierarchy can be examined. Grant Frame notes that in the Neo-Assyrian period from Uruk, witness lists followed a predictable hierarchy. Invariably, the governor (*šākin ṭēmi*) preceded the temple administrator (*šatammu*), who, in turn, preceded the delegate (*qīpu*) of the Eanna-temple and the Eanna-temple scribe.[71] This top-to-bottom ranking – governor, temple administrator, *qīpu*, and temple scribe – is exactly what Frame says should be expected in a witness list, and it is an order that is found in non-witness lists as well. In SAA 10 349, Mār-Issār (his name has been restored in this letter) writes to Esarhaddon that he was unable to check on the 40 minas of gold in the temple treasury:

> ^{28} ^{lu2}ŠA$_3$.TAM ^{lu2}*qe-e-pu u*$_3$ ^{lu2}DUB.SAR E$_2$-DINGIR ^{29}*ša* UNUG^{ki} *pa-an* LUGAL EN-*ia šu-nu*
> $^{r.}$ ^{1}*la e-mu-qa-a-a ba-la-tu-us-šu*$_2$*-nu* ^{2}*re-eš* KUG.GI *la a-na-aš*$_2$*-ši*
>
> The temple administrator, the delegate, and the temple scribe of Uruk are before the king, my lord; without them, I have no authority to inspect the gold. (SAA 10 349:28-r. 2)

Mār-Issār's lack of authority also prevented him from checking on any incoming gold. For the present purposes, whatever authority Mār-Issār had to act on his own is irrelevant; what matters is that his letter mimics a hierarchical arrangement that was common to almost all economic texts relating to real estate transactions at Uruk.[72]

Similarly, Cornelia Wunsch has found regularity in the arrangement of judges in lists. Whereas Frame's survey notes that the hierarchy of witnesses is dependent upon the status of a particular witness's occupation, Wunsch demonstrates that the judicial hierarchy was determined by seniority.[73] This seniority was not determined by a particular judge's familial ties or his age but by how long he had been a royal judge. New judges consistently appeared in the last position of a given witness list and only advanced when a higher-ranking judge died or was dismissed. Because half of her texts in this survey came from a single four-year period, the ninth through twelfth years of Nabonidus's reign, they present a highly uniform picture of individual names climbing from the bottom of the list to the top. Moreover, the turnover rate for

planet Venus and her status compared to other Ištar goddesses, see Meinhold, *Ištar in Aššur*, 76–79, esp. 79, and 114–116.)

71 Grant Frame, "City Administration of Uruk in the Neo-Assyrian Period," (forthcoming), 5.

72 Frame, "City Administration," 6.

73 Cornelia Wunsch, "Die Richter des Nabonid," in *Assyriologica et Semitica: Festschrift für Joachim Oelsner anlässlich seines 65. Geburtstages am 18. Februar 1997*, eds. J. Marzahn and H. Neumann, AOAT 252 (Münster: Ugarit-Verlag, 2000), 572.

the job was quick enough that this process can be seen in just a few texts. The careers of three judges, Nergal-ušallim, Nergal-bānûnu, and Nabû-balāssu-iqbi, and their rank within a set of judge lists illustrate this point (see Table 3.17).

While the divine witness lists display a greater variety and willingness to rearrange their members' hierarchy than do the human witness-list counterparts, the chronological and geographical spans of the divine witness lists under investigation dwarf the Neo-Babylonian judge lists in the same way that gods dwarf humans. Whereas the judicial records spanned just a few years and were restricted to Babylon, the divine witness lists spanned two centuries and represented both the western and southern ends of the Assyrian empire. Nevertheless, Frame's and Wunsch's research on the stability of human witness lists suggest that the stable portions of divine witness lists reflect an accurate and official representation of the divine hierarchy in the Neo-Assyrian period. Those deities who appeared nearer the top of the witness list were the senior or supreme gods, and those deities who appeared nearer the bottom alongside the Sebittu were less important gods and goddesses. This is further strengthened by the structural and hierarchical similarities common to the divine witness lists and other EGLs. Consider, for example, the similarities between the divine witness and adjuration lists and the curse lists in SAA 2 6 (see Table 3.15); these lists differ as one moves from deity to deity, but categories remain stable: Assyrian chief deities, Triad 1, Triad 2, Babylonian chief deities, warrior (and other male) gods, and goddesses.

Consider also the similarities between the composite seventh-century god lists from the reigns of Esarhaddon and Assurbanipal, where this overall structure is still apparent. The two main differences among these various genres of EGL are the lack of interest in Triad 1 deities and the seemingly haphazard placement of warrior (and other male) gods in these lists. The absence of Triad 1 deities, which has already been observed by Barré in treaties and other god lists, is almost complete in Assurbanipal's royal inscriptions EGLs.[74] They are also lacking in the blessings of letters from Assyrian and Babylonian scholars (in SAA 10) and are underrepresented in the curses. The warrior (and other male) gods, however, can be found ascending and descending the ranks in these composite god lists. In addition to appearing either before or after the isolated goddesses near the bottom of the lists, Ninurta, Nergal, and Nusku are occasionally listed among Triad 2 deities and before planets and the Babylonian chief deities. Despite these exceptions that challenge the observed rules governing these god lists and their overarching official hierarchy, these rules are quite simple and make themselves readily apparent to scholars who encounter them while reading the tablets for other purposes.

74 Barré, *God-List*, 23.

3.5 Personal and Royal Correspondence

The greetings and blessing sections in personal and royal correspondence provide another genre of EGLs against which divine hierarchies and arrangements can be checked. According to Frame, the gods who appear in personal correspondence tend to reflect the local divine hierarchy, or at least reflect an attempt to demonstrate loyalty to the king.[75] For example, letters from the Sealand include the divine trio Assur, Šamaš, and Marduk, all of whom are praised by Tiglath-pileser III in locally placed royal inscriptions. Significantly, the Sealand-letter tradition lists the deities in this specific order, placing the imperial god Assur first, Šamaš second as a member of Triad 2, and Marduk third as the Babylonian chief deity. As Frame suggests, this Sealand tradition includes these three deities in this same order. Despite Marduk's local importance, he was listed after Šamaš, which resembles Marduk's relatively late placement in all of SAA 2 6's EGLs (see Table 3.15).[76] Letters can also reflect a bias towards local gods in another way; Assyrian scribes tended to place Nabû before Marduk in their letters when the two deities were invoked together in a blessing, whereas Babylonian scribes placed Marduk, the Babylonian chief deity, first.[77]

A survey of EGLs derived from the blessing section of letters provides the same basic hierarchy that has already been observed in the royal inscription god lists. However, because letters are more personal in nature than royal inscriptions, deities unknown from royal inscriptions or treaty curse lists can appear in blessings in letters (e.g., Lord-Crown in SAA 13 187:6), as can the occasional temple (e.g., the Ešarra-temple in SAA 13 162:4).[78] The following composite god list has been built from letters collected in SAA 13, 16, and 18 (see Table 3.6 for a full explanation of this composite god list)[79]:

---

75 Grant Frame, "My Neighbour's God: Aššur in Babylonia and Marduk in Assyria," *CSMS Bulletin* 34 (1999): 17.

76 In SAA 2 6, the treaty concerns itself primarily with the rule of Esarhaddon's chosen heir Assurbanipal over the entire empire, which is why Marduk played a lesser role than he did in SAA 2 9, a treaty between Assurbanipal and his Babylonian allies. In the latter text, Marduk's promotion to second deity, following only Assur, was an exercise in securing an alliance with the Babylonians.

77 Porter, "What the Assyrians Thought," 255.

78 Assur and the Ešarra-temple appear together in the first of two blessings in SAA 13 162 and 163, which are letters from Babylon about the reconstruction of the Esagil-temple. The second blessing in each letter includes Marduk, Zarpānītu, Nabû, Tašmētu, and Nanaya. Likewise, the scribe Bēl-iddina included Lord-Crown (^{d}EN.AGA) as the final entity in a three-member EGL (following Assur and Ningal) in SAA 13 187.

79 This reconstructed god list has been created from the EGLs from the following Esarhaddon- and Assurbanipal-period letters collected in SAA 13, 16, and 18: SAA 13 9, 10, 12, 15, *37*, 56, 57,

Assur
  Mullissu (Ištar)
Ešarra
Anu
Enlil
  Mullissu
Ea
Sîn
  Ningal
Lord-Crown
Nusku
Šamaš
  Aya
Adad
  Šala
Marduk
  Zarpānītu
  Lady-of-Babylon
Nabû
  Tašmētu
  Nanaya
Ninurta
  Gula
Zababa
Nergal
  Laṣ
Madānu
Ištar-of-Nineveh
Ištar-of-Kidmuri
Ištar-of-Arbela
Queen-of-Nakkanti.

The Assyrian chief deity and his family and temple begin the composite god list and are followed by Triad 1 and Triad 2 members and their consorts (and,

58, 60, 61, 63, 64, 65, 66, 68, 69, 80, 92, 102, 132, 140, *147*, 156, 161, 162, 163, 187, and 188; SAA 16 14, 15, 17, 18, 31, 33, 49, 52, 59, 60, 61, 65, 72, 86, 105, 106, 117, 126, 127, 128, 153, and 193?; and SAA 18 85, 131, 182, and 185. Other EGLs that nearly fit this reconstruction are noted in subsequent footnotes and explained below. If a text number has been italicized, the divine name Nabû immediately precedes Marduk in an EGL within that text.

in the cases of Sîn and Adad, some members of their entourage because some letters focused on their temples). The Babylonian chief deities and their consorts then follow and are themselves followed by warrior (and other male) gods and various goddesses.

Momentarily overlooking Queen-of-Nakkanti, the Ištar goddesses at the end are quite noticeable in this seventh-century composite god list.[80] Although Ištar goddesses tend to appear near the end of god lists in other genres (see Tables 3.14 and 3.16 for royal inscription and witness god lists, respectively), the curse EGL located in SAA 2 6 (and SAA 2 5, see Tables 3.9 and 5.4) presents the Ištar goddesses before Gula. In contrast, this letters-based composite has Gula and Laṣ before Ištar-of-Nineveh, Ištar-of-Kidmuri, and Ištar-of-Arbela. It must be noted that of those letters used to build this composite god list, neither Gula nor Laṣ actually appears in an EGL with any Ištar goddess. Theoretically, Gula, Laṣ, and the localized Ištar goddesses could be grouped without rank following the warrior (and other male) gods. The ranking presented here, however, has been determined by the EGLs in three separate letters: SAA 16 52, 126, and 128. The first letter is a petition written within the Assyrian heartland by an unknown scribe, and the other two are written by Itti-Šamaš-balāṭu from the western reaches of the empire. The extant portion of SAA 16 52 begins with an invocation of paired deities in the blessing:

> [1] [^{d}]EN *u*$_{3}$ ^{d}GAŠAN-*ia* ^{d}AG ^{d}*taš-me-tu*$_{4}$ [2][^{d}]⸢MAŠ⸣ *u*$_{3}$ ^{d}*gu-la* ^{d}U.GUR ^{d}*la-*⸢*aṣ*⸣ [3]DINGIR^{meš} *an-nu-te* GAL^{meš} *a-na* ^{md}AG–[x x x] [4]*lik-ru-bu-ka*
>
> "May Bēl and Bēltiya, Nabû (and) Tašmetu, Ninurta and Gula, Nergal (and) Laṣ, these great gods, bless you, O PN!"

The male deities have been paired with their respective consorts in this letter, so Gula is listed immediately after Ninurta in the EGL, and Laṣ follows Nergal for the same reason. Had the goddesses not been paired with their consorts and ranked according to their husbands' positions, their relative status among the goddesses in the composite god list could not have been determined; they could have been placed either before or after the localized Ištar goddesses. Of

80 In SAA 13 186:5–6, Aplāia of Kurbail invokes Adad with Šala and Šarrat-nakkanti (Queen-of-the-Treasury) to create this three-member EGL of the gods in the Edurhenunna-temple in Kurbail. Theoretically, because she only appears at the end of this one three-member EGL, Queen-of-Nakkanti could be located anywhere after Šala in this composite god list. She has been placed at the end of this composite god list because she is a solitary goddess and solitary goddesses seem to have lower ranks than localized Ištar goddesses (see, for example, SAA 2 6:414–465 and 5 iv 1′–5′). Of course, as discussed above, because she is the last of the three-member EGL, we have no way to know how late in the list she belongs after Šala.

course, if we had chosen to construct this composite god list without considering divine consort pairs in a way reminiscent of SAA 2 6 16–20 (see Table 3.15), then we would be forced to rely on composite god lists compiled from other genres, such as the treaty tradition and SAA 2 6 to figure out a best arrangement for Gula, Laṣ, and the localized Ištar goddesses. Taking this alternative route, we see that Gula and Laṣ receive a higher status when joined with their consorts than when contrasted with the consort-less localized Ištar goddesses, but when considered by themselves as goddesses, Gula and Laṣ take on a lower status than the localized Ištar goddesses.

In contrast, Itti-Šamaš-balāṭu sent his blessings in a purely serial format so that our EGL format does not hide any alternations in divine status:

SAA 16 126:4–6		**SAA 16 128:4–5**	
Assur	^{d}*aš-šur*	Assur	^{d}*aš-šur*
Šamaš	^{d}UTU	Šamaš	^{d}UTU
Bēl	^{d}EN	Bēl	^{d}EN
Nabû	^{d}PA	Nabû	^{d}PA
Nergal	^{d}U.GUR	Nergal	^{d}U.GUR
Ištar-of-Nineveh	^{d}15 *ša* NINA^{ki}	Ištar-of-Nineveh	^{d}15 *ša* ⸢NINA⸣^{ki}
Ištar-of-Kidmuri	^{d}15 *ša e*$_{2}$*-kad-mu-ru*		
Ištar-of-Arbela	^{d}15 *ša arba-il*$_{3}$^{ki}	Ištar-of-Arbela	^{d}15 *ša* ^{uru}*arba-*⸢*il*$_{3}$⸣.

In these two EGLs, the only significant difference is the absence of Ištar-of-Kidmuri in the second list. In both letters, the final male deity Nergal is listed before all the localized Ištar goddesses. Once the EGL from SAA 16 52 is combined with those from SAA 16 126 and 128, a composite god list is created: Assur / Šamaš / Bēl / Bēltiya / Nabû / Tašmētu / Ninurta / Gula / Nergal / Laṣ / Ištar-of-Nineveh / Ištar-of-Kidmuri / Ištar-of-Arbela. Regardless of Gula's and Laṣ's relative position compared to the other goddesses, the fact that three distinct localized Ištar goddesses are listed together must be stressed.

Another collection of seventh-century letters produces a somewhat similar yet noticeably different divine hierarchy. This second letter collection is drawn from SAA 10, *Letters from Assyrian and Babylonian Scholars*, and is treated separately from the material in SAA 13, 16, and 18 in order to highlight the treatment of deities, divine names, and their hierarchies by ancient scholars writing to the royal court. The astrologers, exorcists, and other court scholars who wrote this collection can be included among the most educated scribes of the Neo-Assyrian period. They received specific training in their respective fields of interest, which often included access to esoteric and other select texts. Despite this extra training, the EGLs and divine hierarchies produced by the scholars that have been collected in SAA 10 more closely resemble those written by the other scribes whose letters are collected in SAA 13, 16, and 18 than they do the god lists and hierarchies found in lexical god list traditions. Moreover, the localized Ištar goddesses whom they invoked are consistently linked to specific locations so that nowhere does (the unspecified) Ištar appear in this collection.

The differences in the divine hierarchy in this second collection of EGLs are noteworthy. As in the EGLs in Assurbanipal's royal inscriptions, members of Triad 1 are noticeably absent. The one exception is the invocation of Enlil and his consort Mullissu in SAA 10 286 (see Table 3.7), which is all the more an exception because these two deities are listed before Assur. A second difference is the presence of four planets in an EGL from SAA 10 197 (see Table 3.8) and select other letters.[81] The fact that the planets appear in SAA 10 is no surprise because, as astrologers and diviners, several of these scholar-scribes would have been concerned with the motion or influence of the planets.

Although Nusku appears earlier than normal in SAA 10 197, further similarities between the SAA 10 composite and that of SAA 13, 16, and 18, as well as other lists, should be noted. (See Table 3.6 for a comparison of the SAA 10 with the SAA 13, 16, and 18 composite god list.) First, Ninurta and Nergal have been paired with their respective consorts, Gula and Laṣ. Second, Ištar-of-Nineveh consistently appears before Ištar-of-Arbela whenever the two divine names are included in the same EGL. This also resembles what is found in the witness lists and oath lists of SAA 2 2, 6, and 10 (following the restoration of SAA 2 10) of the Neo-Assyrian treaties.[82] Likewise, Lady-of-Kidmuri's location between two other Ištar goddesses is anticipated from other EGL genres. However, the placement of the localized Ištar goddesses before the warrior (and other male) gods and their consorts differs from the SAA 13, 16, and 18 composite god list, the Neo-Assyrian treaty curse lists, and several Sargonid period royal inscriptions, as well as the witness list that appears in SAA 2 6. Although the fact that the goddesses are listed before the male gods may not feel surprising, we would not have predicted this for any given individual EGL. However, this difference between the relative rankings for the localized Ištar

81 Oddly enough, these deities and planets are not listed as a single group in SAA 10 197 but have been broken up in two pairs: Jupiter and Venus interrupt the typical sequence of Triad 2-Babylonian chief deities, whereas Saturn and Mercury appear between the Babylonian deities and the localized Ištar goddesses.

82 Cultic texts from Sennacherib's reign also show this arrangement (e.g., BM 121206 ix and x), as does the list of gods in two generic curse statements in Sennacherib's Succession Treaty (SAA 2 3:7′–10′ and r. 2′–8′).

goddesses in different EGL genres should not overshadow the fact that even the scholar-scribes with their additional training and direct access to the king still made distinctions between the localized Ištar goddesses.

3.6 Cultic Texts and EGLs

In contrast to lexical god lists, the EGLs examined so far in this chapter function pragmatically, which is how they resemble another group of texts containing EGLs: offering lists and ritual texts. The main difference between these texts and the EGLs examined above is that the latter are the products of, and are primarily used by, the priests serving the gods in their temples. These offering lists and ritual texts provide records of which deities a state or city supported in the temple complexes and how they were supported. *A priori*, there is little reason to assume that these texts would reflect the lay Mesopotamian's conceptions of the divine as opposed to the theological speculations of those priests and scribes who administered to the gods. A survey of a few offering and ritual texts indicates that cultic texts do not reflect the theology of the lexical god lists and esoteric texts. Rather, they provide a theological middle ground between the EGLs already examined in this chapter and the lexical god lists, and they provide further insight about a divine world that was perceived by those people closest to that world, that is, its servants. In addition to the scant Neo-Assyrian material collected, a brief survey of cultic texts from Neo-Babylonian Uruk is first offered.

In his study of the pantheon, or subset of officially revered deities, at Neo-Babylonian Uruk, Beaulieu presents a dozen previously unpublished offering lists, each of which includes the number of animals offered to various deities in and around Uruk.[83] These texts provide an opportunity to compare the hierarchy reflected in them and their use of divine names against the EGLs already examined. Beaulieu finds five exceptions to what otherwise appears to be a fixed divine hierarchy: Divine-Chariot appears before Lady-of-Eanna in NCBT 862; Temple-of-Marduk appears after Uṣur-amāssu and Gula in PTS 2942; Ninurta precedes Nergal in PTS 2042; Šamaš is placed between Uṣur-amāssu and Gula in PTS 3242; and Sîn is placed between Lady-of-Rēš and Uṣur-amāssu in PTS 3210. Otherwise, the regularity within these EGLs prompts Beaulieu to propose the following hierarchy that "reflects their relative theological importance in the local pantheon": Symbol-(or Altar-)of-Bēl / Lady-of-Uruk /

83 Beaulieu, *Pantheon of Uruk*, 41.

Symbol-(or Altar-)of-Nabû / Nanaya / Lady-of-Rēš / Temple-of-Marduk / Uṣur-amāssu / Urkayītu / Gula / *Palil* / Lady-of-Eanna / *Palil*-of-Udannu / Divine-Chariot / *bīt-ḫilṣi* / Nergal / Ninurta / Nusku / Šamaš / Aya (see Table 3.18).[84]

Four of these nineteen entities are not typically thought of as divine residents of Uruk: Šamaš and Aya are from Larsa, and Lady-of-Eanna and *Palil* are the patron deities of Udannu.[85] According to Beaulieu, precisely because deities from Larsa and Udannu appear in these Urukian offering lists, we have evidence of a central administration in charge of all the shrines and temples in Uruk. In this regard, these texts are evidence of a state-run religion with the authority resting in a regional city. This is why local deities dominate the hierarchy of these offering lists; these are the deities about which local priests and administrators were primarily concerned.

Attention should again be paid to the divine names in these EGLs as they reflect not the theological speculations of scholar-scribes but the cultic reality of the local temple administrators. Beaulieu notes that the localized Ištar goddess in these Neo-Babylonian Uruk texts is Lady-of-Uruk, who was worshipped in the city's main temple, the Eanna-temple.[86] As indicated in these offering lists, she was considered distinct from Lady-of-Eanna and Urkayītu, both of whom are also considered localized Ištar goddesses by some scholars.[87] Furthermore, the goddess known as Lady-of-Eanna-of-Udannu (*ša*$_2$ UBARA^{ki} ^{uru}*u*$_2$*-dan-nu*) did not reside in the Eanna-temple in Udannu; rather, she was a resident of the *Palil*-temple (e.g., E$_2$ ^{d}IGI.DU ^{uru}*u*$_2$*-dan-ni*, YBC 11546:4, and *ša*$_2$ ^{d}IGI.DU *ša*$_2$ ^{uru}*u*$_2$*-dan-nu*, YOS 7 137:8).[88] Curiously, then, although the localized Ištar goddess who actually resided in the Eanna-temple in Uruk was never

84 Beaulieu, *Pantheon of Uruk*, 73. Beaulieu notes that PTS 2097, *SWU* 161, and the collection that he terms "group B," which are not included among the 12 previously unpublished texts, conform to his proposed hierarchy (ibid., 74 and 87–95).

85 Beaulieu, *Pantheon of Uruk*, 73. Ištar-of-Uruk, Nanaya, Lady-of-Rēš, Uṣur-amāssu, Gula, *Palil*, and the symbols and altars of Bēl and Nabû all resided in the Eanna-temple. Marduk, Sîn, Nergal, Ninurta, Nusku, and Divine-Chariot resided in small sanctuaries in Uruk, and the *bīt-ḫilṣi* is probably a shrine in the Eanna-temple.

86 Beaulieu, *Pantheon of Uruk*, 119–123.

87 As the primary temple in Uruk for millennia, the Eanna-temple is the ancient home of Uruk's patron goddess Inanna/Ištar. Thus, we might expect that Lady-of-Eanna is one of Ištar-of-Uruk's epithets; however, in these texts, the divine name Lady-of-Eanna is expressly treated to ensure that we do not interpret it as an epithet. The divine name is preceded by a divine determinative in the offering lists and it is contrasted with the divine name Ištar-of-Uruk. According to Beaulieu, Lady-of-Eanna-of-Udannu is probably also a localized Ištar goddess (Beaulieu, *Pantheon of Uruk*, 290).

88 Beaulieu notes that there is no syllabic spelling of this goddess's name, so her name could have been Šarrat/Queen-of-Eanna (Beaulieu, *Pantheon of Uruk*, 290 n. 44).

referred to as Lady-of-Eanna in the Neo-Babylonian archives, the goddess who resided in the *Palil*-temple in Udannu went by the divine name Lady-of-Eanna.[89] If scholars prefer to interpret a divine name with an appended geographic epithet as merely indicating where the deity was worshipped (e.g., Ištar-of-Arbela was the Ištar worshipped at Arbela), then a deity worshipped at a location that does not match the epithet or divine last name should be a problem. In this case, those scholars would need to conclude that Lady-of-Eanna-of-Udannu was not a goddess worshipped in the Eanna-temple but a goddess named Lady-of-Eanna worshipped in Udannu; however, they must also accept that she was recognized as Lady-of-Eanna-of-Udannu by the priests who administered the Eanna-temple. As YBC 9135:4–5 demonstrates, the administrators made sure that Lady-of-Uruk (along with her consort [Symbol-of]-Bēl) received an ox, a sheep, a bird, a lamb, and a turtledove on the 16th of Ulūlu at Uruk's Eanna-temple; likewise, they made sure Lady-of-Eanna received a sheep and a turtledove (l. 13).[90] These names and epithets suggest an interesting history for this deity. She seems to have originated in the Eanna-temple as an epithet of either Ištar-of-Uruk or (the unspecified) Ištar, and she subsequently relocated from the Eanna-temple at Uruk to Udannu. Not only did she retain her epithet-based name in the process, but she also gained a geographic epithet in the move. To complicate the matters, another distinct deity with the same first name took her place at Uruk and appears in the same texts and lists as the first epithet-based goddess. Significantly, the priests at Uruk readily acknowledged this.[91] One might be inclined to compare the

89 After the Kassite period, inscriptions refer to the localized Ištar goddess by the epithet Lady-of-Eanna, which lacks a divine determinative (Ištar//Lady-of-Eanna, ^{d}⸢innin⸣ nin.e$_2$.an.⸢na⸣, A 3519:1–2; ^{d}innin nin.e$_2$.an.na, *UVB* 1, plate 26, no. 12 ll. 1–2 and *UVB* 1, plate 27 n. 15); the divine name Lady-of-Eanna does not reappear until the late eighth century when Merodach-Baladan II called the localized Ištar goddess by this epithet (*a-na* ^{d}*iš-tar be-*⸢*let*⸣ KUR.KUR *šur-bu-*[*t*]*i* DINGIR^{meš} *qa-rit-ti* ^{d}NIN-E$_2$.AN.NA *a-šib-*⸢*ti*⸣ [U]NUG^{ki} *ša*$_2$ *kul-lat* [*pa*]*r*$_2$*-ṣi* *ḫa-am-mat*, "For Ištar//Lady-of-the-Lands//Greatest-of-the-Gods//Valiant-One//Lady-of-Eanna//Who-Resides-(in)-Uruk, who usurped all of the divine offices," RIMB 2 B.6.21.1:1–2 and B.6.21.3:1–2). Aside from these attestations, which notably predate the offering texts from Nabonidus's reign by approximately a century-and-a-half, no Urukian goddess is identified as Lady-of-Eanna (Beaulieu, *Pantheon of Uruk*, 117).

90 Oddly, in YBC 9135:14–15, *Palil*-of-Udannu receives a lamb and an ox. The first name [*Palil*] appears in l. 14, where the lamb is indicated, while the last name *ša*$_2$ [^{uru}*u*$_2$*-dan*]*-nu* appears in l. 15, where the ox is indicated.

91 Likewise, if (the unspecified) *Palil* who was worshipped in the Eanna-temple at Uruk was identified with the *Palil*-of-Udannu (YBC 9135:14–15 and NCBT 6702:13–14) who was worshipped at the *Palil*-temple in Udannu by administrators who oversaw both cults, then why would the administrators double up the offerings to this singular *Palil* deity but still keep them separate (and separated by Lady-of-Eanna) in the records?

implications of YBC 9135 with the Hittite text, *Adlocation of the Goddess of the Night* (see chapter 2.2) because both suggest the movement of a goddess from one temple to an additional temple and the possibility that she could be worshipped simultaneously at both places. Such a comparison is not warranted by these texts, however, because YBC 9135 represents two distinct divine names, i.e., Lady-of-Eanna and Lady-of-Eanna-of-Udannu, whereas *Adlocation of the Goddess of the Night* may only deal with one divine name, Goddess-of-the-Night (DINGIR GE$_6$).

Just as the Neo-Babylonian offering lists provide a fixed order in their presentation, they also solve another potential concern because they explain the relationship between the quantity of sacrificial animals received by a deity and that deity's position in an offering list. All previous work in this chapter focused on a god's position in an EGL as an indicator of relative rank rather than the amount of sacrifices that that deity received. However, the Uruk material reveals a strong correlation between a god's position in offering lists and the amount of offering received. In each of the twelve texts used to determine the Urukian hierarchy, the quantity of sacrificial animals consistently diminished as the lists progress. Potential exceptions to the diminishing offerings are NCBT 1213:8; NBC 4801:10; and YBC 9445:10; however, in these instances an increased offering relates to a pair of deities receiving double portions together after an individual deity who had receive a single portion.[92] NBC 4801 serves as an example:

1	**GU$_4$.ME**	**UDU.NITA$_2$**	**MUŠEN.ḪA$_2$**	**SILA$_4$**	**TU.KUR$_4$$^{mušen.me}$ ...**	
4	1	2	2	2	2	IGI *šu-bat* ^{d}EN
5						*u* $^{d!}$GAŠAN *ša*$_2$ UNUG^{ki}
6	1	2	2	2	2	IGI *šu-bat* ^{d}NA$_3$
7						*u* ^{d}*na-na-a*
8		1	1	1	1	IGI ^{d}GAŠAN *ša*$_2$ SAG
9		1	1	1	1	IGI E$_2$ ^{d}AMAR.UD
10	1	2	2	2	2	IGI ^{d}URI$_3$-INIM-*su*
11						*u* ^{d}UNUG^{ki}-*i-ti*
12		1	1	1	1	IGI ^{d}*gu-la*

92 One qualification must be made here before the texts are closely examined. In YBC 9135, Šamaš and Aya, who appear as the last entry in this EGL, received three turtledoves (and one sheep and one lamb), while the first eight entries received one and the subsequent three received none. Šamaš and Aya received their offerings as a team rather than as individual gods. In NCBT 1213:17 and YBC 9445:19, Šamaš received double offerings as the last member of these EGLs, and Aya was not present. In these three texts, the final deity, who was worshipped outside of Uruk at Larsa, received an extra portion.

oxen	sheep	birds	lambs	turtledoves	
1	2	2	2	2	before Altar-of-Bēl and (before) Lady-of-Uruk
1	2	2	2	2	before Altar-of-Nabû and (before) Nanaya
	1	1	1	1	before Lady-of-Rēš
	1	1	1	1	before Temple-of-Marduk
1	2	2	2	2	before Uṣur-amāssu and Urkayītu
	1	1	1	1	before Gula (NBC 4801:1 and 4–12).

Just as Altar-of-Bēl and Altar-of-Nabû received their offerings with Lady-of-Uruk and Nanaya, so too did Uṣur-amāssu with Urkayītu, but the single recipients Lady-of-Rēš and Temple-of-Marduk received their offerings in between these sets of paired deities. Thus, the perceived increase of offerings in l. 10 is not actually an increase when considered on a per-recipient basis.

A larger collection of texts – Beaulieu's Groups 1, 2, 3, 5, and PTS 2097 – also provides an answer for any questions concerning the correlation between a deity's position in an EGL and the quantity of offerings received. According to PTS 2097, Lady-of-Uruk received more sacrificial animals than each of the other goddesses, which, according to Frame, serves as a sign that Lady-of-Uruk was the most revered deity in Uruk:

> As "owner" of Eanna, Lady-of-Uruk generally received larger quantities of goods than the other three deities in PTS 2097. The amounts assigned to the other two goddesses were often similar and much smaller than those assigned to the first two goddesses [i.e., Bēltu-ša-Rēš and Uṣur-amassu].[93]

In PTS 2097, specifically, Lady-of-Uruk (whom both Frame and Beaulieu identify as Ištar) received 10 *mašīḫus* of barley, 3 5/6 *mašīḫus* of dates, 1 5/6 *mašīḫus* of emmer, and 3 *qûs* (*ina rabīti*) of Dilmun-dates, whereas Nanaya received 93 %, 100 %, 73 %, and 100 % of those amounts:

	Barley		Dates (*mašīḫus*)	
Lady-of-Uruk	10 *mašīḫu*	100 %	3 5/6 *mašīḫu*	100 %
Nanaya	9 1/3 *mašīḫu*	93 %	1 1/3 *mašīḫu*	100 %
Lady-of-Rēš	5 3/4 *mašīḫu*	53 %	1 1/3 ⟨...⟩	87 %
Uṣur-amāssu	4 5/6 *mašīḫu*	48 %	1 1/4 ⟨...⟩	87 %

93 Grant Frame, "Nabonidus, Nabû-šarra-uṣur, and the Eanna Temple," *ZA* 81 (1991): 50.

	Emmer		Dilmun Dates	
Lady-of-Uruk	1 5/6 *mašīḫu*	100 %	3 *qû ina rabīti*	100 %
Nanaya	1 1/3 ⟨...⟩	73 %	3 *qû ina rabīti*	100 %
Lady-of-Rēš	1 1/3 ⟨...⟩	73 %	1 1/2 *qû ⟨...⟩*	50 %
Uṣur-amāssu	1 1/4 ⟨...⟩	68 %	1 1/2 *qû ⟨...⟩*	50 %

As shown in Frame's table, the third goddess in the ELG, Lady-of-Rēš, received 53 %, 87 %, 73 %, and 50 % of Lady-of-Uruk's offerings, and the fourth goddess Uṣur-amāssu received a slightly smaller total than Lady-of-Rēš.[94]

Unfortunately, offering data from Neo-Babylonian Uruk are incomplete and complicated because the texts deal with different deities and relationships at the local rather than imperial level, but they still reflect a reality in which the most important deities were listed earlier and received a greater volume of offerings. Moreover, this is a reality in which geographic last names were appended to first names to distinguish them from other deities with the same first name, such as *Palil* and *Palil*-of-Udannu.

Returning to Assyria, Govert van Driel notes that not many texts have survived that inform us about the daily aspects of the Assyrian temple cult, especially ones that relate to the Neo-Assyrian period.[95] He suggests that so little is known about the Assyrian temple cult because the priests never kept records of their daily activities in a descriptive series as did their neighbors to the south in Babylonia. Instead, the cult material that has survived relates to cultic rites performed during the year. The texts of particular interest to Assyriologists are food-offering texts (e.g., *STT* 88 x 5 ff., VAT 8005), the *tākultu*-ritual texts (VAT 10126, VAT 8005, *KAR* 214, and K 252), the Assyrian *Akītu*-ritual text (e.g., *KAR* 215, BM 121206, *KAV* 49, and VAT 13597 + 13999), New Year's ritual texts (e.g., K 2724 + 8207, Bu 91–5–9,104, K 13325, Assur Photos 4132[f] and 4123[a], A 126, *KAR* 146, VAT 13717, and VAT 10598), and the *Götteradressbuch* of Assur (GAB).[96]

94 Frame, "Nabonidus," 51.

95 Grovert van Driel, *The Cult of Aššur* (Assen: van Gorcum, 1969), 51; see also Walter Farber, review of *The Cult of Aššur*, by G. van Driel, *BiOr* 30 [1973]: 433–434.

96 van Driel, *Cult of Aššur*, 52; Rintje Frankena, *Tākultu: de Sacrale Maaltijd in Het Assyrische Ritueel: Met een overzicht over de in Assur Vereerde Goden* (Leiden: Brill, 1954); Menzel, *Assyrische Tempel*, 2:T113–125, no. 54, T138–144, no. 61, and T146–166; George, *Babylonian Topographical Texts*, 176–184. Frankena suggests that the *tākultu*-ritual was actually a part of the *Akītu*-festival due to the high degree of similarities between *KAR* 215, VAT 8005, and *STT* 88 (Rintje Frankena, "New Materials for the Tākultu Ritual: Additions and Corrections," *BiOr* 8 [1961]: 202). For locations that hosted the *Akītu*-festival, see Pongratz-Leisten, "Interplay of Military," 246.

Porter notes that many of the god lists in these texts are difficult to interpret because they are "not simply listing gods," and because divine names often repeat and can be combined with other divine names and because we are uncertain about how to interpret these double divine names (e.g., Ninurta-Assur, Assur-Ištar-of-Arbela, Assur-Ištar, and even Assur-Assur).[97] Because of the confusing and uncertain nature of the lists in these texts, our analysis of Neo-Assyrian cultic texts is presently limited to BM 121206.

BM 121206 is a ritual text from Assur's temple that describes numerous rites in its seven surviving columns.[98] Column iv is so unintelligible and untranslatable that Brigitte Menzel does not supply any portion for transliteration and interpretation.[99] Column v contains a list of gods and provides the total number of gods named in that list (v 11′). The total number of gods is said to be 15, but determining which divine names make up that total of fifteen is difficult.[100] The remainder of column v through column viii describes various

---

97 Porter, "Anxiety," 231–232 and 235 n. 43. Transliterated into Latin characters, these double divine names seem to resemble the ancient Egyptian inhabiting (an alternative name for "syncretism" in Egyptology; see Excursus), but such an interpretation would be no more secure than any other interpretation.

98 van Driel, *Cult of Aššur*, 81–103; Farber, review, 435–436; and Menzel, *Assyrische Tempel*, 2:T59–72, no. 35. Regarding the actual find spot of BM 121206, van Driel simply says that the "text must have turned up in the course of the excavations at Aššur" (van Driel, *Cult of Aššur*, 74).

99 Menzel, *Assyrische Tempel*, 2:T59.

100 $^{\text{4′giš}}$GIGIR ^{giš}⸢TUKUL⸣ [*s*]*e-b*[*t-t*]*u* ^{d}*ḫa-ia*$_3$ ^{d}KU$_3$.SU$_3$ ^{d}MAŠ *ša*$_2$ BAD$_3$
$^{\text{5′d}}$TIŠPAK ^{d}*man-*[*d*]*a-nu* ^{d}PA.TUG$_2$ ^{d}*ka*$_3$(GA)-*ka*$_3$(GA)
$^{\text{6′}}$AŠ$^{!}$ *ḫ*[*e-p*]*i*$_2$ [*ḫ*]*e-p*[*i*$_3$]
$^{\text{7′d}}$⸢30 ^{d}⸣NI[N.G]AL ^{d}UTU ^{d}*a-a* ^{d}EN.LIL$_2$
$^{\text{8′d}}$15 NINA^{ki} ^{d}*ka*$_3$(GA)-*ka*$_3$(GA) ^{d}⸢PA⸣.TUG$_2$
$^{\text{9′}}$PAP [*š*]*a bit-a-*⸢*ni*⸣ ^{d}GUR$_2$-KUR *ina re-eš* ^{d}⸢EN-MAN⸣$^{?}$
$^{\text{10′}}$*ina* TUR$_3$ ^{d}*ḫa-ia* ^{d}KU$_3$.SU$_3$ *i*[*na*] GUB$_3$-*ša*$_2$
$^{\text{11′}}$PAP 15 DINGIR^{meš} *ša*$_2$ ZAG

Chariot, Weapon, the Sebittu, Ḫaja, KUSU, Ninurta-of-the-Wall,
Tišpak, Ma[d]ānu, Nusku,
(broken) (broken)
⸢Sîn,⸣ Ni[ng]al, Šamaš, Aya, Enlil,
Ištar-of-Nineveh, Kakka, Nusku
Total: for the interior – Kippat-māti *in front of* ⸢EN-MAN⸣;
In the courtyard – Haja, (with) KUSU on her left.
Total: 15 gods (who stand) to the right (of Assur). (Menzel, *Assyrische Tempel*, 2:T59, no. 35 v 4′–11′, my translation; see also Farber, review, 435)

If this set of fifteen gods begins with Chariot, then the Sebittu are not in their usual place; they are nearer the beginning rather than at the end of a list of Assyrian deities. Beginning with Chariot and discounting the multiple attestations of divine names totals more than fifteen

rites on various days and concerns multiple gods – and Assur and Mullissu appear to be deities of interest – but other deities and planets also appear here. Columns vii and viii are less cohesive as they present information concerning other deities and various dates, and as Porter has noted about other ritual texts, divine names may appear throughout BM 121206 v-viii, but often there are too few names to produce EGLs.[101]

God lists do seem to be important elements in the final two columns of BM 121206. Column ix 5′–6′ prepares us for the "gods that Sennacherib, king of Assyria, [through div]ination made stand beside one another" ($^{5'}$[DINGIR^{m}]^{eš} *ša*$_2$ ^{md}30-PAP^{meš}-SU$^{!}$ MAN KUR *aš-šur* $^{6'}$[*ana b*]*i-ri ina re-eš a-ḫe-iš* ⸢*u*$_2$*-še*$^{!}$*-te*⸣$^{!}$*-qa*$^{!}$*-an*$^{!}$*-ni*), who are listed in ll. 7′–23′.[102] These seventeen lines (ll. 7′–23′) cannot be considered to contain an EGL because individual divine names frequently recur; however, each single line does act as its own EGL. It appears that the full force of ll. 7′–23′ provides the physical layout of the deities' cult statues, indicating their relative positions in the ritual. Lines 9′–11′ make this clear:

> $^{9'}$ ^{d}15 NINA^{ki} SAG ^{d}*ku-ta-ta-te* SAG ^{d}KURNUN
> $^{10'}$ ^{d}*ku-ta-ta-te* SAG ^{d}KURNUN SAG ^{d}PA.TUG$_2$
> $^{11'}$ ^{d}KURNUN SAG ^{d}PA.TUG$_2$ ^{d}15 NINA^{ki} SAG ^{d}PA.TUG$_2$
>
> Ištar-of-Nineveh is ahead of Kutatate (who) is ahead of Tašmētu; Kutatate is ahead of Tašmētu (who) is ahead of Nusku; Tašmētu is ahead of Nusku; Ištar-of-Nineveh is ahead of Nusku. (BM 121206 ix 9′–11′)[103]

Visualizing this linearly, these three lines of text provide a simple arrangement of four statues: Ištar-of-Nineveh / Kutatate / Tašmētu / Nusku. The redundant aspects of these lines ensure that the reader fully understands their relative positions in the ceremony; in this case, "ahead of" (SAG) is visually represented by moving to the left in the following table, and "below" (KI.TA), to the right. Although van Driel claimed that "[a]n acceptable reconstruction of the

---

deities. If the count begins after the Sebittu – with Mullissu (^{d}NIN.LIL$_2$) restored to l. 6, as Meinhold maintains (Meinhold, *Ištar in Aššur*, 203 n. 1213), and Nusku and Kakka are counted only once despite the double attestations of these names – the resultant number is fifteen, assuming only one other divine name appears with Mullissu in l. 6.

101 In addition to BM 121206 v 4′–11′ and 13′–17′, each of which claim to list 15 divine names, EGLs can be derived from vi 24′–25′; vii 38′; viii 4′–8′, 39′, and 55′–57′.

102 This translation is based, in part, on Oppenheim's idiomatic rendering of *ina rēš aḫeiš* (A. Leo Oppenheim, "Idiomatic Accadian (Lexicographical Researches)," *JAOS* 61 [1941]: 255). van Driel noted that this idiom may also refer to rank among the deities (van Driel, *Cult of Aššur*, 114).

103 Menzel, *Assyrische Tempel*, 2:T65, no. 35 ix 9′–11′.

order in which the gods were arranged cannot be drawn,"[104] if our interpretation of ll. 9′–11′ is accurate, these seventeen lines suggest the following arrangement of statues listed in ix 7′–23′:

← ("ahead," SAG) ("below," KI.TA) →					
Aya	Bēl	Kippat-māti	Sîn	Anu	
		Šerū'a		DN_1 DN_2	
		Ištar-of-Nineveh	Kutatate	Tašmētu	Nusku
		Adad	Ea	Kakka	
		Sumuqan	Enlil	Šamaš	Nabû[105]
	Gula	Queen-of-Nipḫa	Bēlet-ekalli	Tišpak.[106]	

Regardless any potential layout reconstruction, each divine name in this series is of interest. In particular, within this complex of divine names, the only time that the name Ištar appears, a last name is provided: Ištar-of-Nineveh in ll. 9′ and 11′. Indeed, here the name Ištar-of-Nineveh is treated in the same way as Kippat-māti, Queen-of-Nipḫa, and Bēlet-ekalli; all the elements are needed to distinguish the individual goddess from other goddesses. Porter notes that BM 121206's author demonstrated a "preoccupation with protocol" and an implied "anxiety" that each great Assyrian god and goddess was to be understood by his or her own nature.[107] Otherwise, the precise location of each statute would have been inconsequential for this ritual.

Although no other explicitly localized Ištar goddess besides Ištar-of-Nineveh appears in the complex of BM 121206 ix 7′–23′, four distinct localized Ištar goddesses appear in the following section (ll. 27′–34′), in a list of gods venerated publicly by Sennacherib: Ištar-of-Heaven, Ištar-of-Nineveh, Ištar-of-Arbela, and Assyrian-Ištar (see Table 3.11). Moreover, Mullissu appears alongside Assur as the chief deity's consort and not with the other goddesses. Just as Mullissu is distinct in many, if not most, non-cultic EGLs from the localized Ištar goddesses in the Sargonid period, she is also distinct from them in this ritual text. This distinction is all the more significant because this EGL

104 van Driel, *Cult of Aššur*, 115.

105 Menzel reads the final sign as "PA?," allowing for an otherwise missing Nabû (Menzel, *Assyrische Tempel*, 2:T65, no. 35).

106 BM 121206 ix 19′–21′ provides no relative position between the gods listed in this final row and the others.

107 Porter, "Anxiety," 263–264.

(ll. 27′–34′) is intentionally described as a list of deities that Sennacherib sought to "publicly ... raise their veneration":

> $^{24'}$ DINGIR^{meš} *ša*$_2$ ^{md}30-PAP^{meš}-SU MAN KUR *aš-šur* $^{25'}$ *ana*$^{!}$ *bi-ri ana* GU$_2$.ZI^{meš} *ku-ba-di-šu*$_2$*-nu* $^{26'}$ *man-zal-ta-šu*$_2$*-nu ina pi-i* UKU$_3$^{meš} *ik*$^{!}$*-ru-ru-ni*
>
> The gods whose places Sennacherib, the king of Assyria, established publicly by divination in order to raise their veneration.[108]

The point of these rituals was to ensure that everyone involved in (or witnessing) the event realized the importance of each singular deity present, including the goddess known specifically as Ištar-of-Nineveh.

Cultic realities influenced the discussions and arrangement of the deities' cult statues for the ritual described in BM 121206 xi, but non-cultic tendencies common to EGLs in royal inscriptions, personal correspondence, and curse list are also prevalent in this EGL. These include: placing Assur as the chief deity at the beginning of the EGL in ix 27′; keeping two the members of Triad 2 and their consorts together while being more relaxed about the cohesiveness of Triad 1 deities (which, incidentally, are who interrupt the cohesion of the Triad 2 deities); distinguishing between the goddess Mullissu, who is Assur's consort, and the various localized Ištar goddesses who appear nearer the end of the EGL (though not as near the end as we might expect); and explicitly including geographic epithets as necessary parts of a deity's full name, even when no other deity shared the deity's first name (e.g., Kippat-māti in l. 29′). These are not properties common to the scholar-scribe tradition seen in lexical god lists. Even though the scribes who produced this cultic text likely had little expectation that a lay population would ever have had access to it, in many ways the materials that they created are more similar to those created by palace scribes (including the scholars of SAA 10) than they are to the speculative theological materials of the scholar-scribes. This is true not only for the Sennacherib-period BM 121206, but also for the Neo-Babylonian texts at Uruk examined by Frame and Beaulieu.

3.7 Implications for the Present Study

Throughout this chapter, the primary objective has been to examine the nature and roles of the many EGLs found in Neo-Assyrian texts, including those

108 Menzel, *Assyrische Tempel*, 2:T65, no. 35 ix 24′–26′. The translation of BM 121206 ix 24′–26′ as an explanation for the following EGL in 27′–34′ is based on van Driel's translation, who describes these lines "very difficult to understand" (van Driel, *Cult of Aššur*, 98–99 and 115). Likewise, *CAD* K says the word *kubātu* ("honors") is "in [a] difficult context" (*CAD* K, *kubātu*).

obtained from royal inscriptions, personal letters, state treaties, administrative documents, and ritual texts. The underlying assumption of this chapter's methodology has been that if a scribe listed or addressed a deity by a particular name, then that particular name identified a specific deity who was considered distinct from all the other deities in that EGL. In essence, this assumption attempts to take the ancient scribes at their word and interprets a name as a defining aspect of each deity.[109] A second objective stressed throughout this chapter has been the relative stability of the divine hierarchy in this period. Although variations existed within the EGLs in the texts surveyed, hierarchical arrangements are relatively predictable. The major or most important gods appear first, often following the pattern: Assyrian chief deity, Triad 1, Triad 2, the Babylonian chief deities, warrior (and other male) gods, goddesses, and the Sebittu. Typically, deities with common first names and distinct last names appear later in the EGLs. These two factors suggest that deities whose identities are bound up by both a first and a last name are less important deities than those who are known by only one name. In fact, on the rare occasion when a divine name that lacked a geographic epithet appeared in the same EGL as that same divine name with a geographic epithet, the unspecified divine name appeared earlier in the EGL. See, for example, SAA 2 6:414–465; SAA 2 2 vi 7–20; and SAA 3 34:72–73 and 35:70.

Recognizing this, the argument cannot be made that multiple attestations of a divine first name indicate that the status of a singular deity by that name has been promoted, as some scholars have claimed. When multiple localized Ištar goddesses appear near the end of an EGL, they appear there because they were less important than the gods preceding them in that EGL. Had the scribes' envisioned only one Ištar who was so important that she deserved to be mentioned numerous times with various epithets, the question should be asked: Why do the multiple localized Ištar goddesses appear at the end of most EGLs with the lesser deities rather than nearer the beginning with the major gods? Conversely, if the scribes considered repetition of a divine first name, each with a unique last name, as an appropriate way to honor a major god, why do major gods, like Assur and Marduk, lack the name repetition in non-cultic EGLs? If a last name is simply a way to indicate that a deity is venerated

---

109 In regard to Roman religion in the Near East, Kaizer suggests that we follow the "Millar Axiom," which states that "the god is what the *worshipper* says he is" (Kaizer, "Identifying the Divine," 118; italics in the original; see also Fergus Millar, *The Roman Near East: 31 BC - AD 337* [Cambridge: Harvard University Press, 1995], 270). Thus, by demonstrating that the Neo-Assyrian worshipper said that Ištar-of-Nineveh and Ištar-of-Arbela are distinct and separate entities, modern scholars should also recognize them as distinct and separate.

at a specific location – be it an important town or temple – then other major gods could have also appeared multiple times in the EGLs with multiple designations placing them throughout Assyria, Babylonia, or west of the Euphrates. For instance, Šamaš had major cults in Larsa and Sippar, but he is simply known as Šamaš, not Šamaš-of-Larsa and Šamaš-of-Sippar, in these texts.

The methodology applied in this chapter recognizes that scribes often treated epithets (i.e., geographic last names affixed to titles like Queen or Lady) in the same manner as they treated divine names in EGLs, as indicated by the use of a divine determinative before the epithet. For example, ^{d}15 refers to a goddess whom the scribe knew as (the unspecified) Ištar, whereas ^{d}15 *ša*$_2$ *arba-il*$_3$ refers to a goddess whom the scribe knew as Ištar-of-Arbela, and ^{d}GAŠAN-*ki-di-mur-ri* refers to a goddess known as Lady-of-Kidmuri. This is not to suggest that a scribe or devotee would or could not invoke a single entity by more than one name or epithet. Nor does this assume that the scribe would never refer to Ištar-of-Arbela as Ištar without providing her geographic epithet; rather, it assumes that he chose to make such a distinction between Ištar-of-Arbela and (an unspecified) Ištar in that text.[110] This EGL methodology respects that decision. This methodology also allows for the possibility that multiple names and epithets can be used to refer to a singular deity, but those names are expected to appear in succession in an EGL, or explicitly linked with each other elsewhere in the text, rather than interspersed throughout a list of numerous other divine names. For example, in SAA 10 227:3–6, Adad-šumu-uṣur listed Mullissu immediately after Assur, and only later did he write out the divine names Ištar-of-Nineveh and Ištar-of-Arbela in his fifteen-member EGL that includes a dozen other deities who were undoubtedly independent entities:

Assur
  Mullissu
Sîn
Šamaš
Adad
Marduk
  Zarpānītu
Nabû

110 For example, F. Mario Fales suggests that (the unspecified) Ištar, whose cult statue will arrive for the *Akītu*-festival at Milqia on the following day in SAA 13 149, should be interpreted as a statue of Ištar-of-Arbela (F. Mario Fales, *Guerre et paix en Assyrie Religion et impérialisme*, Les conférences de l'École Pratique desHautes Études, 2 [Paris: Éditions du Cerf, 2010], 93).

Tašmētu
Ištar-of-Nineveh
Ištar-of-Arbela
Ninurta
Gula
Nergal
Laṣ.

There is nothing in SAA 10 227 to suggest that Mullissu is either Ištar-of-Nineveh or Ištar-of-Arbela in this letter to the king. Although some modern scholars argue otherwise – that Mullissu was equated with Ištar in seventh-century Assyria – neither this EGL, the other EGLs examined in this chapter, nor those examined in the following chapter suggest that Mullissu should be equated with either Ištar-of-Nineveh or Ištar-of-Arbela in the scribe's theological world. Just as we cannot ignore the fact that repeated divine first names with different last names are likely to appear near the end of an EGL and cannot claim that the repetition of a divine name is evidence of an elevated status in the divine hierarchy, we cannot argue that a deity has been addressed by multiple unique divine names (e.g., Mullissu and Ištar-of-GN) sporadically throughout an EGL unless something within that particular text suggests those names represent the one same deity.

4 The Ištar Goddesses of Neo-Assyria

The major deities of the Neo-Assyrian Empire have already been introduced in chapter 3 in the discussions of the lexical god-list traditions and, more importantly, the embedded god lists (EGLs) found in royal inscriptions, treaty witness lists, blessing and curse lists, and cultic and ritual texts. Armed with this firm grasp of the Neo-Assyrian divine hierarchy that has been derived from these numerous EGLs, we concluded that localized Ištar goddesses are among the least important of the major Assyrian deities, followed only regularly by the Sebittu and irregularly by other localized deities and independent goddesses (e.g., SAA 2 6:414–465; Table 3.9). This was because their names typically appear as the last or near-last names in these EGLs. Looking back, we can also see that there is an Ištar hierarchy in which Ištar-of-Nineveh outranks Ištar-of-Arbela and several other localized Ištars, including Ištar-of-Kidmuri (see Table 3.6) and Assyrian-Ištar (see Table 3.11); however, Ištar-of-Nineveh has a lower rank than Ištar-of-Heaven (see Table 3.11). We can now more closely examine the localized Ištar goddesses of Neo-Assyria as a group or collection of deities and as individuals. Moreover, we can explore the various name formulas by which these goddesses are identified in EGLs and securely conclude that each formula does, in fact, invoke the same goddesses without creating needless or spurious identifications. For example, because we know that we can expect Ištar-of-Nineveh to appear in a particular position within an EGL, we can also observe that Ištar//Lady-of-Nineveh, Ištar//Who-Resides-(in)-Nineveh, and Lady/Queen-of-Nineveh tend to appear in the same position as Ištar-*ša*-Nineveh and are simply synonyms for Ištar-*ša*-Nineveh.[1] These conclusions allow us to move beyond the EGLs in administrative texts, treaties, and letters to the more theologically sophisticated texts, such as hymns and oracles, which still distinguish between the multiple localized Ištar goddesses worshipped in the Neo-Assyrian period. Finally, we will compare these distinct goddesses who share a common first name with goddesses who

---

1 Two parallel lines (//) are used here and elsewhere to indicate that a proper name and epithet are acting together with the force of a full name (e.g., Ištar//Lady-of-Nineveh, Ištar//Lady-of-Arbela, and Astarte//Name-of-Baal). With reference to the cuneiform evidence, these parallel lines indicate that the first name is preceded by a divine determinative, but the epithet is not. When an epithet is preceded by a divine determinative, that epithet – typically "Lady" (*bēlet*) or "Queen" (*šarrat*) – will instead be written out separately from any specific first name without the parallel lines. For example, "Ištar, Lady-of-Babylon" represents two goddesses. The first is (the unspecified) Ištar, and the second is the esteemed goddess of Babylon. In contrast, "Ištar//Lady-of-Babylon" represents one goddess.

have been historically associated with them but who have their own unique divine first name. As we will see, these comparisons will help us define what it means to be an Ištar goddess in the Neo-Assyrian period, and it highlights why several scholars resist the possibility that these goddesses are distinct and independent deities.

4.1 The Ištar Goddesses by Several Other Names and Titles

Although the Ištar who appears in most of the Assyrian royal inscriptions between the fourteenth and eighth centuries B.C.E. is unspecified, which is to say that no geographic epithet specifies her location, the geographically specific goddesses Ištar-of-Nineveh and Ištar-of-Arbela are the most frequently attested localized Ištar goddesses in Sargonid royal inscriptions and other state documents from the eighth and seventh centuries. In many of these texts, their names are written out in the typical DN-of-GN (i.e., DN-*ša*-GN) formula.[2] Not all texts follow this pattern, however, including Assurbanipal's hymn to the two Ištars (SAA 3 3), which addresses them by the title Lady-of-GN. Moreover, in the eighth-century treaty between Assur-nērārī V and Mati'-ilu of Arpad

2 As a formula, this DN-of-GN looks identical to the one used for Baal deities from Ugarit; however, there is a slight grammatical difference between the two. In Ugaritic, as well as in the other Northwest Semitic languages surveyed in chapters 5 and 6, DN-of-GN usually represents two nouns linked in a construct chain. Literally, Baal-of-Ugarit appears in Ugaritic texts as "Baal . Ugarit" (*b*ʿl . *'ugrt*). Grammatically, this construct chain can occur in Akkadian and could be used to construct divine full names (e.g., ⸢15⸣ *arba-il*$_{3}$, RINAP 4, Esar. 1006:11), but the preferred Akkadian formation for divine full names includes the particle *ša*$_{(2)}$, which *CAD* defines as "of, that, which, that of (introducing a genitive or a subordinate clause)" (*CAD* Š/1, *ša* mng. a). So the Akkadian divine name ^{d}15 *ša*$_{(2)}$ $^{(uru)}$*ni-nu-a*$^{(ki)}$ can be translated, literally, as "Ištar of Nineveh" or "Ištar, that of Nineveh," but both options relate the same meaning as their Northwest Semitic counterparts.

The formula DN-of-GN (DN *ša* GN) is the most frequently written form for localized Ištar goddesses in Esarhaddon's royal inscriptions. When Ištar-of-Nineveh is identified by her full name in these texts, the divine number 15 usually indicates the first name Ištar. Less often, the logogram INANNA or a variation of the syllabic writing *iš-tar* is used. Similarly, the geographic name Nineveh takes many forms. Regardless of the writing, each of the following instances adheres to the standard DN-of-GN formula in Akkadian inscriptions:

^{d}15 *ša*$_{(2)}$ $^{(uru)}$NINA/*ni-nu-a*$^{(ki)}$:	**^{d}INANNA *ša*$_{2}$ NINA^{ki}:**	***^{d}iš-tar ša*$_{2}$ ^{uru}*ni-na-a*:**
RINAP 4, Esar. 1 i 6,10, 45, 59, ii 45, iv 78, v 34, and vi 44; 2 i 9 and iv 22; 3 iv 21′; 5 i 3′; 6 i 5′; 8 [ii′ 4′]; 70:3; 71:3; 77:12; 78:[11]; 79:[11] and [6′]; and 93:5 and 26.	RINAP 4, Esar. 33 (tablet 2) iii 11′; and 71:3	RINAP 4, Esar. 48:25

(SAA 2 2 vi 15–16), the goddesses Ištar-of-Nineveh and Ištar-of-Arbela are addressed using neither the DN-of-GN formula nor the Lady-of-GN formula. In each line, the first name Ištar is followed by an epithet consisting of a noun clause rather than the more common *ša*-clause: ^{d}15 NIN ^{uru}*ni-na-a* KI.MIN ^{d}INNIN NIN ^{uru}*arba-il*$_{3}$ KI.MIN ("Ištar//Lady-of-Nineveh, Ditto! Ištar//Lady-of-Arbela, Ditto!" 15–16). The fact that Ištar//Lady-of-Nineveh and Ištar//Lady-of-Arbela are theologically synonymous with Ištar-*ša*-Nineveh and Ištar-*ša*-Arbela, as well as with Lady-of-Nineveh and Lady-of-Arbela, may be obvious. However, it is also methodologically reliable given that these two goddesses who appear near the end of this EGL in SAA 2 2 also appear together in similar positions in the EGLs in SAA 2 6:16–20 (= ll. 25–30, see Table 3.15) and 10 r. 9′–10′, the letter SAA 10 286 (see Table 3.7), and several other letters in SAA 10, 13, and 16 (see Table 3.6).[3] Although the insertion of NIN (*bēlet*, "lady") between the goddesses' first and last names disrupts what we have been calling their divine "full names" and creates new epithets in SAA 2 2 vi 15–16, no divine determinative separates either of these epithets (NIN ^{uru}GN) from the first name Ištar preceding them, so we can be confident that these epithets do not represent new deities who should be contrasted with (the unspecified) Ištar immediately preceding them. Nor do these epithets undermine the fact that the geographic information conveyed in them is still an essential aspect of the goddess's identification. The form of Ištar-of-Nineveh and Ištar-of-Arbela's full names in SAA 2 2 may be unusual for an EGL, but it is not problematic and should be treated as nothing more than an alternative, and slightly more complex, formula to DN-of-GN: DN//title-of-GN.

Admittedly, the divine name formula DN//title-of-GN for Ištar//Lady-of-Nineveh looks awkward at first, especially compared to the way it is usually written in scholarship, "Ištar, Lady of Nineveh." However, in his discussion of Ištar-of-Babylon and Lady-of-Babylon at Uruk, Beaulieu stresses that punctuation matters when we translate these divine names and epithets, and our slants-and-dashes punctuation has been built upon his dash punctuation.[4] In his book *The Pantheon of Uruk during the Neo-Babylonian Period*, he uses hyphens between words to indicate that there is a divine determinative in the cuneiform and to indicate that the words represent a single divine entity. For instance, Lady-of-Babylon (e.g., ^{d}*be-let* KA$_{2}$.DINGIR.RA^{ki}, SAA 16 49:3)

3 The texts comprising this table include the following: SAA 10 82:6; 83:4; 130:6; 174:18; 227:5; 228:4; 245:5; 249:2′; 252:7; 286:6; 293:4; and 294:3; and SAA 13 9:7; 10:7; 12:6; 15:7; 56:6; 57:7; 58:6; 60:6; 61:6; 62:6; 64:6; 65:6; 66:6; 67:5; 68:6; 140:5; 156:6; and 187 r. 5′; and SAA 16 1:10; 33:6; 49:4; 59:3; 60:3 and 10′; 61:3; and 128:5.

4 Beaulieu, *Pantheon of Uruk*, 75 n. 10.

represents a divine entity by name in the same way that Ištar-of-Babylon represents a divine entity by name. Conversely, he uses words without hyphens to indicate that there is no divine determinative in the cuneiform, and the words should be interpreted as an epithet. For Beaulieu, "Lady of Babylon" (*be-let* KA_2.DINGIR.RA^{ki}) is an epithet. Often these epithets immediately follow a divine name, like "Ištar, Lady of Babylon," and he uses the comma to indicate that the epithet is nothing more than an appositive of the divine name Ištar. If we apply Beaulieu's punctuation to SAA 2 2 vi 15–16, we get "Ištar, Lady of Nineveh," and "Ištar, Lady of Arbela," but as part of a larger EGL, his punctuation becomes too visually complicated:

> Assur, Anu, Antu, Enlil, Mullissu, Ea, Damkina, Sîn, Ningal, Šamaš, Aya, Adad, Šala, Marduk, Zarpānītu, Nabû, Tašmētu, Ninurta, Gula, Uraš, Bēlet-ekalli, Zababa, Bau, Nergal, Laṣ, Madānu, Ningirsu, Ḫumḫummu, Išum, Erra, Nusku, Ištar, Lady of Nineveh, Ištar, Lady of Arbela, Adad-of-Kurbail, Hadad-of-Aleppo, Palil, and the Sebittu. (ll. 6–20)

Because the word Ištar is separated from "Lady of Nineveh" in the same manner that it is separated from Nusku, we cannot immediately recognize that the first Ištar name belongs with the "Lady of Nineveh" phrase. Our slants-and-dashes punctuation makes this relationship more readily recognizable:

> Assur, Anu, Antu, Enlil, Mullissu, Ea, Damkina, Sîn, Ningal, Šamaš, Aya, Adad, Šala, Marduk, Zarpānītu, Nabû, Tašmētu, Ninurta, Gula, Uraš, Bēlet-ekalli, Zababa, Bau, Nergal, Laṣ, Madānu, Ningirsu, Ḫumḫummu, Išum, Erra, Nusku, Ištar//Lady-of-Nineveh, Ištar//Lady-of-Arbela, Adad-of-Kurbail, Hadad-of-Aleppo, Palil, and the Sebittu. (ll. 6–20)

Beaulieu's punctuation works well when discussing one or two divine names, but our punctuation is needed for 37 different names. Thus, we write Ištar//Lady-of-Nineveh and Ištar//Lady-of-Arbela for visual simplicity.[5]

In addition to the alternative formula DN//title-of-GN, wherein title-of-GN is syntactically an appositive and epithet of DN, we can identify two other alternatives to the standard DN-of-GN formula in Neo-Assyrian inscriptions. The second and similar formula is title-of-GN, in which "title" is preceded by a divine determinative and represents only a couple of select possibilities: *šarrat*

5 As seen in chapter 3.1, a formula resembling DN//title-of-GN occasionally accompanies (the geographically unspecified) Ištar in EGLs in royal inscriptions: DN//title-of-X. For example, RINAP 4, Esar. 98:9 mentions a geographically unspecified Ištar as the Ištar//Lady-of-War-and-Battle (^{d}INANNA *be-let* $MURUB_4$ *u* ME_3). See Zsolnay's appendices A, B, C, and D for her treatment of Ištar's epithets in various Middle and Neo-Assyrian royal inscriptions that follow this DN//title-of-X formula (Zsolnay, "Function of Ištar," 217–289).

("queen of") and *bēlet* ("lady of").[6] This formula is only slightly more common than DN//title-of-GN in EGLs, but it is more common outside of EGLs, appearing in court poetry, prophetic texts, and literary miscellanea, including Assurbanipal's hymn.[7] The fact that title-of-GN as a divine name refers to the same deity or deities as DN-of-GN can easily be demonstrated by comparing EGLs.

The best example to demonstrate that title-of-GN represents the same deity as the localized Ištar goddess designated by DN-of-GN is found in SAA 10 174:7–16. The king's chief haruspex Marduk-šumu-uṣur wrote this letter to the king in order to inspire and praise him for his surpassing wisdom and to remind him of Assyria's glorious victories in Egypt. Framing the body of this letter are two EGLs. The first is a six-member EGL comprising three blessings, each of which includes two divine names, and the second is an eleven-member EGL that lists all of the divine names in one blessing:

First Blessing:	**(ll. 4, 5, and 6)**	**Second Blessing:**	**(ll. 17–18)**
		Assur	AN.ŠAR$_2$
Sîn	^{d}30	Sîn	^{d}30
Šamaš	^{d}UTU	Šamaš	^{d}UTU
		Adad	^{d}IŠKUR
Nabû	^{d}AG	Bēl	^{d}EN *u*$_3$
Marduk	^{d}AMAR.UTU	Nabû	^{d}AG
		Ninurta	^{d}MAŠ
		[Nergal]	[^{d}U.GUR] *u*$_3$
		Nusku	^{d}PA.TUG$_2$
Lady-of-Nineveh	^{d}GAŠAN NINA^{ki}	Ištar-of-Nineveh	^{d}15 *ša*$_2$ NINA^{ki}
Ištar-of-Arbela	^{d}15 *ša*$_2$ ^{uru}*arba-il*$_3$	Ištar-of-Arbela	^{d}15 *ša*$_2$ ^{uru}*arba-il*$_3$.

The second blessing is an expanded version of the first because all of the deities who are listed in the first blessing also appear in the second. With this expansion, it adds the Assyrian chief deity, completes Triad 2 by adding Adad, and inserts three warrior gods. As mentioned in chapter 3.3, Nabû is often

---

6 Beaulieu notes that the two divine names Ištar-of-Babylon and Lady-of-Babylon were "functionally equivalent in first millennium theology" (Beaulieu, *Pantheon of Uruk*, 121). According to him, this is proven by analogy by AN : *Anum* IV 128, which equates ^{d}INNIN *a-ga-de*$_3$^{ki} (Ištar-of-Akkad) with *be-let ak-*⌜*ka*⌝-[*di*] (Lady-of-Akkad) rather than with goddesses actually located at Babylon.

7 Frances Reynolds proposed the restoration of the divine name Lady-of-Nineveh for a five+-member EGL in SAA 18 16:1′–4′: [GAŠAN-*ni*]-⌜*na*$^{?}$⌝-a^{ki} (l. 3′).

listed before Marduk in EGLs and in blessings that only invoke the two of them, even when Marduk appears before Nabû elsewhere in the same text, so this minimal difference between the two lists is not problematic.[8] The remaining difference between these EGLs is the divine name associated with Nineveh. In the first EGL, the goddess is addressed by the divine name formula title-of-GN (i.e., Lady-of-Nineveh), but in the second EGL, she is addressed by the normal DN-of-GN formula (i.e., Ištar-of-Nineveh). Both are preceded by a divine determinative, and both appear immediately before Ištar-of-Arbela, who is the last deity in each EGL, as expected (see also Table 3.4).

Other examples of this title-of-GN formula are known for localized Ištar goddesses. Ištar-of-Kidmuri (SAA 16 105:5; 126:5; and 127:5) is called Queen-of-Kidmuri in SAA 10 197:11 between Queen-of-Nineveh and Queen-of-Arbela (see Table 3.8) and in SAA 16 106:6 between Mullissu and Ištar-of-Arbela (^{d}NIN.LIL$_2$ ^{d}GAŠAN *ki-di-mu-ri* ^{7} ^{d}15 *ša* ^{uru}*arba-il*$_3$).[9] The goddess appears as Lady-of-Kidmuri in SAA 16 105 after she had already been identified as Ištar-of-Kidmuri in l. 5. In this second inscription, she is only paired with Mullissu, which means this is not an EGL. However, the two goddesses are both praised as the king's loving mothers. Significantly, the logogram for mother is followed by the plural marker meš, and the verb is morphologically feminine-plural, indicating that two distinct goddesses involved: "the protection of Mullissu (and) of Lady-of-Kidmuri, who (are) the mothers who love you" (*ki-din-nu ša* ^{d}NIN.LIL$_2$ ^{13}*ša* ^{d}GAŠAN *ki-di-mu-ri* ^{14}*ša* AMA^{meš} *ša i-ra-ma-ka-a-ni*, SAA 16 105 r. 12–14).[10] Ištar-of-Kidmuri also appears between Ištar-of-Nineveh and Ištar-of-

8 As noted elsewhere, a text and line number are written in italics (e.g., SAA 13 *126:4*) indicates that Nabû is listed before Marduk in an EGL in that text.

9 In SAA 16 105:5, Ištar-of-Kidmuri is listed after Ištar-of-Nineveh and is last in a four-member EGL. In SAA 16 126:5 and 127:5, she appears between Ištar-of-Nineveh and Ištar-of-Arbela in eight- and nine-member EGLs, respectively. (Note that the Kidmuri-temple is spelled *kad-mu-ru* in SAA 16 126:5.) This goddess also appears with other localized Ištar goddesses in EGLs from more esoteric texts, such as SAA 3 34:73 and 35:70.

As indicated by these EGLs from the seventh century, Lady-of-Kidmuri became more relevant when the Assyrian capital moved to Nineveh, where one of her temples was located (Julian Reade, "The Ištar Temple at Nineveh," *Iraq* 67 [2005]: 384). A Kidmuri-temple was also rebuilt in Calaḫ by Assurnāṣirpal II in the ninth century when he moved the Assyrian capital there (George, *House Most High*, 113, no. 645; see also Julian Reade, "The Ziggurrat and Temples of Nimrud," *Iraq* 64 [2002]: 135–216).

10 Ištar-of-Kidmuri appears in an EGL listing the precious items assigned to each cult statue (^{d}15 E$_2$ *kid-mu-*⌜*ri*⌝, SAA 7 62 ii 2′). Ištar-of-bīt-Eqi is the next goddess listed (^{d}15 E$_2$ *e-qi*, ii 7′), and Mullissu appears much later (^{d}NIN.LIL$_2$, iv 9′), far removed from Assur who is the first extant divine name in this text (^{d}*aš*$^{!}$*-šur*, i 6′). For a discussion of Ištar-of-bīt-Eqi, see Meinhold, *Ištar in Aššur*, 97–98, 124, 154–160, and 183.

Arbela in EGLs in Assurbanipal's royal inscriptions (see Table 3.14). Even though the other two Ištar goddesses' first names are usually written 15 to indicate "Ištar," the Kidmuri goddess is typically addressed by the title-of-GN pattern (e.g., Lady-of-Kidmuri, *BIWA* 33 A ii 27, and Queen-of-Kidmuri, 36 A iii 13). Lady-of-Babylon also appears in an EGL. In a petition written by the maidservant Sarai, Lady-of-Babylon (^{d}*be-let* KA.DINGIR.RA^{ki}) is the third deity in a seven-member EGL in SAA 16 49:3–5: Bēl / Bēltīya / Lady-of-Babylon / Nabû / Tašmētu / Ištar-of-Nineveh / Ištar-of-Arbela.[11] Her placement in this EGL between Marduk and son his Nabû suggests that she was envisioned as Marduk's consort.

In each of these title-of-GN name formulas, the relevant goddess is identified by a title rather than a proper name, but the title is treated like a proper name. The fact that these Ištar goddesses can be referred to as "queens" or "ladies" of a particular place – be it a city or a temple – instead of just as Ištars of that place suggests that these titles should be interpreted as names or nicknames in much the same way that Baal (literally, "lord") came to function as a name or nickname for storm-gods in Ugaritic and other Northwest Semitic languages (see chapter 5.3). This is especially significant because *bēlet* ("lady"; the feminine form of *bēl*) has roughly the same semantic range as *šarrat* ("queen"), and both *bēlet-* and *šarrat-* can be written with the same logogram, GAŠAN. Indeed, aside from Mesopotamia's most famous "Baal," Bēl/Marduk, and his consort Bēltīya/Zarpānītu, deities who lack geographic last names in EGLs are only addressed by their first names, not by potential nicknames. That this variability is allowed only for these select localized Ištar goddesses in EGLs (and Marduk and Zarpānītu) cannot be overstressed, nor can the ease by which we are able to identify reliably Ištar-of-Nineveh with Lady/Queen-of-Nineveh and Ištar-of-Arbela with Lady/Queen-of-Arbela.

The final alternative formula for localized Ištar goddesses in EGLs is the DN//Who-Resides-(in)-GN formula. This formula appears in EGLs in state treaties, private votive donations, and legal documents:

---

11 Lady-of-Uruk appears in two letters from Uruk to the king (^{d}GAŠAN *ša*$_{2}$ UNUG^{ki}, SAA 18 79:5; $^{⌜d⌝}$GAŠAN *ša*$_{2}$ UNUG$^{⌜ki⌝}$ and ^{d}GAŠAN ⌜*ša*$_{2}$⌝ UNUG^{ki}, SAA 18 82:20′ and r. 6′). Technically, these are not EGLs since only Nanaya accompanies her in these blessings, but as blessings in a letter these more closely resemble EGLs than court poetry and prophecy. Notably, the divine name Lady-of-Uruk is a hybrid between the standard DN-of-GN and title-of-GN since the *ša*-particle is used to mark the relationship between the two nouns instead of the use of the construct state. For a discussion of the variant divine names used to identify the localized Ištar goddess in Uruk during the first millennium, see Beaulieu, *Pantheon of Uruk*, 123 ff. One goddess is identified as Ištar//Lady-of-Uruk on stamped bricks from the Eanna-temple during Sargon II's reign: ^{1} ^{d}inanna ^{2}nin unug^{ki}-ga-ta (RIMB 2 B.6.22.5:1–2; Frame, RIMB 2, 150).

Text:	Divine Name:	Cuneiform:
SAA 2 5 iv 1′	[Mullissu//Who-Resides-(in)-Nineveh]	^{d}[NIN.LIL$_2$ *a-ši-bat* ^{uru}NINA^{ki}]
and iv 2′	Ištar//Who-Re[sides-(in)-Arbela]	^{d}*iš-tar* ⸢*a*⸣-[*ši-bat* ^{uru}*arba-il*$_3$]
SAA 2 6:457	Mullissu//Who-Resides-(in)-Nineveh	^{d}NIN.LIL$_2$ *a-ši-bat* ^{uru}NINA^{ki}
and 459	Ištar//Who-Resides-(in)-Arbela	^{d}*iš-tar a-ši-bat* ^{uru}*arba-il*$_3$
SAA 2 9 r. 24′	Ištar//Who-Resides-(in)-Arbela	^{d}INNIN *a-ši-bat arba-il*$_3$^{ki}
SAA 12 93:4	Ištar//Who-Resides-(in)-[Arbela]	^{d}*iš-tar a-ši-bat* ^{uru}[*arba-il*$_3$]
SAA 12 97 r. 2	Ištar//Who-Resides-(in)-Arbela	^{d}*iš-tar a-šib-bat* ^{uru}*arba-il*$_3$
SAA 14 204:8′	[Ištar//Who-Resid]es-(in)-Nineveh	[^{d}15 *a-ši*]-⸢*bat*⸣ ^{uru}NINA
SAA 14 294 r. 4	[Ištar//Who-Resides-(in)]-Nineveh	[^{d}15 *a-ši-bat*] ^{uru}NINA^{ki}
SAA 14 466:6′	[Ištar//Who-Resid]es-(in)-Arbela	⸢^{d}⸣[15 *a-ši*]-*bat* ^{uru}*arba-il*$_3$

This formula could rightly be considered an epithet following a divine name, rather than a last name, because *āšibat* is a participial form of the verb (*w*)*ašābu* ("to reside/live/have domicile"), and our chose of punctuation reflects this.[12] Thus, the phrase can be translated as "DN, (the one) who resides (in) GN," which is precisely how Parpola and Kazuko Watanabe translate ^{d}NIN.LIL$_2$ *a-ši-bat* ^{uru}NINA^{ki} and ^{d}*iš-tar a-ši-bat* ^{uru}*arba-il*$_3$: "Mullissu, who resides in Nineveh" and "Ištar, who resides in Arbela" (SAA 2 6:457 and 459). The comma that they placed between the divine name and the participial phrase in each line indicates that the latter has been interpreted as an epithet, rather than the last part of a full name. In some situations, like SAA 2 6, the choice to translate *āšibat*-GN as an epithet rather than strictly as a last name is reasonable. For instance, SAA 2 6:457 and 459 name deities who are part of the eighteen-member EGL that comprises the curse list near the end of the treaty (see Table 3.9). Each curse in this EGL begins with a divine name that is followed by an epithet. Nergal and Gula, who appear in the curses immediately before and after this Mullissu and this Ištar, receive the respective epithets "hero of the gods" (*qar-rad* DINGIR, l. 455) and "the great physician" (*a-zu-gal-la-tu*$_2$ GAL-*tu*$_2$, l. 461). When considered in this context, Mullissu's "who resides (in) Nineveh" and Ištar's "who resides (in) Arbela" make sense interpreted as epithets, even if dwelling somewhere sounds significantly less impressive than being a great hero or physician.[13] It becomes even more evident that this residing formula serves as the equivalent of a full name formula when Moon-

12 *CAD* A/2, *ašābu* mng. 2a1′.

13 The Ištar who is identified as "the one who resides in [Arbela]" (^{d}*iš-tar a-ši-bat* ^{uru}[*arba-il*$_3$]) in SAA 12 93 r. 4 is one of only two divine names followed by an epithet in this EGL, which was derived from a curse list: Ninurta / Gula / Adad//Canal-Inspector-of-Heaven-and-Earth / Nabû / Ištar//Who-Resides-(in)-[Arbela].

God-of-Ḫarrān is mentioned in royal inscriptions. In RIMA 3 A.0.104.2:12, Moon-God//Who-Resides-(in)-Ḫarrān is the final divine name in a six-member EGL: Assur / Adad / Bēr / Assyrian-Enlil / Assyrian-[Mullis]su / Moon-God// Who-Resides-(in)-Ḫarrān.[14] To reiterate, gods whose names are supplemented with geographic epithets in EGLs tend to be the least important gods in those EGLs. If this Ḫarrān-based deity had been identified as Sîn, the Mesopotamian moon-god, then we would have expected his name to appear before Adad in the EGL.[15] Because the ancient scribes recognized that Moon-God-of-Ḫarrān was not the same deity as (the unspecified) Sîn, the Ḫarrānian deity does not benefit from Sîn's status, just as Hadad-of-Aleppo and Adad-of-Kurbail did not benefit from (the unspecified) Adad's status in SAA 2 2 vi 17–18.

We can empirically demonstrate that the formula DN//Who-Resides-(in)-GN is the equivalent to the standard DN-of-GN formula, rather than simply being a divine name followed by an epithet, by an examination of legal texts. Although legal transactions of the royal court typically lack EGLs, many of those that mention deities adhere to a general structure:

I Space for stamp seal or fingernail impressions.
II The owner sells objects/persons/land to the buyer for a price.
III Statement that the price has been paid completely.
IVa "Should anyone in the future ever appear in court"
IVb "he shall place X mina of metal(s) in the lap of DN"
IV(c) The transgressor may be required to donate horses to other deities.

14 Moon-God//Who-Resides-(in)-Ḫarrān appears in EGLs in two other royal inscriptions: RIMA 3 A.0.104.2:17 and A.0.105.1:20.

15 According to Lipiński, the cult of Moon-God-of-Ḫarrān existed already in the early second millennium (Lipiński, *Aramaeans*, 620). Rubio notes that despite the fact that King Nabonidus appointed his daughter to be the high priestess of Sîn at Ur, which was a very ancient – if not antiquated and obsolete – Mesopotamian tradition dating back to the third millennium, his reverence for the Ḫarrānian moon-god "exhibited attributes and cultic features that depart from the traditional (i.e., Mesopotamian) worship of Sîn" (Gonzalo Rubio, "Scribal Secrets and Antiquarian Nostalgia: Tradition and Scholarship in Ancient Mesopotamia," in *Reconstructing a Distant Past: Ancient Near Eastern Essays in Tribute to Jorge R. Silva Castillo*, ed. Diego A. Barreyra Fracaroli and Gregorio del Olmo Lete, Aula Orientalis – Supplementa 25 [Barcelona: Editorial AUSA, 2009], 161). If the worship of this Aramean moon-god, whose Aramaic name was Śahr/Śehr known from the Zakkur stele (*KAI* 202 B 24 = TSSI 2 5 B 24) can be connected to other Western Asian moon-gods, then this deity's name could be reflected in the following names: the third-millennium Eblaite Sanugaru (written either *sa-nu-gar-ru* or ITI in the cuneiform), Šaggar from Deir 'Alla (*šgr*, Combination I, 14 (16)), the South-Arabian *S²hr*, the Arabic *Šahr*, and ᵈ*še-e-ri* in one of Šalmaneser III's royal inscriptions (RIMA 3 A.0.102.92:1; Lipiński, *Aramaeans*, 621–622).

IVd “shall pay ten times the price to the owner”
IVe “Should he initiate with legal proceedings, he shall not win.”
IV(f) Guarantee against seizures and fraud.
V Witnesses.

Of particular interest are section IV and its subsections a-f, although not all six of the subsections appear in every legal text or in this particular order. In addition to suggesting that the threat of massive penalties reduced the number of broken contracts or future lawsuits during the Neo-Assyrian period, section IV provides several opportunities to compare how divine names are treated in these penalty clauses. Subsection IVb indicates where the offending party had to pay his fine for contesting the contract, which is a separate penalty from his repayment to the other party. Usually, the offending party paid his fine to a local temple, as indicated by the regular statement that the payment shall be placed “in the lap of” (*ina bur-ki*) a particular deity, which is a reference to the deity’s cult statue at the temple. The local temple receiving the fine is designated by the deity in whose lap the gold and silver were placed. By designating the deity as the DN//Who-Resides-(in)-GN (or as DN-of-GN), potential confusion over which temple to deliver the fine is avoided.

Of those late eighth- and seventh-century texts collected in SAA 6 and 14 that required the offending party to pay a fine, the deity most commonly mentioned is Ištar-of-Nineveh (see Table 4.1). Ištar-of-Arbela, Ninurta-of-Calaḫ, and Moon-God-of-Ḫarrān are also mentioned, as are numerous Adads-of-GN (see Table 4.2). More often than not, these deities are identified by the DN//Who-Resides-(in)-GN formula, but the standard DN-of-GN formula is also relatively common. Apart from the choice of formula for the divine name, the sentence that describes the fine is fairly stable. SAA 6 85 and 87 serve as examples for comparison because both involve “the governess of the central city Harem” as the purchaser:

SAA 6 85:14-r. 4	subsection	SAA 6 87:5′-r. 6
^{14}[*man*]-⸢*nu*⸣ *ša ina ur-kiš ina ma-te-ma* ^{15}[*i-zaq-qu-pa*]-⸢*ni*⸣	IVa	$^{5′}$*man-nu ša ina ur-kiš* $^{6′}$*ina ma-te-e-ma i-zaq-qu-pan-ni*
		$^{7′}$*lu-u* PN$_1$ *lu-u* DUMU^{meš}-šu$_2$ $^{8′}$*lu-u* ⸢DUMU⸣ DUMU^{meš}-*šu*$_2$ *lu-u* ŠEŠ^{meš}-*šu*$_2$ *lu-u* DUMU^{meš} ŠEŠ^{meš}-*šu*$_2$
		$^{9′}$*ša* TA$^{!}$ ^{f}*ša*$_2$-*kin*$_2$-*tu*$_2$ DUMU^{meš}-*šu*$_2$ DUMU DUMU^{meš}-*šu*$_2$ $^{10′}$*de*-⸢*e*⸣-*nu* DUG$_4$.DUG$_4$ *ub-ta-’u-u-ni*
4 MA.NA KUG.UD ^{16}[LUḪ-*u* x MA.NA KUG].GI *sak-ru*	IVb	$^{r.\ 1}$10 ⸢MA⸣.NA KUG.UD LUḪ-*u* 1 MA.NA KUG.GI *sak-ru*
$^{r.\ 1}$*ina bur-ki* ^{d}15 *ša*$_2$ ^{uru}NINA GAR-*an*		^{2}*ina bur-ki* ^{d}*iš-tar a-ši-bat* ^{uru}NINA *i-šak-kan*

	IVc	^{3}2 ANŠE.KUR.RA^{meš} BABBAR^{meš} *ina* GIR$_3$^{II} *aš-šur* *i-rak-kas* ^{4}4 ANŠE-*ḫur-ba-kan-ni ina* KI.TA ^{d}ŠEŠ.GAL *u*$_2$*-še-rab*
^{2}*kas-*⸢*pu*⸣ [*a-na* 10]^{meš}*-te a-na* EN-*šu*$_2$ ^{3}GUR-⸢*ra*⸣	IVd	^{5}*kas-pu a-na* 10^{meš}*-te a-na* EN^{meš}*-šu*$_2$ GUR-*ra*
[*ina de*]*-ni-šu*$_2$ DUG$_4$.DUG$_4$*-ma* ^{4}*la i-laq-qi*$_2$	IVe	^{6}*ina de-ni-šu*$_2$ DUG$_4$.DUG$_4$*-ma la i-laq-qi*
Should [anyo]ne in the future ever appear in court,	IVa	Should anyone in the future ever appear in court – be it PN$_1$, his sons, grandsons, brothers, or nephews – and attempts to initiate legal proceedings against the governess, her! sons, or grandsons,
he shall place 4 minas of [pure] gold [and x mina of] refined [silv]er in the lap of Ištar-of-Nineveh.	IVb	he shall place 10 minas of pure gold and 1 mina of refined silver in the lap of Ištar//Who-Resides-(in)-Nineveh,
	IVc	shall tie 2 white horses at Assur's feet, and shall bring 4 donkeys? into Nergal('s temple).
He shall pay ten times the price to the owner.	IVd	He shall pay ten times the price to the owner.
Should he initiate [with legal pr]oceedings, he shall not win.	IVe	Should he initiate with legal proceedings, he shall not win.

SAA 6 87:5′-r. 6 explicitly states who should not challenge whom over this purchase and contains stronger deterrents than does SAA 6 85:14-r. 4, but the role that the deity who would receive the gold and silver plays in both texts is identical. In fact, in most of the texts listed in Table 4.1, there is no discernable difference in meaning between the formula choice DN-of-GN and DN//Who-Resides-(in)-GN; in most instances they are interchangeable. Pragmatically, the first name and subsequent epithet function in the same manner as the standard full name. This is true not only when Ištar-of-Nineveh is the deity but also when other deities are mentioned. The only discernable difference between a given text's use of either formula is that legal transactions containing subsection IVc – in which horses are delivered to the gods (usually) Assur and Nergal – always identify the deity in subsection IVb with the DN//Who-Resides-(in)-GN formula. Why this formulaic difference exists is unclear to me, but this includes fewer than ten percent of the legal texts examined.

In addition to these full name formulas, Ištar goddesses who are recognized as the patron deity of their local city are often said to be identified by a feminized derivative form of the city name. For instance, instead of referring to the patron goddess of Arbela as Ištar-of-Arbela, she might have also been known as Arbilītu, literally, "the (female) one from Arbela."[16] Similarly, Ištar-of-Nineveh appears to be identified as Ninua'ītu by Šalmaneser I and by Tukulti-Ninurta I (^{d}*ni-nu-a-it-ti*, RIMA 1 A.0.77.7:7; ^{d}*nu-na-i-te*, RIMA 1 A.0.78.17:5), and Assyrian-Ištar might have been identified as Assurītu (^{d}15-*šu* ^{d}*aš$_2$-šu-ri-tu$_4$*, "his goddess Assurītu," King, *BMS*, no. 2 n. 8; cf. plate 5 n. 4) in one copy of a *Prayer to Ninurta*, where the divine name Assurītu replaces the generic term *annannītu* (King, *BMS*, 17:26: ^{d}15-*šu* NENNI-*tu$_4$*, "his goddess So-and-so").[17] These are not the only divine names that scholars have identified as localized Ištar goddesses because they are derived from city names.[18] Other Ištar goddesses who have been identified by these city-based nicknames include but are not limited to: Lagabītum, Kītītu, Kišītu, Ḫišamītu, and finally Ulmašītu, whose name is actually derived from the Ulmaš-temple in Akkad rather than the city.[19]

16 Scurlock interprets *ur$_2$-bi-li-ti* in DPS III A 15–16 as an equivalent of Arbilītu for the divine name Ištar-of-Arbela (Scurlock and Andersen, *Diagnoses*, 159).

17 Meinhold, *Ištar in Aššur*, 170–171 and 51. This feminized derivative method of renaming a localized Ištar goddess was not limited to Assyria. According to AN : *Anum* IV, the tablet in the series that identifies the numerous alternative names and epithets for Inanna/Ištar, Ištar-of-Uruk is identified with Aš[ka'ītu] (or Urkayītu, ^{d}INANNA UNUG^{ki} = *aš-*[*ka-i-tu*], l. 117), and Ištar-of-Kiš is identified as Kiš[ītu] ($^{d⌜}$INANNA KIŠ$^{⌝ki}$ = *kiš-*[*i-tu*], l. 119).

In 1923, F. Böhl recognized the divine name Aška'ītu (for Urkyaītu) as an alternative name for Ištar-of-Uruk (F. Böhl, "Älteste keilinschriftliche Erwähnungen der Stadt Jerusalem und ihrer Göttin?" *Acta Orientalia* 1 [1923]: 76–79). He also noted that AN : *Anum* IV 128–133 equate other localized Ištar manifestations with goddesses whose names are feminized derivatives of the local city. Most notable of Böhl's observations is that the Ištar who resides in the city of Silim (i.e., Jerusalem) was Šulmanītu (^{d}INANNA ^{uru}SILIM.MA = *šul-ma-ni-tu*, l. 132).

18 Lambert contemplated the possibility that male patron deities could also take on city-based or temple-based nicknames. For example, he identified the Old Babylonian personal name Urum-šemi, which literally means "(the city of) Ur hears," as a circumlocative reference to Sîn, the patron deity of Ur (W. G. Lambert, "The God Aššur," *Iraq* 45 [1983]: 83). Likewise, he offered the Old Babylonian name Ebabbar-tukultī, which literally means "the Ebabbar-temple is my help," as a reference to Šamaš.

19 Leemans, *Ishtar of Lagaba*, 35; Maria deJong Ellis, "The Archive of the Old Babylonian Kītītum Temple and other Texts from Ishchali," *JAOS* 106 (1986): 759 n. 9 and 762; Dietz Otto Edzard, "Pantheon und Kult im Mari," in *Rencontre Assyriologique Internationale XVe*: *La Civilisation de Mari*: *Colloque international tenu à l'Univerité de Liège dy 4 au 8 juillet 1966*, ed. J. R. Kupper (Paris: Belles letters, 1967), 61; and Karin B. Gödecken, "Bermerkungen zure Göttin Annuītum," *UF* 5 (1973): 146.

As a divine name, Ištar-of-Nineveh is interchangeable with the other full name formulas, including Lady-of-Nineveh, Ištar//Lady-of-Nineveh, and Ištar//Who-Resides-(in)-Nineveh, of which the latter two consist of a first name followed by the epithet, and perhaps a feminized city name. Pragmatically, Lady-of-Nineveh, Ištar//Lady-of-Nineveh, and Ištar//Who-Resides-(in)-Nineveh can be interpreted as divine full names because scribes treated them as a divine full names. Moreover, like the standard formula DN-of-GN and the other two alternative formulas, the geographic information provided in these names was indispensable to that deity's identity, whether the deity was being explicitly contrasted with another same-named deity in an EGL or implicitly contrasted by designating to which temple payments should be delivered. Whether identified as Ištar-of-Nineveh, Ištar//Who-Resides-(in)-Nineveh, Lady-of-Nineveh, or Ištar//Lady-of-Nineveh, this goddess was intentionally being distinguished from the Ištar goddess in Arbela, the one at the Kidmuri-temple, and all the others.

If the divine name formulas Ištar-of-GN_x, Ištar//Who-Resides-(in)-GN_x, Lady-of-GN_x, Ištar//Lady-of-GN_x, and perhaps also GN_x-ītu are all interchangeable and refer to the same goddess, and if the localized Ištar-of-Nineveh is regularly contrasted with Ištar-of-Arbela, then it becomes apparent that the primary distinction between these two goddesses is their location. Put another way, these goddesses' identities come from their last names, the geographic epithets, and not the name Ištar. Just as Assur's identity comes from his name and Marduk's identity comes from his name, Ištar-of-Nineveh's identity comes from her name, or more specifically, her last name. While this may be obvious, stating it leads to the more important observation that it may not matter whether the name Ištar is a proper name or a common noun. If the word Ištar when followed by a geographic epithet is a proper name, then multiple localized Ištar goddesses were treated as separate from and independent of each other and independent of (the unspecified) Ištar in all of these state documents. Whether the Ninevite and Arbelite populations recognized that their own localized Ištar goddesses were once the same goddess as (the unspecified) Ištar and each other in centuries past, by the eighth and seventh centuries their scribes seemed content treating them as different and consistently using geographic epithets to address them. If they were considered derivative Ištars who splintered away from their mother Ištar, as the many "sister" madonnine images had splintered away from the Madonna, this could help explain their relative lack of status within the Neo-Assyrian divine hierarchy. Of course, as we observed in chapter 3.2, (the unspecified) Ištar already had a relatively low rank for a major god in the ninth century. Conversely, if the word *ištar* functioned as the common noun meaning "goddess," then these goddesses apparently did not have their own names, which could help explain their relative status and the fact that *ištar* was interchangeable with *bēlet-* and *šarrat-*.[20] While we could survey each goddess's past to determine whether her personality or attributes resemble those of (the unspecified) Ištar, we must recall that Pongratz-Leisten cautioned against defining gods in this way.[21] Instead, she would have us focus on the fact that a given divine entity helped maintain cosmic order, and the various blessings and curses from which these EGLs are derived demonstrate that localized Ištar goddesses helped maintain divine order. Pragmatically, the difference between Ištar and *ištar* is irrelevant; they were treated as distinct from each other in Neo-Assyrian EGLs as they were from Marduk and Sîn. It might have mattered to the ancient Ninevites and Arbelites that their localized goddesses were Ištars, as opposed to nameless *ištars*, and these goddesses probably really were Ištars as far as everyone else was concerned. More importantly, however, one was from Nineveh, the other was from Arbela, and they were not identifiable or interchangeable with each other.

4.2 Theological Speculations about Ištar Goddesses

Having surveyed the main variations by which Ištar goddesses were identified in EGLs and in legal transactions, three additional formula have been revealed as ways to name the goddess most often identified as Ištar-of-Nineveh, Ištar//Lady-of-Nineveh, Lady-of-Nineveh, and Ištar//Who-Resides-(in)-Nineveh, and all of these names stress the goddess's geographic identity. Moreover, regardless of which formula is used, this goddess is regularly contrasted in EGLs with Ištar-of-Arbela, who can also be identified using any of the alternative formulas. We may now turn from the EGLs contained in state treaties, administrative documents, letters, royal inscriptions, and cultic documents that reflect the writings of the official court scribes and examine "compositions exemplifying and expressing a creative effort" that are the products of the scholar-scribes and are not intended to follow the "day to day religious literature."[22] In addition to *Assurbanipal's Hymn to the Ištars of Nineveh and Arbela* (SAA 3 3), these texts include the *Psalm in Praise of Uruk* (SAA 3 9), the *Mystical Miscellanea* (SAA 3 39), and the various collections of oracles and prophecies delivered to Esarhaddon and Assurbanipal in the name

20 *CAD* I/J, *ištaru*.
21 Pongratz-Leisten, "Divine Agency," 144.
22 Livingstone, SAA 3, XVI.

of Ištar-of-Arbela and Mullissu (SAA 9 1, 2, 5, 7, and 9). Each text has a different theological purpose behind it, and each text reveals a unique aspect of the still salient distinction between Ištar-of-Nineveh and Ištar-of-Arbela, despite the syncretistic tendencies often attributed to these texts by Assyriologists.

In his hymn to the two Ištar goddesses, Assurbanipal called each of them Lady (*bēlet*), using the title-of-GN formula (SAA 3 3:1–2 and r. 14 and 16), and he then declared his praise for them because of their continued support throughout his life. As Porter noted in 2004, Assurbanipal peppered his hymn to the goddesses with feminine plural verbs, pronominal suffixes, and nouns to indicate that he was addressing two distinct goddesses.[23] Indeed, his double entendre in r. 5 removes any lingering doubt about his theological take on the multiplicity of these Ištars. Whether one prefers to interpret ^{d}*iš*$_{8}$*-tar*$_{2}$^{meš}*ia* as a proper or a common noun, Assurbanipal gladly honored the ladies of Nineveh and Arbela in r. 5 as either "my Ištars," calling them by their shared first name, or "my *ištar*s," using their name as a generic term for "goddess." He then proclaimed that "their names are more precious than (other) Ištars/*ištar*s" (*šu-qur zi-kir-ši-na a-na* ^{d}IŠ.TAR^{meš}, l. 4), although a grammatically more accurate translation may be, "their name *is* more precious than (other) Ištars/*ištars*," even if the theology of the statement remains unchanged.[24]

A close reading of the hymn indicates that Assurbanipal not only refused to equate the two goddesses, but he also refused to acknowledge their equal or comparable status. Ištar-of-Nineveh is his favored localized Ištar goddess in this hymn. This is made most obvious in the tablet's colophon where he requested a blessing from Ištar-of-Nineveh alone: "May Lady-of-Nineveh, lady of the song, exalt (my) kingship forever" (^{d}*be-let* ^{uru}NINA *be-let za-ma-ri* LUGAL-⸢*tu*$_{2}$ *li*$^{!}$*-šar*$^{?}$⸣*-bi a-na da-ra-a-ti*, SAA 3 3 r. 19–20). Moreover, although he considered himself a "creation" (*bi-nu-ut*) of both the Emašmaš-temple and the Egašankalamma-temple (l. 10), which belonged to the goddesses in Nineveh and Arbela, respectively, he preceded this by referring to himself as "the great seed of Assur (and) the offspring of Nineveh" (NUMUN$^{!}$ BAL$^{!}$.TIL$^{ki!}$ *ra*$^{!}$⸢*bu*$^{!}$⸣-[*u i-*

23 Porter, "Ishtar of Nineveh," 41.

24 Interpreting *ištar* as the common noun for goddess is most reliably done when the word appears parallel to *ilu* ("god") in a sentence or when a possessive suffix follows the word. For example, one Old Babylonian omen does both: *ilšu u ištaršu ul sanqūšu* ("his god and his goddess are not next to him," Franz Köcher and A. Leo Oppenheim, "The Old Babylonian Omen Text VAT 7525," *AfO* 18 [1957]: 64, l. 38). Other examples of *ištaru* provided in *CAD* as a common noun are less convincing because they lack these cues found in *AfO* 18 64, l. 38. Examples of ^{d}15/*iš-tar*^{meš}*-šu*$_{2}$ following DINGIR^{meš}*-šu*$_{2}$ meaning "his gods and his goddesses" can be found in several of Assurbanipal's royal inscriptions (e.g., *BIWA* 55 A vi 64 and 168 T v 3).

li]*t*$^{!}$-*ti* ^{uru}*ni-na-a*, l. 9).[25] This statement does not explicitly name any deities, but it implicitly proclaims the king as the scion of Assur and Ištar-of-Nineveh.[26] This interpretation is reinforced later in the hymn where the king praised Ištar-of-Nineveh as his birthmother (^{d}*be-let* ^{uru}*ni-na*$_2$*-a um-mu a-lit-ti-ia*, "Lady-of-Nineveh, the mother who bore me," r. 14), whereas he refers to Ištar-of-Arbela as his creator (^{d}*be-let* ^{uru}*arba-il*$_3$ ⸢*ba*$^{!}$⸣-[*ni*]-⸢*ti*⸣-*ia*, "Lady-of-Arbela who created me," r. 16). The participle (*bānītu*) used here to describe Ištar-of-Arbela's role connotes creation, but it lacks the intimacy of the title "mother" (*ummu*) that is given to Ištar-of-Nineveh.[27]

Despite her secondary role as the nurse in Assurbanipal's upbringing,[28] Ištar-of-Arbela is referred to as a mother while Ištar-of-Nineveh is called a wet nurse in the esoteric or mystical texts from Nineveh. *Mystical Miscellanea* (SAA 3 39) refers to Ištar-of-Arbela as the mother of the great god Bēl (l. 22) and calls Ištar-of-Nineveh his wet nurse (l. 19).[29] *Mystical Miscellanea* is a decidedly and self-proclaimed esoteric text that only the initiated are permitted to see (r. 26). In addition to identifying Marduk with Meslamtaea explicitly (r. 7), over the course of five lines this text identifies various goddesses as aspects of each other:

19[^{d}]⸢15⸣ *ša* ^{uru}*dur-na ti-amat ši-i-ma* UM.ME.GA.LA$_2$ *ša*$_2$ ^{d}EN *ši*$^{!}$-*i*$^{!}$-*ma*$^{!}$
20[4 IGI^{II}.M]EŠ-*ša* 4 PI^{IImeš}-*ša*
21A[N.T]A^{meš}-*ša* ^{d}EN KI.TA^{meš}-*ša* ^{d}NIN.LIL$_2$
22 ^{d}NIN ^{uru}LI.BUR.NA *um-m*[*a*$^{?}$] *ša* ^{d}EN *ši-i-ma*
23[S]AR$^{?meš}$ *iš-ru-ka-ši an-tum ši-i-ma kis-pa a-na* ^{d}*a-num i-kas-si-pu*

---

25 George, *House Most High*, 121 (no. 742) and 90 (no. 351).
26 This consort role that Ištar-of-Nineveh plays with Assur is discussed further below.
27 *CAD* B, *banû* A mng. 3a1′ and 2′; see also Botta, "Outlook," 373 n. 63. Ea, Aruru, Narru, Marduk, Ahura Mazda, Nintu, and Erua are all identified as gods who created mankind or individual people.

Although the goddess's divine name does not appear in the oracle, SAA 9 2.1 refers to a goddess, presumably Ištar-of-Arbela given her predominance in the prophetic literature, as the king's creator ([*x x a-na-ku*$^{?}$] ⸢^{d}⸣*ba-ni-tu*, "[I am] Creator," SAA 9 2.1:5′).
28 In SAA 9 1.6, an oracle of encouragement, Ištar-of-Arbela identifies herself as Esarhaddon's midwife and wet nurse: 15′*sa-ab-su-ub-ta-k*[*a*] 16′*ra-bi-tu a-na-ku* 17′*mu-še-ni*[*q*$^{!}$]-*ta-ka* 18′*de-iq-tu*$_2$ *a-na-ku* ("I am your great midwife; I am your capable wet nurse," ll. 15′–18′). She is also identified as Assurbanipal's wet nurse after Mullissu is identified as his mother in SAA 9 7 r. 6: *ma-a ša*$_2$ ^{d}NIN.LIL$_2$ AMA-*šu*$_2$-*ni la ta-pal-laḫ*$_3$ *ša*$_2$ GAŠAN *arba-il*$_3$ *ta-ri-su-ni la ta-pal-laḫ*$_3$ ("Do not fear, you whose mother is Mullissu! Do not fear, you whose wet nurse is Lady-of-Arbela!).
29 See Livingstone's translation in SAA 3 39:19–22 for the identification of Durna with Nineveh (Livingstone, SAA 3, 233; Rocío Da Riva and Eckart Frahm, "Šamaš-šumu-ukīn, die Herrin von Ninive und das babylonische Königssiegel," *AfO* 46–47 [1999/2000], 174; and VAT 13815 r. 17–18).

Ištar-of-Nineveh is Tiāmat; she is Bēl's wet nurse.
She has [four pairs of eye]s; she has four pairs of ears.
Her upper portions are Bēl; her lower portions are Mullissu.
Lady-of-Arbela is Bēl's mother.
He gave her [ga]rdens. She is Antu; they offer funerary offerings to Anu. (SAA 3 39:19–23)

Here, Ištar-of-Nineveh is acknowledged as Bēl's wet nurse, but she is first identified with Tiāmat, the primordial seawaters and (multi-)great-grandmother of all the gods, who serves as Marduk's primary antagonist in *Enūma eliš*.[30] According to Livingstone, as Marduk's wet nurse, Ištar-of-Nineveh unites Marduk's characteristics with Mullissu, with whom she is identified in the same line.[31] By equating Ištar-of-Nineveh with Tiāmat (l. 19) and her "lower portions" with Mullissu, SAA 3 39 presents this goddess as the primordial goddess in order to prove that she outranks Marduk in Assyria.[32] In addition to the tendencies toward hyper-identification of goddesses in ll. 19–23, this esoteric text also presents the geo-political realities and continued aspirations of the composer's world: the goddess who is superior to Babylon's Marduk is from Nineveh. In the metaphoric mind of the Assyrian scribe who composed SAA 3 39, the city of Babylon that could occasionally boast political hegemony in the second millennium and aspired to rule yet again was really a dependent of the Assyrian Empire; after all, the Assyrian goddess nursed the Babylon god.[33]

---

30 According to *Enūma eliš* I 84–86, Marduk's mother is Damkina, Ea's consort, and Marduk nursed at the teats of the *ištars* (^{d}EŠ$_4$.TAR$_2^{meš}$, "goddesses," l. 85), who are also described as his "wet nurses who nursed him" (*ta-ri-tu it-tar-ru-šu*, l. 86). Damkina and these other goddesses are quite distinct in the epic from Tiāmat, whose introduction and progeny appear in I 4 ff. Like Ištar-of-Nineveh in SAA 3 39:20, Marduk is described as having four pairs of eyes and ears in *Enūma eliš* I 95.

31 Livingstone, SAA 3, 234. Livingstone notes that Ištar's celestial aspect as the morning star (i.e., Venus) was identified with the goddess Išḫara and the constellation Scorpio, the latter of which was equated with Tiāmat's serpentine imagery in SAA 3 39 r. 13–16 and *Enūma eliš* I.

32 Likewise, Assur's name is spelled *an-šar*$_{(2)}$ in order to identify him with the god Anšar, who is Anu's father in the epic and Marduk's divine ancestor (*Enūma eliš* I 12–15; see also SAA 3 39 r. 8; Livingstone, *Mystical and Mythological*, 234; and Paul-Alain Beaulieu, "The Cult of AN.ŠÁR/Aššur in Babylonia after the Fall of the Assyrian Empire," SAAB 11 [1997]: 64). Establishing Assur's and Mullissu's genealogical priority over Marduk in the theology of the epic also establishes the cities of Assur and Nineveh's priority over Babylon in the political world, even though the epic explicitly states that Anu's offspring Ea (Nudimmud) surpassed Anšar (*gu-uš-šur ma-a'-diš a-na a-lid* AD-*šu*$_2$ *an-šar*$_3$, "more powerful than Anšar, his father's begetter," l. 19) and that Marduk defeats Tiāmat later in the narrative.

33 Da Riva and Frahm discuss that this motif is also contained in the Assur and Nineveh versions of the Marduk Ordeal (SAA 3 34:44 and 35:39; Da Riva and Frahm, "Šamaš-šumu-ukīn," 173).

Despite this text's tendencies to identity Ištar-of-Nineveh with Mullissu and Tiāmat, SAA 3 39 portrays Ištar-of-Nineveh and Ištar-of-Arbela as distinct as does SAA 3 3, but it reverses their roles. Whereas Ištar-of-Nineveh is explicitly identified as one of Marduk's progenitors because of her identification with Tiāmat, Ištar-of-Arbela is only implicitly and incorrectly identified as one when she is described as Bēl's mother. In SAA 3 39:22–23, Ištar-of-Arbela is identified with Antu, suggesting that the goddess could be identified as Marduk's grandmother, but Antu never actually appears in the genealogy in *Enūma eliš*. Anu is listed as the son of Anšar and Kišar and again as the father of Ea (identified as Nudimmud in *Enūma eliš* I 12 and 16), but unlike previous and subsequent divine generations, Ea is described as the offspring of only one divine parent: "And Anu begot Nudimmud in his (own) image (u_3 ^{d}*a-num tam-ši-la-šu*$_2$ *u*$_2$*-lid* ^{d}*nu-dim*$_2$*-mud*," l. 16). By identifying Ištar-of-Arbela with Antu in SAA 3 39, the scribe undoubtedly considered the goddess to be Ea's birth mother and Marduk's grandmother despite her absence in *Enūma eliš*. Ištar-of-Arbela is Bēl's (grand)mother because she is identified with Antu in this esoteric text that paints the world in terms of Marduk, and Ištar-of-Nineveh is Marduk's nurse and nemesis Tiāmat, but nothing in this text hints at the possibility that Ištar-of-Arbela is Ištar-of-Nineveh (or that Antu is Tiāmat). Indeed, had SAA 3 39 identified these goddesses with each other, the theological complications would have produced mind-numbing consequences in light of the genealogy presented in *Enūma eliš* I. For example, the liberties that the scribe takes in interpreting the epic demand that Ištar-of-Nineveh, who is also Tiāmat, would necessarily become her own ancestor as the great-grandmother of Ištar-of-Arbela, who is also Antu. Sure, esoteric theological texts may require contradictory ideas to be reconciled when put to their logical conclusion, but this complication seems an unnecessary one given the fact that the two goddesses are portrayed as distinct everywhere else. Instead, the preferred interpretation is that *Mystical Miscellanea* simply recognizes one goddess as a mother and the other as a wet nurse.

According to Marten Stol, in ancient Mesopotamia the wet nurse was typically a woman from the lower classes or a slave who was selected to feed the child for the birth mother and who was paid with rations of barley, oil, and wool.[34] Alternatively, a wet nurse could have been the adopting mother if the birth mother was too poor to provide for her own child. There was also a class of *qadištu*-priestesses who performed this task.[35] Stol notes that Old

34 Marten Stol, *Birth in Babylonia and the Bible: its Mediterranean Setting*, Cuneiform Monographs 14 (Gröningen; Styx, 2000), 182.

35 Stol, *Birth*, 183 and 186; see also *CAD* Q, *qadištu*, and the discussion section at the end of the entry.

Babylonian texts from Mari indicate that a "wet nurse" (*tārītu*) could be described as a "mother" (*ummu*), especially if she had a close relationship with the princess for whom she worked at the royal court.[36] Even though the terms "wet nurse" and "mother" could sometimes be used interchangeably at Mari, this does not diminish the probably that the two goddesses are distinct in SAA 3 39 and SAA 9 7 (which refers to a Mullissu, not an Ištar, as the mother who is contrasted with the nurse Ištar-of-Arbela in ll. 6–11) because these terms are only interchangeable in reference to the wet nurse. One can call a wet nurse "mother" as a sign of honor, but no one would refer to the birth mother herself as a child's "wet nurse."

The two terms "mother" and "wet nurse" have been selected for use in *Assurbanipal's Hymn to the Ištars of Nineveh and Arbela* (SAA 3 3) because of their parallel meanings and the intimacy that they invoke between the king and each goddess. Moreover, these terms recognize that someone as important as a crown prince requires superhuman forces to sustain him and legitimize his royal claims.[37] However, nothing necessitates that the two roles be considered identical. Indeed, because Assurbanipal was a prince at the Assyrian royal court, he would have been reared as an infant by both his mother and a wet nurse. The fact that the king and Bēl were envisioned by the scribes responsible for SAA 3 3 and 3 9 (and SAA 9 7) as having both a divine mother and a divine wet nurse is nothing more than imagining the divine world as reflecting the king's daily reality as a child. SAA 3 3 and 39 both attest to the independent existence of Ištar-of-Nineveh and Ištar-of-Arbela. Each goddess performs a slightly different role for the infant, which is exactly the point of the hymns.

4.3 The Goddess at Nineveh

In her discussion on the roles and actions of Mesopotamian goddesses, Scurlock defines an "Ištar" in the Assyrian and Babylonian worlds as the goddess of a particular city, who usually is the daughter of the city's patron god.[38] In one sense, this definition renders the divine name "Ištar" as the virtual equivalent to our English word "goddess," and Scurlock reinforces this

---

36 Stol, *Birth*, 189.

37 Pongratz-Leisten, "When the Gods," 160.

38 JoAnn Scurlock, "Not Just Housewives: Goddesses After the Old Babylonian Period," in *In the Wake of Tikva Frymer-Kensky*, eds. Steven Holloway, JoAnn Scurlock, and Richard Beal (Piscataway: Gorgias, 2009), 68.

generic aspect of the divine name Ištar by listing several examples of Ištar goddesses and their mythological relationships: in Uruk, Ištar was the daughter of Anu; in Ḫarrān, Ištar was the daughter of Moon-God; and in Nippur, Ištar was the daughter of Enlil. Scurlock then refines her definition of "Ištar" by adding that these goddesses were "spoiled brats and extremely dangerous."[39] Using her relationship methodology, this proof-text would come from the lips of a very specific Ištar, Ištar-of-Uruk. In the hymn, the *Self-Praise of Ištar*, the goddess identifies herself as the daughter of Anu (*ma-rat*$^{!}$ ^{d}*a-*[*nim*], r. 4),[40] indicating to Scurlock that this Ištar is best understood as Ištar-of-Uruk.

According to Scurlock, each city's divine daughter is ultimately identifiable with the other divine daughters; the patrons' daughters are the representative of the mythical (the unspecified) Ištar, regardless of each one's unique set of parents. Perhaps the lay populations of Mesopotamia identified their localized Ištar goddesses with the mythical Ištar, and the filial details about their specific Ištar never got in the way should local Ištar goddesses be compared. For Scurlock, temporarily distinguishing between local Ištars is a means that leads her to a different end. The localized mythology is important, but not because it leads us to distinct localized Ištar goddesses but because this relationship-based methodology helps us determine where the various medical diagnoses were developed before they were incorporated into the Diagnostic and Prognostic Series (DPS).[41] If you can isolate the Ištar, you can isolate medical ground zeroes and know where the ancient diagnostics were.

Although Scurlock identifies Ištar-of-Uruk with Ištar-of-Ḫarrān and Ištar-of-Nippur, as well as most other localized Ištar goddesses, she maintains a marked contrast between the goddess known as Ištar-of-Nineveh and others, including Ištar-of-Arbela.[42] Medically, this distinction between the Ninevite Ištar and the others rests upon the nature of the ailment for which the deity was thought to be responsible. According to the Diagnostic and Prognostic Series, Ištar-of-Nineveh was responsible for harmless menstrual cramps, whereas the abdominal pain attributed to other Ištars was typically fatal.[43] In

39 Scurlock, "Not Just Housewives," 68.

40 Carl Frank, *Kultlieder aus der Ischtar-Tamuz-Kreis* (Leipzig: Otto Harrassowitz, 1939), 37.

41 Scurlock and Andersen, *Diagnoses*, 523.

42 Scurlock, "Not Just Housewives," 68.

43 Scurlock and Andersen, *Diagnoses*, 523. Given the evidence that Scurlock provides in *Diagnoses*, this distinction between an Ištar-of-Nineveh and other localized Ištar goddesses is actually difficult to determine. Of the diagnoses and prognoses that discuss abdominal issues and the "hand" of Ištar, none explicitly mention either the geographic name Nineveh or the Hurrian/Hittite divine name Šaušga which is commonly associated with Ištar-of-Nineveh.

One diagnosis does refer to an Ištar goddess as the daughter of Anu: "If he was wounded on his upper abdomen (epigastrium) (and) his hands and his feet are immobilized, 'hand' of

addition to this medical distinction, Scurlock isolates Ištar-of-Nineveh from other localized Ištar goddesses for both historical and theological purposes because she considers this particular Ištar to have originated from the Hurrian goddess Šaušga. According to Scurlock, Ištar-of-Nineveh is not really a native Sumerian or Semitic goddess; instead, she became an Ištar/*ištar* goddess as the result of a syncretistic identification when the Hurrian and Assyrian worlds came into contact in the middle of the second millennium. Because this Ištar really represents another goddess altogether whose Hurrian divine name was Šaušga, Ištar-of-Nineveh can (or should) be differentiated from the native Mesopotamian Ištar goddess(es), who ultimately represent (the unspecified) Ištar, despite their different mythological lineages.

Like Ištar-of-Uruk, whose father was Anu, the Ninevite Ištar was Anu's daughter. Unlike Ištar-of-Ḫarrān, whose brother was Šamaš, this Ištar was the sister of Tešub, son of Anu and head of the Hurrian world.[44] To complicate matters, although no extant text east of the Tigris or in Upper Mesopotamia explicitly labels them as consorts, this Hurrian analog of an Ištar goddess might have been the primary goddess of the official Mitanni Empire and Tešub's consort.[45] For instance, according to Schwemer, this Ištar or Šaušga goddess appeared alongside Tešub often enough in cultic settings that the nature of their relationship in Mitanni might be defined best as consort.[46]

(Ištar), daughter of Anu" (^{d}DUMU.MUNUS ^{d}*a-nim*, 19.159; Scurlock and Andersen, *Diagnoses*, 470). Following Scurlock's methodology, this "daughter of Anu" reference could potentially refer to either Ištar-of-Uruk or Ištar-of-Nineveh because the text provides no explicit prognosis for the abdominal wound it describes. However, its context on Tablet XIII of the DPS suggests that the prognosis probably was death because the surrounding diagnoses are either "death" or "no recovery" (Scurlock and Andersen, *Diagnoses*, 615–616). If so, then this diagnosis and prognosis are probably not to be associated with Ištar-of-Nineveh.

44 Ilse Wegner states that Šaušga was the sister of both Tešub and Tašmišus in Hittite-Hurrian tradition and that both were the children of Anu. In addition to being Anu's child, Tešub also appears as the son of Sîn (^{6}...]x ^{d}U DUMU ^{d}Sîn na-aš[..., *KUB* 33 89), which suggests to Wegner that Sîn could also be the father of Šaušga (Wegner, *Gestalt und Kult*, 43–44). According to Schwemer, the fact that Ištar- or Šaušga-of-Nineveh was Tešub's sister in the Hurrian myths and rituals that were recovered from the Hittite capital Ḫattuša suggests that their relationship was also viewed as one of siblings within the Hittite Empire and North Syria (Schwemer, "Storm-Gods: Part II," 4).

45 Schwemer, "Storm-Gods: Part II," 4. If the deities in the Hittite text *KBo* 4 10 were meant to be presented as two divine couples, this text may indicate that Ištar's consort was the storm-god (presumably Tešub): $^{r.\ 26}$ ... ^{d}U LUGAL *ŠA-ME-E* ^{d}UTU ^{uru}TUL$_2$-*na* GAŠAN KUR.KUR$^{ḫi.a}$ ^{uru}*ḫa-at-ti* ^{27d}LUGAL-*ma-aš* DUMU ^{d}U ^{d}IŠTAR... ("IŠKUR //King-of-Heaven, UTU.MI-of-Arinna// Lady-of-the-Land-of-the-Hittites, Šarruma//Son-of-IŠKUR (and) Ištar ...").

46 Schwemer, "Storm Gods: Part II," 5.

Whether this particular Ištar is understood as Tešub's sister or consort, Ištar- or Šaušga-of-Nineveh's relationship with Tešub markedly differentiates her from the localized Ištars of Assyria and Babylonia and from (the unspecified) Ištar. Indeed, the fact that scholars are uncertain about the full nature of her Hurrian associations and her potential Hurrian origins reminds us not only that Ištar-of-Nineveh was not the typical Mesopotamian Ištar goddess, it also reminds us how little is actually known about this goddess prior to the Middle and Neo-Assyrian periods.

According to Beckman, so little is known about this goddess's early history that the earliest extant reference to her addresses her as neither Ištar nor Šaušga; instead, this goddess was only known by her association with the city of Nineveh.[47] The Sumerian word šauša, from which the name Šaušga might have been derived, is found as an offering recipient in an Ur III inscription from Šulgi's 46th year, but the word might better be interpreted as a title for the temple's divine patron rather than a divine name (^{5}1 sila$_{4}$.niga ^{6d}ŠA.U$_{18}$(^{GIŠ}GAL).ŠA ^{7}ni.nu. a.kam; "1 lamb for Šauša-of-Nineveh," Schneider, 1932, no. 79).[48] Beckman's titular interpretation of this third-millennium text fits with Wegner's suggestion that the divine name Šaušga could be the Hurrian word meaning "the Great/Magnificent One."[49] If so, then the deity who received the lamb was simply addressed by the honorific designation Great-One-of-Nineveh, and this honor only later transformed into the divine name Šaušga-of-Nineveh. This offering recipient might have been the specific Ninevite deity later known as Šaušga, but Beckman's point is instructive: we must be careful when we try to define or identify a deity with the paucity of actual information available to us. Just because a localized Ištar goddess is closely associated with Nineveh centuries later does not mean that this text referred to her.

Moving forward from the Ur III to the Old Babylonian period, the next reference to a potentially localized Ištar-of-Nineveh actually refers further back in time to the Sargonic period. In a dedication inscription, Šamšī-Adad I boasted that he rebuilt "the Emenue-temple, which (is) in the district of the old Emašmaš-temple" (RIMA 1 A.0.39.2 i 7–9), and he claimed that this temple was previously built by Maništūšu, son of Sargon (l. 10–11), "for the goddess

47 Beckman, "Ištar of Nineveh Reconsidered," 1.
48 Beckman, "Ištar of Nineveh Reconsidered," 2.
49 Ilse Wegner, "Der Name der Ša(w)uška," in *Edith Porada Memorial Volume*, eds. D. Owen and G. Wilhelm, SCCNH 7 (Bethesda: CDL Press, 1995), 117.

Ištar in Nineveh" (^{d}INANNA *i-na ni-nu-wa-a*^{ki}, ii 10–11).[50] Whether we should interpret Šamšī-Adad's statement to mean that he credited Maništūšu for being the first king to build Ištar's temple in Nineveh is immaterial. However, we do know that Nineveh was already a leading cult center in northern Mesopotamia by the mid-third millennium, so it is reasonable to conclude that the temple existed prior to Maništūšu's reign.[51] Just as we cannot be certain that this temple to the Ninevite Ištar was a Sargonic innovation, we also cannot know if it was a Hurrian one. We only know that Nineveh's population included Hurrian people prior to Šamšī-Adad's reign, but we do not know when they arrived or how influential they were in the establishment of an Ištar temple and cult in Nineveh.[52] As Beckman rightly suggests, the temple in Nineveh and the deity that it housed in Šamšī-Adad's time were inherited from the city's earlier inhabitants, who could have been Hurrians, Akkadians, or another, unknown and earlier people.[53]

The few attestations of a localized Ištar goddess in Nineveh from the early second millennium are minimal and primarily from Akkadian sources, potentially skewing our perspective on the nature of this goddess away from a Hurrian milieu towards what we know about her from the later Middle and Neo-Assyrian periods. Moreover, these sources appear to relay conflicting information about the Ištar goddess in Nineveh. For instance, the Prologue to the Laws of Ḫammurapi refers to an Ištar in Nineveh at the Emašmaš-temple (LH iv 59–63), whereas Šamšī-Adad I's relatively contemporary building

50 The goddess Ištar is named two additional times in RIMA 1 A.0.39.2, one of which includes the name of the city: Ištar//My-Lady" (^{iii7} ^{d}INANNA *be-el-ti*) and Ištar//Lady-of-Nineveh" (^{iv21} ^{d}INANNA NIN *ni-nu-wa-a*$^{⌜ki⌝}$).

51 Reade, "Ištar Temple," 347; and Fales, *L'impero Assiro*, 37.

52 According to Michael Astour, because of the strong Sargonic presence and development in the region, a Hurrian infiltration of the area must have occurred during the empire's decline or during the Gutian period, which puts the Hurrians arrival in the region sometime between 2150 and 2050 (Michael Astour, "Semites and Hurrians in Northern Transtigris," in *General Studies and Excavations at Nuzi* 9/1, eds. D. Owen and M. Morrison, SCCNH 2 [Winona Lake: Eisenbrauns, 1987], 15–16). Reade places the Hurrian arrival ca. 2000 (Reade, "Ištar Temple," 347; see also Piotr Michalowski, "The Earliest Hurrian Toponymy: A New Sargonic Inscription," *ZA* 76 [1986]: 4–11; and Piotr Michalowski, "Memory and Deed: The Historiography of the Political Expansion of the Akkad State," in *Akkad: The First World Empire: Structure, Ideology, Traditions*, ed. M. Liverani, HANES 5 [Sargon, 1993] 81–82).

53 Beckman, "Ištar of Nineveh Reconsidered," 2. Beckman suggests that it was (the unspecified) Ištar's exalted position in the Sargonic divine hierarchy that resulted in the Ninevite goddess's association with Ištar, whoever the original goddess was (ibid., 2; see also J. J. M. Roberts, *The Earliest Semitic Pantheon: A Study of the Semitic Deities Attestedin Mesopotamia before Ur III* [Baltimore: Johns Hopkins University Press, 1972], 147).

inscription mentions a different temple, the Emunue-temple, which was said to be located in Nineveh's Emašmaš-district (RIMA A.0.39.2 i 7–8). Because the latter places Ištar's temple in the Emašmaš-district and not explicitly in an Emašmaš-temple, as a shrine might be, we should not instinctively identify Šamšī-Adad's Emunue-temple with Ḫammurapi's Emašmaš-temple.[54]

---

54 Beckman, "Ištar of Nineveh Reconsidered," 2. That a single goddess should be expected to serve as the patron deity of two temples in one city may seem problematic on first consideration, but more than one explanation could solve this problem. First, Julian Reade notes that Šamšī-Adad's Emunue-temple (or Ekituškuga-temple) was a ziggurat, separate from the Emašmaš-temple (Reade, "Ištar Temple," 383). This ziggurat might correspond to Šalmaneser I's reference to a temple and a ziggurat in RIMA A.0.77.17:6–9, which Assur-rēša-iši I also boasted about rebuilding after another earthquake hit during Assur-dān I's reign (A.0.86.1–3). Šalmaneser himself boasted of rebuilding the temple that Šamšī-Adad and Assuruballiṭ rebuilt. Despite this, Šamšī-Adad's temple legacy in Nineveh remains muddled; Assurnāṣirpal II mentioned no ziggurat in his inscriptions, Sennacherib mentioned an Ištar ziggurat only once, and Assurbanipal referred to an Ištar ziggurat by the name of Ekibiuga rather than Ekituškuga (Reade, "Ištar Temple," 384). How or if these references correspond to Šamšī-Adad's Emunue-temple is unclear.

A second possibility is that each temple served different ethnic populations in the city, and each population maintained its own cult to a local goddess. These two cults could have been confused by outsider kings such as Ḫammurapi and Šamšī-Adad, who were more interested in boasting about their building projects than about the accuracy of those boasts. As an analogous example, Beckman observes that the Ištar mentioned at Alalaḫ in level-VII texts was never associated with an Assyrian Ištar counterpart (Beckman, "Ištar of Nineveh Reconsidered," 2). This absence of information cannot in any way prove that the Ištar in Nineveh worshipped by Assyrians (including Šamšī-Adad I who explicitly refers to the deity as Ištar//Lady-of-Nineveh in RIMA 1 0.A.39.2 iv 21) is a different deity from the Ištar or Šaušga worshipped by the local Hurrian population, but it may suggest that the local populations would not have readily identified the two goddesses with each other.

Allowing for a primarily ethnic Hurrian population in the first half of the second millennium, a third explanation for reconciling these two different temples presents itself. Perhaps the subset of officially revered Hurrian deities more closely resembled the robust subset of the Hittites – who were the religious heirs of the Hurrians in many ways, borrowing their deities, myths, rituals, and other traditions – whose own subset was more expansive than any heartland Mesopotamian counterpart (see chapter 2.2 for a discussion of Hittite religious traditions). In this vein, perhaps the Hurrian population honored the localized Ištar goddess who was already established in Nineveh, whose temple had once been restored by Maništūšu, and they also honored their own equivalent, yet distinct, localized Ištar goddess in Nineveh. This possibility that a Hurrian population would simultaneously revere multiple localized Ištar goddesses in a manner similar to the Hittites is demonstrated by an "oil offering" list from Nuzi. In this list, Ištar-of-Nineveh is only of only seven Ištar goddesses, which also includes: Ištar-Ḫumella, Ištar-Akkupaweniwe, Ištar-Tupukilḫe, Ištar-Putaḫḫe, Ištar-Allaiwašwe, and Ištar//*bēlat-dūri* (Robert H. Pfeiffer and Ephriam A. Speiser, *One Hundred New Selected Nuzi Texts*, AASOR 16 [New Haven: ASOR, 1936], 35–37 and 99, nos. 46–50 [= SMN 588; 491; 690; 799; and 2153+2154]; and Karlheinz Deller, "Materialien zu den Lokalpantheons des

Whatever the relationship, or lack of the relationship, between the Ištar(s) revered at Šamšī-Adad's Emunue-temple and Ḫammurapi's Emašmaš-temple, the divine name Ištar-of-Nineveh appears in a Hurrian god list from Ugarit (ᵈINANNA *ni-na₂-a*ᵏⁱ, Ugar. V, 220–221, no. 149a), which stresses the importance of this localized goddess in Hurrian theology centuries following the Old Babylonian period. Ištar-of-Nineveh's importance to Hurrian populations is further highlighted in a letter that Tušratta, the king of Mitanni, sent to Amarna:

> ¹³Thus Šaušga-of-Nineveh//Mistress-of-all-Lands: "I wish to go to Egypt, a country that I love, and then return." Now I herewith send her, and she is on her way. ¹⁸Now, in the time, too, of my father ... went to this country, and just as earlier she dwelt there and they honored her, may my brother now honor her 10 times more than before. May my brother honor her, (then) at (his) pleasure let her go so that she may come back. ²⁶May Šaušga// Mistress-of-Heaven, protect us, my brother and me, 100,000 years, and may our mistress grant both of us great joy. And let us act as friends. ³¹Is Šauška for me alone my god(dess), and for my brother not his god(dess)? (EA 23:13–31, William Moran's translation, modified slightly)[55]

Not only did this fourteenth-century king send blessings to Egypt on behalf of Šaušga-of-Nineveh, he sent the goddess's cult statue and ended his message by encouraging the pharaoh to worship Šaušga-of-Nineveh while she was physically there. She was a very important goddess in the official Mitanni traditions, yet her geographic ties to specifically Nineveh remained vital to her identity. Tušratta might have called her just Šaušga or added an epithet so that she was Šaušga//Mistress-of-Heaven (as he does later in the letter), but when Tušratta quoted her, she spoke specifically as Šaušga-of-Nineveh//Mistress-of-all-Lands.

As mentioned in chapter 2.2, this Ninevite goddess also infiltrated the Hittite religious traditions, as Hurrian influences grew in the second half of the second millennium. This Hittite written material now provides us with most of our evidence for this period because the contemporary Assyrian material for Ištar-of-Nineveh is minimal.[56] Beckman notes that the first Middle Hittite appearance of the name Ištar was as a divine witness in an early fourteenth-

---

Königreiches Arrapḫe," *Or* NS 45 [1976], 34 n.6). If this is the case, and this list of goddesses functions similar to a typical Hittite list of goddesses, then each of these divine names represents either a distinct Ištar goddess or a goddess for whom *ištar* serves as a common noun, designating a class of Hurrian goddesses.

55 William Moran, *The Amarna Letters* (Baltimore: Johns Hopkins University Press, 1992). See also EA 21 and 24 § 8 for other occurrences of the divine name Šaušga in the Amarna Letters.

56 Beckman, "Ištar of Nineveh Reconsidered," 3.

century treaty between Arnuwanda I of Ḫatti and Ašmunikkal of Kaška (*CTH* 139 ii 10).[57] During Šuppiluliuma I's reign about twenty years later, the divine name Ištar gained headway in Hittite treaties. In his treaty with Huqqana of Hayasa, the name appears no less than five times in the divine witness list. In addition to Ištar-of-Nineveh, who is the third of the five Ištar goddesses listed, this group includes (the unspecified) Ištar, Ištar-of-the-Countryside, [Ištar]-of-Hattarina, and Ištar//Queen-of-Heaven (*CTH* 42; see Table 2.2, § 8, A i 48–59).[58] Other treaties include these Ištar divine names along with a few others, and Beckman estimates that 25 localized Ištar goddesses appear in the Boğazköy archives.[59] Notably, Ištar-of-Nineveh is never the first of the Ištar goddesses listed in these treaties (see, for example, Tables 2.9 and 2.10), which indicates her lack of primacy in the Hittite religious tradition. Ištar-of-Nineveh does figure prominently in an invocation rite of Queen Taduḫepa and elsewhere, and she is explicitly called Ištar-of-Nineveh//Queen in the Hurrian myth of *Ḫedammu* (^{d}IŠ$_{8}$-TAR ^{uru}*ne-nu-wa-aš* MUNUS.LUGAL, *CTH* 348); however, just because she was called the queen does not mean she was the most important goddess.[60] Because a mythological text like *Ḫedammu* likely reflects the interests or speculations of scholar-scribes, the competing tradition from the treaties should be preferred when determining Ištar-of-Nineveh's status in the Hittite realm.[61]

---

57 Beckman, "Ištar of Nineveh Reconsidered," 3.

58 Beckman, *Hittite Doplomatic Texts*, 29. The goddesses Ninatta and Kulitta, servant goddesses of Ištar/Šaušga, follow these five Ištars, marking the end of the Ištar section in the witness list (for discussion on these goddesses, see Wegner, *Gestalt und Kult*, 76–81). For a discussion of the god lists embedded within Hittite treaties and the nature of Ištar/*ištar* goddesses within those treaties, see chapter 2.2.

59 Beckman, "Ištar of Nineveh Reconsidered," 3. Most of these 25 Ištars did not belong to lands within the Hittite heartland, which suggests that these various localized Ištar goddesses were newly revered by the Hittites as the Hittite Empire expanded into northern Syria and Mitanni (ibid., 4 and n. 39; see also Wegner, *Gestalt und Kult*, 157–196). Other Ištar divine names appearing in Hittite treaties include: The-Proud-Ištar, Ištar//Evening-Star, and Ištar-of-Alalaḫ from Šuppiluliuma I's reign; and Ištar-of-Samuḫa and Ištar-of-Lawazantiya from Ḫattusili III's reign (see also Tables 2.3 and 2.5).

60 Beckman, "Ištar of Nineveh Reconsidered," 3 n. 31: *KUB* 36 18 (*CTH* 364, MH/NS), *KBo* 10 45 (*CTH* 446, MH/LS), and *KBo* 16 97 (*CTH* 571, MS).

61 Two treaties from the thirteenth century differ noticeably from earlier ones, and each differs in its own way. The treaty between Ḫattušili III of Ḫatti and Ulmi-Teššup of Tarḫund contains two distinct divine witness lists. The first of these EGLs (*CTH* 76; see Table 2.9, § 7, obv. 48′–49′) is considerably shorter than the latter (§ 8, obv. 50′- r. 4), invoking only six specific divine names and the thousand gods of Ḫatti as witnesses. The two Ištars in this list are Ištar-of-Šamuḫa (patron goddess of Ḫattušili III) and Ištar-of-Lawazantiya. The second EGL begins by stating that the thousand deities are in assembly to serve as witnesses for the treaty,

According to Beckman, the Ištar-of-Nineveh who was revered by the Hittites was a member of Ḫebat-of-Aleppo's circle (*kaluti*) and received offering along with these deities.[62] Her status as a member of this circle and her relatively low status in the Hittite witness lists reflect her subordinate status within the official Hittite divine hierarchy, which is in marked contrast with her superior rank within the Hurrian divine hierarchy. Further evidence of Ištar-of-Nineveh's lower status in the Hittite divine hierarchy is her lack of close associations with the royal family in Ḫattuša.[63] Although Ištar-of-Nineveh received offerings from the royal family and the queen performed cult rituals for her, it was Ištar-of-Šamuḫa who benefited from her close relationship with the Hittite royal family in the mid-thirteenth century. Indeed, in the *Apology of Ḫattušili III* (*COS* 1.77; *CTH* 81), Ištar-of-Šamuḫa visits her priestess (the future queen) Puduḫepa in her dreams and proclaims that her husband would become king and the goddess' priest.[64]

In sum, the Hittite deity worshipped as Ištar- or Šaušga-of-Nineveh was revered something along the lines of a mid-level high goddess in the official Hittite religion despite the high rank that she had achieved in the Hurrian tradition. In her transition from the Hurrian to the Hittite official religion, her

---

and it contains about four dozen divine names and several summary statements. Four of the deities specified in the first god list reappear in the second; the two who do not are the two Ištar goddesses. Technically, Ištar-of-Nineveh is the first localized Ištar goddess in the god list in which she appears, but her absence in the first list is curious. The second treaty of interest is between Tudḫaliya IV and Kurunta of Tarḫuntassa and only contains one lengthy divine witness list (*CTH* 106; see Table 2.10, § 25, iii 78–iv 15). The thousand gods are called as witnesses, including five specific Ištar divine names: Ištar-of-Šamuḫa, Ištar-of-the-Countryside, Ištar-of-Lawazantiya, Ištar-of-Nineveh, and Ištar-of-Hattarina. Here, the two localized goddesses that appeared in the abbreviated list a generation earlier, during Ḫattušili III's reign, appear before Ištar-of-Nineveh, which suggests that Ištar-of-Šamuḫa had become a more important deity than Ištar-of-Nineveh.

62 Beckman, "Ištar of Nineveh Reconsidered," 6 n. 64. Cultic activities further attest Ištar-of-Nineveh worship there throughout the year, including festivals performed by the queen, who offered apples and washed the cult statues (*KUB* 10 27 VI 1–4; *KUB* 27 16 i 9′–13′; Wegner, *Gestalt und Kult*, 127–130; Beckman, "Ištar of Nineveh Reconsidered," 6). The spring festival for Ištar- or Šaušga-of-Nineveh was celebrated in Ḫurlušša, Šappitta, Kanza-x-na, Iššanašši, Šappagurwanta, and Mallitta. In Šappagurwanta, the festival was also dedicated to Ištar-of-Babylon, and in Mallitta it was also dedicated to Ištar-of-the-Battle (Wegner, *Gestalt und Kult*, 116). Other texts or fragments discussing the worship of Ištar-of-Nineveh include: *CTH* 714–716; *KUB* 41 25; *KUB* 30 76; and *KUB* 5 10, which makes several different references to Ištar-of-Nineveh and her cult.

63 Beckman, "Ištar of Nineveh Reconsidered," 7.

64 J. G. Macqueen, "Hattian Mythology and Hittite Monarchy," *AnSt* 9 [1959], 187 n. 115. As discussed in chapter 2.2, this occurred relatively late in Hittite religious history.

associations with magic remained, but the astral and martial aspects that typically define the Assyrian version of Ištar-of-Nineveh were less important to the Hittites.[65] As Assurnāṣirpal I's eleventh-century hymn indicates, the Hurrian and Hittite associations with healing was still linked to Ištar-of-Nineveh in Assyrian sources. In *Psalm to Ishtar for Assurnasirpal I: (a) On Occasion of Illness*, the king sings praise to the goddess Who-Resides-(in)-the-Emašmaš-temple (*ana a-ši-bat* e_2*-maš-maš*, *AfO* 25 38, l. 3), whom he also identified as Lady-of-Nineveh (*be-let* ^{uru}NINA, l. 5), because he expected her to "drive out my illness, remove my debility" (l. 77, Foster's translation).[66] Although Assurnāṣirpal's hymn refers to this Ištar as the daughter of Sîn (l. 6), which corresponds to a separate Hurrian mythological tradition (e.g., *KUB* 33 89), Scurlock observes that Ištar-of-Nineveh is generally Anu's daughter in Hurrian mythology, which is another part of the reason why Scurlock dismisses different Ištar's lineages. Whatever her divine ancestry, this Ištar- or Šaušga-of-Nineveh remained a healer, even if she inflicted the disease herself: "For how long, Mistress, have you afflicted me with this interminable illness" (l. 71, Foster's translation).[67]

In the second millennium, this localized goddess's cult was not limited to northern Mesopotamia and the Hurrian, Hittite, and Assyrian populations who lived nearby. The Ninevite goddess's influence had spread to Babylon, where her Hurrian role as patron of magic also continued.[68] According to the *Religious Chronicle*, either King Nabû-šumu-libūr of Babylon or his processor referred to "the temple of Lady-of-Nineveh" ([...E_2 ^{d}GA]šan-*ni-nu*$_2$-a, A. K. Grayson, ABC 133 i 6). This reference might have only come from the final few decades of the second millennium – a full three centuries after the Mitanni king Tušratta sent her cult image to Amarna, Egypt – but it suggests that Ištar-of-Nineveh was worshipped in Babylon centuries before the Sargonid kings of Assyria conquered, destroyed, and ruled the city in the seventh century. Moreover, inscriptions from the reigns of Šalmaneser I and Tukultī-Ninurta I that were found in Ištar's temple in Assur mention the temple of Ināyītum (E_2 ^{d}*ni-nu-a-it-ti*, KAH 2 43:6–7; and E_2 ^{d}*nu-na-i-te*$^{!}$, 50:5), which George interprets as a feminized derivative of Nineveh that places the goddess in the Egišḫurankia-temple in Babylon in the thirteenth century.[69]

65 Beckman, "Ištar of Nineveh Reconsidered," 7.

66 Foster, *Before the Muses*, 330; Von Soden, "Zwei Königsgebete," 38; and Beckman, "Ištar of Nineveh Reconsidered," 7.

67 Foster, *Before the Muses*, 330.

68 Da Riva and Frahm, "Šamaš-šumu-ukīn," 171.

69 George, *Babylonian Topographical Texts*, 411.

Regardless of when her cult began in Babylon, we do know that it continued into the seventh century. As the long-established patron goddess of the city that Sennacherib made his imperial capital, it is little surprise that he would promote this cult outside of the Assyrian heartland. In fact, his son Assur-nādin-šumi reorganized the cult of Ištar-of-Nineveh in Babylon during his tenure there from 700 to 694.[70] Sennacherib also deported the cult statues from her Babylonian temple in 689 when he destroyed the city, leaving his son and successor Esarhaddon to later repatriate them to the Egišḫurankia-temple, Lady-of-Nineveh's Babylon temple (*egišḫurankia bīt* ^{d}*bēlet-ninua*^{ki}, Borger, Asarh., 84, AsBbA r. 40 f.).[71] Because we know that Assurbanipal composed and dedicated his hymn to Ištar-of-Nineveh (SAA 3 3), it comes as no surprise that his brother Šamaš-šumu-ukīn would revere a Ninevite goddess, and he did so during his time as king of Babylon.[72] As BM 77612 r 1′ indicates, Šamaš-šumu-ukīn offered a sheep to Lady-of-Nineveh (UDU.NI[TA$_2$ *pa*$^?$-*n*]*i*$^?$ ^{d}GAŠAN-⸢*ni-nu*$_2$-a⸣ x), and another inscription (*VS* 24 110) records that the *Akītu*-festival was celebrated in Babylon in the month of Nisannu involving cult statues of Marduk and Lady-of-Nineveh.[73] Finally, it should be reiterated that this Lady-of-Nineveh and her Egišḫurankia-temple were not just identified with the localized Ištar goddess who was already in Babylon. The city of Babylon had its own localized Ištar goddess Ištar-of-Babylon, whose temple was the Eturkalama-temple. In an inscription pre-dating 652, after boasting that he appointed his brother Šamaš-šumu-ukīn to rule in Babylon, Assurbanipal further boasted that he rebuilt this goddess temple: "At that time, I (re)built anew the Eturkalama-temple, the temple of Ištar-of-Babylon" (*ina u*$_4$-*me-šu*$_2$-*ma* E$_2$.TUR$_3$.KALAM.MA E$_2$ ^{d}INANNA TIN.TIR^{ki} *eš-šiš u*$_2$-*še-piš*, RIMB

70 Da Riva and Frahm, "Šamaš-šumu-ukīn," 171.

71 As George notes, the only cult statues known to have resided in Ištar-of-Nineveh's Babylonian temple are Abtagigi, Abšušu, Kaššītu, and Asakku (George, "Marduk and the Cult," 68 n. 18; see also George, *Babylonian Topographical Texts*, 325). BM 119282:6′ indicates that one of the seven Marduk statues listed belonged to Lady-of-Nineveh's Egišḫurankia-temple in Babylon (*ṣal-mu* ^{d}EN *ša*$_2$ E$_2$.GIŠ.ḪUR.AN.KI.A E$_2$ ^{d}[GAŠAN *ni-nu-a* ... *šum*$_3$-*šu*]), but the name of this statue is not extant, and no indication is given to Marduk's status there (George, "Marduk and the Cult," 66). Finally, a Neo-Babylonian reference to Ištar-of-Nineveh's temple probably appears in Tintir IV 33 (BM 77433): [*bīt* ^{d}*bēlet-n*]*i-nu*$_2$-*a* (George, *Babylonian Topographical Texts*, 224–225).

72 Da Riva and Frahm, "Šamaš-šumu-ukīn," 170.

73 Da Riva and Frahm, "Šamaš-šumu-ukīn," 173. Moreover, the Assur and Nineveh versions of the Marduk Ordeal have Lady-of-Nineveh offer Marduk milk while he is in prison (SAA 3 34:33 and 35:39).

B.6.32.4:13–14a).[74] Even though the Babylonians could have identified the localized Ištar goddess from Nineveh with their own Babylonian one in either the eleventh or seventh centuries, they made a point to distinguish the two and their respective cults.

Even though we do not know the ethnicity of the people who first worshipped her in Nineveh or when they began worshipping her, her intermediate history remains manifest in the guise of her Hurrian and Hittite past when the Assyrian king Sargon II referred to her as Šaušga//Who-Resides-(in)-Nineveh (^{d}*ša-uš-ka a*$^{!}$*-ši-bat ni-nu-wa*, Lyon 1883 9:54). Similarly, perhaps Ištar-of-Nineveh's status as a mid- or-low-level high goddess rather than the high goddesses in the Neo-Assyrian period – a role that predominately belonged to Assur's consort Mullissu until the seventh century – is a remnant of her Hittite legacy, where Ištar-of-Nineveh was a subordinate of the chief deity's consort.

4.4 The Goddess at Arbela

The pre-Neo-Assyrian history of Ištar-of-Nineveh might be sparsely documented, but we can still trace the history of this Ninevite goddess – or, at least, a Ninevite goddess – whom conquering kings eventually identified as Ištar-of-Nineveh. The goddess's prehistory began sometime in the mid-third millennium and continued through the Old Akkadian, the Ur III, the Old Babylonian and Assyrian, the Hurrian Age of the Mitanni Empire, the Middle Hittite Kingdom, and Middle Babylonian periods, and we can connect her to her Neo-Assyrian history. The same cannot be said of the goddess known as Ištar-of-Arbela, whose history is relatively brief and limited to the Middle and Neo-Assyrian periods.[75] The goddess who would be identified as Ištar-of-Arbela had surely been worshipped prior to the thirteenth century, either as (the unspecified) Ištar or as an *ištar* with her own distinct first name that has since been lost to us if it was not Arbilītu. Among the earliest attestations of a potential Ištar-of-Arbela, the epithet "Lady of Arbela" (GAŠAN ^{uru}*arba-il*$_{3}$) was uncovered at Nuzi in a fourteenth-century Babylonian ritual text.

74 Frame, RIMB 2, 203. The divine name Ištar-of-Babylon (^{d}INANNA TIN.TIR^{ki}, ll. 14 and 23) appears twice more in this inscription.

75 Dalley suggests that Ištar-of-Arbela's cult actually continued into the fourth century C.E., as evidenced by the fact that, in 355, a priest of the goddess Sharbel-of-Arbela had been martyred after his conversion to Christianity (Stephanie Dalley, *Esther's Revenge at Susa: From Sennacherib to Ahasuerus* [Oxford: Oxford University Press, 2007], 203). According to Dalley, Sharbel is a variant of Issar-Bēl, which she claims actually represents the name Assyrian-Ištar.

Unfortunately, the mix of Babylonian and Hurrian milieus makes it difficult to determine whether this epithet referred specifically to the goddess later known as Ištar-of-Arbela or any other particular Ištar or Šaušga goddess.[76] Working on the assumption that Hurrian theological influences had affected Assyrian theology, Menzel considers it reasonable to conclude that "Lady of Arbela" was a localized Ištar/Šaušga goddess who later became known as Ištar-of-Arbela.[77]

Our earliest Assyrian attestations of the localized Ištar goddess's cult from the reign of Šalmaneser I, who claimed to have built the goddess a ziggurat in the thirteenth century: "I (re)built Egašankalamma, the temple of Ištar//Lady-of-Arbela, my lady, and her ziggurat" ($^{11'}$E$_2$.GAŠAN.KALAM.MA E$_2$ ^{d}INANNA NIN ^{uru}⸢*ar*⸣-[*ba-il*$_3$$^{?}$] $^{12'}$NIN-*ia u*$_3$ *si-qur-ra-su e-pu-uš*, RIMA 1 A.0.77.16 iii 11′–12′). In addition to this temple and ziggurat in Arbela, Šalmaneser also boasted that he (re)built cult centers for Ištar//Lady-of-Talmuššu (^{d}INANNA NIN ^{uru}*tal-m*[*u-še*], l. 9′) in Talmuššu, Assur in Assur (ll. 13′–14′), and "Adad-of-Kaḫat and Adad-of-Isani, my lords" (^{d}IŠKUR *ša*$_2$ ^{uru}⸢*ka*$^{?}$⸣-*ḫat* ⸢*u*$_3$⸣ ^{d}IŠKUR *ša* ^{uru}*i-sa-ni* EN^{meš}-*ia*, ll. 15′–16′). This inscription creates a five-member EGL that reveals that he distinguished Ištar-of-Arbela from Ištar-of-Talmuššu and that he distinguished multiple Adad deities, referring to them in the plural as "my lords." About a century later, Assur-dān I dedicated a bronze statue to Ištar-of-Arbela in the city of Arbela, and he made it very clear which Ištar he honored: Ištar//Great-Lady//Who-Resides-(in)-Egašankalamma//L[ady]-of-Arbela//Lady-of-X$^{?}$ (^{1d}INANNA NIN GAL-*ti* ^{2}*a-ši-bat* E$_2$.GAŠAN.KALAM.MA *b*[*e*?-*let*?] ^{3} ^{uru}*ar-ba-il* NIN-[*x*], RIMA 1 A.0. 83. 2001:1–3).[78] Even though the cultic context regarding the Egašankalamma-temple in Arbela is clear, the king was careful to make sure Ištar-of-Arbela was the honored goddess.

Because of Arbela's strategic position at the western edge of the Zagros Mountains, Ištar-of-Arbela became increasingly important on the imperial level as the Assyrian Empire expanded.[79] The Milqia shrine that was built just outside of Arbela for the occasional *Akītu*-festival reflects this goddess's growing importance. After describing his successful mid-ninth-century cam-

---

76 Menzel, *Assyrische Tempel*, 6 and n. 19.

77 Menzel, *Assyrische Tempel*, 6 and n. 20; and Volkert Haas, "Remarks on the Hurrian Istar ››Sawuska of Nineveh in the Second Millennium B.C.," *Sumer* 35 (1979): 400 and 398 n. 35. Menzel considers this assumption reasonable because the goddesses Ninatta and Kulitta, assistants to Ištar goddesses in Hurrian and Hittite theology, have been located in the vicinity of Arbela at this time.

78 Grayson, RIMA 1, 307. Grayson follows Deller's preference for ascribing RIMA 1 A.O. 83. 2001 to Assur-dān I of the twelfth century rather than Assur-dān II of the tenth century.

79 Pongratz-Leisten, Ina Šulmi Īrub, 79.

paign against Urarṯu, Šalmaneser III mentioned that he performed the *Akītu*-festival for the Arbelite Ištar in the Milqia shrine (SAA 3 17 r. 27–30), referring to her first as Lady-of-Arbela (*be-let* ^{uru}*arba-il*$_3$, r. 28) and then Ištar (⸢^{d}INANNA⸣, r. 30).[80] Curiously, the goddess was not mentioned by name earlier in the inscription, although the epithet "Lady of Nineveh" (*be-let* ^{uru}NINA^{ki}) appears in the second line of an EGL.[81] Although "Lady of Arbela" and "Lady of Nineveh" appear in the same inscription, we cannot be certain that they were contrasted in it because each name appears in a distinct context within the inscription. Furthermore, because Šalmaneser III only invoked (the unspecified) Ištar in RIMA 3 A.0.102.2, 6, 10, and 14 (see above), it is entirely possible that the Ištar-of-Arbela goddess had not yet fully been thought of as distinct, or having splintered, from another Ištar goddess into her own divine entity. Perhaps the "Lady of Arbela" in the Babylonian ritual text and these royal inscriptions functioned as nothing more than an epithet for an Ištar goddess rather than as part of a divine full name for a localized Ištar goddess.

By the eighth-century, however, Ištar-of-Arbela was increasingly and clearly contrasted with Ištar-of-Nineveh, appearing alongside Ištar-of-Nineveh and other deities in complicated EGLs, including the divine witness list in the treaty between Assur-nērārī V and Mati'-ilu of Arpad (SAA 2 2 vi 15–16). Moreover, she was identified in writing in the inscriptions associated with the famous eighth-century Tel-Barsip relief in northern Syria.[82] Not only is this relief explicitly connected to this geographically specific Ištar, but aspects of her divine personality are very present, even if they all fit the traditional personality of (the unspecified) Ištar of mythology. As Dominique Collon notes, this Ištar-of-Arbela looked very warlike in the relief: she stands on a lion, holds its leash, and is armed with a sword, globe-tipped bow-cases, and a shield.[83]

Pongratz-Leisten notes that the seventh century is really Ištar-of-Arbela's most important century as a deity officially revered by Neo-Assyrian Empire,

---

80 Where Livingstone reads ^{u}[$^{ru?}$*mi-i*]*l*$^{?}$-*qi*$_2$-⸢a$^{?}$⸣ (SAA 3 17 r. 30), Grayson reads only x [x] x^{ki} x (RIMA 3 A.0.102.17:60), leaving out the reference to Milqia.

81 Grayson's translation fills the lacuna that begins line 2 with "[Goddess Ištar]" (RIMA 3 A.0.102.17), whereas Livingstone offers no translation (SAA 3 17).

82 Dalley, *Esther's Revenge*, 51.

83 Dominique Collon, *Catalogue of Western Asiatic Seals in the British Museum: Cylinder Seals V: Neo-Assyrian and Neo-Babylonian Periods* (British Museum Publications, 2001), 130. Collon also attributes the goddess image on various cylinder seals to Ištar-of-Arbela because of the warlike characteristics being portrayed on them; however, because no deity is actually named on those seals, their images should not be used to distinguished Ištar-of-Arbela from (the unspecified) Ištar, Ištar-of-Nineveh, or any other warrior goddess. Thus, the importance of the Tel-Barsip's explicit mention of Ištar-of-Arbela cannot be over stressed when examining this goddess's personality.

owed to her role as a warrior goddess.[84] For instance, although Arbela's location near the Zagros Mountains helps explain her elevated role against Elam and Gambulu during Assurbanipal's reign, her cult statue had already been decorated with spoils from Egypt during Esarhaddon's reign. As a warrior goddess, she was thought to play an active role in subduing or capturing the enemies, so Ištar-of-Arbela was rewarded by Esarhaddon and Assurbanipal with local celebrations of the *Akītu*-festival in her honor.[85] Moreover, her increased honors included a promotion within the divine hierarchy; she was recognized as Assur's daughter and given honorific epithets that reflected "an extraordinarily high rank," such as Lady-of-Ladies (^{d}*be-let* GAŠAN^{meš}, *BIWA* 100 B v 62) and "Honored Queen" (*šar-ra-ti ka-bit-ti*, *BIWA* 99 B v 16).[86] This localized Ištar goddess's eventual elite status is also apparent in Assurbanipal's discussions of his wars against Elam. In *Paean to Assurbanipal after the Conquest of Elam* (SAA 3 22), the king first mentions Mullissu and Lady-of-Arbela while boasting of his own power (l. 11), and then she reappears as the fifth deity in a five-member EGL that concludes the text: Assur / Bēl / Nabû / Mullissu / Lady-of-Arbela (ll. 15–17). This text does not explicitly refer to Ištar-of-Arbela as Assur's daughter, but the other four divine names in this EGL represent the Assyrian and Babylonian chief deities and their consorts, so her inclusion may be suggestive of this new role.[87]

84 Pongratz-Leisten, Ina Šulmi Īrub, 80.

85 Both Pongratz-Leisten and Annus note that the *Akītu*-festival was only "occasionally" celebrated in Arbela, likely because of the victory against Egypt and Elam (Pongratz-Leisten, Ina Šulmi Īrub, 80; and Annus, *Ninurta*, 90–91). The reason that both Esarhaddon and Assurbanipal had to rebuild the *Akītu*-shrine at Milqia was because it had fallen into disuse since Šalmaneser III's celebration there about two centuries earlier.

86 Weissert, "Royal Hunt," 347 n. 23.

87 A similar EGL, adding only Nergal, appears in *Defeat of Teumman and the Annexation of Elam* (SAA 3 31): Assur / Bēl / Nabû / Nergal / Ištar-of-[Nineveh / La]dy-of-Arbela (ll. 14–15). Elsewhere in this inscription, Ištar-of-Arbela's importance is indicated in Assurbanipal's campaigns to the East. Mullissu, who is likely identified with Ištar-of-Nineveh in this text, and Lady-of-Arbela are contrasted as indicated by use of the copula *u* (r. 9).

Ištar-of-Arbela, along with her Egašankalamma-temple, also plays an important role in the *Hymn to the City of Arbela* (SAA 3 8), which begins with praise for the city itself, but the goddess takes an increasingly present role as the hymn progresses. While the goddess is not explicitly identified as Ištar-of-Arbela in the hymn, she is first identified as (the unspecified) Ištar (l. 20), her Egašankalamma-temple (E_2.GAŠAN.KALAM.⌜MA⌝, l. 27) is mentioned by name, and the city name Arbela appears throughout the hymn – 16 times on the obverse and 5 times on the reverse.

When the goddess first appears, she is introduced as residing within the heart of the city (^{d}15 *ina* ŠA_3 *uš-bat*, SAA 3 8:20). This clause conceptually resembles the DN//Who-Resides-(in)-GN formula discussed above, but the differences are grammatically and syntactically

Renowned for her warrior qualities, Ištar-of-Arbela also acted as a divine wet-nurse for the king, as a conduit for prophecy, and as a witness in legal transactions (see Table 4.1). According to Scurlock, she also played a role in medicine. This aspect is reflected in a localized Ištar goddess's alternative divine name that survived in the DPS in two separate diagnoses. In the first, she is blamed for Strachan's Syndrome, a vitamin B deficiency, and the second associates the goddess with "shuddering."[88] Although, the name Ištar-of-Arbela does not actually appear in the Strachan's Syndrome diagnosis, despite Scurlock's translation, the specific association of this localized Ištar goddess with the diagnosis in the DPS is more secure than that of Ištar-of-Nineveh in any given diagnosis:

> [DIŠ UGU-š]*u*$_2$ ⸢GAZ.ME⸣ *ḫi-ḫi-en* KIR$_4$/KA-*šu*$_2$ *i-raš-ši-šu*$_2$ SIG$_2$ GAL$_4$.LA-*šu*$_2$ TAB-*su* ŠU-*šu*$_2$ BAR.ME-*šu* [U]GU-⸢*šu*$_2$ NU⸣ [ŠUB-*ma*] *su*$_2$-*ḫur*? *ina* GI$_8$ DIB.DIB-*su u* NUN^{meš} ŠU ***ur*$_2$-*bi-li-ti***
>
> [If the top] of ⸢his⸣ head continually feels as if split in two, the soft parts of his nose/mouth are reddish, the hair of his pubic region burns him, his hand continually hangs down limply, he does not [lay himself down] ⸢on top of⸣ (a woman), but turns away, it continually afflicts him in the night, and he continually trembles, "hand" of **Ištar-of-Arbela**. (7.17 = DPS III A 15–16 / / C 6–7, Scurlock's translation, emphasis mine)

Perhaps a better translation for *ur*$_2$-*bi-li-ti* would be more literal "the Arbelitess" rather than the more presumptive Ištar-of-Arbela. However, if this is a feminine noun that has been derived from the city name Arbela (*ur*$_2$-*bi-li-ti* = *arbilītu*) as Scurlock suggests, then it could refer to the city's eponymous goddess, who

significant. The form of the verb *wašābu* is stative rather than participial; the clause includes the preposition *ina*; and, finally, the name of the city is not mentioned. Another instance in which the hymn approximates one of the name formulas is r. 22′, which identifies the goddess as Lady-of-the-Temple-of-Arbela (^{d}GAŠAN *ša* E$_2$$^{!!}$ *ša*$_2$ ^{uru}*arba-il*$_3$). This may be described as an expanded variant of the title-of-GN formula: title-of-TN-of-GN (of course, in this text, TN represents the common noun temple rather than a specific temple name).
The goddess is also described as sitting on a lion, an animal often linked with Ištar goddesses (Zsolnay, "Function of Ištar," 48, 97, and 221–222; see also RIMA 2 A.0.101.28 and 32, which were inscribed on stone monumental lions outside the Ištar goddess Queen-of-Nipḫi's [^{d}GAŠAN KUR] temple in ninth-century Calaḫ). So, her name is not explicitly called Ištar-of-Arbela in this text, but it seems reasonable to accept that this hymn specifically praises Ištar-of-Arbela, and not another Ištar goddess.
Notably, this hymn never attempts to identify this Ištar goddess from Arbela with any goddess residing in Nineveh – neither an Ištar nor a Mullissu – but she is identified with Nanaya (^{d}*na-na-a*, ll. 20 and 22) and Irnina (^{d}*ir-ni-na*, l. 21). This text may reveal syncretistic tendencies like those found in *A Sumero-Akkadian Hymn of Nanâ* (K 3933, see Table 3.15), but it does not include the identification between Ištar-of-Nineveh and Ištar-of-Arbela.

88 Scurlock and Andersen, *Diagnoses*, 159 and 708 n. 19.

could theoretically be identified with Ištar-of-Arbela. As an alternative spelling for the divine name Arbilītu, Urbilītu could be compared to other Neo-Assyrian personal names that reference the goddess.[89] In the *Prosopography of the Neo-Assyrian Empire* (*PNA* 1/1–3/1), no less than seven personal names invoke the goddess Ištar-of-Arbela by the city name:

Ana-Arbail-dugul	=	"Look upon [Ištar-of-]Arbela"
Arbail-lāmur	=	"May I see [Ištar-of-]Arbela!"
Arbailītu-bēltūni	=	"The one from Arbela is our lady"
Arbail-ḫammat	=	"[Ištar-of-]Arbela is the mistress"
Arbail-Ilāni	=	"[Ištar-of-]Arbela is my goddess"
Arbail-Šarrat	=	"[Ištar-of-]Arbela is Queen"
Arbail-šumu-iddina	=	"[Ištar-of-]Arbela has given a name."[90]

Names like Ana-Arbail-dugul ("Look upon [Ištar-of-]Arbela") and Arbail-lāmur ("May I see [Ištar-of-]Arbela!") could refer to the city itself, but the other personal names make more sense when the theophoric element is interpreted as a reference to the goddess rather than to the city: Arbailītu-bēltūni ("The [divine] one from Arbela is our lady"), Arbail-ḫammat ("[Ištar-of-]Arbela is the mistress"), Arbail-Ilāni ("[Ištar-of-]Arbela is my god"), Arbail-Šarrat ("[Ištar-of-]Arbela is Queen"), and Arbail-šumu-iddina ("[Ištar-of-]Arbela has given a name").[91]

---

89 It is worth noting, however, that the Arbela element in the other names is typically spelled with the LIMMU$_2$/*arba*-sign and the AN/*il*$_3$-sign. None of these names uses the signs *ur*$_2$-*bi* as an indicator for *arba* in the geographic element.

90 The cuneiform and references for the seven proposed personal names in which Ištar-of-Arbela, or more properly Arbilītu, is the theophoric element (see also *PNA* 1/1 for each of the following) are:

^{f}*ana*-^{uru}*arba*-*il*$_3$-IGI.LAL	(SAAB 5 31 B b.e. 7)
$^{f.uru}$*arba*-*il*$_3$-*la*-*mur*	(ND 2325:4)
arba-*il*$_3$-*tu*$_2$-EN-*tu*$_2$-*ni*	(*Iraq* 41 56, iii 24)
^{f}*arba*-*il*$_3$-*ḫa*-*mat*	(*VS* 1 96:2, r. 3, and 5)
^{m}*arba*-*il*$_3$-DINGIR-*a*-*a*	(SAAB 9 74, iii 12)
^{f}*arba*-*il*$_3$-*šar*$_2$-*rat*	(*ADD* 207:4 and l.e. 1)
^{m}*arba*-*il*$_3$-MU-AŠ	(ND 3466b r. 2).

The fact that most of these personal names are reminiscent of the madonnine epithets presented in chapter 2.1 serves as circumstantial evidence that a goddess rather than a city is being named.

91 Alternatively, Arbilītu could be a goddess associated with the city of Arbela who was distinct from the more frequently named Ištar-of-Arbela. Because the premise of this study involves not identifying distinct divine names as representations of a single deity, such an alternative must be seriously considered. On the one hand, the possibility that a city or location could be considered a divine entity is not unreasonable; see, for example, the

The fact that Scurlock's text 7.17 is the only time an Ištar goddess is singled out as being from a specific location and is not explicitly named "Ištar" is peculiar. The unique treatment seems to indicate that this goddess had established herself as her own distinct personality, so much so that she had to be contrasted with either the generic *ištar* goddesses or (the unspecified) Ištar mentioned elsewhere in the DPS. The fact that the goddess would be rendered in the DPS and personal names as Arbilītu, a name entirely lacking the theophoric element Ištar, could suggest that this goddess was considered her own distinct divine personality. Put another way, because the DPS does not otherwise distinguish between Ištars – just as it does not attempt to distinguish between other localized major gods – a reasonable conclusion is that the scholar-scribe who compiled the DPS viewed Ištar as a singular goddess yet considered Arbilītu/Urbilītu distinct enough from that Ištar that she did not threaten (the unspecified) Ištar's unity. If so, then modern treatments of Arbilītu/Ištar-of-Arbela should be handled in much the same way that scholars treat the post-Old Akkadian goddess Anunītu and the Neo-Babylonian goddess Urkayītu as distinct from their proposed Ištar origins. In short, Ištar-of-Arbela/Arbilītu appears to be evidence of divine splintering in ancient Mesopotamia.[92]

---

mountains and rivers serving as divine witnesses in Hittite treaties (Tables 2.2, 2.7, 2.8, 2.9 and 2.10). Closer to Arbela, the Assyrian chief deity Assur likely took his name from the city of Assur, representing a divine embodiment of the city (Lambert, "The God Aššur," 83). Indeed, in many cuneiform texts, the city/empire name and the divine name are indistinguishable (despite the divine and city determinatives that are often prefixed to the word Assur), so that deciding whether the word is a reference to the city or the god is often based on context. If the male deity Assur could become a divine manifestation of a city, then it is reasonable to conclude that the female deity Arbilītu could also become a divine manifestation of the city of Arbela. Regardless of how reasonable this conclusion might be, I have not encountered any deity known simply as Arbilītu apart from personal names and the DPS. Perhaps this otherwise unknown goddess Arbilītu was worshipped by the laity who recognized her as distinct from the other localized Ištar goddess Ištar-of-Arbela; however, she was not revered within any Assyrian cult or recognized by any of the kings officials. This seems unlikely, so a better explanation is what scholars have already accepted: the divine name Arbilītu is an alternative name for the widely recognized and revered goddess, namely, Ištar-of-Arbela. Of course, the divine name Ištar-of-Arbela could indicate that *an ištar* (i.e., the generic use of the word for "goddess") from Arbela was also known by the specific divine name Arbilītu, which was derived from the city name (the parallel is not exact, but see, for example, Pongratz-Leisten's brief discussion about female deities representing ethnic entities such as Elamītu for the Elamites, Sutītu for the Sutu tribe, and Aḫlamītu for the Aramaic speaking peoples [Pongratz-Leisten, "Comments on the Translatability," 94]). Whichever direction one goes, the identification produces the same result: Arbilītu was Ištar-of-Arbela.

92 For a discussion of Anunītu as splintering off from Inanna/Ištar to become her own goddess, see Roberts, *Earliest Semitic Pantheon*, 147; for a similar discussion of Urkayītu, see Beaulieu, *Pantheon of Uruk*, 255.

Another hint that this feminized derivative of Arbela, Arbilītu, relates to a localized Ištar goddess is the nature of Strachan's Syndrome. It is not actually a venereal disease, but a few of the symptoms listed for Strachan's Syndrome in the DPS do resemble those of venereal diseases: a burning pubic region and a limp "hand," accompanied by the patient's lack of interest in sex.[93] Because of these symptomatic similarities, the syndrome aptly rests alongside actual sexually transmitted diseases in the DPS, which the ancient physicians attributed to an Ištar goddess as a goddess of sexual love.[94] The goddess Arbilītu's retention of this Ištar-associated characteristic, as well as Ištar-of-Arbela's warrior goddess aspect, recalls an analogous situation wherein Anunītu retained her Ištar-associated warrior attributes even after she was recognized as her own distinct personality.[95]

4.5 Who is Mullissu, and when is she Mullissu?

The divine name Ištar is not the only first name for a goddess who is explicitly associated with Nineveh. The divine name Mullissu is also tied with Nineveh in the curse list in Esarhaddon's Succession Treaty as Mullissu//Who-Resides-(in)-Nineveh (^{d}NIN.LIL$_2$ *a-ši-bat* ^{uru}NINA^{ki}, SAA 2 6:457, see Table 3.9; see also the proposed reconstruction in SAA 2 5 iv 1′ and Table 5.4). The name also appears in a purchase document in which Šumma-ilāni, the royal chariot driver, buys slaves (^{d}NIN.[LIL$_2$] ⸢*a*⸣-*ši-bat* ^{uru}*ni-nu-a*, SAA 6 53:14–15).[96] *Assurbanipal's Hymn to Ištar of Nineveh* (SAA 3 7) identifies Ištar-of-Nineveh as the queen of the city, but it also refers to a "Queen Mullissu," and the scribe responsible for the *Psalm in Praise of Uruk* declared, "I love Nineveh, along with Mullissu!" (AG$_2$ ^{uru}*ni-nu-a a*-⸢*di* ^{d}NIN⸣.LIL$_2$, SAA 3 9:14). Finally, *Mystical*

---

93 For example, the diagnosis for gonorrheal urethritis (*mūṣu*) is given in text 4.2:

[DIŠ N]A GIŠ$_3$-*šu*$_2$ *u*$_2$-*zaq-qa-su* U$_4$-*ma* KAŠ$_3$^{meš}-*šu*$_2$ *i-ša*$_2$-*ti-nu re-ḫu-su* ŠUB-*a* [*ni-iš*] ŠA$_3$-*šu*$_2$ *ṣa-bit-ma ana* MUNUS DU-*ka* LAL UŠ$_2$ BABBAR *gi-na-a ina* GIŠ$_3$-*šu*$_2$ (DU-*ak* NA.BI *mu-ṣa* GIG *ana* TI-*šu*$_2$)

"[If] a ⸢person⸣'s penis stings him, he lets his semen fall when he urinates, he is ⸢impotent⸣ and his going to a woman is diminished (and) pus continually flows from his penis" (*BAM* 112 i 17′–19′ // *AMT* 58/6:2–3; *BAM* 112 i 34′–36′, Scurlock's translation [Scurlock and Andersen, *Diagnoses*, 89])

94 Scurlock and Andersen, *Diagnoses*, 89 and 524.

95 Roberts, *Earliest Semitic Pantheon*, 147. Arbilītu/Ištar-of-Arbela, like Anunītu, is a warrior goddess.

96 For an explanation how the name "Ninlil" came to be pronounced "Mullissu" in the late third millennium, see Meinhold, *Ištar in Aššur*, 192.

Miscellanea (SAA 3 39:19–21) mentions a Mullissu and identifies her with Ištar-of-Nineveh/Tiāmat; however, Mullissu is only identified with the lower portions of Ištar-of-Nineveh's body in that text (KI.TA^{meš}-*ša* ^{d}NIN.LIL$_2$, l. 21). Each of these texts represents the gradual identification of Ištar-of-Nineveh with Mullissu, which began when the Assyrian capital moved to Nineveh.[97]

In *Assurbanipal's Hymn to Ištar of Nineveh* (SAA 3 7), Ištar-of-Nineveh is called by each of the divine name formulas. Using the DN//title-of-GN formula, she is "Ištar//Quee[n-of-Nineveh]" (^{d}*iš-tar šar-r*[*a-at* NINA^{ki}], l. 5); using the DN//Who-Resides-(in)-GN formula, she is Mullissu//Queen//Who-Resides-(in)-GN (^{d}NIN.LIL$_2$ *ša*[*r-r*]*a-tu*$_2$ *a-ši*$^{!}$*-bat* [*x*], l. 11; the GN is presumably Nineveh, but it could be the Emašmaš-temple); using the title-of-GN formula, she is Lady-of-Nineveh (^{d}*be-let* NINA^{ki}, l. 12). She is also called the "daughter of Nineveh" (*bi-nat* NINA^{k}[^{i}], l. 1), and although she is never explicitly referred to as Assur's consort in the hymn, the fact that she is identified as Mullissu//Queen//Who-Resides-(in)-[Nineveh] is more than suggestive of this role.

The goddess Mullissu, who was recognized as Enlil's consort in Sumer and Babylonia, made her first appearance as an Assyrian deity in a thirteenth-century Assyrian royal inscription from Šalmaneser I's reign, in which she was paired with Assur: ^{d}*aš-šur u*$_3$ ^{d}NIN.LIL$_2$ *ik-ri-bi-šu i-še-mu-u*$_2$ ("May Assur and Mullissu listen to his prayers," RIMA 1 A.0.77.1:163).[98] Meinhold notes that this pairing does not necessarily imply that Mullissu had yet been recognized as Assur's consort. Instead, she argues that Tukultī-Ninurta I was the first Assyrian king to link Mullissu and Assur as a divine couple when he proclaimed, "May Mullissu, the great wife, your (Assur's) beloved, calm you" (^{d}NIN.LIL$_2$ *ḫi-ir-tu* GAL-*tu na-ra-am-ta-ka li-ni-iḫ-ka*, *MVAG* 23/1 66 r. 29) in his *Psalm to Aššur for Tukultī-Ninurta I* (Ebeling, KAR 128+).[99] According to Meinhold, identifying Mullissu as Assur's wife was possible because Assur had been identified with Enlil; however, numerous EGLs demonstrate that Assur was not identified with Enlil throughout most of Assyrian history.[100] Assur may have been equated with Enlil during Tukultī-Ninurta's reign in the thirteenth century, but the two deities were consistently listed as distinct deities

97 Meinhold, *Ištar in Aššur*, 203.
98 Meinhold, *Ištar in Aššur*, 192.
99 Meinhold, *Ištar in Aššur*, 193.
100 For a fuller discussion on the non-identification of Assur with Enlil at Assyria, see Allen, "Aššur and Enlil," 397–409. For opinions supporting or assuming the identification of Assur with Enlil see Livingstone, "New Dimensions," 167; Menzel, *Assyrische Tempel*, 1:65 and 2:64* n. 812; George, *Babylonian Topographical Texts*, 185–186; Annus, *Ninurta*, 39; and Landsberger and Balkan, "Inschrift des assyrischen Königs," 251.

throughout the Neo-Assyrian period, as several Sargonid EGLs demonstrate (see Tables 3.6, 3.7, 3.9, 3.10, 3.11, 3.13, 3.14, 3.15, and 3.16). Interestingly, Mullissu is not consistently recognized as the Assyrian chief deity's consort during the Neo-Assyrian period, and not all of the texts that recognize Mullissu as Enlil's consort are from Babylonia, where rejecting her as Assur's consort in favor of the local Babylonian god Enlil could imply a rejection of Assyrian hegemony over Babylon. For instance, Šalmaneser III's "Black Obelisk," an inscription that was discovered at Calaḫ, provides Mullissu with an epithet addressing her as Mullissu//Spouse-of-Enlil (^{d}NIN.LIL$_2$ *ḫi-ir-ti* ^{d}BAD, RIMA 3 A.102.14:12),[101] and Assur-nērārī V's treaty with Mati'-ilu of Arpad pairs Mullissu with Enlil, leaving Assur without a consort (SAA 2 2 vi 6–7), but Mati'-ilu's treaty with Barga'yah of KYK (*KAI* 222:7–8) – if Barré's proposed restoration is accepted – recognizes Mullissu as Assur's consort without mentioning Enlil at all.[102]

Mullissu and (the unspecified) Ištar are recognized as distinct goddesses from the thirteenth century into the eighth century, but over time Mullissu resembles an Ištar-like warrior goddess, as evidenced by the "weapons of Mullissu" that are mentioned in a Middle Assyrian ceremony (^{giš}TUKUL^{meš} *ša* ^{d}NIN.LIL$_2$, *MVAG* 41/3 10 ii 15–16).[103] Only during Sennacherib's reign, however, was Mullissu first officially and undeniably equated with Ištar.[104] According to Meinhold, the divine names Mullissu and Ištar were practically synonymous during the reigns of Sennacherib, Esarhaddon, and Assurbanipal, which is why either Mullissu or Ištar could be identified as Assur's consort in the seventh century. For example, Mullissu and Ištar were interchangeable in two of Sennacherib's royal inscriptions: *i-na qi$_2$-bit* ^{d}*aš-šur* AD DINGIR^{meš} *u*$_3$ ^{d}NIN.LIL$_2$ *šar-*[*ra*]*-ti* ("by the command of Assur//Father-of-the-Gods and Mullissu//Queen," Frahm 128 T61) and *i-na qi$_2$-bit* ^{d}*aš-šur a-bu* DINGIR^{meš} *u*$_3$ ^{d}*iš-tar šar-ra-ti* ("by the command of Assur//Father-of-the-Gods and Ištar// Queen," Frahm 121 T36).[105] Similarly, either Mullissu or Ištar could appear alongside Assur and command Assurbanipal to defeat Elam, the Arabs, or Šamaš-šumu-ukīn's Arab allies in a given text: *ina qi$_2$$^{!}$-bit* AN.ŠAR$_2$ ^{d}NIN.LIL$_2$

---

101 The EGL in SAA 10 286:3–7, a text from Babylonia, pairs Mullissu with Enlil. Notably, both deities appear before Assur in this blessing EGL (see Table 3.7).

102 Barré, "First Pair," 210.

103 Meinhold, *Ištar in Aššur*, 199.

104 Meinhold, *Ištar in Aššur*, 200.

105 Meinhold, *Ištar in Aššur*, 200 n. 1190–1191; and Eckart Frahm, *Einleitung in die Sanherib-Inschriften*, AfOB 26 (Vienna: Institut fur Orientalistik, 1997), 128 T61 and 121 T36. Meinhold also cites SAA 13 32 and 36 as evidence that the divine names Mullissu and Ištar were interchangeable because both are paired with Assur in a blessing.

("by the command of Assur [and] Mullissu," *BIWA* 45 A iv 101) and *ina qi₂-bit* AN.ŠAR₂ ᵈ15 ("by the command of Assur [and] Ištar," *BIWA* 49 A v 63).[106]

A letter from Iddin-Ea, a priest of Ninurta in Calaḫ, to the king also identifies Ištar with Mullissu. In his blessing, Iddin-Ea invokes Assur, Ištar, Nabû, and Marduk (SAA 13 126:4). As Tables 3.3, 3.4, and 3.6 indicate, localized Ištar goddesses typically appear near the end of EGLs in letters, whereas Mullissu often appears after her consort Assur at the beginning. The fact that (the unspecified) Ištar has been promoted in this blessing above the Babylonian chief deities Nabû and Marduk is, in itself, evidence of an Ištar's identification with Mullissu.[107] Moreover, the fact that SAA 13 126 is from a priest in Calaḫ indicates that Mullissu's identification with Ištar had moved beyond the court religion in the capital and spread, at least, to the priestly class in nearby Calaḫ.

Just as SAA 13 126 invokes (the unspecified) Ištar, so, too, do most of the texts reflecting Ištar's identification with Mullissu. However, according to Meinhold, (the unspecified) Ištar is really the goddess Ištar-of-Nineveh.[108] She bases her claim on those instances where the first name Mullissu is paired with Ištar-of-Arbela, regardless of whether this pairing is in an EGL. For instance, Mullissu and Ištar-of-Arbela appear together twice in SAA 3 22. First, they appear together as a pair (^{d}NIN.LIL$_2$ *u*$_2$ ^{d}*be-lat* ^{uru}*arba*-[*il*$_3$], r. 11) and then at the end of a five-member EGL: Assur / Bēl / Nabû / Mullissu / Lady-of-Arbela (r. 15–16).[109] Other evidence for this identification, according to Meinhold, includes inscriptions where the first name Mullissu is associated with the city of Nineveh or the Emašmaš-temple: "August Nineveh is the beloved city of Mullissu" (NINA^{ki} URU *ṣi-i-ru na-ram* ^{d}NIN.LIL$_2$, *BIWA* 72 A x 51–52) and "Emašmaš//temple-of-Mullissu" (*e*$_2$*-maš-maš* E$_2$ ^{d}NIN.LIL$_2$, *BIWA* 268 Fuchs, IIT:30).[110]

---

106 See Meinhold, *Ištar in Aššur*, 200 n. 1196 and 201 n. 1197 for a full list of the relevant "by the command of Assur and Mullissu/Ištar" passages.

107 Ištar also appears after Assur and before Marduk/Bēl and Nabû in SAA 13 138:4; *144:5-6*; and 150:3–4, all of which are from Arbela.

108 Meinhold, *Ištar in Aššur*, 202.

109 The placement of (the unspecified) Ištar immediately after Assur in an EGL indicates she has been identified as his consort. In SAA 3 22, Mullissu appears fourth in a five-member EGL. This does not mean, however, that this Mullissu has been demoted and no longer considered Assur's consort. In the witness EGL in SAA 2 6:16–20 (see Table 3.15), Mullissu is separated from Assur by eleven deities, but she is the first goddess in the EGL, positioned like the queen of the goddesses should be. Likewise, Bēl and Nabû appear between Assur and Mullissu in SAA 3 22, but Mullissu is the first of two goddesses in the EGL, which could still be suggestive of her role as Assur's consort.

110 Meinhold, *Ištar in Aššur*, 202. Because Meinhold argues for the identification of Assur with Enlil, other types of evidence for the goddesses' identification include associating Ištar-

Despite this wealth of evidence firmly placing Mullissu in Nineveh as another name for the localized Ištar goddess who had long been associated with the city and her Emašmaš-temple, as well as the numerous inscriptions that implicitly or explicitly identify Ištar(-of-Nineveh) as Assur's consort, the identification between Mullissu and Ištar-of-Nineveh is never complete. Meinhold recognizes this and offers BM 121206 ix as evidence of the distinction between Mullissu and Ištar-of-Nineveh in the cult during Sennacherib's reign (see Table 3.11), along with other texts dating from Esarhaddon's reign to Sîn-šarra-iškun's reign.[111] In each instance, the divine name Mullissu appears alongside her consort Assur at the beginning of the EGL, while the divine name Ištar-of-Nineveh appears near the end with Ištar-of-Arbela.

This seemingly contradictory existence of Ištar-of-Nineveh who is and is not Mullissu can be easily explained, according to Meinhold.[112] By the time Sennacherib moved the Assyrian capital to Nineveh at the start of his reign, Assur's primary temple had been located in the city of Assur for over one thousand years.[113] When the Assyrian capital was moved to Calaḫ and then to Dūr-Šarrukīn in the ninth and eighth centuries, Assur's primary residence remained in Assur. Even though Sargon II did not build Assur a temple in Dūr-Šarrukīn, during Sargon's reign Assur became a primary actor in the *Akītu*-festival at Nineveh alongside the localized Ištar goddess. This provided a cultic foundation upon which Assur's cultic presence in the festival could be built up in Nineveh over the course of the seventh century.[114] Rather than relocate the king back to the city of Assur, the god Assur was brought to the king in Nineveh and provided a local temple. As the patron goddess of Nineveh, it was only natural that Ištar-of-Nineveh should be recognized as the Assyrian chief deity's consort as his divine presence there grew. At Ištar's temple in Nineveh,

---

of-Nineveh with Mullissu's consort: NINA^{ki} URU *na-ram* ^{d}*iš-tar ḫi-rat* ^{d}EN.LIL$_2$ ("Nineveh, beloved city of Ištar, the wife of Enlil," *BIWA* 64 A viii 91–92).

111 Meinhold, *Ištar in Aššur*, 203 and n. 1214.

112 Meinhold, *Ištar in Aššur*, 204.

113 John M. Russell, *Sennacherib's Palace without Rival at Nineveh* (Chicago: University of Chicago Press, 1991), 1 and 266; and Frame, "My Neighbour's God," 12. Frame notes that an Assur temple existed in northern Syria ca. 1900 and that Tukultī-Ninurta I built Assur a temple in his newly built capital city Kār-Tukultī-Ninurta in the thirteenth century; however, little is known about the latter temple's success or how long it was in service to the god.

114 Menzel, *Assyrische Tempel*, 1:120. Menzel also proposes that Assurnāṣirpal II had already built Assur a temple in Nineveh, based on her reading of *VS* 1 66 (1:1 and 120 and 2:118* n. 1639), but a newer edition of this text suggests that the AŠ-sign at the end of l. 2 should be corrected to INANNA (Grayson, RIMA 2, 384; RIMA 2 A.0.101.136:2).

Ištar-of-Nineveh was Assur's consort; however, Mullissu remained his consort at Assur's temple in Assur.[115]

Given this history and cultic development, Meinhold suggests that the identification of Mullissu with Ištar-of-Nineveh was only a localized phenomenon.[116] Most of the texts that dealt with the national deities would continue to distinguish between Mullissu as Assur's consort and Ištar-of-Nineveh.[117] This was accomplished either by an explicit epithet identifying Mullissu as Assur's consort or by placing her after him in EGLs and by simultaneously placing the divine name Ištar-of-Nineveh alongside Ištar-of-Arbela in EGLs. Other texts reflect a Ninevite divine hierarchy and refer to Ištar(-of-Nineveh) as Assur's consort.[118] Because this identification between Mullissu and Ištar-of-Nineveh was incomplete throughout the empire in the seventh century, Meinhold argues that the divine name Mullissu could exist as the first name of two distinct goddesses: one who is the wife of the Assyrian chief deity, and one who is linked with Nineveh and Ištar goddesses. This is exactly what happened in Esarhaddon's Succession Treaty (SAA 2 6), where (the unspecified) Mullissu is the second deity in the curse list and is identified as "his (Assur's) beloved wife" (^{d}NIN.LIL$_2$ *hi-ir-tu na-ram-ta-šu*$_2$, l. 417), and a Mullissu//Who-Resides-(in)-Nineveh (^{d}NIN.LIL$_2$ *a-ši-bat* ^{uru}NINA^{ki}, l. 457) appears much later in the text immediately before Ištar-of-Arbela (see Table 3.9). Elsewhere in this same treaty (ll. 19–20 and 29–30), (the unspecified) Mullissu is the first goddess in the divine witness and adjuration lists, whereas Ištar-of-Nineveh (^{d}15 *ša* ^{uru}NINA^{ki}, ll. 20 and 30) is the fourth of the five goddesses listed (see Table 3.15). By contrasting these two sets of EGLs in SAA 2 6, we can see that Ištar-of-Nineveh is a Mullissu, but Mullissu is not an Ištar goddess on the national level; rather, she is simply the consort of the chief deity (see Table 4.3).

According to Meinhold, this localized identification of an Ištar goddess with Mullissu was not limited to Nineveh. Multiple texts reveal that Ištar-of-

115 Meinhold, *Ištar in Aššur*, 204. The possibility that rival consorts for one god could survive in local traditions is reminiscent of the various local traditions that recognized Ištar as a daughter of Ea, Sîn, Anu, or another patron deity of a city.

116 Meinhold, *Ištar in Aššur*, 205.

117 Pongratz-Leisten says that the identification between Mullissu and a localized Ištar goddess was restricted to Ištar-of-Nineveh (Pongratz-Leisten, "When the Gods," 165–166).

118 Meinhold's proposal to disentangle Mullissu from Ištar-of-Nineveh in seventh-century texts according to their provenance is reminiscent of Barton's methodology (see chapter 1.1 and 1.3). Whereas Barton used the texts' provenance and the king's capital city to determine a local Ištar's characteristics and attributes, Meinhold proposes that a text's (local or imperial) scope can be determined based on its treatment of Mullissu and Ištar-of-Nineveh.

Arbela was also locally identified with Mullissu. While most of these are prophetic texts, one non-prophetic text that identifies Ištar-of-Arbela is the *Psalm in Praise of Uruk* (SAA 3 9). The psalm actually identifies both Ištar-of-Nineveh and Ištar-of-Arbela with Mullissu (ll. 14–15), but the structure indicates that the Mullissu in Nineveh is not the same goddess as the Mullissu in Arbela. In ll. 7–17, with the exception of l. 11, the scribe responsible for this psalm praises Uruk by a KI.MIN placed at the beginning of each line, and he then proclaims his love (AG_2) for a city along with (*adi*) the deity residing there. The psalm's regular structure creates an EGL with the deities arranged geographically, moving away from Uruk (see Table 4.4). In ll. 14–15, Nineveh and Arbela are both praised "along with" (*adi*) Mullissu, but no other deity is listed twice, including Assur, who himself had a significant divine presence in Nineveh by the time this psalm was composed. In the context of an EGL, this double attestation of the divine name Mullissu indicates that these two goddesses were distinct. Two (non-mutually exclusive) explanations are possible for this. Ištar-of-Nineveh and Ištar-of-Arbela have each been locally syncretized with Mullissu while retaining their individual identity, or the first name Mullissu could function as a divine title or nickname, like "Lady" (*bēlet*) or "Queen" (*šarrat*), for local Ištar goddesses in the seventh century.

If forced to choose between these two options, the first seems preferable because the divine name Mullissu-of-Arbela is not extant, whereas Lady-of-Arbela and Queen-of-Arbela are. Despite this explicit lack of the divine name Mullissu-of-Arbela, Meinhold claims that several letters in SAA 13 demonstrate the identification of the national goddess Mullissu with the local city's patron deity Ištar(-of-Arbela).[119] She admits that none of these letters explicitly identify Ištar-of-Arbela as Mullissu, but her process mimics Barton's methodology in which the text's origin can be used to determine which localized Ištar goddess is (the unspecified) Ištar in that text (see chapter 1.1). Because SAA 13 138–146 and 150–153 are all from seventh-century Arbela, which was when Mullissu's potential identification with localized Ištar goddesses occurred, Meinhold suggests that any Ištar who was closely associated with Assur in these letters can be assumed to be his consort. Of these letters, only three definitively identify (the unspecified) Ištar as Assur's consort: SAA 13 138, 144, and 150.[120] In each of these three letters, (the

119 Meinhold, *Ištar in Aššur*, 206 n. 1228. She also notes that Ištar-of-Arbela is closely associated with Assur in VAT 8005 r. 9 (Menzel, *Assyrische Tempel*, 2:T112) but that, in a line referencing the city of Arbela, Assur-Ištar (*aš-šur* ^{d}15) could be interpreted as an esoteric double name rather a consort relationship (see also Porter, "Anxiety," 235 ff.).

120 *A priori*, nothing in SAA 13 140–143, 145–146, and 151–153 indicates that Mullissu has been identified with Ištar-of-Arbela. Indeed, SAA 13 140:5–7 serves as evidence that Ištar-of-Arbela

unspecified) Ištar appears after Assur in an EGL but before Marduk and Nabû, who otherwise typically precede localized Ištar goddesses. However, while these three letters identify an Ištar with Mullissu, only in SAA 13 138 is (the unspecified) Ištar potentially Ištar-of-Arbela. In this letter, Assur-ḫamātū'a complains to the king that Nabû-ēpuš, a priest of Ea, stole a golden object off a table "that is in front of Ištar" in the temple (*ša ina* IGI ᵈ15, SAA 13 138:6–11). If this unnamed temple were specified as Ištar-of-Arbela's Egašankalamma-temple, then the identification of Mullissu with specifically Ištar-of-Arbela would be secure. However, the temple is not specified, and this Ištar, whom Assur-ḫamātū'a likely considered Assur's consort, is not specified as Ištar-of-Arbela, so while Meinhold's argument is plausible, it is circumstantial.

Elsewhere the prophetic texts demonstrate that circumstantial evidence, such as considering the letter's or the letter writer's origin as a link to the localized Ištar goddess, is not a reliable justification for the identification of Ištar-of-Arbela with Mullissu. For instance, just because a prophet who resided in Arbela invoked (the unspecified) Ištar in Arbela, that prophet did not necessarily identify the local deity with the Assyrian chief deity's consort Mullissu. Likewise, just because (the unspecified) Ištar is invoked in a text from Arbela, it does not necessarily mean that Ištar-of-Arbela was the intended referent or Assur's consort. While Meinhold may be correct that (the unspecified) Ištar in SAA 13 138 is Ištar-of-Arbela and her position in the EGL suggests she is Assur's consort in this letter, conclusions should be drawn on a case-by-case basis dependent upon a letter's internal evidence rather than applied over a corpus of texts from a particular location. Indeed, of the other letters that Meinhold offers as evidence for a local identification of Mullissu and Ištar-of-Arbela, SAA 13 139 uses the divine name Mullissu and refers to her as one who raised the king (l. 4), which may be a reference to the goddess's role as mother or wet nurse.[121] However, nothing links this Mullissu with (the unspecified) Ištar who appears with Assur in a blessing at the end of the letter. Moreover, because this Assur-Ištar pairing does not occur in an EGL, there is no reason for us to assume that the letter's author viewed the pair as having a consort relationship. As with SAA 13 141–143, 145–146, 151, and 153, Assur and Ištar could appear together as the national patron deity and the local patron deity rather than as a divine couple, a point Meinhold makes elsewhere about

had not been identified with Mullissu because it lists Ištar-of-Arbela after Ištar-of-Nineveh in the EGL, whereas we would expect the chief deity's consort to be at the beginning of a goddess list (e.g., SAA 2 6:19–20).

121 ⸢*ša*⸣ *tu*$_2$-*ra-bi-i*⸢*ni*⸣, "whom she raised," SAA 13 139:4; compare with SAA 3 3 r. 14–16; and SAA 9 1.6 iii 15′–18′ and SAA 9 7 r. 6

Assyrian-Ištar (^{d}15 *aš-šu-ri-tu*) and Assur in the centuries prior to the identification of Mullissu with any Ištar goddess.[122] A god and a goddess could be "just friends."

Ištar-of-Arbela is also mentioned in several prophetic texts, and many prophets are themselves from Arbela, but not all prophets who potentially identify Ištar-of-Arbela with Mullissu are from Arbela.[123] For example, Urkittu-šarrat, a woman from Calaḫ (SAA 9 2.4 iii 18′), began her message to Esarhaddon with two synonymous phrases, "the word of Ištar-of-Arbela, the word of Queen//Mullissu" (*a-bat* ^{d}15$^{!}$ *ša*$_2$ ^{uru}*arba-il*$_3$ *a-bat šar-ra-ti* ^{d}NIN$^{!}$.LIL$_2$, ii 30′). If the subsequent oracular statements are interpreted as quotes and not as descriptions of the prophet's own actions, then Ištar-of-Arbela was Mullissu: *a-da*$^{!}$*-gal* ("I will see," l. 31′), *as-sa-nam-me* ("I will listen carefully," l. 31′), *u*$_2$*-ḫa-a-a-ṭa*$^{!}$ ("I will investigate," l. 32′), *a-ša*$_2$*-kan* ("I will set," l. 33′), *a-da*$^{!}$*-ab-ub* ("I will speak," l. 34′), and *a-*⌜*ba*$^{!}$⌝*-an-ni* ("I will create," l. 37′). This prophecy was delivered with first person singular verbs, indicating that the prophet was speaking for only one goddess, and this one goddess was Ištar-of-Arbela, whom the prophet from Calaḫ seemed to identify with Mullissu. Another text in which the prophet seems to identify Ištar-of-Arbela with Mullissu is an oracle to the queen mother (SAA 9 5). Like SAA 9 2.4, this text begins with "the word of Ištar-of-Arbela" (*a-bat* ^{d}15 *ša*$_2$ ^{uru}*arba-il*$_3$, SAA 9 5:1). The name Mullissu appears twice in this oracle, and while the name is not definitively tied to Ištar-of-Arbela in either line, it does appear to refer to her rather than another goddess. In the first instance, the prophet reported that "Mullissu [listened] to the cry [of her young animal]" (^{d}NIN.LIL$_2$ *a-na kil-li* [*ša mu-ri-ša*$_2$ *ta-se-me*], l. 3), and in the second instance, the prophet commanded that Mullissu be glorified (^{d}NIN.LIL$_2$ ⌜*dul*$^{!}$⌝*-la* [*x x x x x x*], "Glorify [...] Mullissu [...]," r. 6). We might say that the oracle is ambiguous about this identification, but Pongratz-Leisten notes that Mullissu is not the only non-Ištar goddess who serves as a hypostasis of Ištar:

> In another oracle addressed to Esarhaddon Ištar of Arbela speaks also in the guise of Bel-Marduk and Nabû or Urkittu, the Ištar hypostasis of Uruk. In other words, when the divine word transmitted in a prophetic message is at stake, the polytheistic system manifests itself in the idea of divine unity.[124]

---

122 Meinhold, *Ištar in Aššur*, 191.

123 Prophets from Arbela who invoke Ištar-of-Arbela in their pronouncements but do not indicate either an equation with or contrast from Mullissu include Issār-lā-tašīat (SAA 9 1.1), Sinqīša-āmur (SAA 9 1.2), Bayâ (SAA 9 1.4; Bayâ claims to speak for Bēl, Ištar-of-Arbela, and Nabû in a single oracle in ll. 17′, 30′, and 38′), Aḫāt-Abīša (SAA 9 1.8), Lā-dāgil-ili (SAA 9 1.10, 2.3, and 3.4), and Tašmētu-ēreš (SAA 9 6).

124 Pongratz-Leisten, "When the Gods," 166.

Essentially, she suggests that even in an otherwise polytheistic system, a sense of monotheism might have existed in the prophetic realm. In the same way that Ištar-of-Arbela speaks through human messengers (e.g., Urkittu-šarrat in SAA 9 2.4, Bayâ in 9 1.4, and Tašmētu-ēreš in 9 6), Pongratz-Leisten argues that she can also speak through divine messengers (e.g., Marduk, Nabû, or Urkittu). If this interpretation is correct, then any evidence potentially identifying Mullissu with Ištar-of-Arbela from the prophetic realm is meaningless.

Other prophets, however, definitively distinguish Ištar-of-Arbela from Mullissu in varying degrees of explicit statements. For example, Dunnaša-āmur, a woman from Arbela, invoked both goddesses by name and used feminine-plural verbs and possessive suffixes in her *Words of Encouragement to Assurbanipal*:

> ^{1}[*ki-din*]-*nu ša*$_2$ ^{d}N[I]N.LIL$_2$ ^{2}[(*x*) *x x*] *ša* ^{d}GAŠAN ^{uru}*arba-il*$_3$ ^{3}[*ši-na-m*]*a ina* DINGIR.DINGIR *dan-na* ... ^{4}[*i-ra-'*]*a*$^{!}$*-a-ma u* AG$_2$-*ši*$^{!!}$-*na* ^{5}[*a-na*] $^{m!}$AN.ŠAR$_2$-*ba-an*-A DU$_3$-*ut* ŠU^{II}-*ši-na* ^{6}[*il-t*]*a-nap-pa-ra ša*$_2$ TI.LA-*šu*$_2$ ^{7}[*u*$_2$-*ša*$_2$-*a*]*š*$_2$-*ka-na-šu* ŠA$_3$-*bu*
>
> [Proté]gé of Mullissu, [...] of Lady-of-Arbela, [they] are the strongest among the gods; they [lo]ve and they continually send their love to Assurbanipal, the creation of their hands, they [enco]urage him about his life. (SAA 9 9:1–7)[125]

Furthermore, Dunnaša-āmur later placed a copula (*u*) between the two names in order to stress their distinction: $^{r.\ 1'}$[*x*] ^{d}[NIN].⸢LIL$_2$⸣ *u* ⸢^{d}⸣GAŠAN *arba-il*$_3$^{ki} $^{2'}$[*a-na*] ^{m}AN.ŠAR$_2$.DU$_3$.A ⸢DU$_3$⸣-*ut* ŠU^{IImeš}-⸢*ši-na* $^{3'}$⸢*lu*$^{!}$⸣-*u*$_2$-*bal-liṭ-ṭa a-na* [*d*]*a*-⸢*a*⸣-*r*[*i*] ("May [Mul]lissu and Lady-of-Arbela keep Assurbanipal, the creation of their hands, alive for[e]ve[r]," r. 1′–3′). Parpola notes that this encouragement oracle was written during the middle of Šamaš-šumu-ukīn's rebellion against the king (April 16, 650), so the kind words from these two goddesses must have been welcomed by Assurbanipal.[126] Assuming that the two goddesses in SAA 3 3 are the same two goddesses in SAA 3 7, then the Ištar-of-Nineveh in the former is the Mullissu in the latter.

A second text that distinguishes Ištar-of-Arbela from Mullissu is written by Mullissu-kabtat, a woman from Nineveh who was possibly associated with Ištar-of-Nineveh's Emašmaš-temple.[127] This report to the crown prince

125 See *CAD* Š/1, *šakānu* mng. 5a *libbu*.

126 Parpola, SAA 9, LXXI. Parpola suggests that *Assurbanipal's Hymn to the Ištars of Nineveh and Arbela* (SAA 3 3) was written in response to the words of encouragement in SAA 9 9. He also links the *Dialogue Between Aššurbanipal and Nabû* and the *Righteous Sufferer's Prayer to Nabû* (SAA 3 13 and 12) with this historical moment.

127 Parpola, SAA 9, LI.

Assurbanipal identifies Mullissu as his mother and Lady-of-Arbela as his wet nurse: “Do not fear, you whose mother is Mullissu! Do not fear, you whose wet nurse is Lady-of-Arbela” (*ša*$_2$ ^{d}NIN.LIL$_2$ AMA-*šu*$_2$*-ni la ta-pal-laḫ*$_3$ *ša*$_2$ GAŠAN *arba-il*$_3$ *ta-ri-su-ni la ta-pal-laḫ*$_3$, SAA 9 7 r. 6). As might be expected of an oracle written from Nineveh by a prophet whose name includes Mullissu as its theophoric element, this prophet twice declared that the message came from Mullissu rather than Ištar-of-Arbela (*a-bat* ^{d}NIN.LIL$_2$, “the word of Mullissu, l. 2; [^{d}NIN.L]IL$_2$ *taq-ṭi-bi*, “[Mull]issu says,” l. 12).

A final prophetic text, by an unknown prophet from an unknown city, seems to distinguish Mullissu from Ištar-of-Arbela.[128] After opening with “I am Ištar-of-[Arbela]” (*a-na-ku* ^{d}15 *ša* ^{ur}[^{u}*arba-il*$_3$], SAA 9 1.6 iii 7′), in a way reminiscent of SAA 9 7 r. 6, the goddess refers to herself as the king’s wet nurse: $^{15'}$*sa-ab-su-ub-ta-k*[*a*] $^{16'}$*ra-bi-tu a-na-ku* $^{17'}$*mu-še-ni*[*q*$^!$]*-ta-ka* $^{18'}$*de-iq-tu*$_2$ *a-na-ku* (“I am your great midwife; I am your capable wet nurse,” SAA 9 1.6 iii 15′–18′). However, unlike SAA 9 7, this text does not explicitly contrast the “wet nurse” who is Ištar-of-Arbela with the “mother” who is Mullissu because the word “mother” (*ummu*) does not appear in the text. This text does, however, twice refer to Esarhaddon as the “true heir, the son of Mullissu” (^{m}*aš-šur*-PAB-AŠ *ap-lu ke-e-nu* DUMU ^{d}NIN.LIL$_2$, SAA 9 1.6 iv 5–6; ^{m}*aš-šur*-PAB-AŠ DUMU.UŠ *k*[*e-e-nu*] DUMU ^{d}NIN.[LIL$_2$], iv 20–21). As the “son of Mullissu” who also had Ištar-of-Arbela as a wet nurse, we learn that Esarhaddon had the same relationship with Ištar-of-Nineveh and Ištar-of-Arbela as did Assurbanipal in SAA 3 3: the Mullissu who is Ištar-of-Nineveh is the king’s divine mother, and Ištar-of-Arbela is his divine wet nurse. This inscription does not explicitly identify Mullissu with Ištar-of-Nineveh, but we know that Ištar-of-Nineveh and Ištar-of-Arbela often work together as a team, so we can confidently infer that (the unspecified) Mullissu in this text is Mullissu-of-Nineveh, who is the localized Ištar goddess in Nineveh.

No extant text names a Mullissu-of-Arbela alongside an Ištar-of-Nineveh, and no text contrasts a goddess known as Assyrian-Mullissu with another localized Ištar goddess.[129] Although Mullissu and Ištar-of-Nineveh are not

---

128 The oracle mentions the Inner City (i.e., Assur), Nineveh, Calaḫ, and Arbela in its greeting. In the body of the text, the goddess promises, “[I] am your capable shield (in) Arbela” (^{uru}*arba-*⸢*il*$_3$⸣ *a-ri-it-ka de-iq-tu*$_2$ *a-*[*na-ku*], SAA 9 1.6 iv 18–19), but this follows a blessing to the Inner City (iv 15–17), so it is not necessarily indicative of Arbela as its place of origin. Because the goddess speaking throughout this text is Ištar-of-Arbela (iii 7′), the fact that she would have a special relationship with Arbela is not surprising.

129 An Assyrian-Mullissu is named in an EGL derived from one of Adad-nērārī II’s royal inscriptions (^{12}[NIN.LI]L$_2$ *aš-šur-tu*$_2$, RIMA 3 A.0.104.2). In addition to predating the period when Mullissu was identified with any localized Ištar goddesses, this Assyrian-Mullissu appears after Assyrian-Enlil in the EGL, which suggests that she was his consort, not Assur’s:

universally identified in the seventh-century, more texts identify Mullissu with Ištar-of-Nineveh than they do Ištar-of-Arbela, and they do so more explicitly, even outside of Nineveh itself. Because Nineveh was the Assyrian capital in the seventh century, its patron goddess received more attention and was closer to the interests of the empire than was Ištar-of-Arbela, despite the city of Arbela's and its patron goddess's role in Neo-Assyrian prophecy. The same was true for Assyrian-Ištar who was not identified with Mullissu despite their long coexistent history in the capital city at Assur. The fact that numerous texts – including those with EGLs, as well as literary and prophetic texts – replace Ištar-of-Nineveh with Mullissu (or Mullissu-of-Nineveh) and pair this Mullissu with Ištar-of-Arbela reinforces the distinction between these two Ištars through the seventh century. Moreover, because the divine name Mullissu- or Ištar-of-Nineveh regularly precedes Ištar-of-Arbela in EGLs and elsewhere, we see that Ištar-of-Nineveh outranked Ištar-of-Arbela regardless of what she was called.

4.6 Assyrian-Ištar

While Ištar-of-Nineveh was often identified with Mullissu in some fashion by some scribes and prophets in the final century of the Assyrian Empire, and Ištar-of-Arbela was occasionally but much less often identified with Mullissu (if at all), nothing indicates that Assyrian-Ištar (^{d}15 *aš-šu-ri-tu*) was identified with Mullissu, even though she resided near Assur in his capital for hundreds of years and would have presumably made a fitting consort.[130] The full name Assyrian-Ištar is grammatically different from the names Ištar-of-Nineveh and Ištar-of-Arbela because the word *aššurītu*, which follows the first name, is a feminine adjective rather than a city name. Rather than following the full name formula DN-of-GN or one of its alternatives, *aššurītu* is a feminized noun derived from the word Assur (comparable to the adjectival use of "Assyrian" in English). Meinhold argues that *aššurītu* is a reference to the city Assur and

Assur / Adad / Bēr / Assyrian-Enlil / Assyrian-Mullissu / Name-of-Moon-God//Who-Resides-(in)-Ḫarrān (ll. 11–12). Because Assyrian-Enlil and Assur appear as distinct deities in this and other EGLs (see Table 3.5a), this Assyrian-Mullissu should not be identified with (the unspecified) Mullissu who is Assur's consort in other (mostly later) inscriptions. Rather, like the Mullissu listed on the "Black Obelisk" (RIMA 3 A.0.102.14:12), whose epithet associates her with Enlil and not with Assur, Assyrian-Mullissu is associated with Assyrian-Enlil and not Assur.

130 Meinhold, *Ištar in Aššur*, 206–207 and 190–191.

not the Assyrian chief deity Assur because the two deities never had a close relationship.[131]

The goddess's full name first appears in the Old Assyrian period on two votive offerings from the reign of Sargon I of Assur (ca. 1920–1881) and in a treaty between the king of Apum Till-Abnû and the city of Assur.[132] The treaty, which dates to about 1750, contains an oath by which the two parties swore (*tamû*) by Assyrian-Ištar ([^{d}*eš*$_4$]-⸢*tar*$_2$⸣ *a-šu-ri-tam*, Eidem *Fs. Garelli* 195 i 11), Lady-of-Apu, Lady-of-Nineveh ([^{d}]*be*-[*l*]*a-at ni-nu-wa*, l. 13), Ninkarrak, and Išḫara. This five-member EGL plainly indicates that Assyrian-Ištar was treated as a goddess distinct from the Ninevite Ištar already in the early second millennium.[133] This distinction between Assyrian-Ištar and other Ištar goddesses continues into the Middle Assyrian period, as evidenced by offering lists from Kār-Tukultī-Ninurta. In MARV 4 95, the king made an offering to the goddess by her full name (^{d}⸢*iš*$_8$-*tar*$_2$ *aš*$_2$-*šu*⸣-*re-ti*, i 9′), contrasted her with Ištar-of-Heaven (^{d}⸢*iš*$_8$-*tar*$_2$ *ša* AN-*e*⸣, l. 10′), and then summarized the offerings "to the gods" (*a-na* DINGIR^{meš}-*ni*, l. 11′) "and the goddesses/*ištars*/Ištars" (*u*$_3$ ^{d}INANNA^{meš}, l. 12′).[134]

---

131 Meinhold, *Ištar in Aššur*, 51–52; cf. Barton, who identified Assyrian-Ištar as Assur's consort during the second millennium (Barton, "Semitic Ištar Cult," 156–158).

132 Meinhold, *Ištar in Aššur*, 52 and nn. 205–206.

133 Meinhold, *Ištar in Aššur*, 53; and Jesper Eidem, "An Old Assyrian Treaty from Tell Leilan," in *Marchands, Diplomates et Empereurs: Études sur la Civilisation Mésopotamienne Offertes à Paul Garelli*, eds. D. Charpin and F. Joannès (Paris: Éditions Recherche sur les Civilisations, 1991), 195. Meinhold discusses other texts from the Old Assyrian period that refer to Assyrian-Ištar by her full name and by her first name (Meinhold, *Ištar in Aššur*, 53). Meinhold readily equates Assyrian-Ištar with (the unspecified) Ištar from a text that has been found in or relating to the Ištar temple in Assur or the city of Assur, following a methodology first proposed by Barton (see chapter 1.1 and 1.3). The fact that Ištar-of-Nineveh is the goddess identified in Eidem, *Fs. Garelli* 195 i 13 as Lady-of-Nineveh is reinforced by a slightly earlier royal inscription from Šamšī-Adad I wherein he boasts about rebuilding the Emašmaš-temple in Nineveh and calls upon Ištar//Lady-of-Nineveh in a curse (^{d}INANNA NIN *ni-nu-wa-a*⸢^{ki}⸣, RIMA 1 A.0.39.2 iv 21).

The earliest invocation of the goddess Assyrian-Ištar by her full name in a royal inscription does not appear until Puzur-Assur III's reign in the early fifteenth century, in which the divine full name is linked with Ilu-šumma's temple (^{5}E$_2$ ^{d}INANNA ^{6}*aš-šu-ri-tim ša* DINGIR-*šum-ma* ^{7}*ru-ba-u*$_2$ *e-pu-šu*, "temple of Assyrian-Ištar, which Ilu-šumma the prince built," RIMA 1 A.0.61.2:5–7).

134 Ištar-of-Nineveh (^{d}*iš*$_8$-*tar*$_2$ *ša* ^{uru}*ni-nu-a*) is contrasted with Ištar-of-Heaven (^{d}*iš*$_8$-*tar*$_2$ *ša* AN-*e*) in an offering list from Tukultī-Ninurta's reign (MARV 3 75:1–2), in which each goddess received a male sheep as an offering. In a later section of the tablet, (the unspecified) Ištar and Šamaš each received a sheep (ll. 5–6), and (the unspecified) Ištar is mentioned again in l. 14.

Another offering text, MARV 8 56, contrasts Assyrian-Ištar (^{d}*iš*$_8$-*t*[*ar*$_2$] *aš-šu-ri-t* [*u*], ll. 2–3) with "Lady of Heaven of Kār-Tukultī-Ninurta" (GAŠAN-at AN-⸢e⸣ ša URU.kār-GIŠ.⸢TUKUL-t⸣[i-

In the first millennium, Assyrian-Ištar's role diminishes as Ištar-of-Nineveh, Ištar-of-Arbela, and Mullissu take on greater roles, but Assyrian-Ištar did regularly appear as a witness in land grants and other lower-level administration documents (see Table 3.5a, where she is the probably Assyrian-Enlil's consort and not Assur's).[135] This is partially the result of the movement of the imperial capital away from Assur and, eventually, to Nineveh.[136] Despite this shift away from the city of Assur and Assyrian-Ištar's correspondingly reduced importance, the goddess continued to play an important role in the cult at Assur.[137] The reason that Assyrian-Ištar was never identified with Mullissu is that Assyrian-Ištar was worshipped primarily in the Ištar temple at Assur whereas Mullissu was worshipped primarily in the Assur temple.[138] The fact that Assyrian-Ištar was not identified with Mullissu, even locally in Assur, is demonstrated by the ritual text BM 121206 from Sennacherib's reign. According to this text, Mullissu's statue was placed next to the Assur statue (ix 27′), whereas Assyrian-Ištar's statue was placed alongside other localized Ištar goddesses (xi 30′–31′; see Table 3.11). This distinction between Mullissu and Assyrian-Ištar is likely also maintained in the contemporary text Sennacherib's Succession Treaty (SAA 2 3:7′–10′ and r. 2′–5′). Just as Assyrian-Ištar was listed along with the other Ištar goddesses in BM 121206 ix, she also follows Ištar-of-Nineveh and Ištar-of-Arbela in SAA 2 3's two curse formulas.[139]

d.NIN.URTA], ll. 4–5). This offering list also includes Ass[ur]-of-Kār-Tukultī-Ninurta, making this a 3-member EGL. Curiously, "Lady of Heaven of Kār-Tukultī-Ninurta" is not preceded by a divine determinative, so her name seems to function more as an epithet than a divine name; however, she is undeniably treated as distinct from Assyrian-Ištar as she is from this localized Assur.

135 Meinhold, *Ištar in Aššur*, 58–59.

136 In a royal inscription from mid-eleventh-century Nineveh, Šamšī-Adad IV claims that he rebuilt the towers of Assyrian-Ištar's temple ([*bīt ištar*] *aš$_2$-šu-ri-te*, RIMA 2 A.0.91.1:4). Meinhold argues that this temple [*bīt*] should be interpreted as a shrine within the Emašmaš-temple at Nineveh, which was the temple of the goddess Ištar-of-Nineveh (Meinhold, *Ištar in Aššur*, 64).

137 Meinhold, *Ištar in Aššur*, 59–62. For a full discussion of Assyrian-Ištar, see Meinhold, *Ištar in Aššur*, 51–64.

138 Meinhold also suggests that the lack of evidence connecting Assyrian-Ištar with Mullissu resulted from the various connections Mullissu had established with the other Ištar goddesses in Nineveh and Arbela (Meinhold, *Ištar in Aššur*, 207).

139 Although Mullissu's name is not extant in either curse, assuming that she was placed after Assur, the late placement of Assyrian-Ištar in this EGL indicates that she is not to be associated with the Assyrian chief deity at all.

4.7 Two "Ištar Goddesses" Who are Not Ištar

As discussed in chapter 1.4, there is good reason to accept the distinction between an otherworldly, anthropomorphic deity and a cult statue of that deity or a celestial body associated with that deity. The cases were made that Marduk's statue Asarre was a god in its own right, Assur's Lord-Crown was a god in its own right, and the moon was distinct from the moon-god Sîn. Likewise, there were anthropomorphic goddesses that many Assyriologists recognize as goddesses in their own right. These goddesses received offerings, partook in ritual activities, and were once closely associated with (the unspecified) Ištar. In fact, some of these goddesses actually were once identified with Ištar, but the Ištar theophoric element eventually disappeared from their names. Put another way, the names by which these goddesses became known were originally epithets describing (the geographically unspecified) Ištar, and they became so important that they eventually splintered off to become the names of new goddesses.

Two Ištar-associated goddesses serve as our examples: Anunītu and Dīrītu. For those scholars who tend to minimize multiplicity in the ancient world, if a would-be divine name once served as an epithet or last name for (the geographically unspecified) Ištar, then that divine name forever remained an epithet for that Ištar, regardless of whether it was explicitly associated with the name Ištar in later periods.[140] For other scholars, however, when a divine

---

140 Much of this willingness to identify goddesses whose names lack an Ištar theophoric element, such as Nanaya, results from privileging theologically speculative texts. For example, AN : *Anum* IV from the lexical god-list tradition identifies Inanna/Ištar with the goddesses Lady-of-Eanna, Lady-of-Ešarra, Queen-of-Nippur, Queen-of-Nineveh, and Išḫara (AN : *Anum* IV 13, 15–16, 19, and 276), and *A Sumero-Akkadian Hymn of Nanâ* (K 3933) identifies Nanaya with the goddesses Ištar, Damkina, Gula, Išḫara, Anunītu, and several other goddesses (see Table 1.4). Another reason these goddesses have been identified with (the unspecified) Ištar is because the mythological Ištar has so many characteristics and aspects that can be found among other goddesses. Traditionally, (the unspecified) Ištar is said to have three primary aspects that define her character: she is a warrior goddess, she is a love goddess, and she is the celestial Venus (Jacobsen, *Treasures of Darkness*, 135–143; and Tzvi Abusch, "Ishtar," in *Dictionary of Deities and Demons in the Bible*, eds. Karel van der Toorn, Bob Becking, and Pieter W. van der Horst, 2nd rev. ed. [Leiden: Brill, 1999], 853). Her celestial aspect as Venus is unique to her, but she can also function as a mother goddess, either because of the various seventh-century texts that praise Ištar- or Mullissu-of-Nineveh and Ištar-of-Arbela as a mother and a wet nurse or because of personal names that refer to the goddess as "mother" (*ummu*), such as Ištar-ummu-alīti ("Ištar is my exalted mother") from the Old Babylonian period (Leemans, *Ishtar of Lagaba*, 34). Another reason that some goddesses are identified with (the unspecified) Ištar is because they were associated at one time or another with the name Ištar,

name seems to appear in contrast to (the geographically unspecified) Ištar, that divine name is recognized as an independent and distinct deity.

One warrior goddess who was often associated with (the geographically unspecified) Ištar and worshipped throughout Mesopotamia is Anunītu. According to J. J. M. Roberts, the compound name ^{d}INANNA-*an-nu-ni-tum* should be read as the Akkadian name Eštar-annunītum ("Eštar-the-Skirmisher").[141] The name Anunītu ("She//Who-continually-skirmishes" or "Skirmisher") began as an epithet for Ištar in the Old Akkadian period, but by Šar-kali-šarri's reign (ca. 2175–2150) Anunītu could be used independently. According to Joan Goodnick Westenholz, texts from Narām-Sîn's reign often alternate *an-nu-ni-tum* with INANNA when invoking the goddess, and more than once the two names are separated by the copula *u*: "By the judgment of Ištar and Anunītu, he defeated them in battle [and] triumphed" (^{10}*i-na di-*[*i*]*n iš*$_8$-*tar*$_2$ *u*$_3$ *an-nu-ni-ti*[*m*] ^{11}[*i-na ta*]-*ḫa-zi-tim iš*-ḪA-*ar-šu-nu-t*[*i*] *u*$_2$-[Ḫ]A-*ab-bi-ta*$^{?}$-*am*-[*ma*], A 1252:10–11), suggesting a distinction between the goddesses slightly earlier than the one for which Roberts argues.[142] Westenholz's argument is supported by Narām-Sîn-period texts (ca. 2284–2275) containing EGLs in which other divine names appear between the names Ištar and Anunītu: Ištar / [Ila]aba / Zababa / Anunītu / Šul[lat / Haniš] / Šamaš.[143]

---

in much the same way as Mullissu became associated with the name Ištar in the seventh century.

141 Roberts, *Earliest Semitic Pantheon*, 147. Roberts identifies this goddess with the city goddess of Akkad whose temple was the Eulmaš-temple. Jacobsen had previously proposed that both the name or epithet Anunītu and the name Innin were derived from the Akkadian root *'nn*, "skirmish," reflecting warrior-goddess aspects (Thorkild Jacobsen, *Toward the Image of Tammuz and other essays on Mesopotamian History and Culture*, ed. W. Moran [Cambridge: Harvard University Press, 1970], 323–324 n. 6). I. J. Gelb, on the other hand, claimed that the meaning of *anūnum* cannot be determined, but he admitted that Jacobsen's interpretation is "as good as any" (I. J. Gelb, "Compound Divine Names in the Ur III Period," in *Language, Literature, and History: Philological and Historical Studies presented to Erica Reiner*, ed. F. Rochberg-Halton [New Haven: American Oriental Society, 1987], 132).

142 Joan Goodnick Westenholz, *Legends of the Kings of Akkade: The Texts*, Mesopotamian Civilizations 7 (Winona Lake: Eisenbrauns, 1997), 189 and 234; see also Raphael Kutscher, *The Brockmon Tablets at the University of Haifa: Royal Inscriptions*, Shay series of the Zinman Institute of Archaeology (Haifa: Haifa University Press, 1989), 47.

143 Westenholz, *Legends*, 316 and 320. The *Narām-Sîn and the Enemy Hordes: The Cuthean Legend* (the Standard Babylonian Recension) includes a seven-member EGL near the beginning of the text: [Ištar / Ilaba] / Zaʾbaba / Anunītu / [Šullat / Ḫaniš / Šamaš] (ll. 12–13). This list appears again in the middle of the legend during the omen consultation that identifies these deities as great gods: Ištar / [Ila]ba / Zababa / Anunītu / Šul[lat / Ḫaniš] / Šamaš (ll. 76–77).

At the Sargonic capital Akkad, Anunītu was closely associated with another localized Ištar goddess, namely, Ulmašītu, the goddess of the Eulmaš-temple (K 13228:7′ identifies the goddess by the divine name formula Ištar//Queen-of-Eulmaš ([^{d}]*iš-tar šar-rat e*$_2$-*ul-maš*; ibid.,

By the end of the third millennium, however, Anunītu was recognized as a goddess in her own right, retaining her warrior aspect. I. J. Gelb noted that the name Anunītu first appeared with a divine determinative in the Old Babylonian period, which is consistent with our interpretation of cult statues and other cult objects receiving their own divine names and being considered divine.[144] At Mari, Anunītu's name was already attested in the Ur III period, and by the Old Babylonian period she became a prominent goddess whose own temple was named after her (E_2-Anunītim, "Anunītu's house") and who received a larger sheep offering than most other deities included in the so-called *Pantheon Tablet* from Mari (see Table 4.5).[145] Another indicator of this goddess's rise to prominence during the Old Babylonian period is the increase in the usage of her name as a theophoric element in personal names. Myers notes that near the end of the Old Babylonian period, the name Anunītu appeared in 6.1 % of personal names containing theophoric elements at Sippar, whereas it had appeared as the theophoric element in less than 1 % of the personal names prior to Ḫammurapi's reign.[146] Moreover, the city quarter of Sippar that housed her temple and its complex administrative apparatus was referred to as Sippar-Anunītu (ZIMBIR^{ki} *ša an-nu-ni-tum*, *PBS* 7 100:15) in her honor, and Tiglath-pileser I later referred to Tell ed-Dēr as Sippar-Anunītu, suggesting that the goddess still maintained a major cult in Sippar into the twelfth century.[147] The prominence gained by this goddess eventually waned in Sippar, as indicated by the fact that her divine name was the last included in offering lists from Nabopolassar's reign in the seventh century. However, even though Anunītu's name was last in these offering lists, the divine name still appeared distinct from and in contrast to (the unspecified) Ištar and

---

139). Several scholars have suggested identifying Anunītu with the Ištar at Akkad/Eulmaš (see, for example, Roberts, *Earliest Semitic Pantheon*, 147; and Kutscher, *Brockmon Tablets*, 47–48), while others note that Anunītu is distinguished from Ištar-Ulmašītu, (the unspecified) Ištar, and Ninigizibara (Myers, "Pantheon at Sippar," 98; and F. Joannès, "Les temples de Sippar et leurs trésors a l'Époque néo-Babylonienne," *RA* 86 [1992]: 172).

144 Gelb, "Compound Divine Names," 131.

145 Nakata, "Deities in the Mari Texts," 145; and George, *House Most High*, 162–163 (nos. 1283–1284).

146 Myers, "Pantheon at Sippar," 166. The divine name Ištar was used in approximately 4 % of personal names with theophoric elements before Ḫammurapi's reign and about 5.2 % afterwards.

147 Rivkah Harris, *Ancient Sippar: A Demographic Study of an Old-Babylonian City (1894–1959)*, Utigaven van net Nederlands Historisch-Archaeologisch Instituut te Istanbul 36 (Leiden: Nederlands Historisch-Archaeologisch Instituut te Istanbul, 1975), 150; and Myers, "Pantheon at Sippar," 94 and 179.

another goddess known as Queen-of-Sippar.[148] In Nebuchadnezzar's sixth-century reign, Anunītu regained some of her ancient status in offering lists, appearing as the first of the third-tier deities instead of the final deity, and she maintained this status into the Achaemenid period.[149]

According to Meinhold, Anunītu was identified with Ištar-of-Nineveh in several Assyrian texts, including the Neo-Assyrian *Götteradressbuch* (^{d}15 N[INA]^{ki} ^{d}*a-nu*$^{!}$-*n*[*i-tu*$_4$], GAB l. 94, edition B), a Neo-Assyrian prayer (K 20+:1–2), and various royal inscriptions from the Middle Assyrian period.[150] However, nothing in these texts compels the equation of Anunītu with Ištar-of-Nineveh. According to Meinhold, ll. 94–98 of the GAB likely refer to different names of the goddess Ištar-of-Nineveh, but a better interpretation is that these lines refer to the eight separate deities who were worshipped in the same temple. These deities include Ištar-of-Nineveh, Anunītu, Kubalê, Bēlet-ilī, Nīrītu, Mārat-bīti, Lady-of-Eqi, and Dumuzi.[151] Each of these divine names was associated with the goddess Ištar-of-Nineveh in some fashion, but Dumuzi's presence in this list argues against the actual identification of each divine name with Ištar-of-Nineveh because he was (the mythological) Ištar's consort in multiple mythological texts. Instead, it argues for the possibility that these lines represent a roster of the deities honored in Ištar-of-Nineveh's temple.[152] As

---

148 Myers, "Pantheon at Sippar," 266. Harris notes that Queen-of-Sippar was an epithet for Ištar during the Old Babylonian period but could also be used as an epithet for Anunītu (Harris, *Ancient Sippar*, 150 and 151; and Myers, "Pantheon at Sippar," 113–116).

149 Myers, "Pantheon at Sippar," 319–320 and 355. Beaulieu notes that after the Ur-III period, the goddess Anunītu was not mentioned locally at Uruk until the first millennium, when she was named along with [Kururnn]ītu and *Palil* in a Neo-Assyrian period letter (Beaulieu, *Pantheon of Uruk*, 311). Elsewhere, in a discussion of the goddess Innin, Beaulieu identifies Anunītu and Innin as forms of Ištar (ibid., 122).

150 Meinhold, *Ištar in Aššur*, 177; cf. Menzel, *Assyrische Tempel*, 2:T152, no. 64. See RIMA 1 A.0.77.7:7 (^{d}*ni-nu-a-it-ti*) and RIMA 1 A.0.78.17:5 (^{d}*nu-na-i-te*), where the goddess in Assur is identified by the divine name Ninua'ītu, which is a feminized derivative of the city name Nineveh and which is considered an alternative name for Ištar-of-Nineveh (compare the feminized derivative Arbilītu that is considered an alternative name for Ištar-of-Arbela). Meinhold argues that Nina'ītu is the Middle Assyrian form of the divine name Anunītu, as evidenced by the Middle Assyrian ritual text *KAR* 135+ iii 17–20 and the Neo-Assyrian ritual text no. 13 (Meinhold, *Ištar in Aššur*, 172 n. 997 and 177).

151 Menzel, *Assyrische Tempel*, 2:T152, no. 64:94–98. The names listed here are based on text B, VAT 9932.

152 "Total: 8 deities who (reside in) the temple of Ištar-of-Nineveh" (PAP 8 DINGIR^{meš} *ša*$_2$ E$_2$ ^{d}15 NINA^{ki}, GAB l. 98; Menzel, *Assyrische Tempel*, 2:T152, no. 64). See BM 121206 v 4′–11′ for a similar tally of deities included in the total (Menzel, *Assyrische Tempel*, 2:T59, no. 35; cf. Farber, review, 435).

A second Neo-Assyrian text that Meinhold offers as evidence for the identification of Ištar-of-Nineveh with Anunītu is K 20+:1–8, a prayer to Ištar-of-Nineveh that is sandwiched between ritual texts, ll. 94–98 of the GAB, as well as K 20+ and other texts, are representative of the state religion in Nineveh and the empire, but as the products of scholar-scribe for non-bureaucratic and non-legalistic purposes, there is little reason to conclude that Ištar-of-Nineveh was really identified with Anunītu during the Middle and Neo-Assyrian periods and less reason to generalize this identification beyond a small subset of Ninevite scholar-scribes.

Paul Y. Hoskisson, who agrees that Anunītu was treated as an independent and distinct goddess after the Old Akkadian period, argues that the goddess known as Dīrītu – a divine name derived from the city name Dīr/Dēr located six miles south of Mari (see Map 2) – serves as another example of a goddess who was once a local manifestation of (the unspecified) Ištar but who eventually "established her own identity distinct from other Ištar *Erscheinungsformen* [local manifestations] at Mari, and rose to prominence, perhaps even preeminence, in the pantheon of Mari."[153] By arguing for the independent and distinct existence of the goddess Dīrītu, Hoskisson rejects the idea that a goddess whose name is the feminized derivative of her patron city is nothing more than a local manifestation of (the unspecified) Ištar. Just as others argue for Anunītu's independence after the Old Akkadian period, Hoskisson bases his argument on the fact that, with one notable exception, the name Dīrītu appears without the name Ištar preceding it in the Old Babylonian period.[154] The one exception is ARM 24 263, which begins with a four-member EGL:

---

a prayer to the Sebittu and a prayer to Ištar-of-Arbela. In this brief prayer, Ištar-of-Nineveh is first called by her first name, with her last name appearing after several intermediate epithets, and then she is called Anunītu in the next line:

> 1 ^{d}*iš-tar* GAŠAN GAL-*ti a-ši-bat e*$_2$*-m*[*aš-maš ša*$_2$ *qi*$_2$*-ri*]*b* NINA^{ki}
> 2 ^{d}*a-nu-ni-tu*$_4$ *ša*$_2$ ME$_3$^{meš}-*tu* AŠ^{a}[^{t} *ṭ*]*uḫ-di u meš-re-e*
>
> Ištar//Great-Lady//Who-Resides-(in)-Em[ašmaš in] the midst of Nineveh
> Anunītu-of-Battles, who gives abundance and wealth. (K 20+:1–2)

The prayer ends by invoking the goddess using the standard full name formula DN-of-GN (^{d}*iš-tar ša*$_2$ NINA^{ki}, l. 8). The name Anunītu does appear to function as an epithet for Ištar-of-Nineveh, but Lambert warned that this is a ritual text about which we have no historical or geographic context, and he further lauded the text for its informative and unique nature (Lambert, "Ištar of Nineveh," 37–38). Although this text treats Ištar-of-Nineveh as distinct from Ištar-of-Arbela and treats both of these goddesses as distinct from the Sebittu, the prayers' unique nature could be suggestive of esoteric theological speculations that would not have been familiar to most of the local Ninevite laity (ibid., 39).

153 Paul Y. Hoskisson, "The Scission and Ascendancy of a Goddess: Dīrītum at Mari," *Go to the Land I will show you: Studies in Honor of Dwight W. Young*, eds. J. Coleson and V. Matthews (Winona Lake: Eisenbrauns, 1996), 261.

154 Hoskisson, "Scission and Ascendancy," 263.

[1] ^{d}*eš$_4$-tar$_2$* [2] ^{d}*eš$_4$-tar$_2$ di-ri-tum* [3] ^{d}*an-nu-ni-tum* [4] ^{d}*da-gan* [5]*be-el ma-tim*

Ištar, Ištar-Dīrītu, Anunītu, Dagan//Lord-of-the-Land (ARM 24 263:1–5).[155]

Hoskisson notes that Ištar-Dīrītu cannot be interpreted literally as "Ištar-of-Dīr" because Dīrītu is in the nominative case rather than the genitive.[156] Instead, he prefers the translation Ištar//the-One-of-Dīr, but translating it as Dīrītu- or Dīrian-Ištar – an analog of the feminine adjective Assurītu in the full name Assyrian-Ištar – is preferable. Even though he argues for a distinction between this goddess and the preceding (the unspecified) Ištar, the combination of the first name Ištar and the epithet Dīrītu indicates to Hoskisson that Dīrītu was once a local manifestation of Ištar.[157] However, this localized Ištar goddess quickly grew in stature, and letters from Baḫdi-Lim to Zimri-Lim that discuss the offerings she received at Mari (ARMT 10 142:25–31) indicate that Dīrītu was even worshipped outside of Dīr at Mari and Zurubbān.[158] Furthermore, Dīrītu received seven sheep in the *Pantheon Tablet* from Mari (l. 10), whereas (the unspecified) Ištar only received two sheep (l. 18), and Ištar-of-the-Palace only received one sheep (l. 4; see Table 4.5). Because the goddess Dīrītu was listed before (the unspecified) Ištar and received significantly more sheep than either other goddess in this text, Hoskisson considers the possibility that during Zimri-Lim's reign Dīrītu eclipsed (the unspecified) Ištar, who was otherwise "the most honored deity of Mari."[159]

Because Anunītu and Dīrītu are distinct divine names that lack an Ištar theophoric element, scholars more readily recognize them as distinct and independent deities and not merely another two Ištar manifestations. Historically, Anunītu and Dīrītu were closely associated with the first name Ištar and served as epithets or last names for Ištar, and both of these epithets

---

155 Because the first name Ištar appears twice in succession, the possibility that the full name Ištar-Dīrītu is in apposition with the first Ištar is unlikely.

156 Hoskisson, "Scission and Ascendancy," 262. Compare this epithet-based interpretation with Roberts's interpretation wherein the divine name ^{d}INANNA-*an-nu-ni-tum* acts as a compound name so that the first and last names both exhibit the same case ending (Roberts, *Earliest Semitic Pantheon*, 147).

157 Hoskisson notes that, given the antiquity of Ištar worship at Mari, the worship of a localized Ištar goddess is not surprising (Hoskisson, "Scission and Ascendancy," 263). No evidence exists for this localized Ištar goddess at Dīr prior to the Old Babylonian period (ibid., 262).

158 Hoskisson, "Scission and Ascendancy," 264.

159 (The unspecified) Ištar does not appear in ARM 23 264, which might reflect the needs of the cults at Terqa rather than at Mari, but Dīrītu, Ḫišamītu, and Anunītu are also mentioned in this text (Hoskisson, "Scission and Ascendancy," 266 and n. 27).

came to be used without reference to the Ištar name. Both of these divine names were separated from (the unspecified) Ištar and even contrasted with (the unspecified) Ištar by the eighteenth century, allowing more than one thousand years of Mesopotamian history and theological speculation for each of these goddesses to demonstrate her staying power within the various Mesopotamian pantheons alongside (at least one other) Ištar. Dīrītu and Anunītu are Ištar goddesses whose eventual independent existence demonstrated a multiplicity of Ištar-associated goddesses, or a form of the splintered divine from (the unspecified) Ištar.

In contrast, other Ištar goddesses who retain the first name Ištar, such as Ištar-of-Nineveh and Ištar-of-Arbela, are generally dismissed by scholars as localized versions of (the unspecified) Ištar because of their first names. The full names Ištar-of-Nineveh and Ištar-of-Arbela were used prior to the Neo-Assyrian period (e.g., Ištar-of-Nineveh in EA 23:13, ^{d}INANNA *ša* ^{uru}*ni-i-na-a*), but it was only during the Neo-Assyrian period that these two full names began appearing together regularly in Akkadian inscriptions. Moreover, while these two Neo-Assyrian goddesses often appeared in contrast with (an unspecified) Mullissu or other localized Ištar goddesses, they only appear in contrast with (an unspecified) Ištar in SAA 2 6:453–459, SAA 3 34:73A and 35:70F. Despite these differences, Ištar-of-Nineveh and Ištar-of-Arbela appear in numerous Neo-Assyrian inscriptions and are treated in much the same way as Anunītu and Dīrītu: as distinct from each other as they are from other deities. To deny that Ištar-of-Nineveh and Ištar-of-Arbela are distinct goddesses and insist that they represent two aspects or manifestations of (the unspecified) Ištar ignores or denies what was on the mind of so many Assyrian scribes, priests, and kings during the ninth through seventh centuries.

4.8 Conclusions

Ištar goddesses comprised a special class of deity in the Neo-Assyrian world, especially when examined in light of EGLs. Compared to other deities in EGLs, Ištar goddesses were the only ones who regularly shared a common first name; they were the only ones whose geographic information was truly indispensable to their identities; and, in many instances, they were the only ones whose epithets functioned as last names. (The exception to these rules is found in Assur-nērārī V's treaty with Mati'-ilu of Arpad, SAA 2 2 vi 6–20, where Adad-of-Kurbail and Hadad-of-Aleppo appear near the end of the EGL; see Table 3.10.)

It is precisely this unique treatment that the divine name Ištar received in Neo-Assyrian EGLs that guided our investigation of the different deities. Ištar-of-Nineveh invariably preceded Ištar-of-Arbela when both appear in the same EGL, and the only divine names that interrupt the Ištar-of-Nineveh/Ištar-of-Arbela sequence are other localized Ištar goddesses, which was most often Ištar-of-Kidmuri. Because these localized Ištar goddesses appear together in a regular and predictable arrangement and because they typically appear near the end of EGLs, we can confidently and securely conclude that the various formulas by which these goddesses were known refer to distinct goddesses who are relatively unimportant compared to the other high gods. Excepting only Marduk as Bēl and his consort Zarpānītu as Bēltīya, localized Ištar goddesses are also the only deities who appear in EGLs with alternative name formulas, nicknames, or epithets that lack their first name altogether. Ištar-of-Nineveh could be called Ištar-of-Nineveh, Ištar//Lady-of-Nineveh, Ištar//Who-Resides-(in)-Nineveh, or Lady/Queen-of-Nineveh, this last of which completely lacks her actual first name. Some would also argue that a feminized noun that has been derived from her city name could serve as yet another way to identify this Ištar goddess (e.g., Ninua'ītu is Ištar-of-Nineveh), but this seems more likely to occur in non-EGL settings. Similarly, Ištar-of-Arbela could be called Ištar-of-Arbela, Ištar//Lady-of-Arbela, Ištar//Who-Resides-(in)-Arbela, Lady/Queen-of-Arbela, and probably Arbilītu (or maybe Urbilītu).

Knowing that these goddesses were known by several alternative names in everyday texts, such as administrative documents, loan and purchase documents, and letters, permits us to examine several theologically speculative texts, including hymns of praise, esoteric writings, or oracles, with regard to the status and distinctiveness of these localized Ištar goddesses. Indeed, even in these more speculative texts, Ištar-of-Nineveh was treated as distinct from and contrasted with Ištar-of-Arbela. *Assurbanipal's Hymn to the Ištars of Nineveh and Arbela* (SAA 3 3), the hymn that caught Porter's attention and serves as our introduction into this phenomenon of Ištar-multiplicity is by no means the only theologically speculative text that distinguishes these goddesses from one another. This distinction also appears in several prophetic oracles (e.g., SAA 9) and in esoteric texts that were written as Assyrian propaganda in response to *Enūma eliš* (e.g., SAA 3 39).

Separately, careful examinations of the EGLs, of the different ways Ištar goddesses could be addressed, and of the attestations of the divine name Mullissu indicate that Ištar-of-Nineveh could be locally identified with Assur's consort Mullissu. Ištar-of-Arbela might have also been locally identified with Mullissu, but the divine full name Mullissu-of-Arbela has never been uncovered, whereas Mullissu-of-Nineveh has. Even if both goddesses could be identified with Mullissu in treaties, hymns, or oracles, the two were still distinct from each other in these circumstances. Indeed, they could even be distinct from the goddess Mullissu herself, indicating that in the seventh century the divine name Mullissu became, in some aspects, yet another nickname for these two Ištar goddesses, just like Lady (*bēlet*) or Queen (*šarrat*).

As indicated by texts representing several genres – from loan and purchase documents, state treaties, and letters to ritual texts and mystical texts – Ištar-of-Nineveh and Ištar-of-Arbela were two distinct goddesses. The two goddesses shared a first name, characteristics, the same relatively low status compared to other major deities, and in the seventh century, the ability to be identified as the consort of the Assyrian chief deity in their patron cities, but these goddesses were routinely conceived of as distinct and separate goddesses throughout the Neo-Assyrian world. Moreover, they were distinct and separate from other localized Ištar goddesses, such as Ištar-of-Heaven, Ištar-of-Kidmuri, and Assyrian-Ištar, as well as from Anunītu and Dīrītu. To argue otherwise ignores evidence from hundreds of texts.

5 Geographic Epithets in the West

In ancient Anatolia, the Hittites boasted that they revered more than a thousand deities, and many of these deities were closely tied to their geographic origins. Likewise, the various Mesopotamian cultures revered dozens of gods and invoked hundreds of divine names. Many of these names were not revered so much as they were remembered in the lexical god lists, but some Neo-Assyrian treaties named dozens of different divine names in their divine witness lists and curse sections. Despite the large number of divine names available to the Assyrians and the expanse of gods that these names represented, it was not unusual for inscriptions that addressed only a handful of deities to include common divine names that needed supplemental geographic last names in order to distinguish them from each other. Be it a letter to the king, a hymn of praise, legal transactions, or a prophetic oracle, Ištar-of-Nineveh was still contrasted with Ištar-of-Arbela. Furthermore, it was not unusual for an Ištar goddess to retain her geographic last name even when she was the only Ištar goddess or the only divine name on a tablet. Regardless, once a deity became identified by his or her geography, the geography became indispensable to the deity's identity.

The unique identity provided by a deity's last name seems to have also played an important role in the ancient Levant. At the Mediterranean coastal city of Ugarit (modern Ras Shamra, Syria), the subset of deities officially revered by the state comprised a much smaller number of deities than its second-millennium Hittite and Mesopotamian counterparts. Estimates range from 100 to 265 deities for the number revered at Ugarit, and smaller still were the deities revered in the Levant and neighboring areas in the first millennium.[1] Estimates place the number of the gods worshipped at Ammon,

---

1 According to Gregorio del Olmo Lete, there are approximately 240 divine names and epithets mentioned in Ugaritic texts, which compares well with Dennis Pardee's more recent count of 234 different deities in offering texts, although Johannes C. de Moor's previous count was slightly higher at 265 (Gregorio del Olmo Lete, *Canaanite Religion: According to the Liturgical Texts of Ugarit*, trans. Wilfred G. E. Watson, 2nd rev. ed. [Bethesda: CDL Press, 1999], 78; Dennis Pardee, *Ritual and Cult at Ugarit*, ed. T. J. Lewis, SBLWAW 10 [Atlanta: Society of Biblical Literature, 2002], 222; and Johannes C. de Moor, "The Semitic Pantheon of Ugarit," *UF* 2 [1970]: 216). Despite these estimates in the mid-200s, there are two primary reasons that each scholar assumes that the size of the Ugaritic subset of officially revered deities was significantly smaller. On the one hand, many of these divine names would have been supposedly identified with each other in official Ugaritic religion, and, on the other hand, most divine names only appeared once, so they probably had no actual cultic presence in the city.

Moab, Edom, and the Phoenician city-states at ten or fewer.[2] Yet, even within these small subsets, a few distinct deities shared the first name Baal, so it was necessary to include geographic epithets as last names in offering lists, state treaties, letters, and other inscriptions.

This divine name Baal – or title or nickname as the case may be – is attested throughout the ancient Near East from the third-millennium cuneiform inscriptions found at Ebla to Aramaic texts found at Ḥatra that date to the early centuries of the Common Era. Most of the texts of interest represent a variety of Ugaritic, Phoenician, Punic, Aramaic, and Hebrew, as well as Neo-Assyrian texts. This collection of texts includes royal inscriptions, dedicatory building inscriptions, votive inscriptions, treaties, and biblical narratives, but all of these texts mention at least one Baal deity with a geographic last name. Furthermore, some texts mention multiple Baal deities with distinct last names that represent distinct and separate deities in the EGLs. Those texts that include different Baal divine names are not as numerous as those Akkadian texts that include multiple Ištar divine names (chapters 3 and 4) or Hittite texts that mention the various IŠKUR gods or LAMMA deities (chapter 2.2), but they are examined here in order to show how geographic epithets are used to distinguish deities who were revered by peoples speaking Northwest Semitic languages. Not only does this provide a fuller history for Baal deities, but this survey also provides a regional context for examining the geographic epithets attributed to the Israelite deity Yahweh in the following chapter. Notably, a few of these Baal deities retained their last name in texts that mention no other Baal-named deities, indicating that their last names were as essential to their identity as first names were to most other gods. In many respects, this is reminiscent of the Neo-Assyrian treatments of Ištar-of-Nineveh and Ištar-of-Arbela; the divine names Baal-of-Ṣapun, Baal-Šamêm, and Baal-Ḥamān each appear in EGLs with other Baal-named deities, but each full name also appears when it represents the only male deity in a text.

Before continuing, an explanation should be provided for the nomenclature of these various Baal deities and the other deities whose last names are

---

2 Smith notes that the evidence for these first-millennium states is relatively limited (Mark S. Smith, *The Early History of God: Yahweh and the Other Deities in Ancient Israel*, 2nd ed. [Grand Rapids: Eerdmans, 2002], 60–64). For example, scholars are uncertain whether the Ammonite deity Milkom was identified with El (ibid., 60), and they are unsure of how the divine name Aštar-Chemosh that appears once in the Mesha Inscription (*KAI* 181:17) relates to the Moabite dynastic deity Chemosh (ibid., 60–61). However, even if these names are interpreted as representing distinct deities, each local subset of deities is still significantly smaller than the Hittite, Assyrian, and Ugaritic subsets.

essential to their identification. Grammatically, the Semitic names represented by, for example, Baal-of-Ugarit and Baal-Ṣidon are identical. In the original languages, each full name consisted of two nouns that belong to a construct chain; the first noun is the divine name, which is grammatically a noun whose case is dependent upon its role in the sentence, and the second noun is the geographic last name, which is grammatically a genitival noun.[3] In the Ugaritic material, scholars conventionally translate these construct chains according to the formula DN-of-GN (e.g., Baal-of-Ugarit), whereas the construct chains in Aramaic, Phoenician, Punic, and other texts from the first millennium are conventionally translated as DN-GN (e.g., Baal-Ṣidon). We will follow the conventional practices here except in the case of the divine names Baal-of-Ṣapun and Baal-of-Aleppo. Because these names appear in both Ugaritic and first-millennium Northwest Semitic texts, we retain the conventional Ugaritic translation DN-of-GN throughout the chapter.

This chapter concludes with a survey of Northwest Semitic goddesses whose geographic epithets resemble those epithets associated with Baal divine names. Unlike most of the other epithets in this chapter that follow the DN-of-GN/DN-GN construct-chain pattern, some of these proposed epithets use the *bet*-locative preposition to address the deity's relationship with the named topographical location (i.e., DN-in-GN). Compared with the DN-of-GN/DN-GN usage, the proposed DN-in-GN epithets do not function in the same way. The DN-in-GN pattern never appears in EGLs nor contrasts two deities with the same first name.

5.1 The Baal Deities of Ugarit

One unavoidable consequence of surveying what Dennis Pardee has described as Ugarit's "prescriptive sacrificial ritual" texts is encountering a multiplicity of entities who share a divine first name, either Adad/Hadad or Baal.[4] Indeed, if the so-called *Deity List* or "Canonical List" (e.g., *KTU*^{2} 1.47, 1.118, and 1.148:1–9) represents the same sacrificial rites as the Akkadian text RS 20.024, then we see that the name Adad/Hadad was interchangeable with Baal, and we learn that there were at least seven divine entities at Ugarit associated with the name

3 For a discussion of the construct chain in biblical Hebrew, see Bruce Waltke and M. O'Connor, *An Introduction to Biblical Hebrew Syntax* (Winona Lake: Eisenbrauns, 1990), 137–154.

4 Pardee, *Ritual and Cult*, v.

Baal.[5] Of the Ugaritic texts, *KTU*^{2} 1.118 best preserves this Baal multiplicity because it presents Baal-of-Ṣapun and a series of six Baaluma ("Baals"$^{?}$) entries, and the cuneiform text RS 20.024 explicitly marks the distinctiveness of these storm-gods with a numerical count, which are indicated by Roman numerals in the chart:

***KTU*^{2} 1.118**[6]	**Translation**[7]	**RS 20.024**	**Translation**[8]
1 *'il'ib*	God-of-the-Father	1 DINGIR-*a-bi*	God-of-the-Father
2 *'il*	El	2 DINGIR^{lum}	El
3 *dgn*	Dagan	3 ^{d}*da-gan*	Dagan
4 *b'l ṣpn*	Baal-of-Ṣapun	4 ^{d}IŠKUR *be-el* ḪUR.SAG.*ḫa-zi*	Storm-god//Lord-of-Ṣapun
5 *b'lm*	Baaluma	5 ^{d}IŠKUR II	second storm-god
6 *b'lm*	Baaluma	6 ^{d}IŠKUR III	third storm-god
7 *b'lm*	Baaluma	7 ^{d}IŠKUR IV	fourth storm-god
8 *b'lm*	Baaluma	8 ^{d}IŠKUR V	fifth storm-god
9 *b'lm*	Baaluma	9 ^{d}IŠKUR VI	sixth storm-god
10 *b'lm*	Baaluma	10 ^{d}IŠKUR VII	seventh storm-god
11 *'arṣ w šmm*	Earth-and-Heaven	11 ^{d}IDIM u_3 IDIM.	Mountains-and-the-Abyss

These texts make clear that more than one Baal deity was revered at Ugarit, but they still allow for a large range of interpretative possibilities. The most complicating matter is the *mem*-suffix added to the six entries in KTU^2 1.118:5–10, *b'lm* (Ba'luma or Baaluma). Jonannes C. de Moor suggests that these suffixes are markers of intensity rather than pluralities, with each Baaluma entry highlighting the importance of Baal-of-Ṣapun in l. 4.[9] According to de Moor, priests recognized that there were localized Baal deities, such as Baal-of-Ugarit, Baal-of-Aleppo, and Baal-of-the-field, but they preferred not to

5 Pardee, *Ritual and Cult*, 13.
6 *KTU*^{2} 1.118 begins with a list of the high gods (ll. 1–4) and six b'*lm* (ll. 5–10). One parallel text, *KTU*^{2} 1.47, prefaces its list with the title, "The gods of Mount Ṣapun" (*'il ṣpn*, l. 1). The other, *KTU*^{2} 1.148, designates itself an offering list, "The sacrifices of Mount Ṣapun" (*dbḥ ṣp*n, l. 1).
7 The translations in this table are based on Pardee's translation, modified slightly (Pardee, *Ritual and Cult*, 15).
8 Two parallel lines (//) are used here and elsewhere to indicate that a proper name and epithet are acting together with the force of a full name (e.g., Hadad//Lord-of-Ṣapun, Astarte//Name-of-Baal, Tannit//Face-of-Baal, and Ištar//Lady-of-Nineveh). See chapter 4.1 for a full treatment of divine full name formulas.
9 De Moor, "Semitic Pantheon," 219.

explicitly name them because these deities "were nothing more than some of the manifold manifestations of one god: *b'l ṣpn*, the *b'l* par excellence."[10] For de Moor this intentional sevenfold repetition of the divine name Baal emphasizes Baal-of-Ṣapun as the only Baal, and the point of the Baaluma in ll. 5–10 was to diminish the individuality of localized Baal deities. Pardee takes a noncommittal stance to the Baaluma, translating each entry as "*Ba'luma* (another manifestation of *Ba'lu*)."[11] He considers the possibility that one of these Baaluma entries could represent the famous Baal-of-Aleppo, who appears in an EGL in another canonical list, *KTU*[2] 1.148:26, but he neither offers identifications for the other five Baaluma, nor does he explain what he means when he refers to Baal-of-Aleppo or these other Baaluma as manifestations of (the unspecified) Baal.[12] Referring to a divine name as a manifestation of a deity usually suggests that it is a localized hypostasis of the deity rather than a separate and distinct deity in its own right, but a reader could be tempted to read more into the term.

The interpretation of KTU[2] 1.118 that Gregorio del Olmo Lete offers is appealing, but it does not solve the meaning behind the *mem*-suffixes in ll. 5–10, nor does it adequately explain the lack of epithets for the Baaluma.[13] He suggests that the Baaluma entries are references to cult statues of Baal-of-Ṣapun located in the city, an idea that recalls BM 119282 and the seven different Bēl cult images situated in different temples (see chapter 1.4).[14] In that inscription, each Bēl statue was given its own unique name, whereas each Baaluma entry in KTU[2] 1.118 would be strangely identical in name albeit distinct from the statue known as Baal-of-Ṣapun.[15] As a sacrificial ritual text,

---

10 De Moor, "Semitic Pantheon," 219.

11 Pardee, *Ritual and Cult*, 15.

12 Pardee, *Ritual and Cult*, 24 n. 10; see also Mark S. Smith, "The Problem of the God and His Manifestations: The Case of the Baals at Ugarit, with Implications for Yahweh of Various Locales," in *Die Stadt im Zwölfprophetenbuch*, eds. Aaron Schart and Jutta Krispenz, BZAW 428 (Berlin, de Gruyter, 2012), 224. "*b'l ḫlb* probably corresponds to one of the *b'lm* in lines 6–11 of text 1A and B" (*KTU*[2] 1.47 and 1.118, respectively; Pardee, *Ritual and Cult*, 24 n. 10).

13 del Olmo Lete, *Canaanite Religion*, 75. His reference to these Baaluma as "*seven times god*" recalls de Moor's interpretation of these entries as a reference to Baal as the deity *par excellence* (ibid., 75, emphasis in the original).

14 del Olmo Lete, *Canaanite Religion*, 75 and n. 80; see also Gregorio del Olmo Lete, "The Ugaritic Ritual Texts: A New Edition and Commentary. A Critical Assessment," *UF* 36 (2004), 585 n. 146.

15 Regarding the Akkadian text RS 20.024, del Olmo Lete argues that the numbered IŠKUR entries that also lack geographic epithets indicate to foreigners interested in Baal that each ^{d}IŠKUR or storm-god should be identified with Hadad//Lord-of-Ṣapun (l. 4; del Olmo Lete, *Canaanite Religion*, 75 and 74 n. 79).

this means that the Baal-of-Ṣapun cult statue was the most important of these statues, but it also suggests that he was distinct from them. Not only is his relative rank indicated by the fact that his divine full name was written out in Ugaritic (Baal-of-Ṣapun) and in Akkadian (Hadad//Lord-of-Ṣapun), but he is also the first of these seven entries in the EGL and the only one who is not explicitly numbered in the Akkadian. Tempting as it is to follow Pardee's lead and propose localized Baal deities that these Baaluma represent, such as Baal-of-Aleppo and Baal-of-Ugarit, Smith is correct when he observes that their actual absence in the texts minimizes their relative importance in the cult.[16] Even if Baal-of-Aleppo and Baal-of-Ugarit cult statues were part of this particular sacrificial ritual, they were less than Baal-of-Ṣapun because they were partially nameless. Because of their somewhat marginal treatment (marginal only compared to Baal-of-Ṣapun; after all, they are listed before numerous other deities in these lists; see a comparable list in Tables 5.1 and 5.2, section 3b), the tentative translation that resembles Pardee's "(another manifestation of Ba'lu)" but does not undermine their potential independence as distinct deities would suffice: "(another one of the) Baal deities." We cannot dismiss the fact that whichever gods these Baaluma entities represented, each received his own offering, which indicates that each was treated as equally divine as were the other deities revered at Ugarit who received offerings in this text, including: God-of-the-Father, El, and Dagan.

5.2 Baal-of-Ugarit and the other Baal Deities at Ugarit

Whereas de Moor uses the six Baaluma entries from the *Deity List* to focus attention to Baal-of-Ṣapun, del Olmo Lete focuses instead on a different localized Baal deity. For del Olmo Lete, the Baal of interest is not Baal-of-Ṣapun but Baal-of-Ugarit:

> This deity is central to the Canaanite pantheon: he is the great protector god of Ugarit (*b'l urgt*), the immediate god of whom we spoke above, *seven times god*. His personality is defined by the attribute *ṣpn*, with which are identified all the other possible epithets of circumstance and place, his epiphanies, mentioned in the texts (*b'l urgt*, *ḫlb*).[17]

Curiously, del Olmo Lete's preference for Baal-of-Ugarit over de Moor's preferred Baal-of-Ṣapun has no basis in the text and, in fact, contradicts it, but

16 Smith, "Problem of the God," 225. For Smith's survey of different interpretations of KTU^2 1.118:5–10 and RS 20.024 and the lack of a solid solution, see ibid., 224 f.

17 del Olmo Lete, *Canaanite Religion*, 74–75; cf. Smith, "Problem of the God," 225.

this does reveal the fact that he has identified or equated Baal-of-Ṣapun with Baal-of-Ugarit. If del Olmo Lete had claimed that Baal-of-Ugarit was (the unspecified) Baal within a discussion of *KTU*² 1.119, he would have been arguing from a text that refers to that localized Baal/Hadad deity by the right geographic epithet (see Table 5.3). *KTU*² 1.119 places its ritual within "the temple of Baal-of-Ugarit" (*w bt . bʿl . ʾugrt*, l. 3 and ll. 9–10), and the second section of this tablet consists of a hymn to (the unspecified) Baal that invokes only the deity's first name on eight separate instances (ll. 28–34). Instead, he claims that Baal-of-Ugarit is defined by *ṣpn*, Mount Ṣapun, so that other geographic epithets are unnecessary, including of-Ugarit itself; (the unspecified) Baal is all that is needed. Although del Olmo Lete claims to define the deity according to his mountain, he prefers the location of the deity's temple because that was where his human community revered him.

While some at ancient Ugarit would have identified Baal-of-Ugarit with Baal-of-Ṣapun, as del Olmo Lete claims, this is nowhere made explicit in the texts. Alternatively, the possibility that (the unspecified) Baal could be both Baal-*Par-Excellence* and Baal-of-Ṣapun, as de Moor claims, could be argued for on the basis of some explicit texts. However, this supreme Baal-of-Ṣapun was not identified with Baal-of-Ugarit in the alphabetic cuneiform tablets. de Moor's supreme Baal was, according to the mythology, a deity whose residence was really on Mount Ṣapun but who was worshipped in the temples of Ugarit. To define this deity in terms of Ugarit as del Olmo Lete does, a first name followed by two last names (i.e., *bʿl ʾgrt ṣpn*, Baal-of-Ugarit-of-Ṣapun, or *bʿl ṣpn ʾgrt*, Baal-of-Ṣapun-of-Ugarit) would need to have been found somewhere in the Ugaritic corpus, resembling what actually does appear in Hittite texts: e.g., IŠKUR-of-Aleppo- and Ḫebat-of-Aleppo-of-Ḫattuša and IŠKUR-of-Aleppo- and Ḫebat-of-Aleppo-of-Šamuḫa (*KUB* 6 45 i 43 and 51). Just as no texts explicitly identify these distinct deities with one another, no such full name appears at Ugarit.[18]

del Olmo Lete's take on (the unspecified) Baal at Ugarit is by no means unique within the scholarly community. Schwemer also comments that "[t]he cult distinguishes between Baʿlu of the city of Ugarit and Baʿlu of Mt. Ṣapuna,"[19] but he adds that the Baal temple on the Ugaritian acropolis "could

18 Pardee interprets the *ḫlb* in *KTU*² 1.109:33 as a form of offering ("one/some ḪLB") which is accompanied by an ewe's liver offering. Preceding this word is the divine name Baal-of-Ṣapun, *bʿl ṣpn*, which means that, theoretically, one could argue for the existence of a deity by the name Baal-of-Ṣapun-of-Aleppo (*bʿl ṣpn ḫlb*, ll. 32–33). I am not aware of any scholarly suggestions for such a divine name.
19 Schwemer, "Storm-Gods: Part II," 10.

be called the temple of Ba'lu Ṣapuna, as the mythical home of Ba'lu (of Ugarit) was definitely meant to be Mt. Ṣapuna."[20] This statement fits well with modern scholarship's pro-identification tendencies and seems analogous to the Jerusalemite identification of Mount Ṣapun with Mount Zion as Yahweh's dwelling (i.e., הר-ציון ירכתי צפון, Ps 48:3), but I am unaware of any Ugaritic texts that refer to a local temple as "the temple of Baal-of-Ṣapun."[21]

There is, however, a temple at Ugarit dedicated to the local deity who was explicitly identified as Baal-of-Ugarit, and three related texts state that their rituals take place "in the temple of Baal-of-Ugarit" (e.g., *w b bt . b'l 'ugrt*, *KTU*^{2} 1.109:11; and *bt* [.] b['l .] 'ug*r*[t], *KTU*^{2} 1.130:26).[22] Significantly, and counter to del Olmo Lete's, Schwemer's, and de Moor's preferences, one of these three texts explicitly distinguishes between Baal-of-Ṣapun and Baal-of-Ugarit in the same offering list:

> ^{32} *'lm . 'lm . gdlt . l b'l* ^{33}*ṣpn . ḫlb* x[x]xd . d[q]*t* ^{34}*l ṣpn*[š . l]*b'l . 'u*g[rt š]
>
> On the day after next: a cow for Baal-of-Ṣapun, ḪLB and an e[w]e's [live]r for Mount Ṣapun, (and) [a sheep for] Baal-of-Ugarit. (*KTU*^{2} 1.109:32–34)[23]

Throughout these texts, various Baal deities are repeatedly distinguished from one another.[24] For example, Baal-of-Ugarit appears third in a seven-member

---

20 Schwemer, "Storm-Gods: Part II," 10–11.

21 PRU III 16.276:21–24 is a cuneiform text that refers to a temple of Baal-of-Mount-Ḫazi (*bītum* ^{d}*ba'al ḫuršan* [ḫa-zi]; Michael Heltzer, "Land Grant Along with Tithe Obligations," COS 3.82:201; and Smith, "Problem of the God," 223–224).

22 Pardee, *Ritual and Cult*, 26. *KTU*^{2} 1.46 and 1.130 (= 24.284 in Pardee's edition) are broken in several places, but *KTU*^{2} 1.109 is in good condition. Although these three tablets are not duplicates of each other, they closely resemble one another in structure and format, so that restored signs should be considered quite reliable. Because these texts are so similar, "in the temple of Baal-of-Ugarit" has been restored in *KTU*^{2} 1.46:16 (see also, Pardee, *Ritual and Cult*, 27–28).

23 The translation "an e[w]e's [live]r for Mount Ṣapun" is based on Pardee's restoration of *KTU*^{2} 1.109:33: ⸢*w kb*⸣*d* . ⸢*d*⸣[*q*]⸢*t*⸣ (Pardee, *Ritual and Cult*, 30).

24 Baal-of-Ṣapun appears or has been restored in *KTU*^{2} 1.41:33 and 41; 1.46:12 and 14; 1.109:6, 9, 29, and 32–33; 1.112:22–23; 1.148:2, 10, and 27; 1.130:17 (see Meindert Dijkstra, "The Ritual *KTU* 1.46 (=RS 1.9) and its Duplicats," *UF* 16 [1984], 74) and 22 (RS 24.284:2, 7, and 9 in Pardee's edition [Pardee, *Ritual and Cult*, 32]); as well as in the syllabic deity list RS 92.2004:7.

Baal-of-Ugarit appears or has been restored in *KTU*^{2} 1.41:34–35 and 42; 1.46:16; 1.105:6′; 1.109:11, 16, 34, and 35; 1.112:23; 1.119:3, 9–10, 12, and 22′; and 1.130:10, 24, and 26 (RS 24.284:11 and 23 in Pardee's edition [Pardee, *Ritual and Cult*, 32]).

Baal-of-Aleppo appears or has been restored in *KTU*^{2} 1.109:16; 1.130:11; and 1.148:26; as well as RS 92.2004:6.

The unspecified Baal appears or has been restored in *KTU*^{2} 1.41:15 and 41; 1.46:16; 1.105:17′ and 24′; 1.109:13 and 20; 1.119:6 and 25′ff.; and 1.130:3.

EGL derived from an offering list in *KTU*^{2} 1.130, and Baal-of-Aleppo follows him in the fourth position:

***KTU*^{2} 1.130:**	**no. 6C (Pardee 2002, 32):**	**Translation:**[25]
[8]w šl[m]m	[21]*w šl[m]m*	And as peace-o[fferings]:
[9]*l 'il*⟨'i⟩b [š]	[22]*l 'il*⸢*'i*⸣*[b š]*	for God-of-the-Fa[ther, a sheep];
[10]*l b'l* 'u[grt š]	[23]*l b'l* ⸢*'u*⸣*[grt š]*	for Baal-of-U[garit, a sheep];
[11]*l b'l ḫl*b [š]	[24]*l b'*⸢*l*⸣ *ḫlb [š]*	for Baal-of-Aleppo, [a sheep];
[12]*l yrḫ š*	[25]*l yrḫ š*	for Yariḫu, a sheep;
[13]*l 'nt ṣpn* [l.e. 14] *'alp w š*	[26]*l 'nt ṣpn* [27]*'alp w š*	for Anat-of-Ṣapun, a bull and a sheep;
[15]*l pdr*⟨y⟩ *š*	[28]*l pdr š*	for Pidar, a sheep;
[le.e][w] l *dd*mš . š	[l.e.29]⸢*l*⸣ *ddm*[!]⸢*š.*⸣ *š*	for Dadmiš, a sheep.

Given that this ritual took place in Baal-of-Ugarit's temple (l. 26), the fact that Baal-of-Ugarit precedes Baal-of-Aleppo seems reasonable or expected. What is not expected is the fact that Baal-of-Aleppo precedes or outranks Baal-of-Ṣapun, the only divine full name that appears in the *Deity List* in *KTU*^{2} 1.118, in *KTU*^{2} 1.148:26–27:

> [26]*dgn . š . b'l . ḫlb 'alp w š .* [27]*b'l ṣpn . 'alp . w. š.*
>
> (For) Dagan, a sheep; (for) Baal-of-Aleppo, a bull and a sheep; (for) Baal-of-Ṣapun, a bull and a sheep. (*KTU*^{2} 1.148:26–27)

Nor do we expect either of these localized Baal deities to receive a larger offering than Dagan who precedes them in this EGL, which is derived from a tablet that also contains a version of the *Deity List*.[26] Moreover, an EGL derived from another offering list in *KTU*^{2} 1.46:6–7 includes both (the unspecified) Baal and Baal-Kanapi, whose last name of-the-Wing is a descriptive epithet rather than a geographic epithet:

The Baals (*b'lm*) appear or have been restored in *KTU*^{2} 1.41:18 and 19; 1.119:15$^?$; 1.148:3–4, 11–12, and 44–45.

The non-geographic Baal-Kanapi appears in *KTU*^{2} 1.46:6, and Ba'lu-R'KT appears in 1.119:1.

25 In his edition of RS 24.284, Pardee switches the obverse and reverse found in *KTU*^{2} 1.130, which creates a new numbering system, and he provides new readings to the text itself. The translation given in the third column follows Pardee's edition.

26 God-of-the-Father, Earth-and-Heaven, and El each received one sheep in *KTU*^{2} 1.148:23–25, as did Kôṯarātu, who appeared immediately prior to Dagan. Erasure marks indicate that Kôṯarātu was originally listed as receiving a bull and a sheep ([['*alp w š*]], l. 25).

*KTU*² 1.46:6–7:	Translation:
[6]['i]*l* *š* .	[(For) E]l, a sheep;
b'l *š* .	(for) Baal, a sheep;
'atrt . *š* .	(for) Ašerah, a sheep;
ym . *š* .	(for) Yammu, a sheep;
b'*l* *knp* g[?dlt]	(for) Baal-Kanapi, a c[ow];
[ ]*gdlt* .	(for) [...], a cow;
ṣpn . *dqt* . *šrp* .	(for) Mount Ṣapun, a ewe as a burnt-offering.

(The unspecified) Baal is the second deity in this EGL, whereas the oddly named Baal-Kanapi is the fifth of seven. Later, a third Baal deity appears in another section of this text describing "feast [for Baal-of-Ṣa]pun." Baal-of-Ṣapun received "two ewes and a city-dove" and "[a bul]l's [liver] and a sheep":

> [11]'*šrt* [12][l b'l . ṣ]p*n* d[q]t*m* . *w* [yn]t *qrt* [13][w mtntm . w š .] l *rm*[š .] *kbd* . *w š* [14][l šlm . kbd . 'al]p *w š* . [l] *b'l* . *ṣpn* [15][dqt . l ṣpn . šrp] . *w* šl*mm* . *kmm* [16][w b bt . b'l 'ugr]t
>
> A feast [for Baal-of-Ṣa]pun: two e[w]es and a city-[dov]e; [and two loins/kidneys and a sheep] for RM[Š]; a liver and a sheep [for Šalimu; a bul]l's [liver] and a sheep [for] Baal-of-Ṣapun; [an ewe for Mount Ṣapun as a burnt-offering] and again as a peace-offering. [And in the temple of Baal-of-Ugari]t ... (*KTU*² 1.46:11–16)

In addition to Baal-of-Ṣapun, whose name appears twice in ll. 11–15, three divine names receive offerings in this ritual feast: RMŠ, Šalimu, and Mount-Ṣapun. The divine name Baal-of-Ṣapun only occurs once as a recipient in this offering list, between Šalimu and Mount Ṣapun (both names have been restored). The previous occurrence of the divine full name Baal-of-Ṣapun is in the title of the feast, namely, "a Feast [for Baal-of-Ṣa]pun" (l. 12). Throughout this offering list, the sacrificial victims appeared first and were followed by the deity who received them, so the two ewes and the city-dove are only implicitly listed as an offering to Baal-of-Ṣapun. An alternative interpretation would be that the "Baal-of-Ṣapun" in l. 12 is an example of the Janus Parallelism, in which the name functions distinctly in both phrases: "A feast for Baal-of-Ṣapun" and "for Baal-of-Ṣapun, two ewes and a city-dove."[27]

(The unspecified) Baal in *KTU*² 1.46, 1.109, and 1.130 deserves special attention. Potentially, (the unspecified) Baal could be the primary Baal who was distinct from all other Baal deities and who needed no qualification. Alternatively, assuming that there was only one Baal in the implicit theology

27 For a discussion on Janus Parallelism, see John S. Kselman, "Janus Parallelism in Psalm 75:2," *JBL* 121 (2002): 531–532.

and mythology of the Ugaritic lay population and the priestly cult, it could be argued that the numerous Baal deities were subsumed under the same (unspecified) Baal moniker. This is what most scholars accept. These offering texts demonstrate, however, that if (the unspecified) Baal was to be identified with a localized Baal, that Baal should be Baal-of-Ugarit and only Baal-of-Ugarit. On the face of it, this may resemble the Ištar-based methodology put forth by Barton in the 1890s and again by Meinhold in the 2000s, which assumes that the unspecified deity should be identified with the most local localized deity (see chapter 1.1 and 1.3); however, our tentative localized Baal-based conclusion is based on the intentional divine name contrasts offered in the texts rather than upon any assumptions about those texts. For example, *KTU*^{2} 1.109:11–15 provides five divine names, each receiving a specific offering, and the third name is Baal: God-of-the-Father / El / (the unspecified) Baal / Anat-of-Ṣapun / Pidray. Significantly, this EGL appears after the ritual's locale is specified as "in temple of Baal-of-Ugarit" (*w b bt . b'l . 'ugrt*, l. 11). Likewise, *KTU*^{2} 1.130 r. 26–29 and o. 2–6 probably comprise an eight-member offering list, although much of the text is reconstructed:

***KTU*^{2} 1.130**	**no. 6C[28]**	**Translation**
r. ^{26}*bt* [.] b['l .] 'u*gr*[t]	^{11}*bt* ⸢*b*⸣['*l*] ⸢'*u*⸣*gr*⸢*t*⸣	(In) the temple of Ba[al]-of-Ugarit:
[kbdm ^{27}npš 'il]'*ib* . gd[lt]	^{12}⸢*l*⸣ ['*il*]'*ib* . *gd*[*lt*]	for [God-of-]the-Father, a c[ow];
^{28}[ ]t[ ]	l.e. ^{13}[...]	...
^{29}[...]	^{14}[...]	...
o. ^{2}[l] *š*x[ ]	r. ^{15}⸢*l*⸣ *š*⸢-⸣[...]	for Š ...
^{3}l *b*' [l š]	^{16}*l b*'[*l š*]	for Baa[l, a sheep];
^{4}*l* x[ ]	^{17}l ⸢-⸣[...]	for ...
^{5}*l* '[nt ṣ]p[n] ^{6}'a[lp w š]	^{18}*l* ['*nt ṣpn*] ^{19}⸢'*a*⸣[*lp w š*]	for [Anat-of-Ṣapun,] a b[ull and a sheep];
^{6}*l* p[dry]	^{20}*l* [*pdr*(*y*) *š* <u>*šrp*</u>]	for [Pidray, a sheep as a burnt-offering].

The ritual again takes place in the temple of Ba[al-of]-Ugarit (l. 11), so concluding that (the unspecified) Baal in this text should be identified with Baal-of-Ugarit seems reasonable given the context.[29] These occurrences of (the unspecified) Baal in *KTU*^{2} 1.46:3, 6, and 8 and *KTU*^{2} 1.109:20 are parallel in

28 Pardee's edition of *KTU*^{2} 1.130 is RS 24.284 with the obverse and reverse sides of the tablet switched (Pardee, *Ritual and Cult*, 32).

29 The most likely restoration for *KTU*^{2} 1.46:16–17 ([w b bt . b'l . 'ugr]t[b]⸢'⸣[l]) is based upon these two examples.

these two examples, suggesting that they, too, refer to Baal-of-Ugarit in his own temple.

Elsewhere, when the referent is potentially ambiguous, such as when two localized Baal deities appear in an EGL, the text explicitly clarifies which specific localized Baal deity is being discussed and addresses each deity according to his geographic last name. For example, in *KTU*² 1.109:32–36, when two Baal deities appear in the same EGL, the first is explicitly identified as Baal-of-Ṣapun (ll. 32–33) and the second is identified as Baal-of-Ugarit (ll. 35–36). The location of the ritual is still presumably in the same temple that was last mentioned, Baal-of-Ugarit's temple (l. 11), but the text is careful to specify who is who because this particular ritual is so far removed from l. 11's context. Furthermore, *KTU*² 1.119 mentions multiple times that its rituals take place in the physical context of "the temple of Baal-of-Ugarit" (*w bt . bʿl . ʾugrt*, *KTU*² 1.119:3; 9–10, and 21′–22′; l. 12 mentions Baal-of-Ugarit but lacks a reference to the "temple"). It seems reasonable that a deity could be listed by just his first name in his own temple, but if another localized Baal deity (or Baal deities, as with the *bʿlm* in l. 6) was potentially present, reiterating the deity's full name was necessary. Notably, if our assumption that (the unspecified) Baal refers to Baal-of-Ugarit when the text establishes the location precisely in the temple of Baal-of-Ugarit is incorrect, the case for distinct localized Baal deities at Ugaritic has already been made explicit in the EGLs.[30]

In contrast, whenever Baal-of-Ṣapun appears in these three ritual texts (*KTU*² 1.46, 1.109, and 1.130), these texts make sure that the reader recognizes this particular localized Baal is the one of interest. Unlike with Baal-of-Ugarit, Baal-of-Ṣapun's last name does not disappear when the context would make it unnecessary or even redundant. As mentioned above, the ritual entitled "a

30 The prayer to (the unspecified) Baal that was appended to the ritual and sacrificial discussion in *KTU*² 1.119 could be another example in which this Baal could be identified with Baal-of-Ugarit (compare, Smith, "Problem of the God," 223: "In this case, Baal of Ugarit is the only Baal in view."). This seems plausible for two reasons. The first and more important is the fact that the supplicant performing the prayer and sacrifice would be in the temple of Baal-of-Ugarit, as indicated by the statement in l. 33, "we shall go up to the sanctuary of (the unspecified) Baal" (*qdš bʿl . nʿl*). The second reason is that the tablet itself gives a physical context for the prayer in ll. 25–36. Baal-of-Ugarit was mentioned no less than four times in ll. 1–24, and his temple has been mentioned three of those times in order to reestablish the physical context to the sacrificial rites. While the prayer section is not explicitly linked to the sacrificial rites section, the most recently discussed Baal deity in this text is Baal-of-Ugarit in ll. 21–22 and 25. However, as before, this type of evidence linking (the unspecified) Baal specifically with Baal-of-Ugarit is only secondary to the fact that multiple localized Baal deities have been contrasted with each other in other EGLs derived from Ugaritic alphabetic texts.

feast for Baal-of-Ṣapun" (*ʿšrt l bʿl ṣpn. KTU*² 1.46:11–12 and 1.109:5) includes offerings to RMŠ, Šalimu, Baal-of-Ṣapun, and Mount Ṣapun.[31] Context could suggest that (the unspecified) Baal involved in the feast of Baal-of-Ṣapun would be Baal-of-Ṣapun. However, the texts do not let the context speak for itself because there is no (the unspecified) Baal mentioned in this ritual. Instead, both times that this ritual is presented, the deity is referred to by his first and last name, even though he is followed by the deified Mount Ṣapun. With this Baal deity sandwiched firmly within a Ṣapun milieu, the context could not be clearer, but the scribes who wrote these texts felt compelled to stress specifically which localized Baal deity they intended to receive the offering. This was a ritual dedicated to Baal-of-Ṣapun, and Baal-of-Ṣapun is expressly addressed as such during the ritual. He is not addressed as (the unspecified) Baal, even though the mythical Baal-of-Ṣapun appears to be the most important Baal deity in the *Deity List*. In regards to this particular localized Baal deity's importance, Smith is likely correct that Mount Ṣapun and its god Baal-of-Ṣapun "empower" the city of Ugarit, along with its Baal-of-Ugarit temple and cult, as well as Baal-of-Ugarit himself.[32] Furthermore, he is probably correct to state that Baal-of-Ugarit's origins sprang from the localized worship in the city of Ugarit of the mythical Baal who resides at Mount Ṣapun.[33] In sum, there would surely have been no Baal-of-Ugarit if there had not been a Baal-of-Ṣapun. However, the difference between Smith's interpretation and ours lies in our view that a new deity could splinter off from the original divine personality and be recognized independently of the original as evidenced by being contrasted in EGLs and other contexts.

Whereas Baal-of-Ugarit might have been – but Baal-of-Ṣapun definitely was not – addressed as (the unspecified) Baal in ritual contexts, Baal-of-Ṣapun could be addressed as (the unspecified) Baal in mythical contexts. For example, in the *Baal Cycle* (*KTU*² 1.1–1.6), Baal(-of-Ṣapun) was squarely situated in Ṣapun and could shed his geographic last name precisely because there were no other localized Baal deities in the mythical realm. The context was clear. This Baal identified Ṣapun as his mountain, and he was entertained in its heights:

---

31 The title "a feast for Baal-of-Ṣapun" has been reconstructed from two of the ritual texts:

*KTU*² 1.46:11–12	ʿšrt [l bʿl . ṣ]⌜p⌝n
*KTU*² 1.109:5	ʿšrt . l bʿ [l . ṣpn]
Composite	ʿšrt . l bʿ [l . ṣ]pn.

32 Smith, "Problem of the God," 223.

33 Smith, "Problem of the God," 230–231.

yšr . ġzr . ṭb . ql ʿl . bʿl . b . ṣrrt ṣpn

The hero (with) a good voice sings to Baal on the heights of **Ṣapun** (*KTU*² 1.3 iii 20–22).

b tk . ġry . ʾil . ṣpn b qdš . b ġr . nḥlty b nʿm . b gbʿ . tlʾiyt

… in the midst of my mountain, the divine **Ṣapun**, in the holy (place), in the mountain of my possession, in the good (place), in the hill of my victory. (1.3 iii 29–31)

He was even buried there:

tšmʿ . nrt . ʾilm . špš tšʾu . ʾal ʾiyn . bʿl . l ktp ʿnt . k tšth . tšʿlynh b ṣrrt . ṣp{ʿ}n tbkynh w tqbrnh

Šapaš, the light of the gods, listens (to Anat's plea). She lifts up the mighty Baal onto Anat's shoulders. Having lifted him up, she brings him up onto the heights of **Ṣapun**. She weeps and buries him. (1.6 i 13–17)[34]

When the context is clear that the Baal in question is the Baal who has been geographically identified with Mount Ṣapun, his geographic last name is unnecessary in this myth.

When a scribe had no mythical context to place his specific Baal in his geographic context, however, he provided the last name in order to make sure that his audience understood which specific god was meant. For instance, in his letter to the king (*KTU*² 2.42), an official from Alashia specifically named Baal-of-Ṣap[un] (*bʿl* ṣp[n], l. 6) as the first deity in his blessing.[35] Aside from the divine last name, the letter contains no context to help the reader know which Baal deity was involved, which might be why the chief of Maʾḫadu (*rb* mʾi[ḫd?], l. 2) chose to use the divine full name. Richard Clifford notes that the author used this full name to give Baal-of-Ṣapun a sense of being "the national god of the city of Ugarit" much like Eternal-Šapaš was the national god of Egypt.[36] Baal-of-Ṣapun undoubtedly had more international currency than Baal-of-Ugarit, which is reflected in the deity's international fame. For instance, the Egyptian officer Mami dedicated a statue to Baal-of-Ṣapun and

34 The phrases *ṣrrt ṣpn* (*KTU*² 1.3 iii 20–22; see also 1.6 i 16) and *mrym . ṣpn* (1.3 iv 38) occur several other times throughout the *Baal Cycle*.
35 Baal-of-Ṣapun is the first in this four-member EGL: Baal-of-Ṣapun / Eternal-Šapaš / Aṯtartu / Anat / all-the-gods-of-Alashia (*KTU*² 2.42:6–7). No other EGLs of this length are found in the extant portions of *KTU*² 2.1–2.83.
36 Richard J. Clifford, *The Cosmic Mountain in Canaan and the Old Testament*, HSM 4 (Cambridge: Harvard University Press, 1972), 64.

had it installed in the temple of Baal-of-Ugarit (Louvre AO 13176).[37] Moreover, Baal-Ṣapun functioned as a toponym in the eastern delta in Egypt in the late-second millennium (Exodus 14:2 and 9; Numbers 33:7; see map 1), which was roughly contemporary with Mami's statue, and the deity would become so internationally famous that Mount Ṣapun itself was referred to as Mount-Baal-of-Ṣapun in Neo-Assyrian royal inscriptions during the eighth century (KUR *ba-'a-li-ṣa-pu-na*, e.g., RINAP 1, TP3. 13:6 and 30:2). However, the chief of Ma'ḫadu probably chose to invoke Baal-of-Ṣapun in *KTU*[2] 2.42:6 because of his desire to address an internationally recognized or recognizable deity, who was comparable to the internationally recognized sun-god, whereas his national god Baal-of-Ugarit was little known outside of the patron city. Notably, the chief of Ma'ḫadu was not the only letter writer who specified which localized Baal deity he meant to address. Of the few times that a Baal deity appears in a letter as a divine name, none lack a geographic last name: Baal-of-Byblos (*b*'l . gbl, *KTU*[2] 2.44:8), Baal-of-Ṣapun (*b*'l . *ṣpn*, l. 10, and *b*'[l .]*špn*, 2.23:19), and possibly Baa[l-of-Ugarit] (*b*'l '*u*[rgt?], 2.3:5–6).[38] Perhaps these last names are only needed to distinguish a localized Baal deity from the human ruler (e.g., "lord" or "my lord"), but this requires at least some context, which the deity's first and last name provided.[39] As with these letters, when a scribe located Baal-of-Ṣapun in a particular cultic situation, he proceeded with caution and provided the deity's first and last name. In the cultic context at the temple of Baal-of-Ugarit, (the unspecified) Baal might have been Baal-of-Ugarit, but Baal-of-Ṣapun was just that, Baal-of-Ṣapun. In contrast, in the mythic context, (the unspecified) Baal was certainly Baal-of-Ṣapun.

37 Smith, "Problem of the God," 223. See also ANEP 485 for a picture of Mami's statue, and see ANET 249–250 ("The Egyptians and the Gods of Asia") for a discussion of "Adon-Zaphon, 'Lord of the North'" (i.e., Baal-of-Ṣapun), which was inscribed on a stele depicting Ramses II. Keiko Tazawa lists several other artifacts that suggest the ancient identification between the Egyptian Seth and the Semitic Baal-of-Ṣapun or (the unspecified) Baal (Keiko Tazawa, *Syro-Palestinian Deities in New Kingdom Egypt: The Hermeneutics of their Existence* [Oxford: Archaeopress, 2009], 15–25).

38 This Baal-of-Ugarit possibility depends on whether there is room to restore three missing signs *g-r-t* before the *š-h-r* in *KTU*[2] 2.3:5–6: '*u*[xx]*šhr*[.]. Smith notes that he is unaware of Baal-of-Ugarit appearing in any extant Ugaritic letters, but he has found the divine name in an Akkadian letter: ^{d}IŠKUR *ša* ^{kur}*u*$_2$*-ga-ri-it*, RS 88.2158:15′–16′). This Hadad- or Baal-of-Ugarit is named as part of "a request for help making an image for the temple of Baal of Ugarit" (Smith, "Problem of the God," 226.

39 Most of the time that *b'l* appears in letters, it seems to be a reference to a human king, as is the case in the following examples: *b'ly* ("my lord," *KTU*[2] 2.35:5), *mlk b'ly* ("the king, my lord", 2.33:30–31), *mlk b'lh* ("the king, his lord," 2.47:1–2), and *špš* . *b'lk* ("the Sun, your master," 2.39:11 and 13), among others.

Admittedly, delineating when or why a scribe felt the context was inadequate for determining whether a localized Baal deity should be specified by a last name is, if not complicated, mildly confusing, but their methods did fulfill some need the scribes had.

5.3 Baal: Epithet or Name?

This treatment of the three local Baal deities in the cultic texts, as opposed to the use of (the unspecified) Baal in them, highlights the question of whether Baal should be interpreted as a title instead of a divine name. According to Schwemer, the epithet *bēlu*/*ba'lu* ("lord") can be used "with all sorts of gods," especially when that deity is understood to be the "lord of a place" or when the word can be used to praise a deity as "lord" (of the gods) *par excellence*, as is the case in Babylon with the title Bēl for Marduk.[40] The use of *baal* as a divine title dates to the middle of the third millennium, as evidenced by god lists from Abū Ṣalābīḫ and the list of calendar names from pre-Sargonic Ebla (ITI *be-li*, "month of the-Lord," which Giovanni Pettinato identifies as the first month of the year [TM.75.G.427 iv 2 and r. iii 2]).[41] The identity or identities behind the third-millennium *baal* attestations are difficult to determine, but Schwemer rules out the possibility that the storm-god Hadad was known as Baal at Ebla because the fourth month in the Eblaite "New Calendar" was specifically named after Hadad (ITI NIDBA$_x$ ^{d}'*a*$_3$-*da*, "month of the feast of Hadad," r. i 3 and iii 5). Instead, Dagan was probably the deity called "Lord' (ITI *be-li*, TM.75.G.427).[42]

Along the Levantine Coast, the epithet *baal* developed a special relationship with the mythical storm-god Hadad in the sixteenth and fifteenth

40 Schwemer, "Storm-Gods: Part II," 8.

41 Schwemer, "Storm-Gods: Part II," 8; and Giovanni Pettinato, *The Archives of Ebla: An Empire Inscribed in Clay* (New York: Doubleday, 1981), 150 ff.

42 Pettinato, *Archives of Ebla*, 257. Pettinato notes that Dagan "enjoyed a preeminent position, perhaps the first position" at Ebla (ibid., 246), as suggested by fact that a city quarter and city gate were named after him and the fact that his consort was known as "Lady" (*bēlatu*), which is comparable to the Babylonian *baal*, namely, Bēl/Marduk and his consort Bēltiya/Zarpānītu. Moreover, Dagan's name is often represented by the logogram ^{d}BE/BAD at Ebla, which Pettinato translates as "Lord," whereas Hadad's name is typically written ^{d}'*a*$_3$-*da* (ibid., 248). These data do not definitively prove that Dagan was the *bēli* in question in the month name; after all, Hadad could have had two months named in his honor, but they do suggest that Dagan was a more likely candidate than Hadad.

centuries.[43] Evidence from Ugaritic mythological texts, from cuneiform texts in the Amarna corpus, from texts found at Tell Ta‘anakh, and from Egyptian sources suggest that the divine name Hadad and the epithet Baal had been successfully equated in the West by the mid-second millennium.[44] This equation was inspired by a storm-god Hadad's rise to the top of the various local pantheons in Syro-Palestine. This Hadad, like Marduk in Babylon, had become the lord of the gods, so his epithet needed to reflect this rise to power. Eventually, after this Hadad, who would be identified as the mythical Baal who resides on Mount Ṣapun, successfully maintained his position as the head deity at Ugarit, the epithet Baal began to function with the force of a personal name rather than as a title or epithet. Inversely, the name Hadad began to function as the epithet.[45] This reversal is most salient in the *Baal Cycle*, wherein the name Hadad appears less frequently than Baal, and when Hadad was used, it was the second line of a poetic couplet.[46] For instance, in *KTU*^{2} 1.5 i 22–23, the name Baal is used in the first line of the couplet, and the name Hadad follows in the second: "Invite me Baal with my brothers, call me Hadad with my kin!" (*ṣḥn b‘l* . *‘m ’aḫ*y [.] qr’a*n h*d . *‘m ’aryy*).[47] Again, in 1.4 vi 38–40, the name Baal precedes Hadad in the parallel clauses: "[Baa]l arranged [his] house, Hadad arra[nges his palace]" (*‘dbt* . *bht*[h . b‘]*l y‘db* . *hd* . *‘db* [.‘db*t hklh*]). Reflecting this preference for the name Baal over Hadad, Aicha Rahmouni lists *ġmr hd* ("the annihilator/avenger/champion Hadad," 1.2 i 46) as one of Baal's fourteen epithets and lists none for Hadad in her book *Divine Epithets in the Ugaritic Alphabetic Texts*.[48]

---

43 Schwemer, "Storm-Gods: Part II," 9.

44 Schwemer, "Storm-Gods: Part II," 9. de Moor also notes that the divine names Hadad and Baal were interchangeable in 15th-century Alalaḫ (Johannes C. de Moor, "בעל ba‘al: I-II," in *TDOT* [1988], 2:184).

45 Schwemer, "Storm-Gods: Part II," 9. Pardee notes that while Baal was Hadad's title, "particularly in the coastal area, [Baal] came to function as a divine name" (D. Pardee, "The Ba‘lu Myth," in *COS* 1.86:247 n. 42).

46 Baal does refer to himself in *KTU*^{2} 1.4 vii 38 as Hadad when addressing his audience: *’ib hd* ("enemies of Hadad").

47 Another example of this Baal/Hadad parallelism has been offered by Pardee, whose restoration differs from *KTU*^{2} 1.3 iv 25–27: ^{25}*yšt* ^{26}⸢b š⸣[mm .] *b‘l* . *mdlh* . *yb‘r* ^{27}[hd . mṭ]⸢r⸣ [. – rnh], "May Ba‘lu place his watering devices in [the heavens], may [Haddu] bring the [rain of] his X," (*COS* 1.86:253, Pardee's translation; Pardee, "Ba‘lu Myth," 253 n. 95). Where Pardee proposes [hd . mṭ]⸢r⸣, *KTU*^{2} proposes [rkb . ‘r]pt ("[rider of the clo]uds") as the restoration.

48 Rahmouni notes that some scholars argue that *ġmr hd* is actually a verbal phrase rather than an epithet, but this interpretation is unlikely given that one must ignore the imperative verb *šm‘* earlier in the line (Aicha Rahmouni, *Divine Epithets in the Ugaritic Alphabetic Texts*, trans. J. N. Ford, HO 93 [Leiden: Brill, 2008], 147–149). Pardee translates *ġmr hd* as "Haddu the Avenger" (Pardee, "Ba‘lu Myth," 247 n. 42).

Use of this Hadad's title and epithet "Baal" spread as far east as Emar in the fourteenth and thirteenth centuries, where the storm-god was known as Hadad//Lord-of-Emar (e.g., ^{d}IŠKUR EN ⌜i-mar⌝, Arnaud Emar 6/3 373:133′).[49] However, the epithet did not replace the storm-god's name at Emar as it had at Ugarit, which is indicated by the fact that the storm-god's name was always written IŠKUR at Emar.[50] Daniel Fleming notes that Emar's population was familiar with the storm-god traditions of the Hurrians, Canaanites, and Mesopotamians, but still resisted identifying their local storm-god with the epithet Baal.[51] Another possible factor hindering the spread inland of the alias Baal for Hadad was the composition of locally revered deities and the nature of the relationships between deities in each city. At Emar, for example, the storm-god's consort was Ḫebat and – to a lesser extent, with lesser evidence, and at a later period – Aṯtartu.[52] At Ugarit, Baal was a young god who lacked a consort "in a real sense"; however, the mythological texts suggest that he had "sexual encounters with both 'Aṯtartu and Ba'lu's sister 'Anatu."[53] At Tell Ta'anakh, Ašerah was Baal's consort, even though she was El's consort at

49 Schwemer, "Storm-Gods: Part II," 14. According to Schwemer, this Hadad's identification as Baal made no inroads in Mesopotamian theology because Marduk was already the local Bēl.

Westenholz noted that at Emar Baal was Hadad, who was identified with Tešub, but in her treatment of the hierarchical offering lists, she translated the logogram ^{d}IŠKUR as "Storm god" rather than as "Hadad" (Joan Goodnick Westenholz, "Emar – the City and its God," in *Languages and Cultures in Contact: At the Crossroads of Civilizations in the Syro-Mesopotamian Realm: Proceedings of the 42*[*th*] *RAI*, eds. K. van Lerberghe and G. Voet, OLA 96 [Leuven: Peeters, 1999], 156–158 and 164). Her reluctance to translate the divine name Hadad was likely a response to the fact that ^{d}IŠKUR appears twice in the hierarchical offering lists' EGL (Lord-of-Sagma / ^{d}IŠKUR-of-the-Land-of-Bašime' / Ninurta-of-Repasts / ^{d}IŠKUR//Lord-of-Emar / Ninurta//Lord-of-Kumar; p. 156 nn. 33 and 35); however, elsewhere Westenholz specifically identified ^{d}IŠKUR EN *i-mar* (Hadad//Lord-of-Emar) as Hadad (ibid., 158 and 164).

50 Daniel E. Fleming, *The Installation of Baal's High Priestess at Emar: A Window on Ancient Syrian Religion* (Atlanta: Scholars Press, 1992), 4 n. 6. Fleming further notes that in ritual texts ^{d}IŠKUR is consistently written without any syllabic spelling or phonetic complements at Emar (ibid., 7).

51 Fleming, *Installation*, 71. Schwemer says that the epithet had been treated so that it "came to be established as the proper name of the Syrian storm-god (Ba'lu, Ba'al), a development that sent waves far into the hinterland" (Daniel Schwemer, "The Storm-Gods of the Ancient Near East: Summary, Synthesis, Recent Studies: Part I," *JANER* 7 [2008], 159).

52 Schwemer, "Storm-Gods: Part II," 14; and Fleming, *Installation*, 73–76.

53 Schwemer, "Storm-Gods: Part II," 13. Baal's three "daughters" (*bt*) – Pidray, 'Arṣay, and Tallay – are evidence that the deity had encounters with some goddess, but neither Aṯtartu nor Anat was the mother of these three younger goddesses. The ritual text *KTU*^{2} 1.132.1–3 suggests that Baal is married to his daughter Pidray (Smith, *Origins*, 56).

Ugarit.[54] For André Caquot and Maurice Sznycer, the fact that each local Bronze-Age population had its own understanding of divine relationships indicates that each locale cherished its own ancient traditions, an idea reminiscent of Scurlock's investigation of Ištar goddesses (see chapter 4.3).[55] Local populations or scholar-scribes might not have intentionally paired their local storm-god with a particular goddess or renamed him to indicate his new position within the divine hierarchy and differentiate him from other storm-gods, but the cultic texts do make these distinctions in their descriptions of the rituals: IŠKUR remained the storm-god at Emar and was accompanied by his consort Ḫebat in the NIN.DINGIR-festival, whereas Baal-of-Ugarit was the storm-god at Ugarit with Pidray acting as one of his consorts (*KTU*^{2} 1.132 1–3), and the paramours of the mythical Baal, whose palace was built on Mount Ṣapun, were apparently Aṯtartu and Anat.

Like at Emar, Ḫebat was the consort of the storm-god Hadad(-of-Aleppo).[56] This localized Hadad deity appears in a handful of texts at Ugarit and was identified as one of several localized Baal deities. He appears twice in the *Deity Lists* (*bʿl ḫlb* in *KTU*^{2} 1.148:26 and ^{d}10 *ḫal-bi* in RS 92.2004:6) where he is listed before Baal-of-Ṣapun, and he also appears twice in the ritual texts (bʿ*l ḫlb š* in *KTU*^{2} 1.109:16 and *l bʿ⌜l⌝ ḫlb* [*š*] in *KTU*^{2} 1.130:11) where he is listed after Baal-of-Ugarit. A fifth attestation of Baal-of-Aleppo appears in a tax receipt (*KTU*^{2} 4.728:1–2), indicating that five individuals had paid their oil-tax to Baal-of-Aleppo.[57] Although these attestations at Ugarit are few, Hadad- or Baal-of-Aleppo had a long history in Syria, comparable to the Hadad in Ebla. Already in pre-Sargonic times, great reverence was shown for this storm-god and his relationship with the city of Aleppo. Upon his return from a military campaign against Mari, King Ibbi-zikir of Ebla presented purification offerings specifically to Hadad-of-Aleppo (^{d}*ʾa*$_3$*-da* LU$_2$ *ḫa-lab*$_x$^{ki}, TM.75.G.2426 xi 1).[58]

54 André Caquot and Maurice Sznycer, *Ugaritic Religion* (Leiden: Brill, 1980), 7.

55 Caquot and Sznycer, *Ugaritic Religion*, 7. The fact that Aṯtartu may later replace Ḫebat as the storm-god's consort at Emar suggests that these local variations in the inter-deity relationships are not simply the continued product of ancient traditions being enforced. Indeed, this – as well as the rise of Hadad from a second-tier deity to the active head of the Ugaritic world as "Baal" – change in consorts (or addition of a new consort, if that is a better explanation of Aṯtartu's role) at Emar is itself evidence of a deity's rise or fall in popularity at the local level.

56 Schwemer, "Storm-Gods: Part I," 164.

57 Pardee notes this taxed oil might have been presented to the cult as part of a sacrificial ritual, resembling the ritual in *KTU*^{2} 1.105:18 (Pardee, *Ritual and Cult*, 216).

58 Alfonso Archi and Maria Giovanna Biga, "A Victory over Mari and the Fall of Ebla," *JCS* 55 (2003): 22. This offering consisted of two plates and two bracelets, totaling about four mina of gold. A Hadad-of-Ḫalam (or Ḫalab or Aleppo) is also mentioned in Testo 39 r. xii 21–22: ^{d}*ʾa*$_3$-

Other texts from Ebla point to his temple at Aleppo as the most important temple in northern Syria, and the Hadad temple in Ebla was itself based on the model from Aleppo.[59] The emphasis on this storm-god at Ebla so strongly associated the deity with Aleppo that Schwemer and Alfonso Archi disagree over whether the temple in question in these texts actually stood in Aleppo or Ebla.[60] Contemporary evidence from Mari also reveals that a Hadad-of-Aleppo was worshipped there on the bend of the Euphrates, and Zimri-Lim's Old Babylonian correspondence highlights this localized deity's importance in the area when Zimri-Lim referred to the king of Yamḫad, whose kingdom included the city of Aleppo, as the "beloved of Hadad."[61] Significantly, Hadad-of-Aleppo was not the only localized storm-god that Zimri-Lim recognized. In M.

---

da ^{lu2}*ḫa-lam*^{ki} (Giovanni Pettinato, *Testi amministrativi della biblioteca L. 2769*, Series Maior (Istituto universitario orientale. Seminarior de studi asiatici) 2 [Naples: Istituto Universitario Orientale di Napoli, 1980], 1:268).

In addition to Hadad-of-Aleppo, Francesco Pomponio and Paolo Xella report that Hadad-of-Abati (^{d}'*a*$_3$*-da* LU$_2$ *a-ba-ti*^{ki}, TM.75.G.1764 viii 24–25), Hadad-of-Armi (^{d}'*a*$_3$*-da ar-mi*^{ki}, TM.75.G.10201 r. 10), Hadad-of-Dub (^{d}'*a*$_3$*-da du-ub*^{ki}, TM.75.G.2365 vii 23; 2429 xxiii 5; 2462 xi 21), Hadad-of-Lub (^{d}'*a*$_3$*-da* LU$_2$ *lu-ub*^{ki}/*lu*$_5$*-bu*$_2$^{ki}), Hadad-of-Luban (^{d}'*a*$_3$*-da lu-ba-an*^{ki}, TM.75.G.1464 i 3′–13′), and Hadad-of-Saza (E$_2$ ^{d}'*a*$_3$*-da* LU$_2$ *sa-za*$_x$^{ki}, TM.75.G.2507 ii 34-iii7) are attested at Ebla (Francesco Pomponio and Paolo Xella, *Les dieux d'Ebla: Étude analytique des divinités éblaïtes à l'époque des archives royales due IIIe millénaire*, AOAT 245 [Münster: Ugarit-Verlag, 1997], 527). See pp. 42–48 for a list of 56 attestations of Hadad-of-Aleppo at Ebla; pp. 48–50 for 26 attestations of Hadad-of-Lub at Ebla; and pp. 31–41 for 81 attestations of (the unspecified) Hadad at Ebla. Pettinato also reports that a Hadad-of-Atanni (^{d}'*a*$_3$*-da* '*a*$_3$*-ta-ni*^{ki}) is attested at Ebla (Pettinato, *Archives of Ebla*, 248).

59 Schwemer, "Storm-Gods: Part I," 162. Schwemer notes that the wall foundations of Hadad's temple in Ebla are so thick that the towering temple itself "could be seen from afar in the plain around the city" (ibid., 162).

60 Schwemer, "Storm-Gods: Part I," 163 n.127; and Alfonso Archi, "The Head of Kura – The Head of 'Adabal," *JNES* 63 (2005): 85.

61 Schwemer, "Storm-Gods: Part I," 163; and Jean-Marie Durand, *Le Culte d'Addu d'Alep et l'affaire d'Alahtum*, FM 7, Mémoires de NABÛ 8 (Paris: Société pour l'étude du Proche-orient ancien, 2002). Zimri-Lim also sent a statue of himself to the king of Yamḫad to be placed in the lap of the deity, but Yarim-Lim replied that the statue of the sun-god, which was already in the statue's lap, took priority (Durand, *Le Culte d'Addu*, 14–58 and 44 no. 17 8- l.e. 20; and Schwemer, "Storm-Gods: Part I," 164). Similarly, the king of Elam sent a votive bow to the cult of Hadad-of-Aleppo (Durand, *Le Culte d'Addu*, 11–13 no. 4). Moreover, Zimri-Lim's third regnal year was named after a statue of Hadad-of-Aleppo that he had commissioned (MU *zi-im-ri-li-im* ALAM-*šu a-na* ^{d}IŠKUR *ša ḫa-la-ab u*$_2$*-še-lu*, "Year: Zimri-Lim brought up his statue to Hadad-of-Aleppo," ARMT 25 736:8′–9′; see also ARMT 21 265:9–12). Notably, this tablet lists another of Zimri-Lim's regnal years that was named after Hadad-of-Maḫānu: $^{5'}$MU *zi-*[*im-r*]*i-li-im* ^{giš}GU.ZA GAL $^{6'}$*a-na* ^{d}IŠKUR *ša ma-ḫa-nim u*$_2$*-še-lu-u*$_2$ ("Year: Zi[mr]i-Lim brought up a throne to Hadad-of-Maḫānu," ll. 5′–6′).

7750:3′–5′, Zimri-Lim named three storm-gods in sequence, using IŠKUR as the logogram to represent each first name: $^{3'd}$IŠKUR *ša ša-me-e ta-*[*ma*] $^{4'd}$IŠKUR *be-el ku-um-mi-in*^{ki} *ta-*[*ma*] $^{5'd}$IŠKUR *be-el ḫa-la-ab*^{ki} *ta-*[*ma*]. According to Francis Joannès, the personal names hiding behind these logograms are Hadad-of-Heaven, Tešub-of-Kumme, and Hadad-of-Aleppo.[62]

IŠKUR-of-Aleppo is also attested at Nuzi, Tunip, Emar, and Ḫattuša, as well as in other Anatolian cults, in the middle of the second millennium.[63] Each culture referred to the deity by its usual storm-god name; however, in each instance he retained his geographic epithet of-Aleppo as a last name. For the Eblaites, he was ʾAdu-of-Aleppo; for the Hurrians, he was Tešub-of-Aleppo; for the Hittites, he was IŠKUR-of-Aleppo(-of-Ḫattuša); for the Luwians, he was Tarḫund-of-Aleppo; for the Assyrians, he was IŠKUR(=Adad)-of-Aleppo (see SAA 2 2 vi 18); at Sefire (*KAI* 222), he was Hadad-of-Aleppo; and at Ugarit, he was Baal-of-Aleppo.[64] This diversity of divine first names for the same storm-god demonstrates that the last name was more important an aspect for invoking the deity than the first name, resembling the situation with the localized Ištar goddesses in Neo-Assyrian texts. The last name could have been dropped on occasion when the context made it clear, like in a specific temple or in a mythological text, but the last name itself marked this particular localized Baal deity as especially deserving of reverence for over two thousand years. To dismiss him as just another local manifestation of a supreme mythical storm-god, equivalent to the very regional Baal-of-Ugarit, overlooks the pervasive and persistent honor that the deity received in the ancient Near East

62 Francis Joannès, "Le traité de vassalité d'Atamrum d'Andarig envers Zimri-Lim de Mari," in *Marchands, Diplomates et Empereurs: Etudes sur la civilization mésopotamienne offertes à Paul Garelli*, eds. D. Charpin and F. Joannès (Paris: Éditions Recherche sur les Civilisations, 1991), 176.

63 Schwemer, "Storm-Gods: Part I," 165. The *Puḫānu Chronicle* (*CTH* 16b) places IŠKUR-of-Aleppo at Ḫattuša in the reign of Ḫattušili I. During Muwatalli II's festival reorganization, IŠKUR-of-Aleppo was identified as IŠKUR-of-Aleppo-of-Ḫatti. Muršili III considered IŠKUR-of-Aleppo as his personal protective deity (Schwemer, "Storm-Gods: Part I," 166).

64 Worship of IŠKUR-of-Aleppo survived in northern Syria and Anatolia after the fall of the Hittite Empire (Schwemer, "Storm-Gods: Part I," 167). Luwian Prince Taita renovated the temple of Tarḫunza-of-Aleppo ca. 1100. This temple was destroyed about 200 years later, and a new temple was rebuilt. Later, in the mid-ninth century, Šalmaneser III of Assyria offered sacrifices in Aleppo (^{udu}SISKUR^{meš} *ana* IGI ^{d}IŠKUR *ša* ^{uru}*ḫal-man* DU$_3$-*uš*, "I made sacrifices before Hadad-of-Aleppo," RIMA 3 A.0.102.2 ii 87 [= A.0.102.6 ii 25–26] and A.0.102.8:15′, which is similar but broken). Hadad-of-Aleppo is also listed in GAB § 1 (^{d}IŠKUR *ša*$_2$ *ḫal-bi*, l. 116), near the end of the *Divine Directory of Assur*, where he appears after Hadad-of-Kumme (^{d}IŠKUR *ša*$_2$ *ku-me*, l. 115), although (the unspecified) Adad (^{d}IŠKUR) appears much earlier than these two divine names in l. 59 (see Menzel, *Assyrische Tempel*, 2:T150 and 154, no. 64).

when addressed by his last name. As with the localized Ištar goddesses, whether we consider his storm-god name Hadad or his title-turned-nickname Baal as his real first name, he was primarily -of-Aleppo.

5.4 The Baal Deities of the First Millennium

By the close of the second millennium, the Hurrians and Mitanni were gone, the Hittite Empire had disintegrated, and the city of Ugarit had been destroyed, but the veneration of several Baal deities survived into the first-millennium world (see Table 5.5 for a list of Baal deities with geographic last names). With the destruction of his city, Baal-of-Ugarit disappeared from the record, but Baal-of-Ṣapun and Baal-of-Aleppo survived to be revered by the peoples of the first millennium.[65] In the seventh-century treaty between Esarhaddon and Baal, king of Tyre, Baal-of-Ṣapun appears as the third of three Baal deities in a six- or eight-member EGL of Tyrian deities: Baal-Šamêm, Baal-Malagê, and finally Baal-of-Ṣapun (*ᵈba-al ša-me-me ᵈba-al-ma-la-ge-e ᵈba-al-ṣa-pu-nu*, SAA 2 5 iv 10′).[66] Because the Akkadian verb used in the curse, *lušatbâ* (*lu-šat-ba*,

65 Sommer suggests that the Baal of Ugaritic mythology "seems to have fragmented into a great number of baal-gods who could be worshipped and addressed separately" (Sommer, *Bodies of God*, 25). Such a statement seems to undermine his assessment that "there are many baal-gods [at Ugarit], and they are listed separately from Baal of Ṣaphon," which he had made in the preceding paragraph. However, these two statements need not be in conflict if Sommer is interpreted as saying that every Baal at Ugarit, except Baal-of-Ṣapun, disappeared after the destruction of Ugarit so that any Baals from later periods are really offshoots of Baal-of-Ṣapun alone. Given that these later gods "show no individuation of personality, character, or function" (ibid., 25), deciding from which specific Ugaritic-period Baal they were derived seems an unnecessary exercise.

66 The proper length of this EGL has been debated because the curse involving Bethel and Anat-Bethel (SAA 2 5 iv 6′–7′) appears between a curse enacted by the Sebittu (l. 5′) and summary curses by the great gods, the gods of Assyria, and the gods of Eber-nāri (ll. 8′–9′). As noted in chapter 3, following Barré's analysis of treaty god lists, the Sebittu invariably close the list of Assyrian deities in Neo-Assyrian treaty EGLs (Barré, *God-List*, 19). However, van der Toorn argues that Bethel and Anat-Bethel should be considered Aramean deities and that, as Aramean deities, they belong within the list of Assyrian deities because they have been incorporated into the Assyrian cultic system (Karel van der Toorn, "Anat-Yahu, Some Other Deities, and the Jews of Elephantine," *Numen* 39 [1992]: 84). Smith agrees with Barré that these should be accepted as Tyrian deities (Smith, *Early History*, 63). Whether one counts them among the Assyrian deities or Tyrian deities – the latter seems more in line with other Neo-Assyrian treaty EGLs – their position in SAA 2 5 is unexpected. Including this pair with the rest of the Tyrian deities, this curse section provides the following EGL: Bethel / Anat-Bethel / Baal-Šamêm / Baal-Malagê / Baal-of-Ṣapun / Melqart / Ešmun / Astarte (SAA 2 5 iv 6′–7′ and 10′–19′; see Table 5.4).

"to make rise," l. 11), is singular and because "no explicit copula" indicates that the three Baal names are not actually separate deities, Sommer argues that these three full names refer to the same deity:

> [T]he translations in Parpola and Watanabe, *Treaties* [= SAA 2], and Pritchard, *ANET*, add the word "and" between Baal Malagê and Baal Saphon, thus implying that the text speaks of three gods. However, no explicit copula appears between Baal Malagê and Baal Saphon, and (more important) the verb *lušatba* (a Š-stem injunctive of *tebû*/*tabā'u*) in iv.10 is clearly in the singular (the plural would be *lušatbû*).[67]

Sommer fails to note, however, that no other paired Phoenician deities in these curses are separated by an explicit copula: ^{d}*ba-a-a-ti*-DINGIR^{meš} ^{d}*a-na-ti-ba-*⌜*a*⌝-[*a-ti*]-⌜DINGIR⌝^{meš} ("Bethel and Anat-Be[th]el," l. 6′) and ^{d}*mi-il-qar-tu* ^{d}*ia-su-mu-nu* ("Melqart and Ešmun," l. 14′).[68] Reading the curse in isolation, one could argue that l. 10′ refers to one Baal deity three times by employing three Baaline epithets, but this ignores the fact that each of the three Baal full names is preceded by a divine determinative. It also completely ignores another verb within the curse, which is decidedly plural, i.e., *lissuḫū*: "may they (the three Baal deities) pull out" (*li-is-su-ḫu*, l. 12′; see Table 5.4).[69] Furthermore, as Barré observed, this would be the only instance in the treaty tradition in which a divine name is followed by two epithets, each with its own divine

Edward Lipiński argues that the name of the second Baal in SAA 2 5, Baal-Malagê, should be interpreted as *b'l mhlk* (*ym*?) in Phoenician, meaning "Baal-of-the-march/voyage-(to-the-sea?)" (Edward Lipiński, *Dieux et Déesses de l'univers Phénicien et Punique*, OLA 64 [Leuven: Peeters, 1995], 243–244).

67 Sommer, *Bodies of God*, 24 and 189 n. 82; see *CAD* T, *tebû* mng. 14. It is very tempting to dismiss the final vowel of *lušatbâ* as ventive marker *-am* without the memation, which would allow us to interpret this as a plural verb. However, according to Jaakko Hämeen-Anttila's grammar of Neo-Assyrian period Akkadian, a third-weak plural verb with a ventive ending would be marked with more than just long a-vowel, i.e., *lušatbûni* rather than *lušatbâ* (Jaakko Hämeen-Anttila, *A Sketch of Neo-Assyrian Grammar*, SAAS 13 [Helsinki: Neo-Assyrian Text Corpus Project, 2000], 92).

68 Likewise, the summary statements that precede the curse in SAA 2 5 iv 10′ consist of four groupings, "the great gods of heaven and earth, the gods of Assyria, the gods of Akkad, the gods of Eber-nāri" (DINGIR^{meš} GAL^{meš} *ša*$_2$ AN-*e* *u*$_3$ KI.TIM DINGIR^{meš} KUR-*aš-šur*^{ki} DINGIR^{meš} KUR.URI^{ki} DINGIR^{meš} *e-bir*-ID$_2$, ll. 8′–9′), which also lack a copula, but no one would argue that these are all restatements of just one collection of deities.

69 I would like to thank Joshua Jeffers for pointing out that the *CAD* tentatively suggests that the three Baal deities are subject of the verb *lissuḫu* (*CAD* T, *tarkullu* mng. a.). Another verb used in this curse, *lipṭur* (*lip-ṭu-ur*, "may he loosen," SAA 2 5 iv 11′) is also a singular verb, but the subject of this verb is probably "evil wind" (TU$_{15}$ *lem-nu*), not the three gods.

determinative.[70] A preferred interpretation would be that the verb in question is singular but that the three deities are acting as a unanimous collective. This is how the seven deities who are the Sebittu, the Pleiades, function in the treaty as evidenced by the fact that their curse also includes a singular verb (*liš-kun*, "may *he/she* establish, l. 5′), even though they are described as "heroic gods" (DINGIR^{meš} *qar-du-te*, l. 5′) in the plural! Scholars generally accept that a divine determinative indicates that the marked divine name is distinct from the divine name that precedes it; rarely do they consider it an epithet of the previous divine name. The same should be expected to hold true in Esarhaddon's treaty with King Baal of Tyre.

Sommer's Baal is not the only storm-god in the first-millennium Neo-Assyrian treaties.[71] Hadad-of-Aleppo appears in the ninth-century treaty between kings Assur-nērārī III and Mati'-ilu of Arpad (SAA 2 2 vi 18) as the thirty-fifth divine name in a thirty-seven-member EGL. In fact, this Hadad-of-Aleppo (^{d}IŠKUR *ša*$_2$ ^{uru}*ḫal-la-ba*) is the third IŠKUR deity in the adjuration list (vi 6–26; see Table 3.10), appearing long after (the unspecified) Adad of Triad 2 (l. 9, who is the twelfth deity in this EGL) and immediately after Adad-of-Kurbail (^{d}IŠKUR *ša*$_2$ ^{uru}*kur-ba-il*$_3$, l. 17, who is thirty-fourth in this EGL).[72] Hadad-of-Aleppo ([*hdd ḥ*]*lb*, Sefire i A 10–11 [*KAI* 222]) probably also appears as the penultimate divine name in the Sefire Treaty, following sixteen Assyrian deities and "the gods of the open country and [cultivated] ground" (see Tables 3.12 and 3.13), preceding only the Sebittu.[73] A Baal deity served as the patron

70 Barré, *God-List*, 55. Sommer's interpretation also ignores the fact that Baal-of-Ṣapun and Baal-Šamêm appear alongside other Baal divine names in various other EGLs, be they from Ugaritic texts or Phoenician and Aramaic texts (see Tables 5.2 and 5.6).

71 This Baal, whom Sommer argues is represented by Baal-Šamêm, Baal-Malagê, Baal-of-Ṣapun, is probably not even the only Baal or storm-god in this particular treaty. Mullissu is the first divine name that is extant in the curse list of SAA 2 5 only because several preceding lines of the text have been destroyed. If the entire text were extant, surely the divine name (the unspecified) Adad (^{d}IŠKUR) would appear earlier in the curse list, along with Sîn and Šamaš as part of Triad 2, as is the case in SAA 2 2.

72 (The unspecified) ^{d}IŠKUR (SAA 2 2 vi 24) appears outside of the Assyrian god list in SAA 2 2, as the seventh divine name in a possible ten-member EGL of deities revered at Arpad (see Table 3.10). The fact that this deity belongs in Arpad and not Assyria is secured by his post-Sebittu position in this text (see Barré, *God-List*, 25). This deity's relation with the other Hadad deities, which is to say, Northwest Semitic storm-gods as opposed to the Mesopotamian storm-god Adad, in the treaty is uncertain. For this reason, a non-committal translation "IŠKUR" is preferable to "Adad" or "Hadad" because it retains the same ambiguity provided in translations of Hittite treaties.

73 According to Schwemer, the Phoenicians and biblical authors always call the storm-god "Baal" in the late-second and first millennia, whereas the Arameans in Upper Mesopotamia and Syria call their storm-gods "Hadad" (Schwemer, "Storm-Gods: Part II," 15). In addition to

god at Ugarit in the second millennium, but storm-gods seem to have lost the prominence of their namesakes in the first millennium, at least in the treaty tradition.[74]

With the demotion of these storm-gods in the treaty tradition, a new storm-god appeared at the forefront in the West, Baal-Šamêm/Šamaim/Šamayn, whose name could be translated, Lord-of-Heaven. According to both Klaus Koch and Herbert Niehr, the earliest attestation of Baal-Šamêm as a proper divine name was in the tenth-century inscription of King Yeḥimlk of Byblos (*KAI* 4), in which Baal-Šamêm (בעל־שמם, l. 3) is listed along with Lady-of-Byblos (Baalat-Byblos) and the gods of Byblos (בעלת־גבל and אל־גבל קדשם, ll. 3–4).[75]

---

his appearance in SAA 2 5, Baal-of-Ṣapun's name is found on a sixth-century amulet from Tyre (Lipiński, *Dieux et Déesses*, 247), as well as in Hebrew and Egyptian sources (e.g., B'r D̲pn, p.244; see Table 5.5).

74 This is not to suggest that (the unspecified) Baal/Hadad was an unimportant deity in the West in the first millennium; indeed, (the unspecified) Hadad was an especially important deity for the Aramaic speaking peoples. (The unspecified) Hadad is the first of the deities in the *Hadad Inscription* (*KAI* 214; the five-member EGLs are in ll. 2, 2–3, 11, and 18) and in the *Panamuwa Inscription* (*KAI* 215; the four-member EGL is in l. 22) from the mid-eighth century. Both *KAI* 214 and 215 are Panamuwa of Y'DY's royal inscriptions (see Table 5.7). Because of these texts, Barré argues that (the unspecified) Hadad was the supreme deity in northern Syria, which was comparable to his position as head deity in Aleppo and in Alalaḫ (Barré, *God-List*, 40 and n. 11). Slightly modifying Barré's argument for multiplicity's sake, a Hadad was the supreme deity in northern Syria, which was comparable to a local Hadad's position as head deity in Aleppo and in Alalaḫ.

Moreover, Hadad-of-Sikan was the primary deity of interest in the ninth-century, bilingual Tell-Fekherye Inscription (הדד סכן, *KAI* 309:1; Jonas C. Greenfield and Aaron Shaffer, "Notes on the Akkadian-Aramaic Bilingual Statue from Tell Fekherye," *Iraq* 45 [1983]: 112), and (the unspecified) Hadad assisted the king in his battle against Israel in the Tel Dan Stele (ויהלך . הדד . קדמי, "Hadad went before me," *KAI* 310:5; Avraham Biran and Joseph Naveh, "An Aramaic Stele Fragment from Tel Dan," *IEJ* 43 [1993]: 87–90), but there is no EGL in either of these inscriptions. Of course, in addition to the numerous other extra-biblical inscriptions from the first millennium in which a Baal appears, Baal worship was also present in Israel (e.g., 1 Kings 18).

75 Klaus Koch, "Baal Ṣapon, Baal Šamem and the Critique of Israel's Prophets," in *Ugarit and the Bible: Proceedings of the International Symposium on Ugarit and the Bible: Manchester, September 1992*, eds. G. J. Brooke, A. H. W. Curtis, and J. F. Healey, UBL 11 (Münster: Ugarit-Verlag, 1994), 159; and Niehr, *Ba'alšamen*, 37. Lipiński traces the evidence for a Baal-Šamêm back to the Amarna Period, following Hugo Gressman's suggestion from 1918 (Lipiński, *Dieux et Déesses*, 81; and Hugo Gressmann, "Hadad und Baal nach den Amarnagriefen und nach ägyptischen Texten," in *Abhandlungen zur semitischen Religionskunde und Sprachwissenschaft*, eds. W. Frankenberg and F. Küchler, BZAW 33 [Berlin: Graf von Baudissin, 1918], 213). They appeal to the fourteenth-century letter from Abi-Milku, king of Tyre, as evidence: "the king, my lord, (is) like the sun/Šamaš; you (are) like IŠKUR-in-Heaven" ([6]LUGAL *be-li-ia ki-i-ma* ^{d}UTU [7]*ki-ma* IŠKUR *i-na ša-me at-ta*, EA 149); "who gives his thunder in Heaven like IŠKUR" ([13]*ša id-din ri-ig-ma-šu i-na ša-mi*$_2$ [14]*ki-ma* IŠKUR, EA 147); and "the king, who exists like IŠKUR

Koch summarizes three popular theories regarding the origin of this deity: Baal-Šamêm was another name for Baal-of-Ṣapun, having moved from Mount Ṣapun to Heaven; Baal-Šamêm was another ancient deity who represented a personified Heaven; and Baal-Šamêm was a new deity who resided in Heaven but manipulated life on earth.[76] Koch suggests that the third theory, originally proposed by Otto Eissfeldt in 1939, is the only persuasive one of the three.[77] Because both divine names appear in contrast with each other in SAA 2 5, Koch is correct that Baal-Šamêm should not be identified with Baal-of-Ṣapun. Second, Kock's and others' inability to connect this deity with an ancient counterpart suggests that Baal-Šamêm was not simply a reinvented deity from hoary antiquity, so his conclusion that the deity was a relatively new one who jumped to the top of various regional divine hierarchies in the first millennium does seem the most reasonable of the three options.[78] According to Niehr, although Baal-Šamêm had characteristics that resembled those of the second-millennium storm-gods, Baal-Šamêm was a new deity who appeared during a creative period in Phoenician religious history, a period which also witnessed the appearance of the gods Ešmun and Melqart.[79] However, unlike his second-millennium storm-god predecessors and his first-millennium contemporaries, who were linked with geographic cults, Baal-Šamêm was a celestial god who acted on behalf of different nations throughout the first millennium.[80]

Schwemer suggests that Baal-Šamêm's association with the celestial realm aided his rise in importance because his cosmic epithet was "supposed to bind

---

and the sun/Šamaš-in-Heaven" ([9]*šar*$_3$-*ri ša ki-ma* [d⌜]IŠKUR⌝ [10]*u*$_3$ [d]UTU *i-na ša-me i-ba-ši*, EA 108). Note that these lines have been translated to reflect Gressman and Lipiński's desire to link this second-millennium Hadad with the proposed last name in-Heaven; however, the preposition "in" (*ina* in Akkadian and *bet* in Hebrew and other Northwest Semitic languages) followed by a geographic name should not be interpreted as part of a divine last name (see, Allen, "Examination," 61–82).

76 Koch, "Baal Ṣidon," 160.

77 Koch, "Baal Ṣidon," 164; see also Otto Eissfeldt, "Ba'alšamem und Jahwe," *ZAW* 57 (1939): 1–31.

78 See also Niehr, *Ba'alšamen*, 31. Baal-Šamêm's sudden appearance and rise to the top of a local divine hierarchy is supported by the analogous rise of Yahweh's sudden appearance and rise to the top of Israel's at roughly the same period.

79 Niehr, *Ba'alšamen*, 32–33. Baal-Šamêm's origins differ from Melqart's, a divinized, deceased king, and Ešmun's, a healing deity, but all three deities were products of this same period of religious innovation.

80 Lipiński identifies Baal-Šamêm with (the unspecified) Hadad because they never appeared together in an EGL (Eward Lipiński, *Studies in Aramaic Inscriptions and Onomastics II* [Leuven: Uitgeverij Peeters, 1994], 196). He also argues that this god was identified as *Caelus aeternus* in Latin inscriptions found at Rome and as Zeus Οὐράνιος (Zeus-of-Heaven) in Greek inscriptions found at Damascus (see Philo of Byblos, *PE* 1.10.7).

people from different regions."[81] Supposedly, all peoples could relate to and appeal to this sky-based deity precisely because of his lack of an earthly geographic last name. If so, the motivation behind giving Baal-Šamêm a higher status over other Baal deities resembles giving Ištar-of-Heaven a higher status, which is indicated by the fact that Ištar-of-Heaven's name precedes the other three localized Ištar goddesses in BM 121206 ix (see Table 3.11 for Ištar-of-Heaven and Table 5.6 for Baal-Šamêm). Unlike Baal-of-Ṣapun, who appears after God-of-the-Father, El, and Dagan in the *Deity List* from Ugarit and who never appears in any extant Aramaic texts, Baal-Šamêm occasionally is listed in the top position in the West. For example, in addition to the Phoenician text *KAI* 4, Baal-Šamêm is the first deity in EGLs in the Phoenician Azatiwada Inscription (*KAI* 26 A iii 18), the Aramaic inscription of Zakkur, King of Ḥamath (*KAI* 202 B 23–26), and a Punic votive inscription from Carthage (*KAI* 78 2–4; see Table 5.6).[82] Notably, the EGL from *KAI* 78 contrasts Baal-Šamêm with two other Baal deities: Baal-Ḥamān and Baal-Magnim. Even in this third-century B.C.E. inscription, multiple Baal deities are listed separately just as they had been in SAA 2 5 (Table 5.4), and because the goddess Tannit's name is the second deity in this four-member EGL, the other two Baal names in the third and fourth position in the EGL cannot be interpreted as additional epithets for Baal-Šamêm. Tannit effectively severs these potential epithets from the deity. However, as already noted, in Esarhaddon's treaty with King Baal of Tyre (SAA 2 5 iv 6′–7′), Baal-Šamêm had a lower rank than Bethel and Anat-Bethel, regardless of their somewhat problematic location in this EGL (see Table 5.4).[83] Finally, by the start of the Common Era at Ḥatra, Baal-Šamêm had lost his top status to Our-Lord (מרנ, the Aramaic semantic equivalent to בעלנ) and to

81 Schwemer, "Storm-Gods: Part II," 15.

82 Throughout the Azatiwada Inscription (*KAI* 26), (the unspecified) Baal (A i 1, 2, 3, 8, ii 6, 10, 12, iii 11, and C iv 12) and a Baal-KRNTRYŠ (A ii 19, iii 2, 4, C iii 16, 16–17, 19, and iv 20) are named. The divine name Baal-KRNTRYŠ first appears in Azatiwada's discussion about rebuilding the city of Azitiwadiya and making the deity dwell in it (A ii 17–19), which Philip Schmitz recognizes as a reference to the deity's cult statue (Philip C. Schmitz, "Phoenician KRNTRYŠ, Archaic Greek *ΚΟΡΥΝΗΤΗΡΙΟΣ, and the Storm God of Aleppo," KUSATU 11 [2009]: 121). Baal-KRNTRYŠ's name was written more often than (the unspecified) Baal's name until the end of the inscription. Several potential deities have been proposed as identifications for Baal-KRNTRYŠ. In addition to (the unspecified) Baal, John Emerton suggested that this deity was a non-Hadad storm-god, and Schmitz recently proposed that he should be identified with Hadad-of-Aleppo (John A. Emerton, "New Light on Israelite Religion: The Implications of the Inscriptions from Kuntillet 'Ajrud," *ZAW* 94 [1982]: 11; and Schmitz, "Phoenician KRNTRYŠ," 131 and 140). Regardless of the identification, both Baal-KRNTRYŠ seems to be distinct from Baal-Šamêm, who only appears in the curse section (A iii 18–19).

83 Barré, *God-List*, 20, 46 and 135.

members of that deity's family (*KAI* 245–248; see Table 5.6 and Map 2). Baal-Šamêm's top-rank status also disappeared in the last extant attestation of his divine full name, Kölner Mani-Codex 49,3–5.[84] Having been incorporated into the Manichaean traditions of the third century C.E. and following, he became an angel who reveals an apocalypse to Adam: "I am Balsamos//the-Greatest-Angel-of-Light" (εγω ειμι Βαλσαμος ό μεγιστος αγγελος του φωτος, Kölner Mani-Codex 49,3–5).[85]

Another point of contrast between Baal-Šamêm and Baal-of-Ṣapun, who is known in different Ugaritic texts as the son of both Dagan and of El, Baal-Šamêm had no known genealogy or consort.[86] The goddess Atargatis (אתרעתא) appears after Baal-Šamêm in *KAI* 247 and 248, which could be suggestive of a consort relationship; however, these texts belong to a very late period, so projecting any possible relationship between the god and goddess back 1000 years is problematic. Moreover, Koch warns that because this goddess lacks an explicit connection with Baal-Šamêm elsewhere, these texts could indicate a divine rivalry as easily as they could a consort relationship. Koch's warning is justified because two other goddesses appear after Baal-Šamêm in inscriptions: Baalat-Byblos (*KAI* 4) and Tannit (*KAI* 78). Theoretically, each local population could have recognized a different goddess as Baal-Šamêm's consort with its own unique divine name or epithet, which had been the case in the second millennium at Emar and the rest of the Levant. However, we cannot assume that a goddess who was listed after a god in only one or two texts is that god's consort without any explicit indication, and the same can also be said of divine rivalries. Just as Assur could be paired with Mullissu or another Ištar goddess who was not his paramour because of a common martial aspect, there are numerous possible reasons that a goddess was paired with Baal-Šamêm in any given EGL. In all likelihood, Baal-Šamêm had no relationship with Tannit in *KAI* 78 because we know that Tannit was considered Baal-Ḥamān's consort, who was listed after her in this EGL.

In addition to Baal-Šamêm's appearance in Phoenician, Aramaic, Akkadian, and Punic texts over the course of more than a thousand years, Herbert Donner and Wolfgang Röllig suggest that the Punic text from third-century B.C.E. Sardinia (*KAI* 64:1) attests a Baa⟨l⟩-Šamêm who was located on Hawk

84 Wolfgang Röllig, "Baal-Shamem בעל־שמם, בעל־שמין" in *Dictionary of Deities and Demons in the Bible*, eds. Karel van der Toorn, Bob Becking, and Pieter W. van der Horst, 2nd rev. ed. (Leiden: Brill, 1999),151.

85 A. Henrichs, H. Henrichs, and L. Koenen, "Der Kölner Mani-Kodex (P. Colon inv. Nr. 4780) Περὶ τῆς γέννης τοῦ σώματος αὐτοῦ: Edition der seiten 1–72," *ZPE* 19 (1975): 48–49.

86 Koch, "Baal Ṣidon," 164.

Island (modern San Pietro, Sardinia; see Map 4).[87] This text is especially interesting because the divine full name is followed by a *bet*-locative phrase: to Baa⟨l⟩-Šamêm on-Hawk-Island (לבעשממ באינצמ). In his examination of potential localized Yahweh deities in the Hebrew Bible, McCarter has offered the possibility that the *bet*-locative could serve as an epithet in Hebrew in the same way that *ša* functions in Akkadian epithets.[88] If so, *KAI* 64:1 could then be interpreted as naming a specific localized Baal-Šamêm who resided on the Hawk Island: Baa⟨l⟩-Šamêm-on-Hawk-Island. Like IŠKUR-of-Aleppo-of-Ḫattuša and IŠKUR-of-Aleppo-of-Šamuḫa (*KUB* 6 45 i 43 and 51), this would be a name with three elements. Such an interpretation would mean that Baal-Šamêm-on-Hawk-Island is a different deity from (the otherwise unspecified) Baal-Šamêm. However, because Baal-Šamêm-on-Hawk-Island never appears in a context where he is distinguished from (the otherwise unspecified) Baal-Šamêm, drawing this conclusion would go beyond the methodology presented in chapter 3.3.[89] The preferred interpretation is that this deity is Baal-Šamêm who was worshipped at the cult on Hawk Island, which is invariably how the name is interpreted.

Another text from the first millennium B.C.E. that mentions multiple Baal deities is the Phoenician Kulamuwa Inscription (*KAI* 24) from the late ninth century. Baal-Ṣemed and Baal-Ḥamān, who are followed by the deity Rakib-El, first appear at the end of the inscription in a curse against anyone who would damage it (ll. 15–16). Baal-Ṣemed's last name is not geographic in nature; it means "lord-of-the-mace/club." According to John Gibson, the name is suggestive of the mythical Baal's victory over Yammu in the Ugaritic *Baal Cycle*,[90] but Lipiński claims that "mace" does not relay the divine name's real

87 Donner and Röllig, *KAI* 2, 80.

88 McCarter, "Aspects," 140–142; and Barré, *God-List*, 186 n. 473; cf. Allen, "Examination," 75 and 82. See chapter 4.1 for a discussion of *ša* as it pertains to localized Ištar goddesses.

89 Donner and Röllig do not interpret *KAI* 64:1 as invoking a deity known as Baal-Šamêm-on-Hawk-Island, as indicated by their lack of quotation marks around the whole phrase (Donner and Röllig, *KAI* 2, 80), and McCarter does not actually mention this text in his study (McCarter, "Aspects").

90 Gibson, *TSSI* 3, 39. Gibson notes that the phrase following Baal-Ṣemed is "who belongs to Gabbar" (אש . לגבר, l. 15), which indicates that official worship of this deity at Sam'al began during the reign of Gabbar, a previous king who, according to this text, accomplished nothing (ובל . פ[על], l. 2).

A Ṣedem-Baal (צדמבעל) appears in *KAI* 62, a text from Malta that has been dated between the fourth and second centuries (see Map 4). If Baal-Ṣemed and Ṣedem-Baal are the same deity as Donner and Röllig posit (Donner and Röllig, *KAI* 2, 78), then this deity is the first deity in both EGLs in which he is present: Baal-Ṣemed / Baal-Ḥamān / Rakib-El (*KAI* 24:15–16) and Baal-Ṣemed / DN / Aštart / DN. Alternatively, Ṣedem-Baal could be a mistake for צלמבעל,

meaning.[91] Despite Lipiński's objections, this translation makes sense because the deity is later called upon to smash the offender's head (ישחת . ראש . בעל . צמד, *KAI* 24:15), and a mace would suit this need nicely. In further support of Gibson's mace interpretation, Philip Schmitz recently proposed that the KRNTRYŠ element in the divine name Baal-KRNTRYŠ, the deity whose cult statue Azatiwada installed in his city (*KAI* 26 C iii 17–19), is related to the archaic Greek word *KOPYNH, which means "mace."[92] Using a matrix of Luwian, Greek, Phoenician, and Syrian textual, iconographic, and monumental evidence, he argues that the famous Hadad-of-Aleppo was closely associated with maces and equates the deity Baal-KRNTRYŠ from the eighth-century Azatiwada inscription (*KAI* 26) with the ancient Hadad- or Baal-of-Aleppo.[93] While this identification is appealing, Hadad-of-Aleppo was a deity whose identity was intimately bound to his geographic last name, so the idea that his devotee Azatiwada would neglect this geographic last name in exchange for the new name Baal-KRNTRYŠ is somewhat problematic. For Philip, this is not a problem because he considers Hadad-of-Aleppo just one of the various manifestations of (the unspecified) Hadad.[94] However, even if we disagree with Philip's specific identification between Baal-KRNTRYŠ and Baal-of-Aleppo or (the unspecified) Hadad/Baal, we can readily accept his proposed meaning for the name Baal-KRNTRYŠ as Baal//the-Mace-Bearing. Following Guy Bunnens' suggestion, we can also connect this deity with Kulamuwa's ninth-century Baal-Ṣemed (*KAI* 24:15), whose name similarly means Baal-of-the-Mace.[95] This need not mean that we would equate Baal-KRNTRYŠ with Baal-Ṣemed or that we would equate either one with a specific localized storm-god because these mace-related names could just as easily have represented deified maces associated with a localized or mythical Hadad as they could an

meaning "image of Baal," in which case, no relationship between this divine name and Baal-Ṣemed can be established.

91 Lipiński, *Studies in Aramaic*, 207 n. 25.

92 Schmitz, "Phoenician KRNTRYŠ," 119. The extant word closest to his proposal is ΚΟΡΥΝΗΤΗΡΙΟΣ, which is a Greek masculine adjective that has been derived from a substantive ending that means "mace-bearing" (ibid., 125 and 127).

93 Schmitz, "Phoenician KRNTRYŠ," 129, 140–141, and plate 1.

94 Philip C. Schmitz, personal communication, 02/24/2014.

95 Guy Bunnens, "The Storm-God in Northern Syria and Southern Anatolia from Hadad of Aleppo to Jupiter Dolichenus," in *Offizielle Religion, locale Kulte und individuelle Religiosiät: Akten des religionsgeschichtlichen Symposiums "Kleinasien und angrenzende Gebiete vom Beginn des 2. bis zur Mitte des 1. Jahrtausends vor Chr." (Bonn, 20.-22. Februar 2003)*, eds. M. Hutter and S. Hutter-Braunsar, AOAT 318 (Münster: Ugarit-Verlag, 2004), 63–64; Philip, "Phoenician KRNTRYŠ," 139; and Schwemer, "Storm-Gods: Part II," 18 n. 43.

anthropomorphized deity. Moreover, if either of these Baal names represents weapons that had been deified rather than localized storm-gods, then these two names probably represented two distinct deities.

Whatever our interpretation of the meaning behind the name Baal-Ṣemed, the important thing to remember is that Baal-Ṣemed is not Baal-Ḥamān, the second deity mentioned in *KAI* 24:15–16. Baal-Ḥamān's last name places his origin in the mountains near the Phoenician coast. According to Gibson, Mount Ḥamān should be identified with Umm El-'Amed, which is between Tyre and Acco, but Lipiński wants to identify it with the Mount Amanus on the border of Sam'al, near where Kulamuwa's inscription was found, which seems preferable (see Map 3).[96] Like Mount Ṣapun, Mount Ḥamān was considered divine at Ugarit, which was indicated by its use as the theophoric element in the personal name "Servant of Ḥamān" (*'bd . ḫmn, KTU*^{2} 4.332:12; ^{m}ARAD-*ha-ma-nu*, *PRU* II 223 and *PRU* III 240). This name also belonged to a tenth-century Tyrian (Ἀβδήμουνος, Josephus, *Against Apion* I 120) and a seventh-century Assyrian (^{m}*ab-di-ḫi-mu-nu*, SAA 6 283:15′; *PNA* 1/1 5; see also Ḫammāia in *PNA* 2/1 448), and Ḥamān appears without the element Baal on three steles from Carthage (*CIS* 1 404, 405, and 3248; see Map 4). The mountain is well attested if it was not completely synonymous with the deity. In addition to the Phoenician text *KAI* 24, the divine name Baal-Ḥamān appears in numerous Punic and Neo-Punic texts (where the name might have been pronounced Baal-Ḥamoon), many of which present Baal-Ḥamān alongside the goddess Tannit. The divine name also appears in Greek and Latin texts as *ΒΑΛΑΜΟΥΝ* and *Balamoni* (see Table 5.5).

According to Frank Moore Cross, Baal-Ḥamān was already identified with El in a Ugaritic hymn that praises El as "El the One of the Mountain/Ḫamān" (*'il pbnḫwn* [[xxx]]*ḫmn, KTU*^{2} 1.128:9–10, Cross's translation).[97] He traced this identification into the late first millennium by noting that the Punic iconography of Baal-Ḥamān from Hadrumetum (Sousse) resembles El's iconography at Ugarit: each deity has a long beard, sits on a throne, and wears a conical crown, with a winged sun-disc placed above.[98] If Baal-Ḥamān can be

---

96 Gibson, *TSSI* 3, 39 and 118; and Lipiński, *Studies in Aramaic*, 207 n. 24. For a full discussion of the various mountains with which this deity has been identified and their role in Ugaritic mythology, see Xella, *Baal Hammon*, 143–166. As a place name, Ḥammon (חמון) appears in Joshua 19:28 along with Ebron, Rehob, Kanah, and the great Ṣidon.

97 Frank Moore Cross, *Canaanite Myth and Hebrew Epic: Essays in the History of the Religion of Israel* (Cambridge: Harvard University Press, 1973), 28. Cross admitted that the syntax is unclear in this line and that Ḥamān is probably parallel to the first half of the line (ibid., 28 n. 85).

98 Cross, *Canaanite Myth*, 35. According to Cross, the scenes on two scarabs from Sardinia also resemble these portraits.

identified with El, then, following scholarly syncretistic traditions, Baal-Ḥamān could also be identified with the Greek god Kronos and Latin Saturnus, which is exactly what happens in the scholar-scribe tradition. After discussing the Phoenician secret ritual in which children were slaughtered as a propitiatory sacrifice to the gods, the first-century C.E., Phoenician historian Philo of Byblos explicitly identified El with Kronos: "Now Kronos, whom the Phoenicians call El, who was in their land and who was later divinized after his death as the star of Kronos" (*PE* 1.10.44, H. W. Attridge and R. A. Oden's translation).[99] Already in the fifth century B.C.E., Sophocles had equated Baal-Ḥamān with Kronos (Sophocles, *Andromeda*, fragment 126) because "the barbarians" (βαρβάροις) made infant sacrifices to Kronos, which seems to correspond with Baal-Ḥamān's infant victims at Carthage.[100] So if Baal-Ḥamān and Kronos were syncretized by Sophocles, El and Kronos were syncretized by Philo of Byblos, Cross's modern identification of Baal-Ḥamān with El seems reasonable.

By comparing the EGLs found within the eighth-century *KAI* 24 and *KAI* 215, the argument could be advanced that Baal-Ḥamān was also identified with El in a non-scholar-scribe tradition (see Table 5.7).[101] Both divine names are second in their respective EGLs, and both are followed by Rakib-El, the dynastic deity at Sam'al:[102]

***KAI* 214:2:**	***KAI* 214:2–3:**	***KAI* 24:15–16:**
Hadad	Hadad	Baal-Ṣemed
El	El	Baal-Ḥamān
Rašap		
Rakib-El	Rakib-El	Rakib-El
Šamaš	Šamaš	
	Rašap.	

Furthermore, if Baal-Ṣemed can be identified with (the unspecified) Hadad, as Gibson suggests, then these two lists correspond perfectly, allowing for the fact

99 Attridge and Oden, *Philo of Byblos*, 62–63. This passage, like the rest of Philo of Byblos's work is preserved in Eusebius's *Praeparatio evangelica*, is also reminiscent of Kronos's swallowing the stones while thinking he was eating Zeus in Hesiod's *Theogony* (*Theogony* 485–491).

100 Lipiński, *Dieux et Déesses*, 257 and 260–261.

101 For a list of EGLs in which Baal-Ḥamān appears, see Table 5.8

102 Rakib-El is identified as "Lord of the Dynasty" (בעל . בית) in *KAI* 24:16 and *KAI* 215:22. Rakib-El, whose name means Chariot-Driver-of-El, also appears in the Kulamuwa scepter inscription (*KAI* 25:4 and 5–6) and in the Bar-Rakib Inscription (*KAI* 216:5).

that a Rašap deity appears in a different position in each of the first three EGLs in *KAI* 214 and is completely absent in the final EGL.[103] If so, and if Baal-Ḥamān was identifiable with El in both scholar-scribe and non-scholar-scribe traditions, then this first-millennium Baal is definitely not a Baal that should be identified with any of the other first-millennium Baal deities who were storm-gods. Moreover, this same conclusion can be drawn from these EGLs even if we reject Gibson's identification of Baal-Ṣemed with (the unspecified) Hadad. Just because two divine names serve as absolute anchor points in an EGL does not mean that those names represent the same deity (see chapter 3.3).

5.5 Why is a Baal Deity's Geography Important?

Like their third- and second-millennia counterparts, several first-millennium Baal deities had different geographic last names. In some instances, *baal* likely

103 Gibson, *TSSI* 3, 39. Already predisposed to this identification between El and Baal-Ḥamān because of Philo of Byblos's and Sophocles's writings, a few scholars have offered further textual evidence for this identification. Gibson, for example, argues that in two Phoenician texts from the third century B.C.E. the two adjacent words אל and חמן constitute the divine name El-Ḥamān (אל חמנ, *KAI* 19:4 = *TSSI* 3 31:4 and *TSSI* 3 32:1), which he identifies with Baal-Ḥamān (ibid., 120):

> [1]ערפת כברת מצא שמש וצ[2]פלי אש בנ האלמ מלאכ מלכ[3]עשתרת ועבדי בעל חמנ [4]לעשתרת באשרת אל חמנ [5]בשת 26
> לפתלמיס ...[6]בנ פת[7]למיס וארסנאס
>
> The portico in the western quarter and its object[?], which the god (literally: "the son of the gods") Angel-of-Milkastart and his servants the citizens[!] (literally: Baal) of Ḥamān (built) for Aštart in the sanctuary of El-Ḥamān, in the 26th year of Ptolemy ... son of Ptolemy and Arsinoë. (*KAI* 19/*TSSI* 3 31:1–7)

In *TSSI* 3 32, the divine name Milkastart and El/god-of-Ḥamān appear together:

> [1]לאדני למלכעשתרת אל חמנ כפרת חרצ מתמ אש יתנ עבדכ [2]עבדאדני בנ̇ ע̇בדאלנמ ב[נ] עשת[ר]תעזר ב[-?]על
> חמנ כמאשי[3]להאלנמ מלכעשתרת ומלאכ מלכעשתרת כ שמע קל יברכ
>
> To my lord, to Milkastart//El-Ḥamān, an atonement offering, which your servant 'Abd'adoni son of 'Abdel'onum son of 'Aštar[t]'azara, citizen of (Baal) Ḥamān as his gift to the gods Milkastart and Angel-of-Milkastart because he heard his voice. May he bless him. (*TSSI* 3 32:1–3)

According to Gibson, this potential El deity and Milkastart represent "a fusion of two deities, El ('the king') and Astarte," and he compares it to the compound divine name Kôṯaru-wa-Ḫasīsu at Ugarit (Gibson, *TSSI* 3, 120). His interpretation that El is referred to as "king," overlooks the fact that the word "king" precedes Aštart, not El. A better interpretation would understand *el* (אל) as the common noun "god," functioning in this text as the title in the epithet "God of Ḥamān." This is how Henri Seyrig, Sznycer, and Donner and Röllig each interpret the two words אל and חמן (Henri Seyrig, "Antiquités Syriennes," *Syria* 40 [1963]: 27; Maurice Sznycer, "Une inscription punique trouvée a Monte Sirai [Sardaigne]," *Semitica* 15 [1965]: 43;

served as the title for a god who is well associated with a locale, like Moon-God-of-Ḫarrān who could also be addressed as Baal-Ḫarrān (בעלחרן, *KAI* 218:1, see also Tables 4.2 and 5.5).[104] Similarly, if Philo of Byblos, Sophocles, and modern scholars can be trusted to relate more than just theological speculations, Baal-Ḥamān was identified by the ancients with the Canaanite deity El and the Greek deity Kronos and not identified as yet another storm-god whose title represents (the unspecified) Hadad. However, many first-millennium Baal deities were Hadad-style storm-gods. At Cyprus, a Baal-Lebanon appeared in an eighth-century B.C.E. text (*KAI* 31:1), and a Hadad-Lebanon appeared more than a millennium later in a fourth-century C.E. Greek text. Considering Hadad's association with Baal in the second and first millennia B.C.E., the identification of Baal-Lebanon and Hadad-Lebanon is reasonable, but not definitive considering the huge chronological gap. Of course, any equation of these deities should only be tentative. Finally, there was the storm-god Baal-Šamêm who lacked an earthly geographic epithet and any known divine family but whose heavenly associations seem to have been an integral aspect of his personality.[105] Several of these Baal deities are contrasted with each other, and for some the geographic last name seems to be a more important marker for the deity's identity than is the first name.

When a deity's geographic last name plays such an important role in fixing that deity's identity, which seems to be the case with Baal-Šamêm and other first-millennium localized Baal deities, examining the nature of the relationship between the god and the place could become a worthwhile endeavor. For example, a survey of the deities with geographic last names in the SAA 2 2 treaty (see chapter 3.2) suggested that a city's legacy could cause a patron deity to assume the city as a last name. Both Nineveh and Arbela became increasingly important political and military cities within the Neo-Assyrian Empire in the eighth and seventh centuries about the same time as their two localized Ištar goddesses became regularly identified by their last names. This is not to deny that the divine name Ištar-of-Nineveh appeared prior to Sennacherib's moving the capital to Nineveh or that the divine name Ištar-of-Arbela did not exist prior to Šalmaneser III's successful campaigns against Urarṭu. Rather, it suggests that their value as individual goddesses, distinct from each other and (the unspecified) Ištar, increased more dramat-

---

and Donner and Röllig, *KAI* 2, 27–28). Thus, the words in *TSSI* 3 32:1 should be translated to indicate one deity with one epithet, King-Aštart//God-of-Ḥamān.

104 For discussions on Moon-God-of-Ḫarrān as a western rather than Mesopotamian deity, see Lipiński, *Aramaeans*, 620–623; and Rubio, "Scribal Secrets," 161–163.

105 Niehr, *Ba'alšamen*, 33.

ically when their patron cities' value went up, even if these localized Ištar goddesses were typically among the least important major Assyrian deities.

Returning from the world of Ištar goddesses to that of Baal deities, Hadad-of-Aleppo was also the patron deity of a city with an ancient theological legacy, even if his city was of no political and military importance to the Neo-Assyrian Empire. As he survived from the third to the second millennia, Hadad-of-Aleppo's importance continued alongside the orbit of the Hurrian and Hittite religious traditions, and Hadad-of-Aleppo's devotees lived in a world populated with numerous other storm-gods, some of whom were also called Hadad and some Baal. These other storm-gods were not necessarily rival gods, but they, including Baal-of-Ugarit and Baal-of-Ṣapun, served as contrasts, giving his devotees reason to invoke him by his full name.

Like the Ištars of Nineveh and Arbela, some of these other Baal deities were worshipped in a cult in important regional cities, like Baal-of-Ugarit in the second millennium and Baal-Ṣidon and Baal-Tyre in the first millennium. Still other deities were closely associated with a particular location because that location represented the deity's mythical home, such as Baal-of-Ṣapun. The significance of other geographic last names, such as Pe'or and Me'on, for localized Baal deities might be less obvious, but these, too, could relate to the locations' political or military importance for a people. Alternatively, if a location's importance rests in the deity's mythical background, that location could represent the deity's otherworldly home or his this-worldly primary residence (e.g., his preferred *axis mundi*), as was the case with Baal-of-Ṣapun or the Olympian Zeus on their respective mountains.[106] The mythical importance of a cult site could relate to the place of the deity's birth, such as Zeus *Kretagenes* ("Crete-born"), or another important moment in a deity's life. Furthermore, a location's mythical background could represent a cultic etiology that relates a human experience rather than just a deity's experience. Many of such etiological examples can be found in Genesis, where the mythology associated with a place has been stripped away and was replaced by the human experience of the divine there. For example, Genesis 28:10–22 describes the Israelite patriarch's experience at Bethel with a deity called Elohim ("God") and explains why Jacob changed the place's name from Luz to Bethel (v. 19), even though it does not relate any mythology about a deity known as Bethel.[107]

---

106 Regarding mythological homes and storm-gods, Cross observed, "we are embarrassed with the plenitude of deities associated with mountains in the Canaanite and Amorite pantheons" (Cross, "Yahweh and the God of the Patriarchs," *HTR* 55 [1962]: 247).

107 In addition to the appearance of Bethel and Anat-Bethel in the seventh-century treaty between Esarhaddon and Baal of Tyre (SAA 2 5 iv 6′), the divine name Bethel also appears in

Likewise, some biblical narratives provide a historical, rather than mythological, Israelite experience of the divine for the explanation behind the name Baal-Pe'or. These passages could be pointing to a memory of the location's pre-Israelite cultic significance. If the tradition remembered in Numbers 25:1–2 and elsewhere can be trusted, then Baal-Pe'or was a deity revered by the Moabites whose sacrificial feasts were performed in Pe'or, an unidentified mountain in the Abarim range.[108] Numbers 25 retells the episode in which Moabite women seduced Israelite men into worshipping the deity by feasting and sleeping with them. However, Yahweh's wrath was stirred up by these misdeeds, and he responded by killing 24,000 people with a plague (v. 9). Phinehas stopped the plague by killing the Simeonite Zimri and his Midianite paramour Cozbi, whom he caught *in flagrante*, by throwing a spear through them (vv. 7–8 and 13–15). In a previous episode, the Moabite king Balak had hired the prophet Balaam to curse the Israelites. Balaam built seven altars and sacrificed seven bulls and rams on "the top of (Mount) Pe'or" (ראש הפעור, 23:28) in order to effect his curse against Israel (vv. 28–30).[109] The fact that Pe'or was identified as an active cult site in each episode – with Moabites engaging in a raucous feast to Baal-Pe'or and Balaam offering sacrifices there – cannot be overlooked.[110] A reasonable conclusion would be that Baal-Pe'or was the locally important god whose cult was located in Pe'or.

---

the late sixth/early fifth-century letter from Memphis to Elephantine (שלמ בית בתאל ובית מלכת שמינ, "Peace [to] the temple of Bethel and the temple of the Queen-of-Heaven," *TAD* A2.1:1).

As noted above, after Jacob awoke from his dream, he renamed the place previously known as Luz to Bethel because "this place is nothing but the house of God" (המקום הזה אין זה כי אם־בית אלהים, Genesis 28:17), even though the name Beth-elohim would have fit the narrative better than Bethel. The point is made again just a few verses later, when Jacob identified the deity as Elohim a second time: "He named that place Bethel ... 'Now this stone that I set up as a pillar will be the house of God,'" ([19]ויקרא את־שם־המקום ההוא בית־אל ... [22]והאבן הזאת אשר־שמתי מצבה יהיה בית אלהים, vv. 19 and 22). In another episode, however, the Israelite deity himself uses El in reference to the god of Bethel: "I am the god (El) of Bethel (אנכי האל בית־אל, 31:13).

108 J. Milgrom, *Numbers*: *The Traditional Hebrew Text with the New JPS Translation*, JPS Torah Commentary 4 (Philadelphia: Jewish Publication Society, 1990), 201 and 480.

109 Balak had previously taken Balaam to other sites. He first took him to Bamoth-baal (במות בעל, Numbers 22:41), which Milgrom noted was probably a shrine, as evidenced by the singular noun stele in the LXX: τὴν στήλην τοῦ Βαάλ ("the cult platform of Baal," which would mean the Hebrew should be vocalized *bamat-baal* [i.e., במת בעל]; Milgrom, *Numbers*, 193). The next site was "Sedehzophim, on the top of (Mount) Pisgah" (23:14).

110 Numbers 22–24 never actually says to whom Balaam offered the sacrifices, but Yahweh did speak with him directly on more than one occasion (e.g., 23:12 and 16–18).

Another Pe'or-based geographic name is Beth-Pe'or (בית פעור, Deuteronomy 3:29), which is where the Israelites camped when Moses was denied entrance into Canaan and Joshua was appointed his successor. Cross identified Beth-Pe'or with Baal-Pe'or and suggested that the

A second localized Baal deity to consider in this vein is Baal-Me'on. Like Pe'or, the place known as Baal-Me'on was located within Moabite territory.[111] Although the name Baal-Me'on never actually appears as a direct reference to a deity, it was regularly used as a toponym (e.g., the Mesha Inscription [*KAI* 181:9] and Numbers 32:38) and even appeared as a gentilic adjective in the Samaria Ostraca corpus: "Baala, the Baal-Me'onite" (בעלא.בעלמעני, *Samr* 27:3).[112] Despite the lack of an actual deity who is known by this name, the fact that the area can also be referred to as either Beth-Baal-Me'on (*KAI* 181:30; Joshua 13:17) or Beth-Me'on (Jeremiah 48:23) is intriguing. Because Beth-Baal-Me'on can be translated as "the house of Baal-Me'on" or "the temple of the (divine) lord of Me'on," this suggests that the deity Baal-Me'on had a cultic presence in Me'on. Similar arguments have been proposed for the places Bethel and Pithom, whose names mean "house of El" and "house of Atum," respectively, with the ideas being that El and Atum had originally been worshipped in those cities.[113]

---

full name of this place was Beth-Baal-Pe'or, "the temple of Baal-of-Pe'or" (Frank Moore Cross, "Reuben, First-Born of Jacob," *ZAW* 100 [1988]: suppl. 50). Cross also proposed that the location of Pe'or was a "Reubenite shrine beneath Mount Nebo, over against Mount Ba'l Pĕ'ōr" (ibid., 51–52); however, a later Aaronid prohibition against the Transjordan tribes, including the Reubenites, treated this shrine to Yahweh as one to Baal, which was, he argued, why only the divine name Baal was associated directly with Pe'or in biblical tradition (ibid., 57). Because the priestly tradition replaced the divine name Yahweh with Baal at the Pe'or cult site, Cross contended, no evidence of a Yahweh-of-Pe'or survived.

111 Baal-Me'on was probably located southwest of Madaba, Jordan (Milgrom, *Numbers*, 275).

112 The LXX of 2 Chronicles 20:1 and 26:8 has *Minaioi* where the MT has "the Ammonites" (העמונים), and Ernst Knauf notes that "the Ammonites" makes little sense in these passages – especially in 20:1, where "the sons of Ammon" have already been mentioned and were contrasted with the Minaioi/Ammonites (Ernst A. Knauf, "Meunim," in *Anchor Bible Dictionary*, ed. David Noel Freedman [New York: Doubleday, 1992], 4:801–802; see also Sara Japhet, who argues that the MT is "certainly corrupt" in reference to the former verse and problematic in the latter [Sara Japhet, *I & II Chronicles: A Commentary*, Old Testament Library (Louisville: Westminster/John Knox, 1993), 785 and 880]). Instead, these *Minaioi* should be identified with the inhabitants of the place Ma'on, which Knauf suggests is probably to be identified with Baal-Me'on.

113 Bezalel Porten, *Archives from Elephantine: The Life of an Ancient Jewish Military Colony* (Berkeley: University of California Press, 1968), 167; van der Toorn, "Anat-Yahu," 85; and Carol Redmount, "Bitter Lives: Israel in and out of Egypt," in *The Oxford History of the Biblical World*, ed. M. Coogan (Oxford: Oxford University Press, 2001), 65. Other places with divine names following house/temple include Beth-Anat (Joshua 19:38; Meir Lubetski, "Beth-Anath," in *Anchor Bible Dictionary*, ed. David Noel Freedman [New York: Doubleday, 1992], 1:680), Beth-Dagon (Joshua 19:27; Wade Kotter, "Beth-Dagon," in *Anchor Bible Dictionary*, ed. David Noel Freedman [New York: Doubleday, 1992], 1:683), Bethlehem (Ruth 1:1 and elsewhere; Henri Cazelles, "Bethlehem," in *Anchor Bible Dictionary*, ed. David Noel Freedman [New York:

Although not enough is known about each of the potential localized Baal deities and goddesses that are listed in Tables 5.5 and 5.9, as a general rule, it seems that the geographic last name placed the deity somewhere with an important cult devoted to that deity. At some places, the cult might have entailed an entire temple, as was the case for Baal-Ṣidon at Ṣidon, whose temple is mentioned explicitly (בת לבעל צדן, *KAI* 14:18). Other places might only have had a cult statue in another deity's temple in the city in order to maintain a divine presence, while still others might have had a primarily mythological tie to a place, as was the case for Baal-of-Ṣapun at Mount Ṣapun. Whatever the reasons that tied a deity to a place, these ties were so strongly felt that they not only defined the deities, but they did so by distinguishing each deity from others who shared a common first name. The geographic last name served not so much as a reminder of the location's importance to that god but as a reminder of what defined that god in distinction to other similar-named gods.

5.6 First-millennium Goddesses in Northwest Semitic Texts

Just as the divine first name Baal appears in both second and first millennia texts associated with geographic last names, a select few goddesses were also associated with geographic names. Specifically, these goddesses include localized Anat deities, Ašerah deities, Aštart/Astarte deities, and Tannit deities (see Table 5.9 for a list of goddesses and their geographic epithets).

First, two Anat deities appear in *KTU*² 1.109, one of the tablets that describe a set of rituals for a single month. These goddesses are Anat-of-Ṣapun (ll. 13–14, 17, and 36) and Anat-of-HLŠ (l. 25).[114] Because of this inscription's ritual context, its interest in making sure that offerings are given to a particular deity at specific times and circumstances is expected. Each deity who was conceivably important enough to receive an offering should receive an offer-

Doubleday, 1992], 1:712), Beth-Pe'or (Deuteronomy 3:29; Cross, "Reuben," 50–57, esp. 51–52), and, as Yigael Yadin proposed, Beth-habaal, whose name means the-house-of-the-(divine)-Lord (2 Kings 10:25; Yigael Yadin, "The 'House of Ba'al of Ahab and Jezebel in Samaria, and that of Athalia in Judah," in *Archaeology in the Levant: Essays for Kathleen Kenyon*, eds. R. Moorey and P. Parr [Warminster: Aris & Phillips LTD, 1978], 129). Lubetski says of Beth-Anat: "The adoration of the goddess Anath was already popular in Canaan prior to the Israelite conquest and settlement, and her sanctuary is the town's focal point" (Lubetski, "Beth-Anath," 680).

114 Pardee, *Ritual and Cult*, 26. In addition to these two divine full names, *KTU*² 1.109 also includes Baal-of-Ṣapun (ll. 5, 9, 29, and 32–33), Baal-of-Ugarit (ll. 11, 16, 34, and 35–36), and Baal-of-Aleppo (l. 16).

ing, and each deity present should be included in the ritual. Anything less would potentially insult the excluded deity. Thus, whatever roles that these goddesses played in the cultic life of ancient Ugarit might be uncertain, but the inclusion Anat-of-Ṣapun and Anat-of-ḪLŠ in *KTU*^{2} 1.109 is reminiscent of the multiple LAMMA deities included in *The Festival for All the Tutelary Deities* (*KUB* 2 1 §§ 31′–33′; see chapter 2.2 and Table 2.4), as well as the Ištar goddesses in the rituals contained in the *Pantheon Tablet* from Mari (see Table 4.5) and BM 121206 ix from Sennacherib's reign (see Table 3.11).

Another Ugaritic text, one which would not necessarily be expected to pair a deity with a geographic epithet, is the legendary *Kirta Epic*. In this text, Kirta made a vow as he prepared to lay siege to the city Udum in his search for a wife:

> [38]*ʾi* [[*ṯ*]] *ʾiṯt . ʾaṯrt . ṣrm* [39]*w ʾilt . ṣdynm* [40]*hm . ḥry . bty* [41]*ʾiqḥ . ʾašʿrb . ġlmt* [42]*ḥẓry . ṯnh .* k[!]*spm* [43]*ʾatn . w . ṯlṯth . ḫrṣm*
>
> [38]Certainly, by the lives of Ašerah-of-Tyre [39]and Goddess of Ṣidon,
> [40]if I take Ḥurāya into (my) house, [41](that is, if) I bring the girl into my [42]courts,
> [43]I will pay twice her (worth) in silver and triple her (worth) in gold. (*KTU*^{2} 1.14 iv 38–43)[115]

Prior to making the vow, the narrative had already referred to these goddesses as Ašerah-of-Tyre and "Goddess of Ṣidon" (ll. 35–36). Later in the epic, when Kirta had yet to fulfill his vow, (the unspecified) Ašerah cried out when she remembered the unfulfilled vow, and she was joined by another goddess, presumably the one associated with Ṣidon in iv 35–36 and 39. Unfortunately, the text is broken, so the goddess is anonymous: "And Ašerah remembers his vow, Goddess of X" (*w tḫss* . ʾaṯrt *ndrh w . ʾilt* . x[xx], *KTU*^{2} 1.15 iii 25–26).

Because the epic nowhere explicitly provides "Goddess of Ṣidon" with a first name, given Ugaritic poetry's famous use of synthetic parallelism, the argument that this goddess Ašerah in *KTU*^{2} 1.14 iv 35 is also the goddess in Ṣidon in l. 36 could be advanced. In light of synthetic parallelism, Kirta's house (l. 40) and court (l. 42) are parallel, the individual Ḥurāya (l. 40) and the girl (l. 41) are parallel, and the silver and gold are parallel (l. 43). So, too, are Ašerah-of-Tyre and "Goddess of Ṣidon" parallel. There is no reason to deny that Ḥurāya is the girl in the following line, nor is there reason to deny that

115 The translational value "by the life of" for *ʾiṯ* in l. 38 is derived from an existential particle meaning "there is" (Daniel Sivan, *A Grammar of the Ugaritic Language*, HO 28 [Leiden: Brill, 2001], 187). Pardee acknowledges this possible translation, which he equates with "as she lives," but he prefers the translation "gift" from the hollow root *ʾt* that refers to the silver and gold in the subsequent lines (Pardee, "The Kirta Epic," in *COS* 1.102:336 n. 34).

Kirta's house and his court represent the same location. However, identifying the Ašerah goddess with the goddess associated with Ṣidon is more along the lines of identifying the silver with the gold. Silver and gold both represent a purchase price, but they are not the same metal, nor are their values comparable. In the same way that the metals serve to advance the epic poetically rather than reveal the market values and exchange rates in ancient Ugarit, the couplets that mention the goddesses serve a poetic rather than theological purpose. As reflected in the translation above, Kirta made his vow to two goddesses who were worshipped in two separate towns. One goddess was Ašerah-of-Tyre, who also seems to be (the unspecified) Ašerah later in 1.15 iii 25, and the other goddess was not named, unless 'Ilat should be interpreted as a proper name or title comparable to Baal, in which case her divine name was 'Ilat- or Goddess-of-Ṣidon.

Both Anat and Astarte should be considered as the potential candidate behind the goddess associated with Ṣidon because they both appear elsewhere in the epic. Indeed, Anat and Ašerah are probably presented later in the epic where Kirta's son is described as nursing on Ašerah's milk and suckling from the other goddess's breast: "He will nurse on Ašerah's milk, he will suckle from the maiden [Anat]'s breast" (^{26}ynq . ḥlb . 'a[ṯ]rt ^{27}mṣṣ . ṯd . b*tlt* . ['nt], *KTU*^{2} 1.15 ii 26–27). Although Anat's name is not extant in these lines, according to Rahmouni, *btlt* ("maiden") is "the most common epithet of the goddess" Anat, so the proposed restoration Anat for l. 27 is the reasonable restoration.[116] (Separately, the motif related here in which two goddesses are responsible for nursing Kirta's infant son highly resembles the motif common to *Assurbanipal's Hymn to the Ištars of Nineveh and Arbela* [SAA 3 3 r. 14–16] and *Mystical Miscellanea* [SAA 3 39:19–23].)

Anat and Ašerah were not the only goddesses acting in this epic. Astarte is mentioned after Anat when Kirta compares Ḥurāya's qualities to these two goddesses: "Her goodness is like Anat's, her beauty is like Astarte's" (*k . n'm . 'nt . n'mh km . tsm . 'ṯtrt .* tsmh, *KTU*^{2} 1.14 iii 41–42; and again in vi 26–28). The divine name Astarte also appears near the end of the epic, where she is given the name Name-of-Baal (Astarte//Name-of-Baal, *'ṯtrt . šm . b'l*, *KTU*^{2} 1.16 vi 56), which has also been restored in the *Baal Cycle* (*'ṯtrt* . š[m . b'l], *KTU*^{2} 1.2 i 8). This specific divine full name also reappears several centuries later in the fifth-century Ešmunazar Inscription (Astarte//Name-of-Baal, עשתרת שמ בעל, *KAI* 14:18), a text that also associates this goddess with Ṣidon: "[Astar]te (who is) in-Ṣidon//Land-by-the-Sea" ([עשתר]ת בצדנ ארצ ימ, l. 16). If Astarte is identified as

116 Rahmouni, *Divine Epithets*, 133; see also *KTU*^{2} 1.17 vi 34 and 1.92:29.

Name-of-Baal in a (mythological) text from Ugarit and nearly a millennium later in the Ṣidonian royal inscription, the possibility that she is the goddess hiding behind the epithet "Goddess of Ṣidon" in *KTU*^{2} 1.14 iv 35–36 and 39 should be tentatively considered. Furthermore, the phrase "Astarte (who is) in-Ṣidon" also appears in a seventh-century Ammonite seal (עשת⟨רת⟩ בצדן), indicating that this goddess was associated with this city by three different peoples in three different centuries.[117] If Kirta swore his vow to two goddesses in *KTU*^{2} 1.14 iv 38–39, Astarte, not Anat, was probably the second goddess.

In addition to the temples built for Baal-Ṣidon (בעל צדן) and Astarte//Name-of-Baal, *KAI* 14:14–16 mentions that Ešmunazar and his mother Amotastarte built other temples: one for "[Astar]te (who is) in Ṣidon//Land-by-the-Sea" (l. 16) and one for "Astarte-of-the-Lofty-Heavens" (עשתרת שממאדרם, l. 16).[118] The fact that three separate temples or shrines were built to Astarte in the city of Ṣidon may be significant, indicating that the "Astarte (who is) in-Ṣidon" might have also been Astarte//Name-of-Baal but was distinguished from Astarte-of-the-Lofty-Heavens. This "Astarte (who is) in-Ṣidon" should be considered (the unspecified) Astarte who is associated with the city of Ṣidon, which is to say that she was not known either by the divine full name Astarte-of-Ṣidon or Astarte-Ṣidon. Reading *KAI* 14 literally, this goddess is "in" Ṣidon, not "of" it, so the full-name methodology developed in chapters 3 and 4 is not applicable here. "Goddess of Ṣidon" was probably an epithet belonging to Astarte, who also happened to be known as Name-of-Baal, but no evidence suggests that this goddess was recognized by the full name Astarte-of-Ṣidon. (How or

---

117 Regarding *WSS* 876, Nahman Avigad suggested that עשת is an abbreviation for the divine name Astarte (עשתרת), which he also identified as the theophoric element in various Phoenician personal names (Nahman Avigad, *Corpus of West Semitic Stamp Seals* [Jerusalem: the Israel Academy of Sciences and Humanities: the Israel Exploration Society: the Institute of Archaeology: the Hebrew University of Jerusalem, 1997], 328), whereas Kent Jackson notes that the missing רת- at the end of the goddess's name is the result of haplography (Kent P. Jackson, *The Ammonite Language of the Iron Age*, HSM 27 [Chico: Scholars Press, 1983], 77). Although Avigad originally identified this as a Phoenician seal because of the vocabulary and the word Ṣidon (Nahman Avigad, "Two Phoenician Votive Seals," *Israel Exploration Journal* 16 [1966]: 248), more recently he decided that the seal is actually Ammonite (Avigad, *Corpus*, 328).

According to Larry Herr, the paleography of *WSS* 876 is a great example of late seventh-century Ammonite writing, with "perfect Ammonite forms" for the ע, ת, צ, כ, and ה (Larry G. Herr, *The Scripts of Ancient Northwest Semitic Seals*, HSM 18 [Missoula: Scholars Press, 1978], 71). Moreover, the personal name Abinadab (עבנדב) "is also happy Ammonite." In contrast to these opinions, Manfred Weippert identifies עשת as the Hurrian deity Asiti (Manfred Weippert, "Über den asiatischen Hintergrund der Göttin 'Asiti,'" *Orientalia* NS 44 [1975]: 13).

118 Donner and Röllig offer an alternative reading of *KAI* 14:16 – עשתרת שממאדרם – which would mean "Glorify Astarte there!" (Donner and Röllig, *KAI* 2, 22).

whether she is related to Astarte-of-the-Lofty-Heavens is unclear.) This is why Kirta made his vow to "Goddess of Ṣidon" and not to Astarte-of-Ṣidon by name. This divine name did not exist, perhaps because it had no competing Astarte from which she needed to be differentiated.

Astarte's Name-of-Baal is closely related in form to Tannit's Face-of-Baal (פנ בעל). References to Face-of-Baal are most often found in texts from Carthage, but there are two texts from Constantine in modern Algeria that contain the name (see Map 4). As the English translation indicates, scholars typically interpret this to indicate that Tannit is a representation, or hypostasis, of (the unspecified) Baal; she is an aspect of him, namely, his face.[119] However,

---

119 Cross noted that Tannit//Face-of-Baal and Astarte//Name-of-Baal, are semantically equivalent and that they are, in fact, suggestive of the goddesses' status as hypostases of their consort (Cross, *Canaanite Myth*, 30). Cross also noted that despite these semantically equivalent full names and their explicitly named relationship with Baal, we have reason to deny the identification of Tannit with Astarte because of the sixth-century text from Carthage (*KAI* 81:1). This text mentions both divine names as it dedicates new temples to them: לרבת לעשתרת ולתנת בלבננ מקדשמ חדשמ, "to the ladies, to Astarte and to Tannit (who are) in Lebanon: new temples." Despite their distinctiveness in this inscription, other scholars have pointed to a contemporary text from Sarepta as evidence for the identification of the two goddesses. This sixth-century text includes the compound divine name Tannit-Astarte (תנת עשתרת; James B. Pritchard, *Recovering Sarepta, A Phoenician City: Excavations at Sarafund, Lebanon, 1969-1974, by the University Museum of the University of Pennsylvania* [Princeton: Princeton University Press, 1978], 104–106).

Using a compound name as evidence for the identification of the individual deities can be problematic. For example, the purpose and meaning of the compound names of Assyrian deities, such as Assur-Enlil and Assur-Adad (K 252 iv 20–21), who are contained in the *tākultu*-ritual texts are uncertain (Menzel, *Assyrische Tempel*, 2:T 117). These compound names appear to be treated as though they belonged to a single deity, but the second divine name could also be interpreted as descriptive rather than equative (Porter, "Anxiety," 237; for a comparison with purpose and meaning of the compound divine names in ancient Egyptian religion, see Excursus). Following Porter, the divine names Assur-Enlil and Assur-Adad could signify that Assur had taken on a leadership position as Assur-Enlil and that he had taken on the attributes of a warrior or storm-god, respectively. Indeed, other potential compound divine names in this text indicate that the second name functions adjectivally, such as Assur-Dayyāni (Assur-the-divine-judge, *aš-šur* DI.$KU_5$$^{\cdot meš}$, K 252 i 16 and 22), which boasts of Assur's judicial attributes akin to the group of gods known as "the Divine Judges."

Returning to the Northwest Semitic deities, Maria Giulia Guzzo Amadasi notes that the Tannit-Astarte double name could indicate that Tannit is an associate of Astarte rather than the same goddess (Maria Giulia Guzzo Amadasi, "Tanit – 'ŠTRT *e* Milk – 'ŠTRT: *ipotesi*," *Or* NS 60 [1991]: 82–91, esp. 88–90). Applying Porter's evaluation of the *tākultu*-ritual texts' compound names, the Sarepta text could be describing the goddess Tannit in terms of attributes more commonly associated with Astarte. Of course, other possible interpretations should not be ruled out.

Lipiński suggests that it should be interpreted adverbially, which would mean that the goddess stands *before* (פנ) Baal, a reference to her original role as lamenter in the storm-god's cult.[120] This role, he argues, is reflected in the verbal form of the goddess's name, which is a piel form of the verb t-n-y (תני) that literally means "the lamenter."[121] Lipiñiski's interpretation not only makes historical sense of Face-of-Baal, but it also allows him to treat the goddess as a deity in-and-of herself, and all evidence suggests that she was a deity in her own right. This goddess had devotees who included her divine name in the fifth-century Ṣidonian personal name עבדתנת ("Servant-of-Tannit," *KAI* 53:1), in two sixth-century groups of devotees (גרתנת, "faithful-of-Tannit") at Ṣidon and Kition, in multiple Lebanese toponyms (i.e., *'Aqtanīt*, *'Aïtanīt*, *Kfar Tanīt*), and in various iconographic media, such as the "sign of Tannit."[122]

Of the fourteen times that Tannit is identified as Face-of-Baal, she appears before Baal-Ḥamān eight times (*KAI* 78:2; 79:1; 85:1; 86:1; 87:2[!]; 88:2; 94:1; and 97:1[!]); after Baal-Ḥamān four times (*KAI* 102:1–2; 105:1; 164:1; and 175:2–3); after Kronos once (*KAI* 176:1–3); and after (the unspecified) Baal once (*KAI* 137:1).[123] According to Sommer, because Tannit's full name Tannit//Face-of-Baal appeared only when she was "alongside Baal," she must have been considered Baal's consort and had "little independent existence," which is reminiscent of Cross's earlier hypostasis theories about the goddess.[124] Sommer also claims that the second invocation of the goddess in *KAI* 79:10 as Tannit//Face-of-Baal reinforces the fact that "she is somehow also a part of Baal, at least much of the time."[125] This interpretation, however, necessarily ignores the fact that the goddess was venerated throughout the Mediterranean world for centuries without constant explicit connections with Baal or, much more often, with

120 Lipiński, *Dieux et Déesses*, 199–201; see also Choon Leong Seow, "Face פנים, II," in *Dictionary of Deities and Demons in the Bible*, eds. Karel van der Toorn, Bob Becking, and Pieter W. van der Horst, 2nd rev. ed. (Leiden: Brill, 1999), 322; and Sommer, *Bodies of God*, 26. Seow further includes the phrase *smlb'l* in his discussion (סמל בעל, "Image of Baal," *KAI* 12:3–4; consider also the personal name פנסמלת in *KAI* 57 which means "face of the image"). These comparisons inevitably focus on the physical aspect of the epithets.

121 Lipiński, *Dieux et Déesses*, 199; see also Judges 11:40.

122 Lipiński, *Dieux et Déesses*, 202 and n. 68. Lipiński notes that גרתנת is the patronym of a group dating back to the sixth century (ibid., 202 n. 67). The "sign of Tannit" appears on figurines, amulets, seals, funerary monuments, mosaics, and statues. For a fuller discussion of Tannit, see Lipiński, *Dieux et Déesses*, 199–215.

123 Face-of-Baal is spelled with a yod (i.e., פין בעל) four times: *KAI* 94:1; 97:1; 102:1; 105:1. In the two Greek texts, it is transliterated as Φανεβαλ (*KAI* 175:2) and Φενηβαλ (*KAI* 176:2–3).

124 Sommer, *Bodies of God*, 26; and Cross, *Canaanite Myth*, 30.

125 Sommer, *Bodies of God*, 26.

Baal-Ḥamān.[126] She might have stood before (the unspecified) Baal or Baal-Ḥamān in a cultic setting as Lipiński suggests, and the fact that Baal-Ḥamān is typically present when Face-of-Baal is used might emphasize such a historical role, but this does not undermine her individuality as an independent goddess.

The fact that Tannit's name is listed prior to Baal-Ḥamān's name in most of the extant texts is noteworthy, and this could be suggestive of her independence from him or indicate that she outranked him in the divine world. If Tannit was Baal-Ḥamān's consort, then we should expect her name to appear after his, as is most often the case in the Mesopotamian EGLs examined in much of chapter 3. For instance, Ningal follows her husband Sîn in EGLs, Aya follows Šamaš, Šala follows Adad, Zarpānītu follows Marduk, and Tašmētu follows Nabû (see Tables 3.6, 3.7, 3.9 through 3.14, and 3.16). Moreover, devotees honored Tannit on her own as a goddess at least as much they honored her as Baal-Ḥamān's consort. In addition, concluding that Tannit was Baal's consort, as Sommer does, is mildly problematic if for no other reason than a lack of precision. She only appears in one text with (the unspecified) Baal, whereas she was paired with Baal-Ḥamān about a dozen times.[127] For Sommer, this is not an issue because he claims that he cannot distinguish distinct personalities or functions for the various Baal deities. He considers all Baal deities one, even if Baal-Ḥamān is identified as El/Kronos rather than with a storm-god like other Baal deities.[128]

Face-of-Baal is not the only potential full name of interest for this goddess. Another is found in *KAI* 81, a text from Carthage that locates Tannit in Lebanon (ולתנת בלבננ), which Donner and Röllig interpret as a divine full name: Tannit-in-Lebanon.[129] They also note that Lebanon indicates not the Syrian mountains, in general, but specifically the hills on which shrines to Ceres/Demeter

---

126 Cross suggested that the earliest inscription bearing the divine name Tannit was actually Proto-Sinaitic Text 347, which appears on a sphinx in the Hathor temple (Cross, *Canaanite Myth*, 32). Unlike Lipiński, who associates her name with "lamentation," Cross argued that the word Tannit is a feminine derivative of *tannīn* ("serpent"), which prompted him to identify Tannit with the Ugaritic goddess Ašerah.

127 *KAI* 87:1 and 97:2 have both been corrected by Donner and Röllig to read Baal-Ḥamān in the translations. The divine name is actually written as בחלמנ in *KAI* 87:1 and as בעל המנ in *KAI* 97:2.

128 Sommer, *Bodies of God*, 25; see also Cross, *Canaanite Myth*, 26, 30 and 35; Smith, *Origins*, 138–139; and Smith, *God in Translation*, 64, 248, and 253.

129 Donner and Röllig, *KAI* 2, 98–99. Barré and McCarter both interpret בלבננ ("in-Lebanon") as an epithet or last name for Tannit (Barré, *God-List*, 186 n. 473; McCarter, "Aspects," 141; cf. Allen "Examination," 75 and 81).

and Proserpina/Persephone were built in Roman times. If correct, this means that this Carthaginian text places the goddess at home in a very distant cult from its place of composition. As with the other topographic names governed by *bet*-locatives prepositions in Northwest Semitic texts that Barré and McCarter have proposed as divine epithets, this interpretation is not convincing for *KAI* 81. Unlike the multiple localized IŠKUR deities, LAMMA deities, and IŠTAR goddesses in Hittite treaties, the multiple localized Baal deities in Ugaritic and Northwest Semitic texts, this Tannit who is associated with Lebanon in *KAI* 81 is not distinguished from any other Tannit in this text, just as the Baal-Šamêm who was revered on Hawk Island was not distinguished from any other Baal-Šamêm in *KAI* 64:1. No Northwest Semitic text lists (the unspecified) Tannit alongside a Tannit-in-Lebanon, and no text distinguishes (the unspecified) Baal-Šamêm from Baal-Šamêm-on-Hawk-Island. Tannit is distinguished from Astarte in *KAI* 81, however, which argues against the identification of these two goddesses, as Cross noted.[130] Given the lack of other explicit connections between Tannit and Lebanon, this *bet*-locative could be interpreted as referring to both Tannit and Astarte, except Astarte had a strong association with cults in Ṣidon (e.g., *KAI* 14:16) rather than the specific mountain that Donner and Röllig have located in Lebanon. When considering translations for *KAI* 81:1, "To the ladies, to Astarte and to Tannit who *are* in Lebanon: new temples" is just as reasonable a translation of לרבת לעשתרת ולתנת בלבננ מקדשמ חדשמ as is "To the ladies, to Astarte and to Tannit, who *is* in Lebanon: new temples."

5.7 Conclusions

Although the number of deities officially revered at Ugarit was significantly smaller than the number of Assyrian and Hittite deities, and the local Phoenician, Punic, and Aramaic numbers were smaller still, they included distinct deities who shared the common first name Baal, a name that seems to have functioned less like a title in the latter second and first millennia and more like a name or nickname for the gods. Typically, but by no means exclusively, Baal functioned as another name for distinct storm-gods otherwise known as Hadad. At Ugarit, Baal-of-Ṣapun appeared alongside Baal-of-Ugarit and Baal-of-Aleppo in offering and ritual texts as one of the several (or seven, according to KTU^2 1.118:4–10 and RS 20.024:4–10) storm-gods who were

130 Cross, *Canaanite Myth*, 30.

worshipped in the city's temples. Applying the methodology from chapter 3 to the various EGLs from Ugarit, it can be argued with confidence that these three localized Baal deities were treated and perceived as three distinct deities by the priests and several members of the laity.

While the storm-god Baal-of-Ugarit was only attested in texts found at or near Ugarit, the storm-god Hadad- or Baal-of-Aleppo was attested as early as the third millennium and was still attested into the first millennium. His last name of-Aleppo was more important for his identification than either of his first names, which makes sense because he had two interchangeable first names. Likewise, the divine name Baal-of-Ṣapun continued beyond the second millennium and appeared in texts ranging from seventh-century Assyria to sixth-century Egypt and third-century Marseilles (in modern France; see Table 5.5 and Map 4). Moreover, Baal-of-Ṣapun and Baal-of-Aleppo were not the only Baal deities revered in the first millennium. Others with geographic last names included Baal-Šamêm, Baal-Ḥamān, Baal-Lebanon, and Baal-Kition, and many of these localized Baal deities appeared alongside each other in EGLs, demonstrating that they were envisioned as distinct Baal deities (see Table 5.6). Some, including Baal-Ḥamān, often appeared as the only male deities in a text, yet they still retained their full name, which indicates how important the geographic last name was to those localized Baal deities.

Additionally, there were localized Baal deities whose names did not appear in EGLs or in texts that mentioned another Baal deity, but we may still consider the possibility that they were envisioned as distinct from the other Baal deities discussed in this chapter. Using Baal-Ḥamān as an example of a deity whose last name was stressed even when no other potential Baal is referenced, we must at least entertain the possibility that other localized Baal deities were considered distinct from (the unspecified) Baal and other well-known localized Baal deities. For instance, the divine name Baal-Pe'or is mentioned in four different books in the Hebrew Bible, but nothing in those passages indicates that he was contrasted with (the unspecified) Baal or other geographically specific Baal deities. Perhaps this Baal deity was considered a distinct and independent Baal by his devotees and their Israelite neighbors, or maybe the location of the idolatrous event was too important to the Israelite scribes to let it be forgotten. Because Baal-Pe'or never appears in an EGL with other Baal deities, we cannot definitively decide which it was, but we may tentatively consider the likelihood that he was his own distinct deity based on analogy with Baal-Ḥamān and other localized Baal deities.

The Neo-Assyrian evidence, along with Hittite, Hurrian, and other non-Assyrian evidence from the Mesopotamian heartland, demonstrate that deities with geographic epithets were typically distinguished from each other in the same manner that other deities were distinguished from each other. The divine name Ištar-of-Nineveh was no more or less representative of a deity than was the divine name Ištar-of-Arbela, Aya, or Šamaš. Likewise, even though there were substantially fewer deities of interest in the first-millennium West than in Assyria, the divine name Baal-of-Ṣapun was no more or less representative of a deity than was the divine name Baal-of-Heaven, Baal-Ḥamān, Astarte, or Tannit.

6 A Kuntillet ʿAjrud Awakening

The first name Baal was relatively common for deities throughout the Levant and Mediterranean, and it typically served as an alternative name or nickname for storm-gods, for whom Hadad/Adad was their original first name. There were exceptions, however, including Baal-Ḫarrān, which was a nickname for the western Moon-God-of-Ḫarrān, and Baal-Ḥamān, who has been identified with the Canaanite or Ugaritic El by modern scholars and whom Philo of Byblos and others identified with the Greek god Kronos. Because the common noun *baal* means "lord" or "master," many deities were known by this nickname, including Marduk and Dagan. Similarly, the divine name Ištar was relatively common name among Mesopotamian goddesses, and it could function as a common noun in Akkadian literature, where it was used to mean "goddess" as early as the Old Babylonian period.[1] Unlike the name Baal, however, the name Ištar seemed to serve as each goddess's primary name rather than as her nickname. As discussed in chapter 4.1, other titles or nicknames by which Ištar goddesses were known include "Lady" (*bēlet*) and "Queen" (*šarrat*). There is no reason to suspect that the name Ištar replaced other goddess names in the same way that Baal replaced Hadad and Adad names.

In contrast to the divine first names Baal and Ištar, little about the divine name Yahweh suggests that it should be interpreted as a common noun. Indeed, because the origin and meaning of the name Yahweh have eluded scholarly consensus, making an appeal to *yahweh* as a common noun is exceptionally difficult.[2] This would be true whether the appeal considered the possibility that a divine first name had become a common noun, as with Ištar/*ištar*, or the possibility that a common noun had become a title and divine nickname, as with *baal*/Baal. Also in contrast to the names Baal and Ištar, no extant texts contrast one Yahweh deity with another Yahweh deity in an individual text, and no Israelite text includes an embedded god list to suggest that there were other deities to contrast with (the unspecified) Yahweh. For these reasons, the methodology followed in chapter 3 cannot be used to determine whether the ancient Israelites distinguished one Yahweh associated with a particular location from another Yahweh at another location. However,

---

1 *CAD* I/J, *ištaru*; and Emerton, "New Light," 7.

2 For a recent discussion of possible meanings of the name Yahweh and its extra-biblical attestations, see Karel van der Toorn, "Yahweh," in *Dictionary of Deities and Demons in the Bible*, eds. Karel van der Toorn, Bob Becking, and Pieter W. van der Horst, 2nd rev. ed. (Leiden: Brill, 1999), 913–916; see also Frank Moore Cross, "Yahweh and the God of the Patriarchs," *HTR* 55 (1962), 250–256.

our examinations of divine name formulas in the Neo-Assyrian and various Levantine texts (i.e., DN-of-GN, title-of-GN, DN//title-of-GN, and DN//Who-Resides-(in)-GN; see chapters 4 and 5) provide us with a template for evaluating the likelihood of whether previously proposed Yahweh names could have represented potentially independent and distinct localized Yahweh deities.[3]

Prior to the discovery of the texts at Kuntillet ‘Ajrud (Ḥorvat Teman; see Map 1) in the 1970s, no compelling reason existed for considering Yahweh as the first name of more than one deity. Within the Hebrew Bible, Yahweh had numerous epithets that were attributed to him, including “God of Israel” (e.g., Psalm 68:36) and “God of Heaven” (e.g., Psalm 136:26), but consensus held that these were strictly epithets. With the discovery of the texts at Kuntillet ‘Ajrud, new evidence introduced the possibility that the divine name Yahweh might not just be one of the several names ascribed to the ancient Israelites’ national deity; Yahweh might have been the first name of different locally manifest deities. Now, we know that someone worshipped a deity that he addressed as Yahweh-of-Samaria, and he did this at a shrine dedicated to Yahweh-of-Teman. Since the discovery, a handful of other phrases have been reinterpreted as full names of various localized Yahweh deities, including the Yahweh-in-Hebron and Yahweh-in-Zion. This final chapter examines the Yahweh full names that have been proposed since 1975 and explains whether they should be considered legitimate divine full names. This chapter also explains why even legitimate full names are not necessarily indicative of multiple independent and distinct Yahweh deities in the same way that Northwest Semitic and Akkadian full names indicate the existence of multiple, distinct and independent localized Baal deities and Ištar goddesses.

6.1 “Hear, O Israel, Yahweh//our-God”

Whenever biblical scholars have the opportunity to consider multiple localized Yahweh deities, they tend to do so in light of Deuteronomy 6:4, commonly known by its incipit as “the Shema”: שמע ישראל יהוה אלהינו יהוה אחד. For this reason, we begin our examination of Yahweh full names by considering the potential theological and syntactical meanings of this verse. This verse has

3 “Yahweh deities/deity” should be understood as a multiplicity-neutral phrase indicating that the first name Yahweh has been paired with a specific last name. It is not intended to suggest that each Yahweh-of-GN was necessarily a distinct and independent localized Israelite god.

several possible translations, which also means that many theological possibilities exist. One translation, in particular, and its meaning go back to at least the Septuagint and Vulgate: "Hear, O Israel, the Lord our God is one Lord" (Ἄκουε Ἰσραὴλ Κύριος ὁ θεὸς ἡμῶν Κύριος εἷς ἐστι, LXX; and *audi Israhel Dominus Deus noster Dominus unus est*, Vulgate). In Yahwistic terms, this means that the deity is Israel's deity and that he is one Yahweh. The question then becomes "what does 'one Yahweh' mean?" In his 1910 article, "Monojawhismus des Deuteronomiums," William Bade advocated this ancient interpretation of the verse and argued that the Shema was intended as a polemical warning against the poly-Yahwism that had taken hold in ancient Israel.[4] Writing more than 65 years prior to the discovery of the divine names Yahweh-of-Samaria and Yahweh-of-Teman at Kuntillet 'Ajrud, Bade had no extra-biblical evidence to prompt this discussion; instead, his argument revolved around the twin issues of the centralization of Yahwistic worship in Jerusalem and the identification of Yahweh with Baal as Israelite and Canaanite religious traditions syncretized.[5]

Bade viewed the Canaanite religious communities as localized Baal fertility cults.[6] When Israelites encountered the Canaanites, he argued, they adopted the local practices and began worshipping Yahweh at cults that had been previously dedicated to Baal. Because Bade considered each Baal its own distinct deity and believed that Yahweh had been locally identified with each Baal, he envisioned a poly-Yahwism that had permeated Israelite religious thought.[7] This poly-Yahwism, he argued, not only threatened the Israelite deity's oneness but also threatened the Israelite people's oneness and promoted a tribalism that undermined the monarchy.

In response to this threat, Bade argued that the Deuteronomist sought to strengthen Israel as a united people and focus their worship on a central cult with just one national Yahweh. This was accomplished by the advent of pilgrimages to the central cult (e.g., Deuteronomy 16:16 f.), which was now considered the only legitimate place of worship.[8] In order to further sever Israelite ties to the local cults where each community worshipped its own

4 William F. Bade, "Der Monojahwismus des Deuteronomiums," *ZAW* 30 [1910]: 81.
5 Bade, "Monojahwismus," 88 and 83.
6 Bade, "Monojahwismus," 82.
7 Bade's poly-Yahwism in which different localized Baal deities are individually equated with a national deity like Yahweh may be comparable to Meinhold's proposed identification of different localized Ištar goddesses with the national Assyrian goddess Mullissu (Meinhold, *Ištar in Aššur*, 203 f.; see also chapter 4.5).
8 Bade, "Monojahwismus," 87.

localized Yahweh deity, the Deuteronomist reminded Israel that they were a unique people in a unique relationship with their deity (4:7–8). Whereas the Canaanites and other nations of the world had been allotted their gods (4:19) and could worship them wherever they wanted (12:8–16), the Israelites were only permitted to worship at the national cult, a place chosen specifically by Yahweh (12:5).[9] Bade noted that this sentiment was also espoused by the prophets Hosea and Amos, who specifically condemned the Israelite worship of Baal at illegitimate cult sites.[10] For instance, after a verbal attack against Samaria, Amos denounced worship at the famous Dan and Beersheba cult sites in Israel:

הנשבעים באשמת שמרון ואמרו חי אלהיך דן וחי דרך באר־שבע ונפלו ולא־יקומו עוד

> The ones who swear by the guilt of Samaria and say, "By the life of your God, O Dan," and "By the life of the way of Beersheba." They shall fall and not get up again. (Amos 8:14)

Amos blatantly condemned illicit worship at illegitimate cult sites because it undermined legitimate Yahwism, and Hosea explicitly blamed Israel/Ephraim for worshipping Baal in place of Yahweh (Hosea 13:1 ff.), or as Bade argued, worshipping Baal as a localized form of Yahweh. In contrast to these two prophets, the Deuteronomist decided against a negative campaign about Baal worship and instead formulated a positive call intended to inspire the Israelites to worship the singular Yahweh at his only legitimate cult site. Of course, Bade would not have denied that the Deuteronomist implemented negative campaigns against other non-Israelite deities and "foreign" cultic or idolatrous practices; after all, Deuteronomy 16:21–22 flatly forbids ašerah/Ašerah trees and stone pillars as legitimate forms of Israelite worship. However, because Bade believed that localized Baal deities had been locally equated with the national deity Yahweh, he concluded that the Deuteronomist could not explicitly condemn Baal worship without implicitly disapproving Yahweh worship in his audience's mind. For this reason, the Deuteronomist's campaign was a positive call, and that call was Deuteronomy 6:4, which Bade translated as "(Hear, O Israel,) Yahweh our God is *one Yahweh*," not the many Yahweh deities who are also many Baal deities.[11]

Like Bade, Albrecht Alt was interested in localized worship in ancient Israel and contrasted the national Yahwistic cult with regional tribal cults

---

9 Bade, "Monojahwismus," 90.
10 Bade, "Monojahwismus," 85.
11 Bade, "Monojahwismus," 81, emphasis mine.

devoted to other deities. Instead of focusing on the numerous localized Baal deities that were identified with the Israelite Yahweh, Alt focused on the relationships between the divine name Yahweh and the various alternative divine epithets that are presented in the Patriarchal narratives in Genesis. Guided by the Elohist (Exodus 3:1, 4b, 6, 9–14, and 18–23) and Priestly (6:2–8) accounts that claimed that the name Yahweh had not been known previous to Moses' theophany at the burning bush, Alt examined the pre-Yahwistic epithets (e.g., God-of-the-Father) and determined that these represented independent patron deities.[12] These pre-Yahwistic and pre-Israelite deities often lacked their own unique divine names and were instead identified by their relationship with humanity.[13] For example, the independent god known as God-of-Abraham was first worshipped by Abraham (Genesis 31:42); Fear-of-Isaac was first worshipped by Isaac (v. 42); and Mighty-One-of-Jacob was first worshipped by Jacob (49:24).[14] Centuries later when the Yahwistic Israelite tribes entered Canaan and interacted with the native Canaanite cults, Yahweh was first promoted as the new national deity and the patron deities remained independent. Eventually, worship of the national god Yahweh encroached upon the regional patron gods at the local sanctuaries, and each deity was identified with him.[15] Alt admitted that we cannot know when the many God-of-the-Father religions coalesced into a single Yahwistic national religion, but he believed that it was completed by the time the Elohist and Yahwist accounts were written down. If we were to apply Alt's theory to Deuteronomy 6:4, then the Shema would represent a final step in which the Israelite audience is reminded of Yahweh's singularity. As with Bade, Alt's historical reconstruction begins with distinct regional or tribal deities who became identified with the new Israelite deity on a one-by-one basis. The once independent gods were finally united in the nationally revered figure, Yahweh. Bade's and Alt's theories differ according to their perceived levels of religious tolerance in the Shema. Whereas Alt would have reckoned "Yahweh is one" as a culmination of religious syncretism on a national level, Bade envisioned Deuteronomy 6:4 and its call for a singular Yahweh as an implicit rejection of localized Baalism for the Israelites that was plaguing Israelite society and its earlier pristine Yahwism.

---

12 Albrecht Alt, "The God of the Fathers," in *Essays on Old Testament History and Religion*, trans. R. A. Wilson (Oxford: Basil Blackwell, 1966), 11–12 and 30.
13 Alt, "God of the Fathers," 31.
14 Alt, "God of the Fathers," 47 and 55.
15 Alt, "God of the Fathers," 59–60.

In the century since Bade's article, the meaning and historical context of the Shema have been reexamined numerous times. While the possibility of multiple localized Yahweh deities continues to be noted, the focus on the role that Baal played in the Shema's creation has diminished or disappeared, largely because of the texts from Kuntillet ʻAjrud. In the 1960s, Gerhard von Rad viewed Deuteronomy 6:4 as a confession that distinguished Yahwistic Israelite worship from the Canaanite cult(s) devoted to Baal and as a proclamation meant to undermine divergent Yahwistic shrines and traditions, an idea reminiscent of Bade's poly-Yahwism.[16] Likewise, in the early 1970s before the discovery of Kuntillet ʻAjrud, Georg Fohrer suggested that the centralization of the Yahweh cult at the single sanctuary in Jerusalem occurred in response to the fear that "the conception of Yahweh might split up and finally produce several Yahwehs."[17] More than two decades after the discovery of Kuntillet ʻAjrud, Andrew Mayes, Jeremy Hutton, and Shmuel Aḥituv, Esther Eshel, and Ze'ev Meshel have also interpreted the declaration of Deuteronomy 6:4 as a response to different localized manifestations of Yahweh within Israel with little to no interest in the Yahweh-Baal equation that concerned Bade.[18]

Comprising six words, the verse has no certain interpretation. The first two words, "Hear, O Israel," prepare the audience for the rest of the sentence, of which there are several possible translations and interpretations. Because three of the four Hebrew words are nouns, and the last word is an adjective, the Shema's translation depends on where the linking verb, or the copula, is placed:

i) Yahweh is our God, Yahweh alone.
ii) Yahweh our God is one Yahweh.
iii) Yahweh our God, Yahweh is one.
iv) Yahweh is our God, Yahweh is one.[19]

---

16 Gerhard von Rad, *Deuteronomy: A Commentary*, trans. Dorothea Barton, Old Testament Library (Philadelphia: Westminster Press, 1966), 63.

17 Georg Fohrer, *Introduction to Israelite Religion*, trans. David E. Green (Nashville: Abingdon, 1972), 297.

18 Andrew D. H. Mayes, "Kuntillet ʻAjrud and the History of Israelite Religion," in *Archaeology and Biblical Interpretation*, ed. J. R. Bartlett (London: Routledge, 1997), 62; Jeremy Hutton, "Local Manifestations of Yahweh and Worship in the Interstices: A Note on Kuntillet ʻAjrud," *JANER* 10 (2010): 179–180 and 206; and Shmuel Aḥituv, Esther Eshel, and Ze'ev Meshel, "The Inscriptions," in *Kuntillet ʻAjrud (Ḥorvat Teman): An Iron Age II Religious Site on the Judah-Sinai Border*, ed. Ze'ev Meshel (Jerusalem: Israel Exploration Society, 2012), 130.

19 R. W. L. Moberly, "'Yahweh is One': The Translation of the Shema," in *Studies in the Pentateuch*, ed. J. A. Emerton, VTSup 41 (Leiden: Brill, 1990), 210; and Jeffrey H. Tigay, *Deuteronomy: The Traditional Hebrew Text with the New JPS Translation*, JPS Torah Commentary 5 (Philadelphia, Jewish Publication Society, 1996), 76 and 440.

Option i stresses the relationship between Yahweh and the people of Israel, whereas options ii and iii stress Yahweh's nature. Option iv, which employs two linking verbs, closely resembles option iii, and suffers from the compounded problems with the interpretations of options i and iii.[20]

By stressing the relationship between Yahweh and the Israelites, option i is in keeping with a main Deuteronomic theme, Yahweh is to be Israel's only deity. This theme is already expressed in Deuteronomy 5 as one of the Ten Commandments: "You shall not have other gods besides me" (לא־יהיה לך אלהים אחרים על־פני, 5:7). Likewise, the verses following the Shema reinforce this interpretation. According to the charge in 6:5, each Israelite must love Yahweh with "all your heart, soul, and might" (בכל־לבבך ובכל־נפשך בכל־מאדך), and vv. 13–14 remind each Israelite that he may revere, serve, and swear only by Yahweh and that he may not follow any other gods; after all, Yahweh is a "jealous God" (אל קנא, v. 15). This thematic unity between the Shema's proclamation and the rest of Deuteronomy 6 is the strongest argument in favor of option i, "Yahweh is our God, Yahweh alone."[21]

Nevertheless, there are problems with option i. First, nowhere else in Deuteronomy are the words Yahweh (יהוה) and my/our/your-God (אלהי־) juxtaposed with the latter functioning predicatively, meaning "Yahweh (is) my/our/your God."[22] The Deuteronomist paired these two words as a unit nearly 300 times, and, according to R. W. L. Moberly, it is unlikely that Deuteronomy 6:4 would be the only instance in which these two words would have to be split by a linking verb in translation. Moreover, option i requires a special nuance of the Shema's final word אחד, which normally means "one" rather than "alone." The usual biblical Hebrew word for "alone" is לבד-, as it is used, for example, in 2 Kings 19:15: יהוה אלהי ישראל ישב הכרבים אתה־הוא האלהים לבדך (Yahweh//God-of-Israel//Who-Sits-(on)-the-Cherubim-(Throne), you alone are God").[23] There are a few other passages in which אחד can take on the meaning "alone," according to some scholars. [24] For example, 1 Chronicles 29:1 makes

---

20 Moberly, "Yahweh is One," 210; and Tigay, *Deuteronomy*, 439.

21 Tigay, *Deuteronomy*, 76 and 440; cf. Moberly, "Yahweh is One," 211.

22 Moberly, "Yahweh is One," 213–214.

23 This "alone" (לבד-) appears again in 2 Kings 19:19; Psalm 86:10; and Isaiah 2:11 and 17.

24 Tigay, *Deuteronomy*, 358 n. 10. Tigay also suggests that אחד "possibly" means "alone" in Joshua 22:20 (see also Job 23:13) and compares the use of *'aḥdy* in Ugaritic as "I alone" (KTU^2 1.4 vii 49). Likewise, Moshe Weinfeld noted that a Sumerian dedicatory inscription says, "Enlil is the lord of Heaven and Earth, he is king alone (literally: his oneness)" (^{d}en.lil$_2$ an.ki.šu lugal.am$_2$ aš.ni lugal.am$_2$, RIME 4 E4.1.4.6:1–3), and he also noted that some Greek texts that contain the phrase Εἷς Θεός that might be better translated as "God alone" than as "one god" (Moshe Weinfeld, "The Loyalty Oath in the Ancient Near East," *UF* 8 [1976]: 409 n. 266). Other classical deities that he mentioned who appear with the word "one" when "alone" might be a

sense when "alone" is used in place of "one": שלמה בני אחד בחר בו אלהים ("Solomon, my son, God chose him alone"). Only Solomon, or Solomon alone, is Yahweh's choice as the next king. In this vein, only Yahweh, or Yahweh alone, is Israel's God. Judah Kraut notes, however, that although an "alone" translational value for אחד works in 1 Chronicles 29:1, neither in this verse nor elsewhere does אחד mean "alone" indisputably; "one" makes just as much sense.[25] 1 Chronicles 29:1 works as "Solomon my son is (the) one whom God chose," and because "one" is the normal and expected meaning of the word, it should be preferred to "alone" as a translational value. The simpler possibility is the better possibility.[26] Moberly also rejects the value of אחד as "alone" rather than "one" in 29:1 because it introduces a contrast between Solomon and David's other sons that had not been addressed elsewhere in the passage.[27]

Zechariah 14:9 also seems to use אחד to indicate that Yahweh alone is God – not just the one or only God for Israel but the only God for all mankind: "Yahweh will become king over all the earth. On that day, it will be Yahweh alone and his name alone" (והיה יהוה למלך על־כל־הארץ ביום ההוא יהיה יהוה אחד ושמו אחד). Literally, the last five words of the verse can be translated, "Yahweh will-be one, and-his-name one," but interpreting these "one"s as anything other than a substitute for "alone," "only," or possibly "the one" feels awkward in English.[28] Tigay argues that the wording at the end of Zechariah 14:9 is based upon the Shema, which means that option i is the only above interpretation of the Shema that is documented within the Hebrew Bible.[29] Regardless, relying

preferred translation include Isis (*omnia*), Hermes (*omnia solus et unus*), and Zeus (Εἶς), and William F. Arndt and F. Wilbur Gingrich include the definitions "single, only one" (mng. 2b) and "alone" (mng. 2c) in their discussion of "εἷς, μία, ἕν" (William F. Arndt and F. Wilbur Gingrich, *A Greek-English Lexicon of the New Testament and other Early Christian Literature* [Chicago: University of Chicago Press, 1957], 230). They parenthetically cite Deuteronomy 6:4 in mng. 2c.

25 Judah Kraut, "Deciphering the Shema: Staircase Parallelism and the Syntax of Deuteronomy 6:4," *VT* 61 [2011]: 585 n. 8.

26 Kraut also considers this "one"/"alone" possibility in Joshua 22:20; Isaiah 51:2; Ezekiel 33:24 and 37:22; and Zechariah 14:9, and he concludes, "None of these examples, however, represents an unequivocal precedent in which *'eḥad* must be translated as 'alone'" (Kraut, "Deciphering the "Shema," 585 n. 8).

27 Moberly, "Yahweh is One," 212.

28 The NRSV and NJPS translations reflect this idea: "the Lord will be one and his name one" (NRSV) and "there shall be one Lord with one name" (NJPS). NJPS adds a footnote, however, that the verse really means "the Lord alone shall be worshiped and shall be invoked by His true name."

29 Tigay, *Deuteronomy*, 76 and 439.

on a rare and disputed meaning of אחד and breaking up the fixed pair "Yahweh our-God" with a linking verb make option i a less than ideal translation.

This brings us to option ii, the option favored by Bade, even though the plain sense reading of the verse lacks the Yahweh-is-Baal motif that Bade envisioned: "Yahweh our God is one Yahweh." This option seems more plausible today than it did a century ago in light of the Kuntillet 'Ajrud texts that invoke Yahweh-of-Samaria and Yahweh-of-Teman, but it is still problematic. On the one hand, these now extant divine names only predate Deuteronomy 6 by about a century, so the Shema could have been written in response to Israelites who thought that Yahweh-of-Samaria was distinct from Yahweh-of-Teman, (the unspecified) Yahweh, or any other localized Yahweh deity. If this were the case, then the Israelites' view of poly-Yahwism would have matched the contemporary Neo-Assyrians view regarding multiple localized Ištar goddesses. On the other hand, neither the concept of multiple Yahweh deities nor of Yahweh's non-singular nature is addressed anywhere else in the Hebrew Bible.[30] No other biblical writers showed concern about the possibility that more than one Yahweh existed. No prophets protested poly-Yahwism, nor did the authors and editors of the Deuteronomic histories list poly-Yahwism among the many sins of the Israelite or Judahite kings. Not even Deuteronomy mentions the topic of poly-Yahwism anywhere else. The rest of Deuteronomy 6 is concerned with Israel's exclusive relationship with Yahweh and, contrary to Bade's argument, Deuteronomy 12 never hints that regional Yahwistic shrines would have been a threat to Yahweh's unity.[31] If the Deuteronomist had felt that poly-Yahwism was an issue worth addressing, he would not have introduced it so conspicuously in the Shema and never approached the topic again. Throughout the Hebrew Bible, worshipping Yahweh incorrectly or worshipping other gods was a constant threat to the biblical authors, but worshipping more than one Yahweh or the wrong Yahweh was never a real concern.

Moberly does not address this poly-Yahwism issue as it relates to option ii. Instead, he focuses on his preferred option: option iii. For him, the Shema was a statement about Yahweh's nature, not his relationship with Israel. Because of the stative verb that appears in Zechariah 14:9 (יהיה), Moberly concludes that Zechariah interpreted the final two words of the Shema as a nominal sentence (i.e., "Yahweh will become one"), a conclusion that is noticeably different from Tigay's "alone" theory, and he retrojects this meaning back in time to the

30 Tigay, *Deuteronomy*, 439.
31 McCarter, "Aspects," 142–143.

Deuteronomist's call.[32] According to Moberly, Deuteronomy 6:4 should be interpreted to mean, "Yahweh our-God, Yahweh is one." However, despite Moberly's support, option iii still has a syntactic problem; the second occurrence of the name Yahweh is superfluous. If the point of the verse were to declare that Yahweh is one, it could have said simply "Yahweh our-God is one."[33]

Judah Kraut proposes a solution to deal with option iii's seeming redundancy. He suggests that we reinterpret the Shema as an instance of staircase parallelism.[34] Unlike synonymous (or antithetic) parallelism where the second colon restates (or negates) the first, staircase parallelism involves the repetition of one element in both cola, and the full thought is not completed without reading both cola as one idea.[35] Structurally, staircase parallelism follows an AB//AC pattern, which is a rhetorical flourish for the more common ABC pattern for a tricola. This pattern fits the Shema perfectly:

A	B	//	A	C
Yahweh (יהוה)	our-God (אלהינו)		Yahweh (יהוה)	one (אחד)

equals, or can be interpreted to mean:

A	B			C
Yahweh (יהוה)	our-God (אלהינו)	(is)		one (אחד).[36]

32 Moberly, "Yahweh is One," 215.

33 Tigay, *Deuteronomy*, 439.

34 Kraut, "Deciphering the Shema," 590–591.

35 Kraut notes that staircase parallelism is restricted to direct speech and usually appears at the beginning of a spoken address (Kraut, "Deciphering the Shema," 599). Significantly, Tigay notes that "as the first paragraph of the Instruction that God gave Moses on Mount Sinai [the Shema] is, in a sense, the beginning of Deuteronomy proper," and Kraut argues that, given the significance of Moses's speech to the Israelites, this seems like the perfect place to employ staircase parallelism (Tigay, *Deuteronomy*, 76; and Kraut, "Deciphering the Shema," 600).

36 This staircase parallelism that Kraut observes in the Shema is present in two other verses that also praise Yahweh (Kraut, "Deciphering the Shema," 599):

	MT with staircase parallelism:		without staircase element:
Exodus 15:3	יהוה איש מלחמה יהוה שמו Yahweh//Man-of-War, Yahweh is his name.	→	יהוה איש מלחמה שמו Yahweh//Man-of-War is his name.
Hosea 12:6	יהוה אלהי הצבאות יהוה זכרו Yahweh//God-of-Hosts, Yahweh is his name.	→	יהוה אלהי הצבאות זכרו Yahweh//God-of-Hosts is his name.

Kraut's punctuation for Yahweh-Man-of-War and Yahweh-God-of-Hosts has been modified slightly according to the normal divine name plus epithet formula used throughout this study. As elsewhere, two parallel lines (//) are used to indicate that a proper name and epithet are

In Deuteronomy 6:4, the second attestation of the name Yahweh is the repeated element that can be ignored in order to clarify the verse's underlying meaning. Because this interpretation effectively reduces the Shema to three words, it also simplifies our translational and interpretative possibilities. Given the frequent pairing of the divine name Yahweh (יהוה) with the epithet my/our/your-God (אלהי-) in Deuteronomy, the only reasonable place for a linking verb among these three nouns is between "our-God" and "one," which is why we can ignore option iv altogether. Kraut's interpretation, "Yahweh//our-God is one," which neutralizes the seeming redundancy of the second Yahweh, seems to be the best way to understand these three words and supports option iii.

Moberly notes this "resumptive use of *yhwh*" but attributes its origins to a pre-Deuteronomistic cultic formula rather than solve the problem syntactically as Kraut does.[37] He argues that if there were a pre-Deuteronomist cult formula behind the Shema, it involved the two words Yahweh (יהוה) and one (אחד), which the Deuteronomist expanded by prefacing it with Yahweh//our-God (יהוה אלהינו אחד). This preface was added because the phrase Yahweh//our-God (יהוה אלהינו) is the Deuteronomist's "customary idiomatic way" to refer to the Israelite deity, and he could not leave out this "intrusive use" of the epithet in this ancient declaration.[38] The result is that Moberly dismisses the Shema's redundancy as editorial clumsiness and creates a historical context in which the declaration no longer fits. We are left with "Yahweh (our-God) is one."

However, option iii still leaves us with the question: what does "Yahweh is one" actually mean? Moberly makes no attempt at solving this issue and merely promises to explore this question in a future essay:

> I conclude, therefore, that the Shema cannot legitimately be rendered "Yahweh is our God, Yahweh alone", but should best be translated "Hear, O Israel: Yahweh our God, Yahweh is one". It is not, therefore, a statement about Israel's exclusive relationship with Yahweh, although that exclusive relationship is indeed presupposed by the words "Yahweh our God". Rather, it is a statement about Yahweh; though precisely what it means to say that Yahweh is "one" is an issue to which I hope to return on another occasion.[39]

This conclusion is an admission that no persuasive answer to this question had been found.[40] If the earlier historical context that Moberly proposes did, in

acting together with the force of a full name (e.g., Yahweh//God-of-Hosts and Ištar//Lady-of-Nineveh).

37 Moberly, "Yahweh is One," 214.

38 Moberly, "Yahweh is One," 214.

39 Moberly, "Yahweh is One," 215.

40 The solutions proposed by philosophers, as opposed to philologists, are beyond the purview of this study.

fact, exist, it seems unlikely that the original historical context behind the creation of “Yahweh is one” would have been Bade’s anti-poly-Yahwism referendum. It is unlikely because the issue was never made explicit in sources from the biblical world. If Deuteronomy 6:4 had not existed, Bade would have had no reason to imagine poly-Yahwism in the first place. It also seems unlikely that “Yahweh is one” was meant to serve as a uniting refrain for the incorporation of the God-of-the-Father cults located throughout Canaan into the national Yahwistic cult, as Alt might have argued. According to Alt, the national Yahweh cult had already come to identify Yahweh with the patron deities of the land before the Elohist and Yahwist accounts recorded their accounts of ancient Israelite history. According to Alt, the Elohist and Yahwist only needed to treat the patron gods as epithets for the national deity in order to identify them with “Elohim” and “Yahweh.”[41] Furthermore, if the entirety of the Shema was original to the Deuteronomist as is generally assumed, then we must return to the issue of Yahwistic multiplicity in which Deuteronomy has no interest when making sense of the phrase “Yahweh our-God (is) one.”

In our review of the possible interpretations of the Shema we find: option i (“Yahweh is our-God, Yahweh alone”) entails syntactic and lexical difficulties; option ii (“Yahweh our-God is one Yahweh”) entails historical difficulties and a lack of biblical interest; our modified option iii (“Yahweh our-God is one”) entails a conceptual difficulty that seems to move the discussion nowhere; and option iv has many of the same problems as options i and iii. Of these options, option ii is the option that is most consistent with the syntax and lexicography of the Shema, and its main difficulty is essentially an argument from silence. Perhaps the epigraphic references to Yahweh-of-Samaria and Yahweh-of-Teman demonstrate that there was a certain amount of poly-Yahwism that the Deuteronomist wished to counter, and perhaps the Deuteronomist felt that the Shema’s declaration was sufficient enough to make further discussions on the topic unnecessary. In this vein, Jeremy Hutton recently suggested that Deuteronomy 6:4 “may have been designed precisely in order to draw attention to the impropriety, both syntactic and theological, of differentiating between local manifestations of Yahweh.”[42] Perhaps, even if different localized Yahweh manifestations were each recognized as the one singular and solitary Yahweh revered by the Deuteronomist and his contemporary Israelites, this was still too fragmented, or non-one, in the Deuteronomist’s theology. This is a possibility that we must now consider if we are going to keep the famous Shema as a proof text for or against poly-

41 Alt, “God of the Fathers,” 24 and 29.
42 Hutton, “Local Manifestations,” 206.

Yahwism, even if the Deuteronomist and authors and editors of the historical books reveal no concern about this issue elsewhere in their writings. We begin by examining the divine names Yahweh-of-Teman, Yahweh-of-Samaria, and potential evidence that could suggest a Yahwistic cult site in either of those places. Then we consider a known Yahwistic cult site, Jerusalem and Zion, and look in vain for a geographic last name related to that site. Finally, other proposed Yahweh full names are considered (and rejected).

6.2 The Geographic Origin of Yahweh: Teman

The Deuteronomist placed the Shema on Moses's lips near the beginning of his final speech to the Israelites before they entered into Israel near the end of their long journey from Egypt, but the Hebrew Bible contains indications that Yahweh was not native to the land of Israel or a Sinai that was part of a direct route from Egypt to Moab's Mount Nebo. Recently, Joseph Blenkinsopp revisited the possibility that both Yahweh's and the people of Judah's origins can be located in the land of Edom, and Karel van der Toorn suggests that Yahweh was originally not a Northwest Semitic deity but one of proto-Arabic origin.[43] Along these same lines, Martin Rose entertains the possibility that Yahweh was previously an Edomite deity, which he claims explains the "religious cohesion" of the Israelites, Judahites, and Edomites.[44] Beyond the cohesion claims, a handful of ancient texts and biblical verses do suggest that Yahweh's origins can be traced to somewhere southeast of ancient Israel in the Arabah.

Apart from Mitchell Dahood's belief that the divine name Yahweh was among the theophoric elements common to personal names from third-millennium Ebla, the earliest known attestations of the name Yahweh actually appear as geographic rather than divine names.[45] Of these texts, the most notable is the thirteenth-century text from Ramses II's reign that associates the name Yahweh with the cities Seir (*s'rr*), Laban (*rbn*), Payaspayas (*pyspys*, which

43 Blenkinsopp, "Midianite-Kenite Hypothesis Revisited and the Origins of Judah," *JSOT* 33 (2008): 131–153; and van der Toorn, "Yahweh," 910–911; see also Smith, *Early History*, 25 and 81.

44 Martin Rose, "Yahweh in Israel – Quas in Edom?" *JSOT* 4 (1977): 31.

45 Mitchell Dahood, "Afterword: Ebla, Ugarit, and the Bible," afterward to *The Archives of Ebla*: *An Empire Inscribed in Clay*, by Giovanni Pettinato (New York: Doubleday, 1981), 277; and van der Toorn, "Yahweh," 911. Raphael Giveon notes that the earliest text dates to the 11th Dynasty in Egypt but lacks a specific geographic context (Raphael Giveon, "'The Cities of our God' [II Sam 10 12]," *JBL* 83 [1964]: 415).

lacks a modern identification), Samath (*smt*), Turbil/r (⟨*t*⟩*wrbr*, or modern Wadi Hasa; see Map 3) in the land of the Shasu.[46] Because Seir and Laban are known

46 Donald B. Redford, *Egypt, Canaan, and Israel in Ancient Times* (Princeton: Princeton University Press, 1992), 272; Raphael Giveon, *Les Bédouins Shosou des documents Égyptiens* (Leiden: Brill, 1971), 76; and William F. Albright, review of "L'épithète divine Jahvé Seba'ôt: Étude philogique, historique et exégétigue," by B. N. Wambacq, *JBL* 67 (1948): 380. This Ramesside inscription provides six geographic names in the land of the Shasu (Kenneth A. Kitchen, *Ramesside Inscriptions: Translated & Annotated: Translations* [Oxford: Blackwell Publishers, 1996], 2:75):

line:	**Transcription:**	**Translation:**
92	*t3-šs sʻrr*	Shasu-land: Seir
93	(*t3-šs*) *rbn*	Shasu-land: Laban
94	*t3-šs pyspys*	Shasu-land: Payaspayas
95	*t3-šs smt*	Shasu-land: Samata
96	*t3-šs yhw*	Shasu-land: Yahwe
97	(*t3-šs*) ⟨*t*⟩*wrbr*	Shasu-land: ⟨T⟩urbil/r
...	...	...
103	*knʻn*(ʻ)	Canaan
104	*rḥb*	Reḥob.

("Amara West, Temple: Syrian List II," Kitchen's translation)

This thirteenth-century Ramesside inscription is actually a copy of a fourteenth-century text that dates to Amenhotep III's reign and was found at Soleb in Nubia. Note that the corresponding lines have been reversed from this earlier text:

line:	**Transcription:**	**Translation:**
B 1	*bt* ʻ [*nt*]	Beth A[nat]
A 1	*t3-šs trbr*	Shashu-land: Turbil/r
2	*t3-šs yhw*	Shasu-land: Yahwe
3	*t3-šs smt*	Shasu-land: Samata.

(doc 6, Giveon, *Les Bédouins Shosou*, 27)

Redford notes that the doubled *r* in Seir (*sʻrr*) in the Ramesside inscription reflects late Egyptian orthography (Redford, *Egypt, Canaan, and Israel*, 272 n. 67), so its identification is secure. He also notes that Laban can probably be identified with Libona, which is south of Amman, whereas Kenneth Kitchen suggests identifying it with the Libna that is mentioned in Numbers 33:20–21 (and Laban in Deuteronomy 1:1; Redford, *Egypt, Canaan, and Israel*, 272; and Kenneth A. Kitchen, *Ramesside Inscriptions: Translated & Annotated: Notes and Comments* [Oxford: Blackwell Publishers, 1999], 2:129). Samata can be identified with the Kenite family the Shimeathites, who are mentioned in 1 Chronicles 2:55 (שמעתים), which Kitchen locates in the Arabah Valley, south of the Dead Sea (Kitchen, *Notes and Comments*, 2:129). The location of Payaspayas (*pyspys*) is uncertain, and the identification of the final name Turibal/r is more problematic. Kitchen notes that the *wrbr* that appears in l. 97 of the Ramesside inscription is a mistake for Turbil/r, which is how the name appears in the earlier text. He locates Turbil/r in either the Beqaʻ or north Lebanon. Redford, however, interprets *wrbr* as a variant of *ybr*, which is the transliteration of the Canaanite word "dry wadi bed" (*'ubal*), and he identifies *ybr* with Wadi Hasa, one of the major east-west wadis that leads into the Jordan rift (Redford, *Egypt, Canaan, and Israel*, 272 n. 69).

to have been located in the southern Transjordan region, a region that is generally identified with the land of Edom, Raphael Giveon and other scholars conclude that the toponym Yahweh must have been located in this region during the second millennium.[47] These texts, however, associate Yahweh not with the Israelites but with the Shasu, a second-millennium Egyptian designation for Bedouin-like peoples, who lived in the plains of Moab and northern Edom and who were associated with lawlessness, plundering, raiding, and cattle herding.[48]

Moshe Weinfeld noted that the locations Seir and Laban were associated with the Midianites and Kenites, so they should not be located in the area near Edom. Instead, he argued that Seir and Laban denote a range of mountains west of the Arabah and south of the Dead Sea, a region much larger than the limited area known as Edom.[49] Wherever Seir actually was within the Transjordan region, Weinfeld's analysis of these geographic names fits with the Midianite-Kenite Hypothesis, which maintains that (the unspecified) Yahweh deity was first worshipped by the Midianite and Kenite tribes in the Transjordan and only later introduced to the Israelites by Moses and his father-in-law Jethro, a Midianite priest (Exodus 2:16).[50]

---

47 Giveon, "'The Cities'", 415; Tigay, *Deuteronomy*, 4, 319, and 421; van der Toorn, "Yahweh," 911; Redford, *Egypt, Canaan, and Israel*, 273; Kitchen, *Notes and Comments*, 2:129; and Moshe Weinfeld, "The Tribal League at Sinai," in *Ancient Israelite Religion: Essays in Honor of Frank Moore Cross*, eds. Patrick D. Miller, Paul D. Hanson, and S. Dean McBride (Philadelphia: Fortress, 1987), 304.

48 Redford, *Egypt, Canaan, and Israel*, 271–272 and 278.

49 Weinfeld, "Tribal League," 304 and 310. Weinfeld noted that EA 288:26 mentions the "lands of Seir" (KUR_2. KUR_2 *še-e-ri*^{ki}; see also Joshua 11:17 and 12:7), so he located Seir near the southern border of the Jerusalemite kingdom of the Amarna Period (ibid., 304). More recently, Blenkinsopp has argued that Seir is synonymous with Edom and proposes that it simply refers to the area west of the Arabah, whereas "[t]he original Edomite homeland was east of the Arabah" (Blenkinsopp, "Midianite-Kenite Hypothesis," 136–137). Thus, Blenkinsopp also argues against limiting the potential location of Seir – and, thus, against limiting the potential location of the place Yahweh – to the land east of the Arabah. As noted above, Redford views the land of the Shasu as encompassing both northern Edom and the land of Moab (Redford, *Egypt, Canaan, and Israel*, 273). Further expanding the potential Shasu realm, Kitchen includes northern Syria and Lebanon within the "land of the Shasu" (Kitchen, *Notes and Comments*, 2:128–129); however, he agrees with everyone else that the place Yahweh was most likely located around the Sinai, Negev, Edom, or even southern Syria.

50 Weinfeld, "Tribal League," 310; van der Toorn, "Yahweh," 912; Klaus Koch, "Jahwäs Übersiedlung vom Wüstenberg nach Kanaan: Zur Herkunft von Israels Gottesverständnis," in "*Und Mose Schreib dieses Lied auf*": *Studien zum Alten Testament und zum alten Orient: Festschrift für Oswald Loretz zur Vollendung seines 70. Lebensjahres mit Beiträgen von Freunden, Schülern, und Kollegen* (Münster: Ugarit-Verlag, 1998), 441; and Blenkinsopp, "Midianite-Kenite Hypothesis," 133–136.

Yahweh’s pre-Israelite association with Seir and the Transjordan region in these Egyptian texts offers extra-biblical evidence that corresponds well with the biblical evidence that locate (the unspecified) Yahweh deity in the region south and east of Israel. Of particular interest among these passages is the early poetry that is contained in Deuteronomy 33:2 and Judges 5:4–5, which describe Yahweh as coming from Seir.[51] Judges 5:4 explicitly associates Yahweh with Seir and the land of Edom, and the next verse associates the deity with Sinai:

[4]יהוה בצאתך משעיר בצעדך משדה אדום ארץ רעשה גם־שמים נטפו גם־עבים נטפו מים
[5]הרים נזלו מפני יהוה זה סיני מפני יהוה אלהי ישראל

> Yahweh, when you came out from Seir, when you marched out from the field of Edom, the earth shook, the heavens dripped, and the clouds dripped water. The mountains quaked before Yahweh-of-Sinai, before Yahweh//God-of-Israel. (Judges 5:4–5)

Aḥituv, Eshel, and Meshel recently proposed interpreting the זה in יהוה זה סיני as a possessive pronoun rather than a demonstrative pronoun, which significantly alters the syntax and meaning of the verse.[52] This proposal also produces a potential localized Yahweh name: Yahweh//One-of-Sinai, or informally Yahweh-of-Sinai. Notably, Yahweh-of-Sinai does not represent the DN-of-GN formula (i.e., the construct chain) that is typical of Hebrew and Northwest Semitic languages; rather, it more closely resembles the DN-*ša*-GN form that we find in Akkadian inscriptions. This by itself should not deter us from accepting this interpretation; however, there are two other mutually exclusive reasons to reject this reading. Contrary to the syntax created by the Masoretic punctuation, which is also preserved in the LXX and Vulgate, this proposed interpretation removes the parallelism and balance present in the traditional syntax of 5:5:

	Subject:	**Verb:**	**Preposition:**	**DN:**
5α:	Mountains (הרים)	Quaked (נזלו)	before (מפני)	Yahweh (יהוה)
5β:	This Sinai (זה סיני)	(Quaked)	before (מפני)	Yahweh//God-of-Israel (יהוה אלהי ישראל).[53]

51 Frank Moore Cross and David Noel Freedman date Deuteronomy 33:2 and Judges 5:4 to the late second millennium (Frank Moore Cross and David Noel Freedman, *Studies in Ancient Yahwistic Poetry*, new ed. [Livonia: Dove Booksellers, 1997], 3–4).
52 Aḥituv, Eshel, and Meshel, “The Inscriptions,” 130. This interpretation seems to have been anticipated by Cross (Cross, “Yahweh and the God,” 239 n. 61; see also Robert G. Boling, *Judges*, AB [Garden City: DoubleDay, 1975], 108).
53 The interpretation offered by Aḥituv, Eshel, and Meshel does retain a sense of parallelism with its A B C_1 C_2 form:

Second, the phrase "this Sinai" (זה סיני) may be a gloss from the theophany in Exodus 19:18 that was later inserted into Judges 5:5 (see the comment "frt add" in BHS). As a gloss, the potential reference to Yahweh-of-Sinai is incidental and cannot be attributed to the ancient author. If we prefer the Masoretic punctuation to the newly offered reading, we lose the Yahweh full name, but, significantly, we do not lose the association that Sinai and Yahweh share with Seir and Edom. Alternatively, if we were to accept this DN-of-GN formula as an interpretation of יהוה זה סיני then this would be the only biblical attestation of a localized Yahweh deity.

Deuteronomy 33:2 also identifies Yahweh as the one who "shone from Seir" (וזרח משעיר) and also proclaims Yahweh as the one from Sinai, Mount Paran, and Ribeboth-kodesh:

> יהוה מסיני בא וזרח משעיר למו הופיע מהר פארן ואתא מרבבת קדש מימינו אשדת למו
>
> Yahweh came from Sinai; he shone from Seir upon them; he shone forth from Mount Paran; and he came from Ribeboth-kodesh, from the south (literally, "his right") of them the slope. (Deuteronomy 33:2)[54]

In this verse, just as in Judges 5:4, Yahweh is not associated with his famous, fiery manifestation at Sinai (see Deuteronomy 5:4) and Seir, Paran, and Ribeboth-kodesh because of his covenant with Israel. Rather, the verse states that he came from those places in order to help Israel against its enemies.[55] The thrust of these three verses is that Yahweh left his home to assist Israel before Israel entered Canaan in Deuteronomy (33:2) and after they entered the land in Judges (5:4–5). Although the Egyptian texts identify Yahweh as a place and the biblical texts identify Yahweh as a god, both groups of texts locate the name in the same general area, the mountains south or southeast of Israel, and in the same general period, the late second millennium.

Biblical and extra-biblical texts from the early first millennium also locate Yahweh in the Transjordan region. The ninth-century Mesha Inscription (*KAI* 181) is the earliest extant extra-biblical text to mention Yahweh as a divine name, and it associates him with the people/nation of Israel, stating that he

---

Subject:	**Verb:**	**Preposition:**	**DN:**
Mountains (הרים)	Quaked (נזלו)	before (מפני)	Yahweh-of-Sinai (יהוה זה סיני)
		before (מפני)	Yahweh//God-of-Israel (יהוה אלהי ישראל).

The verbal balance that the Masoretic punctuation provides is more satisfying.

54 Tigay, *Deuteronomy*, 320; BDB אשדה; see also Deuteronomy 3:17 and 4:49 for the relative locations of the Arabah and Pisgah.

55 Tigay, *Deuteronomy*, 319; and Weinfeld, "Tribal League," 306.

was their deity.[56] The inscription commemorates Mesha’s military victory over Israel at Nebo, a border town in northwestern Moab, and it mentions Yahweh in the course of reporting on Mesha’s capture of the “[ves]sels of Yahweh” (א[ת כ]לי יהוה, *KAI* 181:17–18) as part of the booty that he took from Israel and presented to his god Chemosh.[57] Although the inscription relates events that took place in the Transjordan, this text does not associate Yahweh with the region as far south as Edom; instead, it places an Israelite Yahwistic cult where Weinfeld located the Shasu, just east of the Dead Sea.

A body of extra-biblical evidence that represents the earliest Israelite writing of the divine name Yahweh links the deity with the southern Transjordan: the collection of texts from Kuntillet ‘Ajrud.[58] Of the many separate texts from the site, three refer to a deity as Yahweh-of-Teman:

1 [י]. ארכימם. וישבעו [...] יתנו. ל[ ]הוה [.] תימנ. ולאשרתה 2[ ].היטב יהוה. התי[...]

[May] he lengthen their days, and may they be satisfied [...] may they be given by [Ya]hweh-of-Teman by [his] ašerah/Ašerah [and] Yahweh-of-the-Te[man] favored... (*Meshel* 4.1.1:1–2, ink-on-plaster)[59]

ברכתכ. לי 6הוה תמנ 7ולאשרתה 5

I bless you by [Ya]hweh-of-Teman and by his ašerah/Ašerah. (*Meshel* 3.6:5–7, Pithos B)

1[ ]ליהוה. התמנ ולאשרתה. 2[ ]כל אשר ישאל מאש חננ הא ואמ̇ פתה ונתנ לה יהו 3כלבבה.

To Yahweh-of-the-Teman and to his ašerah/Ašerah ... all that he asks from a man, he (will give) generous(ly). And if he persuades, may Yahwe(h) give to him according to his wishes. (*Meshel* 3.9:1–3, Pithos B)[60]

---

56 Van der Toorn, “Yahweh,” 911.

57 Kent Jackson notes that the proposed restoration “vessels” ([כ]לי) fits the context but is uncertain (Kent P. Jackson, “The Language of the Mesha Inscription,” in *Studies in the Mesha Inscription and Moab*, ed. Andrew Dearman, SBLABS 2 [Atlanta: Scholars Press, 1989], 116). van der Toorn, however, prefers the restoration ’[*r*’]*ly*, which he leaves untranslated, but the word has been proposed as a “military term denoting more than one person,” “altar hearth,” “lion figure,” “certain type of priest,” or “cherub” (van der Toorn, “Yahweh,” 911; and *DNWSI*, *’r’l* mngs. 1 and 2).

58 Emerton, “New Light,” 2.

59 While the word Teman is more often spelled at Kuntillet ‘Ajrud using the “expected northern orthography,” i.e., a collapsed */ay/* diphthong “(*tmn* = */tēman/* ⟨ **tayman*)” (Hutton, “Local Manifestations,” 202), in *Meshel* 4.1.1:2, the word is once spelled as though the diphthong had not collapsed (e.g., התי[מנ]), reflecting a local, but not necessarily Judahite, (i.e., an eighth-century Edomite) pronunciation of the geographic name: */tayman/* (ibid., 200). The divine names Yahweh-of-Teman (l. 1) and Yahweh-of-*the*-Teman (l. 2) seem to be functionally equivalent, with the latter including the definite article “the” (-ה) prefixed to the geographic name.

60 This translation is based on the translation by Aḥituv, Eshel, and Meshel (Aḥituv, Eshel, and Meshel, “The Inscriptions,” 100). They translate חננ as “will give him generously,” in light

The role of "his ašerah/Ašerah" has been the focus of much debate since the discovery of these texts and Ze'ev Meshel's 1979 article, "Did Yahweh Have a Consort? The New Religious Inscriptions from Sinai," but the place name Teman is our present interest.[61] Both Amos 1:11–12 and Ezekiel 25:13 associate the nation of Edom with the city or region known as Teman, and Shalom Paul notes that the city of Teman served as a "common metonymic appellation for the entire country" of Edom, so we can confidently maintain that these texts place this Yahweh deity in the region of and surrounding Edom, even if Kuntillet 'Ajrud is too far in the west to have been a part of Edom.[62] Of course, the divine name Yahweh-of-Teman is not the only Yahweh full name that has been uncovered at Kuntillet 'Ajrud. Yahweh-of-Samaria also appears in one text:

[1]ברכת אתכמ [2]ליהוה.שמרנ.ולאשרתה

I bless you by Yahweh-of-Samaria and by his ašerah/Ašerah. (*Meshel* 3.1:1–2)[63]

At first, the appearance of the divine name Yahweh-of-Samaria at Kuntillet 'Ajrud is somewhat problematic because it relates to the northern Israelite state and its capital city even though no other evidence directly associates a Yahwistic cult with the city. At the same time, however, this text has played an instrumental role in informing scholars' conclusions about local worship and religious tolerance in ancient Israel.

The site of Kuntillet 'Ajrud is about forty miles south of Kadesh-barnea on a road that connects Kadesh-barnea with the Gulf of Aqaba. Located in the

---

of Psalm 37:12, where the verb is paired with "give" (חונן ונתן ,נתן). They offer "urge" (and "entreat," "entice," "coax," and "implore") for פתה; "persuades" was chosen in light of Proverbs 25:15: בארך אפים יפתה קצין.

61 Ze'ev Meshel, "Did Yahweh Have a Consort? The New Religious Inscriptions from Sinai," BAR 5, no. 2 (1979): 24–34; and Ze'ev Meshel, *Kuntillet 'Ajrud (Ḥorvat Teman): An Iron Age II Religious Site on the Judah-Sinai Border* (Jerusalem: Israel Exploration Society, 2012).

62 Shalom Paul, *Amos: A Commentary on the Book of Amos*, Hermeneia (Minneapolis: Fortress, 1991), 67. See also Jeremiah 49:7 and 20; Obadiah 9; and Habakkuk 3:3 for further examples of this metonymic use.

63 Meshel originally rejected the possibility that שמרנ in this text referred to the geographic name Samaria, preferring instead to translate the word as the epithet "(the one who) protects us" because the divine name Yahweh never appears in the Hebrew Bible as part of a construct chain with a geographic name (Meshel, "Did Yahweh," 31).

Citing *KAI* 50:2–3 ("I have blessed you by Baal-of-Ṣapun," ברכתכ לבעל צפנ), Emerton noted that even though ברכת is a perfect verb that would normally be translated "I have blessed," because it represents a continual wish, a better translation would be, "May you be blessed" (Emerton, "New Light," 2).

eastern Sinai, it has served as a water source for travelers since antiquity.[64] Meshel, who was the primary dig excavator in the mid-1970s, suggests that Kuntillet 'Ajrud was a religious center or "wayside shrine" that served as a stop for travelers.[65] In contrast, because of the obvious lack of a temple layout and objects for ritual sacrifice at the site, Judith Hadley argues against the interpretation that there was a shrine at Kuntillet 'Ajrud, be it an official, state-run one or a foreign-sponsored heterodox one.[66] More recently, although Meshel admits that no sacrifices were performed at the site, he advances the idea that the nearby tree grove might have increased the sanctity of the area, a *bamah*-platform ("high place") might have been located in Building B, and four *maṣṣebot*-like cultic stones that were found in Building A might betray a religious nature at the site.[67] However, Brian Schmidt has warned against continuing the religious-versus-secular debate surrounding Kuntillet 'Ajrud,

---

64 Meshel, "Did Yahweh," 27–28; and Meshel, "Kuntillet 'Ajrud," in *Anchor Bible Dictionary*, ed. David Noel Freedman (New York: Doubleday, 1992), 4:103.

65 Meshel, "Did Yahweh," 34; and Meshel, "The Nature of the Site and its Biblical Background," in *Kuntillet 'Ajrud (Ḥorvat Teman): An Iron Age II Religious Site on the Judah-Sinai Border*, ed. Ze'ev Meshel (Jerusalem: Israel Exploration Society, 2012), 65 f. In contrast to Meshel's proposed links between Kuntillet 'Ajrud and the northern state of Israel, which is an idea that McCarter considers (McCarter, "Aspects," 140), John Holladay notes that the shrine at Kuntillet 'Ajrud lacked any major architectural structures resembling the cultic architecture at state-run shrines in Israel and Judah, such as Megiddo, Dan, or Lachish, and he concludes that neither Israel nor Judah were responsible for the shrine at Kuntillet 'Ajrud (John S. Holladay, "Religion in Israel and Judah under the Monarchy: an Explicitly Archaeological Approach," in *Ancient Israelite Religion: Essays in Honor of Frank Moore Cross*, eds. Patrick D. Miller, Paul D. Hanson, and S. Dean McBride [Philadelphia: Fortress, 1987], 259 and 272).

66 Judith M. Hadley, "Kuntillet 'Ajrud: Religious Centre or Desert Way Station?" *PEQ* 125 (1993): 117. She views the site as a "way station" that provided water for travelers and their animals from the nearby wells and offered housing for those passing by (ibid., 122). Some of these travelers left blessings behind as a thanksgiving for their shelter from the surrounding wilderness. The lack of local pottery – most of the pottery found at the site was from the coastal region of Judah and the north of Israel (ibid., 119; see also Jan Gunneweg, Isadore Perlman, and Ze'ev Meshel, "The Origin of the Pottery," in *Kuntillet 'Ajrud (Ḥorvat Teman): An Iron Age II Religious Site on the Judah-Sinai Border*, ed. Ze'ev Meshel [Jerusalem: Israel Exploration Society, 2012], 279) – and lack of cult vessels suggest to her that the site did not support a permanent priestly population, although long-term residents, such as a "hostel-keeper" could not be ruled out (Hadley, "Kuntillet 'Ajrud," 120). According to Meshel, the fine linen fabrics found at the site and the 400-pound bowl found in the bench room, inscribed with a blessing that invokes (the unspecified) Yahweh (*Meshel* 1.2), are more indicative of a priestly population living there than of a lay population (Meshel, "Did Yahweh," 32–34; and Meshel, "Nature of the Site," 68). However, because of the lack of cult materials, Meshel is forced to speculate that the priests took everything with them when they abandoned the site.

67 Meshel, "Nature of the Site," 65–66.

pointing out that a fortified trade center's design could include the incorporation of religious function and ritual in the architecture.[68] He then points out that the architectural layout, texts, drawings, and physical contents of Deir 'Alla, a contemporary site in the eastern Jordan Valley, was also a mix of religious and secular usages.[69] Like Deir 'Alla, we can consider the fortified trade stop at Kuntillet 'Ajrud an atypical cult center in that worship was not the site's primary function, but, as Schmidt notes, specific rooms "were set aside and decorated ... to facilitate the cultic observances of both the locals ... and travelers."[70] Also allowing for a mixture of (the modern compartmentalization of) religious and secular usages at Kuntillet 'Ajrud, Othmar Keel and Christoph Uehlinger emphatically state, "We ought to abandon the notion, once and for all, that the site was a pilgrimage shrine or some other kind of religious center;" rather, "[t]he architecture and decoration at the site both characterize it much more clearly as a state-run caravanserai."[71] The architects responsible for Kuntillet 'Ajrud made it possible for travelers to worship their preferred deity or deities and leave offerings and texts to them, even though they would have traveled to the site for other purposes.

For paleographic reasons and because of the style of pottery upon which many texts were written, these texts – and, consequentially, the occupation of the entire site – have been dated to roughly 800 B.C.E.[72] Meshel suggests that Kuntillet 'Ajrud was occupied during the reign of Israel's King Joash/Jehoash (ca. 801–786).[73] After capturing Judah's King Amaziah, tearing down the city

---

68 Brian B. Schmidt, "The Iron Age pithoi drawings from Horvat Teman or Kuntillet 'Ajrud: Some New Proposals," *JANER* 2 (2002): 103.

69 The architectural layout at Deir 'Alla includes benches for receiving offerings; the textual evidence includes the famous Balaam text in the same room as the benches; the drawings include a picture of a sphinx located near the Balaam text; and the physical contents include cooking supplies, household pottery, and materials for weaving fabric (Schmidt, "Iron Age pithoi," 103).

70 Schmidt, "Iron Age pithoi," 104.

71 Othmar Keel and Christoph Uehlinger, *Gods, Goddesses, and Images of God in Ancient Israel*, trans. T. H. Trapp (Minneapolis: Fortress, 1998), 247.

72 Aḥituv, Eshel, and Meshel, "The Inscriptions," 73; Etan Ayalon, "The Pottery Assemblage," in *Kuntillet 'Ajrud (Ḥorvat Teman): An Iron Age II Religious Site on the Judah-Sinai Border*, ed. Ze'ev Meshel (Jerusalem: Israel Exploration Society, 2012), 205; Israel Carmi and Dror Segal, "^{14}C Dates from Kuntillet 'Ajrud," in *Kuntillet 'Ajrud (Ḥorvat Teman): An Iron Age II Religious Site on the Judah-Sinai Border*, ed. Ze'ev Meshel (Jerusalem: Israel Exploration Society, 2012), 61–63; Hadley, "Kuntillet 'Ajrud," 119; Keel and Uehlinger, *Gods, Goddesses*, 248; and Smith, *Early History*, 118. For an epigraphic analysis of the texts from Kuntillet 'Ajrud compared to the Samaria Ostraca, see Christopher A. Rollston, "Scribal Education in Ancient Israel: The Old Hebrew Epigraphic Evidence," *BASOR* 344 (2006): 55–60.

73 Meshel, "Did Yahweh," 34; and Meshel, *Kuntillet 'Ajrud* (2012), XXI–XXII.

walls of Jerusalem, and seizing the temple and palace treasuries (2 Kings 14:13–16), this Israelite king could afford to exert military and political control over Judah and beyond its borders, including down to Kuntillet ‘Ajrud.[74] Meshel contends that King Joash had the site built in order to provide Israelite merchants a stop on their way to the Red Sea. This, he argues, explains why Yahweh-of-Samaria's name was invoked in the blessing on Pithos A and why Israelite personal names – as indicated by the spelling of the Yahwistic theophoric element that matches the spelling in the Samaria Ostraca – were found throughout the site.[75] Indeed, the theophoric and personal names point to a predominately northern (or Israelite), rather than a southern (or Judahite), population residing at or passing through Kuntillet ‘Ajrud.

Within this predominantly northern element at Kuntillet ‘Ajrud, the extant texts' nature still reveals that multiple individuals were responsible for them. One obvious distinction among these is the divine name or names included in each text. When considering the Yahweh full names, there are two groups of texts: those that mention Yahweh-of-Teman (*Meshel* 4.1.1, 3.6, and 3.9) and the one that mentions Yahweh-of-Samaria (*Meshel* 3.1). The three that explicitly mention the deity's associations with Teman place him in the southern Transjordan region near and around Edom, and the one that explicitly mentions the deity's associations with Samaria places him in the heart of the northern Israelite kingdom. Another way to group these texts is by their find spots. Two were found inside the so-called "bench room": one was found on Pithos A (*Meshel* 3.1), and the other was part of a plaster text that was presumably on the bench room wall (*Meshel* 4.1.1).[76] The other two were found

74 Meshel also entertains the possibility that the occupation of Kuntillet ‘Ajrud belonged to the reigns of Jehoram, Ahaziah, or Athaliah in Judah during the mid-ninth centuries (Meshel, "Did Yahweh," 34; and Meshel, "Kuntillet ‘Ajrud," 4:109). Zevit prefers to interpret the texts, artifacts, and the site's location as evidence Judahite investment and construction at Kuntillet ‘Ajrud, but he admits that none of the evidence "disallows the presence of Israelians" in its construction or maintenance (Ziony Zevit, *The Religions of Ancient Israel: A Synthesis of Parallactic Approaches* [London: Continuum, 2001], 378). If the site were a product of Athaliah's reign, then her ties to the northern kingdom of Israel as the daughter of Ahab could explain why Yahweh-of-Samaria was invoked at the site whereas no Yahweh-of-Jerusalem, Yahweh-of-Judah, Yahweh-of-Zion, or Yahweh-of-Hosts was. Her northern background and influences could also explain the presence of personal names with Yahwistic theophoric elements that conform to Israelite spellings (i.e., יוה, which was likely pronounced "yau") rather than contemporary Judahite spellings (i.e., יהו, which was likely pronounced "yahu").
75 Meshel, "Did Yahweh," 32; and Aḥituv, Eshel, and Meshel, "The Inscriptions," 128; see also the discussion of the Yahwistic theophoric elements and citations in Dobbs-Allsopp, et al., *Hebrew Inscriptions*, 283–298, and Keel and Uehlinger, *Gods, Goddesses*, 247.
76 Aḥituv, Eshel, and Meshel, "The Inscriptions," 86 and 105; and Schmidt, "Iron Age pithoi," 93.

on Pithos B (*Meshel* 3.6 and 3.9), which was found outside the bench room and on the opposite side of the wall where the plaster-based texts were found. The third way in which these texts can be grouped is particularly revealing – official and non-official texts – especially when this grouping system is contrasted against the divine-name groupings and the find-spot groupings.

According to Keel and Uehlinger, the ink-on-plaster texts are official inscriptions, which is to say that *Meshel* 4.1.1 and its Yahweh-of-Teman "seem to have an official character about them" because they were commissioned by the state.[77] The two other officially sanctioned ink-on-plaster texts that were found in the bench room are *Meshel* 4.3 and 4.2, which further bolster the "official character" of *Meshel* 4.1.1. Unfortunately, although it was discovered *in situ* on a door jamb, *Meshel* 4.3 is too faded and is no longer legible.[78] Fortunately, *Meshel* 4.2 is legible, but like *Meshel* 4.1.1, it was found in pieces on the floor. Using *Meshel* 4.3's location as a hint, had *Meshel* 4.2 been discovered *in situ*, it would have probably been at a different door jamb in the same room because it was uncovered near the bench room's western entrance.[79] This text relates the theophany of a warrior god, who seems to be identified as El/God (אל, *Meshel* 4.2:1), the Most High (עלי[ן], l. 4), Baal/Lord (בעל, l. 5), and perhaps also Name-of-El/God (שמ אל, l. 6).[80] Although Aḥutiv,

77 Keel and Uehlinger, *Gods, Goddesses*, 245. Keel and Uehlinger compare the character of the ink-on-plaster inscriptions and drawings in the bench room at Kuntillet 'Ajrud with the contemporary Assyrian palace reliefs and paintings, noting that the bench room pictures are "thematically reminiscent" of their Assyrian counterparts with representations of enthroned princes and lotus blossoms (ibid., 245; compare figure 237, which is from the bench room, with figure 238a, which is an Assyrian drawing, both of which are on p. 246). Likewise, Hutton compares the quality of the official drawings on the plaster in the bench room with the "relative impermanence" of the *ad hoc* drawings on pithoi A and B (Hutton, "Local Manifestations," 199).

Hutton also agrees with Keel and Uehlinger that the official and non-official texts represent two distinct sets of individuals. The ink-on-plaster inscription of *Meshel* 4.1.1 (and the theophany described in *Meshel* 4.2) was written by a scribe with Israelite and/or Phoenician training, as indicated by his predominately northern orthographic conventions that occasionally includes uncollapsed */ay/* diphthongs (for example, *hyṭb* for the expected *hṭb* and *tymn* for the expected *tmn* in *Meshel* 4.1.1:2; Hutton, "Local Manifestations," 200). The individuals responsible for *Meshel* 3.6 and 3.9 on Pithos B were native Israelite travelers, and so was the individual responsible for *Meshel* 3.1 on Pithos A, and they all demonstrated a northern consistent orthography (ibid., 202).

78 Aḥituv, Eshel, and Meshel, "The Inscriptions," 115; and Allsopp, et al., *Hebrew Inscriptions*, 286.

79 Aḥituv, Eshel, and Meshel, "The Inscriptions," 110.

80 Allsopp et al. interpret Baal and Most High as epithets of a Yahweh deity (Allsopp, et al., *Hebrew Inscriptions*, 287 and 289), and they suggest that Name-of-God "is the deity's hypostatic presence," meaning it represents an external aspect of the Yahweh deity that is reminiscent of

Eshel, and Meshel recently suggested that "Y]HW[H" begins a new sentence at the end of l. 2, noting "no other restoration seems possible,"[81] the name Yahweh is not part of the extant text and might not have ever been part of the text. However, as Brian Mastin notes, there is nothing in this text that does not fit the biblical titles and descriptions of the biblical deity Yahweh, or perhaps some local Yahweh deity (i.e., the Yahweh-of-Teman in *Meshel* 4.1.1).[82] Further adding to *Meshel* 4.1.1's official character are the fact that it makes no appeal for private blessings from the deity and the fact that *Meshel* 4.1.1 had a permanent presence in the bench room as an ink-on-plaster text that doubled as a decoration.[83] In contrast, *Meshel* 3.1, 3.6, and 3.9 all included private blessings and were written on the very mobile pottery shards of Pithoi A and B.

Considering all three groupings at once, we observe the following: the official *Meshel* 4.1.1 inscription with its Yahweh-of-Teman was found in the same bench room as the unofficial *Meshel* 3.1 text with its Yahweh-of-Samaria, whereas the unofficial *Meshel* 3.6 and 3.9 texts with their Yahweh-of-Teman were found in an adjacent room at the site. Using this grouping matrix and the assumption that the ink-on-plaster inscription was the first text written and

---

Astarte//Name-of-Baal and Tannit//Face-of-Baal as hypostases of Baal (ibid., 289; Cross, *Canaanite Myth*, 30).

81 Aḥituv, Eshel, and Meshel, "The Inscriptions," 111.

82 Brian A. Mastin, "The Inscriptions Written on Plaster at Kuntillet ʻAjrud," *VT* 59 (2009): 114. Being careful not to assume *a priori* that *Meshel* 4.2 was written by an Israelite scribe, Mastin notes that while we do not know how the Phoenicians would have described a theophany, everything about this inscription fits within what we know of ancient Israelite descriptions (ibid., 113). He also notes that we cannot completely rule out the possibility that *Meshel* 4.2 and its El and Baal divine names were not representative of a Canaanite, as opposed to Phoenician and Israelite, theophany. However, because *Meshel* 4.1.1 and 4.2 are both officially sponsored inscriptions in what would have been in close proximity on the wall, Mastin ultimately identifies the deity in *Meshel* 4.2 with an Israelite Yahweh deity.

Allsopp, et al, note further connections between the Yahweh-of-Teman mentioned in *Meshel* 4.1.1 and the theophany revealed in *Meshel* 4.2 (Allsopp, et al., *Hebrew Inscriptions*, 287). The first extant word in *Meshel* 4.2 is "and when he shone forth" (ובזרח, l. 1), which is the verbal root that also appears in Deuteronomy 33:2 ("and he shone from Seir upon them," וזרח משעיר למו), a verse that uses Seir, Paran, and Sinai to locate Yahweh in the region near Teman (see also Habakkuk 3:3).

83 Keel and Uehlinger, *Gods, Goddesses*, 245. Whereas Keel and Uehlinger compared the ink-on-plaster inscriptions and drawings with contemporary Assyrian artwork as proof of Kuntillet ʻAjrud's government-controlled origins, Hutton compares the inscriptions of *Meshel* 4.1.1 and 4.2 and the nearby drawings with the "well-planned plasters of Deir ʻAlla" that were recently discovered and the command to set up stones covered in plaster in Deuteronomy 27:2–4 and 8 (Hutton, "Local Manifestations," 199).

available to all worshippers, Hutton makes several conclusions about worship and religious tolerance at Kuntillet 'Ajrud. First, because the bench room contained an officially sanctioned ink-on-plaster reference to Yahweh-of-Teman, that room must have been officially and "deliberately claimed for the worship of a single specific regional – if not local – divine manifestation, Yahweh of Teman."[84] According to Ziony Zevit, this act of officially designating a place of worship for the local Temanite Yahweh served to inspire travelers into leaving offerings and other gifts for Yahweh-of-Teman at the Kuntillet 'Ajrud site.[85] Zevit's assertion is reasonable; each (literate) Israelite merchant or traveler who entered the bench room would have presumably read *Meshel* 4.1.1 and taken to heart that Yahweh-of-Teman along with his ašerah/Ašerah was prepared to lengthen the traveler's days and provide him with other blessings. Furthermore, if the traveler identified Yahweh-of-Teman with the divine names or epithets presented in Meshel 4.2's theophany, then he would have further reason to believe that this deity was potent enough to ensure that the individual would be blessed. The state-sponsored ink-on-plaster drawings in the bench room would have similarly inspired illiterate travelers. The two unofficial texts that invoke Yahweh-of-Teman (*Meshel* 3.6 and 3.9) reinforce the idea that Israelite travelers would be inspired to revere the local Yahweh. Second, because *Meshel* 3.6 and 3.9 were found outside out the bench room, Hutton concludes that there were several different loci of sacred space at Kuntillet 'Ajrud.[86] Had there been a prohibition against revering a deity outside of his delineated space, these texts would have been left inside the bench room. This also demonstrates that the travelers believed that the deity could receive offerings and effect blessings regardless of where in the complex he was revered. Third, even though the bench room was officially dedicated to Yahweh-of-Teman, the devotee who invoked Yahweh-of-Samaria in *Meshel* 3.1 apparently felt no need to limit his petition to the officially sanctioned divine name.

This divine name distribution leads Hutton to several possible conclusions. There were no prohibitions against worshipping a "competing" deity in the shrine of another deity (i.e., worshipping a Yahweh-of-Samaria in a room officially dedicated to Yahweh-of-Teman); the dedications and offerings that were left by travelers were not thoroughly vetted by overseers at the site; and an ancient "ecumenical mindset" recognized the "fundamental fluidity

84 Hutton, "Local Manifestations," 202.
85 Zevit, *Religions of Ancient Israel*, 374.
86 Hutton, "Local Manifestations," 202. For a discussion on how a temple or locus comes to be seen as sacred in the ancient Near East, see Pongratz-Leisten, "Reflections on the Translatibility," 417 ff.

between such fragmentary local manifestations” in ancient Israelite religious practice.[87] Hutton seems to prefer the first two (non-mutually exclusive) possibilities over the third, but he rules nothing out because of our limited evidence and because we can reconstruct the *ad hoc* unofficial texts’ histories.[88] Acknowledging these limitations, Hutton concludes that the two divine names uncovered at Kuntillet ‘Ajrud represent deities who “seem to have led separate lives in the experience of the worshippers,” contrary to an interpretation of Deuteronomy 6:4 that maintains that “Yahweh is one.”[89]

Whether Yahweh-of-Teman and Yahweh-of-Samaria were wholly distinct deities like their full-named Assyrian counterparts (e.g., Ištar-of-Nineveh and Ištar-of-Arbela) or simply local manifestations of one singular Yahweh, at first glance their geographic last names reflect reverence from two distinct communities.[90] On the one hand, Yahweh-of-Teman and his shrine at Kuntillet ‘Ajrud are located near the Temanite/Edomite region. On the other hand, Yahweh-of-Samaria’s shrine would presumably have been located in Samaria,

87 Hutton, “Local Manifestations,” 204. Following Sommer’s fluidity model that Hutton references, it should be observed that even if Yahweh-of-Samaria and Yahweh-of-Teman are, in one sense “competing” deities or manifestations, in another sense, the two localized Yahweh deities are similar enough that the merchant/traveler-devotee from Samaria had no problem revering his hometown Yahweh in a shrine devoted to another Yahweh who was actually geographically closer to the shrine. Likewise, the two localized Yahweh deities were similar enough to each other that the overseer had no reason to resist the Samarian traveler’s offering on behalf of the local Temanite Yahweh. Similarly, Emerton supposed that they were so similar that the devotee would have considered the both divine names as representative of the same deity (Emerton, “New Light,” 13).

88 Hutton, “Local Manifestations,” 205.

89 Hutton, “Local Manifestations,” 205 and 206.

90 Meshel, Holladay, and Michael Coogan each envision Kuntillet ‘Ajrud as a site representing various different cultural and ethnic strands, including Judahite, Israelite, and Phoenician ones (Meshel, “Did Yahweh,” 34; Holladay, “Religion in Israel and Judah,” 258; and Michael Coogan, “Canaanite Origins and Lineage: Reflections on the Religion of Ancient Israel,” in *Ancient Israelite Religion: Essays in Honor of Frank Moore Cross*, eds. Patrick D. Miller, Paul D. Hanson, and S. Dean McBride [Philadelphia: Fortress, 1987], 118). Although Coogan suggests that Kuntillet ‘Ajrud represents different ethnicities and their religious practices, he warns against concluding that the site was a syncretistic cult (ibid., 119). The religious views might have been concurrent but they were not all necessarily espoused by each worshipper. Likewise, Hadley espouses the view that travelers – and even a few pilgrims – of “any ethnic background” stayed at and left the blessings behind at Kuntillet ‘Ajrud (Hadley, “Kuntillet ‘Ajrud,” 122). As noted above, Hutton’s focus on the inscriptions’ orthography suggests to him a predominately northern or Israelite population, and while Mastin notes we cannot rule out a Canaanite population, he also notes that nothing contained in the Kuntillet ‘Ajrud texts is inconsistent with an Israelite population (Hutton, “Local Manifestations,” 200; and Mastin, “Inscriptions Written on Plaster,”113).

which is in Israel. If the unofficial texts had been the only texts discovered at Kuntillet ʿAjrud, then the existence of a local community who worshipped a Yahweh deity in Teman would have been a reasonable inference. However, scholarly consensus now holds that this was not the case, and the divine name Yahweh-of-Teman and his shrine have confidently been interpreted as the result of an Israelite initiative. No native Temanite community need be assumed. It could have existed, but it need not be assumed.[91]

With the Temanite cult established and maintained by a Samarian community, the various texts could represent not only a single orthographic tradition, but they could also represent a single community's religious tradition, namely one from the northern state of Israel. Theoretically, this community could have simultaneously revered multiple Yahweh deities in much the same way that Assurbanipal revered both Ištar-of-Nineveh and Ištar-of-Arbela (and even Ištar-of-Kidmuri). Yahweh-of-Samaria might have been revered as the deity whose primary residence was the nation's political capital, while Yahweh-of-Teman was simultaneously revered at the nation's newly established outpost and trading stop, a place that the biblical authors also associated with their Yahweh. Ideally, such a conclusion would be based on a text that contrasted both divine full names, as was the case with the localized Ištar divine names in numerous royal inscriptions from the eighth and seventh centuries. For instance, the following would have made a fantastic addition to the argument regarding poly-Yahwism:

יתנו. ארכ.יממ ליהוה.תמנ ליהוה.שמרנ ולאשרתמ והיטבו.יהוה.ה תמנ ליהוה.שמרנ

> May they be given longevity by Yahweh-of-Teman, by Yahweh-of-Samaria, and by their ašerah/Ašerah, and may Yahweh-of-the-Teman and Yahweh-of-Samaria favor ...

Because no comparable text is known to exist, it would be methodologically unsound to conclude that the Israelite scribes responsible for *Meshel* 4.1.1, 3.1, 3.6, and 3.9 considered the possibility that these two divine names represented two distinct and independent Yahweh deities. Before we conclude that Yahweh-of-Teman and Yahweh-of-Samaria would have necessarily been identified with each other by ancient Israelites or the state of Israel, we should not dismiss the fact that that our investigation of localized Baal deities in chapter 5 found that it was not unusual in the first millennium for a scribe to

91 Emerton acknowledged the role the Kenite Hypothesis could play in Yahweh's nomadic origins and subsequent development into the Israelite deity, but he doubted that a Yahwistic cult continued in Teman or Edom from the late second millennium as late as ca. 800 (Emerton, "New Light," 10).

provide a full Baal divine name when no other Baal deity was mentioned in the text. In several of these instances, it seemed as though the full names were implicitly contrasting the named deity with other deities sharing the same name. The most salient example is Baal-Ḥamān, who was contrasted with Baal-Šamêm and Baal-Magnim in a third-century votive inscription from Carthage (e.g., *KAI* 78; see Table 5.8), but who was also fully Baal-Ḥamān as the only male deity named (e.g., *KAI* 79) or the only deity named at all (e.g., *KAI* 114?; see Table 5.5). Whatever motivated the scribes who were responsible for *KAI* 79 and 114 and other relevant texts to identify this deity Baal-Ḥamān by his full name even when they knew that no competing localized Baal deities would appear in these texts, similar motivations could also have been behind the identification of Yahweh-of-Samaria by his full name in *Meshel* 3.1. In a decidedly polytheistic population, like the various Phoenician or Punic ones considered in chapter 5, distinguishing one Baal from another by including a geographic last name removed potential ambiguity. Whether this would also be true in an Israelite context is uncertain because scholars have not reached a consensus regarding the fully polytheistic or highly monolatrist tendencies of Israel in the first half of the first millennium. If we concede that the Israelite community from Samaria was either a monolatrist community – which is to say that the ancient Israelites revered one deity without denying the existence of other (foreign) gods – or a monotheistic community, then this Baal-Ḥamān analogy serves little purpose. If, however, we concede that this Israelite community consisted of polytheists either at the official, royal level or possibly also the lay level, then our Baal-Ḥamān example is quite illustrative: even though Yahweh-of-Samaria is never explicitly contrasted with Yahweh-of-Teman, the mere presence of the geographic last names in a text is suggestive of poly-Yahwism.

Writing before scholars had settled on the northern state of Israel’s role in overseeing the site at Kuntillet ‘Ajrud, McCarter asserted that the scribe responsible for *Meshel* 3.1 and the divine name Yahweh-of-Samaria was from Samaria and had called upon his hometown or regional god for a blessing.[92] McCarter then offered multiple reasons underlying the relationship between the scribes who invoked Yahweh-of-Teman in *Meshel* 3.6 and that deity, whose geographic name is a synonym for “south.” They could have called upon Yahweh-of-Teman specifically because they had come from “farther south” where they had previously worshipped him or because the deity was already the established localized Yahweh within the region at the time.[93] If the former,

92 McCarter, “Aspects,” 140.

93 McCarter, “Aspects,” 140. McCarter notes that the geographic name Samaria in Yahweh-of-Samaria’s full name could designate the capital city of Israel or the larger region containing

Yahweh-of-Teman could rightly be considered the scribe's localized Yahweh deity in much the same way that Yahweh-of-Samaria was the localized Yahweh deity for the scribe of *Meshel* 3.1. If the latter, then Yahweh-of-Teman's cult site could actually have been Kuntillet 'Ajrud. Because Hadley rejects the possibility that Kuntillet 'Ajrud could have been Yahweh-of-Teman's shrine, she rejects the possibility that there was any shrine at the site, which she claims is evidenced by a lack of cult vessels.[94] Moreover, she rejects the possibility that Yahweh-of-Teman was the local deity because the name should indicate that he was from somewhere other than the shrine at Kuntillet 'Ajrud.[95]

Hadley's conclusion leads us to a third alternative that must also be considered in light of our survey of localized Baal deities and their associated places. The geographic name Teman is associated with the divine name Yahweh in these texts not because the scribe or cult originated in Teman, but because Yahweh's mythical home was Teman. The divine name Baal-of-Ṣapun

---

that city (ibid., 139; see also Hutton, "Local Manifestations," 191). However, given his preference for Teman as a region rather than a specific site or mountain in Transjordan (or even further south), if he envisions the two different Yahweh full names as reflecting parallel information, he should prefer to interpret Samaria as the region rather than the capital city. Because the GN in most other DN-of-GN full names examined in chapters 3 through 5 represent a specific place (e.g., a particular city or mountain), the Samaria in *Meshel* 3.1 should be interpreted as designating the capital city rather than the region. Similarly, the Teman in *Meshel* 4.1.1, 3.6, and 3.9 should probably be understood as a particular mountain or place rather than a region (cf. Emerton, "New Light," 9).

It should be noted, however, that Yigael Yadin would likely have agreed that the Samaria in the divine name Yahweh-of-Samaria was a reference to the region and not the capital city. This is based on his premise that there was no temple of Baal in the capital city of Samaria (Yigael Yadin, "The House of Ba'al of Ahab and Jezebel in Samaria, and that of Athalia in Judah," in *Archaeology in the Levant: Essays for Kathleen Kenyon*, eds. R. Moorey and P. Parr [Warminster: Aris & Phillips LTD, 1978], 129). Instead, because no archaeological evidence of a temple in the city of Samaria has been discovered, Yadin suggested that Baal's temple and its "huge *temenos*" were built in either the region of Samaria, Jezreel, or Mount Carmel (see 1 Kings 18). Wherever the exact location of this temple was, Yadin surmised that it was called "the *city* of the house of Ba'al" (עיר בית-הבעל, 2 Kings 10:25). Presumably, if there were no Baal temple in the capital, then there would have been no Yahweh temple there either.

94 Hadley, "Kuntillet 'Ajrud," 120. The 400-pound bowl is a potential exception to her inability to locate objects with cultic function (see Meshel, "Did Yahweh," 32–33). However, even though Hadley rejects the possibility that this site was a functioning religious shrine, she does not rule out the possibility that "there was a religious or emotive ambiance to the site" (Judith M. Hadley, *The Cult of Asherah in Ancient Israel and Judah: Evidence for a Hebrew Goddess* [Cambridge: Cambridge University Press, 2000], 111).

95 Hadley, "Kuntillet 'Ajrud," 119; and Hadley, *Cult of Asherah*, 111.

represents a localized Baal deity, who was internationally famous and whose mythical home was on Mount Ṣapun (cf. *KTU*² 1.1–6), and this deity could be venerated as such by a scribe, priest, or king from Ugarit, Tyre, or as far away as Egypt (i.e., *KAI* 50 is from Saqqāra).[96] Likewise, the divine name Yahweh-of-Teman could represent a localized Yahweh deity residing at his mythical home, and he, too, could be venerated by anyone, regardless of their geographic proximity. In addition to *Meshel* 4.1.1, 3.6, and 3.9, Habakkuk 3:3 links the God of Israel with Teman:

אלוה מתימן יבוא וקדוש מהר־פארן

God comes from Teman; the Holy One from Mount Paran. (Habakkuk 3:3)

Cross considered this verse's reference to Teman an "archaic tradition preserved in part of the hymn."[97] Antiquity and mythology often fit well together. Notably, this verse mentions Mount Paran, which is also mentioned in Deuteronomy 33:2 along with Seir and other geographic names in the southern Transjordan region.

Eventually, the biblical Yahweh made his home at the temple in Jerusalem during the monarchic period in Judah. According to the historical books and Amos, he was also revered within the northern kingdom of Israel at the illicit cult sites in Dan and Bethel. Presumably, but by no means definitively, Yahweh had some sort of residence in Samaria; after all, it was the capital of the northern Israelite state and *Meshel* 3.1 places the deity there. In addition to these traditions, multiple ancient texts from Egypt, the Hebrew Bible, and Kuntillet 'Ajrud come together to suggest that a Yahweh once resided somewhere among the mountains south and east of the Dead Sea in Edom. Yahweh-of-Teman could have resided at a particular mountain known as Teman in this region.[98] Perhaps these ancient associations between Yahweh and Teman led the northern state of Israel to adopt the divine name Yahweh-of-Teman for worship in the bench room shrine at Kuntillet 'Ajrud. Such an association

96 The name Baal-Ṣapun (בעל צפן) appears in Exodus 14:2 as a geographic name in Egypt near Pi-hahiroth, Migdol, and the Mediterranean Sea (see Maps 47 and 48 in Yohanan Aharoni et al., *The Macmillan Bible Atlas* [3d ed.; New York: Macmillan, 1993], 45).

97 Cross, *Canaanite Myth*, 70–71. He also translated "pestilence" and "plague" as the ancient Canaanite deities Dabr and Rašp, respectively, in order to highlight Habakkuk 3's association with the polytheistic Canaanite population. He capitalized Deep, Sun, and Moon for the same purpose.

98 Weinfeld suggested that there were, in fact, several mountains rather than one with multiple names that various nomadic groups closely associated with Yahweh: Paran, Edom, Midian, Kushan, Horeb, and Sinai (Weinfeld, "Tribal League," 306).

would lend an additional sense of authority and power to the deity's presence and his ability to effect blessings; moreover, this would likely result in more and larger offerings at the site. Choosing such a powerful name is especially important if there were some external sense of a competing Yahweh, at Jerusalem, Zion, Samaria, or elsewhere. Not only would this deity's shrine be run by the relatively powerful state of Israel – at least compared to Judah and the other, smaller Transjordan peoples – but this Yahweh-of-Teman would also be the ancient, local storm-god whose influence rose beyond the immediate desert region. Regardless of where the historical Teman had been, during the Israelite occupation at Kuntillet 'Ajrud, Teman was here at the site were Yahweh-of-Teman could be revered.

6.3 Yahweh and the Kingdom of Israel: Samaria

Whereas three texts at Kuntillet 'Ajrud explicitly link Yahweh with Teman, only one text links Yahweh with Samaria:

[1]ברכת. אתכמ. [2]ליהוה. שמרנ. ולאשרתה

I bless you by Yahweh-of-Samaria and by his ašerah/Ašerah. (*Meshel* 3.1:1–2)

This text, like the ink-on-wall plaster inscription (*Meshel* 4.1.1), was found in the bench room at Kuntillet 'Ajrud, a room that the northern state of Israel had officially dedicated to Yahweh-of-Teman.[99] Unlike *Meshel* 4.1.1, however, the divine name inscribed on *Meshel* 3.1 (Pithos A) does not correspond to the divine name officially associated with that room. Hutton argues that this disconnect between the Yahweh-of-Samaria on Pithos A and its find spot, which was in an area devoted to Yahweh-of-Teman, indicates a religious tolerance between "competing" deities at the site, and he likens this tolerance to deities who were revered in the same sacred space in Mesopotamian temples.[100] In the same way that Mesopotamian deities were often revered together or would receive offerings in a temple devoted to another deity, Yahweh-of-Samaria could receive offerings in a room or shrine dedicated to Yahweh-of-Teman. This analogy is somewhat inexact or limited, however, because of the lack of modern consensus regarding the nature of Israel's worldview. Because the Assyrian worldview was decidedly polytheistic, and the state needed to honor multiple gods and goddesses in order to ensure military, economic, and agricultural

99 Hutton, "Local Manifestations," 203–204.
100 Hutton, "Local Manifestations," 203.

success, the idea of revering one deity in another's temple or any other form of sacred space does not so much reveal a religious tolerance as it does a religious norm. Assuming for a moment that the officials in Israel who oversaw the shrine at Kuntillet ʻAjrud were polytheists, there was no real sense of competition between Yahweh-of-Teman and Yahweh-of-Samaria. If they had been perceived as different deities, analogous to Ištar-of-Nineveh and Ištar-of-Arbela, they would have surely been perceived as friendly deities, which is probably why Hutton uses quotes around "competing." After all, Yahweh-of-Teman was being locally promoted by the same state where Yahweh-of-Samaria's name suggests he resided. Assuming that these officials were monolatrists or monotheists, it also seems unlikely that those in charge of the shrine would have viewed Yahweh-of-Samaria anything other than the same deity as Yahweh-of-Teman. Whichever theological lens we use, we would expect that Yahweh-of-Samaria was welcomed at the Yahweh-of-Teman shrine at Kuntillet ʻAjrud.[101]

Yahweh's associations with Samaria likely began in the ninth century when King Omri of Israel established his capital at Samaria (1 Kings 16:24).[102] However, the biblical narrative never credits Omri for building a temple to Yahweh at Samaria, insisting instead that he erected an altar and temple to Baal (v. 32) and installed an ašerah pole (v. 33). Despite this lack of biblical evidence, along with a lack of archaeological evidence, several scholars have argued that there was a temple, or at least a cult presence, dedicated to Yahweh in Samaria during the Omride Dynasty. Some base their argument upon the text from Kuntillet ʻAjrud, while others argue for a Yahwistic cult presence or temple in response to the peculiarities that they find in 1 Kings 16–18.[103]

101 However, if the overseers belonged to a super-monotheistic party, like the one that Hutton suggests could have been responsible for the "Yahweh is One" declaration (Hutton, "Local Manifestations," 206), then they might have envisioned this localized fragmentation as a threat to the singular and solitary Yahweh, whom they preferred to call Yahweh-of-Teman.

102 Lawrence Stager suggests that Omri's ancestral ties as a member of the tribe of Issachar made his purchase of Shemer's estate possible (Lawrence Stager, "Shemer's Estate," *BASOR* 277/278 [1990]: 103–104). The history of the estate itself goes back no further than the eleventh century.

103 Saul M. Olyan's suggestion that there was a shrine devoted to Yahweh in Samaria is based on the Yahweh-of-Samaria invoked at Kuntillet ʻAjrud (Saul M. Olyan, *Asherah and the Cult of Yahweh in Israel*, SBLMS 34 [Atlanta: Scholars Press, 1988], 35). In contrast, McCarter notes that the last name Samaria in *Meshel* 3.1:2 could be a reference to either Samaria the capital city of Israel or the general region surrounding Samaria (McCarter, "Aspects," 139). If Samaria is understood as a region rather than a city, then its usage is parallel with Teman in *Meshel* 4.1.1, 3.6, and 3.9, which he argues "seems to have always been a region designation" (ibid., 139).

Tikva Frymer-Kensky, for example, found it improbable that an altar to Baal would have been built in Samaria alongside an ašerah pole.[104] She reinforced this disconnect between Baal and Ašerah with a reference to the cultic battle that Elijah waged against Baal's prophets in 1 Kings 18. The goddess and her 400 prophets are only mentioned once (v. 19), whereas Baal and/or his 450 prophets are mentioned several times (vv. 19, 21, 22, 25, 26, and 40). After his victory, the Yahwist Elijah ordered that Baal's prophets be seized and killed (v. 40), but he said nothing about the goddess's prophets. Moreover, an ašerah pole accompanied Yahweh's cult in the official cult at Bethel (2 Kings 23:15), and Frymer-Kensky expected that this same pairing existed in what was surely an official cult in the capital city Samaria. Smith emphasizes this unlikely historical pairing of Ašerah with Baal, noting, "Asherah is not attested anywhere in coastal Phoenicia during the Iron Age," much less alongside a Baal deity.[105] As a princess from Phoenician Tyre, Ahab's wife Jezebel would not have promoted Ašerah's cult of as part of her worship of Tyrian deities because Ašerah was not a Tyrian deity. Smith suggests that when the divine name Ašerah is associated with Baal, as is the case in 1 Kings 18:19 and elsewhere within the historical books, we should substitute the Phoenician goddess Astarte for Ašerah to make better historical sense of the cultic situation.[106] Similarly, Frymer-Kensky would have had us substitute Yahweh for Baal in the Samarian cult when Ašerah is paired with Baal. Because of the association of Yahweh-of-Samaria with his ašerah/Ašerah in *Meshel* 3.1 and the general lack of connections between Baal and Ašerah as consorts in Ugaritic and Phoenician religious traditions, Frymer-Kensky's expectation seems reasonable.[107]

Similarly, Niehr argues for a Yahwistic cult in the capital city of Samaria. Niehr offers several arguments and forms of evidence, including the idea that the state's primary deity would surely have been worshipped in the capital city or royal court.[108] However, his most convincing argument for the presence of

---

104 Tikva Frymer-Kensky, *In the Wake of the Goddesses: Women, Culture and the Biblical Transformation of Pagan Myth* (New York: Fawcette Columbine, 1992), 157.

105 Smith, *Early History*, 126. Smith's discussion of Ašerah is found on pp. 126–133.

106 Smith, *Early History*, 126.

107 At Ugarit, Ašerah was El's consort, not Baal's (Smith, *Origins*, 47–49 and 55).

108 Herbert Niehr, "The Rise of YHWH in Judahite and Israelite Religion," in *The Triumph of Elohim: From Yahwisms to Judaisms*, ed. D. V. Edelman (Grand Rapids: Eerdmans, 1995), 56. Niehr presents a twofold argument to explain that Yahweh was worshipped in the Omride capital city of Samaria. He first argues that the state's primary deity would surely have been worshipped in the royal city, "especially in the royal court," and he then suggests that dedicating an altar to a deity within his own temple is religiously incomprehensible (ibid., 56). Neither of these arguments is convincing. Whereas the first argument seems reasonable in

a Yahwistic cult in Samaria is based upon Sargon II's *Nimrud Prism*.[109] In this inscription, Sargon claimed to have removed "gods" from Samaria, but he did not explicitly state that he took a statue of Yahweh or his ašerah/Ašerah. Instead, he only said, "I counted the gods, their helpers, as booty" (DINGIR^{meš} *ti-ik-li-šu$_2$-un šal-la-*[*ti-iš*] *am-nu*, *Iraq* 16 179, iv 32–33, translation mine).[110] Whereas Niehr is interested in this inscription in his search for a Yahwistic cult presence in Samaria, several other scholars are more interested in the nature or number of the statues as evidence of Israelite polytheism. For instance, according to Uehlinger, "it seems plausible" that Yahweh and Ašerah would be among the anthropomorphic statues that Sargon took with him back to Assyria.[111]

---

light of Yahweh's worship in the Davidic capital city Jerusalem and Assur's worship in the Assyrian capital cities Assur and Nineveh, it is not wholly compelling because there is no evidence that Assur had a temple in Calaḫ or Dūr-Šarrukīn when the Assyrian capital was moved from Assur in the ninth century and before it was moved to Nineveh at the end of the eighth century (Frame, "My Neighbour's God," 12). A chief deity need not have a temple in a capital city.

Moreover, Yadin argued against Niehr's other argument, saying that an altar (re)dedicated to the primary deity of a temple seems perfectly normal – "Obviously, if Ahab built a temple for Ba‘al it comprised an altar" – although he noted that 1 Kings 16:32 originally indicated that the altar was dedicated to Ašerah (Yadin, "House of Ba‘al," 129). Niehr's argument is based on more than redundancy, however. He appeals to the supposed *Vorlage* for the LXX to 1 Kings 16:32, where the Greek has "the house of his abominations" (οἴκῳ τῶν προσοχθισμάτων) in place of the Hebrew's "the house of Baal" (בית הבעל). Rather than accept that this change was a deliberate interpretation by the translator, he believes that this difference between the LXX and MT indicates that the temple in Samaria was known as "the house of Elohim" (בית אלהים), in keeping with the Psalms and Pentateuchal sources that refer to the Israelite national deity as "Elohim" (God) rather than "Yahweh" (Niehr, "Rise of YHWH," 56). This argument is not compelling either.

109 Niehr, "Rise of YHWH," 57. Niehr also appeals to the ninth-century Mesha Inscription's presentation of Yahweh as the supreme Israelite God, the invocation of a Yahweh-of-Samaria in *Meshel* 3.1, and fifth-century papyri from Elephantine that supposedly venerates Yahweh as Beth-El in Samaria as evidence of a Yahwistic cultic presence in the Omride capital of Samaria (ibid., 58).

110 Cyril J. Gadd, "Inscribed Prisms of Sargon II from Nimrud," *Iraq* 16 (1954): 179.

111 Christoph Uehlinger, "Anthropomorphic Cult Statuary in Iron Age Palestine and the Search for Yahweh's Cult Image," in *The Image and the Book: Iconic Cults, Aniconism, and the Rise of Book Religion in Israel and the Ancient Near East*, ed. Karel van der Toorn, CBET 21 (Leuven: Peeters, 1997), 125. In contrast to Uehlinger, who is focused on the physical nature of the statues, Niehr is more interested in Gadd's suggestion that this *Nimrud Prism* is evidence of polytheism in Samaria, whereas Bob Becking is equally interested in both the iconic nature of the statues and the polytheism they represent (Niehr, "Rise of YHWH," 59; and Bob Becking, "Assyrian Evidence for Iconic Polytheism in Ancient Israel?" in *The Image and the Book: Iconic*

Both Nadav Na'aman and Tigay caution against using Sargon's *Nimrud Prism* as evidence for Israelite polytheism in the eighth century, as far as the nature or the number of cult statues carried away from Samaria is concerned.[112] Whereas Bob Becking had previously suggested that Sargon's claim about despoiling Samaria of its gods was *not* merely a "literary topos," or literary flourish, but it was a real event, Na'aman maintains that the *Nimrud Prism*'s account is a "literary embellishment" and denies that the inscription is historically reliable.[113] The destruction of Samaria took place ca. 720, but the *Nimrud Prism* was not written until ca. 706, long after most of Sargon's other inscriptions. This delay gave the scribe time to "improve" the narrative.[114] Weighing data from Sargon's *Nimrud Prism* against the earlier inscriptions, Na'aman notes that the prism inflated the numbers of horses, cavalry, and deportees by two- to fourfold. If the scribe responsible for the *Nimrud Prism* had the freedom to manipulate numerical data, as well as chronological and other data, then he could have easily added the despoiling of the Samarian gods – a detail not found in earlier accounts about Samaria – with a similar lack of concern for historical accuracy. This point should be emphasized: none of Sargon's earlier records described despoiling Israelite or Samarian gods during his ca. 720 campaign.

Throughout his treatment of the *Nimrud Prism*, Na'aman is primarily concerned with the idea that Sargon's took the anthropomorphic "gods" (DINGIR^{meš}) as booty. He also concedes that cult vessels and theriomorphic or aniconic objects could have been taken from Samaria, a concession that should undermine his objection to the prism's historical reliability. For example, he notes that calf-shaped pedestals could have been looted at this time and that even the local Israelites could have mistaken these for gods.[115] Why he speculates at length about the form of the objects that could have been taken from the cult at Samaria and the Israelites' interpretation of those objects, while he simultaneously argues against Sargon's *Nimrud Prism* historical reliability is puzzling. If the claims about Sargon's taking booty from Samaria

---

Cults, Aniconism, and the Rise of Book Religion in Israel and the Ancient Near East, ed. Karel van der Toorn [Leuven: Peeters, 1997], 161).

112 Jeffrey H. Tigay, *You Shall Have No Other Gods: Israelite Religion in the Light of Hebrew Inscriptions*, HSS 31 (Atlanta: Scholars Press, 1986), 35; and Nadav Na'aman, "No Anthropomorphic Graven Image: Notes on the Assumed Anthropomorphic Cult Statues in the Temples of *YHWH* in the Pre-Exilic Period," *UF* 31 (1999): 395–398.

113 Becking, "Assyrian Evidence," 165; and Na'aman, "No Anthropomorphic," 398.

114 Na'aman, "No Anthropomorphic," 396–398.

115 Na'aman, "No Anthropomorphic," 413.

in this inscription are not historically reliable, then why bother speculating what exactly was taken as booty in the first place?

In his discussion of the *Nimrud Prism*, Tigay does not question the statement that cult objects were taken as booty. Instead, he argues that although the carried-away objects were characterized as gods (DINGIR^{meš}) by the undoubtedly polytheistic Assyrian scribe who wrote the prism, we should not necessarily assume that this outsider correctly identified what the local Israelites thought that they were. For example, the objects carried away from Samaria could have resembled the calves that Jeroboam I placed at Bethel and Dan (1 Kings 12:25–33), as Na'aman noted, but the local Samarian devotee of Yahweh could have envisioned the calves as Yahweh's pedestal rather than as Yahweh himself. The Assyrians would likely have been ignorant of this local tradition and would naturally have interpreted the objects according to what they already knew about their cults and cult objects at home. Regardless of the nature of the objects that Sargon took, any Assyrian eye could have mistaken them for gods because the Assyrian worshipped both anthropomorphic statues and non-anthropomorphic objects, such as crowns, drums, or chariots, as divine beings. Following Tigay's warning about the *Nimrud Prism* and what its author interpreted as "gods" (DINGIR^{meš}), we can only say that some objects that could be characterized as gods were removed from the state cult at Samaria. These objects could have been iconic or aniconic Yahwistic cult objects that had been promoted by the Israelite kings and their cult in the capital, or they could have been cult statues or other objects that were used in the state's service of non-Yahweh deities, like a Baal or Ašerah deity.[116]

For Tigay, this warning against assuming that the DINGIR^{meš} should be identified with actual Israelite gods – be they anthropomorphic or any other officially sanctioned shaped object (consider Deuteronomy 5:8 and 4:16–18) – fits with his larger argument that most Israelites were exclusively Yahwistic during the monarchic period. His evidence for a primarily Israelite monolatrist

116 While no definitive textual, pictorial, or archaeological evidence has turned up indicative of an iconic Yahwistic cult image, Na'aman notes that several Yahwistic shrines have yielded aniconic images or cult vessels (Na'aman, "No Anthropomorphic," 405–408). For example, the Lachish Reliefs depicting Sennacherib's campaign to Judah in 701 indicate no graven images, but they do show cult objects, including bronze incense burners among the booty (ibid., 405). Likewise, in the Mesha Inscription (*KAI* 181:17–18), the Moabite king boasted about despoiling the vessels of Yahweh from Nebo but did not mention any cult statues. In the destruction layer at the fortress in Arad, which Na'aman tentatively dates to Sennacherib's campaign, one *maṣṣebah* (standing stone) was found (ibid., 408). The *maṣṣebah* could have been a physical object representing Yahweh's presence, but because it was a blank stone it is considered aniconic by scholars.

or monotheistic population rests on the almost exclusive use of the divine name Yahweh as the theophoric element in both biblical and inscriptional Israelite personal names.[117] Tigay also warns against taking the classical prophets or the historical books' accusations of Israelite idolatry too literally, even though such accusations are plentiful.[118] After all, when the classical prophets accused the Israelites of idolatry or fetishism, they could have been employing a polemic against Samaria (or, on occasion, Jerusalem) in order to denigrate their devotion to Yahweh in light of their other moral failings.[119]

Regardless of our interpretation of the objects that Sargon took in the late eighth century, their presence in Samaria probably points to the veneration of some Yahweh deity in the capital city of Samaria. On the one hand, if the ancient Israelites were predominantly monolatrists or monotheists, as Tigay contends, then the objects would have been Yahwistic in nature because Yahweh would have been the only deity of concern to most Israelites. On the other hand, if the ancient Israelites were polytheists, then we could expect that at least one of the despoiled objects was Yahwistic in nature. Polytheists are religiously tolerant, so surely a Yahweh deity would have been venerated even in Samaria where they had a temple devoted to Baal. This tolerance for a Yahweh in Samaria – or the Yahweh-of-Samaria – should be all the more expected given that King Ahab, whom the books of Kings blamed for the Baal Temple in Samaria (1 Kings 16:32), was himself a Yahwist. He gave his two sons and successors and his daughter who ruled as queen mother in Jerusalem names containing Yahwistic theophoric elements: Ahaziah (אחזיה, "Yahweh holds," 2 Kings 1:2), Jehoram (יהורם, "Yahweh is exalted," v. 17), and Athaliah (עתליהו, "Yahweh has manifest his glory" or "Yahweh is just", 8:26).[120] Several

117 Tigay, *You Shall Have*, 19–20.

118 Several biblical texts refer to idols in Samaria: Isaiah 10:10–11; Hosea 4:17; 10:5–6; 13:2; Amos 5:26; and Micah 1:7; and 5:12 (Tigay, *You Shall Have*, 35 n. 71). Of these, Isaiah 10:10–11 (פסיליהם, "their images," v. 10; אליליה, "her worthless images," and עצביה, "her idols" v. 11) and Hosea 10:5–6 (עגלות בית און, "calves of Beth-aven") most closely resemble Sargon's *Nimrud Prism* in that they discuss sending Israelite idols from Samaria to Assyria. Similarly, Micah 1:7 (כל-פסיליה, "all her images") and 5:12 (פסיליך, "your images," and מצבותיך, "your sacred pillars") refer to the destruction of cult objects in Samaria. Hosea 4:17 (עצבים, "idols") and 13:2 (מסכה, "molten image," and עצבים, "idols") refer to objects of local devotion in Ephraim rather than their removal from Samaria, with Baal mentioned in 13:1.

119 Consider, in this vein, 1 Samuel 15:22; Isaiah 1:11–17; Hosea 6:5–6; and Amos 2:6–16.

120 Athaliah is listed as the daughter of Omri in 2 Kings 8:26 but as the daughter of Ahab in v. 22. She is also the first woman documented with the theophoric element Yahweh in her name (Winfried Thiel, "Athaliah in *Anchor Bible Dictionary*, ed. David Noel Freedman [New York: Doubleday, 1992], 1:511). Thiel notes that the non-theophoric element in Athaliah's name is not from a Hebrew verbal root. The meaning "Yahweh has manifest his glory" depends upon

post-Omride Israelite kings also had Yahwistic theophoric elements in their names, including Pekahiah (פקחיה, "Yahweh has opened [his eyes]," 15:23), whose reign was only a few decades before the destruction of Samaria. Unless one of the final two kings of Israel, Pekah or Hoshea, was an ardent anti-Yahwist, which seems highly unlikely given that the Yahwistic cult at Bethel survived into Josiah's late seventh-century reign (see 23:15) despite them, Sargon almost certainly took some kind of Yahwistic object(s) from Samaria as booty.

While Sargon's *Nimrud Prism* gives reason to assume that there was a Yahwistic cult at Samaria, an appeal to the Yahweh-of-Samaria in *Meshel 3.1* as evidence must be evaluated under an entirely different set of circumstances. The *Nimrud Prism* was officially commissioned for the Neo-Assyrian state on behalf of the king as a propagandistic piece, whereas *Meshel 3.1* has been described as an *ad hoc* inscription dedicated to a divine name not officially recognized by the shrine in which it was deposited. As an unofficial text, we cannot presume how representative it was of Israelite religiosity. Perhaps only the scribe who wrote it and his caravan companions revered a deity by the name of Yahweh-of-Samaria, but he could just as easily be representative of his entire community in Samaria or, at least, the royal court and its priests.

Ideally, the value of the *Meshel 3.1* and its Yahweh-of-Samaria would be weighed against comparable, i.e., *ad hoc*, texts. Unfortunately, none of the first-millennium inscriptions that list Baal deities are clearly non-official. They appear to have been produced by state-sponsored scribes or commissioned by state officials for cultic use.[121] Despite this difference, these Northwest Semitic inscriptions are the closest analogies to *Meshel 3.1* and Yahweh-of-Samaria available to us, so they should be considered anyway. As discussed in chapter 5, one way to describe the relationship between a deity and his or her geographic last name included mythological and/or historical cultic ties. Baal-of-Ṣapun served as the best representative of this kind of relationship as both the *Baal Cycle* and biblical tradition (e.g., Psalm 48:3) have made his divine home at Mount Ṣapun famous. Likewise, the power of Teman's mythical background could be responsible for Yahweh-of-Teman's association with his place. On a related note, although the biblical narrative has been stripped of

---

the Akkadian root for a solution, and the meaning "Yahweh is just" is based upon an Aramaic root. The meaning "Yahweh is abundant" is based upon an Arabic root.

121 Perhaps personal names containing Bēl-Ḫarrān as the theophoric element (e.g., Bēl-Ḫarrān-issē'a, a dependent farmer from Que, *PNA* 1/2, 303) could be used as evidence for the DN-of-GN formula in non-official usage, where the divine name for the moon-god is intimately associated with a place containing a cult to that deity.

its mythical layers, it does contain many historical narratives that tie divine names to a particular place. Two different episodes in Numbers 22–23 and 25, which are also recalled elsewhere, relate major theological events in the early history of the people of Israel. These cult-related events took place at or near Pe'or, and because these narratives survived, the divine name Baal-Pe'or survived.

As discussed in chapter 3.2, the DN-of-GN (or the semantic equivalent in Akkadian, DN-*ša*-GN) also seems to represent a deity who was venerated at an official cult in the city that bears its last name, and these cities were often politically or militarily significant in the Neo-Assyrian Empire. This is true of Ištar-of-Nineveh, Ištar-of-Arbela, and Adad-of-Kurbail, who are all mentioned in Assur-nērārī V's treaty with Mati'-ilu of Arpad (SAA 2 2 vi 15–17). This is by no means the only reason a deity received a geographic last name (consider, for example, Ištar-of-Heaven in Table 3.11, and the Babylonian god *Palil*-of-Udannu in Table 3.18), but it is telling. Of course, most of the Neo-Assyrian texts with these DN-of-GN names are state treaties, administrative documents, and letters to the court, whereas *Meshel* 3.1 is not and so would not necessarily reflect the political and military concerns of the state. However, during the mid-ninth century, Samaria was a military and political stronghold from which Ahab led his military campaigns against Damascus and coalitions against Assyria.[122] If an Israelite DN-of-GN formulation is in any way comparable to its Neo-Assyrian counterparts, then it is not surprising that Samaria, of all ancient Israelite cities or places, would become home to a localized Yahweh deity. This being the case, it is all the more surprising that *Meshel* 3.1 is the only text providing such a formula for Samaria.

When considering the nature of Yahweh-of-Samaria's relationship with the city or region of Samaria, nothing suggests that Yahweh-of-Samaria had a mythological tie to Samaria. Also, no evidence explicitly claims that a Yahweh had a small yet significant presence in the temple at Samaria – a presence that Sargon II likely despoiled in the eighth century – but if there were cult objects for Sargon to despoil, at least some of these objects surely belonged to a Yahweh deity. Likewise, no evidence explicitly places a major cult of Yahweh in Samaria, even though several scholars have suggested that the Baal temple mentioned in 1 Kings 12:32 was actually a temple dedicated to Yahweh. However, Samaria was a powerful military capital during Ahab's reign in the mid-ninth century, and he expanded his political power and influence into

122 Mordechai Cogan, *I Kings*, AB 10 (New York: Doubleday, 2001), 498.

Judah and the Transjordan. A couple of generations later, Joash again extended his influence into and beyond Judah. Perhaps the otherwise unattested divine name Yahweh-of-Samaria from *Meshel* 3.1 reflects a militaristic or nationalistic association between the deity and the city in the same way that the divine name Ištar-of-Nineveh does. Apart from *Meshel* 3.1, no evidence directly links a Yahweh with Samaria, but indirect evidence – including, perhaps, the 1 and 2 Kings' silence concerning a Yahwistic cult presence at Samaria while focusing on Baal at Samaria in 1 Kings 16:32 and focusing on Yahweh at Dan and Bethel (12:29) – and the fact that Sargon carried off cult objects of some fashion from Samaria hint that a Yahweh had a cultic presence in Samaria. Indeed, the deity known as Yahweh-of-Samaria could have been the primary divine presence in Samaria ca. 800 or throughout Samaria's tenure as a capital city.

6.4 Yahweh and the Kingdom of Judah: Zion and the Hosts

In stark contrast to the Hebrew Bible's silence on any Yahwistic cult presence in Samaria, the Jerusalem cult in Judah played a central role in biblical history and theology from David's conquest of the city (2 Samuel 5) to Ezra's supervision of the temple's rebuilding (Ezra 7–8) several centuries later. After capturing the city from the Jebusites (2 Samuel 5:8–9), David relocated the ark of Yahweh to Jerusalem (6:15) but left the building of a permanent temple to his son Solomon (7:13). Once Solomon built Yahweh a temple in Jerusalem (1 Kings 6), the Davidic dynasty and the Yahwistic cult became intertwined, and the Davidic dynasty ruled from Jerusalem for more than four hundred years until the exile of Zedekiah in 586 (2 Kings 25:7). With the force of the state religion of Judah behind the relocation of Yahweh's cult from Shiloh to Jerusalem during David's reign (see 1 Samuel 4; 2 Samuel 6; and Jeremiah 7:12–20), the royal Yahwistic cult in the capital city became the shrine for legitimate Yahwistic worship.

During the monarchic period, Jerusalem and the hilltop near the city of David, namely, Zion (e.g., 2 Samuel 5:7), became Yahweh's holy mountain and his dwelling place. In the first millennium, Zion was to Yahweh as Mount Ṣapun had been to (the unspecified) Baal in the Ugaritic *Baal Cycle*:

[2]נודע ביהודה אלהים בישראל גדול שמו [3]ויהי בשלם סוכו ומעונתו בציון

> God is known in Judah; in Israel, his name is great. In (Jeru)Salem his tent came to be. And his dwelling is in Zion. (Psalm 76:2–3)

Indeed, one psalmist literally likens Yahweh's abode in Zion to Mount Ṣapun in Psalm 48:2–3:

2 גדול יהוה ומהלל מאד בעיר אלהינו הר־קדשו ... 3 הר־ציון ירכתי צפון קרית מלך רב

> Great is Yahweh, and he is very praiseworthy in the city of our God, his holy mountain ... Mount Zion, the peak of Ṣapun, city of the great king.

Because Mount Ṣapun is located to the north of Israel, its name became synonymous with the cardinal direction "north" in biblical Hebrew, which is why the phrase "the peak of Ṣapun" (ירכתי צפון) in this verse is often translated something along the lines of "the extreme north."[123] If we recognize צפון in v. 3 as (Mount) Ṣapun, Psalm 48 not only celebrates Mount Zion as Yahweh's beautiful abode, but it also praises Yahweh by associating him with Ṣapun and, thereby, appropriating Baal-of-Ṣapun's attributes.[124] This association between Yahweh and Ṣapun became so well known that other biblical authors could allude to it through common Baal motifs.[125] Isaiah 3:1 and Zechariah 14:4 tell of Yahweh getting ready for battle on Mount Zion, and 2 Esdras 13:35 (and elsewhere) contains language that is reminiscent of Baal's getting ready for battle against the sea (Yam) on Mount Ṣapun. Other Psalms, including 74:2 and 135:21, also praise Yahweh for having chosen Zion and Jerusalem as his dwelling place.[126] The deity and his mountain in Jerusalem were closely associated in the minds of many biblical authors.

Extra-biblical graffiti found in a cave at Khirbet Beit Lei – which Cross dated to the early sixth century, and André Lemaire dates to ca. 700 – also associates Yahweh with Jerusalem.[127] Although Cross, Lemaire, and Joseph Naveh offer different readings of the text, all agree that the divine name Yahweh appears in the first line and Jerusalem is the last word of the two-line

---

123 Edward Lipiński, "צפון *ṣāp̱ôn*; צפוני *ṣᵉp̱ônî*," in *TDOT* (2003), 12:440–441. This phrase appears as "in the far north" in NRSV, and "*on* the sides of the north" in KJV, but as "summit of Zaphon" in NJPS.

124 Smith, *Early History*, 88–91.

125 Smith, *Early History*, 89.

126 Psalm 74:2: הר־ציון זה שכנת בו ("Mount Zion, you dwelt upon it").
Psalm 135:21: ברוך יהוה מציון שכן ירושלם ("Blessed be Yahweh from Zion, who resides [in] Jerusalem").

127 Frank Moore Cross, "The Cave Inscriptions from Khirbet Beit Lei," in *Near Eastern Archaeology in the Twentieth Century: Essays in Honor of Nelson Glueck*, ed. J. Sanders (New York: Doubleday 1970), 304; and André Lemaire, "Prières en temps de crise: Les inscriptions de Khirbet Beit Lei," *RB* 83 (1976): 565.

inscription.[128] In contrast to Cross, who interpreted Jerusalem as the object of the sentence – “yea, I [Yahweh] will redeem Jerusalem” (וגאלתי . ירשלם, *BLei* 5) – both Lemaire and Naveh interpret Jerusalem as the geographic element in an epithet that refers to Yahweh: “to ‘God of Jerusalem’” (לאלהי . ירשלם).[129] Whichever reading is the better interpretation, this text demonstrates that Yahweh’s ancient association with Jerusalem had expanded beyond the interests of the state cult and biblical authors to members of the lay population. The locals around Jerusalem appealed to this deity in time of trouble, which, if *BLei* 5 dates to ca. 700, could be a reference to Sennacherib’s besiegement of Jerusalem in 701.

Yahweh’s association with Zion and Jerusalem became so strong that it far outlived the Davidic dynasty. In Ezra 1:3–4, Cyrus’s decree twice addresses Yahweh as “the God who is in Jerusalem (יהוה ... האלהם אשר בירושלם), even though Yahweh’s temple had been destroyed almost fifty years earlier during Nebuchadnezzar’s reign (2 Kings 25:8–9). Likewise, in the letter that he wrote to commission Ezra to rebuilt the temple in Jerusalem (Ezra 7:12–26), Artaxerxes locates the deity in Jerusalem no less than four times. The divine name Yahweh never actually appears in the letter, but the place is unambiguous:

v. 15	לאלה ישראל די בירושלם משכנה	to “the God of Israel” whose dwelling (is) in-Jerusalem
v. 16	לבית אלההם די בירושלם	of the house of their-God who (is) in-Jerusalem
v. 17	די בית אלהכם די בירושלם	of the house of your-God who (is) in-Jerusalem
v. 19	קדם אלה ירושלם	before the “God of Jerusalem.”

In addition to the epithets “God of Israel” and “God of Jerusalem,” the deity is also called “God of Heaven” (אלה שמיא, 7:12, 21, and twice in 23).

Although these passages locate Yahweh in Zion or Jerusalem, the first name Yahweh never appears in the formula DN-of-GN in which the GN refers to Jerusalem. There is no good Jerusalem counterpart (i.e., Yahweh-of-Jerusalem) to Yahweh-of-Samaria or Yahweh-of-Teman. At best, if we ignore the Masoretic punctuation, Isaiah 60:14 could be translated, “they will call you, ‘the city of Yahweh-of-Zion//the-Holy-One-of-Israel’” (ויקראו לך עיר יהוה ציון קדש ישראל). However, turning Yahweh-of-Zion into a divine name followed by the

128 Cross, “Cave Inscriptions,” 301; Lemaire, “Prières en temps de crise,” 559; and Joseph Naveh, “Old Hebrew Inscriptions in a Burial Cave,” *IEJ* 13 (1963): 84.

129 Lemaire, “Prières en temps de crise,” 559; Naveh, “Old Hebrew Inscriptions,” 84; cf. Cross, “Cave Inscriptions,” 301. Dobbs-Allsopp et al. follow Cross’s reading, whereas Aḥituv does not indicate a preferred reading, and in 2001 Naveh maintained his own reading (Dobbs-Allsopp, et al., *Hebrew Inscriptions*, 128; Shmuel Aḥituv, *Echoes from the Past: Hebrew and Cognate Inscriptions from the Biblical Period*, trans. A. F. Rainey [Jerusalem: Carta, 2008], 233–235; and Joseph Naveh, “Hebrew Graffiti from the First Temple Period,” *IEJ* 51 [2001]: 197).

epithet "the Holy One of Israel" is not a satisfying translation because it minimizes the role of the city in this verse. This artificial emendation should be rejected because the current Masoretic punctuation provides a more balanced unit, setting up a city-deity pattern in each colon: City-of-Yahweh = Zion-of-the-Holy-One-of-Israel.

Nevertheless, as we have seen in chapter 4.1, there are alternative formulas that express the relationship between deities and their cities, so we should consider whether there are any such formulas connecting Yahweh with Jerusalem. Of the three alternative full name formulas used for the various Ištar goddesses in Neo-Assyrian inscriptions (i.e., title-of-GN, DN//title-of-GN, and DN//Who-Resides-(in)-GN), none of them can be found in the Hebrew Bible as a potential Yahweh full name. Only a combination of two formulas DN//title-of-GN, where "title" here represents "God" (אלהי־), and DN-(Who)-Resides-(in)-GN resembles any pattern that could potentially be considered a Yahweh full name. As the following analysis and discussion demonstrate, there is no compelling instance of a Yahweh full name that places the deity in Jerusalem.

In response to his examination of Yahwistic epithets from the fifth-century Aramaic texts at Elephantine (see Table 6.1 and Map 1), Bezalel Porten notes several comparable epithets from the Hebrew Bible. For example, the Yahweh full names and epithets Yahweh-of-Hosts, Yahweh//God, and "God of Heaven" were common to both the Elephantine texts and the Hebrew Bible.[130] Other epithets from Elephantine that located the deity in the local Elephantine temple, (e.g., YHW//the-God in-the-Elephantine-Fortress [יהו אלהא ביב בירתא]; YHW//the-God-(who)-resides-(in)-the-Elephantine-Fortress [יהו אלהא שכנ יב ברתא]) inspired Porten to consider various biblical analogies: Yahweh//(who)-resides-(in)-Jerusalem (יהוה ... שכן ירושלם, Psalm 135:21)[131]; Yahweh-of-Hosts//(Who)-resides in-Mount Zion" (יהוה צבאות השכן בהר ציון, Isaiah 8:18); and Yahweh//your-God//(Who)-resides in-Zion (יהוה אלהיכם שכן בציון, Joel 4:17),

130 Porten, *Archives from Elephantine*, 106–109.

131 Porten, *Archives from Elephantine*, 107. The epithet that Porten cites in Psalm 135:21 does not immediately follow the divine name Yahweh because the phrase "from-Zion" (מציון) separates them. Porten probably associates "from-Zion" with the phrase "blessed is" (ברוך) at the beginning of the verse, which he would translate as something along the lines of "Blessed is Yahweh, (he) who resides (in) Jerusalem, from Zion" (ברוך יהוה מציון שכן ירושלם). This sentence structure (i.e., verb / subject / prepositional-phrase) is also found in Psalm 110:2; 128:5; and 134:3:

Verse:	Hebrew:	Literal Translation:	Idiomatic English Translation:
110:2	ישלח יהוה מציון	Will-send Yahweh from-Zion	Yahweh will send from Zion
128:5	יברכך יהוה מציון	May-bless-you Yahweh from-Zion	May Yahweh bless you from Zion

among others.[132] I should stress that Porten was not proposing these as Yahweh full names; he was only noting them as epithets because of their structural resemblance to those discovered at Elephantine.

Because these epithets somewhat resemble a combination of the full name formulas found in Neo-Assyrian inscriptions, we, too, should consider them as potential Yahweh full names, if only for argument's sake. In particular, Joel 4:17 and 21 and Psalm 135:21 each contain the participial form of the verbal root ש-כ-ן ("to reside/dwell"), which corresponds to the Akkadian *āšib/āšibat-*.[133] Even if we allow for the combined formula, DN//title//Who-Resides-(in)-GN, none of these examples matches the Neo-Assyrian models. In Joel 4:17, the divine name is separated from the geographic name by the *bet*-locative preposition: Yahweh//your-God (who)-resides in-Zion. A *bet*-locative also interrupts the (who)-resides element from the geographic element in v. 21: Yahweh (who)-resides in-Zion (יהוה שכן בציון). Finally, in Psalm 135:21, the formula is again interrupted by another geographic element: Yahweh from-Zion (who)-resides-(in)-Jerusalem. None of these three verses provides a good correspondence to the Akkadian formula DN//Who-Resides-(in)-GN. Two contain a *bet*-locative phrase that interrupts the potential full name, and the third is interrupted by yet another prepositional phrase.

Although the Yahweh whose cult site was in Jerusalem was not known by any full names that included the geographic last name Jerusalem or Zion, the full name Yahweh-of-Hosts was closely associated with the cult in Jerusalem and should be considered as a possible reference to a specific Yahweh deity.

Verse:	**Hebrew:**	**Literal Translation:**	**Idiomatic English Translation:**
134:3	יברכך יהוה מציון עשה שמים וארץ	May-bless-you Yahweh from-Zion maker of-heaven and-earth	May Yahweh maker of heaven and earth bless you from Zion
135:21	ברוך יהוה מציון שכן ירושלם	Blessed-is Yahweh from-Zion Who-resides (in)-Jerusalem	Blessed from Zion is Yahweh who resides in Jerusalem.

Notably, like Psalm 135:21, 134:3 has an epithet after the "from-Zion" phrase that describes Yahweh. Regardless of how the syntax of Psalm 135:21 is parsed, however, the inclusion of the phrase "from-Zion" interrupts the potential full name formula DN//Who-Resides-(in)-GN (i.e., Yahweh//Who-Resides-(in)-Jerusalem), which would resemble the formulas used to name goddesses in Neo-Assyrian inscriptions.

132 None of these texts (i.e., Joel 4:17 and 21; Isaiah 8:18; and *TAD* B3.12:2) represent an actual Yahweh full name (Allen, "Examination," 77–78).

133 According to Tryggve Mettinger, ש-כ-ן ("to reside/dwell") is more generalized in its usage with the divine name than is its synonym י-ש-ב ("to sit/dwell/reside"), which is used to designate Yahweh's sitting upon his cherubim throne (Tryggve Mettinger, *The Dethronement of Sabaoth: Studies in the Shem and Kabod Theologies*, trans. F. Cryer [Lund: Willin & Dalholm, 1982], 94).

According to Tryggve Mettinger, Yahweh-of-Hosts comprises two nouns in a construct chain, so grammatically it resembles the standard pattern, but as a non-geographic word it more closely resembles the non-geographic Hittite divine epithets used for LAMMA deities and other classes of gods (e.g., ^{d}LAMMA-^{kuš}*kuršaš*, The-tutelary-deity-of-the-hunting-bag; see also Tables 2.4 and 2.5).[134] This genitive relationship between the two nouns seems to be presupposed by the occasional Greek translation of the name: Κυρίον τῶν δυνάμεων, (Lord-of-Hosts, e.g., 2 Samuel 6:2).[135] However, Mettinger's grammatical interpretation of this Yahweh full name is only one of several possibilities. Other proposed interpretations include treating the name as two nouns in apposition (i.e., "Yahweh, the-Hosts"); as a nominal sentence (i.e., "Yahweh [is] the-Hosts"); and as a sentence in which the name Yahweh is reinterpreted as the verb (i.e., "He who creates the [heavenly] hosts/armies").[136] Whatever the grammatical and syntactical meaning of the name, Isaiah 47:4 explicitly identifies Yahweh-of-Hosts as divine full name when it states "Yahweh-of-Hosts is his name" (יהוה צבאות שמו), and Amos 4:13 and 5:27 indicate to us that the epithet and title "God" (אלהי־) can interrupt the full name without significantly altering the meaning: "Yahweh//God-of-Hosts is his name" (יהוה אלהי־צבאות שמו).[137] With this addition of "God" (אלהי־), Yahweh//God-of-Hosts syntactically resembles the full name formula DN//title-of-GN and the full name Ištar//Lady-of-Nineveh.[138]

---

134 Tryggve Mettinger, *In Search of God: the Meaning and Message of the Everlasting Names*, trans. F. Cryer (Philadelphia: Fortress, 1988), 135; and McMahon, *Hittite State Cult*, 4–5. Mettinger and Emerton both claim that the Yahweh DN-of-GN names at Kuntillet 'Ajrud reinforce this interpretation of the grammatical relationship between Yahweh and Hosts as comprising a construction chain (Mettinger, *In Search of God*, 135; and Emerton, "New Light," 8).

135 H.-J. Zobel, "*ṣ^{e}ḇā'ôṯ*," *TDOT* (2003), 12:219.

136 Matitiahu Tsevat, "Studies in the Book of Samuel," *HUCA* 36 (1965): 55; Zobel, "ṣebā'ôt," 219; van der Toorn, "Yahweh," 914; Cross, *Canaanite Myth*, 70; and Cross, "Yahweh and the God," 252–256. Cross rejected the possibility that Yahweh-of-Hosts could be a construct chain and the possibility that it could be an adjective or participle because Hosts is plural and does not agree with the singular Yahweh. Emerton, however, approved of the construct chain interpretation in light of the Kuntillet 'Ajrud texts (Emerton, "New Light," 8). As van der Toorn points out, there are several verbal roots from various different languages that could be behind the name Yahweh (van der Toorn, "Yahweh," 915–916), which means that interpreting Yahweh-of-Hosts as a sentence has at least as many possible translation values as the meaning of the word Yahweh itself has.

137 See also Isaiah 48:2; 51:15; and 54:5; and Jeremiah 10:16; 31:35; 32:18; 46:18; 48:15; 50:34; and 51:57.

138 Although I have treated Yahweh//God-of-Hosts as a lengthened form of the name Yahweh-of-Hosts, the name Yahweh-of-Hosts could also be viewed as an abbreviated form of Yahweh//God-of-Hosts.

By Mettinger’s count, the full name Yahweh-of-Hosts occurs 284 times in the Hebrew Bible, and the full name is most commonly associated with the cults at the Israelite shrine in Shiloh and the Judahite shrine in Jerusalem.[139] Mettinger, J. P. Ross, and H.-J. Zobel each locate the origins of the full name Yahweh-of-Hosts in the cult at Shiloh because of the references to the deity (1 Samuel 1:3 and 11) and the Ark of the Covenant (4:4) there during Samuel’s life.[140] However, once David moved the Ark to Jerusalem in 2 Samuel 6, most of the biblical attestations of the full name appear in Judahite rather than Israelite contexts.[141] Approximately half of the attestations of Yahweh-of-Hosts occur in collections of the Judahite prophets Isaiah, Haggai, Zechariah, and Malachi.[142] Ross notes that the northern prophets Elijah and Elisha only used the full name Yahweh-of-Hosts four times, and Zobel considers the reference in Hosea 12:6 a later insertion.[143] Thus, even though the name Yahweh-of-Hosts has an Israelite origin, it was eventually more widespread in a Jerusalemite context; at least, this is what the extant biblical evidence that passed through Judahite hands suggests. The name Yahweh-of-Hosts is also attested in four extra-biblical texts, one of which is in Hebrew, and the others are in Aramaic.[144]

---

139 Tryggve Mettinger, “Yahweh Zebaoth,” in *Dictionary of Deities and Demons in the Bible*, eds. Karel van der Toorn, Bob Becking, and Pieter W. van der Horst, 2nd rev. ed. (Leiden: Brill, 1999), 920; J. P. Ross, “Jahweh Ṣ^{E}B̲Ā’ÔT̲ in Samuel and Psalms,” *VT* 17 [1967]: 82; Tsevat, “Studies,” 49; and Zobel, “ṣebā’ôt,” 215.

140 Mettinger, *In Search of God*, 149; Ross, “Jahweh,” 80; and Zobel, “ṣebā’ôt,” 222. Ross suggests that the god “Hosts” was originally a Canaanite deity at the Shiloh cult because 1 Samuel 1:4 is the first biblical occurrence of the name Yahweh-of-Host (Ross, “Jahweh,” 79).

141 Citing 1 Samuel 4:4, William Albright argued that the name Yahweh-of-Host could not be conceptually severed from the Ark of the Covenant (Albright, “L’épithète divine Jahvé Seba’ôt,” 378).

142 Mettinger, “Yahweh Zebaoth,” 921. Because the name Yahweh-of-Hosts appears less frequently in Ezekiel, the Deuteronomistic History, and the Torah, Mettinger concludes that this full name was most popular in Jerusalem prior to the exile.

143 Ross, “Jahweh Ṣ^{E}B̲Ā’ÔT̲,” 82 and 91; and Zobel, “ṣebā’ôt,” 227 and n. 94.

144 The Hebrew text is unprovenanced, but because its script resembles the script of the Khirbet el-Qôm inscription, it has been similarly dated to the first half of the seventh century (Dobbs-Allsopp, et al., *Hebrew Inscriptions*, 575). The inscription, a curse against Ḥarip, consists of two lines: [1]ארר חרפ בנ חגב ליהוה [2]צבאת (“Cursed be Ḥarip, the son of Ḥagab, by Yahweh-of-Hosts,” *Nav** 1:1–2). The three Aramaic texts are from the Elephantine ostraca dating to the fifth century, and Yahweh’s first name is spelled YHH in each (Porten, *Archives from Elephantine*, 106). In contrast to the strong relationship between Yahweh-of-Hosts and Jerusalem/Zion in the Bible, nothing from these three ostraca indicates that this Yahweh-of-Hosts should be disassociated from the Elephantine Fortress and the Yahweh temple (אגרא/בית) there. These three attestations of the name could suggest that the Elephantine Yahwists were from Judah rather than Israel.

When used as a common noun in Hebrew, צבא means "army, war, warfare," which is why צבאות has traditionally been translated as "Hosts" in reference to the heavenly armies accompanying Yahweh or to his earthly Israelite armies.[145] However, Mettinger, Ross, and Zobel agree that as a divine name Yahweh-of-Hosts acts more royally than militarily in the epithet.[146] According to Ross, the royal aspect of the full name Yahweh-of-Hosts is most apparent in Psalm 84, which praises the deity who dwells in Zion without any significant military language.[147] This psalm praises Yahweh-of-Hosts (vv. 2, 4, 9, and 13) as the one who is "my king and my God" (מלכי ואלהי, v. 4), who is "God in Zion" (אלהים בציון, v. 8), and in whose courts a day is a thousand times better than anywhere else (v. 11).[148] The closest the psalm comes to anything martial is the mention

---

145 BDB, צבא mng. 1–2 and 4; and Tryggve Mettinger, "YHWH Sabaoth – The Heavenly King on the Cherubim Throne," in *Studies in the Period of David and Solomon and other Essays: Papers Read at the International Symposium for Biblical Studies, Tokyo, 5–7 December, 1979*, ed. T. Ishida (Winona Lake: Eisenbrauns, 1979), 109–110.

146 Mettinger, *Dethronement of Sabaoth*, 24; Ross, "Jahweh," 84; and Zobel, "ṣebā'ôt," 224. Mettinger lists more than 20 instances in which Yahweh-of-Hosts is depicted as a king (Exodus 15:18; Isaiah 24:33; 33:22; 52:7; Jeremiah 8:19; Micah 4:7; Zephaniah 3:15; Zechariah 14:9, 16, 17; and Psalms 10:16; 48:3; 68:25; 74:12; 84:4; 93:1; 95:3; 96:10; 97:1; 99:1; 146:10; and 149:2), along with another dozen setting him on a throne with Zion-based theology (Isaiah 6:1; 66:1; Jeremiah 3:17; 17:12; Ezekiel 1:26; and Psalm 9:5 and 8; 47:9; 89:15; 93:2; and 103:19; Mettinger, *Dethronement of Sabaoth*, 24).

Ross claims that the strongest military connotations for Yahweh-of-Hosts is 1 Samuel 17:45, where David explains that Yahweh-of-Hosts//the-God-of-the-Ranks-of-Israel (יהוה צבאות אלהי מערכות ישראל) is a superior weapon to Goliath's sword, spear, and javelin (Ross, "Jahweh," 81), although he notes that this passage could be a later writer applying a popular etymology to the divine name. The most militaristic occurrence of the full name in the Psalms is Psalm 24:8, where the deity is praised as Yahweh//Hero-of-Battle (יהוה גבור מלחמה) and later called Yahweh-of-Hosts in v. 10 (ibid., 88). The author of Samuel prefers to present Yahweh as a divine king rather than a military general, but Yahweh-of-Hosts occurs relatively infrequently in Samuel and Kings and only in a non-royal context in 1 Samuel 17:45 (ibid., 83 and 89). Other verses that place Yahweh-of-Hosts in military contexts include Isaiah 1:24 and 21:10 and Zephaniah 2:9. Although Yahweh is not called Yahweh-of-Hosts in Numbers 10:24, this verse has been offered as a parallel to Yahweh-of-Hosts because of its earthly war associations (see, for example, Milgrom, *Numbers*, 81).

147 Ross, "Jahweh," 87.

148 Other Zion psalms include Psalm 46 and 48. The name Zion is not used in the former psalm, but Yahweh-of-Hosts appears in vv. 8 and 12. Zion appears three times in the latter psalm (vv. 3, 12, and 13), and Yahweh-of-Hosts appears in v. 9. Both of these psalms describe the deity as a refuge for the troubled. Psalm 46:10 proclaims that Yahweh-of-Hosts will put an end to wars by breaking bows and shattering spears, whereas Psalm 48 drops military language in favor of a discussion of Zion's defenses: citadels (vv. 3 and 14), towers (v.13), and ramparts (v. 14).

of shields (מגן) in vv. 10 and 12. Similarly, Isaiah's vision of Yahweh-of-Hosts in the temple in Jerusalem pictures him as accompanied by a heavenly court:

> [1]בשנת־מות המלך עזיהו ואראה את־אדני ישב על־כסא רם ונשא ושוליו מלאים את־ההיכל [2]שרפים עמדים ממעל לו ...
> [3]וקרא זה אל־זה ואמר קדוש קדוש קדוש יהוה צבאות מלא כל־הארץ כבודו
>
> In the year when the king Uzziah died, I saw my lord sitting upon a high and lofted throne, his robes' filling the temple, (and) seraphim standing around him ... each calling to one another, "Holy, holy, holy is Yahweh-of-Hosts. His glory fills the earth." (Isaiah 6:1–3)

Isaiah's famous vision depicts a Yahweh-of-Hosts who is decked out in royal robes that spill into the earthly temple and who is surrounded by a chorus of heavenly beings, praising the king (v. 3) and helping visitors prepare for their audience with him (v. 6).[149] By locating this vision in the temple in the capital city of Jerusalem, Isaiah presents the Jerusalem temple as an *axis mundi* that connected the heavens with earth.[150] Because Isaiah described the temple as the place where Yahweh-of-Hosts' robes rest below his throne, the temple was no longer merely a building wherein a deity resides but a portal between the divine and human worlds.[151]

Perhaps this interconnectedness between the divine full name Yahweh-of-Hosts and the temple in Zion/Jerusalem prevented the development of Yahweh-of-Jerusalem and Yahweh-of-Zion as divine full names. Indeed, the complete absence of a simple DN-of-GN formulation for these potential Yahweh full names suggests that, even though the divine name Yahweh appears in the Hebrew Bible over 6000 times, the deity was never known as Yahweh-of-Jerusalem or Yahweh-of-Zion. Theoretically, later scribes could have excised these full names from the biblical tradition, but we might expect that at least one vestigial Yahweh-of-Jerusalem or Yahweh-of-Zion full name would have

149 A similar description of the heavenly court is presented in 1 Kings 22:19, in which (the unspecified) Yahweh sits on his throne with "all the Host-of-Heaven standing alongside him, on his right and left" (וכל־צבא שמים עמד עליו מימינו ומשאלו). Whereas those functioning as attendants are named seraphim in Isaiah 6:2 and the Host-of-Heaven ("Host" is singular) in 1 Kings 22:21 (and "the spirit" [הרוח], who is among the Host-of-Heaven, answers Yahweh's question in v. 21), in both instances, the attendants are described as standing around or beside Yahweh. For a fuller treatment of the beings who comprise the Hosts-of-Heaven and survey of scholarship on the topic, see Zobel, "ṣebāʾôt," 218–220.

150 Jon D. Levenson, *Sinai & Zion: An Entry into the Jewish Bible* (San Francisco: HarperCollins, 1985), 122.

151 Mettinger also identifies Amos 1:2 and Psalm 11, 14, and 24 as passages reinforcing this *axis mundi* aspect of the Zion/Jerusalem and Yahweh-of-Hosts complex (Mettinger, "Yahweh Zebaoth," 923).

been left behind (comparable to the potential Yahweh-of-Sinai in Judges 5:5) or that either of these names would have eventually appeared among the extra-biblical Hebrew and Aramaic texts. We now have an extra-biblical attestation of the name Yahweh-of-Samaria from Kuntillet ʻAjrud even though we have no explicit extant reference to a temple to Yahweh in Samaria, but we do not have a single reference to Yahweh-of-Jerusalem or Yahweh-of-Zion.

This complete absence of geographic last names in biblical texts, supposing we reject the Judges 5:5 proposed by Aḥituv, Eshel, and Meshel, could indicate that the biblical authors envisioned a singular Yahweh. This would be especially true for those authors living after Jerusalem became the only legitimate Yahwistic cult site. If Yahweh's only legitimate temple was in Jerusalem, or if Yahweh's name or glory resided in the temple in Jerusalem while Yahweh himself resided in heaven, then there was no need to distinguish this Yahwistic cult and its deity from others that lacked legitimately from a state sponsor, especially after the fall of Israel and Samaria in the late eighth century.[152] Unlike the numerous Ištar goddesses and Baal deities whose geographic last names were indispensable to their identification, a singular or incomparable Yahweh needed no geographic markings from a Jerusalemite or Judahite perspective. The full name Yahweh-of-Hosts did not locate the deity but extolled his character, so the name did not reinforce the idea that the deity's sovereignty was limited geographically or was confined to the earthly realm in the same way that the names Yahweh-of-Jerusalem and Yahweh-of-Zion might have.

Those post-exilic biblical texts that explicitly locate Yahweh in Jerusalem or as the deity associated with Jerusalem are credited to the Persian kings Cyrus and Artaxerxes. Each king acknowledged that Yahweh was the God who was in heaven, but each also located the deity specifically in Jerusalem.[153] In Cyrus's decree, the deity is first mentioned as Yahweh//God-of-Heaven (Ezra

---

152 Weinfeld noted that the Deuteronomistic Historian does not envision Yahweh as dwelling in the temple in Jerusalem; rather, Yahweh is in heaven (e.g., 1 Kings 8:17–20, 30, 39, 43–44, and 48–49), and "Yahweh's name" is in the temple (שם יהוה, vv. 17 and 20; שמי, "my name," vv.18 and 19; שמך, "your name," vv. 44 and 48; Moshe Weinfeld, *Deuteronomy and the Deuteronomic School* [Winona Lake: Eisenbrauns, 1992], 193). Similarly, the Priestly scribes and Ezekiel expressed Yahweh's earthly presence with his glory's presence (e.g., Exodus 16:10; 29:43; Numbers 14:10; 16:19; 17:7; 20:6; and Ezekiel 8:4; 11:23; 43:4–5; and 44:4; Mettinger, "YHWH Sabaoth," 137).

153 Blenkinsopp notes that the epithet "God of Heaven" corresponds to an epithet used for the Zoroastrian deity Ahura Mazda, but he further notes, however, that we do not know with certainty that Cyrus was a Zoroastrian (Joseph Blenkinsopp, *Ezra-Nehemiah: A Commentary*, Old Testament Library [Philadelphia: Westminster, 1988], 75).

1:2), then as Yahweh//God-of-Israel and the-God//Who-(is) in-Jerusalem (v. 3). Because the pronouns, verbs, and pronominal suffixes in vv. 2–4 are all masculine singular, each of these three divine names or epithets can be interpreted as referring to the same deity: Yahweh//God-of-Heaven was Yahweh//God-of-Israel, who was also the-God//Who-(is) in-Jerusalem. Likewise, in Artaxerxes's letter, Ezra's deity, who was mentioned as "the God of Heaven" at the beginning of the letter (7:12) and identified as Yahweh by the narrator in the previous verse (v. 11), was "the God of Jerusalem" (7:19; with variations in vv. 15, 16, and 17). In both instances, the deity's relationship with the to-be-rebuilt temple in Jerusalem was of primary importance. The association is made between the deity and the city, but no proper name is attested in the biblical texts.

Similarly, the Judeao-Arameans living in fifth-century Elephantine at the first cataract of the Nile occasionally referred to their deity Yahweh (spelled either YHW or YHH) as "God of Heaven" and as the deity residing in the local temple.[154] Of the slightly more than three dozen occurrences of the divine name Yahweh in the Elephantine corpus (excluding the theophoric element in personal names), eight mention (the unspecified) Yahweh; sixteen mention Yahweh//the-God; two mention Yahweh//God-of-Heaven; three mention Yahweh-of-Hosts; and ten associate Yahweh with Elephantine (יב; see Tables 6.1 and 6.2).[155] For example, in *TAD* A4.7, the deity was identified as Yahweh//

---

154 Angela Rohrmoser describes the populations who revered Yahweh in Elephantine as "Judäo-Aramäer" because these Yahwists likely arrived there from Syria, Samaria, and Judah between the eighth and fifth centuries (Angela Rohrmoser, *Götter, Tempel und Kult der Judäo-Aramäer von Elephantine: Archäologische und schriftliche Zeugnisse aus dem persezeitlichen Ägypten*, AOAT 396 [Münster: Ugarit-Verlag, 2014], 374; see also Botta, "Outlook," 368–369, who contrasts Aramean and Jew, with the former serving as "an ethnic-administrative designation," wheveras the latter is "an ethnic-communal designation"). The worship of Yahweh in fifth-century Elephantine differed both from the Yahwism of the monarchic period in Samaria and Judah and the Yahwism of contemporary Jerusalem. Rohrmoser notes, for example, that Syrian or Samarian populations in Elephantine brought with them the worship of Anat and Ašim(a) in the late eighth century, which is to say that these Yahwists should not be identified as monotrous or monotheists and that they were more religiously tolerant of non-Yahweh deities than their contemporaries in Judah who had recently returned from exile in Babylon.

155 A handful of texts use more than one Yahweh divine name, and none give us reason to assume that multiple Yahweh deities are intended. For example, the late fifth-century text *TAD* A4.3 names Yahweh//the-God in l. 1 and "God of Heaven" in ll. 2–3. This alternation of divine names is quite reminiscent of those in Cyrus's decree and Artaxerxes's letter, especially because one epithet is "God of Heaven" and the other identifies the deity as Yahweh. A second letter, *TAD* A4.7, first refers to the deity "God of Heaven" (l. 2), then as Yahweh//Lord-of-Heaven (l. 15), and finally as Yahweh//God-of-Heaven (ll. 27–28; A4.8, a duplicate of this text,

the-God three times (ll. 6, 24, and 26), one of which is immediately followed by "who (is) in the Elephantine Fortress" (יהו אלהא זי ביב בירתא, l. 6). Also common to Cyrus and Artaxerxes and the Elephantine archives is the use of the *bet*-locative to place the deity in his residence.

6.5 Yahweh and the *bet*-Locative

Over the past thirty years, the role of the *bet*-locative has become a central issue in analyzing divine full names in Northwest Semitic texts. In the wake of the discovery of the full names Yahweh-of-Samaria and Yahweh-of-Teman at Kuntillet ʿAjrud, scholars began looking for other potential localized Yahweh deities, but because the divine name Yahweh never occurs in a construct chain with a geographic name in the biblical texts, alternative divine name formulas were sought. In addition to the standard name formula DN-of-GN examined in chapters 3 through 5, the three alternative formulas introduced in chapter 4 include DN//Who-Resides-(in)-GN, title-of-GN, and DN//title-of-GN. As already mentioned, the first of these has no exact correspondence in the Hebrew Bible, but if we designate "God" (either אל־ or אלהי־) as the title in these formulas, then representatives of these two remaining alternatives – title-of-GN and DN//title-of-GN – can be found in the Hebrew Bible and at Elephantine. These representatives include Yahweh//God-of-Israel (e.g., 2 Chronicles 32:17) and "God of Jerusalem" (i.e., v. 19).[156] Despite the fact that Yahweh//God-of-Israel and "God of Jerusalem" parallel their contemporary Neo-Assyrian divine name formulas, I am unaware of scholars who interpret such references as potential names for a localized Yahweh deity. Instead, they prefer interpreting the word "Israel" in the epithet "God of Israel" as an ethnic name rather than geographic one and dismiss "God of Jerusalem" as an epithet for the previously named Yahweh. Finding no satisfactory biblical parallel to the Neo-Assyrian full

contains more lacunae, and the divine names found within it are not included in the tallies above).

156 This attestation of "God of Jerusalem" in 2 Chronicles 32:19 belongs to a summary of the words spoken by Sennacherib's men meant to undermine the Jerusalemites' confidence in their god Yahweh. For a full list of "God of Israel" and Yahweh//God-of-Israel in the Bible, see אלהי־ nos. 1254–1370, 1375–1404, 1426–1432, and 1569 (Abraham Even-Shoshan, *A New Concordance of the Bible: Thesaurus of the Language of the Bible, Hebrew and Aramaic, Roots, Words, Proper Names Phrases and Synonyms* [Jerusalem: Kiryat-Sefer, 1998], 72). For Yahweh-of-Hosts//God-of-Israel, see אלהי־ nos. 1452–1488; for "God of Heaven," see אלהי־ nos. 1180–1187. Psalm 68:36 and 136:26 use the element אל־ in the title-of-GN formula, producing "God of Israel" and "God of Heaven."

names, scholars have instead explored the few instances in the Hebrew Bible where the name Yahweh is followed by a geographic name contained in a *bet*-locative phrase.

In the endnotes of his study of embedded god lists in state treaties, Barré considers the various alternatives to the standard DN-of-GN formula.[157] In addition to DN-of-GN, he proposes three alternatives for Northwest Semitic divine names: the *bet*-locative DN-in-GN (e.g., Tannit-in-Lebanon, *KAI* 81:1), a variant on the *bet*-locative DN//Who-Resides-in-GN (e.g., Yahweh//Who-Resides-in-Zion, Joel 4:21), and DN//title-of-GN (e.g., Melqart//Lord-of-Tyre, *KAI* 47:1).[158] Of Barré's alternatives, the last one resembles the naming of localized Ištar goddesses in Neo-Assyrian inscriptions, but in no instance does the DN-in-GN formula or DN//Who-Resides-in-GN formula serve as divine full name in Hebrew or in Northwest Semitic texts. Furthermore, these two formulas never contrast the named deity with another full-named deity who shares that first name.

Of Barré's proposed alternatives, McCarter is especially attracted to the DN-in-GN option because, he says, "[i]n Biblical Hebrew the expression DN *b*-GN ('DN-in-GN') seems to be equivalent to DN GN at ʿAjrud."[159] Using the DN-in-GN formula, McCarter retranslates Psalm 99:2, a verse already noted by Barré, so that the verse praises the deity Yahweh-in-Zion:

יהוה בציון גדול ורם הוא על־כל־העמים

> Yahweh-in-Zion is great! And he is exalted above all other gods! (Psalm 99:2, McCarter's translation, modified slightly)[160]

The words יהוה בציון גדול have traditionally been interpreted as a nominative sentence, and it makes perfect sense as one: "Yahweh is great in Zion." This

157 Barré, *God-List*, 186 n. 473. He also includes DN-from-GN as a variant form of DN-of-GN, so that Psalm 135:21 is reinterpreted as blessing Yahweh-from-Zion//Who-Resides-(in)-Jerusalem (יהוה מציון שכן ירושלם). This proposed *min*-locative divine name, like the *bet*-locative divine name examined here, should be rejected.

158 Barré also has a variant form of the DN-in-GN formula in which the *bet*-locative is replaced by a locative *he* that has been suffixed to the GN. He provides textual examples representing the same proposed divine name Milk-in-ʿAštart: *mlk bʿṯtrt* (*KTU*[2] 1.107.42) and *mlk ʿṯtrth* (*KTU*[2] 1.100:41; Barré, *God-List*, 186 n. 473). Smith provides an updated catalogue of potential divine-full-name formulas that, in addition to the Northwest Semitic, Ugaritic, and Akkadian names listed by Barré, includes Eblaite, Egyptian, and Epigraphic South Arabian divine names and their respective geographic names (Smith, "Problem of the God," 208–218). Smith's list of *bet*-locative possibilities can be found on pp. 214–215.

159 McCarter, "Aspects," 140.

160 McCarter, "Aspects," 141.

is precisely how NJPS, NRSV, and KJV all interpret and translate the phrase (allowing, of course, for the traditional English use of "the LORD" as a substitution for the divine name). As noted above, several psalms, classical prophets, and historical passages link Yahweh with Mount Zion in Jerusalem, such as Psalm 110:2; 128:5; 134:3; 135:21; and Joel 4:17–21. In Psalm 99:2, Yahweh is praised as the one in-Zion, but this seems to be a reference to the same deity who is called (the unspecified) Yahweh in the previous verse. Put another way, specifically in a way that rejects the idea that in Zion is Yahweh's last name, (the unspecified) Yahweh of v. 1 is the same deity as the Yahweh in v. 2 who has been located in-Zion. Verse 1's Yahweh is the king before whom the people tremble and who sits on a cherubim throne. In vv. 5, 8, and twice in 9, this deity is praised as Yahweh//our-God, and throughout the psalm all the pronouns, verbs, adjectives, and suffixes are masculine singular (the person switches between third and second person in the psalm), indicating that these different references to Yahweh all refer to a single, individual deity. Psalm 99, like numerous other psalms, locates Yahweh in Zion, but it makes no attempt to distinguish its Yahweh of interest from any other Yahweh who might be located outside of Zion.

The syntax of Psalm 99:2 also suggests that Yahweh and in-Zion should be interpreted as two distinct parts of the sentence rather than one. In other passages that contain similar elements – i.e., a name, a *bet*-locative phrase, and an adjective (specifically גדול) – the *bet*-locative phrase cannot be interpreted as part of the name, even when it follows the divine name. For instance, in Esther 9:4, in the phrase גדול מרדכי בבית המלך ("Mordecai was great in the king's house"), the person Mordecai is said to be an important figure within the palace administration. He has not been renamed Mordecai-in-the-king's-house, a man who also happens to be great. This verse is different from Psalm 99:2 because it involves a personal name followed by the *bet*-locative phrase rather than a divine name, but this difference is superficial and should not be discounted because the syntax is the same.[161]

There are several other verses containing the proposed divine name Yahweh-in-Zion in which a *bet* functions with non-locative purposes, and these too should be rejected as potential divine names. For example, the divine name Yahweh is followed by in-Zion in two other verses where the *bet* in the sentence functions as the direct object marker for the verb: בחר יהוה בציון ("Yahweh chose Zion," Psalm 132:13), and שכח יהוה בציון ("Yahweh forgot Zion," Lamentations

161 Although proper names do not appear in Psalm 76:2 and Malachi 1:11, the syntax of the *bet*-locative is comparable to that contained in Psalm 99:2 and Esther 9:4 (Allen, "Examination," 70–71).

2:6). In both verses, if the phrase in-Zion were interpreted as an element in a Yahweh deity's full name, the sentences would be grammatically complete, but the meaning of the sentences would be incomplete: "Yahweh-in-Zion chose" and "Yahweh-in-Zion forgot." Reading Psalm 99:2 in light of its own internal contexts and compared to the syntax of similar verses makes accepting the proposed Yahweh-in-Zion as a Yahweh full name highly problematic. Like all other proposed *bet*-locative full names found in Northwest Semitic texts, "Yahweh in Zion" does not function like a full name. Yahweh's devotees at the Jerusalem/Zion cult knew a deity named Yahweh, but they did not know this deity by the name Yahweh-in-Zion.

McCarter also suggests the possible divine name Yahweh-in-Hebron, which is invoked by Absalom in 2 Samuel 15:7.[162] After his lengthy house arrest, David's son asks his father for permission to return to Hebron so that he may fulfill the vow that he had had made to a Yahweh deity:

[7]אלכה נא ואשלם את־נדרי אשר נדרתי ליהוה בחברון [8]כי־נדר נדר עבדך
בשבתי בגשור בארם לאמר אם־ישיב ישיבני יהוה ירושלם ועבדתי את־יהוה

> "Let me go fulfill the vow I made to Yahweh-in-Hebron, for your servant made a vow when I was living in Aram-geshur, as follows: 'If Yahweh will bring me back to Jerusalem, I shall serve Yahweh!'" (2 Samuel 15:7–8, McCarter's translation)[163]

McCarter correctly argues that in-Hebron cannot refer to the place where the vow had been made because that took place in Aram-geshur, which is in the opposite direction from Jerusalem than Hebron. Neither can in-Hebron refer to where Absalom wants to go and fulfill his vow because, as McCarter notes, "it is most awkward as a modifier of 'Let me go.'"[164] The *bet*-locative phrase in-Hebron in v. 7 is, indeed, an awkward modifier for "Let me go" because we would expect to-Hebron (ל/אל־חברון) to accompany the verb "go." However, the verse makes more sense if we understand the phrase as modifying "and I will fulfill" (ואשלם): "and I will fulfill my vow ... in Hebron." Because McCarter incorrectly associates in-Hebron with the wrong verb, his resulting interpretation is awkward, forcing him into the only option remaining for in-Hebron, one that modifies Yahweh: "Although Yahweh is worshipped in Jerusalem, Absalom has to go to Hebron to fulfill his vow, because it was to the

162 Smith also spends a few pages exploring the possibility of a deity known as Yahweh-in-Hebron (Smith, "Problem of the God," 241–243).

163 McCarter, "Aspects," 141. McCarter does *not* entertain the possibility that Absalom named Yahweh-of-Jerusalem in 2 Samuel 15:8, so that the verse might be translated, "If Yahweh-of-Jerusalem will bring me back, I will serve Yahweh."

164 McCarter, "Aspects," 141.

Hebronite Yahweh (*yhwh bḥbrwn*) that the vow was made."[165] Rather, these verses make more sense when Yahweh is understood as (the unspecified) non-localized Yahweh deity.

Because Absalom's vow predates the cultic reforms of Hezekiah and Josiah, there were no restrictions preventing where he could legitimately worship Yahweh. Absalom's decision to worship Yahweh in Hebron, where David had reigned for several years before relocating his capital to Jerusalem (2 Samuel 5:5) and where Absalom is said to have been born (3:3), is likely due to his familial ties to that local cult. McCarter is undoubtedly correct that Absalom's vow was cult specific in much the same way that the fines imposed in Neo-Assyrian legal transactions were paid to deities who were explicitly connected to a city or temple cult (e.g., SAA 6 87; see chapter 4.1). His treatment of in-Hebron as a geographic last name for the deity Yahweh, however, is not the best or easiest solution. Absalom makes his vow to a Yahweh who is worshipped in Hebron, whom he mentions three times in these two verses as (the unspecified) Yahweh, but he did not know this deity as Yahweh-in-Hebron.

Even if we momentarily consider the possibility that Absalom did identify (the twice unspecified) Yahweh in 2 Samuel 15:8 with a deity that he knew as Yahweh-in-Hebron in v. 7, this identification is still problematic in light of our examination in chapters 4 and 5 of the various localized Ištar goddesses and Baal deities in roughly contemporaneous texts. In order to consider whether a localized Ištar or Baal full name represented an independent and distinct deity, we must determine whether the deity's geographic last name serves as an integral aspect of that deity's identity. Ištar-of-Arbela is considered an independent and distinct goddess from Ištar-of-Nineveh and other localized Ištar goddesses precisely because her geographic last name was indispensable to her identity. Her full name was used when she was the only goddess whose first name was Ištar in an embedded god list or in a prophetic oracle (e.g., *BIWA* 278 Fuchs, IIT:104; 286 Fuchs, IIT:148 and 152; and 288 Fuchs IIT:164; and SAA 9 7 and 9). Moreover, she was often called Ištar-of-Arbela when she was the only goddess mentioned in a text (e.g., SAA 9 2.3). Similarly, we consider Baal-of-Ugarit distinct from both Baal-of-Ṣapun and Baal-of-Aleppo because he was treated as though he was distinct from these other Baal deities in the ritual texts. As shown in chapter 5.2, Baal-of-Ṣapun and Baal-of-Ugarit each received their own offerings in *KTU*^{2} 1.109:32–34, and Baal-of-Ugarit and Baal-of-Aleppo each received their own offerings in an earlier section of the

---

165 McCarter, "Aspects," 141.

tablet (l. 16). In contrast, because Absalom never treated Yahweh-in-Hebron (2 Samuel 15:7) as a distinct deity from (the unspecified) Yahweh (v. 8) or any other potential localized Yahweh deity, and because Hebron does not seem to define this deity in any particular way in other texts, we cannot consider Yahweh-in-Hebron an independent or distinct Yahweh. If Absalom had vowed to make a sacrifice to Yahweh-in-Hebron – or better yet, Yahweh-of-Hebron (יהוה חברון) – *and* to Yahweh-of-Hosts, or an otherwise unattested Yahweh-of-Jerusalem or Yahweh-of-Zion, only then would we argue for potential localized Yahweh deities using 2 Samuel 15:7–8 as a proof text. Even though Absalom did not give an offering to a deity whom he called Yahweh-in-Hebron, these two verses do tell us that Hebron was once home to a local Yahwistic cult, a cult that might have been where Israel's elders made their covenant with David before Yahweh (5:3). Yahweh was in Hebron, but there was no localized entity Yahweh-in-Hebron.

Other divine names with the proposed DN-in-GN formula that Barré and McCarter mention include Tannit-in-Lebanon (*KAI* 81:1), Astarte-in-Sidon (*KAI* 14:16), and Dagan-in-Ashdod (1 Samuel 5:5).[166] The proposed divine name Tannit-in-Lebanon has already been discussed in chapter 5.6, and it should be rejected as a divine name for several reasons. Neither *KAI* 81 nor any other text contrasts a localized Tannit-in-Lebanon goddess with any other Tannit goddess. Also, this Punic text from Carthage only names two deities, and Tannit is the second of the two, so it is impossible to determine whether the *bet*-locative is intended for just Tannit or for both goddesses. "To the ladies, to Astarte and to Tannit who *are* in Lebanon: new temples" is just as reasonable a translation of לרבת לעשתרת ולתנת בלבננ מקדשמ חדשמ as is "to the ladies, to Astarte and to Tannit, who *is* in Lebanon: "new temples." If the text listed a third or fourth deity, then we could derive an embedded god list and determine how similar or dissimilar Tannit's treatment is compared to the others. If Tannit were the second of four deities and the only deity associated with a *bet*-locative phrase, this unique aspect would better favor the interpretation that Tannit-in-Lebanon was considered a full name by the scribe. Alternatively, if the two

166 Barré, *God-List*, 186 n. 473; and McCarter, "Aspects," 141; see also Smith, "Problem of the God," 214. In addition to the several potential Ugaritic divine full names that Smith includes in his *bet*-locative/locative *he* listing, he also offers two Phoenician/Punic texts with *bet*-locative phrases that I have not had the opportunity to examine for this article: Astarte-in-Lapethos (*ʿštrt blpš*, Lapethos 6), and Baal-Ḥamān-in-Althiburus (*bʿl ḥmn bʾltbrš*, Hr. Medeine N 1:1; Smith, "Problem of the God," 214–215). An Astarte-in-*GW* (*ʿštrt bgw*) also appears in his list, but this potential divine full name is based upon a reading offered in Krahmalkov's *Phoenician-Punic Dictionary* (p. 391), which differs from that offered in *KAI* 17:2: לעשתרת אש בגו ("Astarte, who is in *GW*"; ibid., 215 n. 62).

divine names had been reversed so that the temples were dedicated "to the ladies, to Tannit in Lebanon and to Astarte: new temples," then it would be clear that in-Lebanon only referred to Tannit and not Astarte. With only two divine names mentioned in *KAI* 81 and with Tannit as the second name, concluding that there was a goddess known as Tannit-in-Lebanon is, at best, tentative and syntactically questionable.

Likewise, there is no doubt that Astarte had a cultic presence in Ṣidon, which is indicated by both Phoenician and biblical evidence. In addition to the fifth-century Ṣidonian text *KAI* 14:16, which mentions that Ešmunazar and his mother Amotastarte (re)built her temple in Ṣidon, 1 Kings 11:5 and 33 (and 2 Kings 23:13) note that the Ṣidonians worshipped Astarte and that Solomon also worshipped her as a result of marrying his many foreign wives. Astarte could have been one of the goddesses whom Kirta had in mind when he addressed "Ašerah-of-Tyre and 'Goddess of Ṣidon'" in his vow in the Ugaritic text the *Kirta Epic* (*'aṯrt . ṣrm w 'ilt . ṣdynm*, *KTU*² 1.14 iv 38–39). Regardless, the proposed divine full name Astarte-in-Ṣidon that has been derived from the seventh-century Ammonite text *WSS* 876:2 (Ast⟨arte⟩ in Ṣidon, עשת⟨רת⟩ בצדן) and *KAI* 14:16 ([Astar]te in Ṣidon//Land-of-the-Sea, [עשתר]ת בצדן ארץ ים) is still problematic for syntactic reasons (see chapter 5.6 and Table 5.9). As with Tannit's cultic presence in Lebanon, Astarte's cultic presence in Ṣidon is not in doubt, but the idea that the goddess was known as Astarte-in-Ṣidon is.

The final divine name with a *bet*-locative element that McCarter proposes is Dagan-in-Ashdod. Aside from this proposed attestation in 1 Samuel 5:5, (the unspecified) Dagan appears nine other times in vv. 1–5, three of which indicate that the deity had a cultic presence in Ashdod. Dagan's temple (בית־דגון, vv. 2 and 5) is mentioned twice, and Dagan's priests (כהני דגון, v. 5) are mentioned once. As with the other proposed full names with *bet*-locative elements, nothing in this passage suggests that these first nine unspecified attestations should be contrasted with the proposed Dagan-in-Ashdod at the end of the passage. Moreover, because the passage serves as an etiology for a local priestly custom in the Dagan temple that is practiced "to this day" (עד היום הזה, v. 5), the placement of in-Ashdod as the final thought in the legend makes more sense as a reminder of the story's setting than as the final element in a divine name. 1 Samuel 5 indicates that this custom is unique to the Dagan cult in Ashdod, but he does not contrast this particular Dagan with any other known Dagan deity.

We can conclude with two potential divine full names with a *bet*-locative element, which McCarter does not propose and which resemble the Dagan situation in 1 Samuel 5:5. These are Chemosh-in-Qarḥō ((כמש.בקרחה, *KAI* 181:3) and Chemosh-in-Kerioth (כמש.בקרית, l. 13), which both appear in the Mesha

Inscription.[167] Near the beginning of the inscription, Mesha claimed that he built a "high place" (במת, l. 3) for Chemosh in Qarḥō (ואעש.הבמת.זאת.לכמש.בקרחה, l. 3) because the deity saved him from his enemies. After he defeated and slew the Israelites living in Ataroth (l. 11), Mesha claimed, "I brought the cult object$^{(?)}$ from there and I dragged it before Chemosh in Kerioth" [12]ואשב.משם. את.אראל. דודה.וא[ס][13]חבה.לפני.כמש.בקרית.[168] If *bet*-locative phrases were elements found in divine names in Northwest Semitic texts, then Mesha could be thought of as contrasting these two localized Chemosh deities with (the unspecified) Chemosh, who appears in ll. 5, 9, 12, 14, 18, 19, 32, and 33.[169]

---

167 The city Kerioth is mentioned in Amos 2:2 and Jeremiah 48:24 in oracles delivered against the Moabites.

168 Regarding the "vessels$^{(?)}$ of Yahweh" (כ[לי].יהוה, *KAI* 181:17–18), the meaning of אראל is uncertain. The meaning of דודה (l. 12) is also uncertain, although possibilities along the lines of "noun denoting deity or comparable divine being," "defeat," and "champion" have all been offered (*DNWSI*, dwd_3 mngs. 1–4). For this reason, the phrase אראל . דודה has simply been translated "cult object$^{(?)}$" here.

169 Gibson suggests that Qarḥō was possibly a city quarter within Diban rather than a distinct town (Gibson, *TSSI* 1, 78), whereas Dearman finds it more likely that Qarḥō was a suburb of Diban with a royal administrative center (Andrew J., "Historical Reconstruction and the Mesha Inscription," in *Studies in the Mesha Inscription and Moab*, ed. Andrew Dearman, SBLABS 2 [Atlanta: Scholars Press, 1989], 173). If Qarḥō were a royal administrative center, then it makes sense that the king would build a shrine (במת, "high place," l. 3) to Chemosh there. In another inscription, Mesha mentions a "temple of Chemosh" (בת.כ[מש], Roland E. Murphy and O. Carm, "A Fragment of an Early Moabite Inscription from Dibon," *BASOR* 125 [1952]: 22; [ב]ת.כמש, *TSSI* 1 17:2), which Dearman places in Diban as a separate structure from the high place in the adjacent suburb of Qarḥō (Dearman, "Historical Reconstruction," 229).

A final attestation of the divine name Chemosh appears as the second element in what looks to be a compound divine name, Aštar-Chemosh (עשתר.כמש, l. 17). Gerald Mattingly notes that two general theories have been posited for the compound name Aštar-Chemosh. The first is that Aštar-Chemosh was an Ištar goddess who was Chemosh's consort (Gerold L. Mattingly, "Moabite Religion and the Meshaʻ Inscription," in *Studies in the Mesha Inscription and Moab*, ed. Andrew Dearman, SBLABS 2 [Atlanta: Scholars Press, 1989], 219). The alternative is that this compound name was indicative of the assimilation of the Northwest Semitic male deity Aštar and the national Moabite deity Chemosh (ibid., 221). Because the compound name only appears in *KAI* 181:17, neither theory is certain. If we consider the Assyrian compound names that were listed in the *tākultu*-ritual texts, then the second divine name could be interpreted as defining a (new) divine attribute for the first divine name (Porter, "Anxiety," 237). In this case, Aštar would be redefined in terms of the Moabite deity Chemosh.

Yet another interpretive possibility that has been built upon other Northwest Semitic divine compound names deals with consort relationships. For example, Anat-Bethel (^{d}*a-na-ti-ba-*⌜*a*⌝-[*a-ti*]-⌜DINGIR⌝^{meš}) appears after her (presumably) consort Bethel in King Baal of Tyre's treaty with Esarhaddon (SAA 2 5 iv 6). If Aštar-Chemosh was a female deity, then Anat-Bethel's presence after Bethel could suggest an analogous consort relationship for Aštar-Chemosh and Chemosh. A second compound divine name, which also begins with the name Anat, is Anat-

Chemosh-in-Qarḥō and Chemosh-in-Kerioth could be thought of as independent deities and distinct from (the unspecified) Chemosh, and each would have had his own cult site.[170]

The preferred alternative is that (the unspecified) Chemosh was venerated at both Qarḥō and Kerioth, which is, of course, what is universally accepted. First, Mesha built Chemosh a high place in Qarḥō, and later he brought offerings to that same deity at the cult site at Kerioth, which was several miles from Diban, nearer the Israelite city of Ataroth.[171] Next, Mesha slew the Israelites as an "offering/spectacle for Chemosh" (רית.כמש, l. 12) and brought the cult object (אראל.דודה, l. 12) to Chemosh at Kerioth, at which point Chemosh commanded the king to attack Nebo (l. 14).[172] Moreover, it makes more sense to interpret in-Kerioth as the place in the story to which Mesha dragged (וא[ס]חבה, ll. 12–13) the offering.[173] If either of these potential Chemosh deities had lacked the *bet*-locative element so that the first name Chemosh belonged to a construct chain with Qarḥō or Kerioth, then arguing for their distinctness from (the unspecified) Chemosh would be more tempting. The switch between (the unspecified) Chemosh and Chemosh-Kerioth and back in ll. 11–14, however, would still be suggestive of the identification of these two divine names with each other. Regardless, in each instance, the *bet*-locative makes more sense as a general locative phrase that indicates where these events

---

Yahu, who appeared in the late fifth-century Elephantine papyrus text B7.3:3 after a deified Ḥerem and a "place of prostration" (בח[רמ.אלה]א.במסגדא.ובענתיהו, "(PN swore) "by Ḥe[rem] the [-god], by the place of prostration, and by Anat-Yahu"). McCarter, however, prefers the restoration בי[הו.אלה]א to בח[רמ.אלה]א in this text, which makes Yahu/Yahweh the first deity in a very unusual embedded god list: Yahu (Yahweh) / Place-of-Prostration / Anat-Yahu (McCarter, "Aspects," 154 n. 60). If McCarter were correct, then the divine name Anat-Yahu would serve as further evidence that Aštar-Chemosh was Chemosh's consort, if Aštar was, in fact, a goddess. Recently, Rohrmoser retained Porten's reading, but this does not necessarily alter the consort relationship between Anat-Yahu and Yahu at Elephantine because, she observes, the Judeao-Arameans at Elephantine were not monolatrists or monotheists (Rohrmoser, *Götter, Tempel und Kult*, 426 and 150–151). Another reason to prefer Porten's reading over McCarter's restoration is the fact that this text would contain the only embedded god list that I have encountered that includes the divine name Yahweh.

170 The theoretical Chemosh-Qarḥō: [3] ואעש.הבמת.זאת.לכמש.קרחה ("I built this high place for Chemosh-Qarḥō"). The theoretical Chemosh-Kerioth: [12] אשב.משמ.את.אראל.דודה.וא[ס][13]חבה.לפני.כמש.קרית ("I brought from there the cult object[?], and I dragged it before Chemosh-Kerioth," ll. 11–12).

171 Dearman, "Historical Reconstruction," 179.

172 Jackson notes that there is no consensus for the meaning of רית in l. 12 (Jackson, "Language," 111–112).

173 This is in contrast to McCarter's evaluation of 2 Samuel 15:7–8, where he argues that in-Hebron makes sense neither as the place where Absalom made his vow nor as the place where he was requesting to go (McCarter, "Aspects," 140–141).

happened than as a geographic element in a distinct localized Chemosh deity's full name.

If we consider the syntax of the *bet*-locative phrases in relation to the divine name Chemosh in the Mesha Inscription (*KAI* 181:3 and 13), we find that they appear at the end of their respective verbal clauses. The divine name Chemosh precedes the *bet*-locatives because the divine name is the indirect object of the verb, not because Chemosh is being defined in relation to the place. Given the typical sentence structure Verb / Subject / Direct-Object / Indirect-Object common to Northwest Semitic languages, the structural patterns we that find in *KAI* 181:3 and 13 are exactly what we should expect.[174] This is also true for in-Ṣidon in WSS 876:2, the various *bet*-locative phrases in *KAI* 14:15–18, the in-Ashdod in 1 Samuel 5:5, and the in-Hebron in 2 Samuel 15:7. The *bet*-locative plays the same syntactic role in each of these texts:

[3]ואעש.הבמת.זאת.לכמש.בקרחה

I built this high place for Chemosh in-Qarḥō. (*KAI* 181:3)

[12]ואשב.משמ.את.אראל. דודה.וא[ס][13]חבה.לפני.כמש.בקרית

I brought from there the cult object[(?)], and I dragged it before Chemosh in-Kerioth. (ll. 12–13)

[1]ש נד[2]ר לעשת בצדנ

That (Abinadab) vowed to Astarte[!] in-Ṣidon. (*WSS* 876:1–2)

[15]בננ אית בת [16]אלנמ אית [בת עשתר]ת בצדנ ארצ ימ ... [17]ואנחנ אש בננ בתמ [18]לאלנ צדנמ בצדנ ארצ ימ

We built the house of the gods, the [house of Astar]te in-Ṣidon//Land-by-the-Sea and we (are the ones) who built houses for the gods of the Ṣidonians in-Ṣidon//Land-by-the-Sea. (*KAI* 14:15–18)

[5]על-כן לא-ידרכו כהני דגון וכל-הבאים בית-דגון על-מפתן דגון באשדוד

Therefore, none of Dagan's priests or anyone entering Dagan's temple tread upon the threshold of Dagan in-Ashdod. (1 Samuel 5:5)

Returning to McCarter's take on 2 Samuel 15:7, we see that its sentence structure also places the *bet*-locative phrase after the indirect object Yahweh.

174 Note also that the six examples of *bet* used in the spatial sense (11.2.5b) in Waltke and O'Connor's *Biblical Hebrew Syntax* have the *bet*-locative phrase at the end (Waltke and O'Connor, *Biblical Hebrew Syntax*, 196). *Bet*-prepositional phrases seem to fit well at the end of their clauses after all the important parts of the clause have already been presented.

Repayment is the action, Absalom is the actor, the vow is the direct object, Yahweh is the indirect object, and in-Hebron is the location of the action.

[7]אלכה נא ואשלם את-נדרי אשר נדרתי ליהוה בחברון

Let me go fulfill my vow that I vowed to Yahweh in-Hebron. (2 Samuel 15:7)

This sentence structure is also used in 1 Samuel 1:3 and 2 Kings 23:23:

[3]ועלה האיש ההוא ... להשתחות ולזבח ליהוה צבאות בשלה

That man went up ... to prostrate himself and offer sacrifices to Yahweh-of-Hosts in-Shiloh. (1 Samuel 1:3)[175]

[32]נעשה הפסח הזה ליהוה בירושלם

This Passover was made to Yahweh in-Jerusalem. (2 Kings 23:23)

Furthermore, when there is no verb in the sentence, the *bet*-locative phrase still appears at the end of the thought, such as "in-Lebanon" in *KAI* 81:1 and "on-Hawk-Island" in *KAI* 64:1:

לרבת לעשתרת ולתנת בלבננ מקדשמ חדשמ

To the ladies, to Astarte and to Tannit, (who are/is) in-Lebanon: new temples. (*KAI* 81:1)

לאדנ לבע⟨ל⟩שממ באינצמ נצבמ וחנוטמ שנמ 2 אש נדר בע[2]לחנא

To the/my lord, to Baa⟨l⟩-Šamêm on-Hawk-Island: (these are) the stele and the 2 *ḥnwṭ* that Baalḥana vowed. (*KAI* 64:1–2)

Bet-locative phrases follow divine names not because they are elements in those divine names; rather, the scribes placed the phrases at the end of their respective clause or phrase in accordance with the customary syntax of Northwest Semitic languages.

Just because a deity was worshipped in or associated with one or more temples in a city, that deity was not necessarily known by that location. According to the *Götteradressbuch* of Assur (GAB) § 4, Nabû had a cultic presence at both Nineveh and Assur (ll. 161–163).[176] Despite this plethora of cultic presences in Assur and the deity's temples in his native Borsippa and

---

175 In 1902, D. Karl Budde proposed that this Yahweh-in-Shiloh might have served as a divine name that distinguished the local manifestation of Yahweh from that worshipped at other cult sites, namely, Hebron (D. Karl Budde, *Die Bücher Samuel* [Tübingen: Verlag von J. C. B. Mohr, 1902], 4).
176 Menzel, *Assyrische Tempel*, 2:T159, no. 64; George, *Babylonian Topographical Texts*, 179.

Babylon, the deity is not called Nabû-of-Assur in Neo-Assyrian texts as opposed to Nabû-of-Borsippa or Nabû-of-Babylon, and he is definitely not called Nabû-in-Assur; he is simply Nabû. Likewise, just because Dagan had a cultic presence in Ashdod, Tannit had one in Lebanon, and Yahweh had one in Hebron, we should not expect that these deities had divine full names corresponding to those cultic presences. Attestations of DN-of-GN full names for non-Baal deities are relatively rare in Northwest Semitic texts and the Hebrew Bible, yet they do exist. The Kuntillet ʿAjrud texts that mention the divine full names Yahweh-of-Samaria and Yahweh-of-Teman could theoretically indicate such a localized phenomenon occurred in ancient Israel, but none of the DN-in-GN names with *bet*-locative phrases that have been proposed are convincing as actual divine full names for syntactic and other methodological reasons.

6.6 Conclusions

Unlike the localized Baal and Ištar full names discussed in chapters 3 through 5, the Yahweh full names discussed in this chapter are never contrasted with each other. Texts that were found in and next to the bench room at the Kuntillet ʿAjrud shrine mention either a Yahweh-of-Samaria (*Meshel* 3.1) or Yahweh-of-Teman (*Meshel* 3.6 and 3.9), but we cannot know who deposited these *ad hoc* inscriptions or what they thought about the localized Yahweh deity that they addressed compared to any other localized Yahweh deity. It is certainly possible that devotees of Yahweh-of-Teman saw the text on Pithos A that invoked Yahweh-of-Samaria (*Meshel* 3.1) after it was deposited in the bench room. It is also possible that the Yahweh-of-Samaria devotee who wrote *Meshel* 3.1 saw the texts on Pithos B (*Meshel* 3.6 and 3.9) in the adjacent room or the ink-on-plaster (*Meshel* 4.1.1) that mentions Yahweh-of-the-Teman. Moreover, it is possible that both localized Yahweh names were revered within the same Israelite communities. Yet, these are only possibilities, and because no text bears more than one Yahweh full name, no positive conclusions about the distinctness of Yahweh deities can be drawn. At most, we can say that *Meshel* 3.9:1–2 seems to identify Yahweh-of-the-Teman with (the unspecified) Yahweh. Three of these texts (i.e., *Meshel* 4.1.1, 3.6, and 3.9) could indicate that Teman represented the biblical Yahweh's mythical (mountain) home just as (the unspecified) Baal of the *Baal Cycle* was at home on Mount Ṣapun, whereas the fourth text strengthens the possibility that a Yahweh had some sort of cultic presence in Samaria.

Potentially both Yahweh-of-Teman and Yahweh-of-Samaria were revered by Israelites from the northern kingdom, which we know because the personal names and the texts at Kuntillet 'Ajrud generally conform to northern Israelite orthography. In contrast to northern traditions, the official Judahite Yahweh was known as Yahweh-of-Hosts and was the deity worshipped at the Jerusalemite temple on Mount Zion. Like Yahweh-of-Teman, Yahweh-of-Hosts could be identified with (the unspecified) Yahweh (e.g., Psalm 99), which is also true of the Yahweh revered in Elephantine (see Table 6.2). This indicates either that the identification of these Yahweh deities were not as wrapped up in their geography as were many of their Neo-Assyrian and Levantine counterparts, or it means that each localized Yahweh deity was never envisioned in contrast to any other Yahweh. For example, Yahweh-of-Hosts had a history at Shiloh that predated his placement in Jerusalem, but his associations with Jerusalem and the Davidic Dynasty there became so strong during the monarchic period that Jerusalem came to be viewed as his new mythical home, the *axis mundi* between heaven and earth.

The focus of this chapter has been on Yahweh full names and not on possible additional members of an (official) Israelite or Judahite cultic system, such as his Ašerah (e.g., *Meshel* 4.1.1:1; 3.1:2; 3.6:7; and 3.9:1; and 2 Kings 16:33) or Baal (e.g., 1 Kings 16:32).[177] For this reason, conclusions about whether Israelites or Judahites, whether in official or lay circles, worshipped other deities cannot and should not be drawn from this study. When considering the evidence for potentially distinct localized Yahweh deities, this chapter routinely considered the material in light of both possible monolatrist/ monotheistic and possible polytheistic populations. On the one hand, because Yahweh full names do not appear together, there is no evidence that any individual Israelite revered more than one localized Yahweh deity in the same way that Assyrians could and would revere more than one localized Ištar goddess or Northwest Semitic speakers could and would revere more than one localized Baal deity. On the other hand, given the nature and implications of the geographic last name in Assyria and the Levant, we may also conclude that any Assyrian or non-Israelite who might have encountered the divine names Yahweh-of-Samaria and Yahweh-of-Teman would have expected that these names represented two distinct localized Yahweh deities.

177 Although the ašerah/Ašerah was addressed in *Meshel* 3.1, 3.6, and 3.9 in the blessing along with the two localized Yahweh deities, this does not necessarily mean that the scribes responsible for these texts considered ašerah/Ašerah a goddess. Tigay observed that the altar in the Second Temple was invoked after the deity in by Rabbi Eliezer, "To Yāh and to you, O Altar!" (M. *Sukkah* 4:5; Jeffrey H. Tigay, "A Second Temple Parallel to the Blessings from Kuntillet 'Ajrud," *IEJ* 40 [1990]: 218). Needless to say Rabbi Eliezer was a monotheist and did not recognize the Temple's altar as divine in and of itself.

7 Conclusions

The question "What is a god?" has been asked several times in studies of ancient Near Eastern religions. In 2009, Porter edited a volume of essays by this very title that explored the nature of Mesopotamian non-anthropomorphic deities, which included a discussion by Rochberg on the relationship between the gods and celestial bodies and a discussion by Porter that looked at the role of deified cult objects that received their own offerings in temple ritual texts. Similarly, in his book *The Origins of Biblical Monotheism*, Smith retells how Hurowitz's question "what is an *ilu*?" (*ilu* being the Akkadian word for "god"), served as a springboard for his treatment of the divine at Ugarit and Israel. Answers to this question can involve defining what it means to be divine in a particular culture; determining what qualities set divine beings apart from the rest of the universe; understanding the relationship between a god and humanity; or contemplating what shape or form a god's body takes. These are all issues that Rochberg, Porter, and Smith regularly consider in their bodies of work. These issues are important, which is why the question "What is a god?" served as a foundational question during our examination of various ancient Near Eastern traditions, and, to a lesser extent, modern Italy.

As important as the question "What is a god?" has been to this study, the real question that this study aimed to answer is "Who is a god?" More precisely, the question is "Who is a *distinct* god?" Rather than define what it means to be a god according to any set theological criteria in a given religious tradition, this study approached each religious tradition by identifying the major gods and determining how they were treated by their respective communities and scribes and by modern scholars. The treatment of those undisputed gods was compared with the treatment of the gods who shared first names but had different geographic last names. Often, modern scholars deny the individuality of these gods, but as this study has demonstrated, the ancient sources embraced their individuality.

7.1 Summary

No Assyriologist would deny the fact that Assur, Enlil, Marduk, and (the unspecified) Ištar were considered gods by the ancient Assyrians. However, they might deny that Assur and Enlil were distinct, separate deities during the Middle and Neo-Assyrian periods. Likewise, they might deny that deities who shared first names were considered distinct from each other in religious thought. Specifically, many argue that the deity known as Ištar-of-Nineveh, or

"Ištar, the one of Nineveh," by her devotees was the same goddess as the deity called Ištar-of-Arbela, or "Ištar, the one of Arbela." Furthermore, they argue that Baal-of-Ṣapun was really Baal-Šamêm, which is to say, that the Baal who was associated with Mount Ṣapun was also known as the Baal who resided in Heaven, and Ugarit, and Aleppo. Likewise, the scribe who called upon the deity Yahweh-of-Samaria is thought by many biblical scholars to have invoked the same deity, Yahweh-of-Teman, in whose shrine the scribe deposited his text.

In Mesopotamia, the scholarly lexical god lists do not address these issues, but some royal or esoteric hymns do. The author of the Middle Assyrian *Psalm to Aššur for Tukultī-Ninurta I* (Ebeling, KAR 128+) identified Assur with Enlil. A Neo-Assyrian scribe wrote in the bilingual *Sumero-Akkadian Hymn of Nanâ* (K 3933) that the goddess Nanaya identified herself with the goddesses Ištar and Anunītu, as well as Šerū'a, Adad's consort Šala, Marduk's consort Zarpānītu, and numerous other goddesses. Likewise, there are no scholarly texts from Ugarit, the Phoenician city-states, Moab, or elsewhere in Western Asia that discuss whether Baal-of-Ṣapun was identified with Baal-of-Ugarit or with Baal-Šamêm, but the six tablets of the *Baal Cycle* leave the impression that there was only one Baal found along the Levantine coast in the mid-second millennium. And, of course, while the Hebrew Bible associates Yahweh with Teman on a handful of occasions, no verse would have caused biblical scholars to surmise that the deity could have been addressed as Yahweh-of-Teman. Nor would they have guessed that Yahweh-of-Samaria was worshipped by that name because the Hebrew Bible never associates the Israelite deity with a cult in this Israelite capital city.

In Assyria, Assur, Marduk, and Enlil were recognized as gods, and various myths and hymns attest to their treatment as gods by their devotees. They could receive praise and offerings, control aspects of the physical world, and interact with other gods, as well as with humans. As Pongratz-Leisten reminds us, apart from their more specific roles in the myths, these major gods were expected to maintain the order of the universe, and they had additional help from the divine statues, drums, crowns, and other objects that also served a purpose sustaining cosmic order. More common than the myths and hymns are the numerous royal inscriptions, state treaties and administrative documents, personal letters, and ritual texts that indicate how the major deities, like Assur, Šamaš, and Marduk, maintained the universe by assisting kings and nations in war, serving as witnesses in human affairs, effecting blessings and curses, and receiving praise and offerings. As shown throughout chapter 3, Neo-Assyrian kings and scribes called upon the famous Assur, Šamaš, Marduk, and numerous other deities in blessings and curses, and priests made arrangements for them and their cult statues in temple rituals and other ceremonies. Likewise, scribes often called upon these deities in an orderly and regular fashion, in which the more important deities appeared first in these inscriptions, and the lesser deities appeared later. Throughout this study, we have referred to these lists of deities as embedded god lists, or EGLs, because they were derived from existing texts whose primary functions were to do something besides list gods. Significantly, throughout this study, we have encountered deities who shared common first names and who were only distinguishable from each other because they had different geographic last names.

The ideal embedded god list, which is based upon the list of thirty-seven Assyrian deities by whom Mati'-ilu swore in his treaty with Assur-nērārī V (SAA 2 2 vi 6–26; see Table 3.10), includes the Assyrian chief deity Assur, the ancient high gods Anu, Enlil, and Ea, and their consorts, the Babylonian chief deity Marduk and his consort and family, warrior (and other male) gods, and goddesses. All but a handful of the deities in this list were identified by a single name, including Assur, Sîn, Marduk, and Nergal, but the handful that are identified by more than a single name were treated in the same way in every other respect. They had the same expectations thrust upon them by Assur-nērārī and Mati'-ilu as did the rest of the deities. Among this handful were two goddesses near the end of the list who were identified by the name Ištar plus a geographic epithet: Ištar//Lady-of-Nineveh and Ištar//Lady-of-Arbela (^{d}15 NIN ^{uru}*ni-na-a* and ^{d}INNIN NIN ^{uru}*arba-il*$_{3}$, ll. 15–16). We can be confident that the text meant to distinguish them from each other precisely because of the context that the embedded god list provides. The great gods Assur, Sîn, Marduk, and Nergal only appear once in this list, and they appear significantly earlier in the list. It is unlikely that the Assyrian and Babylonian chief deities would only be mentioned once whereas the one Ištar would be mentioned twice near the bottom. If we are to interpret this list of gods consistently, then we are forced to recognize that Assur-nērārī recognized (and expected Mati'-ilu to recognize) that Ištar//Lady-of-Nineveh was distinct from Ištar//Lady-of-Arbela. Otherwise, he would have included only (the unspecified) Ištar in his oath, and he would have done so only once.

Similarly, the ritual text BM 121206 describes the physical arrangement in which several cult statues are to be placed (see Table 3.11). More than two dozen statues of Assyrian gods are listed in ix 27′–34′, and all but four of these are identified by one name. The four who are identified by more than a single name all have the first name Ištar, and all of them appear in the middle of the list: Ištar-of-Heaven (^{d}15 *ša*$_{2}$ AN-*e*), Ištar-of-Nineveh (^{d}15 *ša*$_{2}$ NINA^{ki}), Ištar-of-Arbela (^{d}15 *ša*$_{2}$ *arba-il*$_{3}$), and Assyrian-Ištar (^{d}15 *aš-šu-ri-tu*). Again, if we are to interpret this list of gods consistently, then we are forced to recognize that the priests in Assur distinguished these four localized Ištar goddesses from one another. If these four names were supposed to refer to one Ištar who was so important that she could be mentioned by name more often than Assur and his consort Mullissu or any other deity, then we would probably expect her to play a more central role in the ritual or expect that her different names would appear earlier in the list. As chapters 3 and 4 demonstrate, each of the individual localized Ištar goddesses was treated like any other individual deity, and this treatment was not unique to state treaties such as SAA 2 2 or to ritual texts, like BM 121206. This phenomenon was also common to state administrative documents and personal letters. The goddess Ištar-of-Nineveh was treated as distinct from Ištar-of-Arbela and the other localized Ištar goddesses by Neo-Assyrian scribes as she was from Šerū'a, Zarpānītu, and Gula, or any other deity with a distinct name. Because the Neo-Assyrian scribes treated Ištar-of-Nineveh and Ištar-of-Arbela the same way that they treated other deities, the question "Who is a god?" includes an answer that indicates that not only Assur, Šamaš, and Marduk were distinct gods, or that rituals texts reveals that statues, drums, and crowns were each considered independent and distinct gods, but we also need an answer that allows Ištar-of-Nineveh and Ištar-of-Arbela to be considered independent and distinct goddesses. The same can also be said of Ištar-of-Kidmuri and various other Ištar goddesses, regardless of exactly how their name is written out, as long as the geographic name was regularly present.

Significantly, each goddess is an answer to this question regardless of whether she was originally identified with the mythical Ištar and eventually splintered away to become her own personality or if she was a goddess with a unique (and now lost to us) name that was later replaced with the common name Ištar, which is not necessarily synonymous with the common noun *ištar*. As the evidence from modern Italy made clear in chapter 2.1, sister madonnine images could be considered separate from each other, even if the lay population recognized that each madonnine image ultimately could trace her origins back to the singular Madonna in heaven. Moreover, if Hittite scribes could use Sumerian and Akkadian first names to denote a class or category of deity in Hittite inscriptions, then when we encounter a list of deities with multiple IŠKUR, LAMMA, and IŠTAR first names or labels combined with distinct geographic last names, these could be representing specific deities from specific places whose personal names have been lost to us. We might not know if a given IŠKUR, LAMMA, or IŠTAR first name represents a personal divine name or a category of deity, but we do know that each divine full name represents a unique deity. Returning to the Assyrian heartland, a scribe might have recognized that Ištar-of-Nineveh was a goddess formerly known as Ninua'ītu who later adopted the name Ištar-of-Nineveh and that Ištar-of-Arbela was once known as (the unspecified) Ištar. Perhaps it was the other way around with (the unspecified) Ištar in Nineveh and Arbilītu in Arbela, or some other combination. What was important to him was that when he addressed them, he primarily made sure that their geographic names were in place. He would call them Ištar, Lady, Queen, or One-Who-Resides-(in), but he made sure to include consistently where they resided.

Similarly, a survey of Ugaritic and other Northwest Semitic texts reveals that more than one deity was named or nicknamed Baal. The embedded god lists in which many of these Baal deities appear are significantly shorter than those from Neo-Assyrian texts, but several texts still indicate that more than one deity was locally known by the first name Baal. At Ugarit, Baal-of-Aleppo and Baal-of-Ṣapun were listed together in the offering list *KTU*[2] 1.148:23–45, a list which also includes the deities God-of-the-Father, El, Dagan, Ašerah, and Šapaš, among others (see Table 5.2). In this and other offering lists, if each individual name in the list received its own offerings, then each individual divine name was treated as an individual god by the ancient priests, and each individual name should be considered an individual deity by scholars today. Likewise, embedded god lists appear in Aramaic royal inscriptions and Akkadian treaties from the early first millennium (e.g., *KAI* 24 and SAA 2 5) and in Punic votive inscriptions from the third century (i.e., *KAI* 78). When texts include more than one localized Baal deity and do not treat those divine names any differently than they do the other divine names – aside from the fact that they include a geographic last name – we should accept that the scribes responsible for these texts viewed these localized Baal deities as individual and distinct gods. Moreover, in many instances the geographic last names were indispensable to their identity and were included in the text even when only one individual deity appeared in the text (e.g., *KAI* 50). Occasionally, a text's context might have made it clear which particular localized Baal deity was under discussion. For instance, much of the mythical *Baal Cycle* took place on Mount Ṣapun, so the deity only needed to be referred to as (the unspecified) Baal. This might have also been the case in ritual texts that were performed in the temple of Baal-of-Ugarit. It is possible that when Baal-of-Ugarit was the only deity or only Baal deity involved in a particular ritual and the scribe has explicitly set the context in his temple, then he, too, could be referred to as (the unspecified) Baal. However, without these explicit and specific contexts, these deities needed the identity that their geographic last names provided. Baal-of-Ṣapun was addressed as such in letters, and Baal-of-Ugarit was called just that in a ritual that also involved Baal-of-Aleppo. The scribes treated each localized Baal deity like they did any other independent and distinct god, including Dagan, Arṣay, and Mount Ṣapun, when providing offerings. They also expected the same things from each localized Baal deity as they did from other independent and distinct gods; they expected them to maintain the cosmic order. For these reasons, we, too, should consider each localized Baal deity an independent and distinct god. Just as each localized Ištar goddess is a unique answer to the question "Who is a god?" so is each localized Baal deity another unique answer. Each localized Baal deity was a separate and distinct god.

Whereas both the various localized Ištar goddesses and Baal deities could be explored against the background of their divine peers with whom they shared a first name, the few Yahweh full names that we examined do not appear in embedded god lists and cannot be explored by following the same methodology. There are no embedded god lists that include either a localized or (the unspecified) Yahweh deity, and no texts clearly distinguish one localized Yahweh deity from another. Moreover, because the name Yahweh-of-Samaria appears in only one text and the city of Samaria is not known to have been a Yahwistic cult site, we cannot determine how indispensable the place Samaria was to this particular Yahweh deity's identity. The other localized Yahweh name from Kuntillet ʿAjrud is Yahweh-of-(the)-Teman. This full name appears in three different texts, one of which was an official inscription commissioned by the northern state of Israel (*Meshel* 4.1.1). Unlike Samaria, biblical evidence associates Yahweh with Teman in Habakkuk 3:3, so this geographic name is at least pertinent to the deity's identity, especially if Teman and Sinai were so close to each other that they were virtually synonymous terms, along with Seir and Paran in Deuteronomy 33:2 and Judges 5:4–5. However, we cannot be sure if this geographic last name was indispensable to the deity's personality because he is simply called (the unspecified) Yahweh in *Meshel* 3.9:2 and because the scribe responsible for *Meshel* 3.1 did not mind leaving a text addressing Yahweh-of-Samaria at Yahweh-of-Teman's shrine. Perhaps the context of *Meshel* 3.9 was clear enough to its author, comparable to Baal-of-Ugarit in KTU^2 1.109 or 1.119, so that Yahweh-of-Teman was naturally understood to be (the unspecified) Yahweh, but we cannot be certain. Similarly, the Samarian-based scribe responsible for *Meshel* 3.1 might have recognized the oneness of his Yahweh and naturally assumed that Yahweh-of-Samaria should be identified with Yahweh-of-Teman. The third Yahweh full name that we encountered is known from biblical and extra-biblical sources, Yahweh-of-Hosts. This divine full name appears about 300 times in the Hebrew Bible and is often identified with (the unspecified) Yahweh (e.g., Psalm 84), but the last name "of-Hosts" is admittedly not a geographic last name. Because these Yahweh full names lack the context used to determine the individuality and distinctness of other deities with full names, we cannot confidently respond to the question "Who is a god?" by declaring that Yahweh-of-Teman, Yahweh-of-Samaria, and Yahweh-of-Hosts are unique answers. If we accept the possibility, as many scholars believe, that the Israelites were not monotheists during the monarchic period, then we may suppose that these were unique answers. A polytheistic Israelite who was familiar with both of the divine names Yahweh-of-Samaria and Yahweh-of-Teman could easily have considered them distinct and independent deities. This conclusion is made by analogy: just as their Neo-Assyrian counterparts considered Ištar-of-Nineveh distinct from Ištar-of-Arbela or as the Phoenicians considered Baal-Ṣidon distinct from Baal-of-Ṣapun, polytheistic Israelites considered Yahweh-of-Samaria distinct from Yahweh-of-Teman. In this regard, we can confidently suppose that any Neo-Assyrian or Phoenician polytheists who might have encountered the divine names Yahweh-of-Samaria and Yahweh-of-Teman would have considered these names as representing two distinct localized Yahweh deities, based on their understanding of localized Ištar goddesses and Baal deities. (For a list of divine full names with geographic last names that are discussed in this study and would likely have been recognized as distinct deities by their ancient devotees, see Table 7.1).

7.2 Implications

Despite this lack of context for determining whether any ancient Israelites distinguished between Yahweh deities, the origins behind each Yahweh full name can still be sought. In Assyria, the two major localized Ištar goddesses were Ištar-of-Nineveh and Ištar-of-Arbela. Each goddess's patron city was a political, military, economic, and theological stronghold in the Neo-Assyrian Empire. Likewise, Assyrian-Ištar played a greater role in state administrative documents when Assur was still the capital, and Ištar-of-Kidmuri became more relevant when the capital moved to Nineveh, where one of the Kidmuri-temples was located. Similarly, Baal-of-Aleppo was the patron deity of the ancient city of Aleppo in the west, and Baal-of-Ṣapun was the deity associated with the mythical home of (the unspecified) Baal in the *Baal Cycle*. Each geographic last name located its deity in a significant place that was indispensable to the deity's identity.

In the case of the localized Yahweh deities, the significance of the location is probably equally important, but there is not enough evidence to be as certain. As the capital city of the northern state of Israel, Samaria was a political powerhouse, especially during the Omride dynasty in the mid-ninth century. *Meshel* 3.1 is the only piece of textual or archaeological evidence that explicitly links Yahweh with Samaria and a cult site there, but despite the biblical and archaeological silence on the subject, the deity likely had some sort of cultic presence in the capital city. According to 1 Kings, King Jeroboam I of Israel established shrines at the northern and southern extremes of his kingdom, at Dan and Bethel (1 Kings 12:29–30).[1] He built these and other cult sites in order to prevent the Israelites from worshipping Yahweh in Jerusalem and, as a result, politically returning to the kingdom of Judah (vv. 26–27 and 31).[2] 1 Kings also accuses Jeroboam of using inappropriate cult imagery for a Yahwistic cult (i.e., calves, not cherubim, v. 28) and of imposing a new religious calendar on the Israelites (vv. 32–33).[3] According to 1 and 2 Kings, there was a political rivalry between Israel and Judah throughout most of their history, and 1 Kings 12 indicates that there was also a religious rivalry. While neither these cultic innovations nor any other evidence explicitly places a Yahwistic cult in Samaria, if a religious rivalry existed between Israel and Judah before and after Samaria was the Israelite capital city, then either the Omride kings or some later Israelite king could have fueled this political and religious rivalry by honoring Yahweh there.

As some scholars have suggested, the area of Kuntillet ʻAjrud was likely under Samaria's political control and not too far from Teman and Edom, but at first glance, the full name Yahweh-of-Teman does not appear to have been coined for the benefit of the northern state. Unlike Yahweh's (supposed) associations with Samaria, his associations with Teman are textually and biblically based. Teman was no political stronghold, but it was probably important for mythical reasons. In Habakkuk 3:3, the Israelite God is described as coming from Teman (אלוה מתימן יבוא). Other verses locate the deity in the southern Transjordan, and second-millennium Egyptian texts associate the geographic name Yahweh with this region. If Yahweh had been known as Yahweh-of-Teman by more than just the scribes and overseers at Kuntillet ʻAjrud, then this full name should be interpreted along the lines as the name

---

1 Cross pointed out that the cults at Dan and Bethel existed prior to Jeroboam I and claimed that "Jeroboam's real sin was his establishing a rival to the central sanctuary in Jerusalem, not in the introduction of a foreign god or pagan idol (Cross, "Yahweh and the God," 258).

2 Jeroboam's capital probably contained one of the "high places" (בית־במות), with a commissioned priesthood, that are mentioned in 1 Kings 12:31. It should be stressed, however, that his capital was Shechem, not Samaria.

3 According to Cross, Jeroboam I reintroduced Israel to worship of the god El by using the calf images (Cross, "Yahweh and the God," 258).

Baal-of-Ṣapun, a divine name with mythic associations. From this perspective we can reconsider the benefits that the divine name Yahweh-of-Teman provided the northern state of Israel. Israel had interest in demonstrating its power over its neighboring peoples, especially Judah whose national deity was also known as Yahweh and was probably even the same Yahweh. It is one thing to control a fortress or trade-stop in the desert far from the capital, but it is another thing to oversee a shrine there and proclaim, identify, or equate it with Yahweh's ancient, mythical home. If the state of Israel wanted to lord its dominance over Judah and Yahweh's newer home in Jerusalem and Zion, then what better way to do this than take control of the original home of Yahweh? Israel did not need to control the historical and specific Teman, wherever that actually was in or near Edom or Mount Sinai, but by officially sanctioning the shrine at Kuntillet 'Ajrud, Israel identified the shrine with Teman and effectively took control of Yahweh's home. Because Kuntillet 'Ajrud was only occupied for a generation, we should probably not consider this a successful attempt at undermining Jerusalem's claims on Yahweh at Zion, but the intent of the program is still worth consideration.

The third Yahweh deity of interest, Yahweh-of-Hosts, lacks a geographic last name, but he was intimately associated with the Judahite capital Jerusalem. Mimicking Teman's mythical associations with Yahweh, the cult site at Jerusalem developed its own mythical associations, which is made evident by the reinterpretation of Mount Zion as Yahweh's own Mount Ṣapun in the city of David. Despite the political and religious center that Jerusalem became and the fact that Yahweh could be referred to as "God of Jerusalem" in the post-exilic period (i.e., 2 Chronicles 32:17 and Ezra 7:19), the local Yahwistic cult never referred to Yahweh as the Yahweh-of-Jerusalem or the Yahweh-of-Zion.

If the Israelites had been polytheists, then they presumably would have composed texts from which embedded god lists could be derived, just as their Assyrian, Aramaic, Phoenician, and other neighbors did in their treaties, royal inscriptions, and the greetings in letters. It is true that we have no extant Israelite treaties or royal inscriptions in which to look for potential embedded god lists, but the greetings in the letters are suggestive of an Israelite Yahwistic monolatry or monotheism.[4] As mentioned in chapter 6, the concept of multiple Yahweh deities or distinct and independent localized Yahweh deities is not a topic that was addressed by the authors and editors of the historical books, the prophets, or any other biblical authors. Their lack of concern about the

4 In contrast, the embedded god lists in the Assyrian letters SAA 10 197:7–14 and 286:3–7 (see Tables 3.7 and 3.8) name multiple deities, including multiple Ištar goddesses.

topic suggests that they were aware of few, if any, Israelites who recognized the Yahweh divine names that they encountered as representing distinct and independent deities. Notably, some scholars have appealed to the declaration in Deuteronomy 6:4, "Yahweh is one" (יהוה אחד), as evidence that Israelites did recognize distinct Yahweh deities, or at least, they distinguished between multiple localized manifestations of the one singular (the unspecified) Yahweh. The ancient Israelites might have known or encountered the names Yahweh-of-Samaria and Yahweh-of-Teman, but there is nothing to suggest from the textual or biblical evidence that they thought of these as different Yahweh deities.

The presence of multiple localized Yahweh deities with geographic last names is not necessarily evidence of polytheism or poly-Yahwism among Israelites. Nor is the absence of multiple Assur deities with geographic last names evidence of monolatry or monotheism among the Assyrians. But it could be evidence that Assur never splintered into multiple Assur deities. The contexts in which these divine full names appear matter. They should guide how we interpret the names and determine whether we can confidently respond to the question "Who is a (distinct) god?" by answering Ištar-of-Nineveh, Ištar-of-Arbela, Baal-of-Ṣapun, and Baal-Šamêm, answers with which ancient Assyrians, Arameans, and Phoenicians would surely have agreed.

Bibliography

Abusch, Tzvi. "Ishtar." In *Dictionary of Deities and Demons in the Bible*. Edited by Karel van der Toorn, Bob Becking, and Pieter W. van der Horst. 2nd rev. ed. 452–456. Leiden: Brill, 1999.

Aharoni, Yohanan, Michael Avi-Yonah, Anson F. Rainey, and Ze'ev Safrai. *The Macmillan Bible Atlas*. New York: Macmillan, 1993.

Aḥituv, Shmuel. *Echoes from the Past: Hebrew and Cognate Inscriptions from the Biblical Period*. Translated by A. F. Rainey. Jerusalem: Carta, 2008.

Aḥituv, Shmuel, Esther Eshel, and Ze'ev Meshel. "The Inscriptions." In *Kuntillet ʻAjrud (Ḥorvat Teman): An Iron Age II Religious Site on the Judah-Sinai Border*. Edited by Ze'ev Meshel. 73–142. Jerusalem: Israel Exploration Society, 2012.

Albertz, Rainer. "Household in the Ancient Near East." In *Household and Family Religion in Antiquity*. Edited by J. Bodel and S. Olyan. 89–112. Malden: Blackwell, 2008.

Albright, William F. Review of "L'épithète divine Jahvé Seba'ôt: Étude philogique, historique et exégétigue," by B. N. Wambacq. *JBL* 67 (1948): 377–381.

Alexander, Robert L. "Šaušga and the Hittite Ivory from Megiddo." *JNES* 50 (1991): 161–182.

Allen, James P. *The Ancient Egyptian Pyramid Texts*. Edited by P. Der Manuelian. Writings from the Ancient World 23. Atlanta: Society of Biblical Literature, 2005.

Allen, Spencer L. "Aššur and Enlil in Neo-Assyrian Documents." In *Organization, Representation, and Symbols of Power in the Ancient Near East Proceedings of the 54th Rencontre Assyriologique Internationale Proceedings of the 54th Rencontre Assyriologique Internationale at Würzburg 20–25 July 2008*. Edited by G. Wilhelm. 397–409. Winona Lake: Eisenbrauns, 2012.

Allen, Spencer L. "An Examination of Northwest Semitic Divine Names and the *Bet*-locative." *JESOT* 2 (2013): 61–82.

Allen, Spencer L. "Rearranging the Gods in Esarhaddon's Succession Treaty (SAA 2 6:414–465)." *Die Welt des Orients* 43 (2013): 1–24.

Alt, Albrecht. "The God of the Fathers." In *Essays on Old Testament History and Religion*. Translated by R. A. Wilson. 1–66. Oxford: Basil Blackwell, 1966.

Annus, Amar. *The God Ninurta in the Mythology and Royal Ideology of Ancient Mesopotamia*. SAAS 14. Helsinki: The Neo-Assyrian Text Corpus Project, 2002.

Archi, Alfonso. "The Head of Kura–The Head of ˀAdabal." *JNES* 63 (2005): 81–100.

Archi, Alfonso, and Maria Giovanna Biga. "A Victory over Mari and the Fall of Ebla." *JCS* 55 (2003): 1–44.

Arnaud, Daniel. *Recherches au pays d'Astata: Emar* 6/3. Paris: Editions Recherche sur les Civilisations, 1986.

Arndt, William F., and F. Wilbur Gingrich. *A Greek-English Lexicon of the New Testament and other Early Christian Literature*. Chicago: University of Chicago Press, 1957.

Assmann, Jan. *Egyptian Solar Religion in the New Kingdom: Re, Amun and the Crisis of Polytheism*. Translated by A. Alock. London: Kegan Paul International, 1995.

Astour, Michael. "Semites and Hurrians in Northern Transtigris." In *General Studies and Excavations at Nuzi* 9/1. Edited by D. Owen and M. Morrison. SCCNH 2. 3–68. Winona Lake: Eisenbrauns, 1987.

Atti e decreti del concilio diocesano di Pistoia dell'anno 1786. Vol. 1. Florence: L. S. Olschki Editore, 1986.

Attridge, Harold W., and Robert A. Oden. *Philo of Byblos: The Phoenician History; Introduction, Critical Texts, Translation, and Notes*. CBQMS 9. Washington, D.C.: Catholic Biblical Association of America, 1981.

Avigad, Nahman. "Two Phoenician Votive Seals." *IEJ* 16 (1966): 243–251.

Avigad, Nahman. *Corpus of West Semitic Stamp Seals*. Jerusalem: the Israel Academy of Sciences and Humanities: the Israel Exploration Society: the Institute of Archaeology: the Hebrew University of Jerusalem, 1997.

Ayalon, Eton. "The Pottery Assemblage." In *Kuntillet ʻAjrud (Ḥorvat Teman): An Iron Age II Religious Site on the Judah-Sinai Border*. Edited by Ze'ev Meshel. 203–274. Jerusalem: Israel Exploration Society, 2012.

Bade, William. F. "Der Monojahwismus des Deuteronomiums." *ZAW* 30 (1910): 81–90.

Baines, John. "Egyptian Deities in Context: Multiplicity Unity and the Problem of Change." In *One God or Many? Concepts of Divinity in the Ancient World*. Edited by Barbara N. Porter. Transactions of the Casco Bay Assyriological Institute 1. 9–78. Casco Bay Assyriological Institute, 2000.

Banfield, Edward. *The Moral Basis of a Backward Society*. Glencoe: The Free Press, 1958.

Barré, Michael L. *The God-List in the Treaty between Hannibal and Philip V of Macedonia: a study in Light of the Ancient Near Eastern Treaty Tradition*. Baltimore: Johns Hopkins University Press, 1983.

Barré, Michael L. "The First Pair of Deities in the Sefire I God-List." *JNES* 44 (1985): 205–210.

Barton, George A. "The Semitic Ištar Cult." *Hebraica* 9 (1893): 131–165.

Barton, George A. "The Semitic Ištar Cult (Continued)." *Hebraica* 10 (1893–1894): 1–74.

Beal, Richard H. "Dividing a God." In *Magic and Ritual in the Ancient World*. Edited by Paul Mirecki and Marvin Meyer. 197–208. Leiden: Brill, 2002.

Beaulieu, Paul-Alain. "The Cult of AN.ŠÁR/Aššur in Babylonia after the Fall of the Assyrian Empire." SAAB 11 (1997): 55–73.

Beaulieu, Paul-Alain. *The Pantheon of Uruk During the Neo-Babylonian Period*. Leiden: Brill, 2003.

Becking, Bob. "Assyrian Evidence for Iconic Polytheism in Ancient Israel?" In *The Image and the Book: Iconic Cults, Aniconism, and the Rise of Book Religion in Israel and the Ancient Near East*. Edited by Karel van der Toorn. Contributions to Biblical Exegesis and Theology 21. 157–171. Leuven: Peeters, 1997.

Beckman, Gary. "Ištar of Nineveh Reconsidered." *JCS* 50 (1998): 1–10.

Beckman, Gary. *Hittite Diplomatic Texts*. Edited by H. A. Hoffner. Writings from the Ancient World 7. Atlanta: Scholars Press, 1999.

Beckman, Gary. "Plague Prayers of Muršili II (1.60)." In *The Context of Scripture: Canonical Compositions from the Biblical World*. Edited by William W. Hallo. 1:156–160. Leiden: Brill, 2003.

Beckman, Gary. "Pantheon. A. II. Bei den Hethitern." *RlA* 10/3–4 (2004): 308–316.

Berlinerblau, Jacques. *Official Religion and Popular Religion in Pre-exilic Ancient Israel*. Cincinnati: Department of Judaic Studies, University of Cincinnati, 2000.

Bevan, Edwyn. *Holy Images: An Inquiry into Idolatry and Image-Worship in Ancient Paganism and in Christianity*. London: G. Allen & Unwin, 1940.

Biran, Avraham, and Joseph Naveh. "An Aramaic Stele Fragment from Tel Dan." *IEJ* 43 (1993): 81–98.

Blenkinsopp, Joseph. *Ezra-Nehemiah: A Commentary*. Old Testament Library. Philadelphia: Westminster, 1988.

Blenkinsopp, Joseph. "The Midianite-Kenite Hypothesis Revisited and the Origins of Judah." *JSOT* 33 (2008):131–153.
Boeckh, Augustus. *Corpus inscriptionum graecarum*. 4 vols. Berlin, 1828–1877.
Boehmer, Rainer M. "Die Datierung des Puzur/Kutik-Inšušinak und einige sich daraus ergebende Konsequenzen." *Or* NS 35 (1966): 345–376.
Böhl, F. "Älteste keilinschriftliche Erwähnungen der Stadt Jerusalem und ihrer Göttin?" *Acta Orientalia* 1 (1922–1923): 76–80.
Boling, Robert G. *Judges*. AB. Garden City: Doubleday, 1975.
Bonnet, Hans. "Zum Verständnis des Synkretismus." *ZÄS* 75 (1939): 40–52.
Bonnet, Hans. "On Understanding Syncretism." Translated by J. Baines. *Or* NS 68 (1999): 189–199.
Borger, Riekele. *Beiträge zum Inschriftenwerk Assurbanipals: Die Prismenklassen A, B, C = K, D, E, F, G, H, J und T sowie andere Inschriften: Mit einem Beitrag von Andreas Fuchs*. Wiesbaden: Harrassowitz Verlag, 1996.
Botica, Aurelian. "The Theophoric Element Ba'al in Ancient Phoenician Inscriptions." *Perichoresis* 10 (2012): 67–93.
Botta, Alejandro F. "Outlook: Aramaeans Outside of Syria: Egypt." In *The Aramaeans in Ancient Syria*. Edited by Herbert Niehr. 366–377. HdO 106. Leiden: Brill, 2014.
Bottéro, Jean. *Religion in Ancient Mesopotamia*. Translated by T. L. Fagan. Chicago: University of Chicago, 2001.
Brown, F., S. R. Driver, and C. A. Briggs. *A Hebrew and English Lexicon of the Old Testament: with an appendix containing the Biblical Aramaic, based on the lexicon of William Gesenius as translated by Edward Robinson*. Oxford: Clarendon, 1962.
Bryce, Trevor. *The Kingdom of the Hittites*. Oxford: Oxford University Press, 1999.
Bryce, Trevor. *Life and Society in the Hittite World*. Oxford: Oxford University Press, 2002.
Bryce, Trevor. *The World of the Neo-Hittite Kingdoms: A Political and Military History*. Oxford: Oxford University Press, 2012.
Buccellati, Giorgio. "The Descent of Inanna as a Ritual Journey to Kutha?" *Syro-Mesopotamian Studies* 4 (1982): 3–7.
Budde, D. Karl. *Die Bücher Samuel*. Tübingen: Verlag von J. C. B. Mohr, 1902.
Budin, S. L. "A Reconsideration of the Aphrodite-Ashtart Syncretism." *Numen* 51 (2004): 95–145.
Bunnens, Guy. "The Storm-God in Northern Syria and Southern Anatolia from Hadad of Aleppo to Jupiter Dolichenus." In *Offizielle Religion, locale Kulte und individuelle Religiosiät: Akten des religionsgeschichtlichen Symposiums "Kleinasien und angrenzende Gebiete vom Beginn des 2. bis zur Mitte des 1. Jahrtausends vor Chr." (Bonn, 20.–s22. Februar 2003)*. Edited by M. Hutter and S. Hutter-Braunsar. AOAT 318. 57–81. Münster: Ugarit-Verlag, 2004.
van Buren, Elizabeth D. "The *ṣalmê* in Mesopotamian Art and Religion." *Or* NS 10 (1941): 65–92.
Caquot, André, and Maurice Sznycer. *Ugarititc Religion*. Leiden: Brill, 1980.
Carmi, Israel, and Dror Segal, "^{14}C Dates from Kuntillet 'Ajrud." In *Kuntillet 'Ajrud (Ḥorvat Teman): An Iron Age II Religious Site on the Judah-Sinai Border*. Edited by Ze'ev Meshel. 61–63. Jerusalem: Israel Exploration Society, 2012.
Carroll, Michael. *The Cult of the Virgin Mary: Psychological Origins*. Princeton: Princeton University Press, 1986.
Carroll, Michael. *Catholic Cults & Devotions: A Psychological Inquiry*. Montreal: McGill-Queen's University Press, 1989.

Carroll, Michael. *Madonnas that Maim: Popular Catholicism in Italy since the Fifteenth Century*. Baltimore: Johns Hopkins University Press, 1992.
Carroll, Michael. *Veiled Threats: The Logic of Popular Catholicism in Italy*. Baltimore: Johns Hopkins University Press, 1996.
Cazelles, Henri. "Bethlehem." In *Anchor Bible Dictionary*. Edited by David Noel Freedman. 1:712–715. New York: Doubleday, 1992.
Cesare D'Engenio, D. *Napoli Sacra*. Napoli: Ottavio Beltrano, 1623.
Christian, William. *Local Religion in Sixteenth-Century Spain*. Princeton: Princeton University Press, 1981.
Clifford, Richard J. *The Cosmic Mountain in Canaan and the Old Testament*. HSM 4. Cambridge: Harvard University Press, 1972.
Cogan, Mordechai. *I Kings*. Anchor Bible 10. New York: Doubleday, 2001.
Cole, Steven W., and Peter Machinist. *Letters from Assyrian and Babylonian Priests to Kings Esarhaddon and Assurbanipal*. SAA 13. Helsinki: Helsinki University Press, 1998.
Coogan, Michael. "Canaanite Origins and Lineage: Reflections on the Religion of Ancient Israel." In *Ancient Israelite Religion: Essays in Honor of Frank Moore Cross*. Edited by Patrick D. Miller, Paul D. Hanson, and S. Dean McBride. 115–124. Philadelphia: Fortress, 1987.
Collins, Billie Jean. "The First Soldiers' Oath (1.66)." In *The Context of Scripture: Canonical Compositions from the Biblical World*. Edited by William W. Hallo. 1:165–167. Leiden: Brill, 2003.
Collins, Billie Jean. "Establishing a New Temple for the Goddess of the Night (1.70)." In *The Context of Scripture: Canonical Compositions from the Biblical World*. Edited by William W. Hallo. 1:173–177. Leiden: Brill, 2003.
Collon, Dominique. *Catalogue of Western Asiatic Seals in the British Museum: Cylinder Seals V: Neo-Assyrian and Neo-Babylonian Periods*. British Museum Publications, 2001.
Cooper, Jerrold S. *The Return of Ninurta to Nippur*: an-gim dím-ma. Analecta orientalia 52. Rome: Pontificium Institutum Biblicum, 1978.
Cooper, Jerrold S. Review of "Assyrian Prophecies, the Assyrian Tree, and the Mesopotamian Origins of Jewish Monotheism, Greek Philosophy, Christian Theology, Gnosticism, and Much More," by Simo Parpola. *JAOS* 120 (2000): 430–444.
Corpus inscriptionum latinarum. 17 vols. Berolini: G. Reimerum, 1862 ff.
Corpus inscriptionum semiticarum. 5 vols. Parisiis: E Reipublicae Typographeo, 1881 ff.
Corrain, Cleto, and Pierluigi Zampinim. *Documenti etnografici e folkloristici nei diocesani italiani*. Bologna: Forni, 1970.
Cross, Frank Moore. "Yahweh and the God of the Patriarchs." *HTR* 55 (1962): 225–259.
Cross, Frank Moore. "The Cave Inscriptions from Khirbet Beit Lei." In *Near Eastern Archaeology in the Twentieth Century: Essays in Honor of Nelson Glueck*. Edited by J. Sanders. 299–306. New York: Doubleday 1970.
Cross, Frank Moore. *Canaanite Myth and Hebrew Epic: Essays in the History of the Religion of Israel*. Cambridge: Harvard University Press, 1973.
Cross, Frank Moore. "Reuben, First-Born of Jacob." *ZAW* 100 (1988): Supplement, 46–65.
Cross, Frank Moore, and David Noel Freedman. *Studies in Ancient Yahwistic Poetry*. New ed. Livonia: Dove Booksellers, 1997.
Cruz, Jean Carroll. *Relics: The Shroud of Turin, the True Cross, the Blood of Januarius... History, Mysticism, and the Catholic Church*. Huntington: Our Sunday Visitor, 1984.
Da Riva, Rocío, and Eckart Frahm. "Šamaš-šumu-ukīn, die Herrin von Ninive unddas babylonische Königssiegel." *AfO* 46–47 (1999/2000): 156–182.

Dahood, Mitchell. "Afterword: Ebla, Ugarit, and the Bible." Afterward to *The Archives of Ebla: An Empire Inscribed in Clay*. Written by Giovanni Pettinato. 217–321. New York: Doubleday, 1981.

Dalley, Stephanie. *Myths from Mesopotamia: Creation, The Flood, Gilgamesh, and Others*. Oxford: Oxford University Press, 1998.

Dalley, Stephanie. *Esther's Revenge at Susa: From Sennacherib to Ahasuerus*. Oxford: Oxford University Press, 2007.

Dearman, Andrew J., ed. *Studies in the Mesha Inscription and Moab*. Archaeology and Biblical Studies 2. Atlanta: Scholars Press, 1989.

Dearman, Andrew J."Historical Reconstruction and the Mesha Inscription." In *Studies in the Mesha Inscription and Moab*. Edited by Andrew J. Dearman. Archaeology and Biblical Studies 2. 155–210. Atlanta: Scholars Press, 1989.

Deighton, Hilary. *The 'Weather-God' in Hittite Anatolia: An Examination of the Archaeological and Textual Sources*. Oxford: British Archaeological Reports International Series, 1982.

Deimel, Anton. *Codex Ḫammurapi*. Rome: Sumptimus Pontificii Instituti Biblici, 1930.

Delitzsch, F. *Vorderasiatische Schriftdenkmäler der Königlichen Museen zu Berlin*. Leipzig: J. C. Hinrichs, 1907 ff.

Deller, Karlheinz. "Materialien zu den Lokalpantheons des Königreiches Arrapḫe." *Or* NS 45 (1976): 33–45.

Deller, Karlheinz, F. Mario Fales, and Liane Jakob-Rost. "Neo-Assyrian Texts from Assur Private Archives. Part 2." SAAB 9 (1995): 3–137.

Dick, Michael. Review of *Die Theologie der Bilder: Herstellung und Einweihung von Kultbildern in Mesopotamien und die alttestamentliche Bilderpolemik*, by Angelika Berlejung. *JAOS* 120 (2000): 257–258.

Dietrich, Manfried, Oswald Loretz, and Joaquín Sanmartín. *The Cuneiform Alphabetic Texts from Ugarit, Ras Ibn Hani and other Places (KTU: second, enlarged edition)*. Abhandlungen zur Literatur Alt-Syrien-Palästinas und Mesopotamiens 8. Münster: Ugarit-Verlag, 1995.

Dijkstra, Meindert, "The Ritual *KTU* 1.46 (=RS 1.9) and its Duplicates." *UF* 16 (1984): 69–76.

Dobbs-Allsopp, F. W., J. J. M. Roberts, C. L. Seow, and R. E. Whitaker. *Hebrew Inscriptions: Texts from the Biblical Period of the Monarchy with Concordance*. New Haven: Yale University Press, 2005.

Donbaz, Veysel, and Simo Parpola. *Neo-Assyrian Legal Texts in Istanbul*. Saarbrücken: In Kommission bei SDV Saarbrücker Druckerei und Verlag, 2001.

Donner, Herbert, and Wolfgang Röllig. *Kanaanäische und Aramäische Inschriften*. Vol. 1. 5th ed. Wisebaden: Otto Harrassowitz, 2002.

Donner, Herbert, and Wolfgang Röllig. *Kanaanäische und Aramäische Inschriften: Kommentar*. Vol. 2. Wisebaden: Otto Harrassowitz, 1964.

Dossin, Georges. "Benjaminites dans les texts de Mari." In *Mélanges syriens offert à M. René Dussaud*. 2:981–996. Paris: Librairie Orientaliste Paul Geuthner, 1939.

Dossin, Georges. "Le Panthéon de Mari." In *Studia Mariana: Publiées sous la direction de Andreé Parrot*. 41–50. Leiden: Brill, 1950.

van Driel, Govert. *The Cult of Aššur*. Assen: van Gorcum, 1969.

Durand, Jean-Marie. *Le Culte d'Addu d'Alep et l'affaire d'Alahtum*. Florilegium Marianum 7, Mémoires de NABU 8. Paris: Société pour l'étude du Proche-orient ancien, 2002.

Ebeling, Erich. *Quellen zur Kenntnis der babylonischen Religion*. Mitteilungen der Vorderasiatischen Gesellschaft 23. Vol. 1. Leipzig: J. C. Hinrichs, 1918.

Ebeling, Erich. *Keilschrifttexte aus Assur religiösen Inhalts*. Ausgrabungen der Deutschen Orient-Gesellschaft in Assur. E, Inschriften 2. Leipzig, 1919–1923.
Ebeling, Erich. *Die Akkadische Gebetsserie "Handerhebung": Von Neuem Gesammelt und Herausgegeben*. Veröffentlichung 20. Berlin: Akademie-Verlag, 1953.
Edzard, Dietz Otto. "Pantheon und Kult im Mari." In *Rencontre Assyriologique Internationale XVe: La Civilisation de Mari: Colloque international tenu à l'Univerité de Liège dy 4 au 8 juillet 1966*. Edited by J. R. Kupper. 51–71. Paris: Belles letters, 1967.
Eidem, Jesper. "An Old Assyrian Treaty from Tell Leilan." In *Marchands, Dipliomates et Empereurs: Études sur la Civilisation Mésopotamienne Offertes à Paul Garelli*. Edited by D. Charpin and F. Joannès. 185–207. Paris: Éditions Recherche sur les Civilisations, 1991.
Ellis, Maria deJong. "The Archive of the Old Babylonian Kītītum Temple and other Texts from Ishchali." *JAOS* 106 (1986): 757–786.
Emerton, John A. "New Light on Israelite Religion: The Implications of the Inscriptions from Kuntillet 'Ajrud." *ZAW* 94 (1982): 2–20.
Even-Shoshan, Abraham. *A New Concordance of the Bible: Thesaurus of the Language of the Bible, Hebrew and Aramaic, Roots, Words, Proper Names Phrases and Synonyms*. Jerusalem: Kiryat-Sefer, 1998.
Faist, Betina. *Alltagstexts aus neuassyrischen Archiven und Bibliotheken der Stadt Assur*. Studien zu den Assur-Texten 3. Wiesbaden: Harrassowitz Verlag, 2007.
Fales, F. Mario. *L'impero Assiro: Storia e Amministrazione (IX-VII Secolo A.C.)*. Collezione storica. Rome: Editorio Laterza, 2001.
Fales, F. Mario. *Guerre et paix en Assyrie Religion et imperialism*. Les conférences de l'École Pratique desHautes Études, 2. Paris: Éditions du Cerf, 2010.
Fales, F. Mario, and Liane Jakob-Rost. "Neo-Assyrian Texts from Assur, Private Archives in the Vorderasiatisches Museum of Berlin. Part 1 (with two appendixes by K. Deller)." SAAB 5 (1991): 3–157.
Fales, F. Mario, and J. N. Postgate. *Imperial Administrative Records, Part I: Palace and Temple Administration*. SAA 7. Helsinki: Helsinki University Press, 1992.
Farber, Walter. Review of *The Cult of Aššur*, by Govert van Driel. *BiOr* 30 (1973): 433–436.
Ferron, J. "Dédicace latine á Baal-Hammon." *CdB* 3 (1953): 113–118.
Fleming, Daniel. E. *The Installation of Baal's High Priestess at Emar: A Window on Ancient Syrian Religion*. HSS 42. Atlanta: Scholars Press, 1992.
Fohrer, Georg. *Introduction to Israelite Religion*. Translated by David E. Green. Nashville: Abingdon, 1972.
Foster, Benjamin. *Before the Muses: An Anthology of Akkadian Literature*. Bethesda: CDL Press, 2005.
Frahm, Eckart. *Einleitung in die Sanherib-Inschriften*. AfO Beiheft 26. Vienna: Institut fur Orientalistik, 1997.
Frahm, Eckart. "Wie „christlich" war die assyrische Religion? Anmerkungen zu Simo Parpolas Edition der assyrischen Prophetien." *WdO* 31 (2000/2001): 31–45.
Frame, Grant. "Nabonidus, Nabû-šarra-uṣur, and the Eanna Temple." *ZA* 81 (1991): 37–86.
Frame, Grant. *Rulers of Babylonia: From the Second Dynasty of Isin to the End of Assyrian Domination (1157-612 BC)*. RIMB 2. Toronto: University of Toronto Press, 1995.
Frame, Grant. "My Neighbour's God: Aššur in Babylonia and Marduk in Assyria." *CSMS Bulletin* 34 (1999): 5–22.
Frame, Grant. "City Administration of Uruk in the Neo-Assyrian Period." (Forthcoming).
Frank, Carl. *Kultlieder aus der Ischtar-Tamuz-Kreis*. Leipzig: Otto Harrassowitz, 1939.

Frankena, Rintje. *Tākultu: de Sacrale Maaltijd in Het Assyrische Ritueel: Met een overzicht over de in Assur Vereerde Goden*. Leiden: Brill, 1954.
Frankena, Rintje. "New Materials for the Tākultu Ritual: Additions and Corrections." *BiOr* 8 (1961): 199–207.
Frayne, Douglas. *Old Babylonian Period (2003-1595 B.C.)*. RIME 4. Toronto: University of Toronto Press, 1990.
Frayne, Douglas. *Ur III Period (2112-2004 B.C.)*. RIME 3/2. Toronto: University of Toronto Press, 1997.
Freedman, David Noel, ed. *Anchor Bible Dictionary*. 6 vols. New York: Doubleday, 1992.
Fresnel, F. "Inscriptions trilingues trouvées à Lebdah." *JA* 8 (1846): 349–355.
Freydank, H. *Spätbabylonische Wirtschaftstexte aus Uruk*. Veröffentlichung 71. Berlin: Akademie Verlag, 1971.
Frymer-Kensky, Tikva. *In the Wake of the Goddesses: Women, Culture and the Biblical Transformation of Pagan Myth*. New York: Fawcette Columbine, 1992.
Fuchs, Andreas. *Die Inschriften Sargons II. Aus Khorsabad*. Göttingen: Cuvillier Verlag, 1994.
Fuchs, Andreas. *Die Annalen des Jahres 711 v. Chr. nach Prismenfragmenten aus Ninive und Assur*. SAAS 8. Helsinki: The Neo-Assyrian Text Corpus Project, 1998.
Gadd, Cyril J. "Inscribed Prisms of Sargon II from Nimrud." *Iraq* 16 (1954): 173–201 and plates XLIV-LI.
Gelb, I. J. *The Assyrian Dictionary of the Oriental Institute of the University of Chicago*. 21 volumes. Chicago: University of Chicago Press, 1956 ff.
Gelb, I. J. "Compound Divine Names in the Ur III Period." In *Language, Literature, and History: Philological and Historical Studies presented to Erica Reiner*. Edited by F. Rochberg-Halton. 125–138. New Haven: American Oriental Society, 1987.
Genouillac, H. de. "Grande liste de noms divins sumériens." *RA* 20 (1923): 89–106.
George, A. *Babylonian Topographical Texts*. OLA 40. Leuven: Department Orientalistiek, 1992.
George, A. *House Most High: The Temple Lists of Ancient Mesopotamia*. Mesopotamian Civilizations 5. Winona Lake: Eisenbrauns, 1993.
George, A. "Marduk and the Cult of the Gods of Nippur at Babylon." *Or* NS 66 (1997): 65–70.
Gibson, John C. L. *Textbook of Syrian Semitic Inscriptions*. 3 vols. Oxford: Clarendon, 1971–1982.
Giveon, Raphael. "'The Cities of our God' (II Sam 10 12)." *JBL* 83 (1964): 415–416.
Giveon, Raphael. *Les Bédouins Shosou des Documents Égyptiens*. Leiden: Brill, 1971.
Gödecken, Karin B. "Bermerkungen zure Göttin Annuītum." *UF* 5 (1973): 141–163.
Grayson, A. Kirk. *Assyrian and Babylonian Chronicles*. TCS 5. Locust Valley: J.J. Augustin, 1975.
Grayson, A. Kirk. *Assyrian Rulers of the Third and Second Millennia BC I (to 1115)*. RIMA 1. Toronto: University of Toronto Press, 1987.
Grayson, A. Kirk. *Assyrian Rulers of the Early First Millennium BC I (1114-859)*. RIMA 2. Toronto: University of Toronto Press, 1991.
Grayson, A. Kirk. *Assyrian Rulers of the Early First Millennium BC II (858-745)*. RIMA 3. Toronto: University of Toronto Press, 1996.
Green, Alberto. R. W. *The Storm-God in the Ancient Near East*. Biblical and Judaic Studies 8. Lake Winona: Eisenbrauns, 2003.
Greenfield, Jonas C., and Aaron Shaffer. "Notes on the Akkadian-Aramaic Bilingual Statue from Tell Fekherye." *Iraq* 45 (1983): 109–116.
Gressmann, Hugo. "Hadad und Baal nach den Amarnagriefen und nach ägyptischen Texten." In *Abhandlungen zur semitischen Religionskunde und Sprachwissenschaft*. Edited by W. Frankenberg and F. Küchler. BZAW 33. 191–216. Berlin: Graf von Baudissin, 1918.

Gunneweg, Jan, Isadore Perlman, and Ze'ev Meshel. "The Origin of the Pottery." In *Kuntillet 'Ajrud (Ḥorvat Teman): An Iron Age II Religious Site on the Judah-Sinai Border*. Edited by Ze'ev Meshel. 279–287. Jerusalem: Israel Exploration Society, 2012.

Gurney, Oliver R., and J. J. Finkelstein. *The Sultantepe Tablets*. 2 vols. London: British Institute of Archaeology at Ankara, 1957–1964.

Guzzo Amadasi, Maria Giulia. "Tanit – 'ŠTRT *e* Milk – 'ŠTRT: *ipotesi*." *Or* NS 60 (1991): 82–91.

Guzzo Amadasi, Maria Giulia, and V. Karageorghis. *Fouilles de Kition: III. Inscriptions Phéniciennes*. Nicosia: Published for the Republic of Cyprus by the Department of Antiquities, 1977.

Haas, Volkert. "Remarks on the Hurrian Istar››Sawuska of Nineveh in the Second Millennium B.C." *Sumer* 35 (1979): 401–397.

Haas, Volkert. *Geschichte der hethitschen Religion*. Leiden: Brill, 1994.

Hadley, Judith M. "Kuntillet 'Ajrud: Religious Centre or Desert Way Station?" *PEQ* 125 (1993): 115–124.

Hadley, Judith M. *The Cult of Asherah in Ancient Israel and Judah: Evidence for a Hebrew Goddess*. Cambridge: Cambridge University Press, 2000.

Hallo, William W., ed. *The Context of Scripture*. 3 vols. Leiden: Brill, 2003.

Hämeen-Anttila, Jaakko. *A Sketch of Neo-Assyrian Grammar*. SAAS 13. Helsinki: Neo-Assyrian Text Corpus Project, 2000.

Harris, Rivkah. *Ancient Sippar: A Demographic Study of an Old-Babylonian City (1894–1959)*. Utigaven van net Nederlands Historisch-Archaeologisch Instituut te Istanbul 36. Leiden: Nederlands Historisch-Archaeologisch Instituut te Istanbul, 1975.

Heltzer, Michael. "Land Grant Along with Tithe Obligations (3.82)." In *The Context of Scripture: Archival Documents from the Biblical World*. Edited by William W. Hallo. 3:201. Leiden: Brill, 2003.

Henrichs, A., H. Henrichs, and L. Koenen, "Der Kölner Mani-Kodex (P. Colon inv. Nr. 4780) Περὶ τῆς γέννης τοῦ σώματος αὐτοῦ: Edition der seiten 1–72." *ZPE* 19 (1975): 1–85.

Herodotus. *Books 1-9*. Translated by A. D. Godley. LCL 117–120. Cambridge: Harvard University Press, 1922–1969.

Herr, Larry G. *The Scripts of Ancient Northwest Semitic Seals*. HSM 18. Missoula: Scholars Press, 1978.

Hesiod. *Theogony*; *Works and Days*; *Testimonia*. Edited and translated by Glenn W. Most. LCL 57. Cambridge: Harvard University Press, 2006.

Hoffner, Harry A. *Hittite Myths*. Edited by G. Beckman. Writings from the Ancient World 2. Atlanta: Scholars Press, 1998.

Hoffner, Harry A. *Letters from the Hittite Kingdom*. Edited by G. Beckman. Writings from the Ancient World 15. Atlanta: Society of Biblical Literature, 2009.

Hoftijzer, Jacob, and Karel Jongeling. *Dictionary of the North-West Semitic Inscriptions*. Leiden: Brill, 1995.

Holladay, John S. "Religion in Israel and Judah under the Monarchy: an Explicitly Archaeological Approach." In *Ancient Israelite Religion: Essays in Honor of Frank Moore Cross*. Edited by Patrick D. Miller, Paul D. Hanson, and S. Dean McBride. 249–299. Philadelphia: Fortress, 1987.

Holloway, Steven W. *Aššur is King! Aššur is King!: Religion in the Exercise of Power in the Neo-Assyrian Empire*. CHANE 10. Leiden: Brill, 2002.

Hornung, Erik. *Conceptions of God in Ancient Egypt*. Translated by J. Baines. Ithaca: Cornell University Press, 1982.

Horowitz, Wayne. *Mesopotamian Cosmic Geography*. Mesopotamian Civilizations 8. Winona Lake: Eisenbrauns, 1998.

Hoskisson, Paul Y. "The Scission and Ascendancy of a Goddess: Dīrītum at Mari." In *Go to the Land I will show you: Studies in Honor of Dwight W. Young*. Edited by J. Coleson and V. Matthews. 261–266. Winona Lake: Eisenbrauns, 1996.

Houwink ten Cate, Philo H. J. "The Hittite Storm God: His Role and his Rule According to Hittite Cuneiform Sources." In *Natural Phenomena: Their Meaning, Depiction, and Description in the Ancient Near East*. Edited by D. J. W. Meijer. 83–148. Amsterdam: North-Holland, 1992.

Hundley, Michael. Review of *Reconsidering the Concept of Revolutionary Monotheism*, by Beate Pongratz-Leisten, ed. *RBL* (http://www.bookreviews.org) (2012): 4.

Hundley, Michael. *Gods in Dwellings: Temples and Divine Presence in the Ancient Near East*. Edited by Amélie Kuhrt. Writings from the Ancient World Supplement Series 3. Atlanta: Society of Biblical Literature, 2002.

Hundley, Michael."Here a God, There a God: Conceptions of the Divine in Ancient Mesopotamia." AoF 40 (2013): 68–107.

Hunger, Hermann. *Astrological Reports to Assyrian Kings*. SAA 8. Helsinki: Helsinki University Press, 1992.

Hurowitz, Victor, and Joan Goodnick Westenholz. "LKA 63: A Heroic Poem in Celebration of Tiglath-Pileser I's Musru-Qumanu Campaign." *JCS* 42 (1990): 1–49.

Hutton, Jeremy. "Local Manifestations of Yahweh and Worship in the Interstices: A Note on Kuntillet 'Ajrud." *JANER* 10 (2010): 177–210.

Jackson, Kent P. *The Ammonite Language of the Iron Age*. HSM 27. Chico: Scholars Press, 1983.

Jackson, Kent P. "The Language of the Mesha Inscription." In *Studies in the Mesha Inscription and Moab*. Edited by Andrew J. Dearman. Archaeology and Biblical Studies 2. 96–130. Atlanta: Scholars Press, 1989.

Jacobsen, Thorkild. *Toward the Image of Tammuz and Other Essays on Mesopotamian History and Culture*. Edited by W. Moran. HSS 21. Cambridge: Harvard University Press, 1970.

Jacobsen, Thorkild. *The Treasures of Darkness: A History of Mesopotamian Religion*. New Haven: Yale University Press, 1976.

Jacobsen, Thorkild. "The Graven Image." In *Ancient Israelite Religion: Essays in Honor of Frank Moore Cross*. Edited by Patrick D. Miller, Paul D. Hanson, and S. Dean McBride. 15–32. Philadelphia: Fortress, 1987.

Jacobsen, Thorkild. *The Harps that Once...Sumerian Poetry in Translation*. New Haven: Yale University Press, 1987.

Japhet, Sara. *I & II Chronicles: A Commentary*. Old Testament Library. Louisville: Westminster/John Knox Press, 1993.

Joannès, Francis. "Le traité de vassalité d'Atamrum d'Andarig envers Zimri-Lim de Mari." In *Marchands, Diplomates et Empereurs: Etudes sur la civilization mésopotamienne offertes à Paul Garelli*. Edited by D. Charpin and F. Joannès. 167–177. Paris: Éditions Recherche sur les Civilisations, 1991.

Joannès, Francis. "Les Temples de Sippar et Leurs Trésors a l'Époque Néo-Babylonienne." *RA* 86 (1992): 159–184.

Johns, C. H. W. *Assyrian Deeds and Documents*. 4 vols. Cambridge: Deighton, Bell and Co., 1898–1923.

Johnson, Elizabeth A. "Saints and Mary." In *Systematic Theology: Roman Catholic Perspectives*. Edited by F. Schüssler Fiorenza and J. Galvin. 2:145–177. Minneapolis: Fortress Press, 1991.

Josephus. *The Life*; *Against Apion*. Translated by H. St. J. Thackery. LCL 186. Cambridge: Harvard University Press, 1997.

Kataja, Laura, and R. M. Whiting. *Grants, Decrees and Gifts of the Neo-Assyrian Period*. SAA 12. Helsinki: Helsinki University Press, 1995.

Kaizer, Ted. "Identifying the Divine in the Roman Near East." In Panthée: *Religious Transformations in the Graeco-Roman Empire*. Edited by Laurent Bricault and Corinne Bonnet. Religions in the Graeco-Roman World 177. 113–128. Leiden: Brill, 2013.

Keel, Othmar, and Christoph Uehlinger. *Gods, Goddesses, and Images of God in Ancient Israel*. Translated by T. H. Trapp. Minneapolis: Fortress, 1998.

Keilschrifttexte aus Boghazköi. WVDOG 30, 36, 68–70, 72, 73, 77–80, 82–86, 89–90. Leipzig, 1916–1980.

Keilschrifturkunden aus Boghazköi. Berlin: Akademie-Verlag, 1921ff.

King, Leonard W. *Babylonian Magic and Sorcery*: *Being "The Prayers of the Lifting of the Hand*." London: Luzac and Company, 1896.

Kitchen, Kenneth A. *Ramesside Inscriptions*: *Translated & Annotated*: *Translations*. Vol. 2. Oxford: Blackwell Publishers, 1996.

Kitchen, Kenneth A. *Ramesside Inscriptions*: *Translated & Annotated*: *Notes and Comments*. Vol. 2. Oxford: Blackwell Publishers, 1999.

Knauf, Ernst A. "Meunum." In *Anchor Bible Dictionary*. Edited by David Noel Freedman. 4:801–802. New York: Doubleday, 1992.

Knudtzon, Jörgen A. *Die El-Amarna-Tafeln mit Einleitung und Erläuterungen*. Aalen: Otto Zeller, 1964.

Koch, Klaus. "Baal Ṣapon, Baal Šamem and the Critique of Israel's Prophets." In *Ugarit and the Bible*: *Proceedings of the International Symposium on Ugarit and the Bible*: *Manchester*, *September 1992*. Edited by G. J. Brooke, A. H. W. Curtis, and J. F. Healey. Ugaritisch-biblische Literatur 11. 159–174. Münster: Ugarit-Verlag, 1994.

Koch, Klaus. "Jahwäs Übersiedlung vom Wüstenberg nach Kanaan: Zur Herkunft von Israels Gottesverständnis." In "*Und Mose Schreib dieses Lied auf*": *Studien zum Alten Testament und zum alten Orient*: *Festschrift für Oswald Loretz zur vollendung seines 70. Lebensjahres mit Beiträgen von Freunden*, *Schülern*, *und Kollegen*. 437–474. Münster: Ugarit-Verlag, 1998.

Koch-Westenholz, Ulla. *Mesopotamian Astrology*: *an Introduction to Babylonian and Assyrian Celestial Divination*. CNI Publications 19. Denmark: Museum Tusculanum Press, 1995.

Köcher, Franz. *Die babylonisch-assyrische Medizin in Texten und Untersuchungen*. 7 vols. Berlin: W. De Gruyter, 1963ff.

Köcher, Franz, and A. Leo. Oppenheim. "The Old Babylonian Omen Text VAT 7525." *AfO* 18 (1957): 62–77.

Köcher, Franz, and L. Rost. *Literarische Keilschrifttexte aus Assur*. Berlin: Akademie-Verlag, 1953.

Kotter, Wade. "Beth-Dagon." In *Anchor Bible Dictionary*. Edited by David Noel Freedman. 1:683. New York: Doubleday, 1992.

Kraut, Judah. "Deciphering the Shema: Staircase Parallelism and the Syntax of Deuteronomy 6:4." *VT* 61 (2011): 582–602.

Kselman, John. S. "Janus Parallelism in Psalm 75:2." *JBL* 121 (2002): 531–532.

Kuhrt, Amélie. *The Ancient Near East*: *c. 3000-330 BC*. 2 vols. London: Routledge, 1998.

Kutscher, Raphael. *The Brockmon Tablets at the University of Haifa*: *Royal Inscriptions*. Shay series of the Zinman Institute of Archaeology. Haifa: Haifa University Press, 1989.

Kwasman, Theodore. *Neo-Assyrian Legal Documents in the Kouyunjik Collection of the British Museum*. Rome: Eitrice Pontificio Istituto Biblico, 1988.

Kwasman, Theodore, and Simo Parpola. *Legal Transactions of the Royal Court of Nineveh, Part I: Tiglath-Pileser III through Esarhaddon*. SAA 6. Helsinki: Helsinki University Press, 1991.

Lambert, Wilfred G. *Babylonian Wisdom Literature*. Oxford: Clarendon, 1960.

Lambert, Wilfred G. "Götterlisten." *RlA* 3/6 (1969): 473–479.

Lambert, Wilfred G. "The Historical Development of the Mesopotamian Pantheon: A Study in Sophisticated Polytheism." In *Unity and Diversity: Essays in the history, literature, and religion of the ancient Near East*. Edited by H. Goedicke and J. J. M. Roberts. 191–200. Baltimore: Johns Hopkins University Press, 1975.

Lambert, Wilfred G. "The God Aššur." *Iraq* 45 (1983): 82–86.

Lambert, Wilfred G. "Ancient Mesopotamian Gods: Superstition, Philosophy, Theology," *Révue de l'histoire religions* 207 (1990): 115–130.

Lambert, Wilfred G. "Syncretism and Religious Controversy in Babylonia." AoF 24 (1997): 158–162.

Lambert, Wilfred G. "Ištar of Nineveh." *Iraq* 66 (2004): 35–39.

Landsberger, B., and K. Balkan. "Die Inschrift des assyrischen Königs Īrișum, gefunden in Kültepe 1948." *Belleten* 14 (1950): 171–268.

Laroche, Emmanuel. "Le Panthéon de Yazilikaya." *JCS* 6 (1952): 115–123.

Laroche, Emmanuel. "Le Dieu Anatolien Sarrumma." *Syria* 40 (1963): 277–302.

Laroche, Emmanuel. *Catalogue des Textes Hittites*. Etudes et commentaries 75. Paris: Klincksiech, 1971.

Laroche, Emmanuel. "Panthéon national et pantheons locaux chez les Hourttites." *Or* NS 45 (1976): 94–99.

Lebrun, Rene. *Samuha: Foyer religieux de l'empire Hittite*. Louvian-la-Neuve: Institut Orientaliste, 1976.

Leemans, Wilhelmus François. *Ishtar of Lagaba and her Dress*. Studia ad tabulas cuneiformas callectas a F.M.Th. de Liagre Böhl pertinentia 1/1. Leiden: Brill, 1953.

Leichty, Erle. *Royal Inscriptions of Esarhaddon, King of Assyrian (680-669)*. RINAP 4. Winona Lake: Eisenbrauns, 2011.

Lemaire, André. "Prières en temps de crise: Les inscriptions de Khirbet Beit Lei." *RB* 83 (1976): 558–568.

Lemaire, André. "Outlook: Aramaeans Outside of Syria: Anatolia." In *The Aramaeans in Ancient Syria*. Edited by Herbert Niehr. 319–328. HdO 106. Leiden: Brill, 2014.

Lesko, Leonard H. "Ancient Egyptian Cosmogonies and Cosmology. In *Religion in Ancient Egypt: Gods, Myths, and Personal Practice*. Edited by Byron E. Shafer. 88–122. Ithaca: Cornell University Press, 1991.

Levenson, Jon D. *Sinai & Zion: An Entry into the Jewish Bible*. San Francisco: HarperCollins, 1985.

Lewis, Theodore J. "The Identity and Function of El/Baal Berith." *JBL* 115 (1996): 401–423.

Lipiński, Edward. *Studies in Aramaic Inscriptions and Onomastics II*. OLA 57. Leuven: Peeters, 1994.

Lipiński, Edward. *Dieux et Déesses de l'univers Phénicien et Punique*. OLA 64. Leuven: Peeters, 1995.

Lipiński, Edward. "צפון *ṣāp̱ôn*; צפוני *ṣᵉp̱ônî*." In *Theological Dictionary of the Old Testament*. Edited by G. Johannes Botterweck, Helmer Ringgren, and Heinz-Josef Fabry. Translated by John T. Willis. 12:435–443. Grand Rapids: Eerdmans, 1974 ff.

Lipiński, Edward. *The Aramaeans: Their Ancient History, Culture, Religion*. OLA 1000. Leuven: Peeters, 2000.

Litke, Richard L. *A Reconstruction of the Assyro-Babylonian God-lists, AN: ᵈA-NU-UM and AN: ANU ŠÁ AMĒLI*. Texts from the Babylonian Collection 3. New Haven: Yale Babylonian Collection, 1998.

Liverani, Mario. *International Relations in the Ancient Near East, 1600-1100 B.C.* New York: Palgrave, 2001.

Livingstone, Alasdair. *Mystical and Mythological Explanatory Works of Assyrian and Babylonian Scholars*. Oxford: Clarendon Press, 1986.

Livingstone, Alasdair. *Court Poetry and Literary Miscellanea*. SAA 3. Helsinki: Neo-Assyrian Text Corpus Project, 1989.

Livingstone, Alasdair. "New Dimensions in the Study of Assyrian Religion." In *Assyria 1995: Proceedings of the 10th Anniversary Symposium of the Neo-Assyrian Text Corpus Project, Helsinki, September 7–11, 1995*. Edited by Simo Parpola and R. M. Whiting. 165–177. Helsinki: Neo-Assyrian Text Corpus Project, 1997.

Lloyd-Jones, Hugh. "Ancient Greek Religion." In *Proceedings of the American Philosophical Society* 145. 456–464. Philadelphia: The American Philosophical Society, 2001.

Lozachmeur, Hélène. *La Collection Clermont-Genneau: Ostraca, épigraphs sur jarred, étiquettes de bois*. 2 vols. Paris: Diffusion de Boccard, 2006.

Longo, Bartolo. *Storia del santuario di Pompei*. Vol 1. Pompei: Pontificio santuario di Pompei, 1890.

Lubetski, Meir. "Beth-Anath." In *Anchor Bible Dictionary*. Edited by David Noel Freedman. 1:680–681. New York: Doubleday, 1992.

Luckenbill, Daniel D. *Ancient Records of Assyria and Babylonia*. 2 vols. Chicago: University of Chicago Press, 1926–1927.

Luckenbill, Daniel D. *The Annals of Sennacherib*. Reprint. Eugene: Wipf & Stock Publishers, 2005.

Luft, U. H. "Religion." *The Oxford Encyclopedia of Ancient Egypt*. Edited by Donald Redford. 3:139–145. Oxford: Oxford University Press, 2001.

Luukko, Mikko, and Greta van Buylaere. *The Political Correspondence of Esarhaddon*. SAA 16. Helsinki: Helsinki University Press, 2002.

Lyon, D. G. *Keilschrifttext Sargon's Königs von Assyrien (722–705 v. Chr.) nach den Orginalen neu herausgegeben, umschrieben, üebersetzt und erklärt*. Assyriologische Bibliothek 5. Leipzig: J. C. Hinrichs, 1883.

Macqueen, J. G. "Hattian Mythology and Hittite Monarchy." *AnSt* 9 (1959): 171–188.

Macqueen, J. G. "Nerik and its Weather God." *AnSt* 30 (1980): 179–187.

Markus, Robert. "How on Earth Could Places Become Holy?" *Journal of Early Christian Studies* 2 (1994): 257–271.

Mastin, Brian A. "The Inscriptions Written on Plaster at Kuntillet 'Ajrud." *VT* 59 (2009): 99–115.

Mattila, Raija. *Legal Transactions of the Royal Court of Nineveh, Part II: Assurbanipal Through Sin-šarru-iškun*. SAA 14. Helsinki: Helsinki University Press, 2002.

Mattingly, Gerald L. "Moabite Religion and the Mesha' Inscription." In *Studies in the Mesha Inscription and Moab*. Edited by Andrew J. Dearman. Archaeology and Biblical Studies 2. 211–238. Atlanta: Scholars Press, 1989.

Mayes, Andrew D. H. "Kuntillet 'Ajrud and the History of Israelite Religion." In *Archaeology and Biblical Interpretation*. Edited J. R. Bartlett. 51–66. London: Routledge, 1997.

McBrien, Richard P. *Catholicism*. 2 vols. Minneapolis: Winston Press, 1980.

McCarter, P. Kyle. "Aspects of the Religion of the Israelite Monarchy: Biblical and Epigraphic Data." In *Ancient Israelite Religion: Essays in Honor of Frank Moore Cross*. Edited by Patrick D. Miller, Paul D. Hanson, and S. Dean McBride. 137–155. Philadelphia: Fortress, 1987.

McMahon, Gregory. *The Hittite State Cult of the Tutelary Deities*. AS 25. Chicago: The Oriental Institute of the University of Chicago, 1991.

Medica, Giacomo. *I santuari mariani d'Italia*. Torino: Leumann, 1965.

Meinhold, Wiebke. *Ištar in Aššur: Untersuchung eines Lokalkultes von ca. 2500 bis 614 v. Chr.* AOAT 367. Münster: Ugarit-Verlag, 2009.

Menzel, Brigitte. *Assyrische Tempel*. Studia Pohl. Series maior 10. 2 vols. Rome: Biblical Institute, 1981.

Meshel, Zeev. "Did Yahweh Have a Consort? The New Religious Inscriptions from the Sinai." *BAR* 5, no. 2 (1979): 24–34.

Meshel, Zeev. "Kuntillet 'Ajrud." In *Anchor Bible Dictionary*. Edited by David Noel Freedman. 4:103–109. New York: Doubleday, 1992.

Meshel, Zeev. ed. *Kuntillet 'Ajrud (Ḥorvat Teman): An Iron Age II Religious Site on the Judah-Sinai Border*. Jerusalem: Israel Exploration Society, 2012.

Meshel, Zeev. "The Nature of the Site and its Biblical Background." In *Kuntillet 'Ajrud (Ḥorvat Teman): An Iron Age II Religious Site on the Judah-Sinai Border*. Edited by Ze'ev Meshel. 65–69. Jerusalem: Israel Exploration Society, 2012.

Mettinger, Tryggve. "YHWH Sabaoth – The Heavenly King on the Cherubim Throne." In *Studies in the Period of David and Solomon and other Essays: Papers Read at the International Symposium for Biblical Studies, Tokyo, 5-7 December, 1979*. Edited by T. Ishida. 109–138. Winona Lake: Eisenbrauns, 1979.

Mettinger, Tryggve. *The Dethronement of Sabaoth: Studies in the Shem and Kabod Theologies*. Translated by F. Cryer. Coniectanea biblica. Old Testament Series 18. Lund: Willin & Dalholm, 1982.

Mettinger, Tryggve. *In Search of God: the Meaning and Message of the Everlasting Names*. Translated by F. Cryer. Philadelphia: Fortress Press, 1988.

Mettinger, Tryggve. "Yahweh Zebaoth." In *Dictionary of Deities and Demons in the Bible*. Edited by Karel van der Toorn, Bob Becking, and Pieter W. van der Horst. 2nd rev. ed. 920–924. Leiden: Brill, 1999.

Michalowski, Piotr. "The Earliest Hurrian Toponymy: A New Sargonic Inscription." *ZA* 76 (1986): 4–11.

Michalowski, Piotr. "Memory and Deed: The Historiography of the Political Expansion of the Akkad State." In *Akkad: The First World Empire: Structure, Ideology, Traditions*. Edited by M. Liverani. HANES 5. 69–90. Pavoda: Sargon, 1993.

Milgrom, Jacob. *Numbers: The Traditional Hebrew Text with the New JPS Translation*. JPS Torah Commentary 4. Philadelphia: Jewish Publication Society, 1990.

Millar, Fergus. *The Roman Near East: 31 BC–AD 337*. Cambridge: Harvard University Press, 1995.

Miller, Jared L. *Studies in the Origins, Development and Interpretation of the Kizzuwatna Rituals*. STBoT 46. Wiesbaden: Harrassowitz, 2004.

Miller, Jared L. "Setting up the Goddess of the Night Separately." In *Anatolian Interfaces: Hittites, Greeks, and their Neighbors: Proceedings of an International Conference on Cross-cultural Interaction, September 17–19, 2004, Emory University, Atlanta, GA*. Edited by Billie Jean Collins, Mary R. Bachvarova, and Ian Rutherford. 67–72. Oxford: Oxbow Books, 2008.

Miller, Patrick D., Paul D. Hanson, and S. Dean McBride, eds. *Ancient Israelite Religion: Essays in Honor of Frank Moore Cross*. Philadelphia: Fortress, 1987.

Mittelassyrische Rechtsurkunden und Verwaltungstexte. Vorderasiatische Schriftdenkmäler der Staatlichen Museen zu Berlin 3, etc. Berlin: Akademie-Verlag, 1976–1982.

Mitteilungen der Vorderasiatisch-Aegyptischen Gesellschaft. Vols. 1–44. 1896–1939.

Moberly, R. W. L. "'Yahweh is One': The Translation of the Shema." In *Studies in the Pentateuch*. Edited by J. A. Emerton. Supplements to Vetus Testamentum 41. 209–215. Leiden: Brill, 1990.

de Moor, Johannes. C. "The Semitic Pantheon of Ugarit." *UF* 2 (1970): 196–226.

de Moor, Johannes. C. "בעל ba'al: I-II." In *Theological Dictionary of the Old Testament*. Edited by G. Johannes Botterweck, Helmer Ringgren, and Heinz-Josef Fabry. 2:181–192. Grand Rapids: Eerdmans, 1974 ff.

Moran, William. *The Amarna Letters*. Baltimore: Johns Hopkins University Press, 1992.

Murphy, Roldand E., and O. Carm. "A Fragment of an Early Moabite Inscription from Dibon." *BASOR* 125 (1952): 20–23.

Myers, Jennie. "The Pantheon at Sippar: A Diachronic Study." Ph.D. diss., Harvard University, 2002.

Na'aman, Nadav. "No Anthropomorphic Graven Image: Notes on the Assumed Anthropomorphic Cult Statues in the Temples of *YHWH* in the Pre-Exilic Period." *UF* 31 (1999): 391–415.

Nakata, Ichiro. "Deities in the Mari Texts: Complete Inventory of All the Information on the Deities Found in the Published Old Babylonian Cuneiform Texts from Mari." Ph.D. diss., Columbia University, 1974.

Naveh, Jospeh. "Old Hebrew Inscriptions in a Burial Cave." *IEJ* 13 (1963): 74–93.

Naveh, Jospeh. "Hebrew Graffiti from the First Temple Period." *IEJ* 51 (2001): 194–207.

Niehr, Herbert. "The Rise of YHWH in Judahite and Israelite Religion." In *The Triumph of Elohim: From Yahwisms to Judaisms*. Edited by D. V. Edelman. 45–72. Grand Rapids: Eerdmans, 1995.

Niehr, Herbert. *Ba'alšamem: Studien zu Herkunft, Geschitchte und Rezeptionsgeschichte eines phönizischen Gottes*. OLA 123. Leuven: Peeters, 2003.

Niehr, Herbert. ed. *The Aramaeans in Ancient Syria*. HdO 106. Leiden: Brill, 2014.

del Olmo Lete, Gregorio. *Canaanite Religion: According to the Liturgical Texts of Ugarit*. Translated by Wilfred G. E. Watson. 2nd rev. ed. Bethesda: CDL 1999.

del Olmo Lete, Gregorio. "The Ugaritic Ritual Texts: A New Edition and Commentary. A Critical Assessment." *UF* 36 (2004): 539–648.

Olyan, Saul M. *Asherah and the Cult of Yahweh in Israel*. SBL Monograph Series 34. Atlanta: Scholars Press, 1988.

Oppenheim, A. Leo. "Idiomatic Accadian (Lexicographical Researches)." *JAOS* 61 (1941): 251–271.

Pardee, Dennis. "The Ba'lu Myth (1.86)." In *The Context of Scripture: Canonical Compositions from the Biblical World*. Edited by William W. Hallo. 1:241–274. Leiden: Brill, 2003.

Pardee, Dennis. "The Kirta Epic (1.102)." In *The Context of Scripture: Canonical Compositions from the Biblical World*. Edited by William W. Hallo. 1:333–343. Leiden: Brill, 2003.

Pardee, Dennis. *Ritual and Cult at Ugarit*. Edited by T. J. Lewis. Writings from the Ancient World 10. Atlanta: Society of Biblical Literature, 2002.

Parpola, Simo. *The Correspondence of Sargon II, Part I: Letters from Assyria and the West*. SAA 1. Helsinki: Helsinki University Press, 1987.

Parpola, Simo. *Letters from Assyrian and Babylonian Scholars*. SAA 10. Helsinki: Helsinki University Press, 1993.
Parpola, Simo. "The Assyrian Cabinet." In *Vom Alten Orient zum Alten Testament: Festschrift für Wolfram Freiherrn von Soden zum 85. Geburtstag am 19. Juni 1993*. Edited by M. Dietrich and O. Loretz. AOAT 240. 379–401. Kevelaer: Verlag Butzon & Bercker, 1995.
Parpola, Simo. *Assyrian Prophecies*. SAA 9. Helsinki: Helsinki University Press, 1997.
Parpola, Simo. "Monotheism in Ancient Assyria." In *One God or Many? Concepts of Divinity in the Ancient World*. Edited by Barbara N. Porter. Transactions of the Casco Bay Assyriological Institute 1. 165–209. Casco Bay Assyriological Institute, 2000.
Parpola, Simo, and Kazuko Watanabe. *Neo-Assyrian Treaties and Loyalty Oaths*. SAA 2. Helsinki: Helsinki University Press, 1988.
Parpola, Simo, and R. M. Whiting, eds. *Assyria 1995: Proceedings of the 10th Anniversary Symposium of the Neo-Assyrian Text Corpus Project, Helsinki, September 7–11, 1995*. Helsinki: Neo-Assyrian Text Corpus Project, 1997.
Paul, Shalom. *Amos: A Commentary on the Book of Amos*. Hermeneia. Minneapolis: Fortress Press, 1991.
Percival, H. R. "The Decree of the Holy, Great, Ecumenical Synod, the Second of Nice." In *The Seven Ecumenical Councils of the Undivided Church: Their Canons and Dogmatic Decrees, Together with the Canons of all the Local Synods which have Received Ecumenical Acceptance*. Edited by P. Schaff and H. Wace. NPNF 14. 549–551. Grand Rapids: Eerdmans, 1983.
Pettinato, Giovanni. *Testi Amministrativi della Biblioteca L. 2769*. Vol 1. Naples: Istituto Universitario Orientale, 1980.
Pettinato, Giovanni. *The Archives of Ebla: An Empire Inscribed in Clay*. New York: Doubleday, 1981.
Pfeiffer, Robert H., and Ephraim A. Speiser. *One Hundred New Selected Nuzi Texts*. AASOR 16. New Haven: ASOR, 1936.
Pomponio, Francesco, and Paolo Xella. *Les dieux d'Ebla: Étude analytique des divinités éblaïtes à l'époque des archives royales due IIIe millénaire*. AOAT 245. Münster: Ugarit-Verlag, 1997.
Pongratz-Leisten, Beate. Ina Šulmi Īrub: *die Kulttopographische und ideologische Programmatik der akītu-Prozession in Babylonien und Assyrien im 1. Jahrtausend v. Chr.* Baghdader Forschungen 16. Hainz am Rhein: Philipp von Zabern, 1994.
Pongratz-Leisten, Beate. "The Interplay of Military Strategy and Cultic Practice in Assyrian Politics." In *Assyria 1995: Proceedings of the 10th Anniversary Symposium of the Neo-Assyrian Text Corpus Project, Helsinki, September 7–11, 1995*. Edited by Simo Parpola and R. M. Whiting. 254–252. Helsinki: Neo-Assyrian Text Corpus Project, 1997.
Pongratz-Leisten, Beate. *Herrschaftswissen in Mesopotamien: Former der Kommunikation zwischen Gott und König im 2. und 1. Jahrtausend v. Chr.* SAAS 10. Helsinki: The Neo-Assyrian Text Corpus Project, 1999.
Pongratz-Leisten, Beate. "When the Gods are Speaking: Toward Defining the Interface between Polytheism and Monotheism." In *Propheten in Mari, Assyrien und Israel*. Edited by Matthias Köckert and Martti Nissinen. FRLANT 201. 132–168. Göttingen: Vandenhoeck & Ruprecht, 2003.
Pongratz-Leisten, Beate. "Reflections on the Translatability of the Notion of Holiness." In *Of God(s), Trees, Kings, and Scholars: Neo-Assyrian and Related Studies in Honour of Simo Parpola*. Edited by Mikko Luukko, Saana Svärd, and Raija Mattila. Studia Orientalia 106. 409–427. Helsinki: Finnish Oriental Society, 2009.

Pongratz-Leisten, Beate, ed. *Reconsidering the Concept of Revolutionary Monotheism.* Winona Lake: Eisenbrauns, 2011.

Pongratz-Leisten, Beate. "A New Agenda for the Study of the Rise of Monotheism." In *Reconsidering the Concept of Revolutionary Monotheism*. Edited by Beate Pongratz-Leisten. 1–40. Winona Lake: Eisenbrauns, 2011.

Pongratz-Leisten, Beate. "Divine Agency and Astralization of the Gods in Ancient Mesopotamia." In *Reconsidering the Concept of Revolutionary Monotheism*. Edited by Beate Pongratz-Leisten. 137–187. Winona Lake: Eisenbrauns, 2011.

Pongratz-Leisten, Beate. "Comments on the Translatability of Divinity: Cultic and Theological Responses to the Presence of the Other in the Ancient Near East." In *Les représentations des dieux autres*. Supplemento a Mythos 2. Rivista di Storia delle Religioni. Edited by Corinne Bonnet, Amandine Declercq, and Iwo Slobodzianek. 83–111. Caltanisseta: Salvatore Sciascia Editore, 2012.

Pope, Marvin, and Jeffrey H. Tigay, "A Description of Baal." *UF* 3 (1971): 117–130.

Popko, Maciej. "Zum Tempel des Teššup von Ḫalap in Ḫattuša." AoF 29 (2002): 73–80.

Porten, Bezalel. *Archives from Elephantine: The Life of an Ancient Jewish Military Colony.* Berkeley: University of California Press, 1968.

Porten, Bezalel, and Ada Yardeni. *Textbook of Aramaic Documents from Ancient Egypt: Newly Copied, Edited and Translated into Hebrew and English.* 4 vols. Jerusalem: Hebrew University, Department of the History of the Jewish People, 1986–1999.

Porter, Barbara N. "What the Assyrians Thought the Babylonians Thought about the Relative Status of Nabû and Marduk in the Late Assyrian Period." In *Assyria 1995: Proceedings of the 10th Anniversary Symposium of the Neo-Assyrian Text Corpus Project, Helsinki, September 7–11, 1995.* Edited by Simo Parpola and R. M. Whiting. 253–260. Helsinki: Neo-Assyrian Text Corpus Project, 1997.

Porter, Barbara N., ed. *One God or Many? Concepts of Divinity in the Ancient World.* Transactions of the Casco Bay Assyriological Institute 1. Casco Bay Assyriological Institute, 2000.

Porter, Barbara N. "The Anxiety of Multiplicity: Concepts of Divinity as One and Many in Ancient Assyria," In *One God or Many? Concepts of Divinity in the Ancient World.* Edited by Barbara N. Porter. Transactions of the Casco Bay Assyriological Institute 1. 211–271. Casco Bay Assyriological Institute, 2000.

Porter, Barbara N. "Ishtar of Nineveh and Her Collaborator, Ishtar of Arbela, in the Reign of Assurbanipal." *Iraq* 66 (2004): 41–44.

Porter, Barbara N., ed. *What is a God? Anthropomorphic and Non-Anthropomorphic Aspects of Deity in Ancient Mesopotamia.* Transactions of the Casco Bay Assyriological Institute 2. Winona Lake: Casco Bay Assyriological Institute, 2009.

Porter, Barbara N. "Introduction." In *What is a God? Anthropomorphic and Non-Anthropomorphic Aspects of Deity in Ancient Mesopotamia.* Edited by Barbara N. Porter. Transactions of the Casco Bay Assyriological Institute 2. 1–13. Winona Lake: Casco Bay Assyriological Institute, 2009.

Porter, Barbara N. "Blessings from a Crown, Offerings to a Drum: Were There Non-Anthropomorphic Deities in Ancient Mesopotamia?" In *What is a God? Anthropomorphic and Non-Anthropomorphic Aspects of Deity in Ancient Mesopotamia.* Edited by Barbara N. Porter. Transactions of the Casco Bay Assyriological Institute 2. 153–194. Winona Lake: Casco Bay Assyriological Institute, 2009.

Postgate, J. N. "Kurba'il." *RlA* 6/5–6 (1983): 367–368.

Pritchard, James B. *The Ancient Near East in Pictures Relating to the Old Testament.* Princeton: Princeton University Press, 1954.

Pritchard, James B. *Ancient Near Eastern Texts Relating to the Old Testament.* 3rd rev. ed. with supplement. Princeton: Princeton University Press, 1969.

Pritchard, James B. *Recovering Sarepta, A Phoenician City: Excavations at Sarafund, Lebanon, 1969–1974, by the University Museum of the University of Pennsylvania.* Princeton: Princeton University Press, 1978.

The Prosopography of the Neo-Assyrian Empire. Vols. 1/1–3/1. Finland: Neo-Assyrian Text Corpus Project, 1998–2002.

Provitera, Gino. "L'edicola votive e le sue funzioni." In *Questione meridionale, religione, e classi subalterne.* Edited by F. Saija. 337–345. Napoli: Guida, 1978.

Publications of the Babylonian Section, University Museum, University of Pennsylvania. 16 vols. Philadelphia: University Museum, 1911–1930.

von Rad, Gerhard. *Deuteronomy: A Commentary.* Translated by Dorothea Barton. Old Testament Library. Philadelphia: Westminster, 1966.

Radner, Karen. "The Assur-Nineveh-Arbela Triangle: Central Assyria in the Neo-Assyrian Period." In *Between the Cultures: The Central Tigris Region from the 3rd to the 1st Millennium BC: Conference at Heidelberg, January 22nd–24th, 2009.* Edited by Peter Miglus and Simone Mühl. HSAO 14. 321–329. Heidelberg: Heidelberger Orientverlag, 2011.

Radner, Karen. "The Neo-Assyrian Empire." In *Imperien und Reiche in der Weltgeschichte: Epochenübergreifende und globalhistorische Vergleiche, Teil 1: Imperien des Altertums, Mittelalterliche und frühneuzeitliche Imperien.* Edited by M. Gehler and R. Rollinger. 101–120. Wiesbaden: Harrassowitz Verlag, 2014.

Rahmouni, Aicha. *Divine Epithets in the Ugaritic Alphabetic Texts.* Translated by J. N. Ford. HdO 93. Leiden: Brill, 2008.

Reade, Julian. "The Ziggurrat and Temples of Nimrud." *Iraq* 64 (2002): 135–216.

Reade, Julian. "The Ištar Temple at Nineveh." *Iraq* 67 (2005): 347–390.

Redford, Donald B. Review of "Conceptions of God in Ancient Egypt: The One and the Many," by Erik Hornung, translated by John Baines. *American Historical Review* 88 (1983): 1250–1251.

Redford, Donald B. *Egypt, Canaan, and Israel in Ancient Times.* Princeton: Princeton University Press, 1992.

Redmount, Carol. "Bitter Lives: Israel in and out of Egypt." In *The Oxford History of the Biblical World.* Edited by M. Coogan. 58–89. Oxford: Oxford University Press, 2001.

Reiner, Erica. "A Sumero-Akkadian Hymn of Nanâ." *JNES* 33 (1974): 221–236.

Reynolds, Frances. S. *The Babylonian Correspondence of Esarhaddon and Letters to Assurbanipal and Sin-šarru-iškun from Northern and Central Babylonia.* SAA 18. Helsinki: Helsinki University Press, 2003.

de' Ricci, Scipinoe. *Memorie di Scipinoe de'Ricci: Vescovo di Prato e Pistoia.* Vol 2. Florence: Felice Le Monnier, 1865.

Richter, Daniel S. *Cosmopolis: Imagining Community in Late Classical Athens and the Early Roman Empire.* Oxford: Oxford University Press, 2011.

Roberts, J. J. M. *The Earliest Semitic Pantheon: A Study of the Semitic Deities Attested in Mesopotamia before Ur III.* Baltimore: Johns Hopkins University Press, 1972.

Rochberg, Francesca. "Personifications and Metaphors in Babylonian Celestial Omina." *JAOS* 116 (1996): 475–485.

Rochberg, Francesca. *The Heavenly Writing: Divination: Divination, Horoscopy, and Astronomy in Mesopotamian Culture*. Cambridge: Cambridge University Press, 2004.

Rochberg, Francesca. "'The Stars Their Likenesses': Perspectives on the Relation Between Celestial Bodies and Gods in Ancient Mesopotamia." In *What is a God? Anthropomorphic and Non-Anthropomorphic Aspects of Deity in Ancient Mesopotamia*. Edited by Barbara N. Porter. Transactions of the Casco Bay Assyriological Institute 2. 41–91. Winona Lake: Casco Bay Assyriological Institute, 2009.

Rochberg, Francesca. "The Heavens and the Gods in Ancient Mesopotamia: The View from a Polytheistic Cosmology." In *Reconsidering the Concept of Revolutionary Monotheism*. Edited by Beate Pongratz-Leisten. 117–136. Winona Lake: Eisenbrauns, 2011.

Rohrmoser, Angela. *Götter, Tempel und Kult der Judäo-Aramäer von Elephantine: Archäologische und schrftliche Zeugnisse aus dem persezeitlichen Ägypten*. AOAT 396. Münster: Ugarit-Verlag, 2014.

Röllig, Wolfgang. "Baal-Shamem בעל־שמם, בעל־שמין." In *Dictionary of Deities and Demons in the Bible*. Edited by Karel van der Toorn, Bob Becking, and Pieter W. van der Horst. 2nd rev. ed. 149–151. Leiden: Brill, 1999.

Rollston, Christopher A. "Scribal Education in Ancient Israel: The Old Hebrew Epigraphic Evidence." *BASOR* 344 (2006): 47–74.

Rose, Martin. "Yahweh in Israel – Quas in Edom?" *JSOT* 4 (1977): 28–34.

Ross, J. P. "Jahweh Ṣ^{E}ḆĀʾÔṮ in Samuel and Psalms." *VT* 17 (1967): 76–92.

Rubio, Gonzalo. "Scribal Secrets and Antiquarian Nostalgia: Tradition and Scholarship in Ancient Mesopotamia." In *Reconstructing a Distant Past: Ancient Near Eastern Essays in Tribute to Jorge R. Silva Castillo*. Edited by Diego A. Barreyra Fracaroli and Gregorio del Olmo Lete, Aula Orientalis – Supplementa 25. 155–182. Barcelona: Editorial AUSA, 2009.

Rubio, Gonzalo. "Gods and Scholars: Mapping the Pantheon in Early Mesopotamia." In *Reconsidering the Concept of Revolutionary Monotheism*. Edited by Beate Pongratz-Leisten. 91–116. Winona Lake: Eisenbrauns, 2011.

Russell, John M. *Sennacherib's Palace without Rival at Nineveh*. Chicago: University of Chicago Press, 1991.

Saggs, H. W. F. "Historical Texts and fragments of Sargon II of Assyria: 1. The 'Assur Charter.'" *Iraq* 37 (1975): 11–20.

Schmidt, Brian B. "The Iron Age Pithoi Drawings from Horvat Teman or Kuntillet 'Ajrud: Some New Proposals." *JANER* 2 (2002): 91–125.

Schmitz, Philip C. "Phoenician KRNTRYŠ, Archaic Greek *ΚΟΡΥΝΗΤΗΡΙΟΣ, and the Storm God of Aleppo." *KUSATU* 11 (2009): 119–60.

Schneider, Nikolaus. *Die Drehem- und Djohatexte im Kloster Monserrat*. AnOr 7. Rome: Biblical Institute, 1932.

Schneider, Tammi J. "A New Analysis of the Royal Annals of Shalmaneser III." Ph.D. diss., University of Pennsylvania, 1991.

Schroeder, Otto. *Keilschrifttexte aus Assur verschiedenen Inhalts*. Ausgrabungen der Deutschen Orient-Gesellschaft in Assur. E. Inschriften 3. Leipzig: J. C. Hinrichs, 1920.

Schwemer, Daniel. "The Storm-Gods of the Ancient Near East: Summary, Synthesis, Recent Studies: Part I." *JANER* 7 (2008): 121–168.

Schwemer, Daniel. "The Storm-Gods of the Ancient Near East: Summary, Synthesis, Recent Studies: Part II." *JANER* 8 (2008): 1–44.

Scurlock, JoAnn. "Not Just Housewives: Goddesses After the Old Babylonian Period." In *In the Wake of Tikva Frymer-Kensky*. Edited by S. Holloway, J. Scurlock, and R. Beal. Gorgias précis portfolios 4. 59–70. Piscataway: Gorgias, 2009.

Scurlock, JoAnn, and Burton Andersen. *Diagnoses in Assyrian and Babylonian Medicine: Ancient Sources, Translations, and Modern Medical Analyses*. Urbana: University of Illinois Press, 2005.

Selz, Gebhardt J. "The Holy Drum, the Spear, and the Harp. Towards an Understanding of the Problems of Deification in the Third Millennium Mesopotamia." In *Sumerian Gods and Their Representations*. Edited by I. L. Finkel and M. J. Geller. Cuneiform Monographs 7. 167–213. Gröningen: Styx Publications, 1997.

Seow, Choon Leong. "Face ,פנים II." In *Dictionary of Deities and Demons in the Bible*. Edited by Karel van der Toorn, Bob Becking, and Pieter W. van der Horst. 2nd rev. ed. 322–325. Leiden: Brill, 1999.

Seyrig, Henri. "Antiquités Syriennes." *Syria* 40 (1963): 17–32.

Singer, Itamar. "'The Thousand Gods of Hatti': The Limits of an Expanding Pantheon." In *Concepts of the Other in Near Eastern Religions*. Edited by I. Alon, I. Gruenwald, and I. Singer. 81–102. Leiden: Brill, 1994.

Singer, Itamar. *Hittite Prayers*. Edited by H. A. Hoffner. Writings from the Ancient World 11. Atlanta: Society of Biblical Literature, 2002.

Sivan, Daniel. *A Grammar of the Ugaritic Language*. HdO 28. Leiden: Brill, 2001.

Smith, Mark S. *The Origins of Biblical Monotheism: Israel's Polytheistic Background and the Ugaritic Texts*. Oxford: Oxford University Press, 2001.

Smith, Mark S. *The Early History of God: Yahweh and the Other Deities in Ancient Israel*. 2nd ed. Grand Rapids: Eerdmans, 2002.

Smith, Mark S. *God in Translation: Deities in Cross-Cultural Discourse in the Biblical World*. Grand Rapids: Eerdmans, 2010.

Smith, Mark S. "The Problem of the God and His Manifestations: The Case of the Baals at Ugarit, with Implications for Yahweh of Various Locales." In *Die Stadt im Zwölfprophetenbuch*. Edited by Aaron Schart and Jutta Krispenz. BZAW 428. 205–250. Berlin: de Gruyter, 2012.

von Soden, Wolfram. "Zwei Königsgebete an Ištar aus Assyrien." *AfO* 25 (1974): 37–49.

Sommer, Benjamin. *The Bodies of God and the World of Ancient Israel*. Cambridge: Cambridge University Press, 2009.

Sophocles. *Fragments*. Edited and translated by H. Lloyd-Jones. LCL 483. Cambridge: Harvard University Press, 1996.

Stager, Lawrence. "Shemer's Estate." *BASOR* 277/278 (1990): 93–107.

Starcky, Jean. "Inscriptions Archaïques de Palmyre." In *Studi Orientalistici in onore di Giorgio Levi Della Vida*. 2:509–528. Rome: Istituto per L'oriente, 1956.

Stol, Marten. *Birth in Babylonia and the Bible: Its Mediterranean Setting*. Cuneiform Monographs 14. Gröningen; Styx, 2000.

Strassmaier, Johann N. *Inschriften von Nabonidus, König von Babylon (555–538 v. Chr.) von den Thontafeln des Britischen Museums copirt und autographirt*. Leipzig: E. Pfeiffer, 1889.

Sumption, Jonathan. *The Age of Pilgrimage: the Medieval Journey to God*. Mahwah: Hidden Spring, 2003.

Sznycer, Maurice. "Une Inscription Punique Trouvée a Monte Sirai (Sardaigne)." *Semitica* 15 (1965): 35–43.

Tadmor, Hayim, and Shigeo Yamada, *The Royal Inscriptions of Tilgath-pileser III (744–727 BC) and Shalmaneser V (726-722), Kings*. RINAP 1. Winona Lake: Eisenbrauns, 2011.

Tallqvist, Knut. *Akkadische Götterepitheta, mit einem Götterverzeichnis und einer Liste der prädikativen Elemente der sumerischen Götternamen*. Studia Orientalia 7. Helsingforsiae: Societas orientalis fennica, 1938.

Taracha, Piotr. *Religions of Second Millennium Anatolia.* DBH 27. Wiesbaden: Barrassowitz, 2009.

Tazawa, Keiko. *Syro-Palestinian Deities in New Kingdom Egypt: The Hermeneutics of their Existence.* Oxford: Archaeopress, 2009.

Thiel, Winfried "Athaliah." In *Anchor Bible Dictionary.* Edited by David Noel Freedman. 1:511–512. New York: Doubleday, 1992.

Thureau-Dangin, François. "Rois de Kiš et rois d'Agadé." *RA* 9 (1912): 33–37.

Tigay, Jeffrey H. *You Shall Have No Other Gods: Israelite Religion in the Light of Hebrew Inscriptions.* HSS 31. Atlanta: Scholars Press, 1986.

Tigay, Jeffrey H. "A Second Temple Parallel to the Blessings from Kuntillet 'Ajrud." *IEJ* 40 (1990): 218.

Tigay, Jeffrey H. *Deuteronomy: The Traditional Hebrew Text with the New JPS Translation.* JPS Torah Commentary 5. Philadelphia: Jewish Publication Society, 1996.

van der Toorn, Karel. "Anat-Yahu, Some Other Deities, and the Jews of Elephantine." *Numen* 39 (1992): 80–101.

van der Toorn, Karel, ed. *Family Religion in Babylonia, Syria, and Israel: Continuity and Change in the Forms of Religious Life.* Studies in the History and Culture of the ancient Near East 7. Leiden: Brill, 1996.

van der Toorn, Karel, ed. *The Image and the Book: Iconic Cults, Aniconism, and the Rise of Book Religion in Israel and the Ancient Near East.* Contributions to Biblical Exegesis and Theology 21. Leuven: Peeters, 1997.

van der Toorn, Karel. "Yahweh." In *Dictionary of Deities and Demons in the Bible.* Edited by Karel van der Toorn, Bob Becking, and Pieter W. van der Horst. 2nd rev. ed. 910–919. Leiden: Brill, 1999.

van der Toorn, Karel, Bob Becking, and Pieter W. van der Horst, eds. *Dictionary of Deities and Demons in the Bible.* 2nd rev. ed. Leiden: Brill, 1999.

Tremlin, Todd. *Minds and Gods: The Cognitive Foundations of Religion.* New York: Oxford University Press, 2010.

Tsevat, Matitiahu. "Studies in the Book of Samuel." *HUCA* 36 (1965): 49–58.

Uehlinger, Christoph. "Anthropomorphic Cult Statuary in Iron Age Palestine and the Search for Yahweh's Cult Image." In *The Image and the Book: Iconic Cults, Aniconism, and the Rise of Book Religion in Israel and the Ancient Near East.* Edited by Karel van der Toorn. Contributions to Biblical Exegesis and Theology 21. 92–155. Leuven: Peeters, 1997.

Vleeming, Sven P., and Jan W. Wesselius. "An Aramaic Hymn from the Fourth Century B.C." *BiOr* 39 (1982): 501–509.

Vleeming, Sven P., and Jan W. Wesselius.*Studies in Papyrus Amherst 63.* Vol 1. Amsterdam: Juda Palache Instituut, 1985.

Walker, Christopher, and Michael Dick. *The Induction of the Cult Image in Ancient Mesopotamia: The Mesopotamian* Mīs Pî *Ritual: Transliteration, Translation, and Commentary.* SAALT 1. Helsinki: The Neo-Assyrian Text Corpus Project, 2001.

Waltke, Bruce, and M. O'Connor. *An Introduction to Biblical Hebrew Syntax.* Winona Lake: Eisenbrauns, 1990.

Wearzeggers, Caroline. *The Ezida Temple of Borsippa: Priesthood, Cult, Archives.* Achaemenid History 15. Leiden: Nederlands Instituut voor Het Nabije Oosten, 2010.

Wegner, Ilse. *Gestalt und Kult der Ištar-Šawuška in Kleinasien.* AOAT 36. Kevelaer: Butzon und Bercker, 1981.

Wegner, Ilse. "Der Name der Ša(w)uška." In *Edith Porada Memorial Volume.* Edited by D. Owen and G. Wilhelm. SCCNH 7. 117–120. Bethesda: CDL Press, 1995.

Weinfeld, Moshe. "The Loyalty Oath in the Ancient Near East." *UF* 8 (1976): 379–414.

Weinfeld, Moshe. "The Tribal League at Sinai." In *Ancient Israelite Religion: Essays in Honor of Frank Moore Cross*. Edited by Patrick D. Miller, Paul D. Hanson, and S. Dean McBride. 303–304. Philadelphia: Fortress, 1987.

Weinfeld, Moshe. *Deuteronomy and the Deuteronomic School*. Winona Lake: Eisenbrauns, 1992.

Weippert, Manfred. "Über den asiatischen Hintergrund der Göttin 'Asiti.'" *Or* NS 44 (1975): 12–21.

Weissert, Elnathan. "Royal Hunt and Royal Triumph in a Prism Fragment of Ashurbanipal (82-5-22, 2)." In *Assyria 1995: Proceedings of the 10th Anniversary Symposium of the Neo-Assyrian Text Corpus Project, Helsinki, September 7–11, 1995*. Edited by Simo Parpola and R. M. Whiting. 339–358. Helsinki: Neo-Assyrian Text Corpus Project, 1997.

Westenholz, Joan Goodnick. *Legends of the kings of Akkade: The Texts*. Mesopotamian Civilizations 7. Winona Lake: Eisenbrauns, 1997.

Westenholz, Joan Goodnick. "Emar – the City and its God." In *Languages and Cultures in Contact: At the Crossroads of Civilizations in the Syro-Mesopotamian Realm: Proceedings of the 42th* [sic] *RAI*. Edited by K. van Lerberghe and G. Voet. OLA 96. 145–167. Leuven: Peeters, 1999.

Wunsch, Cornelia. "Die Richter des Nabonid." In *Assyriologica et Semitica: Festschrift für Joachim Oelsner anlässlich seines 65. Geburtstages am 18. Februar 1997*. Edited by J. Marzahn and H. Neumann. AOAT 252. 557–597. Münster: Ugarit-Verlag, 2000.

Xella, Paolo. *Baal Hammon: Recherches sur l'identité et l'histoire d'un dieu phénico-punique*. Contributi alla storia della religione fenicio-punica 1. Rome: Consiglio Nazionale Delle Ricerche, 1991.

Yadin, Yigael. "The 'House of Ba'al of Ahab and Jezebel in Samaria, and that of Athalia in Judah." In *Archaeology in the Levant: Essays for Kathleen Kenyon*. Edited by R. Moorey and P. Parr. 127–135. Warminster: Aris & Phillips LTD, 1978.

Zevit, Ziony. *The Religions of Ancient Israel: A Synthesis of Parallactic Approaches*. London: Continuum, 2001.

Zobel, H.-J. צבאות" *ṣᵉḇāʾôṯ*." In *Theological Dictionary of the Old Testament*. Edited by G. Johannes Botterweck, Helmer Ringgren, and Heinz-Josef Fabry. Translated by John T. Willis. 12:215–232. Grand Rapids: Eerdmans, 1974 ff.

Zsolnay, Ilona. "The Function of Ištar in the Assyrian Royal Inscriptions: A Contextual Analysis of the Actions Attributed to Ištar in the Inscriptions of Ititi through Šalmaneser sIII." Ph.D. diss., Brandeis University, 2009.

Maps

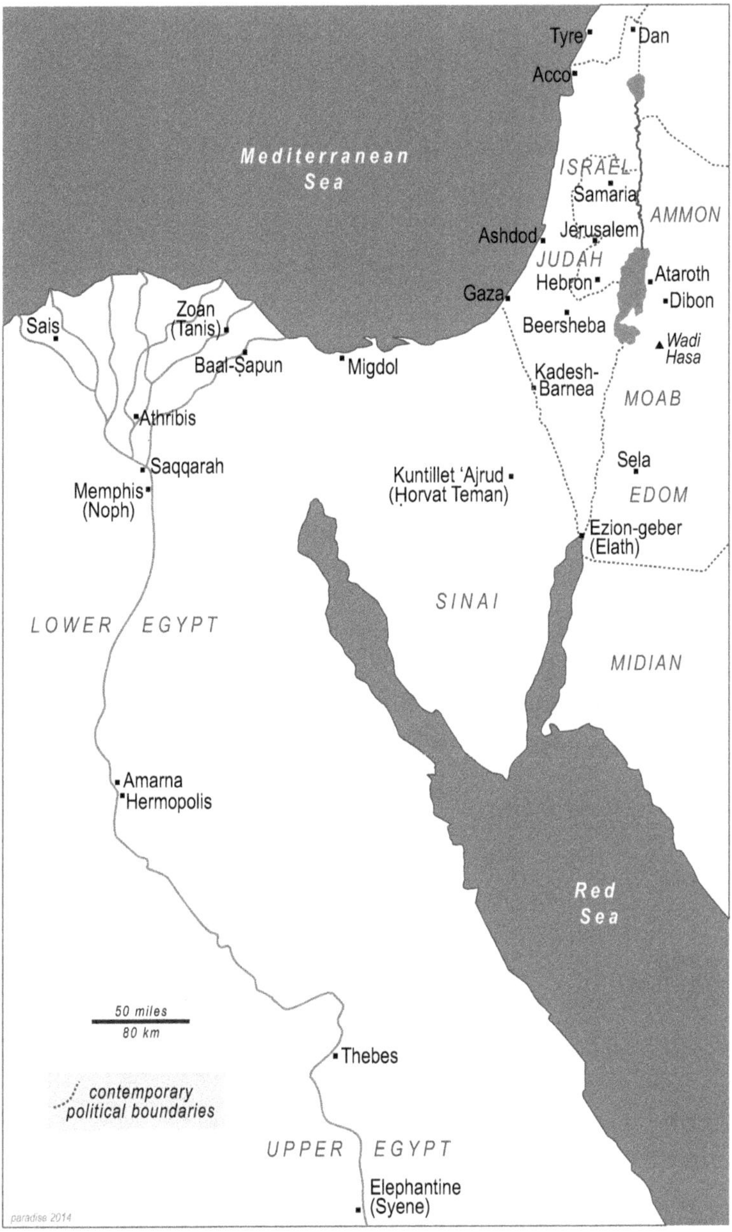

Map 1: Egypt and Juda

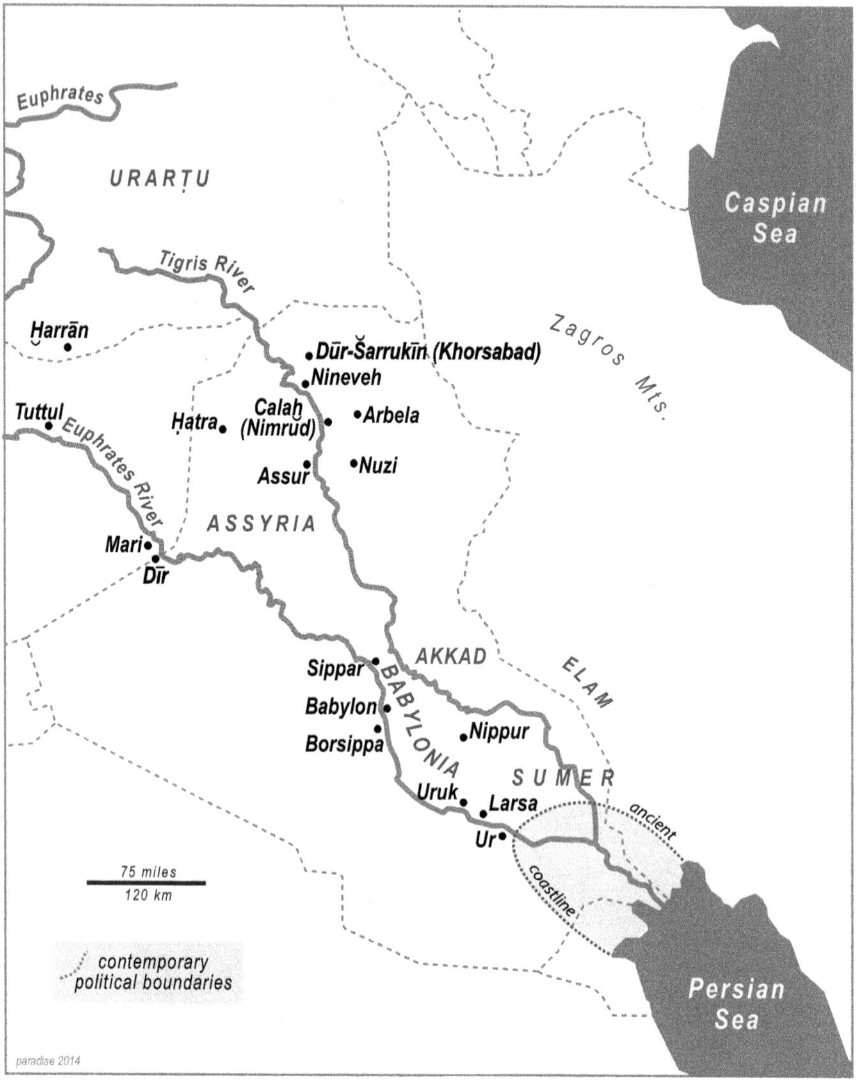

Map 2: Mesopotamia

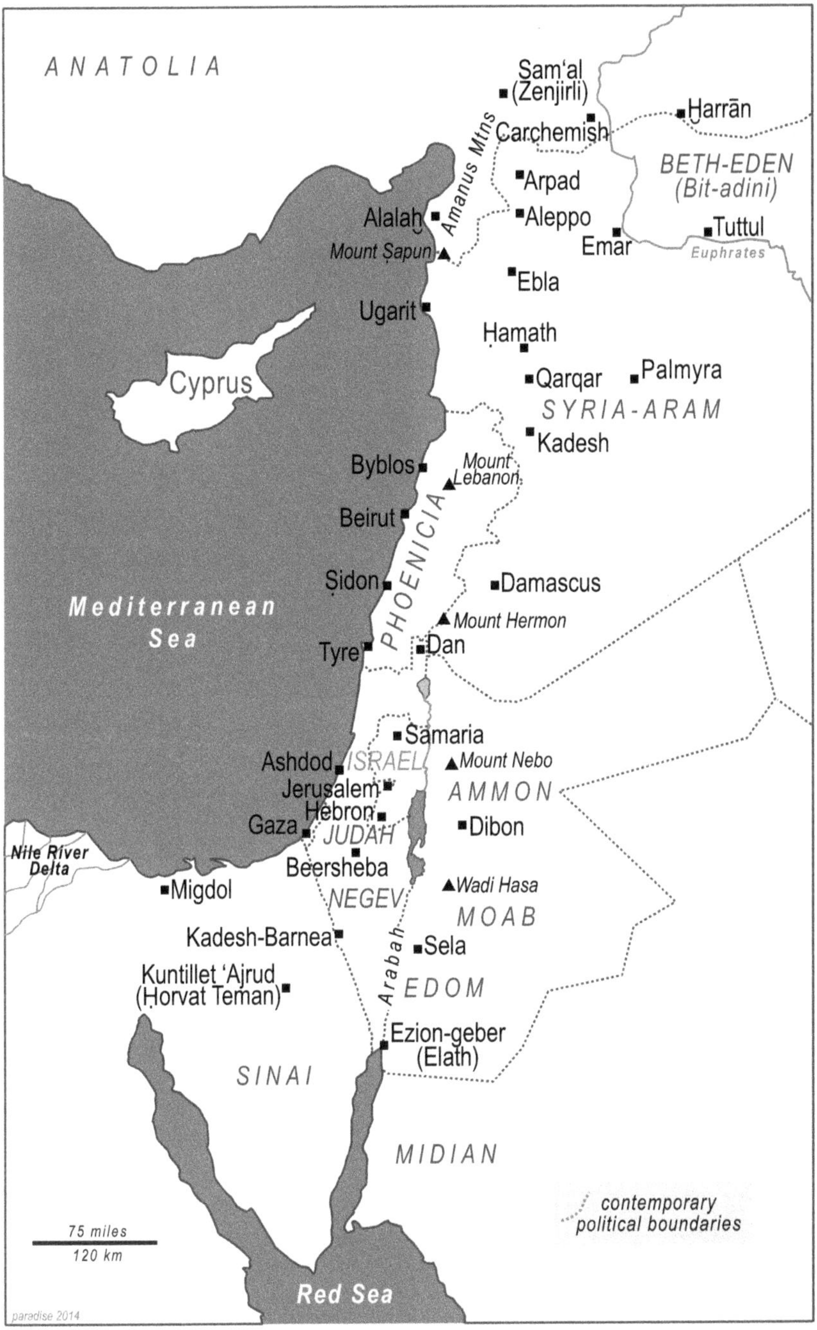

Map 3: Israel and the Levant

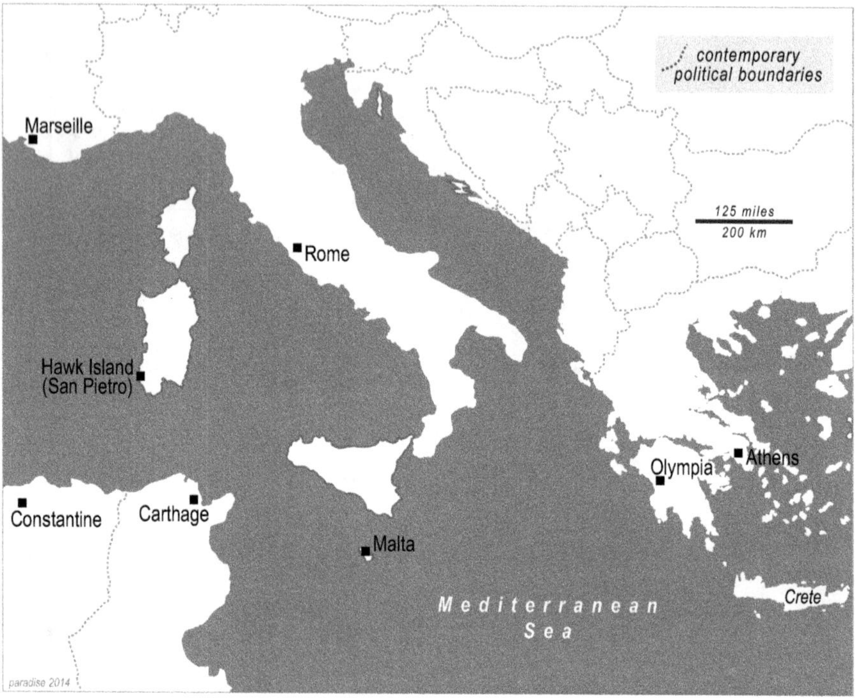

Map 4: Around The Mediterranean Sea

Appendix: Tables 1.1–7.1

Table 1.1: *Syncretic Hymn to Marduk* (Erich Ebeling, *KAR* 25 ii 3–17).[1]

line:	Deity:	attribute:
3	Sîn	your divinity
	Anu	your royalty
4	Dagan	your lordship
	Enlil	your kingship
5	Adad	your supremacy
	Ea	your wisdom[2]
6	Nabû	your ability
7	Ninurta	your pre-eminence
	Nergal	your strength
8	Nus[ku]	your august advice
9	Šamaš	your judgeship
10	Marduk	your important name
11	a merci[less li]on	your terrible arrow
13	the Sebittu	those who walk at your sides
15	the Igigū	your greatness
	Irnini	your leadership(?)[3]
16	the depths (Apsu)	your (plural) cave
17	the netherworld	your ...

Table 1.2: BM 47406:1–14 (Simo Parpola, "The Assyrian Cabinet," 399; based on Parpola's translation, modified slightly).[4]

line:	Deity:		attribute:
1	Uraš (is)	Marduk of	Planting
2	Lugalakida (is)	Marduk of	the Ground Water
3	Ninurta (is)	Marduk of	the Hoe
4	Nergal (is)	Marduk of	War
5	Zababa (is)	Marduk of	Battle
6	Enlil (is)	Marduk of	Lordship and Deliberation
7	Nabû (is)	Marduk of	Accounting
8	Sîn (is)	Marduk of	Illuminator of the Night
9	Šamaš (is)	Marduk of	Justice
10	Adad (is)	Marduk of	Rain
11	Tišpak (is)	Marduk of	Hosts
12	Ištarān (is)	Marduk of	...
13	Šuqamuna (is)	Marduk of	The container
14	[Ma]mi (is)	Marduk of	[the Potte]r's clay.

Table 1.3: *Syncretic Hymn to Ninurta* (Erich Ebeling, *KAR* 102:10–33).[5]

line:	God:	Body Part:
10	Šamaš	Face
	[Nisaba]	Locks (Shape)
11	Enlil and [Mullissu]	Eyes
12	Gula and Bēlet-ilī	Eyeballs (Pupils)
13	Sîn [and Šamaš]	Eyelids (Green of eyes = Iris)
14	corona of the sun (rays of Šamaš)	Eyebrows (Eyelashes)
15	Ištar-kakkabi	Mouth's shape (Appearance of mouth)
16	Anu and Antu	Lips
	[Nusku]	Speech
17	Pabilsag	Tongue
18	Circumference of Heaven and Earth	Roof of Mouth
19	the Sebittu	Teeth
20	Rising of bri[lliant] stars	Cheeks
21	Ea and Damkina	Ears
22	Adad	Head
23	Šala	Brow (Forehead)
24	Marduk	Neck
25	Zarpānītu	Throat
26	Šullat (Nabû)	Chest
27	Haniš	Upper Back
28	Uta'ulu	Right Side
29	Ninpanigarra	Left Side
30	[ ]	Fingers
31	Dagan	[ ]
32	[ ]	Navel
33	Zababa	[ ]

Table 1.4: *A Sumero-Akkadian Hymn of Nanâ* (K 3933+, derived from Table 1 in Reiner, "Sumero-Akkadian," 232).

Strophe:	Goddess:	Consort:
I–II	(Ištar)	
III	Irnina, Damkianna	Ea
IV	Šuluḫḫītu	Enzag and Meskilak
V	Gula/Ninkarrak, Bau	[ ]
VI	Ungal-Nibru	[ ]
VII	Išḫara, Bau	Zababa
VIII	[ ]	[ ]
IX	Zarpānītu	Marduk
X	Nanaya	Nabû
XI	Nanaya	---
XII	Anunītu	---
XIII	Šala	Adad
XIV	Manzat?	[Ištarān]
XV	[Nisaba]	Ḫ[aya]
XVI	Mammītu	Meslamtaea
XVII	A[...]	[ ]
...		
ε	Šimalia	---
ζ	Pirigal	---
η	Šerū'a	Assur
θ	Ištar	[ ]

Table 2.1: The Hittite-Hurrian Deities at Yazilikaya and the *Itkalzi*-Ritual (Emmanuel Laroche, "Le Panthéon de Yazilikaya," *JCS* 6 [1952]: 121).

line:	Hittite equivalent:	Cuneiform:
42	Tešub(-of-Heaven)	^{d}10 (AN)
	Nanni-Ḫazzi	KUR KUR
41	Tešub-of-Ḫattuša	^{d}10 *ḫa*^{ki}
40	Grain	NISABA = *ḫalki*
39	Ea	^{d}*A*
38	Šaušga	^{d}*sa+us-ga*
37	Ninatta	[*ni*$^{??}$]-*na*$^{?}$-*ta*
36	Kulitta	[*ku*]-*li*$^{?}$-*ta*
35	Kušuh	^{d}NANNA
34	Šimegi	^{d}UTU AN
33	Aštabi	^{d}[*a*]*s-ta-pi*
32	LAMMA	^{d}LAMA
31	?	^{d}*tu+ta*$^{??}$
30	Ḫešui??	^{d}U.GUR
	eše-	AN
29–28	Šerri -Ḫurri	GUD GUD
	ḫawur-ni	KI
43	Ḫebat	^{d}*ḫe-pa-tu*
44	Šarruma	^{d}LUGAL-*ma*
47	Ḫutena	[^{d}*ḫu*]-*ti*$^{?}$-*na*
48	Ḫutellurra	^{d}*ḫu-ta-lx+ra*
49	Nabarbi	^{d}*na?-par*$^{?}$-*pi*
56	Šaušga	? ^{d}*sa+us-ga*

Table 2.2: Divine Witness List between Šuppiluliuma I and Ḫuqqana of Ḫayasa (*CTH* 42).

§ 7 (A i 41–47)
UTU-of-Heaven
UTU.MI$_2$-of-Arinna
IŠKUR-of-Heaven
IŠKUR-of-Ḫatti
IŠKUR-of-Aleppo
IŠKUR-of-Arinna
IŠKUR-of-Zippalanda
IŠKUR-of-Sapinuwa
IŠKUR-of-Nerik
IŠKUR-of-Hisashapa
IŠKUR-of-Sahpina
IŠKUR-of-the-Army
IŠKUR-of-the-Market$^{(?)}$
IŠKUR-of-Uda
IŠKUR-of-Kuzzuwatna
IŠKUR-of-Pittiyarik
IŠKUR-of-Šamuḫa
[IŠKUR]-of-Sarissa
IŠKUR-of-Ḫurma
IŠKUR-of-Lihzina
IŠKUR-of-Ruin-Mound
IŠKUR-[of ...]
IŠKUR-of-Hulasa
Ḫebat-of-Uda
Ḫebat-of-Kizzuwatna
§ 8 (A i 48–59)
LAMMA
LAMMA-of-Ḫatti
Zithariya
Karzi
Ḫapantaliya
LAMMA-of-Karaḫna
LAMMA-[of-the-Countryside]
LAMMA-of-the-Hunting-Bag
Aya

§ 8 (continued.)
Ištar
Ištar-of-the-Countryside
Ištar-of-Nineveh
[Ištar]-of-Ḫattarina
Ištar//Queen-of-Heaven
Ninatta
Kulitta
Warrior-God
Warrior-God-of-Illaya
Warrior-God-[of-Arziya]
All the-Deities-of-the-Army
Marduk
Allatu
[UTU.MI$_2$]-of-the-Earth
Huwassanna-of-Hupisna
Ayabara-of-Šamuḫa
Hantitassu-[of-Hurma]
Katahha-of-Ankuwa
[Ammamma]-of-Tahurpa
Queen-of-Katapa
Hallara-of-Dunna
The-[Mountain-Dweller]-Gods
The-[Mercenary]-Gods
All the-Deities-of-Ḫatti
The-Deities-[...]-of-the-Land
The-Deities-of-Heaven
The-Deities-of-the-Earth
The-Mountains
[The-Rivers]
[The-Springs]
[The-Clouds]
Heaven
The-Earth
The-Great-Sea

Table 2.3: Hittite Deity Categories from Selected Divine Witness Lists (*CTH* 42, 68, 69, 76, and 106; see also Tables 2.6 through 2.10).

Storm-Gods:[6]
Personal-IŠKUR-of-Lightning-of-my-Majesty
The-Powerful-IŠKUR//[King-of-the-Lands]
IŠKUR-of-Heaven
IŠKUR-of-Ḫatti//King-of-the-Lands
IŠKUR-of-Lightning
IŠKUR-of-Market(?)
IŠKUR-of-the-Army
IŠKUR-of-Ḫisašapa
IŠKUR-of-Arinna
IŠKUR-of-Pittiyarik
IŠKUR-of-Zippalanda
IŠKUR-of-Nerik
IŠKUR-of-Aleppo
IŠKUR-of-Uda
IŠKUR-of-Kizzuwatna
IŠKUR-of-Šamuḫa
IŠKUR-of-Sapinuwa
IŠKUR-of-Sahpina
IŠKUR-of-Ḫurma
IŠKUR-of-Sarissa
IŠKUR-of-Liḫzina
IŠKUR-of-Ruin-Mound
IŠKUR-of-Hulasa
IŠKUR-of-Kummanni
IŠKUR-of-Help
The-Piḫaimmi-IŠKUR
IŠKUR-of-Lightning
Šeri
Ḫurri
(Mount-Nanni)
(Mount-Hazzi)

LAMMA Deities:
LAMMA
LAMMA-of-Ḫatti
Ayala
Zithariya
Karzi
Ḫapantaliya
LAMMA-of-Karaḫna
LAMMA-of-the-Countryside
LAMMA-of-the-Hunting-Bag

Ištar Goddesses:
Ištar
Ištar-of-Šamuḫa
Ištar-of-the-Countryside
Ištar-of-Lawazantiya
Ištar-of-Nineveh
Ištar-of-Ḫattarina
Ištar//Queen-of-Heaven
(Ninatta)
(Kulitta)

Warrior Gods:
Warrior-God
Warrior-God-of-Ḫatti
Warrior-God-of-Illaya
Warrior-God-of-Arziya

Table 2.4: *The Festival for All the Tutelary Deities* (*KUB* 2 1 §§ 31′–33′, derived from McMahon, *Hittite State Cult*, 96–115).

	The LAMMA Deities in *KUB* 2 1 §§ 31′–32′:
i 43	LAMMA-of-the-Sky/Heaven
	LAMMA-of-Karaḫna
44	Karši (variant Karzi)
	Ḫapantaliya
45	LAMMA-Alatarma
	LAMMA-of-Mount-Šaluwanda
46	LAMMA-of-Šarpa
47	LAMMA-of-Šulupašša
	LAMMA-of-Tuttuwa
48	LAMMA-of-Ḫarana
49	LAMMA-of-Šarišša
50	LAMMA-of-Mount-Šunnara
	LAMMA-of-the-River-Kummara
51	LAMMA-of-the-River-Šiḫiriya
	LAMMA-of-Ḫallatta
	(about 12 lines missing or largely broken)
ii 13	LAMMA-of-horses-[of-the-Labarna]
14	LAMMA-of-the spear-[of-the-Labarna]
15	LAMMA-of-[M]ount-Iškiša-[of-the-Labarna]
16	LAMMA-of-the-animals-[of-the-Labarna]
17	LAMMA-of-the-strengthening-[of-the-Labarna]
18	LAMMA-of-the-shoulder-[of-the-Labarna]
19	LAMMA-of-the-encircling$^{(?)}$-[of-the-Labarna]
20	LAMMA-of-the-divine-power-[of-the-Labarn]a
21	LAMMA-of-the-life-[of-the-Labarn]a
22	LAMMA-of-the-heroism-[of-the-Labarn]a
23	LAMMA-of-the-army-[of-the-Labar]na
24	LAMMA-of-battle-[of-the-Labar]na
25	LAMMA-of-running-in-front-[of-the-Labar]na
26	LAMMA-of-holding-up-the-hand-[of-the-Laba]rna
27	LAMMA-of-*ḫallašša*-[of-the-Lab]arna
28	LAMMA-of-the-fulfilling-of-the-wish-[of-the-Lab]arna
29	LAMMA-of-the-omen-giving-[of-the-Lab]arna
30	⟨LAMMA-of⟩-the-*ašta-wašta*-[of-the-La]barna
31	LAMMA-of-the-[-]*nanta*-of-the-Labarna
32	LAMMA//Who-[f]ills-the-hunting-bag-of-the-Labarna

Table 2.4: (continued).

33	LAMMA-of-the-strong-of-the-Labarna
34	LAMMA-the-warrior-of-the-Labarna
35	The-Labarna's-LAMMA
36	Fire-Tender-of-the-fire-(and)-hearth
37	LAMMA-of-watching-over-the-body-of-the-Labarna
38	LAMMA-of-Mount-Tudḫaliya
39	LAMMA-of-time
40	LAMMA-of-the-small-place(s)–(and)–(of[?])-setting-a-time-of-the-Labarna
41	LAMMA-of-the-*lapattali*(*ya*)-of-the-Labarna
42	LAMMA-getting-up-of-the-Labarna
43	LAMMA-of-the-field(?)-of-the-Labarna
44	LAMMA-of-the-L[ab]arna's-sitting-down-again(?)
45	LAMMA-of-the-decision-of-the-Labarna
46	LAMMA-of-the-lordliness-of-the-Lab[ar]na
47	LAMMA-of-the-*ḫantiyašša*-of-the-Labarna
48	LAMMA-of-the-*tarpatta*-of-the-Labarna ⟨LAMMA⟩-of-the-*šalubat*[*ta*-]-of-the-same
49	LAMMA-of-the-swiftness-of-the-same (i.e., the Labarna)[7]
50	LAMMA-of-the-brining near-of-the-Laba[rn]a
51	LAMMA-of-the-*išmašuwala*-of-the-Laba[rn]a
52	LAMMA-of-the-*takšatar*-of-the-Laba[rn]a
iii 1	[L]AMMA-of-the-[ ]-of-the-Labarna
2	LAMMA-of-the-*annari*-and-*tarpi*-spirit-of-the-Labarna
3	LAMMA-of-all-the-lands-of-the-[Laba]rna
4	LAMMA-of-the-place-[of-the-L]abarna
5	⌜LAMMA⌝-of-the-*takkuwi*-of-the-Labarna
6	LAMMA-of-the-body-of-the-Labarna
7	[LAMMA-of]-the-righ[t]-should[er]-of-the-Labarna
8	LAMMA-[of]-the-le[f]t-shoulder-of-the-Labarna
9	[LAMMA-of]-Mount-Kitawa[nta]-of-the-Labarna
10–11	LAMMA-of-the-*piḫadda*-of-the-Labarna
11–12	LAMMA-of-praise-of-the-Labarna
13	LAMMA-of-the-weapon-of-the-L[aba]rna
14	LAMMA-of-the-awe-inspiring-ability(?)-of-the-Labarna
16	LAMMA-of-the-*kurraštarra*-of-the-Labarna
17–18	LAMMA-of-the-*paraštarra*-of-the-Labarna
19	LAMMA-of-the-propitious-day-of-the-Labarna

Table 2.4: (continued).

20	LAMMA-of-the-Labarna's-*ḫuwapra*-building
21–22	LAMMA-of-the-Labarna's-"house-of-"Labarna"
22–23	The-Labarna's-LAMMA-of-His-Majesty-Tudḫaliya
	(The Ala Deities in *KUB* 2 1 § 33′)
r. iv 28	Ala-of-Life
29	Ala-of-the-sky
30	Ala-of-the-animals
31	Ala-of-the-countryside
32	Ala-of-kindliness
33	Ala-of-favor
34	Ala-of-Ḫatti
35	Ala-of-the-army
36	Ala-of-the-city-Alatarma
37	Ala-[of]-Mo[unt]-Šarpa
38	Ala-of-Mount-Šakyw[anda]
39	Ala-of-T[u]ttu
40	Ala-of-Šulupašša
41	Ala-of-Ḫarana
42	Ala-of-the-enclosed(?)-countryside
43	Ala-of-*Warwantali(ya)*
44	Ala-of-*Aššatta*
45	Ala-of-encircling(?)
46	Ala-of-"setting-a-time"
47	Ala-of-forcefulness/power
48	Ala-of-[(-)]x-*kutiyatḫita-*
49	Ala-of-*ašta-wašta-*
iv 1	Ala-of-glory
2	Ala-of-praise
3	Ala-of-the-bow
4	Ala-of-the-quiver
4–5	Ala-of-x[...]-of-the-Labarna
6	Ala-of-the-[ ]x-*da*-of-the-Labarna
7–8	Ala-of-the-divine-power-of-the-Labarna
8–9	Ala-of-the-calling-up-of-the-Labarna
10–11	[Ala]-of-the-calling-[ ]x-[of-the-Laba]rna
11–13	Ala-of-holding-[u]p-[the-hand(?) ...]-of-the-[Laba]rna
14	[Ala]-of-the-just
15	[Ala-of-(-)]x-*nugana-*

Table 2.4: (concluded).

16–17	[Ala]-of-the-summer-pastures-[ ]-of-the-Labarna
18–19	[Ala]-of-the-x-*ra*-[of-the-Labarn]a
20	[Ala]-of-the-refuge
21	[Ala]-of-the-[...]x-*ātar*
22	[Ala-of-the ...]-of-the-hunting-bag
	(ll. 23–26 are too broken to identify specific Ala deities)
27	[Ala]-of-running-[in-fr]ont
28	[Ala]-of-covering-the-[ ]-*nu*
	(ll. 29–30 only has traces of text)
31	[Al]a-of-all-the-mountains
32	[Al]a-of-the-rivers
33	[Al]a-of-all-the-*duwaduna*
34–35	Ala-of-all-the-springs$^{(?)}$
35–36	x-*kušnuwanti*-Ala
37	Ala-of-Mount-Šarp[a]
38	[Al]a-of-abundance-of-fruit
39	[Al]a-of-the-propitious-day
40	[Ala-of-the-g]oo[d]-[sp]irit
v 1	Ala-of-the-palace-[of-Tudḫa]liya
2	[Ala$^{(?)}$]-of-Tudḫ[aliya]

Table 2.5: *The Festival of Individual Offerings* (*KBo* 11 40+, derived from McMahon, *Hittite State Cult*, 120–127).

KBo 11 40 i 4′	LAMMA-of-[Šul]upašša
7′	LAMMA-of-[Tu]ttuwa
9′	LAMMA-of-Ḫarana
12′	LAMMA-of-[Mount(?)-Š]arešša
15′	LAMMA-of-[Mount-Šu]nnara
18′	LAMMA-of-[the-river-Kummar]a
KUB 40 108 ii 20′	LAMMA-of-the-river-Kella
22′	LAMMA-of-Ḫallašša
24′	LAMMA-of-Tidanda
26′	LAMMA-of-Anza
KBo 11 40 i 28′	LAMMA-of-[tablet breaks off]
	(traces only)
ii 3′	[LAMMA-of]-Mount-I[škiša]
5′	[LAMMA-of]-the-animals-[of-the-Labarna]
7′	[LAMMA-of]-the-strengthen[ing-of-the-Labarna]
9′	[LAMMA-of]-the-shoulder-[of-the-Labarna]
11′	[LAMMA-o]f-encircling(?)-[of-the-Labarna]
13′	[LAMMA-of]-the-divine-pow[er-of-the-Labarna]
15′	LAMMA-x-of-the-life-[of-the-Labarna]
17′	LAM[MA]-of-the-heroism-[of-the-Labarna]
19′	LAMMA-of-the-army-[of-the-Labarna]
21′	LAMMA-of-x-of-battle-[of-the-Labarna]
23′	[LAMMA-of]-runnin[g-before-of-the-Labarna]
KBo 12 60 x+1	LAMMA-of-[x]
2′	[LAMMA-of]-Mount-Kidawanda-[of-the-Labarna]
4′	LAM[MA]-of-the-*piḫadda*-[of-the-Labarna]
6′	LA[MMA]-of-praise-[of-the-Labarna]
7′	[LAMMA-of-the-weapon-of-the-Labarna]
8′	[LAMMA-of-the-awe-inspiring-ability(?)-of-the-Labarna]
	(tablet breaks off)
KUB 55 25 4′	Ala
6′	Ala-of-x
8′	Ala-[of-the-countryside]
9′	[Ala-of]-kindliness
10′	A[la]-of-favor
11′	Ala-o[f-Ḫatti]

Table 2.5: (concluded).

12′	[Al]a-of-the-arm[y]	
		(tablet breaks off)
KUB 40 108 r. v 2	Ala-[of]-divine-power	
4	Ala-[of]-calling-up	
6	Ala-[of-x]	
		(traces)
KUB 40 101 x+1	[Ala-of-Tud]ḫaliya	
	Ala-[of-the-palace-of-T]udḫaliya	

Table 2.6: Divine Witness List between Muršili II of Ḫatti and Kupanta-Kurunta of Mira-Kuwaliya (*CTH* 68, translation is based on Beckman, *Hittite Diplomatic Texts*, no. 11, 81–82).

§ 29 (I iv 9′–15′)	UTU-of-Heaven
	[UTU.MI$_2$-of-Arinna]
	The-Powerful-IŠKUR
	IŠKUR-of-Heaven
	Šeri
	[Ḫurri]
	Mount-Nanni
	Mount-Ḫazzi
	[...]
	IŠKUR-of-Market$^{(?)}$
	IŠKUR-of-Army
	[IŠKUR-of-Aleppo]
	[IŠKUR-of-Zippalanda]
	IŠKUR-of-Nerik
	IŠKUR-of-[...]
	IŠKUR-of-Uda
	IŠKUR-of-[...]
	IŠKUR-of-Sapinuwa
	The-[IŠKUR-of-]
	The Proud-IŠKUR
	IŠKUR-of-[...]
	(approximately ten line break)

Table 2.7: Divine Witness List between Muršili II of Ḫatti and Manapa-Tarḫund of the Land of the Seḫa River (*CTH* 69, the translation is based on Beckman, *Hittite Diplomatic Texts*, no. 12, 85–86).

§ 14 (A iii 52′–54′; B iv 1–3)
[UTU-of-Heaven]
[UTU.MI_2-of-Arinna]

[IŠKUR]-of-Heaven
The-Powerful-IŠKUR
[...]
[Šeri]
[Ḫurri]
Mount-Nanni
Mount-Ḫazzi
[...]
IŠKUR-of-Market(?)
IŠKUR-of-Army
[IŠKUR-of-]
[IŠKUR-of-Pittiyarik]
IŠKUR-of-Nerik
IŠKUR-of-the-Ruin-Mound
[IŠKUR-of-]
[IŠKUR-of-Aleppo]
IŠKUR-of-Uda
IŠKUR-of-Kummanni

§ 15 (B iv 4–6)
[IŠKUR-of-]
[IŠKUR-of-Ḫisashapa]
IŠKUR-of-Šamuḫa
IŠKUR-of-Sapinuwa
[IŠKUR-of-]
[IŠKUR]-of-Saḫpina
IŠKUR-of-Ḫurma
IŠKUR-of-Sarissa
IŠKUR-[of-]
IŠKUR-of-Help
IŠKUR-of-Zippalanda

§ 16 (B iv 7–13)
LAMMA
LAMMA-of-Ḫatti

Zithariya
Karzi
Ḫapantaliya
LAMMA-of-Karaḫna
LAMMA-of-the-Countryside
LAMMA-of-the-Hunting-Bag
Allatu
Enki
Telipinu
Pirwa
Moon-God//⟨Lord⟩-of-the Oath
Ḫebat//Great-Queen
[...]
Ištar
Ištar-of-the-Countryside
Ištar-of-Nineveh
[Ištar]-of-Ḫattarina
Ninatta
Kulitta
[Išhara]//Queen-of-the-Oath

§ 17 (B iv 14–20)
[Warrior-God]
Warrior-God-of-Ḫatti
Warrior-God-of-Illaya
Warrior-God-of-Arziya
Yarri
Zappana
Abara-of-Šamuḫa
Ḫantitassu-of-Ḫurma
Kataḫḫa-of-Ankuwa
Queen-of-Katapa
Ammamma-of-Taḫurpa
Ḫallara-of-Dunna
Ḫuwassanna-of-Ḫupisna
The-Mountain-Dweller-Gods
All the-Mercenary-Gods-of-Ḫatti

§ 18 (B iv 21–25)
[The-Male-Deities]
and Female-Deities-of-Ḫatti
UTU.MI_2-of-the-Earth (i.e., Ereškigal)
all the-Primeval-Deities:
Nara
Namsara
Minki
Ammunki
[Tuḫusi]
Ammizzadu
Alalu
Kumarbi
Anu
Antu
Enlil
Ninlil

§ 19 (B i 26–27)
[The-Mountains]
[The-Rivers]
The-Springs
The-Great-Sea
[Heaven]
[Earth]
The-Winds
The-Rivers
The-Clouds

Table 2.8: Divine Witness List between Wuwattalli II of Ḫatti and Alaksandu of Wilusa (*CTH* 76, the translation is based on Beckman, *Hittite Diplomatic Texts*, no. 13, 91–92).

§ 17 (A iv 1–9)

[UTU]-of-Heaven//King-of-the-Lands//Shepherd-of-Humankind
UTU.MI$_2$-of-Arinna//[Queen]-of-the-Lands
Personal-IŠKUR-of-Lightning-of-my-Majesty
The-Powerful-IŠKUR//[King-of-the Lands]
[IŠKUR-of-Ḫatti]//King-of-the Lands
IŠKUR-of-Lightning
IŠKUR-of-Zippalanda
[IŠKUR-of-Nerik]
IŠKUR-of-Aleppo
IŠKUR-of-Market$^{(?)}$
[IŠKUR-of]
IŠKUR-of-Arinna
IŠKUR-of-Ḫisašapa
IŠKUR-of-[Sapinuwa]
IŠKUR-of-Šamuḫa
IŠKUR-of-Ḫurma
IŠKUR-of-Sarissa
IŠKUR-of-Liḫzina
IŠKUR-of-Uda
IŠKUR-of-Saḫpina
IŠKUR-of-Help
Šeri
Ḫurri
Mount-Nanni
Mount-Hazzi
Ḫebat//Queen-of-Heaven

§ 18 (A iv 10–16)

LAMMA
LAMMA-of-Ḫatti
Karzi
Ḫapantaliya
LAMMA-of-Karaḫna
LAMMA-of-the-Hunting-Bag
Allatu
Moon-God//Lord-of-the-Oath
Ištar
Ištar-of-the-Countryside
Ištar-of-Nineveh
Ištar-of-Ḫattarina
Ninatta
Kulitta
Išḫara//Queen-of-the-Oath
Warrior-God
Warrior-God-of-Ḫatti
Warrior-God-of-Illaya
Warrior-God-of-Arziya
Yarri
Zappana

§ 19 (A iv 17–23)

Abara-of-Šamuḫa
Ḫantitassu-of-Ḫurma
Kataḫḫa-of-Ankuwa
Queen-of-Katapa
Ammamma-of-Taḫurpa
Ḫallara-of-Dunna
Ḫuwassanna-of-Ḫupisna
The-Mountain-Dweller-Gods
The-Mercenary-Gods
All The-Male and-Female-Deities

§ 19 (continued)

All the-Primeval-Deities:
Nara
Namsara
Ammunki
Tuḫusi
Minki
Ammizzadu
Alalu
Kumarbi
Enlil
Ninlil

§ 20 (A iv 24–30)

Mount-Ḫulla
Mount-Zaliyanu
Mount-Taḫa
The-Mountains
The-Rivers
The-Springs-of-Ḫatti
The-Great-Sea
Heaven
Earth
The-Winds
The-Clouds
All [the-Deities]-of-the-Land-of-Wilusa:
IŠKUR-of-Army
[...]appaliuma
The-Male-Deities
The-Female-Deities
The-Mountains
[The-Rivers]
[The-Springs]
The-Underground-Watercourse$^{?}$-of-the-Land-of-Wilusa

Table 2.9: Divine Witness List between Ḫattušili III of Ḫatti and Ulmi-Teššup of Tarḫund (*CTH* 106, the translation is based on Beckman, *Hittite Diplomatic Texts*, no. 18B, 111–112).

§ 7 (obv. 48′–49′)
IŠKUR-of-Lightning
UTU.MI$_2$-of-Arinna
IŠKUR-of-Ḫatti
IŠKUR-of-Nerik
Ištar-of-Šamuḫa
Ištar-of-Lawazantiya
The Thousand-Gods-of-Ḫatti

§ 8 (obv. 50′-r. 4)
(an new EGL)
The Thousand Gods:
UTU-of-Heaven
UTU.MI$_2$-of-Arinna
IŠKUR-of-Heaven
IŠKUR-of-Ḫatti
IŠKUR-of-the-Army
IŠKUR-of-Ḫisašapa
IŠKUR-of-Zippalanda
IŠKUR-of-Nerik
IŠKUR-of-Aleppo
IŠKUR-of-Uda
IŠKUR-of-Sapinuwa
The-Powerful-IŠKUR
The-Piḫaimmi-IŠKUR
IŠKUR-of-Lightning
Lulutassi
LAMMA
LAMMA-of-Ḫatti
Ayala
Karzi
Ḫapantaliya
Šarrumma
Zithariya

§ 8 (obv. 50′-r. 4, continued)
Ḫebat//Queen-of-Heaven
Ištar
Ištar-of-Nineveh
Ištar-of-Ḫattarina
Ninatta
Kulitta
Ningal
[Išḫara]
Moon-God//Lord-of-the-Oaths
Deity-of-Arusna
Warrior-God
Warrior-God-of-Ḫatti
Warrior-God-of-Illaya
Warrior-God-of-Arziya
Yarri
Zappana
Abara-of-Šamuḫa
Ḫantitassu-of-Ḫurma
Kataḫḫa-of-Ankuwa
Queen-of-Katapa
Ammamma-of-Taḫurpa
Ḫallara-of-Dunna
Ḫuwassanna-of-Ḫupisna
Lelwani
The-Mountain-Dweller-Gods
The-Mercenary-Gods
The-Male-Deities
The-Female-Deities
The-Great-Sea
The-Mountains
The-Rivers
The-Springs-of-Ḫatti and The-land-of-Tarḫund

Table 2.10: Divine Witness List between Tudḫaliya IV of Ḫatti and Kurunta of Tarḫund (*CTH* 106, the translation is based on Beckman, *Hittite Diplomatic Texts*, no. 18C, 121–122).

§ 25 (iii 78-iv 15)
UTU-of-Heaven
UTU.MI$_2$-of-Arinna
IŠKUR-of-Heaven
IŠKUR-of-Ḫatti
IŠKUR-of-the-Army
IŠKUR-of-Ḫisašapa
IŠKUR-of-Zippalanda
IŠKUR-of-Nerik
IŠKUR-of-Aleppo
IŠKUR-of-Uda
IŠKUR-of-Kizzuwatna
IŠKUR-of-Šamuḫa
IŠKUR-of-Sapinuwa
The-Powerful-IŠKUR
IŠKUR-of-Lightning
Lulutassi
LAMMA
LAMMA-of-Ḫatti
Ayala
Karzi
Ḫapantaliya
LAMMA-of-the-Countryside
LAMMA-of-the-Hunting-Bag
Zithariya
Šarrumma
Ḫebat-of-Uda
Ḫebat-of-Kizzuwatna
Ištar-of-Šamuḫa
Ištar-of-the-Countryside
Ištar-of-Lawazantiya
Ištar-of-Nineveh
Ištar-of-Ḫattarina

(cont.)
Ninatta
Kulitta
Moon-God//King-of-the-Oaths
Ningal//Queen-of-the-Oaths
Išḫara
Deity-of-Arusna
Warrior-God
Warrior-God-of-Ḫatti
Warrior-God-of-Illaya
Warrior-God-of-Arziya
Yarri
Zappana
Ḫantitassu-of-Ḫurma
Abara-of-Šamuḫa
Kataḫḫa-of-Ankuwa
Ammamma-of-Taḫurpa
Ḫuwassanna-of-Ḫupisna
Ḫallara-of-Dunna
Lelwani
The-Mountain-Dweller-Gods
The-Mercenary-Gods
The-Male-Deities
The-Female-Deities
Heaven
Earth
The-Great-Sea
The-Mountains
The-Rivers-and-Springs-of-Ḫatti and-the-Land-of-Tarḫund

Table 3.1: AN : *Anum* (Litke, *Reconstruction*, 20–227).[8]

I 1	Anu
I 33	Papsukkal
I 148	Enlil
I 176	Mullissu
I 205	Ninurta
I 294	Nisaba
I 357	Nergal
II 3	Ninḫursaĝa
II 129	Ea
II 173	Damkina
II 185	Marduk
II 236	Zarpānītu
II 242	Nabû
II 247	Tašmētu
III 1	Sîn
III 27	Ningal
III 97	Šamaš
III 126	Aya
III 206	Adad
III 240	Šala
IV 1	Ištar
V 192	Manungal

Table 3.2: AN : *Anu* : *ša amēli* (Litke, *Reconstruction*, 228–241).

1	Anu
13	Enlil
22	Mullissu
24	Sîn
39	Ningal
40	Šamaš
45	Aya
48	Adad
59	Šala
61	Papsukkal
70	Ninurta
76	Nergal
86	Ištar
97	Nisaba
100	Sumuqan
107	Marduk
113	Nabû
119	Ea
149	Manugal

Table 3.3: The Positions of Localized Ištar Goddesses in EGLs in Esarhaddon's Royal Inscriptions (RINAP 4, Esar.).[9]

Text:	DN(s):	position(s):	of total DNs:
1 i 6	^{d}15 *ša* ^{uru}*ni-nu-a* ^{d}15 *ša*$_2$ ^{uru}*arba-il*$_3$	5 and 6	6
1 i 10	^{d}15 *ša*$_2$ ^{uru}*ni-nu-a*^{ki} ^{d}15 *ša*$_2$ ^{uru}*arba-il*$_3$	6 and 7	7
1 i 45	^{d}15 *ša*$_2$ NINA^{ki} ^{d}15 *ša*$_2$ ^{uru}*arba-il*$_3$	6 and 7	7
1 i 59	^{d}15 *ša*$_2$ ^{uru}NINA^{ki} ^{d}15 *ša*$_2$ ^{uru}*arba-il*$_3$	7 and 8	8
1 ii 16	^{d}*iš-tar šar-ra-ti*	7	7
1 ii 38	^{d}*iš-tar be-let* MURUB$_4$ *u* ME$_3$	6	6
1 ii 45–46	^{d}15 *ša*$_2$ NINA^{ki} ^{46} ^{d}15 *ša*$_2$ ^{uru}*arba-il*$_3$	5 and 6	6
1 iv 78–79	^{d}15 *ša*$_2$ NINA^{ki} ^{79} ^{d}15 *ša*$_2$ ^{uru}*arba-il*$_3$	6 and 7	7
1 v 34	^{d}15 *ša*$_2$ NINA^{ki} ^{d}15 *ša*$_2$ ^{uru}*arba-il*$_3$	5 and 6	6
1 vi 44	^{d}15 *ša*$_2$ NINA^{ki} ^{d}15 *ša*$_2$ ^{uru}*arba-il*$_3$	4 and 6	5
2 i 9	^{d}15 *ša*$_2$ NINA^{ki} ^{d}15 *ša*$_2$ ^{uru}*arba-il*$_3$	6 and 7	7
2 iv 22	^{d}15 *ša*$_2$ NINA^{ki} ^{d}15 *ša*$_2$ ^{uru}*arba-il*$_3$	5 and 6	6
3 iv 21′	^{d}15 *ša*$_2$ NINA^{ki} $^{d⸢}$15⸣ [*ša*$_2$] ⸢^{uru}⸣*arba-il*$_3$	5 and 6	6
5 i 3′	^{d}15 *ša*$_2$ *ni-*[*nu-a* ^{d}15 *ša*$_2$ ^{uru}*arba-il*$_3$]	6 and 7	7
6 i 5′–6′	^{d}15 *ša*$_2$ NINA^{ki} $^{6'}$ [^{d}15 *ša*$_2$ ^{uru}*arba-il*$_3$]	7 and 8	8
8 ii′ 4′–5′	[^{d}15 *ša*$_2$ NINA^{ki}] $^{5'}$ ^{d}15 *ša*$_2$ ^{uru}*arba-il*$_3$ $^{d⸢}$*gu-še*⸣-[*a*]	8 and 9	10
33 (tablet 2) iii 11′	^{d}INANNA *ša*$_2$ NINA^{ki} ^{d}INANNA *ša*$_2$ $^{uru⸢}$*arba*⸣*-il*$_3$	8 and 9	10$^{?}$
48:25–26	^{d}*iš-tar ša*$_2$ ^{uru}*ni-na-a šar-ra-tu*$_2$ GAL-*tu*$_2$ [*hi*]-*šiḫ-tu* *ša*$_2$ ^{d}*iš-tar-a-*[*ti ša*$_2$ ^{d}15 *ša*$_2$] ^{uru}*arba-il*$_3$	3 and 4	4
70:3	^{d}15 ⸢*ša*$_2$⸣ NINA$^{⸢ki⸣}$ ^{d}15 *ša*$_2$ ^{uru}*arba-il*$_3$	6 and 7	7
71:3	^{d}INANNA *ša*$_2$ NINA^{ki} ^{d}INANNA *ša*$_2$ ^{uru}*arba-il*$_3$	6 and 7	7
77:12	^{d}15 *ša* NINA^{ki} ^{d}15 *ša* ^{uru}*arba-il*$_3$	6 and 7	7
78:11	[^{d}15] *ša*$_2$ NINA^{ki} [^{d}]15 *ša* ^{uru}*arba-il*$_3$	6 and 7	7
79:11	[^{d}15 *ša* NINA]^{ki} ^{d}15 *ša* ^{uru}*arba-*⸢*il*$_3$⸣	6 and 7	7
79:6′	[^{d}15 *ša* NINA^{ki} ^{d}15 *ša* ^{uru}*arba-il*$_3$]	7 and 8	8
93:5	^{d}15 *ša* NINA^{ki} ^{d}15 *ša* ^{uru}*arba-il*$_3$	6 and 7	7
93:26	^{d}15 *ša* NINA^{ki} ^{d}15 *ša* ^{uru}*arba-il*$_3$	7 and 8	8
98:9	^{d}INANNA *be-let* MURUB$_4$ *u* ME$_3$	9	10
98:22	^{d}*iš-tar i-lat kal gim-ri*	6	6
101 r. 4′	^{d}*iš-tar i-lat kal gim-*[*ri*]	6	6
133:10	^{d}15	11	11
133:14	^{d}15	4	4
1006:11′	⸢^{d}15⸣ *arba-il*$_3$	4	4

Table 3.4: The Positions of Ištar-of-Nineveh and Ištar-of-Arbela in EGLs in Letters (SAA 10, SAA 13, and SAA 16).

Text:		DN(s):	positions:	of total DNs:
SAA 10	82:6–7	^{d}15 *ša* NINA^{ki} ^{7} ^{d}15 *ša* ^{uru}*arba-il*$_{3}$	6 and 7	7
	83:4–5	^{d}15 *ša* [NINA^{ki}] ^{5} [^{d}15] *ša* ^{uru}*arba-il*$_{3}$	3 and 4	4
	130:6–7	^{d}[15] *ša* NINA^{ki} ^{7} ^{d}[15] *ša* ^{uru}*arba-il*$_{3}$	3 and 4	4
	174:6	^{d}GAŠAN NINA^{ki} ^{d}15 *ša*$_{2}$ ^{uru}*arba-il*$_{3}$	5 and 6	6
	l. 18	^{d}15 *ša*$_{2}$ NINA^{ki} ^{d}15 *ša*$_{2}$ ^{uru}*arba-il*$_{3}$	10 and 11	11
	227:5	^{d}15 *ša* ^{uru}NINA^{ki} ^{d}15 *ša* ^{uru}*arba-il*$_{3}$	10 and 11	15
	228:4–5	^{d}15 *ša* ^{uru}NINA^{ki} ^{5} ^{d}15 *ša* ^{uru}*arba-il*$_{3}$	9 and 10	15
	245:5–6	^{d}15 *ša* NINA^{ki} ^{6} ^{d}15 *ša* ^{uru}*arba-il*$_{3}$	7 and 8	8
	249:2′–3′	[^{d}15 *ša*$_{2}$ NINA^{ki}] $^{3'}$ ^{d}15 *ša*$_{2}$ ⸢*arba*⸣-[*il*$_{3}$]	7 and 8	8
	252:7–8	[^{d}]15 *ša* NINA^{ki} ^{d}15 ^{8} ⸢*ša*⸣ ^{uru}*arba*-[*il*$_{3}$]	7 and 8	8
	286:6	[^{d}15 *ša*$_{2}$ ^{uru}NINA^{ki} ^{d}15 *ša*$_{2}$] ^{uru}*arba-il*$_{3}$	14 and 15	19
	293:4	[^{d}15 *ša*$_{2}$ ^{uru}NINA^{ki}] ^{d}15 *ša*$_{2}$ ^{uru}*arba-il*$_{3}$	5 and 6	10
	294:3	[^{d}15 *ša* ^{uru}NINA^{ki} ^{d}15] *ša* ^{uru}⸢*arba*⸣-[*il*$_{3}$]	5 and 6	10
SAA 13	9:7–8	^{d}15 *ša* NINA^{ki} ^{8} ^{d}15 *ša* ^{uru}*arba-il*$_{3}$	6 and 7	7
	10:7–8	^{d}15 *ša* ^{uru}NINA ^{8} ^{d}15 *ša* ^{uru}*arba-il*$_{3}$	6 and 7	7
	12:6	^{d}15 *ša* NINA^{ki} ^{d}15 *ša* ^{uru}*arba-il*$_{3}$	6 and 7	7
	15:7–8	^{d}15 *ša* NINA^{ki} ^{8} ^{d}15 *ša* ^{uru}*arba-il*$_{3}$	6 and 7	7
	56:6	^{d}15 *ša* ^{uru}NINA ^{d}15 *ša* ^{uru}*arba-il*$_{3}$	8 and 9	9
	57:7–8	[^{d}15 *ša* ^{uru}]⸢NINA⸣^{ki} ^{8} [^{d}15 *ša* ^{uru}*arba*]-⸢*il*$_{3}$⸣	8 and 9	9
	58:6–7	^{d}15 *ša* ^{uru}NINA ^{7} ^{d}15 *ša* ^{uru}*arba-il*$_{3}$	8 and 9	9
	60:6	[^{d}15 *ša* ^{uru}NINA ^{d}15 *ša* ^{uru}*arba-il*$_{3}$]	8 and 9	9
	61:6–7	^{d}15 *ša* NINA^{ki} ^{7} ^{d}15 *ša* ^{uru}*arba-il*$_{3}$	7 and 8	8
	62:6–7	^{d}15 *ša* ^{uru}NINA ^{7} ^{d}15 *ša* ^{uru}*arba-il*$_{3}$	8 and 9	9
	64:6–7	[^{d}15 *ša*] ^{7} ^{uru}[NINA ^{d}15 *ša* ^{uru}*arba-il*$_{3}$]	8 and 9	9
	65:6–7	^{d}15 *ša*$_{2}$ NINA^{ki} ^{7} ^{d}15 *ša*$_{2}$ ^{uru}*arba-il*$_{3}$	7 and 8	8
	66:6	^{d}15 *ša*$_{2}$ NINA^{ki} [^{d}15 *ša*$_{2}$ ^{uru}*arba-il*$_{3}$]	8 and 9	9
	67:5–6	^{d}15 [*ša* NINA^{ki}] ^{6} ^{d}[15] ⸢*ša*⸣ ^{uru}*arba-il*$_{3}$	7 and 8	8
	68:6	^{d}15 *ša*$_{2}$ NINA$^{⸢ki⸣}$ [^{d}15 *ša*$_{2}$ ^{uru}*arba-il*$_{3}$]	8 and 9	9
	140:5–7	^{d}15 ^{6} ⸢*ša*⸣ ^{uru}*ni-nu-a* ^{d}15 ^{7} [*ša*] ^{uru}*arba-il*$_{3}$	4 and 5	5
	156:6–7	^{d}15 *ša* ^{uru}*ni-nu-*[*a*] ^{7} ^{d}15 *ša* ^{uru}*arba-il*$_{3}$	4 and 5	5
SAA 16	1:10	^{d}15 *ša* NINA^{ki} ^{d}15 *ša* ^{uru}*arba-il*$_{3}$	6 and 7	7
	33:6–7	[^{d}15 *š*]*a* ^{uru}NINA^{ki} ^{7} [^{d}15 *š*]*a* ^{uru}*arba-il*$_{3}$	6 and 7	7
	49:4–5	^{d}15 *ša* NINA^{ki} ^{5} ^{d}15 *ša* ^{uru}*arba-il*$_{3}$	6 and 7	7
	59:3	^{d}15 *ša*$_{2}$ ^{uru}NINA ^{d}15 *ša*$_{2}$ ^{uru}*arba-il*$_{3}$	5 and 6	6
	60:3	^{d}15 *ša*$_{2}$ [NINA^{ki} ^{d}15 *ša*$_{2}$ ^{uru}*arba-il*$_{3}$]	5 and 6	6
	61:3	[^{d}15 *ša*$_{2}$ ^{ur}]^{u}NINA ^{d}15 *ša*$_{2}$ [^{uru}*arba-il*$_{3}$]	5 and 6	6
	128:5	^{d}15 *ša* ⸢NINA⸣^{ki} ^{d}15 *ša* *arba*-⸢*il*$_{3}$⸣	6 and 7	7

Table 3.5a: EGLs in Land Grants and other Documents from SAA 12.[10]

i	ii	iii	iv	v
13 r. 8′–9′;	14 r. 7′–8′;	10 r. 6′–8′;	25 r.33–34 & 36–37;	35 r. 30;
69 r. 28;	75 r. 11′?	19 r. 22	26 r.33–34 & 36–37;	36 r. 33′;
85:13–14			31 r.33–34 & 36–37;	40 r. 12′–13′;
			34:6′–7′ & 9′–10′	41 r. 3′
Assur	Assur	Assur	Assur	Assur
		Šamaš		
		[Enlil]		Enlil
Adad	Adad		Adad	Adad
Bēr	Bēr		Bēr	Bēr
	Assyrian-Enlil		Assyrian-Enlil	
Assyrian-Ištar	Assyrian-Ištar	Assyrian-Ištar	Assyrian-Ištar	Assyrian-Ištar
		Adad		
		Bēr		
		Nergal		
		Ninurta		
		the Sebittu		

Table 3.5b: The Composite God List derived from EGLs in Documents from Private archives in SAAB 5, SAAB 9, and Faist.[11]

Assur
⟨Ištar⟩[12]
Šamaš
Adad
Bēl
Nabû
    Tašmētu
[Sîn][13]
Nergal[14]
Mullissu
Šerū'a
Ištar-of-Arbela

Legend: ⟨ ⟩ the unspecified DN does not appear in EGLs in royal inscriptions with other same DN-named deities

Table 3.6: Composite God Lists from Seventh-Century Letters.[15]

SAA 13, 16, and 18:[16]	**SAA 10:**[17]
Assur	Enlil[18]
Mullissu[19] (Ištar)[20]	Mullissu
Anu	
Enlil[21]	**Assur**
Mullissu	**Mullissu**[22]
Ea[23]	
Sîn	Sîn
Ningal	Ningal
Nusku[24]	
Šamaš[25]	Šamaš[26]
Aya	Aya
Adad[27]	Adad[28]
Šala	Šala
	Nusku[29]
	Jupiter
	Venus
Marduk	**Marduk**[30]
Zarpānītu	**Zarpānītu**
Lady-of-Babylon	
Nabû[31]	**Nabû**
Tašmētu	**Tašmētu**
Nanaya[32]	
	Saturn
	Mercury
	Ištar-of-Nineveh
	Queen-of-Kidmuri
	Ištar-of-Arbela
Ninurta	Ninurta
Gula	Gula
Zababa	
Nergal	Nergal[33]
Laṣ	Laṣ
Madānu[34]	
Ištar-of-Nineveh[35]	
Ištar-of-Kidmuri	
Ištar-of-Arbela	
Queen-of-Nakkanti[36]	

Table 3.7: SAA 10 286:3–7. An EGL from a Blessing.

Enlil Mullissu	3 ^{d}BAD ^{d}NIN.LIL$_2$
Ass[ur]	^{d}*aš-šur*
[Sîn Ningal]	4[^{d}30 ^{d}NIN.GAL]
[Šamaš] Aya	[^{d}UTU] ^{d}*a-a*
Adad [Šala]	^{d}IŠKUR ^{d}[*ša-la*]
[Marduk Zarpānītu]	5[^{d}AMAR.UTU ^{d}*zar-pa-ni-tu*$_4$]
Nabû Tašmētu	^{d}AG ^{d}*taš-me-tu*$_4$
[Ištar-of-Nineveh Ištar-of]-Arbela	6[^{d}15 *ša*$_2$ ^{uru}NINA^{ki} ^{d}15 *ša*$_2$] ^{uru}*arba-il*$_3$
Ninurta Gula	^{d}MAŠ ^{d}*gu-la*
[Nergal Laṣ]	7[^{d}U.GUR ^{d}*la-aṣ*]
[the Great Gods] who dwell in Heaven and Earth	[DINGIR^{meš} GAL^{meš}] *a-šib* AN-*e u* KI.TIM

Table 3.8: SAA 10 197. Blessing the King, by Adad-šumu-uṣur, the Exorcist.

7	**Assur**	^{d}*aš-šur*
	Sîn	^{d}30
	Šamaš	^{d}UTU
	Adad	^{d}IŠKUR
	Nu[sku]	^{d}*n*[*usku*]
8	**Jupiter**	^{d}SAG.ME.GAR
	Venus	^{d}*dil-bat*
	Marduk	^{d}AMAR.UTU
	[Zarpānītu]	⸢^{d}⸣[*zar-pa-ni-tu*$_4$]
9	**Nabû**	^{d}AG
	Tašmētu	^{d}*taš-me-tu*$_4$
	Sa[turn]	^{d}UDU.[IDIM.SAG.UŠ]
10	**Mercury**	^{d}UDU.IDIM.GUD.DU
	Queen-[of-Nineveh]	^{d}*šar-ra*[*t* ^{uru}NINA^{ki}]
11	**Queen-of-Kidmuri**	^{d}*šar-rat kid-mu-ri*
12	**[Queen]-of-Arbela**	^{d}[*šar-rat*] ^{uru}*arba-il*$_3$
	Ninurta	^{d}NIN.URTA
	[Gula]	⸢^{d}⸣[*gu-la*]
13	**Nergal**	^{d}U.GUR
	Laṣ	^{d}*la-aṣ*
14	The great gods of Heaven and Earth	DINGIR^{meš} GA[L^{meš}] *ša* AN-*e u* KI.TIM

Table 3.9: Curse Lists from the Laws of Ḫammurapi's Epilogue, Neo-Assyrian Treaties, and a Private Votive Offering Inscription (SAA 12 93).

LH xlix 18-li 83	**SAA 2 1:16′-r. 16**	**SAA 2 6:414–465**	**SAA 2 9 r. 5′–25′**	**SAA 2 14 i 28′–ii 2′, ii 16′, and 19′–25′**[37]	**SAA 12 93 r. 6–7 and 15-r. 5**[38]
		Assur	**Assur**	**Assur**	**Assur**
		Mullissu		**Šerū'a**	
				Gods-of-the-Ešarra-temple	
	Marduk		**Marduk**		
	Nabû		**Nabû**		
				( )- [39]	
Anu	[Anu]	Anu		Anu	
				Antu	
Enlil	Enlil			Enlil	
Mullissu	Mullissu			Mullissu	
Ea	Ea				
Šamaš	Šamaš	Sîn	Šamaš		[Sîn]
Sîn	[Sîn]	Šamaš	Sîn		[Šamaš]
			Ea		**Bēl**
Adad	[Adad]		Adad		
		Ninurta	Ninurta		[Nergal]
			Nergal		Ninurta
Zababa	[Zababa]		Zababa		
			Palil		
Ištar		Venus			Gula
Nergal		Jupiter			
		Marduk		**Bēl/Marduk**	
		Zarpānītu	Zarpānītu	**Bēltīya/[Zarpānītu]**	
		Bēlet-ilī			
		Adad			Adad
		Ištar			
		Nergal	Nanaya		**Nabû**
Nintu		Mullissu-of-Nineveh			
Ninkarrak		I-o-A	I-o-A		I-o-[A]
		Gula			
		the Sebittu		the Sebittu	

Legend: I-o-A Ištar-of-Arbela

Table 3.10: SAA 2 2. Assur-nērārī V's Treaty with Mati'-ilu of Arpad.[40]

vi 6	**Assur**	^{d}*aš-sur* MAN AN KI *tum*$_{3}$*-ma-tu*$_{2}$*-nu*
7	Anu and Antu	^{d}*a-nu-um an-tu*$_{4}$ KI.MIN
	Enlil and Mullissu	^{d}BAD ^{d}NIN.LIL$_{2}$ KI.MIN
8	Ea and Damkina	^{d}DIŠ ^{d}*dam-ki-na* KI.MIN
	Sîn and Ningal	^{d}30 ^{d}NIN.GAL KI.MIN
9	Šamaš and Aya	^{d}UTU ^{d}*a-a* KI.MIN
	Adad and Šala	^{d}IŠKUR ^{d}*ša-la* KI.MIN
10	**Marduk** and **Zarpānītu**	^{d}AMAR.UTU ^{d}*zar-pa-ni-tu*$_{4}$ KI.MIN
	Nabû and **Tašmētu**	^{d}AG ^{d}LAL$_{2}$ KI.MIN
11	Ninurta and Gula	^{d}MAŠ ^{d}ME KI.MIN
	Uraš and Bēlet-ekalli	^{d}*uraš* ^{d}NIN.E$_{2}$.GAL KI.MIN
12	Zababa and Bau	^{d}*za-ba*$_{4}$*-ba*$_{4}$ ^{d}*ba*-U$_{2}$ KI.MIN
	Nergal and Laṣ	^{d}U.GUR ^{d}*la-aṣ* KI.MIN
13	Madānu and Ningirsu	^{d}DI.KUD ^{d}NIN.GIR$_{2}$.SU KI.MIN
14	Ḫumḫummu and Išum	^{d}*ḫum-ḫum-mu* ^{d}*i-šum* KI.MIN
15	Erra and Nusku	^{d}GIŠ.BAR ^{d}PA.TUG$_{2}$ KI.MIN
	Ištar//Lady-of-Nineveh	^{d}15 NIN ^{uru}*ni-na-a* KI.MIN
16	Ištar//Lady-of-Arbela	^{d}INNIN NIN ^{uru}*arba-il*$_{3}$ KI.MIN
17	Adad-of-Kurbail	^{d}IŠKUR *ša*$_{2}$ ^{uru}*kur-ba-il*$_{3}$ KI.MIN
18	Hadad-of-Aleppo	^{d}IŠKUR *ša*$_{2}$ ^{uru}*ḫal-la-ba* KI.MIN
19	*Palil*, who marches in front	^{d}IGI.DU *a-lik maḫ-ri* KI.MIN
20	the heroic Sebittu	^{d}7.BI *qar-du-ti* KI.MIN
21	Dagan [and M]uṣuruna	^{d}[*d*]*a-*⌜*gan*⌝ ⌜^{d}⌝[*m*]*u*$^{?}$*-ṣur-u-na* KI.MIN
22	M[elqart and Eš]mun	^{d}*m*[*i-il-qar-tu* ^{d}*ia-s*]*u*$^{!}$*-mu-na* KI.MIN
23	Kub[aba and Kar]ḫuḫa	^{d}*k*⌜*u*$_{2}$⌝$^{!}$*-b*[*a-ba* ^{d}*kar*]*-ḫu-ḫa* KI.MIN
24	Hadad, [...], and Ramman-	^{d}IŠKUR ^{d}[*x*] ⌜*x* $^{d!}$*ra*$^{!}$*-ma*$^{!}$*-nu*$^{!}$⌝
25	of-[Damascus]	*ša* ^{ur}[^{u}*di-maš-qa* KI.MIN]
26	Za ...	^{d}*za-*[*x x x x x x x x*]
	Rest broken away	

Legend: Two parallel lines (//) are used here and elsewhere to indicate that a proper name and epithet are acting together with the force of a full name (e.g., Ištar//Lady-of-Nineveh).

Table 3.11: SAA 2 3 (restored) and BM 121206 ix 27′–34′ (Menzel, *Assyrische Tempel*, 2:T66, no. 35). Sennacherib-Period God Lists.

SAA 2 3 r. 2′–5′ (and obv. 7′–11′):		**BM 121206 ix 27′–34′:**	
[**Assur**]	[*aš-šur*]	**Assur**	^{d}*aš-šur*
[**Mullisu**]	[^{d}NIN.LIL$_2$]	**Mullissu**	^{d}NIN.LIL$_2$
[**Šerū'a**]	[^{d}*še-ru-u-a*]	**Šerū'a**	^{d}*še-ru-u-a*
Sîn	⌜d⌝30	Sîn	^{d}30
Ningal	^{d}NIN.GAL	Ningal	^{d}NIN.GAL
Šamaš	^{d}UTU	Šamaš	^{d}UTU
[Aya]	[^{d}*a-a*]	Aya	^{d}*a-a*
[Anu]	[^{d}*a-num*]	Anu	^{d}*a-nu*
[Antu]	[*an-tu$_4$*]	Antu	^{d}*an-tu$_4$*
		Kippat-māti	^{d}GUR$_2$.KUR
[E]nlil	[^{d}E]N.LIL$_2$	Enlil	^{d}EN.LIL$_2$
Adad	^{d}IŠKUR	Adad	^{d}IŠKUR
Šala	^{d}*ša-la*	Šala	^{d}*ša-la*
[Kippat-māti]	[^{d}GAM.KUR]		
[Ištar-of-Heaven]	[^{d}15 *ša$_2$* AN-*e*]	Ištar-of-Heaven	^{d}15 *ša$_2$* AN-*e*
[Ištar-of-Nineveh]	[^{d}15 *ša$_2$* NINA^{ki}	Ištar-of-Nineveh	^{d}15 *ša$_2$* NINA^{ki}
[Ištar-ofArb]ela	[^{d}15 *ša$_2$ arba*]-*il$_3$*^{ki}	Ištar-of-Arbela	^{d}15 *ša$_2$ arba-il$_3$*
Assyrian-Ištar	^{d}15 *aš-šur*-[*i-tu$_2$*]	Assyrian-Ištar	^{d}15 *aš-šu-ri-tu*
[Zababa]	[^{d}*za-ba$_4$-ba$_4$*]	Zababa	^{d}*za-ba$_4$-ba$_4$*
[Bau]	[^{d}*ba*-U$_2$]	Bau	^{d}*ba*-U$_2$
[Ea]	[^{d}*e$_2$-a*]	Ea	^{d}DIŠ
[Bēlet-ilī][41]	[^{d}MAḪ]	Bēlet-ilī	^{d}MAḪ
[Damkina]	[^{d}*dam-ki-na*]	Damkina	^{d}*dam-ki-na*
---		Ninurta	^{d}MAŠ
[Kakk]a	[^{d}*ka$_3$*]-*ka$_3$*	Kakka	^{d}*ka$_3$-ka$_3$*
Nergal	^{d}U.GUR	Nergal	^{d}U.GUR
---		**Marduk**	^{d}AMAR.UTU

Table 3.12: Sefire i A 7–14 (*KAI* 222). Treaty between Barga'yah of KTK and Mati'-ilu of Arpad.

[before **Assur**][42] and **Mullissu**	*[qdm 'sr]* [8]*wmlš*
before **Marduk** and **Zarpānītu**	*wqdm mrdk wzrpnt*
before **Nabû** [and **Tašmētu**]	*wqdm nb' wt[šmt*
[before **Erra** and **Nus**]**ku**	*wqdm 'r wnš]*[9]*k*
before **Nergal** and **Laṣ**	*wqdm nrgl wlṣ*
before **Šamaš** and **Nur** (=**Aya**?)	*wqdm šmš wnr*
before **Sîn** [and **Ningal**]	*wqdm s[n wnkl*
[be]fore **NKR** and **KD'H**	*wq]*[10]*dm nkr wkd'h*
before Gods of the open country	*wqdmkl 'lhy rḥbh*
and [cultivated] ground	*w'dm[...*
[before **Hadad-of**]-**Aleppo**	*wqdm hdd ḥ]*[11]*lb*
before the **Sebittu**	*wqdm sbt*
before El and Elyon[43]	*wqdm 'l w'lyn*
before **Heaven** [and **Earth**]	*wqdm šmy[n w'rq*
[before **Abyss**] and **Springs**	*wqdm mṣ]*[12]*lh*
	wm'ynn
before **Day** and **Night**	*wqdm ywm wlylh*

Table 3.13: Comparing SAA 2 2 (Table 3.10) and Sefire i A Witness Lists (Table 3.12).

SAA 2 2 vi 6–26:	Sefire i A 7–14 (*KAI* 222):
Assur	[**Assur**] and **Mullissu**
Anu and Antu	
Enlil and Mullissu	
Ea and Damkina	
Sîn and Ningal	
Šamaš and Aya	
Adad and Šala	
Marduk and **Zarpānītu**	**Marduk** and **Zarpānītu**
Nabû and **Tašmētu**	**Nabû** [and **Tašmētu**]
Ninurta and Gula	
	[Erra and Nus]ku
Uraš and Ninegal	
Zababa and Bau	
Nergal and Laṣ	Nergal and Laṣ
Madanu and Ningirsu	
Ḫumḫummu and Išum	
Erra and Nusku	
	Šamaš and Nur (=Aya?)
	Sîn [and Ningal]
	and
Ištar//Lady-of-Nineveh	
Ištar//Lady-of-Arbela	
	Gods of the open country and [cultivated] ground
Adad-of-Kurbail	
Hadad-of-Aleppo	[Hadad-of]-Aleppo
Palil, who marches in front	
the heroic Sebittu	Sebittu
	El and Elyon
Dagan and [M]uṣuruna	
M[elqart and Eš]mun	
Kub[aba and Kar]ḫuḫa	
Hadad, [...], and Ramman-of-[Damascus]	
Za ...	[and]
	[ ] and
	and

Table 3.14: EGLs from Royal Inscriptions.

Tiglath-pileser III:[44]	Sargon:[45]	Sennacherib:[46]	Esarhaddon:[47]	Assurbanipal:[48]
Assur	**Assur**[49]	**Assur**	**Assur**	**Assur**
		[Mullissu][50]	**Mullissu**[51]	**Mullissu**[52]
Šerū'a		**Šerū'a**	**Šerū'a**[53]	
	Anu	Anu	Anu[54]	
		Antu[55]	Antu	
Enlil[56]	Enlil	Enlil	Enlil	
			(Mullissu)[57]	
	Ea	Ea[58]	Ea[59]	Ea[60]
	Ninšiku[61]		Bēlet-ilī	Bēlet-ilī
	Dagan			
	Sîn	Sîn	Sîn	Sîn[62]
	Ningal	Ningal	Ningal	
	Šamaš	Šamaš	Šamaš[63]	Šamaš
		Aya	Aya	
	Adad[64]	Adad	Adad	Adad
		Šala		
	Nabû[65]			
Marduk/Bēl[66]	***Marduk***	**Marduk** (Šamaš)[67]	**Bēl**[68]	**Marduk/Bēl**[69]
Zarpānītu	**Zarpānītu**		**Bēltiya**	**Zarpānītu**
Nabû		**Nabû**	**Nabû**[70]	**Nabû**
Tašmētu	**Tašmētu**		**Tašmētu**	**Tašmētu**
Nanaya			**Nanaya** [71]	**Nanaya**
Lady-of-Babylon [72]				
	Ninurta	Ninurta	Ninurta[73]	
			Gula	

Table 3.14: (concluded).

Tiglath-pileser III:	Sargon:	Sennacherib:	Esarhaddon:	Assurbanipal:
Nergal[74]		Nergal[75]	Nergal	
Laṣ				
	Ištar[76]	⟨Ištar⟩[77]	⟨Ištar⟩[78]	⟨Ištar⟩[79]
		Ištar-of-Nineveh[80]	Ištar-of-Nineveh[81]	Ištar-of-Nineveh
		Ištar-of-Kidmuri[82]		Ištar-of-Kidmuri
		Ištar-of-Arbela	Ištar-of-Arbela	Ištar-of-Arbela
	Consorts[83]	Bēlet-ilī	Gušea/Agušāya[84]	Assyrian-Ištar[85]
Šamaš[86]		Kakka[87]		
[Sîn][88]		Ḫaya		Ninurta
Adad		Kusu		Nergal
Ea		Lumḫa	Nusku	Nusku[89]
Ištar//Lady-of-Battle		Dunga		Išum[90]
		Egalkiba		
the Sebittu		the Sebittu	the Sebittu	
Amurru[91]				
Sumuqan				

Legend: ⟨ ⟩ the unspecified DN does not appear in EGLs in royal inscriptions with other same DN-named deities.

Table 3.15: SAA 2 6. Esarhaddon's Succession Treaty: God List 1, the Witness List.

line:	God:	cuneiform:
13	Jupiter	(*ina* IGI) ^{mul}SAG.ME.GAR
	Venus	^{mul}*dil-bat*
14	Saturn	^{mul}UDU.IDIM.SAG.UŠ
	Mercury	^{mul}UDU.IDIM.GUD.UD
15	Mars	^{mul} *zal-bat-a-nu*
	Sirius	^{mul}GAG.SI.SA$_2$
16	**Assur**	(*ina* IGI) ^{d}*aš-šur*
	Anu	^{d}*a-num*
	Enlil	^{d}EN.L[IL$_2$]
	Ea	^{d}*e*$_2$-*a*
17	Sîn	^{d}30
	Šamaš	^{d}*ša*$_2$-*maš*
	Adad	^{d}IŠKUR
	Marduk	^{d}AMAR.UTU
18	**Nabû**	^{d}PA
	Nusku	^{d}*nuska*
	Uraš	^{d}*uraš*
	Nergal	^{d}U.GUR
19	Mullissu	^{d}NIN.LIL$_2$
	Šerū'a	^{d}*še-ru-u-a*
	Bēlet-ilī	^{d}*be-let*-DINGIR^{meš}
20	Ištar-of-Nineveh	^{d}15 *ša* ^{uru}NINA^{ki}
	Ištar-of-Arbela	^{d}15 *ša* ^{uru}*arba-il*$_3$
21	Gods dwelling in heaven and earth	DINGIR^{meš} *a-ši-bu-ti* AN-*e* KI.TIM
22	Gods of Assyria	DINGIR^{meš} ^{kur}*aš-šur*
	Gods of Sumer and [Akka]d	DINGIR^{meš} ^{kur}*šu-me-ri u* [UR]I.[K]I
23	Gods of the Lands	DINGIR^{meš} KUR.KUR

Table 3.16: Composite Divine Witness List from SAA 12 10 and SAA 2 2 and 6 (Tables 3.5a iii, 3.10, and 3.15, respectively).[92]

Assur[93]
Anu
  Antu
Enlil[94]
  (Mullissu)
Ea
  Damkina
Sîn
  Ningal
Šamaš
  Aya
Adad
  Šala
Marduk
  Zarpānītu
Nabû
  Tašmētu
Ninurta
  Gula
Uraš
  Ninegal
Zababa
  Bau
Nergal
  Laṣ
Madānu
Ningirsu
Ḫumḫummu
Išum
Erra
Nusku
Mullissu
Šerū'a
Bēlet-ilī
Ištar-of-Nineveh
Ištar-of-Arbela
Assyrian-Ištar[95]
Adad-of-Kurbail
Hadad-of-Aleppo
Palil
the Sebittu

Table 3.17: Neo-Babylonian Royal Judge Witness Lists (chart 1, derived from Wunsch, "Richter des Nabonid," 570–571).[96]

Text	Nabonidus's Regnal Year	Nabû-ēṭir	Bēl-zēri mār Rīmût-DN	Esagil-šadûnu	Marduk-šuma-uṣur	Mušēzib-Marduk	Nabû-zēr-kitti	**Nergal-ušallim**	Bēl-uballiṭ	Bēl-zēri mār Eppeš-ilī	**Nergal-bānûnu**
Nbn. 13	0			1	2	3	4	**6**	5		
Nbn. 16	0					1		**2**			**3**
Nbn. 1128	1+x			1	2	3	4	**6**	5		
Nbn. 64	2	1				3		**4**	5	6	**7**
BM 32174	2+x	1	2					**3**	4	5	**6**
BM 34392	3	1	2			3		**4**	5	6	**7**
AJSL 27 216	[x?]	1	2					**3**	4	5	**6**
TCL 12 86	6	1						**2**	3	4	**5**
BM 32157	[x]	1						**2**	3	4	**5**
BM 31546	[9+x]							**1**	2		**3**
MM 363b	(x)							**?**			**1+**
BM 33056	[9]							**1**	2		**3**
BM 32166	[x]							**1**	2		**3**
BM 31961	[9]							**1**			**2**
Nbn. 355	9							**1**			
Nbn. 356	9										**1**
BM 31672	9							**1**			
BM 32023	[11]										**1**
Nbn. 495	11+							**1**			**2**
Nbn. 608	12							**1**			
BM 79049	12							**1**			**2**
Nbn. 668	12							**1**			
BM 34196	12							**1**			**2**
TCL 12 122	1[2]							**1**			**2**
BM 32846	[x]							**?**			**1+**
Nbn. 720	13							**1**			
BM 40263	[x]							**1**			
Nbn. 776	14							**1**			

Table 3.17: Neo-Babylonian Royal Judge Witness Lists (chart 2, derived from Wunsch, “Richter des Nabonid,” 570–571).

Text	Nabonidus’s Regnal Year	**Nergal-ušallim**	Bēl-uballiṭ	Bēl-zēri mār Eppeš-ili	**Nergal-bānûnu**	Nabû-aḫḫē-iddin	Nabû-šuma-ukīn	Bēl-aḫḫē-iddin	Bēl-ēṭir	**Nabû-balāssu-iqbi**
Nbn. 13	0	**6**	5							
Nbn. 16	0	**2**			**3**	4				
Nbn. 1128	1+x	**6**	5							
Nbn. 64	2	**4**	5	6	**7**	8				
BM 32174	2+x	**3**	4	5	**6**	7				
BM 34392	3	**4**	5	6	**7**	8				
AJSL 27 216	[x?]	**3**	4	5	**6**					
TCL 12 86	6	**2**	3	4	**5**	6				
BM 32157	[x]	**2**	3	4	**5**					
BM 31546	[9+x]	**1**	2		**3**		4	5	6	**7**
MM 363b	(x)	**?**			**1+**	2+	3+		4+	**5+**
BM 33056	[9]	**1**	2		**3**		4	5	6	**7**
BM 32166	[x]	**1**	2		**3**		[4?]	5	[6]	**7**
BM 31961	[9]	**1**			**2**		3	4	5	**6**
Nbn. 355	9	**1**					2	3	4	**5**
Nbn. 356	9				**1**	2	3	4	5	**6**
BM 31672	9	**1**				2	3	?	?	**5**
BM 32023	[11]				**1**	2	3	4	5	**6**
Nbn. 495	11+	**1**			**2**		3	4	5	**6**
Nbn. 608	12	**1**					2	3	4	
BM 79049	12	**1**			**2**	3	4	5		**6**
Nbn. 668	12	**1**				2	3		4	**5**
BM 34196	12	**1**			**2**	3	4	5	6	**[7]**
TCL 12 122	1[2]	**1**			**2**	3	4	5	6	**7**
BM 32846	[x]	**?**			**1+**	2+				
Nbn. 720	13	**1**						2		**3**
BM 40263	[x]	**1**						2		**3**
Nbn. 776	14	**1**								
BM 42040	[x]									**1+**
BM 41785	17									**1?**
TBER 60	17									**1**

Table 3.18: Divine Rankings from Neo-Babylonian Offering Lists at Uruk, Group A (Beaulieu 2003, 73).[97]

Symbol/Atlar-of-Bēl[98]
  Ištar-of-Uruk[99]
Symbol/Altar-of-Nabû
  Nanaya
Lady-of-Rēš
Temple-of-Marduk[100]
Uṣur-amāssu
Urkayītu
Gula
Palil[101]
  Lady-of-Eanna
Palil-of-Udannu
Divine-Chariot[102]
bīt-ḫilṣi
Nergal[103]
Ninurta[104]
Nusku
Šamaš
  Aya

Table 4.1: Lists of Ištar//Who-Resides-(in)-GN and Ištar-of-GN in Transactions from SAA 6, SAA 14, SAAB 5, SAAB 9, and Faist.[105]

Deity:	Texts:
Ištar//Who-Resides-(in)-Nineveh	SAA 6 50 r. 8; 51 r. 6; 87 r. 2; 99 r. 2–3; 110 r. 2–3; 118 r. 1′–2′; 163 r. 4′; 201 r. 1; 202 r. 4; 211 r. 2′; 229 r. 1–2; 250 r. 4; **251:16′**; 253 r. 5; 278 r. 4; 301 r. 1; 309 r. 2–3; 314 r. 5; **325 r. 4′**; **326 r. 10**; 328 r. 4; 329 r. 4; **334 r. 16–17**; 335 r. 10; and 349 r. 4; SAA 14 21:18′-r. 1; 24 r. 7–8; 35 r. 3; 40 r. 2; 42 r. 11; 46 r. 6; 49 r. 4; **64:4–5**; 85 r. 5′; 90:15′; 114:12–13; 116 r. 4–5; 154 r. 7; 178 r. 7–8; 198 r. 7–8; 204:8′; **215:11′**; 290:4′–5′; **294 r. 4**; 325:7′–8′; 337 r. 4′–5′; 424:5–6; 425 r. 10; 463 r. 5; 467 r. 3; SAAB 9 127 r. 25; and VAT 9762:28
Ištar-of-Nineveh	SAA 6 31 r. 10; 52 r. 7; 85 r. 1; 165 r. 1; 185 r. 6–7; 254:10′; 310 r. 1; 341:17′; and 346 r. 6–7; SAA 14 1 r. 3; 19 r. 7; 330:0–1′; 435 r. 5; 470 r. 8; and 472 b.e. 9′; SAAB 5 37:12; and SAAB 9 127:33
Ištar-Nineveh	SAA 14 188 r. 2–3
Lady-of-Nineveh	SAA 6 319 r. 2
Mullissu//Who-Resides-(in)-Nineveh	SAA 6 53:14-e. 15
Ištar//Who-Resides-(in)-Arbela	SAA 6 7 b.e. 16–17; 179 r. 7–8; 210 r. 1; and 219 r. 8–9; and SAA 14 36 r. 6; and **466:6′**
Ištar-of-Arbela	SAA 6 3:13′; 34 r. 2; 184:2; and 291:2; SAA 14 265 r.3′; and 443 r. 12; SAAB 5 64:3; SAAB 9 69:5; 87:16; 121:2; 122 A o. 4 and B o. 3; 129:2; and VAT 8274: l. Rd.; 19687:1; and VAT 20822:2
Ištar-Arbela	SAAB 9 123:2; and 138:3
Ištar//Lady-of-Arbela	SAA 14 112 r. 4–5
[Ištar//Who-Resides-(in)-GN]	SAAB 9 134 r. 4′

Table 4.2: Other Divine Names Using the formula DN//Who-Resides-(in)-GN (listed alphabetically by divine name and then geographic name).[105]

Deity:	Text:
Adad//Who-Resides-(in)-Anah	SAA 6 198:4′
Adad//Who-Resides-(in)-Dur-illil	SAA 14 197:10′
Adad//Who-Resides-(in)-GN^(?)	SAA 14 223 r. 6′
Adad//Who-Resides-(in)-[Ḫarrān]	SAA 14 131 r. 4′
Adad//Who-Resides-(in)-Kalizi	SAA 6 289 r. 1
Adad//Who-Resides-(in)-Urraka	SAA 6 96:18
Assur//Who-Resides-(in)-Ezida	SAA 6 200 r. 3′–4′; 283 r. 9; SAA 14 294 r. 2
Bēlanu//Who-Resides-(in)-Ḫirana	SAA 14 162 r. 6–7
DN//Who-Resides-(in)-GN	SAA 6 16 r. 1; **20:5′**^(?); 42:22; and 92 r. 4′–5′; and SAA 14 13 r. 2; 14 r. 2–3; 56 r. 2; 100 r. 2; 196 r. 1′–2′; 257:17′–18′; 302 r. 4′
Nabû//Who-Resides-(in)-Ezida	SAA 12 96:1 and r. 2; and SAA 14 397 r. 1′
Nabû//Who-Resi[des-(in)-GN]	SAA 14 306:3′
Ningal//[Who-Resides-(in)-Ḫarrān]	SAA 14 193 r. 7
Ninurta//Who-Resides-(in)-Calaḫ	SAA 6 6 r. 1–2; **11 r. 5′**; **32 r. 2**; 58 r. 4′ (GN?); 131 r. 2′; 220 r. 6′; 284 r. 4–5; 298 r. 1; and 299:13′; and SAA 14 63 r. 9–10; 219:7^(?); 350 r. 5′; 406:2′; 464 r. 2; and 468 r. 13
Sîn//Who-Resides-(in)-Dūr-šarrukīn	SAA 14 220 r. 3–4
Moon-God//Who-Resides-(in)-Ḫarrān	SAA 6 98 r. 4; and 140:10′; SAA 14 146 r. 1′–2′; 193 r. 8–9; 213:18′; and 344 r. 4′–5′; and SAAB 9 124 r. 14 See also RIMA 3 A.0.104.2:12 and 17; A.0.104.3:23; and A.0.105.1:20
Moon-God-of-Ḫarrān	SAA 6 334 r. 15; and SAA 12 48:6′

Table 4.3: Comparing the EGLs in Esarhaddon's Succession Treaty (SAA 2 6; compare Tables 3.15 and 3.9).[106]

ll. 16-20 and 25-30:	ll. 414-465:
Assur	**Assur**
	Mullissu
Anu	Anu
Enlil	
Ea	
Sîn	Sîn
Šamaš	Šamaš
Adad	
	Ninurta
	Venus
	Jupiter
Marduk	**Marduk**
	Zarpānītu
Nabû	
	Bēlet-ilī
Nusku	Adad
Uraš	Ištar **(**Lady -of-Battle**)**
Nergal	Nergal
Mullissu	
Šeru'a	
Bēlet-ilī	
Ištar-of-Nineveh	*Mullissu //Who-Resides-(in)-Nineveh*
Ištar-of-Arbela	Ištar//Who-Resides-(in)-Arbela
	Gula
	the Sebittu

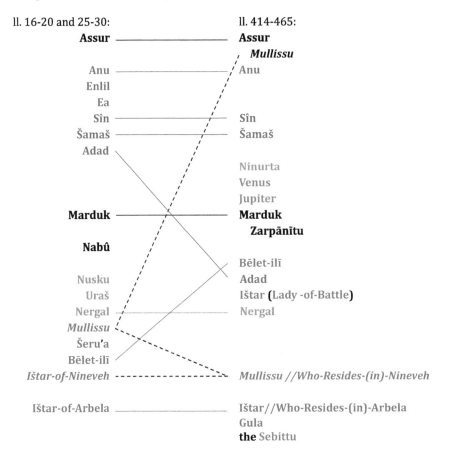

Table 4.4: "Psalm in Praise of Uruk" (SAA 3 9). AG_2 ^uru^GN *a-di* DN ("I love GN, along with DN").

line:	GN:	DN:	elsewhere in SAA 3 9:
1–2	Uruk		(ll. 19–23)
3–5	Babylon		[Mardu]k and Lady-of-Babylon (ll. 24–27)
6–7	Ezida (in Borsippa)	our-Nabû	our-Nabû (r. 1–4)
8	Šapazzu	Bēl-ṣarbi	Bēl-ṣarbi (r. 5–6)
9	Cutha	Nergal	Nergal and Laṣ (r. 7–8)
10	Dēr	Ištarān	Ištarān and Lady-of-Dēr (r. 11–12)
11	Kiš	Eḫursagkalamma (TN)	Zababa and Bau (r. 9–10)
12	Sippar	Šamaš	
13	the Inner City (Assur)	Assur	
14	Nineveh	Mullissu	
15	Arbela	Mullissu	
16	Calaḫ	Ninurta	
17	Ḫarrān	Moon-God	

Table 4.5: The *Pantheon Tablet* from Mari (Georges Dossin, "Le pantheon de Mari," in *Studia Mariana: Publiées sous la direction de Andreé Parrot* [Leiden: E. J. Brill, 1950], 44).

line:	**number of sheep (*immerātu*):**	**for (*ana*) deity:**
1	6	*niqêm*
2		Bēlet-ekalli
3	2	Šamaš-of-Heaven
4	1	**Ištar-of-the-Palace**
5	6	Dagan
6	6	Ninḫursag
7	6	Šamaš
8	2	Sîn
9	6	Itūr-Mēr
10	7	**Dīrītu**
11	6	**Anunītu**
12	[2]	IGI.KUR
13	6	Adad
14	2	N[a]nni
r. 15	2	Ḫ[an]at
16	6	Nergal
17	6	Ea
18	2	**Ištar**
19	2	La[dy]-of-Akkad
20	2	Numušda
21	2	Kīšītu
22	2	Ḫišamītu
23	2	Mārat-altim
24	1	Ninkarrak
25	1	Išḫara
26	1	Lady-of-Ḫiṣāri

Table 5.1: The *Deity List* from Ugarit (*KTU*^{2} 1.47).[107]

1	*'il ṣpn*[108]	The Gods of Ṣapun:
2	*'⸢il'i⸣b*	⸢God-of-the-Fa⸣ther
3	*'i⸢l⸣*	E⸢l⸣
4	*dg⸢n⸣*	Daga⸢n⸣
5	*⸢b'⸣l ṣpn*	⸢B⸣aal-of-Ṣapun
6	*b'lm*	Baaluma
7	*b'lm*	Baaluma
8	*b'lm*	Baaluma
9	*⸢b'⸣lm*	⸢Ba⸣aluma
10	[b]⸢'⸣*lm*	[B]⸢a⸣aluma
11	[b'l]*m*	[Baal]uma
12	['arṣ] *w šm⸢m⸣*	[Earth]-and-Heav⸢en⸣
13	[kṯr]⸢t⸣	[Kôṯarā]⸢tu⸣ (Goddess of Female Reproduction)
14	[yrḫ]	[Yariḫu] (Moon)
15	[ṣpn]	[Mount Ṣapun]
16	[kṯr]	[Kôṯaru] (Skillful)
17	[pdry]	[Pidray] (Fatty)
18	['ṯtr]	[Aṯtaru]
19	[ġrm w 'mqt]	[Mountains-and-the-Abyss]
20	['aṯrt]	[Ašerah]
21	['nt]	[Anat]
22	[šp]⸢š⸣	[Šap]⸢aš⸣ (Sun)
23	['a]*rṣ⸢y⸣*	[A]rṣa⸢y⸣ (Earthy)
24	['u]*šḫr⸢y⸣*	[U]šḫara⸢ya⸣
25	[']*ṯtrt*	[A]starte
26	*'il t'ḏr b'l*	The Auxiliary Gods of Baal
27	*ršp*	Rašap
28	*ddmš*	Dadmiš
29	*pḫr 'ilm*	The Assembly of the Gods
30	*ym*	Yammu (Sea)
31	*'uṯḫt*	Uṯḫatu (Censer)
32	*knr*	Kinnāru (Lyre)
33	*mlkm*	(deceased) Kings
34	*šlm*	Šalimu

Table 5.2: The Main Embedded God Lists in *KTU*^{2} 1.148.[109]

Section 1 (ll. 1–9)	**Section 2a (ll. 10–12)**	**Section 3b (ll. 23–45)**
The Gods of Mount Ṣapun:		
[1][God-of-the-Father]	[10]God-of-the-Father	[23]God-of-the-Father
		[24]Earth-and-Heaven
[2]El	El	[25]El
		Kôṯarātu
[Dagan]	Dagan	[26]Dagan
		Baal-of-Aleppo
[Baal-of-Ṣapun]	Baal[!]-of-Ṣapun	[27]Baal-of-Ṣapun
	(*‘bl-ṣpn*)	
[3](another) Baal	[11]*b‘lm*	
[(another) Baal]	*b‘lm*	
[4](another) Baal	*[b]‘lm*	
(another) Baal	*b‘lm*	
[(another) Baal]	[12]*b‘lm*	
	b‘lm	
[5]Earth-and-Heaven		
Kôṯarā[tu]		[28]Ṯarraṯiya
Yariḫu (Moon)		[29]Yariḫu
[Aṯta]ru		
[6]Mount Ṣapun		Mount Ṣapun
Kôṯaru		[30]Kôṯaru
Pidray		Aṯtaru
Mountains-and-the-Abyss		
[7]Ašerah		[31][A]šerah
Anat		Šaggar-wa-Iṯum
Šapaš		[32][Šap]aš
Arṣay		
Astarte		
[8]Ušḫaraya		
Auxiliary Gods of Baal		
Rašap		Rašap-Idrippi
		[33][----]⌜MṢ⌝R
Dadmiš		[34][Dadmiš]
[9]the Assembly of El		[-(-)]MT

Section 1 (ll. 1–9)	**Section 2a (ll. 10–12)**	**Section 3b (ll. 23–45)**
		$^{35-42}$**[mostly broken]**
Yammu		
		^{43}[The Gods of Al]eppo ([d]d*m*)
		The Gods of Leba[no]n (*lb*[n]n)
		U[t̠ḫatu]
Kinnāru		
		^{44}(another) Baal
		[(another) Baal]
		^{45}[(another) Baal]
		[(another) Baal]
		possible l. 46 broken

Table 5.3: *KTU*[2] 1.119:1–25 (Following Pardee's Divisions [Pardee, *Ritual and Cult*, 52–53]).[110]

Section (line):	Day:	Deity:
IA (1)	7th	(a sheep for) Baal-R'KT[136]
IB (3)		(the temple of) Baal-of-Ugarit
IIB (6) (7)	17th	(the sanctuary of) El (a cow for) Baalim (a cow for) Ġalmu (two ewes and a cow for) ĠLMTM
IIC (9–10)		(the temple of) Baal-of-Ugarit
IIIA (12)	18th	(a bull for) MDGL-of-Baal-of-Ugarit
IIIB (14)		(the temple of) El (a neck for) Baal-[of-xxx]
V (21–22)	5th	(birds and a liver and a sheep as a burnt offering for) Baal-of-Ugarit
VIA (25)	7th	(oil of well-being) Baal (libation-offering for the benefit of) the Malakūma

Table 5.4: SAA 2 5. Esarhaddon's Treaty with Baal, King of Tyre.

line:	God:	cuneiform:	cursing verb and translation:
iv 1′	[Mullissu//Who-Resides-(in)-Nineveh]	^{d}[NIN.LIL$_{2}$ *a-ši-bat* ^{uru}NINA^{ki}]	[*li-ir-ku-su*] ("[may *they* tie]")[111]
2′	Ishtar//W[ho-Resides-(in)-Arbela]	^{d}IŠ.TAR ⸢*a*⸣-[*si-bat* ^{uru}*arba-il*$_{3}$]	[*la i-ša*$_{2}$*-kan*] ("[may *she* not establish]")
3′	Gula	^{d}*gu-la*	GIG ("may she make sick")
5′	the Sebittu	^{d}*si-bit-te*	*liš-kun* ("may *he* establish")
6′	Bethel (and) Anat-Be[the]l	^{d}*ba-a-a-ti*-DINGIR^{meš} ^{d}*a-na-ti-ba-*⸢*a*⸣-[*a-ti*-DINGI]R^{meš}	[*lim-nu-u-k*]*u-nu* ("[may *they* deliver y]ou")
8′	The great gods of Heaven and Earth, the gods of Assyria, the gods of Akkad, (and) the gods of Eber-nāri	DINGIR^{meš} GAL^{meš} *ša*$_{2}$ AN-*e u*$_{3}$ KI.TIM DINGIR^{meš} KUR *aš-šur*^{ki} DINGIR^{meš} KUR.URI^{ki} DINGIR^{meš} *e-bir*-ID$_{2}$	*li-ru-ru-*⸢*ku*⸣*-nu* ("may *they* curse you")
10′	Baal-Šamêm Baal-Malagê Baal-of-Ṣapun	^{d}*ba-al ša-me-me* ^{d}*ba-al-ma-la-ge-e* ^{d}*ba-al-ṣa-pu-nu*	*lu-šat-ba* ("may *he* raise up"); *li-is-su-ḫu* ("may *they* pull out")[112]
14′	Melqart (and) Ešmun	^{d}*mi-il-qar-tu* ^{d}*ia-su-mu-nu*	*li-di-nu* ("may *they* deliver"); [*lis-su-ḫ*]*u*$^{!}$-⸢*ku*$^{!}$*-nu*$^{!}$⸣ ("[may] *they* [uproot] you"); *lu-ḫal-li-qu* ("may *they* banish")
18′	Astarte	^{d}*as-tar-tu*$_{2}$	*li-*⟨*iš*⟩*-bir* ("may *she* break")

Table 5.5: Baal-of-GN epithets in Northwest Semitic Texts.

DN-of-GN:	Spelled:	Text:	Language:	Date, Place:
Baal-of-Ugarit	*b'l 'ugrt*	*KTU*^{2} 1.41:34–35 and 42; 1.46:16; 105.6′; 109:11, 16, 34, and 35; 1.112:23; 1.119:3, 9–10, 12, and 22′; 1.130:10, 24, and 26	Ugaritic	14th–13th Centuries, Ugarit
Baal-of-Aleppo[113]	^{d}'*a*$_3$-*da* LU$_2$ *ḫa-lab*$_x$^{ki}	TM.75.G.2426 xi 1;	Eblaite	3rd Millennium, Ebla
	^{d}'*a*$_3$-*da* ^{lu2}*ḫa-lam*^{ki}	Testo 39 r. xii 21–22;	Eblaite	3rd Millennium, Ebla
	^{d}IŠKUR *ša ḫa-la-ab*	ARMT 25 736:8′-9;	Akkadian	18th Century, Mari
	^{d}IŠKUR *be-el ḫa-la-ab*^{ki}	M. 7750:5′;	Akkadian	18th Century, Mari
	^{d}10 *ḫal-bi*	RS 92.2004:6;	Sumero-Akk.	14th–13th Centuries, Ugarit
	b'l ḫlb	*KTU*^{2} 1.109:16; 1.130:11; 1.148:26; 4.728:1–2;	Ugaritic	14th–13th Centuries, Ugarit
	^{d}IŠKUR *ša* ^{uru}*ḫal-man*	RIMA 3 A.0.102.2 ii 87;	Akkadian	9th Century, Assyria (Kurkh)
	^{d}IŠKUR *ša*$_2$ ^{uru}*ḫal-la-ba*	SAA 2 2 vi 18;	Akkadian	8th Century, Assyria
	^{d}IŠKUR *ša*$_2$ *ḫal-bi*	GAB § 1, l. 116;	Akkadian	7th Century, Assyria
	[הדד ח]לב	Sefire i A (*KAI* 222):10–11	Aramaic	8th Century, Northern Syria
IŠKUR-of-Aleppo[114]		*CTH* 16b; *CTH* 42; 68; 69; 76; and 106	Hittite	14th–13th Centuries, Anatolia
IŠKUR-of-Aleppo-(of-Ḫattuša) IŠKUR-of-Aleppo-(of-Šamuḫa)		*KUB* 6 45 i 43 and 51	Hittite	14th–13th Centuries, Anatolia
Baal-KRNTRYŠ[115]	בעל כרנתריש	*KAI* 26 A ii 19, iii 1, 4, C iii 16 17, 19, and iv 20	Phoenician	8th Century, Karatepe
Baal-of-Ṣapun[116]	*b'l ṣpn*	*KTU*^{2} 1.14:33 and 41; 1.46:12 and 14; 1.109:6, 9, 29, and 32–33; 1.112:22–23; 1.148:2, 10, and 27; 1.130 17 and 22	Ugaritic	14th–13th Centuries, Ugarit

DN-of-GN:	Spelled:	Text:	Language:	Date, Place:
	^{d}10 ḪUR.SAG-*ḫa-zi*	RS 92.2004:6;	Sumero-Akk.	14th–13th Centuries, Ugarit
	^{d}*ba-al-ṣa-pu-nu*	SAA 2 5 iv 10′;	Akkadian	7th Century, Assyria
	בעל צפן	*KAI* 50:2–3;	Phoenician	6th Century, Saqqāra
	בעלצ̊פ̊ן	*KAI* 69:1;	Punic	3rd Century, Marseilles
Mount-Baal-of-Ṣapun[117] (GN)[118]	KUR *ba-*[*ʾa-li*]*-*⌜*ṣa*⌝*-pu-na*	RINAP 1, TP3. 13:6;	Akkadian	8th Century, Assyria
	KUR *ba-ʾa-li-ṣa-*⌜*pu*⌝*-na*	RINAP 1, TP3. 30:2;	Akkadian	8th Century, Assyria
	בעל צפן	Exodus 14:2, 9; Numbers 33:7	Hebrew	8th–5th Century, Israel
Baal-Šamêm[119]	בעל שממ	*KAI* 4:3;	Phoenician	10th Century, Byblos
	[בע]לשמין	*KAI* 202 B 23;	Aramaic	8th Century, Afis (Ḥamath)
	בעל שממ	*KAI* 26 A iii 18;	Phoenician	8th Century, Karatepe
	^{d}*ba-al-sa-me-me*	SAA 2 5 iv 10′;	Akkadian	7th Century, Assyria
	בעלשמין	*KAI* 266:2;	Aramaic	Ca. 600, Saqqāra
	בעלשמין	*KAI* 259:3;	Aramaic	5th/4th Century, Gönze, Anatolia
	bʿl-G šmyn-G	Papyrus Amherst 63 12:18;	Aramaic	4th Century, Egypt
	בעל שממ	*KAI* 78:2;	Punic	3rd Century, Carthage
	בעלשמ(י)ן	*KAI* 244–248;	Aramaic	1st–2nd Centuries C.E., Ḥatra
	Βαλσαμος	Kölner Mani-Kodex 49,3–5	Greek	3rd Century C.E. or later
Baal[!]-Šamêm on-Hawk-Island	לבעשממ באינצמ	*KAI* 64:1	Punic	3rd Century B.C.E., Sardinia
Baal-Meʿon (GN)[120]	בעלמען/נ	*KAI* 181:9;	Moabite	9th Century, Diban
	בית.בעלמען/נ	Numbers 32:38; Ezekiel 25:9; 1 Chronicles 5:8; *KAI* 181:30; Joshua 13:17	Hebrew	8th–4th Century, Israel
the Baal-Meʿonite	בעלמעני	*Samr* 27:3	Hebrew	8th Century, Samaria

DN-of-GN:	Spelled:	Text:	Language:	Date, Place:
Baal-Ḥamān[121]	בעל . חמנ	*KAI* 24:16 ;	Phoenician	late 9th Century, Sam'al
	בעלמנ	*KAI* 114:2;	Punic	3rd–1st Century B.C.E., Constantine (Algeria)
	ΒΑΛ ΑΜΟΥΝ	*KAI* 175:1;	Neo-Punic	?, Constantine
	BALAMONI	*CdB* 3 114, l. 1;	Latin	1st/2nd Century C.E., Carthage
	BEBELLAHAMON	*CIL* 3 7954;	Latin	
El-Ḥamān[122]	אל חמנ	*KAI* 19:4/*TSSI* 3 31:4;	Phoenician	late 3rd Century B.C.E., Umm El-'Amed
		TSSI 3 32:1	Phoenician	
Baal-Ḥarrān[123]	בעלחרנ	*KAI* 218:1;	Aramaic	8th Century, Sam'al
Bēl-Ḫarrān[124]	$^{(d)}$EN.$^{(uru)}$KASKAL-*x-x* ...	*PNA* 1/2 , 300–304;	Akkadian	9th–7th Century, Assyria
Moon-God-of-Ḫarrān[125]	^{d}EN.ZU *ša ḫa-ar-ra-nim*^{ki}	*Mélanges syriens* 986, l. 12;	Akkadian	18th Century, Mari
	^{d}30 *a-šib* ^{uru}KASKAL(*-ni*)	RIMA 3 A.0.104.2:12 and 17;	Akkadian	8th Century, along the Orontes River
	ס(י)נכשר	*TAD* B2.2:19 and B3.9:10;	Aramaic	5th Century, Elephantine
(Hadad-Sikan)	(הדד סכנ)	(*KAI* 309:1)	(Aramaic)	(9th Century, Tell Fekherye)
Baal-Lebanon[126]	בעל לבננ	*KAI* 31:1 and 2	Phoenician	8th Century, Cyprus
Hadad-Lebanon[127]	θεῷ Ἀδάδῳ Λιβανεώτῃ	*Inscriptions Graecae urbis Romae 110*	Greek	4th Century C.E., Cyprus
Baal-Gad (GN)[128]	בעל גד	Joshua 11:17; 13:5	Hebrew	7h Century, Israel
Baal-Harmon (GN)	הר בעל חרמון	Judges 3:3	Hebrew	7th Century, Israel
	בעל חרמון	1 Chronicles 5:23	Hebrew	5th/4th Century, Israel
Baal-Beʳrît	בעל ברית	Judges 8:33; 9:4	Hebrew	7th Century, Israel

DN-of-GN:	Spelled:	Text:	Language:	Date, Place:
El-B^{e}rît	אל ברית	Judges 9:46	Hebrew	7th Century, Israel
Baal-Tāmār (GN)	בעל תמר	Judges 20:33	Hebrew	7th Century, Israel
Baal-Peraṣim (GN)	בעל פרצים	2 Samuel 5:20	Hebrew	7th Century, Israel
Baal-Ḥaṣôr (GN)	בעל חצור	2 Samuel 13:23	Hebrew	7t^{h} Century, Israel
Baal-Šālîšā (GN)	בעל שלשה	2 Kings 4:42	Hebrew	7th Century, Israel
Gûr-Baal (GN)	גור בעל	2 Chronicles 26:7	Hebrew	4th Century, Israel
Baal-Peʻor[129] (GN)	בעל פעור	Numbers 25:1–5; Deuteronomy 4:3; Hosea 9:10; and Psalm 106:28	Hebrew	8th–5th Century, Israel
Baal-Malagê[136]	^{d}*ba-al ma-la-ge-e*	SAA 2 5 iv 10′	Akkadian	7th Century, Assyria
Baal-Ṣidon[130]	בעל צדן	*KAI* 14:18	Phoenician	5th Century, Ṣidon
Baal-Kition[131]	בעל כתי	*Fouilles de Kition* 3, D 37 (plate 16 3)	Phoenician	5th/4th Century, Cyprus
Baal-MRP'K[132]	בעל מרפאכ	*CIS* 1 41:3	Phoenician	4th Century, Cyprus
Melqart Baal-Tyre Hercules	מלקרת בעל צר Ἡραχλεῖ ἀρχηέτει	*KAI* 47:1 *KAI* 47:3	Phoenician Greek	2nd Century, Malta
Baal-Marqod[133]	Βαλμαρκώς Βαλμαρκῶδι Balmarcodes	*CIG* 3 4536:6; *CIL* 3 6668; *CIL* 3 6673:2–3	Greek Latin Latin	2nd Century C.E., Beirut
Baal-Qart [134] (Baal-of-the-City)	ב[עלקרת] Βώνχαρ Boncar	*JA* 8 350, l. 1	Neo-Punic Greek Latin	3rd Century C.E., Carthage

Table 5.6: Baal-Šamêm in EGLs from the 10th Century B.C.E. to the 2nd Century C.E.

KAI 202 B 23–26 Zakkur Inscription late 8th Century B.C.E. Aramaic	*KAI* 26 A iii 18–19 Azatiwada Inscription early 8th Century B.C.E. Phoenician	SAA 2 5 iv 6′–7′ and 10′–19′ Esarhaddon's Treaty with King Baal of Tyre mid-7th Century B.C.E. Akkadian	*KAI* 9 B 5 Son of Šipiṭba'al of Byblos Inscription ca. 500 Phoenician	*KAI* 259:3–4 Gönze, Anatolia 5th/4th Century B.C.E. Aramaic	*KAI* 78:2–4 votive inscription from Carthage 3rd Century B.C.E. Punic	*KAI* 247:1–4 = *KAI* 248:5–7 Ḥatra inscriptions 1st–2nd Centuries C.E. Aramaic
		Bethel				Our Lord (מרן)
		Anat-Bethel[135]				Our Lady (מרתן)
						[Son of our] Lo[rd] (בר מ[רין])
						ŠḤRW
[Ba]al-Šamêm	Baal-Šamêm	Baal-Šamêm	[Baal-Šamê]m	Baal-Šamêm	Baal-Šamêm	Baal-Šam[êm]
						Atargatis
					Tannit//Face-of-Baal	
		Baal-Malagê[136]			Baal-Ḥamān	
		Baal-of-Ṣapun	Baal-'Addir[136]		Baal-Magnim[136]	
	El//Creator-of-Earth			moon-god ŠHR		
Il[wer]				Šamaš		
Šamaš	Šamaš		Baalat			
		Melqart	All the Go[ds of Byblos]			
		Ešmun				
moon-god ŠHR						
		Astarte				
Gods of Heave[n] [God]s of Earth Baal-of-[...].	Whole Generation of Gods					

Table 5.7: EGLs in the Kulamuwa Inscription, the Hadad Inscription, and the Panamuwa Inscription.

Text:	*KAI* 24			*KAI* 214		*KAI* 215a
	ll. 15–16	l. 2	ll. 2–3	l. 11	l. 18	l. 22
	Kulamuwa Inscription			The Hadad Inscription		The Panamuwa Inscription
Period:	late 9th Century			late 8th Century		late 8th Century
Language:	Phoenician			Sam'alian (Aramaic)		Sam'alian (Aramaic)
Deities:	Baal-Ṣemed[136]	Hadad	Hadad	⌜Hadad⌝	Hadad	Hadad
	Baal-Ḥamān	El	El	El	El	El
		Rašap				
	Rakib-El	Rakib-El	Rakib-El	Rakib-El	Rakib-El	Rakib-El//Lord-of-the-Dynasty[137]
		Šamaš	Šamaš	Šamaš	Šamaš	Šamaš
			Rašap	'Arqû-Rašap		
						All the Gods of Y'DY

Table 5.8: Baal-Ḥamān in EGLs from the 9th Century to the 1st Century B.C.E.

Text:	*KAI* 24:15–16 Kulamuwa Inscription	*KAI* 78:2–4 votive inscription from Carthage	*Studi Orientalistici*, vol. 2, 516 Dedicatory inscription from Palmyra	*CIL* 3 7954:1–3[138] Temple Dedicatory Inscription from Syriacorum
Period:	late 9th Century	3rd Century B.C.E.	32 B.C.E.	
Language:	Phoenician	Punic	Palmyra (Aramaic)	Latin
Deities:	Baal-Ṣemed[136]	Baal-Šamêm	Baal[139]	MALAGBEL
		Tannit//Face-of-Baal		
	Baal-Ḥamān	Baal-Ḥamān	Baal-Ḥamān	BEBELLAHAMON[140]
	Rakib-El	Baal-Magnim[136]		BENEFAL (⟨ Face-of-Baal)[141]
			Manawāt	MANAVAT

Table 5.9: Goddess-of / in-GN epithets in Northwest Semitic Texts.

DN-of-GN:	Spelled:	Text:	Language:	Date, Place:
Anat-of-Ṣapun	*'nt ṣpn*	*KTU*^{2} 1.109:13–14, 17, 34	Ugaritic	14th–13th Centuries, Ugarit
Anat-of-ḪLŠ	*'nt ḫlš*	*KTU*^{2} 1.109:25	Ugaritic	14th–13th Centuries, Ugarit
Ašerah-of-Tyre and "Goddess of Ṣidon"	*'aṯrt* [.] *ṣrm w 'ilt . ṣdynm*	*KTU*^{2} 1.14 iv 35–39 (Kirta Epic)	Ugaritic	14th–13th Centuries, Ugarit
Astarte[!] in-Ṣidon	עשת⟨רת⟩ בצדנ	*WSS* 876:2	Ammonite	7th Century, unknown
[Astar]te in-Ṣidon//Land-by-the-Sea	[עשתר]ת בצדנ ארצ ימ	*KAI* 14:16	Phoenician	5th Century, Ṣidon
Astarte-of-the-Lofty-Heavens	עשתרת שממ אדרמ	*KAI* 14:16	Phoenician	5th Century, Ṣidon
(Astarte and) Tannit in-Lebanon	(לעשתרת) ולתנת בלבננ	*KAI* 81:1	Punic	uncertain date, Carthage
Astarte-Kition	עשתרת כת	*KAI* 37:5	Phoenician	4th/3rd Century, Cyprus

Table 6.1: Yahwistic Divine Names at Elephantine (From Bezalel Porten and Ada Yardeni, *Textbook of Aramaic Documents from Ancient Egypt*, vols. 1–4 = *TAD* A-D).[142]

Text:	Date:	Aramaic:	Translation:
			YHH/YHW
TAD D7.21:3	early 5th Century	ברכתכ ליהה ולחנ'מ	I bless you by YHH and Khn^{u}m
TAD D7.16:3	early 5th Century	חיליהו	by the life of YHW
TAD D7.16:7	early 5th Century	חי ליהה	by the life of YHH
TAD D7.18:2–3	early 5th Century	[2]בית [3]יהה	the temple of YHH
TAD D4.9:1	early 5th Century	[בי]ת יהו	[the temp]le of YHW
TAD B2.2:6	Jan 2, 464	ביהו	(swear) by YHW
TAD B2.2:11	Jan 2, 464	ביהו	(swear) by YHW
TAD B3.12:1	Dec 13, 402	זי יהו	of YHW
			YHH/YHW//the-God
TAD B2.7:14	Nov 17, 446	זי יהה אלה	of YHH//the-God
TAD B3.4:3	Sept 14, 437	ליהו אלהא	to YHW//the-God
TAD B3.4:10	Sept 14, 437	יהו ^{אלהא}	(of) YHW//$^{the\text{-}God}$
TAD B3.5:10	Oct 30, 434	זי יהו אלהא	of YHW//the-God
TAD B3.7:2	July 11, 420	זי יהו אלהא	of YHW//the-God
TAD B2.10:6	Dec 16, 416	זי יהו אלהא	of YHW//the-God
TAD B7.1:4	Sept, 413	ביהו אלהא	by YHW//the-God
TAD A4.5:15	ca. 410	ליהו א[להא]	to YHW//[the]-G[od]
TAD A4.7:24–25	Nov 25, 407	[24]על אגורא זי יהו אלהא	upon the temple of YHW//the-God to
(*TAD* A4.8:24)		[25] למבניה ביב בירתא	(re)build it in the Elephantine Fortress

Table 6.1: (continued).

Text:	Date:	Aramaic:	Translation:
TAD A4.7:26 (and *TAD* A4.8:25)	Nov 25, 407	מדבחא די יהו אלהא	the altar of YHW//the-God
TAD A4.10:8–9	after 407	[8]ואגורא זי יהו אלהא זילנ יתבנה [9]ביב בירתא	our temple of YHW//the-God will be rebuilt in the Elephantine Fortress
TAD B3.10:23	Nov 25, 404	זי יהו אלהא	of YHW//the-God
TAD B3.11:17	March 9, 402	זי יהו אלהא	of YHW//the-God
TAD B3.12:10–11	Dec 13, 402	[10]ליהו [11]אלהא	to YHW//the-God
TAD B3.12:33	Dec 13, 402	זי יהו אלהא	of YHW//the-God
TAD A4.3:1	late 5th Century	זי יהו אלהא	of YHW//the-God
			"God of Heaven"
TAD A3.6:1	late 5th Century	[אל]ה שמיא	[May "the Go]d of Heaven" seek
TAD A4.3:2–3	late 5th Century	קדמ[3] אלה שמיא	before "the God of Heaven"
TAD A4.7:2 (*TAD* A4.8:1)[143]	Nov 25, 407	אלה שמיא	"the God of Heaven"
TAD A4.7:27–28	Nov 25, 407	קדמ יהו אלה[28] שמיא	before YHW//God-of-Heaven
TAD A4.7:15	Nov 25, 407	ליהו מרא שמיא	to YHW//Lord-of-Heaven
			YHW//the-God in the Elephantine Fortress
TAD B2.2:4	Jan 2, 464	ביהו אלהא ביב בירתא	(you swore) by YHW//the-God in the Elephantine Fortress
TAD B3.5:2	Oct 30, 434	זי יהו אלהא ביב בירתא	of YHW//the-God in the Elephantine Fortress

Table 6.1: (continued).

Text:	Date:	Aramaic:	Translation:
TAD B3.10:2	Nov 25, 404	ליהו אלהא ביב ברתא	to YHW//the-God in the Elephantine Fortress
TAD B3.11:1–2	March 9, 402	זי 2 יהו אלהא ביב ברתא	of YHW//the-God in the Elephantine Fortress
			YHH/YHW//the-God who (is) in the Elephantine Fortress
TAD B3.3:2	Aug 9, 449	זי יהה אלהא זי ביב בירתא	of YHH//the-God who (is) in the Elephantine Fortress
TAD A4.7:6 (*TAD* A4.8:6–7)	Nov 25, 407	אגורא זי יהו אלהא זי ביב בירתא	the temple of YHW//the-God who/that (is) in the Elephantine Fortress[144]
			YHW//the-God//Who-Resides-(in)-the-Elephantine-Fortress
TAD B3.12:2	Dec 13, 402	זי יהו אלהא שכן יב ברתא	(Tapamet, his wife, a servitor) of YHW//the-God//Who-Resides-(in)-the-Elephantine-Fortress
			YH(W) in Elephantine
TAD A3.3:1	mid-5th Century	[שלמ ב]ית יהו ביב	[Greetings] to the [T]emple of YHW in Elephantine
TAD B3.2:2	July 6, 451	ליהו ביב	to YHW in Elephantine
TAD B3.4:25	Sept 14, 437	ליה ביב	to YH in Elephantine

Table 6.1: (concluded).

Text:	Date:	Aramaic:	Translation:
			Yahweh-of-Hosts
TAD D7.35:1–2 = *Lozachmeur* no. 168	early 5th Century	[1]שלמכ יהה [2][צבאת ישא]ל בכל עדן	May Yahweh-of-[Hosts see]k your well-being at all times.
Lozachmeur no. 175:2 (= **J8**)		כבלכי יהה צבאת	Yahweh-of-Hosts bound you/made you sterile.[145]
Lozachmeur no. 167:1–2		[1][שלמ אחי יה]ה צבאת ישא[2][ל בכל עדן]	May [Yahwe]h-of-Hosts see[k] my brother's well-being [at all times].

Table 6.2: Equations of Yahwistic Divine Names within Individual Texts from Elephantine.

Text:	Date:	Aramaic:	Translation:
TAD A4.3:1	late 5th Century	זי יהו אלהא	of YHW//the-God
ll. 2–3		קדמ[3] אלה שמיא	before "the God of Heaven"
TAD A4.7:2	Nov. 25, 407	אלה שמיא	"the God of Heaven"
l. 6		אגורא זי יהו אלהא זי ביב בירתא	the temple of YHW//the-God who/that (is) in the Elephantine Fortress[143]
ll. 7–8		אגורא זי ביב[8] בירתא[7]	The temple that is in the Elephantine Fortress
l. 13		בנו אגורא זכ ביב בירתא	(they) built that temple in the Elephantine Fortress
l. 15		ליהו מרא שמיא	to YHW//Lord-of-Heaven
ll. 24		על אגורא זי יהו אלהא[25] למבניה	upon the temple of YHW//the-God to
		ביב בירתא	(re)build it in the Elephantine Fortress
l. 26		מדבחא די יהו אלהא	the altar of YHW//the-God
ll. 27–28		קדמ יהו אלה[28] שמיא	before YHW//God-of-Heaven
TAD B2.2:4	Jan 2, 464	ביהו אלהא ביב בירתא	(you swore) by YHW//the-God in the Elephantine Fortress
l. 6		ביהו	(swear) by YHW
l. 11		ביהו	(swear) by YHW
TAD B3.4:3	Sept 14, 437	ליהו אלהא	to YHW//the-God
l. 10		יהו [אלהא]	(of) YHW//the-God
l. 25		ליה ביב	to YH in Elephantine

Table 6.2: (concluded).

Text:	Date:	Aramaic:	Translation:
TAD B3.5:2	Oct 30, 434	זי יהו אלהא ביב בירתא	of YHW//the-God in the Elephantine Fortress
l. 10		זי יהו אלהא	of YHW the-God
TAD B3.10:2	Nov 25, 404	ליהו אלהא ביב ברתא	to YHW//the-God in the Elephantine Fortress
l. 23		זי יהו אלהא	of YHW//the-God
TAD B3.11:1–2	March 9, 402	זי [2] יהו אלהא ביב ברתא	of YHW//the-God in the Elephantine Fortress
l. 17		זי יהו אלהא	of YHW//the-God
TAD B3.12:1	Dec 13, 402	זי יהו	of YHW
l. 2		זי יהו אלהא שכנ יב ברתא	(Tapamet, his wife, a servitor) of YHW//the-God who-resides-(in)-the-Elephantine-Fortress
ll. 10–11		ליהו [11]אלהא	to YHW//the-God
l. 33		זי יהו אלהא	of YHW//the-God

Table 6.3: Proposed Yahwistic Divine Names (see also the various units within Table 6.1).[146]

Text:	Hebrew:	Translation:
		-of-Teman:
Meshel 4.1.1:1	ל[י]הוה.⸢ת⸣ימנ	[Y]ahweh-of-Teman
l. 2	יהוה.התי]מנ	Yahweh-of-the-Teman
Meshel 3.6:5–6	ל[י]^{6}הוה ת⸢מנ⸣	[Y]ahweh-of-Teman
Meshel 3.9:1	ליהוה . התמנ	Yahweh-of-the-Teman
		-of-Samaria
Meshel 3.1:2	ליהוה.שמרנ	Yahweh-of-Samaria
Judges 5:5		**-of-Sinai**
	יהוה זה סיני	Yahweh of Sinai (Yahweh//One-of-Sinai)[147]
		in-Zion
Joel 4:17	יהוה אלהיכם שכן בציון	Yahweh//your-God, who-resides in-Zion
v. 21	ויהוה שכן בציון	Yahweh who-resides in-Zion
Isaiah 8:18	יהוה צבאות השכן הר ציון	Yahweh-of-Hosts, who-resides in-Mount-Zion
*Nav** 1:2	ליהוה צבאות	Yahweh-of-Hosts[148]
Psalm 99:2	יהוה בציון	Yahweh in-Zion
135:21	יהוה מציון שכן ירושלם	Yahweh (from-Zion) who-resides-(in)-Jerusalem
		in-Hebron
2 Samuel 15:7	ליהוה בחברון	Yahweh in-Hebron

Table 7.1: An Alphabetic Listing of Plausible Divine First Names and Geographic Last Names of Deities Mentioned in Chapters 3–6. (Comparable Hittite Divine Names from Chapter 2 can be found in Tables 2.3 and 2.10. All divine names are written in DN-of-GN form, regardless of their treatment elsewhere. Mentioned or hinted identifications are provided; rejected identifications are not provided; uncertain identifications and uncertain divine full names are labeled with a question mark.)[149]

Adad-of-Kurbail
Anat-of-Ṣapun
Astarte-of-Kition
Astarte-of-the-Lofty-Heavens
Ašerah-of-Tyre
Baalat-of-Byblos
Baal-of-Aleppo = Hadad-of-Aleppo
Baal-of-Byblos
Baal-of-Emar
Baal-of-Heaven = Baal-Šamêm
Baal-of-Ḥamān
Baal-of-Ḫarrān = Moon-God-of-Ḫarrān
Baal-of-Kition
Baal-of-KRNTRYŠ
Baal-of-Lebanon = Hadad-of-Lebanon(?)
Baal-of-Marqod
Baal-of-Me'on (as Geographic name only)
Baal-of-MRP'K
Baal-of-Pe'or
Baal-of-Qart
Baal-of-Ṣapun
Baal-of-Ṣidon
Baal-of-Tyre = Melqart(?)
Baal-of-Ugarit
Lady-of-Eanna
Lady-of-Eanna-of-Udannu
Bēl-of-Zabban
Enlil-of-Assyria = Assyrian-Enlil
Hadad-of-Aleppo = Baal-of-Aleppo = 'Adu-of-Aleppo = [Tešub-of-Aleppo] = [Tarḫund-of-Aleppo]
Hadad-of-Armi
Hadad-of-Atanni
Hadad-of-Dub
Hadad-of-Heaven (not Baal-of-Šamêm)
Hadad-of-Kume
Hadad-of-Lub
Hadad-of-Luban
Hadad-of-Maḫānu
Hadad-of-Saza
Hadad-of-Sikan
Ištar-of-Akkad
Ištar-of-Arbela = Arbelītu(?)
[Ištar-of-Assur] = Assyrian-Ištar
[Ištar-of-Babylon]
Ištar-of-Dīr = Dīrītu
Ištar-of-Heaven = Venus(?)
[Ištar-of-Ḫarrān]
Ištar-of-Kidmuri
Ištar-of-Kiš = Kišītu
Ištar-of-Nineveh = Ninua'ītu(?)
[Ištar-of-Nippur]
Ištar-of-the-Palace
Ištar-of-Ulmaš = Ulmašītu
Ištar-of-Uruk
Moon-God-of-Ḫarrān = Baal/Bēl-of-Ḫarrān
Mullissu-of-Assyria = Assyrian-Mullissu
Palil-of-Udannu
Šamaš-of-Heaven
Tešub-of-Kummin
Yahweh-of-Samaria
Yahweh-of-Sinai(?)
Yahweh-of-(the)-Teman

Notes

1 Erich Ebeling, *Die Akkadische Gebetsserie "Handerhebung": Von Neuem Gesammelt und Herausgegeben*, Veröffentlichung 20 (Berlin: Akademie-Verlag, 1953), 14–15; and Foster, *Before the Muses*, 692.
2 Whereas Anu, Enlil, and Ea appear in close proximity to each other, they do not appear in their traditional sequence here. Instead, they are separated by Dagan and Adad. It is worth noting, however, that in this embedded god list, although Anu is second, Enlil is fourth, and Ea is sixth, these divine names end the first three lines in this hymn. Thus, visually they have been grouped together.
3 *CAD* M/1, maššûtu B.
4 Simo Parpola, "The Assyrian Cabinet," in *Vom Alten Orient zum Alten Testament: Festschrift für Wolfram Freiherrn von Soden zum 85. Geburtstag am 19. Juni 1993*, eds. M. Dietrich and O. Loretz, AOAT 240 (Kevelaer: Verlag Butzon & Bercker, 1995), 399; see also Lambert, "Historical Development," 197–198.
5 Erich Ebeling, *Quellen zur Kenntnis der babylonischen Religion*, Mitteilungen der Vorderasiatischen Gesellschaft 23 (Leipzig: J. C. Hinrichs, 1918), 1:47–48; and Foster, *Before the Muses*, 713–714. The table is based on Foster's translation with my alternative translations in parentheses.
6 The composite god lists in this table follow the same methodology that will be established in chapter 3. The names appear here in the same order as they do in the majority of the divine witness lists examined in these treaties. However, because the storm-god divine names are varied and reorganized in each individual EGL, and because so many titles are broken and cannot be dependably restored, no has attempt has been made to faithfully present a full arrangement here.
7 McMahon, *Hittite State Cult*, 105.
8 The tablet and line numbers provided represent the first occurrence of a given deity's section, unless the first occurrence is the tag line at the end of one tablet and thus begins the next (i.e., Sîn in III i and Ištar in IV i).
9 As noted elsewhere, when a text and line number that are written in italics (e.g., SAA 13 *126:4*) Nabû is listed before Marduk in an EGL and blessing in that text.
10 The EGLs contained in the SAA 12 grants can appear twice in one grant. This is particularly true for those grants in column iv of Table 3.5a. The deities are first named to ensure the grant is honored by future kings (e.g., SAA 12 26:33–35: *ni-iš* DNs ... NUN-*u*$_2$ EGIR-*u*$_2$ *ša pi-i dan-ne*$_2$-*te šu-a-tu la u*$_2$-*šam-sak*, "By the life of (five gods), a future prince shall not nullify this tablet's wording"), and they are invoked again in a blessing for the future king (e.g., ll. 36–38: DNs *ik-ri-bi-*⸢*ka i-šem*⸣-*mu-u*$_2$, "may (these five gods) hear your prayer").

Many of the EGLs in these grants are damaged; however, because the grants are so similar within their groupings, the proposed reconstructions of these texts in SAA 12 are reliable. The EGLs presented below are grouped according to their columns in Table 3.5a.

i

SAA 12 13:8′–9′	**SAA 12 69 r. 28**	**SAA 12 85:13–14**
[^{d}*aš*]-*šur*	[^{d}*aš-šur*]	[^{d}*aš-šur*]
^{d}IŠKUR	$^{[d]}$IŠKUR	^{d}IŠKUR
^{d}*be-er*	^{d}*be-er*	^{d}*be-er*
[^{d}IŠ.TAR *aš*$_2$]-*šu-ri-tu*$_2$	^{d}INNIN *aš-šur-tu*$_4$	[^{d}*iš*$_8$.*tar*$_2$ *aš*$_2$-*šu-ri-tu*]

ii

SAA 12 14:7′–8′	SAA 12 75 r. 11′?
^{d}*aš-šur*	^{d}*aš-šur*
^{d}IŠKUR	^{d}[*x x x*]
[^{d}*be-er*]	[^{d}*x-x*]
[^{d}EN.LIL$_{2}$ *aš-šur*^{ki}-*u*$_{2}$]	[^{d}EN].LIL$_{2}$$^{?}$
[^{d}IŠ.TAR *aš*$_{2}$]-*šu-ri-tu*$_{2}$	^{d}IŠ.TAR *aš-šu-*[*ri-tu*]

iii

SAA 12 10 r. 6′–8′	SAA 12 19 r. 22
^{d}*aš-šur*	^{d}*a-šur*
^{d}*ša*$_{2}$-*maš*	^{d}*ša*$_{2}$-*maš*
^{d}[EN.LIL$_{2}$]	
^{d}IŠ.TAR *aš*$_{2}$-*šu-ri-te*	
^{d}IŠKUR	^{d}IŠKUR
	^{d}*be-er*
^{d}MAŠ.MAŠ	
^{d}MAŠ	
^{d}7.BI PAB	(broken)

iv (part 1)

SAA 12 25		SAA 12 26	
r. 33–34	r. 36–37	r. 33–34	r. 36–37
^{d}*aš-šur*	^{d}*aš-šur*	^{d}*aš-šur*	^{d}*aš-šur*
^{d}IŠKUR	^{d}IŠKUR	^{d}IŠKUR	^{d}IŠKUR
^{d}*be-er*	[^{d}*be-er*]	^{d}*be-er*	^{d}*be-er*
^{d}EN.LIL$_{2}$ *aš-šur*^{ki}-*u*$_{2}$	^{d}EN.LIL$_{2}$ *aš-šur*^{ki}-*u*$_{2}$	^{d}EN.LIL$_{2}$ *aš-šur*^{ki}-*u*$_{2}$	^{d}EN.LIL$_{2}$ *aš-šur*^{ki}-*u*$_{2}$
^{d}15 *aš-šur*^{ki}-*i-t*[*u*$_{4}$]	^{d}15 *aš-šur*^{ki}-[*i-tu*$_{4}$]	^{d}15 *aš-šur*^{ki}-*i-tu*	^{d}15 *aš-šur*^{ki}-*i-t*[*u*]

iv (part 2)

SAA 12 31		SAA 12 34	
r. 33–34	r. 36–37	r. 6′–7′	r. 9′–10′
^{d}*aš-šur*	[^{d}*aš-šur*]	^{d}*aš-šur*	$^{[d]}$*aš-šur*
^{d}IŠKUR	$^{[d]}$IŠKUR	^{d}IŠKUR	^{d}IŠKUR
^{d}[*be-er*]	[^{d}*be-er*]	[^{d}*be-er*]	[^{d}*be-er*]
[^{d}EN.LIL$_{2}$] *aš-šur*^{ki}-*u*$_{2}$	[EN.LIL$_{2}$ *aš-šur*^{ki}-*u*$_{2}$]	[^{d}EN.L]IL$_{2}$ *aš-šur*^{ki}-*u*$_{2}$	[^{d}E]N.LIL$_{2}$ *aš-šur*^{ki}-*u*$_{2}$
^{d}15 *aš-šur*[^{ki}-*i-tu*]	^{d}15 [*aš-šur*^{ki}-*i-tu*]	^{d}1[5 *aš-šur*^{ki}-*i-tu*]	^{d}[15 *aš-šur*^{ki}-*i-tu*]

v

SAA 12 35 r. 30	SAA 12 36 r. 33′	SAA 12 40 r. 12′–13′	SAA 12 41 r. 3′
[^{d}AN.ŠAR$_{2}$]	^{d}AN.ŠAR$_{2}$	[^{d}AN.ŠAR$_{2}$]	[^{d}AN.ŠAR$_{2}$]
[^{d}EN.LIL$_{2}$]	^{d}[EN.LIL$_{2}$]	^{d}[EN].LIL$_{2}$	[^{d}EN.LIL$_{2}$]
⸢^{d}IŠKUR⸣	⸢^{d}IŠKUR⸣	^{d}IŠKUR	[^{d}IŠKUR]
^{d}*be-er*	^{d}*be-er*	^{d}*be-er*	^{d}*be-er*
[^{d}15 *aš-š*]*ur-i-tu*$_{2}$	[^{d}15 *aš-š*]*ur-i-tu*$_{2}$	[^{d}15 *aš*]-*šur-i-tu*	[^{d}15 *aš-šur-i-tu*]

11 This composite god list has been built from EGLs in the following inscriptions: SAAB 5 16, 17, 30, 37, 53, and 61; SAAB 9 71, 76, and 99; and Faist 15, 16, 23, 103, and 105.

12 In SAAB 5 53, (the unspecified) Ištar is first in a four-member EGL: Ištar / Šamaš / Bēl / Nabû.

13 In SAAB 9 71, the divine name Sîn has been restored at the end of a six-member EGL: [Assur] / [Šamaš] / Bēl / Nabû / Tašmētu / [Sîn]. Because we would normally expect the divine name Sîn to appear before Šamaš in an EGL, the name's placement in this EGL is more

reminiscent of the placement of Moon-God-of-Ḫarrān; however, there is not enough room in this text to propose all the signs needed for this divine full name.
14 In SAAB 5 37, Nergal is first in a six-member EGL: Nergal / Assur / Šamaš / Mullissu / Šerū'a / Ištar-of-Arbela.
15 As in chapter 3 in EGLs and tables in Akkadian and Sumerian texts, chief deities (i.e., **Aššur**, **Marduk**, and **Nabû**) and their consorts appear in a bold **black**; members of Triad 1 (i.e., **Anu**, **Enlil**, and **Ea**) and their consorts appear in bold **blue**; members of Triad 2 (i.e., **Sîn**, **Šamaš**, and **Adad**) and their consorts appear in bold **red**; warrior (or other male) gods appear in bold **green**; goddesses appear in **pink**; other deities, including deified objects appear in bold ; and celestial objects (e.g., planets/stars) appear in bold **orange**. As elsewhere, consorts are indented when they appear immediately after their (usually) husband.
16 This composite god list has been created from EGLs in the following Esarhaddon- and Assurbanipal-period letters from SAA 13, 16, and 18: SAA 13 9, 10, 12, 15, *37*, 56, 57, 58, 60, 61, 63, 64, 65, 66, 68, 69, 80, 92, 102, 132, 140, *147*, 156, 161, 162, 163, 187, and 188; SAA 16 14, 15, 17, 18, 31, 33, 49, 52, 59, 60, 61, 65, 72, 86, 105, 106, 117, 126, 127, 128, 153, and 193[?]; and SAA 18 85, 131, 182, and 185. Other EGLs that nearly fit this composite go list are noted and explained in subsequent notes.

As noted elsewhere, when a text and line number are written in italics (e.g., SAA 13 *126:4*) Nabû is listed before Marduk in an EGL and blessing in that text. Note also that SAA 13 9, 10, and 12 are all written by the scribe Marduk-šallim-aḫḫē, yet Bēl and Nabû's relative positions are not fixed within even the EGLs created by this individual scribe.
17 This composite god list has been created from EGLs in the following Esarhaddon- and Assurbanipal-period letters from SAA 10 8, 53, 59, 61, 67, 82, 83, 110, 123, 130, 139, 174, 177, 180, 185, 186, 195, 197, 224, 225, 227, 228, 233, 240, 242, 245, 248, 249, 252, 284, 286, 293, 294, 297, 298, 307, 316, 328, *338*, *339*, 345, 346, 371, and 383. EGLs that deviate from this composite god list are explained below.
18 In his letter to the king, Nabû-nādin-šumi lists the divine names of Enlil and his consort Mullissu as the first and second deities in the EGL, and he places Assur as the third deity in the EGL without a consort (SAA 10 286, see Table 3.7). It should be noted that this is the only appearance of a Triad 1 deity in this survey of SAA 10 EGLs. As a southern deity, Enlil's typical promotion is all the more unexpected in this letter because the author is an exorcist at the court in Nineveh, the Assyrian capital.
19 Adad-aḫu-iddina invokes Mullissu in a four-member EGL from the Assyrian letter SAA 13 37:4 (Assur / Mullissu / Nabû / Marduk). In contrast, Mullissu is the fourth member in an EGL from Pūlu of Calaḫ (SAA 13 132), wherein Sîn, Nabû, and Marduk are first invoked in their own blessing, and Mullissu follows in her own blessing.
20 The divine name (the unspecified) Ištar follows Assur and precedes Nabû and Marduk in SAA 13 *126*, 138, *144*, and 150 (Marduk precedes Nabû in SAA 13 138 and 150), which could indicate a local identification of the regional Ištar goddess with Assur's consort Mullissu. If (the unspecified) Ištar in these letters is to be identified with Mullissu as Meinhold suggests (Meinhold, *Ištar in Aššur*, 204–206), then there is no disruption in the hierarchy in these letters compared to the composite god list.
21 The following letters from Babylonia are among the few that include Triad 1 deities: SAA 18 24, 68, 70, 73, [74], 124, 192, 193, 194, 195, [197], 199, [200], 201, 202, and 204. Moreover, SAA 18 192–204 are from Nippur and noticeably promote Enlil and his divine family, including his consort Mullissu and his son Ninurta.
22 Mullissu is paired with Assur in SAA 10 227 and *383*.

23 Ea only appears in one EGL, the "Report on Ubaru" (SAA 18 16). The beginning of the tablet is broken, so it is impossible to know how many deities precede Ea in this EGL. He has been placed here after Enlil and Mullissu because of his traditional association with Triad 1. Furthermore, the EGL in SAA 18 16 is unusual because Ištar-of-Nineveh immediately follows Ea (following F. Reynolds' restoration: $^{3'}$[^{d}GAŠAN *ni-n*]*a*$^{?}$-*a*^{ki}, Lady-of-Nineveh) and is followed by Madānu, [Marduk], and [Zar]pānītu (l. 4′).

An additional invocation of Ea occurs in SAA 17 145, a letter to Sargon from the elders of Nēmed-Laguda. This restored four-member EGL includes two deities, a city, and a temple: E[a / Damkina / Uruk] / the Eanna-temple (ll. 4–5). However, this letter is not included in the current survey because it is an eighth-century letter rather than a seventh-century letter.

24 Bēl-iddina, a priest from Ḫarrān, invokes Lord-Crown and Nusku in his two letters to the king (SAA 13 187–188), which explains Nusku's appearance (as a high-ranking member of Sîn's entourage) before Šamaš in the letters. Note also that on the reverse of SAA 13 187, Bēl-iddina calls upon Ištar-of-Nineveh and Ištar-of-Arbela to bless the king (r. 5′–9′). Note also Nusku's lowly position in Esarhaddon's and Assurbanipal's royal-inscription EGLs following the localized Ištar goddesses and his only somewhat higher placement in Sennacherib's royal-inscription EGLs.

25 Šamaš was listed before Sîn and Ningal in an EGL from Adad-dān to the king: ^{3}[^{d}*aš-šur*] ^{d}*ša*$_{2}$-*maš* ^{d}30 ^{d}NIN.GAL ^{4}*a-na* LUGAL EN-*ia lik-ru-bu* ("May [Assur], Šamaš, Sîn (and) Ningal bless the king, my lord", SAA 16 132:3–4). This letter, along with another written by Adad-dān that invokes only Assur and Šamaš (SAA 16 131:3), originates from "Phoenicia and Transpotamia" (Luukko and Van Buylaere, SAA 16, 111).

26 A four-member EGL (Assur / Šamaš / Bēl / Nabû, SAA 10 316:10) from Urad-Nanaya is located within an atypically formulated blessing wherein the deities are asked not to abandon the king. Another atypical blessing appears in SAA 10 180:5–6: Nabû / Šamaš / Marduk. Here Nāṣiru has already written a standard blessing with Nabû and Marduk and followed it with "Daily, I pray to Nabû, Šamaš, and Marduk for the sake of the life of the crown prince, my lord" (^{5}UD-*mu-us-su* ^{d}PA ^{d}UTU ^{6}*u* ^{d}AMAR.UTU *a-na bul-luṭ* ZI^{meš} ^{7}*ša*$_{2}$ DUMU-LUGAL *be-li*$_{2}$-*ia u*$_{2}$-*ṣal-li*).

27 Adad appears as the penultimate deity in the EGL (Assur / Šamaš / Bēl / Nabû / Nergal / Laṣ / Išum / Adad / Bēr) found in SAA 16 148:3–4, a letter by Assur-ušallim to the crown prince.

28 Adad-šumu-uṣur invokes Adad before Šamaš in the three-member EGL (Assur / Adad / Šamaš) when he blesses the king (SAA 10 185:19). However, in an earlier blessing in this letter, Adad does not appear at all in a probable four-member EGL: Assur / Šamaš / Na[bû / Marduk] (l. 16).

29 Nusku was listed earlier than typically expected in SAA 10 197:7 by Adad-šumu-uṣur, whom the *Prosopography of the Neo-Assyrian Empire* calls "by far the most prolific letter-writer among all the Ninevite scholars" (*PNA* 1/1, 38). This letter also provides the sole invocation of the planets Jupiter, Venus, Saturn, and Mercury (SAA 10 197:8–10), as well as of Queen-of-Kidmuri (l. 11), in the SAA 10 EGLs. The only other appearance Nusku makes in an SAA 10 EGL is in a three-member EGL with Šamaš and Ningal (SAA 10 346:8). Nabû-zeru-iddina of Nineveh (*PNA* 2/2, 908 f., entry 11) invokes the deity in the letter's second EGL blessing, wherein he hopes that the gods will listen to the king's prayers (ll. 8–9). Following the methodology described in chapter 3.3, Nusku enjoys a higher rank in these letter-based composite god lists (see also his placement in SAA 13 187 and 188) than he does elsewhere. This relatively early position is surely a reflection of his association with Sîn rather than his own importance.

30 Bēl and Nabû appeared before Triad 2 deities in SAA 10 53, 59, 82, 110, and *338* (and *339*). In only SAA 10 *338* (and *339*) does Nabû appear before Marduk.

31 Nabû and Marduk often appear paired together in a blessing at the beginning of letters. This blessing has been omitted from these EGLs because both Nabû and Marduk typically appear in the second, larger blessing as well. For example, in SAA 13 102:5–6, Nabû-šumu-iddina invokes Nabû and Marduk on behalf of the king and subsequently blesses him with a seven-member EGL (Assur / Bēl / Nabû / Sî[n] / [Šamaš] / Ninurta / Nergal) in ll. 8–10. Likewise, in SAA 13 92, Nabû-šumu-iddina invokes Nabû and Marduk and then invokes Bēl, Nabû, and Nergal in a second blessing.

Perhaps the blessings in SAA 13 63:4 and 156:5–7 represent a hybrid tradition in which the blessing that includes only Nabû and Marduk has been merged with those blessings that invoke several divine names: Nabû / Marduk / Sîn (63:4) and Nabû / Marduk / Sîn / Ištar-of-Nineveh / Ištar-of-Arbela (156:5–7). Or the appearance of Nabû and Marduk (or Marduk alone, or Marduk's preceding Nabû) could simply reflect their increased honor as chief deities of Babylon. Either way, one or both of these deities move up in within EGLs in SAA 13 10 (from Assur), SAA 13 128 (from Calaḫ), and SAA 16 32, compared to other letters from the eighth and seventh centuries.

32 In SAA 18 55:4–7, a letter from Babylonia, Tašmētu follows Nanaya in a five-member EGL (Bēl / Zarpānītu / Nabû / Nanaya / Tašmētu) in which Nabû-nādin-šumi declares that he prayed for the life of the king. Elsewhere in this letter, Bēl and Nabû are invoked twice in blessings (ll. 11 and r. 1). The fact that Nanaya is listed before Tašmētu in this letter is significant. According to Caroline Waerzeggers, Nanaya has replaced Tašmētu as Nabû's consort at the Ezidu in Borsippa, Nabû's temple in the city where he is the patron deity, during the Neo-Babylonian period (Caroline Wearzeggers, *The Ezida Temple of Borsippa: Priesthood, Cult, Archives* [Achaemenid History 15; Leiden: Nederlands Instituut voor Het Nabije Oosten, 2010], 21). Nabû-nādin-šumi's letter seems to be part of this emerging tradition that had not otherwise taken hold in Assyria during the Neo-Assyrian period. When Nanaya is identified as Nabû's consort in Neo-Assyrian EGLs, as she clearly is in SAA 18 55, her divine name is indented to reflect her status as the consort of a Babylonian chief deity in the resultant EGLs and composites.

33 The relevant letters from SAA 10 inconsistently place Nergal in their EGL hierarchies. The Ninevite astrologer Nabû-aḫḫē-erība (*PNA* 2/2, 794 f.) lists Nergal before the localized Ištar goddesses in SAA 10 82, and Marduk-šākin-šumi, the chief exorcist during Assurbanipal's reign (*PNA* 2/2, 722 f.), likewise lists him before them in SAA 10 248, 249, and 252. However, Adad-šumu-uṣur (SAA 10 197, 227, and 228), Nabû-nādin-šumi (SAA 10 286), and Urad-Gula (SAA 10 293 and 294) each place the goddesses before the warrior gods Ninurta and Nergal. Because these three scribes out-number Nabû-aḫḫē-erība and Marduk-šākin-šumi in both the number of letters and the number of relevant EGLs produced by them, Nergal appears nearer the bottom of this composite god list.

34 Madānu is the penultimate deity in an unusual five-member EGL in a letter from Mardî, the governor of Barḫalza, concerning his debt (SAA 16 29:2–3). Following Mikko Luukko and Greta van Buylaere's proposed restoration, the EGL is [Ninurta] / Zababa / Nergal / Madānu / [Nabû]. If this restoration is correct, then Nabû's late appearance after this collection of warrior (and other male) gods corresponds with Madānu's appearance before [Marduk and Zar]pānītu in SAA 18 16. The EGL Bēl / Nabû / Šamaš (^{d}EN ^{d}PA *u* ^{d}UTU) appears in ll. 9 and 12, where Mardî claims he has prayed to this trio of deities.

35 Ubru-Nabû names Mullissu before Lady-of-Kidmuri and Ištar-of-Arbela in SAA 16 106:6–7, which may suggest that he identified Mullissu with Ištar-of-Nineveh, the localized Ištar goddess in the imperial capital. This identification is explored further in chapter 4.5.

36 In SAA 13 186:5–6, the priest Aplāia of Kurbail invokes Adad with Šala and Queen-of-Nakkanti (Queen-of-the-Treasury) to create this three-member EGL in the Edurhenunna-temple in Kurbail. Steven Cole and Peter Machinist regard Queen-of-Nakkanti as an independent deity and not an epithet for Šala, which fits Beaulieu's observation that epithets tend to lack the divine determinative, which Queen-of-Nakkanti has here (Beaulieu, *Pantheon of Uruk*, 75). Theoretically, because she only appears at the end of this one three-member EGL, Queen-of-Nakkanti could be located anywhere after Šala. She has been placed after the localized Ištar goddesses here because she is an independent goddess.
37 There are three distinct EGLs in the curse lists in SAA 2 14. The first is a ten+-member EGL in i 28′–ii 2′ that is broken in the middle: [Assur] / Šerū'a / gods-of-the-Ešarra-temple / [Anu] / Antu / [Enlil] / Mullissu / ... / Bēl / Bēltīya / the Sebittu. The second is a four-member EGL in ii 16′: Assur / (Lord)-Crown / Anu / Antu. The third is a seven+-member EGL that is broken at the end in ii 19′–25′: Šerū'a / Anu / Antu / Enlil / Mu[lissu] / Marduk / [Zarpānītu] / (?). Because (Lord)-Crown only appears in the second EGL between Assur and Anu, we cannot determine his position relative to Šerū'a and the gods-of-the-Ešarra-temple from the first EGL. Additionally, although Šerū'a has been interpreted as Assur's offspring in other EGLs from Esarhaddon treaties (i.e., the witness and adjuration lists in SAA 2 6), her epithet in SAA 2 14 ii 19′ could suggest that she is his consort here: ^{d}*ši*-EDIN$^{!}$-*u*$_{2}$$^{!}$-*a be-let* DINGIR^{meš} GAL-⌜*ti*⌝ ("Šerū'a, great lady of the gods").
38 Ninurta and Gula are the only two deities in SAA 12 93 who are in both EGLs (a five-member EGL in ll. 15-r. 5 and a seven-member EGL in r. 6–8). Interestingly, Ninurta and Gula appear as the first two deities in the first EGL and the final two deities in the second EGL. Together these two EGLs create a ten-member composite god list wherein Adad and Nabû appear later compared to other curse lists. The fact that Ninurta would appear in both EGLs and begin one EGL makes sense because the tablet opens with a dedication of Nabû-maqtu-šatbi by his father Mannu-deiq to Ninurta (ll. 1–4).
39 The other EGL in which Lord-Crown appears after Assur and Ningal is a blessing on behalf of the king (*aš-šur* ^{d}NIN.GAL ^{d}EN.AGA, SAA 13 187:6).
40 Parpola and Watanabe have transliterated and translated Šamaš's consort's name as ^{d}A.A and *Nur* in SAA 2 2 vi 9. In contrast, the divine name is transliterated as ^{d}*a-a* and translated as Aya in throughout this study when dealing with Neo-Assyrian texts. Presumably, Parpola and Watanabe chose *Nur* because that name appears with Šamaš in Sefire i A 9 (*KAI* 222) (*wqdm šmš wnr*, see Table 3.12).
41 In the EGLs in BM 121206 and the reconstructed curse lists in SAA 2 3, the divine name Bēlet-ilī appears between Ea and his consort Damkina. Although the nature of Ea's relationship with Bēlet-ilī varies in Mesopotamian mythology, the fact that her name separates Ea from his typical consort Damkina suggests that Bēlet-ilī has been identified as Ea's consort in these texts. Moreover, the presence of Damkina in this EGL suggests that the two goddesses have not been identified with each other. Rather, in these texts, Ea has two consorts.
42 This restoration is based on Barré's analysis of the text (Barré, "The First Pair," 210).
43 Cross theorized that the deity known as Elyon who is paired with El in Sefire i A (*KAI* 222:11) and who appears as the epithet for El in Genesis 14:18–22 was originally an aspect or epithet of El who "split apart into a separate cult" (Cross, "Yahweh and the God," 243).
44 EGLs from Tiglath-Pileser III's royal inscriptions have been obtained from the following texts:

Hayim Tadmor and Shigeo Yamada, *The Royal Inscriptions of Tiglath-Pileser III (744-727 BC) and Shalmaneser V (726-722)*, *Kings of Assyria*, RINAP 1 (Winona Lake: Eisenbrauns, 2011): 35

i 1–13, 21–24; 37:1–11; 39:15–16; 47 o. 3 and 12; 51:3. EGLs and texts from this collection are identified "RINAP 1, TP3. x" (e.g., RINAP 1, TP3. 35).

45 EGLs from Sargon II's royal inscriptions have been obtained from the following texts:

Andreas Fuchs, *Die Inschriften Sargons II. aus Khorsabad* (Göttingen: Cuvillier Verlag, 1994): 1.1:1, 58, and 62 (The Cylinder Inscription); 1.2.1:29 (The Bronze Tablet Inscription); 1.2.2:12 (The Silver Tablet Inscription); 1.2.3:14–15 (The Gold Tablet Inscription); 1.2.4:11–12 (The "Antimony" Tablet Inscription); 1.3:17 (The Plattenrückseiten Inscription); 2.1:3, 58–59, and 104–105 (The Bull Inscription); 2.2:2, 21 and 34 (The Small "Grand-Inscription" of Hall XIV); 2.3:304, 305–306, 312, 325, 341, and 426 (The Annals); 2.4:3, 154, 155–156 (The Large "Grand-Inscription"); 2.5.1:6 (Threshold Inscription I); 2.5.2:3 (Threshold Inscription II); 2.5.3:4–5 and 24–25 (Threshold Inscription III); 2.5.4:91–92 (Threshold Inscription IV); and 2.5.5:29–30 (Threshold Inscription V). EGLs from this collection are identified "Fuchs x.x:x" (e.g., Fuchs 1.1:1).

Andreas Fuchs, *Die Annalen des Jahres 711 v. Chr. nach Prismenfragmenten aus Ninive und Assur*, SAAS 8 (Helsinki: The Neo-Assyrian Text Corpus Project, 1998): K 1669:7 (p. 25); K 1673 ii 4 (p. 27); and K 1668+ iv′ 34–35 (p. 46).

H. W. F. Saggs, "Historical Texts and fragments of Sargon II of Assyria: 1. The 'Assur Charter,'" *Iraq* 37 (1975): 11–20.

46 EGLs from Sennacherib's royal inscriptions have been obtained from the following texts:

Daniel D. Luckenbill, *The Annals of Sennacherib*, repr. (Eugene: Wipf & Stock, 2005): "The Rock Inscription on the Jûdî Dâgh" (E3) and "The Bavian Inscriptions" (H3). The EGLs from this collection are identified "Luckenbill's *Sennacherib* E3," "H3," or "20."

Eckart Frahm, *Einleitung in die Sanherib-Inschriften*, AfOB 26 (Vienna: Institut fur Orientalistik, 1997): 28 T16; 136–137 T63; 161–162 T128; 163–165 T129; 177 T145; and 176 T173. EGLs from this collection are identified "Frahm page Tx" (e.g., Frahm 28 T16).

47 EGLs from Esarhaddon's royal inscriptions have been obtained from the following texts: Erle Leichty, *Royal Inscriptions of Esarhaddon, King of Assyria (680-669)*, RINAP 4 (Winona Lake: Eisenbrauns, 2011): 1 i 5–6, 9–10, *17*, 45, 59, ii 16–17, 30–38, 45–46, 56, iii 28, *iv 78–79*, v 33–34, vi 44; 2 *i 8–9*, iv 21–22; 3 i 21′, iv 20′–22′; 5 i 2′–3′ (mostly restored), 10′ (partially restored); 6 i 5′–6′ (mostly restored), ii 44′; 8 ii′ 3′–5′; 12:13, 22; 31:3′–4′ (restored); 33 (tablet 2) r. iii 10′–11′; 38:29′–30′; 43:5–13; 44:1–4; 48:1–12, 22–26, *30a*, 30b, 52–54; 57 i 11–12; 70:3; 71:3; *77:12*; *78:11*; *79:11* (mostly restored), 6′ (restored); 93:5, 26; 98 (found at Zinçirli): 1–10, *18-19, 26, r. 18, 21–22, 25*; 99:5; 101 r. *3′–4′*; 103 (Lebanon):1–2 (first 3 and last 2 restored, middle 5 extant); 104 iii 9; 105 iii 40, v 24–25; 113 (Babylon):2–4, 22; 114 iii 16–17; 115 r. 9; 128:5, 7; 129:13 (restored); 130:6, 9; 133:10, 14; 1015 vi 1–7 (perhaps by Esarhaddon, p. 299); 2003 i 8′–15′ (partially restored), *iii 11′-14′*; and 2004:6′. EGLs from this collection are identified "RINAP 4, Esar. x" (e.g., RINAP 4, Esar. 1).

48 EGLs from Assurbanipal's royal inscriptions have been obtained from Riekele Borger's *Beiträge zum Inschriftenwerk Assurbanipals* (Wiesbaden: Harrassowitz Verlag, 1996). EGLs are cited by page, column, and line. When multiple parallel copies of an inscription exist, only the text with the lowest assigned letter is given. For example, on pp. 35–36, A iii 12; F ii 42; B iii 87; and C iv 110 are all parallel inscriptions that Borger has set together, but only "35–36 A iii 12–13" is listed in the notes below. If there are significant differences in parallel inscriptions, these are noted.

The most common EGL pattern in Assurbanipal's royal inscriptions appears in Borger's prism class A and F: *BIWA* 15 A i 14–17; 16 A i 41–43; 25 F i 48–49; 33 A ii 127–129; 35–36 A iii 12–13; 37–38 A iii 29–31; 43 A iv 46–48; 58 A vi 126–128; 62 A viii 19–22; 63 A viii 52–55; 64 A viii 73–76; 67 A ix 61–64; 68 A ix 97–100; 71 A x 33–36; 72 A x 60–62; and 75 A x 118–119. This

EGL usually consists of twelve members: Assur / Sîn / Šamaš / Adad / Marduk / Nabû / Ištar-of-Nineveh / Ištar-of-Kidmuri / Ištar-of-Arbela / Ninurta / Nergal / Nusku. Mullissu's divine name is extant and is listed second in the EGL in the largely reconstructed *BIWA* 33 K 5433:5′–6′.

The second most common EGL pattern appears in Borger's prism class B and D: *BIWA* 94 B iii 10/C iv 22–23; 98 C v 111–112; 112 B vii 73; 114 B viii 28–29; and 115 B viii 41–42. This EGL usually consists of seven divine names: Assur / Sîn / Adad / Marduk / Nabû / Ištar-of-Nineveh / Ištar-of-Arbela. *BIWA* 110 B vii 40 includes Nergal in place of the two Ištar goddesses, while *BIWA* 117 B viii 74–76 and 119 D viii 77 include Ninurta / Nusku / Nergal after the two localized Ištar goddesses.

The remainder of the EGLs in this composite god list are discussed in the notes below as necessary: *BIWA* 14 A i 3; 14 A i 5–6; 20 A i 81; 33 B iii 31; 82–83 K 2631+10 and 20–22; 84–85 K 2631 r. 7/K 2654 r. 15 and 18 and 20; 106 B vi 47; 125 82–5–22,15 x 80–81; 138 T i 23–24 (the gods of the Esagil-temple); 144 T iii 32; 149 C viii 74–76; 154 C ix 76; 157 22 = k; 162 K 3043+ r.$^{!}$ 9′–11′; 163 C ix 78′–80′; 164 C x 100–101; 165 CKalach X 99–101; 171 TVar1 5; 175 BM 127940+ ii′ 4–8; 187 Inschrift L i 5′–8′; 191–192 H2 ii 8′ and 20′; 192 H3 iii 3; 193 H4:2′; 193–194 J1 iii′ 3–5, 9, and 17–20; 195 J3 ii′ 4–5; 196 J5:24–25; 197 J6:9–10; 198 66–5–19,1:22′–23′; 200 BM 122616+:22′–23′; 203 K 120B+:42–44; 268 Fuchs, IIT:29–30; 270 Fuchs, IIT:40 and 43; 278 Fuchs, IIT:104; 280 Fuchs, IIT:116–117; 281 Fuchs, IIT:119; 286 Fuchs, IIT:148 and 152; 288 Fuchs, IIT:164–165; and 301 A Teumman und Dunanu 10 i 31–32 (ibid., 301) and B r. 1′–2′ (ibid., 306).

49 Determining which deity belongs at the beginning of the composite god list for Sargon's royal inscriptions is a difficult task. Assur would be expected in the first position because he is generally regarded the chief deity of the Assyrian Empire, but Assur and Enlil only appear together in one of these EGLs, which is an EGL found within a list of royal titles (Fuchs 1.1:1). Moreover, Enlil appears before Assur in royal titles that only include these two deities (e.g., Fuchs 1.2.1:1 and 1.2.2:1), which is an ordering that can be found in the royal titulary of several other Assyrian kings: e.g., Erība-Adad I (RIMA 1 A.0.72.2:2–3), Assur-uballiṭ (A.0.73.1:13), Šalmaneser I (A.0.77.1), Tukultī-Ninurta I (A.0.78.26:4), Assur-dān II (RIMA 2 A.0.98.4:2), Adad-nērārī II (A.0.99.2:11), and Esarhaddon (RINAP 4, Esar. 48:22). However, in the so-called "Assur Charter" (*Iraq* 37 14, ll. 12–13), Assur appears before Enlil in a three-member EGL that is also derived from royal titles (Assur / Enlil / Marduk). Assur's primacy has been retained in this composite list because he appears most frequently in Sargon's royal-inscription EGLs.

50 Only one of Sennacherib's royal inscriptions lists Mullissu in a three+-member EGL. In Frahm 177 T145 eighteen deities are identified as images/reliefs (*ṣa-lam*, l. 2) created by the king: Assur / [Mullissu] / Šerū'a / Sîn / Nin[gal] / Šamaš / Aya / Anu / Antu / Adad / Šala / Ištar-of-Kidmuri / Bēlet-ilī / Ḫaya / Kusu / [Lumḫa] / Dunga / Egalkiba (ll. 2–7).

51 Mullissu appears as Assur's consort in RINAP 4, Esar. 1 ii 16; 33 r. iii 10′; and 113:3. In RINAP 4, Esar. 58 i 7; and 59 i 4, she is paired with Assur, but they are the only two deities listed, so these cannot be considered EGLs. Methodologically, Barré determined that a god list must include at least three members (Barré, *The God-List*, 6).

52 Mullissu and Ištar-of-Nineveh appear together in a three- or four-member EGL in *BIWA* 195 J3 ii′: ^{4}*da-na-an an-šar*$_{2}$ ^{d}NIN.[LIL$_{2}$] ^{5} ^{d}15 *ša*$_{2}$ $_{NINA}$^{ki} [...] ^{6}DINGIR^{meš} GAL^{meš} EN^{me}[^{š}-*ia*]. Mullissu is also presented as Assur's consort in *BIWA* 198 66–5–19,1:22′ in an eight-member EGL that concludes with both Ištar-of-Nineveh and Ištar-of-Arbela (l. 23′).

Mullissu appears to have been identified with Ištar-of-Nineveh in several EGLs throughout *BIWA* 278–288 Fuchs, IIT. The EGL Assur / Mullissu / Ištar-of-Arbela reoccurs in ll. 104, 116–117, 119, and 164–165. That Ištar//Who-Resides-(in)-Arbela is not an epithet for Mullissu in these lines is indicated both by the copulas *u*$_{3}$ in ll. 117 and 119 and by the divine determinative before Ištar-of-Arbela's divine name. This identification of Mullissu with Ištar-of-Nineveh is further stressed in the five-member EGL in ll. 148 and 152: Assur / Mullissu / Bēl / Nabû / Ištar-of-Arbela. The fact that Ištar-of-Arbela is the only localized Ištar goddess in this EGL in a royal inscription about the Emašmaš-temple (of the localized Ištar goddess in Nineveh) that likely begins with a dedication to Mullissu ([*a-na* ? ^{d}NI]N.L[I]$^{⌜}$L$_2$$^{⌝}$, *BIWA* 264 Fuchs, IIT:1) reinforces this identification because Ištar-of-Nineveh would be expected to appear at least somewhere in this EGL.

The inconsistent identification of the local Ištar-of-Nineveh with the Assyrian chief deity's consort Mullissu in Assurbanipal's royal inscriptions resembles the inconsistencies in EGLs in other seventh-century inscriptions.

53 Šerū'a appears in RINAP 4, Esar. 33 iii 10′. The following divine name in this EGL is missing, and the next extant name is Ninurta.

54 Anu appears before Assur in RINAP 4, Esar. 43:5. In an EGL (Assur / Nabû / Marduk / Sîn / Anu / Ištar) that is embedded in royal titulary and common to both Esar. 98 r. 21–22 and 101 r. 3′–4′, Anu follows Sîn.

55 Antu only appears in one EGL in Sennacherib's royal inscriptions (Frahm 173–174 T139:4), where she appears as Anu's consort. This eighteen-member EGL is unusual in that Anu is listed after Sîn, Šamaš and their consorts but before Adad and his consort (ll. 3–5). Because Anu is listed along with the other Triad 1 deities more often than not in Sennacherib's royal inscriptions, he and Antu have been placed in his traditional position in this composite god list.

56 Enlil appears before Assur in a three-member EGL, which is derived from the king's titulary: Enlil / Assur / Šerū'a (RINAP 1, TP3. 35 i 21–24).

57 In RINAP 4, Esar. 1015 v 5 – an Assyrian copy of a Babylonian text that is probably from Esarhaddon's reign (Leichty, RINAP 4, 299) – Mullissu is Enlil's consort in an EGL embedded in a series of blessings: Marduk / [Z]arpānītu / Anu / Antu / Enlil / Mullissu / Ea / Bēlet-ilī / Sîn / Šamaš. The fact that Marduk and Zarpānītu begin the EGL reflects its Babylonian origin.

58 Ea is followed by an Enbilulu and an Eneimdu in a three-member EGL describing statues in Luckenbill's *Sennacherib* H3:27–29.

59 When not appearing as a member of Triad 1, the divine name Ea typically appears in EGLs from Esarhaddon's royal inscriptions that are explicit references to the deity's statue: RINAP 4, Esar. 48:87 and 60:36′–41′ (Bēl / Bēltiya / Bēlet-Bābili / Ea / Madānu) and Esar. 60:48′–49′ and 2010:7′–10′ (Ea / Šamaš / Asalluḫi / Bēlet-ilī / Kusu / Ningirima). In Esar. 1015 v 6, he is paired with Bēlet-ilī when they are invoked in a blessing.

60 Found within royal titulary, a twelve-member EGL includes the Triad 1 deity Ea and Bēlet-ilī, as well as Nanaya, whose divine name has been restored and who appears to be a secondary consort for Nabû: Assur / Mullissu / Ea / Bēlet-ilī / Sîn / Šamaš / Adad / Marduk / Zarpānītu / Nabû / Tašmētu / N[anaya?] (*BIWA* 175 BM 127940+ ii′ 5–8). The first seven deities of this EGL (Šamaš and Adad's divine names have been restored) comprise an EGL in *BIWA* 187 Inschrift L i 5′–9′.

61 In Fuchs 1.1:1, Sargon's royal titulary provides a four-member EGL (Enlil / Assur / Anu / Dagan, l. 1), which differs from the traditional ordering Anu / Enlil / Ea in l. 58, when Triad 1 is supplemented by Ninšiku. Separately, Dagan and Ninšiku both appear last in their respective EGLs (Fuchs 1.1:1 and 58, respectively), and both divine names only appear in one EGL, which means that their relative ranks cannot be determined by use of common anchor points. Ninšiku is given priority in this composite list over Dagan because Ninšiku is often considered another name, or epithet, for Ea (Fuchs, *Inschriften Sargons II*, 474).

62 When Ningal and Aya are listed in EGLs in Assurbanipal's royal inscriptions, these EGLs are typically referring to the deities housed in the Sîn-Šamaš double temple in Nineveh: e.g., "the temple of Sîn, Ningal, Šamaš, (and) Aya that (is) inside Nineveh" (E_2 ^{d}30 ^{d}NIN.GAL ^{d}UTU [^{d}*a*]-*a* *ša*$_2$ $_{[qe2}$-*re*]*b* NINA^{ki}, *BIWA* 270 Fuchs, IIT:40).
63 Šamaš is third in an EGL (Assur / Marduk / Šamaš) in RINAP 4, Esar. 1019:18.
64 Šamaš's name is listed before Adad's in Fuchs 1.2.1:28; 1.2.2:12; 1.2.3:15; 1.2.4:12; and 1.3:17, but Adad's name is first in 1.1:62.
65 Nabû consistently appears before Marduk in the three-member EGL (Assur / Nabû / Marduk) found in many of Sargon's royal inscriptions (Fuchs *2.1:3*; *2.2:2* and *21*; *2.3:304* and *305–306*; *2.4:3* and *154*; *2.5.1:6*; *2.5.2:3*; *2.5.3:4–5* and *24–25*; *2.5.4:91–92*; and *2.5.5:29–30*). Marduk and his consort Zarpānītu appear before Nabû and his consort Tašmētu twice in Fuchs 2.3:312 and 325 (the later of which is mostly restored). As noted elsewhere, when a text and line number are written in italics (e.g., SAA 13 *126:4*) Nabû is listed before Marduk in an EGL and blessing in that text.
66 Marduk and Nabû are listed before Šamaš in RINAP 1, TP3. 37:2–5 and in (the reconstructed) RINAP 1, TP3. 35 i 2–4 and 8. Šamaš appears before Marduk in a three-member EGL in RINAP 1, TP3. 47 o. 3; 51:3; and [52:3] (Assur / Šamaš / Marduk).
67 The divine name Marduk has been deliberately replaced by Šamaš's in the twelve-member EGL in Frahm 136–137 T63:1–14, reflecting Sennacherib's political frustration with Babylon ca. 700 (Frahm, *Einleitung in die Sanherib-Inschriften*, 136): Assur / Anu / Enlil / E[a] / [Sîn] / [Šamaš] / Adad / Šamaš / Nabû / Ninurta / [Ištar] / the Sebittu.
68 Marduk and Zarpānītu precede Assur and Mullissu in an EGL embedded in royal titulary in an inscription from Babylon (RINAP 4, Esar. 113:2), but Marduk still appears after Assur, Sîn, and Šamaš in l. 22 of the same inscription. Also, Marduk and Zarpānītu precede Anu and Antu in RINAP 4, Esar. 1015 v 1–7.
69 A five+-member EGL appears in *BIWA* 270 Fuchs, IIT:43 in reference to cult images: Bēlum / [Bēltīya] / Lady-of-Babylon / Ea / Madānu.
70 Nabû is named *mār*-Bēl (DUMU ^{d}EN, "son-of-Bēl") in RINAP 4, Esar. 44:4; 128:7; 129:13 (restored); 130:9; and 133:14.
71 Nanaya appears in RINAP 4, Esar. 113:4, following Tašmētu.
72 Because "Lady of Babylon" (*bēlet-babili*) does not have a divine determinative in the ten-member EGL in RINAP 1, TP3. 39:16, this could be interpreted as an epithet for the goddess Nanaya, who appears before "Lady of Babylon" in this text (l. 15). If so, Nanaya's name and the epithet should be translated Nanaya//Lady-of-Babylon. However, the missing determinative is not a problem because Marduk (here Bēl) is also missing a divine determinative in this EGL (l. 15). Thus, both instances in which *bēlet-*/*bēl* appear as a divine first name (or nickname), the divine determinative is not used. Lady-of-Babylon is typically regarded a consort of Marduk in Babylon and is often identified with Zarpānītu by scholars (see Beaulieu, *Pantheon of Uruk*, 75–76), whereas Nanaya is often considered Nabû's consort in Borsippa (ibid., 77). Alternatively, Lady-of-Babylon could be considered a localized Ištar goddess (Livingstone 1986, 224; and Scurlock and Andersen, *Diagnoses*, 523), which is the option reflected in this composite god list of Tiglath-Pileser III's royal inscriptions.
73 Ninurta appears between Assur and Sîn in an eight-member EGL in RINAP 4, Esar. 2003 iii 11′.
74 According to the proposed new reading in RINAP 1, TP3. 37:10, the divine name Sumuqan follows Amurru, which itself follows the Sebittu, in the twelve-member EGL. The two other royal inscriptions from Tiglath-pileser III's reign that include Nergal in an EGL (RINAP 1, TP3. 39:16) place Nergal at or near the end of those EGLs, with his consort Laṣ, but none of the

deities who are listed after him in RINAP 1, TP3. 35 are listed in these EGLs, so there are no relative anchor points for comparison.

75 Ninurta and Nergal do not both appear in an EGL from Sennacherib's royal inscriptions. Nergal appears in four EGLs (Frahm 161–162 T128:1; 163–165 T129:3; and 28 T16:63; and Luckenbill's *Sennacherib* H3:1). Ninurta is in two EGLs (Luckenbill's *Sennacherib* 20 §§ 63–66e:2 and Frahm 136–137 T63:12). Because Ninurta appears before Nergal in other kings' royal inscriptions, he has been place before him in this composite god list.

76 The divine name Ištar is the final name in the two EGLs in which it appears (K 1669:7 and K 1673 ii′ 4), so the name could be placed anywhere after Adad in the Sargon II composite god list.

77 (The unspecified) Ištar appears in Luckenbill's *Sennacherib* E3:2; Frahm 136–137 T63:13 [reconstructed] and 161–162 T128:1; and Luckenbill's *Sennacherib* H3:1. In none of these EGLs do localized Ištar goddesses appear; however, Ištar-of-Nineveh and Ištar-of-Arbela are mentioned by name and as "[the goddesses]" (proposed reconstruction: [DINGIR.DINGIR^{meš}], l. 60) by Sennacherib in Frahm 161–162 T128:60 in a request for help against his enemies.

78 In two EGLs in RINAP 4, Esar. 1, (the geographically unspecified) Ištar is given the epithets "the queen" (*šar-ra-ti*, ii 17) and "the lady of battle" (*be-let* MURUB$_4$ *u* ME$_3$, ii 38; see also RINAP 4, Esar. 93:9), and she appears with Assur in the closing invocations of vi 65–74. In contrast, Ištar-of-Nineveh and Ištar-of-Arbela appear together in several EGLs in RINAP 4, Esar. 1 (i 6, i 10, i 45, i 59, ii 45–46, iv 78–79, v 33, and vi 44. (The unspecified) Ištar is also listed before Nabû and Marduk in an EGL (Assur / Ninurta / Sîn / Šamaš / Adad / Ištar / Nabû / Marduk), which has the summary statement "the gods dwelling in Nineveh" (DINGIR^{meš} *a-ši-bu-ut* NINA^{ki}, RINAP 4, Esar. 2003 iii 13′).

79 (The unspecified) Ištar appears in a three-member EGL between Assur (*an-šar$_2^!$*) and Nergal in *BIWA* 83 K 2654:7′; both Ištar-of-Nineveh and Ištar-of-Arbela appear in an eight-member EGL in r. 15 (Borger, *BIWA*, 84) that does not include (the unspecified) Ištar.

80 In addition to their invocation in Frahm 161–162 T128:60, which is not an EGL, Ištar-of-Nineveh and Ištar-of-Arbela only appear in the eight-member EGL in Frahm 28 T16:63–64. Neither (the unspecified) Ištar nor Ištar-of-Kidmuri are in this EGL, but their relative positions in this composite god list are based upon EGLs from seventh-century EGLs.

81 Ištar-of-Nineveh is called "the great queen" (^{d}*iš-tar ša*$_2$ ^{uru}*ni-na-a šar-ra-tu*$_2$ GAL-*tu*$_2$, RINAP 4, Esar. 48:25) in an EGL in which she is followed by Ištar-of-Arbela, who is praised as having "shining, upraised eyes" (*ni-iš* IGI^{II}-*ša*$_2$ *nam-ra-a-ti*, l. 26).

82 Ištar-of-Kidmuri is placed between the goddesses from Nineveh and Arbela in accordance with her position in seventh-century EGLs rather than in other Sennacherib period royal inscriptions.

83 In three EGLs, "their great consorts" (*ḫi-ra-ti-šu*$_2$*-nu ra-ba-a-ti*, Fuchs 2.4:156) are mentioned collectively at the end (Fuchs 2.2:[34]; 2.3:[426]; and 2.4:156). The same male gods are listed in each of the three EGLs (Ea / Sîn / Šamaš / Nabû / Adad / Ninurta), but Fuchs has restored the divine name Ningal between the divine names Sîn and Šamaš in 2.2:34. This would mean that she is named explicitly in l. 34 and that she and her consort Sîn are implicitly considered part of the collective at the end of the EGL.

84 Guše[a] appears in RINAP 4, Esar. 8 ii′ 5′ after Ištar-of-Nineveh (restored) and Ištar-of-Arbela. In RINAP 4, Esar. 48:11, Agušāya appears between Nergal and the Sebittu in a twelve-member EGL that contains no other Ištar goddesses (Assur / Anu / Enlil / Ea / Sîn / Šamaš / Adad / Marduk / [Nabû] / [Ner]gal / Agušāya / the Sebittu, ll. 1–12). In this EGL, Agušāya is followed by Lady-of-[War]-and-Battle (^{d}*a-gu-še-e-a* ^{d}GAŠAN [MURUB$_4$] *u* ME$_3$, l. 11). Erle Leichty interprets GAŠAN MURUB$_4$ *u* ME$_3$ as one of two epithets for the goddess in this line, and he parenthetically equates Agušāya with (the unspecified) Ištar (Leichty, RINAP 4, 104). Divine determinatives do not typically precede epithets; rather, they indicate a new and distinct divine name. However, the structure of this EGL does seem to suggest that ᵈGAŠAN $MURUB_4$ *u* ME_3 is an epithet for Agušāya rather than a distinct deity. Each of the first 13 lines in this text begins with a divine name (admittedly, *i-nu-um*, "when," is the first word of the Assur line, but this word sets up the entire EGL in one subordinate clause that ends in l. 13), and the entire line is devoted to that one deity.

85 Assyrian-Ištar (ᵈ15 *aš-šur-i-t*[*u*]) only appears in one EGL in Assurbanipal's royal inscriptions, where she follows Assur and Nergal (*BIWA* 83 Die Nergal-Laṣ-Inschrift:40 = K 2654:24′). She has been placed after the other localized Ištar goddesses in this composite god list, which is where she commonly appears when listed with other localized Ištar goddesses in EGLs and other composite lists, rather than immediately after Nergal.

86 The EGL in RINAP 1, TP3. 37:1–10 consists of ten divine names, each with a line devoted to that deity. Because Nergal is only extant in one EGL in Tiglath-pileser III's royal inscriptions, and Nergal appears before (the reconstructed) Šamaš in that EGL (RINAP 1, TP3. 35 i 5 and [8]), Nergal has been placed before Šamaš in this composite list. Of the few EGLs found within Tiglath-Pileser royal inscriptions, the gods of Babylon receive more attention than would otherwise be expected when comparing these EGLs with those from EGLs from royal inscriptions dating to the Sargonic dynasty.

Šamaš is the first deity mentioned in an unusual three-member EGL in a funerary inscription for Queen Yabâ (RINAP 1, TP3. 2003:1). Because the other two deities do not appear in another EGL from this period (and because this is a funerary inscription and not one of Tiglath-Pileser III's royal inscriptions), Ereškigal and the Anunnakū have not been included in this composite god list. If they had been included, the lack of anchor points would allow these divine names to be placed anywhere after Šamaš.

87 This collection of minor deities is listed in Frahm 177 T145:6–7 and 176 T173:5–6, both of which are EGLs listing cult images (*ṣa-lam*, T145:2) that Sennacherib had created.

88 Šamaš appears before (the reconstructed) Sîn in RINAP 1, TP3. 37:4–5 (ca. 739) and probably appears before him in the lacuna in RINAP 1, TP3. 35 i 7–8. Otherwise, Sîn precedes Šamaš in most royal-inscription EGLs written between Sargon's and Assurbanipal's reigns. Note that this dynamic relationship status between Sîn and Šamaš dates back at least to the Old Babylonian period a thousand years earlier, as witnessed in various portions of the prologue and epilogue to the Laws of Ḫammurapi and in contemporary letters. However, given the limited number of texts used to compile this composite god list for Tiglath-Pileser III's royal inscriptions and the three-member EGL in RINAP 1, TP3. 47 o. 3; 51:3; and [52:3] (Assur / Šamaš / Marduk), Šamaš has been given priority over Sîn here.

89 Nusku is listed after Sîn and Ningal and before Šamaš and Aya in *BIWA* 144 T iii 32.

90 Išum appears in one EGL after Assur and Nergal in *BIWA* 157 22 = k.

91 Amurru and Sumuqan appear after the Sebittu in RINAP 1, TP3. 37:9–10, and Amurru has been restored after the Sebittu in (the restored) RINAP 1, TP3. 35 i 12–13 (Sumuqan probably could be restored in l. 14, which is also broken). Notably, these EGLs would be the only EGLs in which the Sebittu appear where they are not the last Assyrian deities, a phenomenon discussed by Barré in Neo-Assyrian treaties (Barré, *God-List*, 19 ff.; cf. the minority opinion of van der Toorn's analysis of the EGLs in SAA 2 5 iv 6 [van der Toorn, "Anat-Yahu," 84]).

92 SAA 12 10 dates to the reign of Adad-nērārī III (ca. 800); SAA 2 2 dates to the reign of Assur-nērāri V (mid-eighth century); and SAA 2 6 dates to the reign of Esarhaddon (mid-seventh century.

93 Although the six planets (i.e., Jupiter, Venus, Saturn, Mercury, Mars, and Sirius) precede Assur in SAA 2 6's witness list, they are not included here. They are included in Table 3.15.
94 Enlil appears here in the composite witness list, but he appears (though restored) after Šamaš in the Adad-nērārī III land grant (SAA 12 10 r. 6′).
95 The limited nature of the EGLs in this sample provides no contextual reason to place Assyrian-Ištar with such a low rank; however, when she does appear in EGLs with other localized Ištar goddesses, she is typically last (see Table 3.11, which likely resembles the curse EGL in SAA 2 3:7′–10′ and r. 2′–5′). Similarly, she is invariably last when she appears as the only goddess in the four- or five-member EGLs from SAA 12 (see Table 3.5a). For this reason, Assyrian-Ištar has been given a lower rank in this composite list as compared to SAA 12 10, and those following her in SAA 12 10 appear in this composite as they do in SAA 2 2 and SAA 2 6.
96 This table has been derived from the tables in Wunsch, "Richter des Nabonid," 570–571, keeping only those judges and texts that are necessary to relate the rise of Nergal-ušallim mār Šigûa, Nergal-bānûnu mār Rab-banê, and Nabû-balāssu-iqbi mār Amēlû. Their names and serial positions are indicated in bold.

Following Wunsch, the number in each box indicates an individual judge's serial position in a tablet's list of judges. The question mark (?) indicates that a judge's name does not appear in the text, but he might have functioned as a judge in the case. The plus sign (+) indicates that the absolute serial position of a judge is uncertain, so his relative serial position is given from the extant portion of the text. In most cases, the plus sign appears after a question mark, where Wunsch felt a judge's name likely appeared in a lacuna. Finally, the arrangement of the texts in this table are based on Wunsch's chronology, and an "x" – be it representing whole or part of the date – indicates her reconstruction of a text's placement in this chronology.
97 Table 3.18 is based on Beaulieu's proposed "hierarchy of deities in group A" (Beaulieu, *Pantheon of Uruk*, 73).
98 Beaulieu allows for an interchange between Symbol (^{giš}TUKUL) and Altar (*šu-bat*/$^{(\text{d}/\text{giš})}$KI.TUŠ) for these Marduk and Nabû representations.
99 Ištar-of-Uruk can appear joined with Symbol-of-Bēl through the use of the copula "and" (*u*) after the list of offerings (e.g., NCBT 862:4–5), or she can be recorded as receiving her own offering (e.g., YBC 9238:4–5). The same is true of Symbol-of-Nabû with Nanaya, as well as Uṣur-amāssu with Urkayītu (e.g., NBC 4801:10–11).
100 In PTS 2942, Temple-of-Marduk appears after Uṣur-amāssu and Gula. Beaulieu notes that Temple-of-Sîn appears once in this position (Beaulieu, *Pantheon of Uruk*, 73).
101 Beaulieu suggests that *Palil* could be identified with either Ninurta or Nergal (Beaulieu, *Pantheon of Uruk*, 87).
102 Divine-Chariot appears before Lady-of-Eanna in NCBT 862.
103 Or Temple-of-Nergal.
104 Or Temple-of-Ninurta. In PTS 2042, Ninurta appears before Nergal.
105 Legal transactions that include additional deterrents (subsection IVc; e.g., donating horses to a local temple; see the discussion in chapter 4.1) are indicated in bold. For further legal transactions that involve Ištar-of-Nineveh or Ištar-of-Arbela, see Theodore Kwasman, *Neo-Assyrian Legal Documents in the Kouyunjik Collection of the British Museum* (Rome: Eitrice Pontificio Istituto Biblico, 1988) and Veysel Donbaz and Simo Parpola, *Neo-Assyrian Legal Texts in Istanbul* (Saarbrücken: In Kommission bei SDV Saarbrücker Druckerei und Verlag, 2001).
106 For an explanation of the curse list in SAA 2 6:414–465 compared to other curse lists in Neo-Assyrian treaties, see Spencer L. Allen, "Rearranging the Gods in Esarhaddon's Succession Treaty (SAA 2 6:414–465)," *Die Welt des Orients* 43 (2013): 1–25.

107 This table is based on Pardee's edition of *KTU*^{2} 1.47 (= RS 1.1017 = CTA 29) and is supplemented by his edition of the parallel text *KTU*^{2} 1.118 (Pardee, *Ritual and Cult*, 14 f.) to fill in the lacunae of the former.
108 De Moor notes that *'il ṣpn* does not appear at the beginning of the parallel texts and should be equated with mountain *ṣpn* rather than a topical heading (de Moor, "Semitic Pantheon," 218 and 218 nn. 24–25).
109 The pronunciation of the Ugaritic divine names not discussed elsewhere in this book are based on Pardee's transliteration of *KTU*^{2} 1.148 (Pardee, *Ritual and Cult*, 15–19). As with Anat and Ašerah, ‘ and ’ have been discarded for transliteration in these names. The translation of [d]dm in l. 43 is based on Pardee's translation, but my translation of *lb*[n]n as Lebanon is based on the edition in *KTU*^{2} because Pardee only translates it as "*Labana*" (ibid., 19). Finally, the markings for whether the four Baal manifestations in ll. 44–45 have been restored are based on my interpretations of the *KTU*^{2} edition rather than on Pardee's (ibid., 18).
110 Because each section of *KTU*^{2} 1.119, as indicated by a Roman numeral, represents a new day on which sacrifices were offered, the repetition of a divine name in different sections does not represent a new deity by the same name. Section divisions in this table follow Pardee's division of the text (Pardee, *Ritual and Cult*, 52–53).
111 The verb that has been reconstructed in Mullissu//Who-Resides-(in)-Nineveh's curse is plural ([*li-ir-ku-su*], "[may *they* tie]"), but a singular verb (i.e., *lirkus*) would make more sense grammatically.
112 *CAD* T tentatively suggests that the three Baal deities are the subject of the verb *lissuḫu* (*CAD* T, *tarkullu* mng. a.).
113 For a list of 56 attestations of Hadad-of-Aleppo at Elba, see Pomponio and Xella, *Les dieux d'Ebla*, 44–48.
114 Schwemer notes that Hadad-of-Aleppo's cult spread throughout the region in the second half of the second millennium, including cults devoted to the deity at Nuzi, Ugarit, Tunip, Emar, and Ḫattuša (Schwemer, "Storm-Gods: Part I," 165). In each location, the deity takes on the local first name of the storm-god, such as Tešub-of-Aleppo, Tarḫund-of-Aleppo, etc. For a further discussion of Hadad-of-Aleppo's cult in the Hittite capital, see also, Maciej Popko, "Zum Tempel des Teššup von Ḫalap in Ḫattuša," AoF 29 (2002): 73–80.
115 For the identification of Baal-KRNTRYŠ with Hadad-of-Aleppo, see Schmitz, "Phoenician KRNTRYŠ, 139–141 and plate 1 on 143. For the possibility that Baal-KRNTRYŠ was a deified weapon, see Bunnes, "The Storm-God," 63–64.
116 In Egypt, the deity b‘r-ḏpn is eventually identified with Zeus Kasios, the Greek name for Mount Ṣapun (Lipiński, *Dieux et Déesses*, 244 and 247).
117 In addition to these two references to the deity's mountain as Mount-Baal-of-Ṣapun in Tiglath-pileser III's royal inscriptions, the name also appears in a royal inscription from Sargon II's reign (ARAB II:13).
118 Because there is no scholarly consensus for the dates of the Pentateuchal sources, the dates surrounding the Exodus and Numbers verses are intentionally overly general.
119 For a bibliography on the deity Baal-Šamêm and summary of the various attestations of the divine name, related epithets, and potential identifications, see Wolfgang Röllig, "Baal-Shamem בעל־שמם, בעל־שמין," in *DDD* (1999), 149–151.

In addition to Baal-Šamêm, Papyrus Amherst 63 12:11–19 also mentions Yahweh (spelled YHW-G; the G signifies the divine determinative in the Demotic writing system) and the deity Bethel. Most of the hymn is devoted to Yahweh, with Bethel's and Baal-Šamêm's names appearing only in l. 18. According to Sven P. Vleeming and Jan W. Wesselius, Baal-Šamêm's role in this hymn is to "pronounce your benedictions to your faithful" (Sven P. Vleeming and

Jan W. Wesselius, *Studies in Papyrus Amherst 63* [Amsterdam: Juda Palache Instituut, 1985], 51). In an earlier translation of this text, they had interpreted Bethel and Baal-Šamêm as the ones whom "my lord" (*mr*, i.e., Yahweh) would bless: "May the lord bless Betel (and) Ba'al Šamayn" (*bytl b'l šmyn mr ybrk'*, l. 18; Sven P. Vleeming and Jan W. Wesselius, "An Aramaic Hymn from the Fourth Century B.C.," *BiOr* 39 [1982]: 504–505).

Several Baal deities appear in Papyrus Amherst 63. For example, (the unspecified) Baal appears in 13:15 and is asked to bless Yahweh. Baal-Šamêm appears again in 18:3 and is said to have "spoiled and stripped your (the city of Babylon's) cedar-wood." In 8:3, (the unspecified) Baal is asked to bless from Mount Ṣapun, while Bēl (i.e., Marduk) is asked to bless from Babylon and Nabû from Borsippa (ll. 4–5). *Baal* also seems to be used as a title for deities who are not typically thought of as Baal deities. For instance, the god Bethel – identified as such by Vleeming and Wesselius because he is located in Resh, Bethel's city, in this blessing – appears to be referred to as *baal* (8:2; Vleeming and Wesselius, *Papyrus Amherst 63*, 55).

120 The toponym Baal-Me'on, along with its reservoir and the city of Kiriathaim, is described as being rebuilt by Mesha in *KAI* 181:9–10. Baal-Me'on also appears as a toponym in Numbers 32:38; Ezekiel 25:9; and 1 Chronicles 5:8. In *KAI* 181:30, Beth-Baal-Me'on is listed as a grazing place. Beth-Baal-Me'on also appears in Joshua 13:17, and Beth-Me'on appears in Jeremiah 48:23. Japhet dates 1 and 2 Chronicles to the end of the Persian period in the late fourth century (Japhet, *I & II Chronicles*, 27–28).

121 Of the fourteen times that Tannit is identified as Face-of-Baal, her name appears before Baal-Ḥamān eight times (*KAI* 78:2; 79:1; 85:1; 86:1; 87:2$^{!}$; 88:2; 94:1; and 97:1$^{!}$) and after him four times (*KAI* 102:1–2; 105:1; 164:1; and 175:2–3). For a fuller treatment of Baal-Ḫamān, his history from the late-ninth century B.C.E. to the first century C.E., his identification with the Greek god Kronos and the Roman god Saturn, and his iconography, see J. Ferron, "Dédicace latine á Baal-Hammon," *CdB* 3 (1953): 114; Xella, *Baal Hammon*; and Lipińiski, *Dieux et Déesses*, 251–264. For an explanation of BEBELLAHAMON, see Table 5.8 and Xella, *Baal Hammon*, 198.

122 Umm El-'Amed is between Tyre and Acco (Gibson, *TSSI* 3, 118). In *TSSI* 3 32:1, the divine name Milkaštart//God-of-Ḥamān (מלכעשתרת אל חמנ) appears on a sphinx statue (ibid., 121).

123 The first name Baal is likely hiding the original name of the famous Moon-God-of-Ḫarrān in *KAI* 218 (see SAA 2 2 iv 4′: ^{d}30 EN GAL-*u a-šib* ^{uru}KASKAL, Moon-God//Great-Lord//Who-Resides-(in)-Ḫarrān). According to Gibson, "[t]he moon-god (i.e., Baal-Ḫarrān) was doubtless worshipped at Sam'al under his West Semitic name Sahar, but he was not prominent enough to be mentioned in the lists of deities in" the Hadad Inscription (*KAI* 214) and the Panamuwa Inscription (*KAI* 215); Bar-Rakib's introduction of this deity to the cult "was motivated by political considerations" (Gibson, *TSSI* 1, 93). For a fuller discussion of Moon-God-of-Ḫarrān, see Lipiński, *Dieux et Déesses*, 171–192; and Rubio, "Scribal Secrets," 161–163.

124 More than seventeen distinct personal names with the theophoric element Bēl-Ḫarrān are listed in *PNA* 1/2.

125 Georges Dossin, "Benjaminites dans les texts de Mari," in *Mélanges syriens offert à M. René Dussaud* (Paris: Librairie Orientaliste Paul Geuthner, 1939), 2:986.

Moon-God-of-Ḫarrān also appears in SAA 6 334 r. 15 ([^{d}30 *ša*$_{2}$ ^{uru}]KASKAL); SAA 12 48:6′ (⌜^{d}30⌝ *ša*$_{2}$ ŠA$_{3}$ ⌜^{uru}KASKAL$^{!}$⌝^{k}[^{i}]); SAA 14 193 r. 8–9 ([^{d}30] *a-šib* ^{uru}KASKAL); RIMA 3 A.0.104.3:23 (^{d}30 *a-šib* ^{uru}KASKAL); and RIMA 3 A.0.105.1:20 (^{d}30 *a-šib* ^{uru}KASKAL). See also the *Psalm in Praise of Uruk*, which associates Moon-God with Ḫarrān (AG$_{2}$ ^{uru}KASKAL *a*-⌜*di* ^{d}30⌝, "I love Ḫarrān along with Moon-God," SAA 3 9:17).

126 The bowl inscribed with Baal-Lebanon was made at the "new city" in Cyprus (Gibson, *TSSI* 3, 67). Gibson is uncertain whether the cult for Baal-Lebanon was local or if this deity was only revered at the governor's residence.
127 *Inscriptiones graecae urbis Romae*, vol. 1, edited by L. Moretti (Rome: 1968).
128 The following series of Baal divine names that function as toponyms in Hebrew Bible narratives is partially adapted from Hutton, "Local Manifestations," 184 n. 37. The dates provided refer to the first edition of the Deuteronomistic History in the late seventh century.
129 Because there is no scholarly consensus for the dates of the Pentateuchal sources, the dates surrounding the Baal-Pe'or episode in Numbers 25:1–5 are intentionally overly general. Deuteronomy is generally considered a product of the seventh and sixth centuries, and Hosea is generally considered a product of the eighth century.
130 In *KAI* 14:18, there is a temple built for Baal-Ṣidon (בת לבעל צדנ) and another temple built for Astarte//Name-of-Baal (לעשתרת שמ בעל). Gibson notes that the latter shrine is different from the one restored in l. 16 "[the house of Astar]te in-Ṣidon//Land-by-the-Sea" ([בת עשתר]ת בצדנ ארצ ימ), which is dedicated to Astarte-of-Lofty-Heavens (עשתרת שממ אדרמ; Gibson, *TSSI* 3, 109).
131 M. G. Guzzo Amadasi and V. Karageorghis, *Fouilles de Kition: III. Inscriptions Phéniciennes* (Nicosia: Published for the Republic of Cyprus by the Department of Antiquities, 1977), 170–171; and Lipiński, *Dieux et Déesses*, 315. See also Astarte-of-Kition in *KAI* 37:5 (Table 5.9).
132 Lipiński, *Dieux et Déesses*, 308. Lipiński says MRP'K is probably a toponym, which corrects the reading found in *CIS* 1 41:3 (ibid., 60–61), wherein the *k* is separated from *mrp'* by a space. *MRP'*, without the K, has been understood to mean "healer."
133 Lipiński notes that Baal-Marqod was identified with Jupiter Heliopolis of Baalbek (Lipiński, *Dieux et Déesses*, 115–116).
134 F. Fresnel, "Inscriptions trilingues trouvées à Lebdah," *JA* 8 (1846): 350. Only the first letter of the Baal divine name is legible in the Neo-Punic portion of this trilingual text, so the proposed restoration is Fresnel's. Lipiński notes that the phonetic shift from *ba'al* 〉 *bon* in these divine names is also common to the name Hannibaal (*ḥanniba'al* 〉 *anniboni*) and the name Baalmilk (*ba'almilk* 〉 Βονομίλεξ; Lipiński, *Dieux et Déesses*, 361).
135 Bethel and Anat-Bethel actually precede the Assyrian summary statements in SAA 2 5 iv 8′–9′, but because they follow the Sebittu, they should not be considered among the Assyrian deities (Barré, *God-Lists*, 20).
136 Baal-Ṣemed, Baal-Kanapi (Baal-of-the-Wing?), Baal-R'KT, Baal-Malagê, Baal-Magnim, and Baal-'Addir are included in these tables because the have Baal first names, but their last names are not geographic names.
137 Lord-of-the-Dynasty (בעל . בית) is probably an epithet for Rakib-El and not an unexpected new Baal divine name in this text (Gibson, *TSSI* 1, 229); Rakib-El, whose name means (chariot)-driver-of-El, also appears in the Kulamuwa Inscription (*KAI* 24:16), in the Kulamuwa scepter inscription (*KAI* 25:4 and 5–6), and in the Bar-Rakib Inscription (*KAI* 216:5).
138 The conjunction *et* appears between each of these divine names in *CIL* 3 7954.
139 Jean Starcky interprets (the unspecified) Baal as a distinct deity in this EGL rather than as a title for Baal-Ḥamān (Jean Starcky, "Inscriptions Archaïques de Palmyre," in *Studi Orientalistici in onore di Giorgio Levi Della Vida*, Pubblicazioni dell'Istituto per l'Oriente 52 [Rome: Istituto per L'oriente, 1956], 2:516). Xella notes that the appearance of both (the unspecified) Baal and Baal-Ḥamān in the sequence in this inscription is unusual, but he interprets Baal-Ḥamān as a "particular manifestation" (*une manifestation particulière*) of or "a sort of 'fusion'" (*sorte de "fusion"*) with (the unspecified) Baal. Compare this interpretation with Bebellahamon in the following note for its text.

140 Xella interprets the divine name Bebellahamon in *CIL* 3 7954 as the name Baal affixed to the front of the name Baal-Ḥamān, with the "l" of Baal assimilated to the "b" of Baal-Ḥamān (Xella, *Baal Hammon*, 198). Compare this interpretation with (the unspecified) Baal in the previous note for its text.
141 BENEFAL is a scribal mistake for Fenebal, which is how Face-of-Baal (e.g., פנ בעל) occasionally appears in Neo-Punic texts written in Greek or Latin letters (e.g., ΘΙΝΙΘ ΦΑΝΕ ΒΑΛ, Tannit//Face-of-Baal, *KAI* 175:2).
142 The divine name Yahweh is spelled YHW in the papyri and YHH in the ostraca at Elephantine (Porten, *Archives from Elephantine*, 105).
143 *TAD* A = Bezalel Porten and Ada Yardeni, *Textbook of Aramaic Documents from Ancient Egypt*: *Letters*, vol. 1 (1986); *TAD* B = *Contracts*, vol. 2 (1989); *TAD* D = *Ostraca and Assorted Inscriptions*, vol. 4 (1999). The dates given for these texts have been taken from Porten and Yardeni's commentary in *TAD* A–D.

TAD A4.7 is better preserved than A4.8. When significant portions of the text in *TAD* A4.8 are extant, the equivalent lines are provided in parentheses.
144 If Yahweh is the subject of the subordinate clause beginning with זי in *TAD* A4.7:6, then זי should be translated as "who" and this clause should be treated as an epithet or part of the Yahweh full name: Yahweh//the-God. However, if the clause modifies the temple, זי should be translated as "that" or "which," indicating where the temple is located.
145 According to *DNWSI*, kbl_1 (כבל) means "to bind," which, by extension, may also mean "to render barren" when referring to a woman (*DNWSI*, kbl_1) in *Lozachmeur* no. 175. This meaning and interpretation is "uncertain." Hélène Lozachmeur's proposed "Yahweh-of-Hosts has made you sterile/bound you" ("*Yahô-Ṣeba'ôt t'a rendue sterile/t'a liée*") simultaneously extends the uncertain meaning "to be barren" as he renders the primary meaning (Hélène Lozachmeur, *La Collection Clermont-Genneau: ostraca, épigraphs sur jarred, étiquettes de bois* [Paris: Diffusion de Boccard, 2006], 325).
146 Full names are indicated by dashes in the English translation. If the divine name Yahweh is not explicitly connected with the following geographic name by a dash, then that proposed full name has been rejected.
147 As discussed in chapter 6.2, the acceptance of this Yahweh full name depends on whether we reject the Masoretic punctuation and balance in Judges 5:5. If we keep the Masoretic punctuation, then the divine name ends the first colon of the verse, and "the one of Sinai" or "this Sinai" begins the second colon of the verse.
148 This is the only extra-biblical attestation of Yahweh-of-Hosts outside of the Elephantine corpus. See Dobbs-Allsopp, *et al.*, *Hebrew Inscriptions*, 575–576; and Naveh, "Hebrew Graffiti," 206–207.
149 For Hittite Ištar-named goddesses, storm-gods, warrior gods and other categories of deities with geographic last names, see Table 2.3. For Tešub(-of-Heaven) and Tešub-of-Ḫattuša, see Table 2.1. For a list of Hittite LAMMA deities with geographic (and other) last names, see Table 2.4, esp. i 43–51, and Table 2.5. For Neo-Assyrian deities whose names follow the DN//Who-Resides-(in)-GN formula, see Tables 4.1 and 4.2. For the one Yahweh full name that follows the DN//Title//Who-Resides-(in)-GN formula, YHW//God//Who-Resides-(in)-the-Elephantine-Fortress, see Table 6.1.

Divine names that are mentioned but for which no textual evidence is given or available are placed in brackets, e.g., [Ištar-of-Ḫarrān].

Indices

Primary Texts Index

Italic page numbers indicate material in endnotes or footnotes.

Biblical Texts

Northwest Semitic and Eblaite Texts

Non-Semitic and Non-Sumerian Texts

Italian Texts

Latin Texts

General Index

Legend:

DN = divine name
GN = geographic name
RN = royal name
TN = temple name

Adad (DN) viii–ix, 10, 23–25, 34, 77, 94, 99–110, 112–116, 118, 124–125, 136, 139, 144–145, 148–149, 171, 188, 202, 220, 223, 243, 247, 311, 351–354, 369, 372–377, 379–383, 388–389, 391, 413, 415–416, 418, 420–423
Adad-of-Kurbail (DN) viii, 104–106, 108–109, 119, 144, 149, 197, 223, 285, 376, 379, 383, 412
Alalaḫ (GN) 164, 216, 224, 347
Amarna (GN) 165, 168, 216, 224, 261, 345
Anu (DN) viii–ix, 7, 16, 21, 30, 32, 52, 56, 85, 98–101, 103–104, 110, 112–116, 124, 136, 144, 157–158, 160–161, 182, 312, 351, 353, 365, 369, 373, 375–377, 379–380, 382–383, 389, 413, 415, 418, 420–423
Anunītu (DN) 9, 29, 176–177, 191–197, 199, 311, 354, 391
Arbela (GN) 1–2, 12–14, 17, 19, 28, 48, 106–108, 117–118, 130, 152–155, 170–171, 173–177, 180, 183–188, 190, 233–234, 314, 346, 390, 423
Artaxerxes (RN) 288, 295–297
ašerah/Ašerah (DN) 5–6, 209, 217, 237–239, 243, 250, 264–265, 271, 273, 277–280, 282, 303, 309, 314, 392–393, 404, 412, 426
Asherah (DN) 279; see also ašerah/Ašerah
Assur (DN/GN) vii–ix, 2–3, 9, 14–16, 22, 24, 28–30, 33, 35, 37–38, 43–46, 56, 100–116, 118–120, 123–124, 126–127, 133–139, 142, 144–146, 149, 151, 153, 155–157, 164, 168–173, 176, 178–185, 187–191, 194, 197–198, 220, 223, 227, 241, 280, 285, 307–308, 310–313, 316, 319, 346, 354,372–383, 388, 390, 412, 414–418, 420–425
Assurbanipal (RN) 1–3, 12–16, 20, 22, 24–25, 27, 44, 46–48, 95, 116, 122–123, 127, 142, 145, 147, 154–156, 159, 164, 169, 173, 177–179, 186–187, 198, 239, 273, 373, 380–381, 415–417, 419, 421–422, 424
Assurnāṣirpal (RN) 15–16, 107, 146, 164, 168, 181
Assyria (GN) x, 2, 6–7, 15–17, 19, 22, 25, 27, 48, 58, 93, 105–106, 114, 116, 133, 135, 137, 139–140, 145, 157, 162, 168, 178, 220–223, 245–246, 280, 283, 285, 309, 311, 316, 346, 352, 372–373, 375–377, 380–383, 387, 389, 396–401, 412, 417
Astarte (DN) viii, 4–5, 57, 141, 203, 221, 232, 237, 239–241, 244, 246, 270, 279, 302–303, 306–307, 392–393, 396, 400–401, 404, 412, 428; see also Aštarte
Aštarte (DN) 228, 232–233, 237, 298; see also Astarte
Atargatis (DN) 227, 401

Baal (DN) viii, xi, 3–6, 9–11, 25–26, 36, 48, 94, 104, 118, 142, 147, 201–218, 220–230, 232–237, 239–252, 255, 265, 269–270, 278–280, 282–287, 295, 301, 304, 308–309, 311, 314–316, 318–319, 380–381, 392–404, 408–410, 412, 426–429; see also Ba‘lu
(the unspecified) Baal (DN) 204, 206–212, 214–215, 224, 226, 241–243, 245, 286, 308, 314, 316, 398, 403, 427–429
Baal deity/deities 3, 6, 10–11, 25, 48, 94, 142, 201–205, 207–215, 218, 220–223, 226, 228, 232–234, 236–237,

CPSIA information can be obtained
at www.ICGtesting.com
Printed in the USA
LVHW021459030523
745797LV00021BB/321